The
Empowered
Writer

*An Essential Guide to Writing,
Reading, & Research*

Eric Henderson

K.M. Moran

OXFORD
UNIVERSITY PRESS

OXFORD

UNIVERSITY PRESS

8 Sampson Mews, Suite 204, Don Mills, Ontario M3C 0H5
www.oupcanada.com

Oxford University Press is a department of the University of Oxford.
It furthers the University's objective of excellence in research, scholarship,
and education by publishing worldwide in

Oxford   New York

Auckland   Cape Town   Dar es Salaam   Hong Kong   Karachi
Kuala Lumpur   Madrid   Melbourne   Mexico City   Nairobi
New Delhi   Shanghai   Taipei   Toronto

With offices in

Argentina   Austria   Brazil   Chile   Czech Republic   France   Greece
Guatemala   Hungary   Italy   Japan   Poland   Portugal   Singapore
South Korea   Switzerland   Thailand   Turkey   Ukraine   Vietnam

Oxford is a trade mark of Oxford University Press
in the UK and in certain other countries

Published in Canada
by Oxford University Press

Library and Archives Canada Cataloguing in Publication

Henderson, Eric
The empowered writer : an essential guide to writing, reading & research / Eric
Henderson & Kathleen Moran.

Includes index.
ISBN 978-0-19-543161-2

1. Report writing. 2. Academic writing. 3. English language--Rhetoric.
I. Moran, Kathleen M., 1955- II. Title.

PE1408.H388 2010   808'.042   C2010-900355-1

Cover image: Joe McBride/Corbis

This book is printed on permanent (acid-free) paper ∞.

Printed in Canada.

1 2 3 4 — 13 12 11 10

Contents

From the Publisher   xii
Preface   xvii
Acknowledgements   xviii

1 Basic Skills Development for Today's Student: Writing and Reading   1

Thinking, Writing, and Reading: An Integrated Approach   2
Writing and Thinking   2
    Exercise 1.1   3
Writing and Reading   3
The Composing Process   4
    The Traditional Linear Model   4
    Process-Reflective Writing   5
Thinking and Writing + Reading   7
    Scanning versus Focused Reading   10
    Exercise 1.2   12
Critical Thinking   12
    What Is Critical Thinking?   12
    Applying Critical Thinking   13
    Reading and Critical Thinking   14
    Exercise 1.3   15
    Exercise 1.4   17
    Responding Critically and Analytically through Questions   18
    Exercise 1.5   19
    Exercise 1.6   21
Sample Professional Essay (Excerpt): *How More Information Leads to Less Knowledge* by C. Thompson   23
    Exercise 1.7   24
Word Meanings   25
    Exercise 1.8   27
    Chapter Review Questions   28

2 The Writing Situation   29

Writing Purpose   30
    Exercise 2.1   31
"A" Is for Audience   32
    Reader-based versus Writer-based Prose   33
    Exercise 2.2   34
    Exercise 2.3   35
    Audience Factors   35
    Exercise 2.4   35
    Knowledge and Interest   36
    Writer–Reader Relationship   37

Exercise 2.5   **37**
Exercise 2.6   **37**
Audience Orientation   **38**
Exercise 2.7   **39**
Exercise 2.8   **40**
Exercise 2.9   **41**
Stages in Essay-Writing   41
Pre-writing   **42**
Exercise 2.10   **42**
Exercise 2.11   **44**
Research   **47**
Organization   **48**
Exercise 2.12   **49**
Composing: First Draft   50
Revising: Final Draft   52
Chapter Review Questions   **54**

3   Kinds of Essays   55

Rhetorical Modes of Discourse   56
Expository versus Argumentative Essays   **56**
Narration and Description   **57**
Exercise 3.1   **58**
Exercise 3.2   **58**
The In-Class Essay or Examination Essay   **58**
Exercise 3.3   **64**
The Critical Response   **64**
Sample Professional Essay: *An Enviro's Case for Seal Hunt* **by Terry Glavin   66**
Chapter Review Questions   **72**

4   Paragraph Essentials   73

Introducing the Paragraph   74
Topic Sentences   **74**
Paragraph Wraps as Conclusions   **74**
Connecting Paragraphs by Using Transitions   **75**
Exercise 4.1   **75**
Paragraph Unity   **76**
Exercise 4.2   **77**
Exercise 4.3   **78**
Paragraph Coherence   **78**
Exercise 4.4   **82**
Exercise 4.5   **82**
Exercise 4.6   **84**
Chapter Review Questions   **86**

5   Essay Basics   87

Introductions   88
Functions of Introductions   88
Reader Interest: Logical, Dramatic, and Mixed Approaches   **88**
Exercise 5.1   **90**
Introduction Length   92

Starting at the Beginning   **92**
Exercise 5.2   **93**
Thesis Statements   94
Kinds of Thesis Statements   **94**
Effective Thesis Statements   95
Ineffective Thesis Statements   96
Exercise 5.3   **97**
Exercise 5.4   **98**
Exercise 5.5   **98**
Exercise 5.6   **100**
Outlines   101
The Value of Outlines   **101**
Organizing an Outline   **101**
General Guidelines for Outlines   **102**
Developing an Outline with Thesis Statement   **102**
Conclusions   104
Functions of Conclusions   **104**
Two Kinds of Conclusions   **105**
Exercise 5.7   **106**
Exercise 5.8   **108**
Chapter Review Questions   **108**

6 Paragraph Development   109

Developing Your Essay through Substantial Paragraphs   110
Methods for Developing Paragraphs   110
Analysis and Paragraph Development   **111**
Definition—What Is It?   **112**
Chronology—When Did It Occur?   **112**
Description—What Does It Look Like?   **113**
Narration—How Can It Be Told?   **113**
Process—How Does It Work?   **114**
Personal—Why Should It Affect Me?/How Does or Did It Affect Me?   **114**
Classification/Division—What Kinds Are There?   **115**
Cause–Effect—What Is the Cause?   **115**
Question–Answer—What Is the Answer?   **116**
Example/Illustration—How Can It Be Shown?   **116**
Problem–Solution—How Can It Be (Re)Solved?   **117**
Cost–Benefit—What Are the Advantages and Disadvantages?   **117**
Analogy—How Is It Like Something Else?   **118**
Comparison and Contrast—How Is It Like and/or Unlike Something Else?   **118**
Exercise 6.1   **119**
Exercise 6.2   **120**
Chapter Review Questions   **120**

7 The Design of An Essay   121

The Essay: An Analytical Model   122
Kinds of Claims: Fact, Value, and Policy   122
Claims of Fact   **122**
Claims of Value   **122**
Claims of Policy   **123**

Tentative and Conclusive Claims   **123**
Support: Evidence and Credibility   123
Organization of Evidence   **123**
Kinds of Evidence   **124**
Facts and Statistics   **124**
Authorities and Experts   **125**
Examples, Illustrations, Case Studies, Precedents   **125**
Analogies, Description, Personal Experience   **127**
Credibility   **127**
Exercise 7.1   **129**
Exercise 7.2   **130**
Exercise 7.3   **131**
Chapter Review Questions   **131**

The Expository Essay   132

Expository Writing   133
Types of Expository Essays   133
Exercise 8.1   **136**
The Process Analysis Essay   136
Planning Process Essays   **137**
Writing Process Essays   **137**
Sample Process Essay   139
The Definition Essay   141
Exercise 8.2   **141**
Sample Definition Essay   142
Exercise 8.3   **143**
Exercise 8.4   **143**
The Comparison and Contrast Essay   143
Block and Point-by-Point Methods   **144**
Sample Comparison and Contrast Essay   145
Exercise 8.5   **147**
Exercise 8.6   **147**
Points to Remember   147
Exercise 8.7   **147**
Sample Professional Essay: *The Origins of Leadership* by Mark van Vugt   148
Chapter Review Questions   **152**

Summaries   153

What Is a Summary?   154
Terms Related to Summarizing   154
How to Write Summaries   155
Summary Length   **155**
Main Features of a Summary   **155**
Sample Sentence Summaries   **155**
Exercise 9.1   **156**
Exercise 9.2   **157**
Main Features of an Extended Summary   **157**
Extended Summary Writing Steps   **157**
Summarizing Your Sources   **159**

Summaries and Argument **159**
Using Signal Phrases **159**
Extended Summary Samples **160**
Sample Professional Essay: *Fighting Hockey Violence Will Give You a Concussion* by Jeffrey Simpson 160
Paraphrase and Other Types of Summaries 164
Paraphrase **164**
Exercise 9.3 **165**
Abstract **165**
Exercise 9.4 **165**
Annotated Bibliography **166**
Exercise 9.5 **166**
Summarizing at the Workplace 166
Exercise 9.6 **167**
Chapter Review Questions **168**

10 Research 169

Developing Research Skills 170
Research—Finding and Exploring **171**
Synthesis I—Integration **172**
Organization—Arranging **173**
Synthesis II—Composing **173**
Documenting—Following Rules **174**
What Is Research? 174
Who Are These Experts . . . And Where Can You Find Them? 175
A Note about the Internet 176
Researching Your Topic 177
Exploring **177**
Research Note-Taking **178**
Organizing Research Notes **178**
Cross-Referencing **179**
Some Useful Research Strategies **179**
Using Contradictory Evidence **180**
Sources of Research Material 181
Primary and Secondary Sources **181**
Start Your Research by Looking at Secondary Sources **181**
Internet Searches **183**
Notes on Library Research **186**
Alternative Information Sources **187**
Chapter Review Questions **187**

11 Using Your Research 189

Outlines for Research Essays 190
Plagiarism 194
What Is Plagiarism? **194**
To Cite or Not to Cite? **195**
Integrating Secondary Sources 197
Summary, Paraphrase, Direct Quotation, Mixed Format **197**
Signal Phrases, Ellipses, and Brackets **200**

Documentation: Citations   **203**
    Necessary versus Unnecessary Citations   **203**
Sample Student Research Essay   **203**
    Exercise 11.1   **209**
    Exercise 11.2   **209**
    Chapter Review Questions   **210**

12 APA and MLA Documentation Styles   211

Choosing Your Citation Style   **212**
The Major Documentation Styles   **213**
    APA Citation Style   **213**
    Sample Student Research Essay (APA)   **225**
    MLA Citation Style   **231**
    Sample Student Essay Using MLA Style   **244**
    Exercise 12.1   **251**
Sample Academic Essay   **252**
Sample Academic Essay: *Institutional "Incompleteness": The Challenges in Meeting the Needs of Canada's Urban Aboriginal Population* **by Jack Jedwab**   **253**
    Chapter Review Questions   **261**

13 The Argumentative Essay   262

Emotional versus Logical Arguments   **263**
    Argument, Opinion, and Facts   **265**
    Exercise 13.1   **266**
    Exercise 13.2   **267**
    Exercise 13.3   **267**
    Exercise 13.4   **271**
    Exercise 13.5   **272**
    Exercise 13.6   **278**
    Exercise 13.7   **284**
Sample Professional Argumentative Essay   **284**
Sample Professional Argumentative Essay: *The Beauty of Wind Farms* **by David Suzuki**   **285**
    Exercise 13.8   **288**
    Sample Argumentative Essays   **288**
    Exercise 13.9   **291**
    Chapter Review Questions   **297**

14 Sentence Essentials   298

Grammatical Groundwork   **299**
    Exercise 14.1   **299**
    Exercise 14.2   **299**
The Grammar of Reading and Writing   **300**
Introducing . . . the Parts of Speech   **300**
    The Parts of Speech at Work   **301**
    Nouns and Pronouns   **301**
    Verbs   **304**
    Modifiers: Adjectives and Adverbs   **305**

Joiners: Prepositions and Conjunctions   **306**
Exercise 14.3   **308**
Exercise 14.4   **309**
Introducing . . . the Sentence   309
What Is a Sentence?   **309**
The Invisible-Subject Sentence   **311**
Exercise 14.5   **312**
Four Errors of Incompletion   **312**
Exercise 14.6   **313**
Exercise 14.7   **315**
Exercise 14.8   **316**
Exercise 14.9   **318**
Introducing . . . Phrases and Clauses   318
Phrases   **318**
Exercise 14.10   **320**
Clauses   **321**
Sentence Patterns   **321**
Exercise 14.11   **322**
Exercise 14.12   **324**
Exercise 14.13   **324**
Errors of Combining   **325**
Exercise 14.14   **328**
Exercise 14.15   **328**
Exercise 14.16   **330**
Chapter Review Questions   **330**

15

Commas and Other Forms of Punctuation   331

Do Commas Matter?   332
Rule Category 1: Use Commas to Separate Items in a Series   332
Rule Category 2: Use Commas to Separate Independent Clauses   333
Rule Category 3: Use Two Commas to Separate Parenthetical Information   335
Rule Category 4: Conventional and "Comma Sense" Uses   337
Exercise 15.1   **339**
Exercise 15.2   **340**
Exercise 15.3   **341**
Other Forms of Punctuation   342
Semicolons   **342**
Exercise 15.4   **345**
Colons   345
Dashes and Parentheses   347
Exercise 15.5   **348**
Exercise 15.6   **350**
Exercise 15.7   **351**
Punctuation Prohibitions   352
No-Comma Rules   **352**
No-Semicolon Rules   **353**
Apostrophes   353
Exercise 15.8   **356**
Exercise 15.9   **357**
Chapter Review Questions   **358**

16

Agreement, Pronoun, and Sentence Structure Errors   359

Agreement   360
Subject–Verb Agreement   **360**
Pronouns at Work   365
Pronoun–Antecedent Agreement   **365**
Problematic Pronouns: Inclusive Language   **367**
Exercise 16.1   **368**
Exercise 16.2   **368**
Exercise 16.3   **369**
Other Problems with Pronouns   370
Pronoun Reference   **370**
Exercise 16.4   **370**
Exercise 16.5   **374**
Exercise 16.6   **374**
Exercise 16.7   **375**
Pronoun Case   **376**
Exercise 16.8   **380**
Pronoun Consistency   **381**
Exercise 16.9   **381**
Sentence Construction Errors   382
Misplaced Modifiers   **382**
Dangling Modifiers   **385**
Exercise 16.10   **387**
Exercise 16.11   **387**
The Parallelism Principle   **389**
Exercise 16.12   **395**
Exercise 16.13   **396**
Exercise 16.14   **398**
Exercise 16.15   **400**
Exercise 16.16   **402**
Chapter Review Questions   **403**

17

Achieving Clarity and Depth in Your Writing   404

Effective Style: Clarity   405
Exercise 17.1   **406**
Exercise 17.2   **406**
Cutting for Conciseness   **407**
Exercise 17.3   **409**
Writing Directly   **411**
Exercise 17.4   **412**
Exercise 17.5   **414**
Exercise 17.6   **417**
Exercise 17.7   **418**
Exercise 17.8   **419**
Working Toward Precision: Wise Word Choices   **419**
Exercise 17.9   **420**

Exercise 17.10 **423**
Exercise 17.11 **424**
Exercise 17.12 **424**
Exercise 17.13 **425**
Providing Depth: Variety and Emphasis 425
Sentence Variety **425**
Exercise 17.14 **426**
Exercise 17.15 **426**
Creating Emphasis **427**
Proofreading: Perfection *Is* Possible 429
Proofreading Methods **430**
Guidelines for Proofreading **430**
Common Errors **431**
Essay Presentation 431
Common Words That Confuse 433
Exercise 17.16 **440**
Chapter Review Questions **441**

Appendices

A **Tense Encounters with Verbs: A Summary 442**
1. Present Tenses 442
2. Past Tenses 443
3. Future Tenses 443
Exercise **444**

B **A Checklist for EAL Writers 446**
Adjectives 446
Adverbs 448
Articles—*A, An, The* 449
Nouns 453
Verbs 455
Additional Commonly Confused Words and Idioms 464

C **Peer Edit Forms 470**
Peer Edit Form: Formal Outline 470
Peer Edit Form: Argumentative Essay First Draft 472
Peer Edit Form: Research Essay First Draft 474

D **Partial Answer Key 476**
Chapters 14, 15, 16 Exercise Answers 476

E **Glossary of Important Terms 495**

Index 510

From the Publisher

Oxford University Press is delighted to introduce *The Empowered Writer*, an original text with an innovative approach to the writing process.

Tailored specifically to college and university students in undergraduate composition courses, *The Empowered Writer* offers a detailed and widely applicable method for developing skills in research and writing as well as in personal and business communication. Key principles are illustrated through sample professional and student essays and reinforced through carefully crafted, classroom-tested exercises that encourage students to empower themselves as writers in training: to actively participate in honing their skills, to make informed choices, and to think deeply and critically about how—and why—they write.

We hope that as you browse through the pages that follow, you will see why we believe *The Empowered Writer* is the most exciting and innovative new textbook for Canadian students of writing and composition.

◎ Exceptional Features of *The Empowered Writer*

- **Abundant exercises**. Well over a hundred exercises designed to be completed individually or in groups provide students with ample opportunity to practise and refine their skills. Exercises include
  - pre- and post-reading exercises
  - end-of-chapter review questions
  - documentation exercises
  - grammar exercises
  - collaborative assignments.

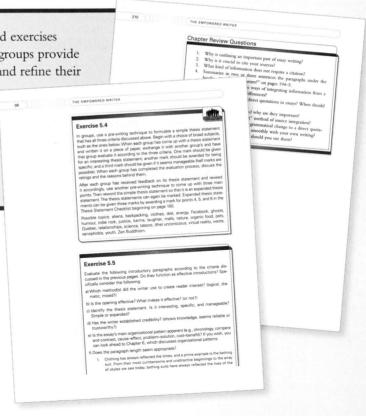

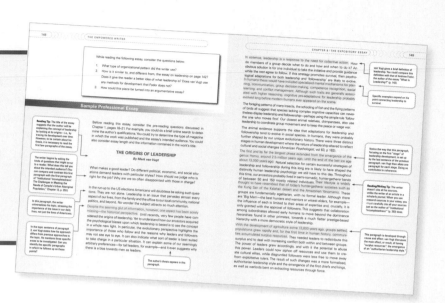

■ **High-interest professional essays.** Accessible selections by working writers cover topics of particular interest to students— including wind farms and hockey violence—encouraging readers to engage with the material. Marginal annotations highlight techniques for students to follow.

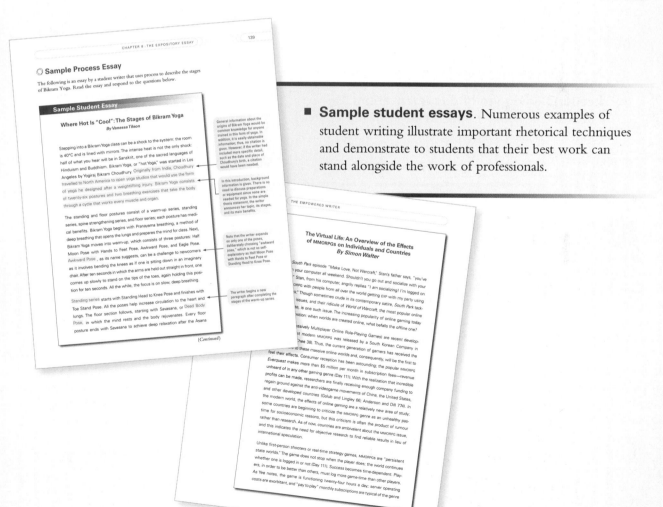

■ **Sample student essays.** Numerous examples of student writing illustrate important rhetorical techniques and demonstrate to students that their best work can stand alongside the work of professionals.

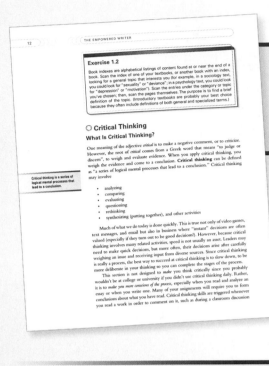

- **Critical thinking focus**. The authors encourage students to think critically about their plans and purposes for writing in order to better structure their work and carry out research more effectively.

- **Thorough coverage of documentation**. The authors outline both MLA and APA documentation styles, making the book a valuable resource for students in a wide variety of disciplines.

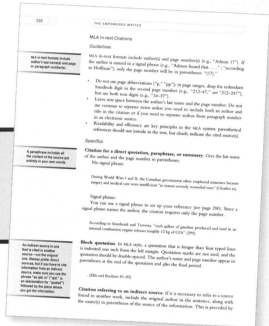

- **Checklist for EAL writers**. Students of English as an additional language will benefit from an appendix that clarifies common idiomatic words and phrases and matters of usage that native English speakers often take for granted.

- **Helpful marginal notes** provide useful writing tips, summaries of content, and a running glossary. Marginal definitions, together with definitions that appear in the running text, are compiled in a glossary for handy reference.

- **Explanatory visuals** present key concepts in ways designed to assist student comprehension.

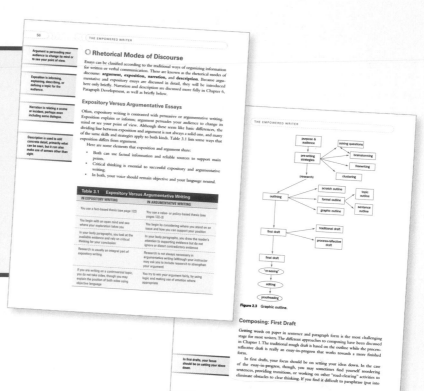

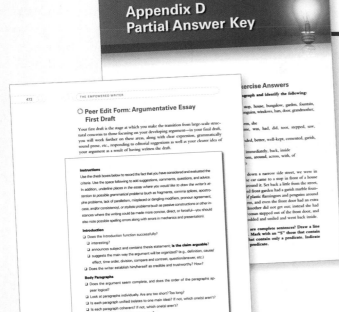

- **Peer editing forms** are provided to assist students in evaluating the work of their classmates.

- **Partial answer key** enables students to check their progress but leaves some exercises unsolved so that they may be assigned as graded coursework.

◎ For More Information: Online Resources

The Empowered Writer is but the central element in a comprehensive package of learning and teaching tools that includes resources for both students and instructors.

For Instructors

- An **instructor's manual** features chapter overviews and summaries, examples of key concepts, suggestions for in-class and take-home writing assignments, suggested print and online resources, and much more.

- A comprehensive **test generator** enables instructors to sort, edit, import, and distribute hundreds of questions in multiple-choice, short-answer, and essay formats.

For Students

- Student exercises include self-grading quizzes, consisting of multiple-choice and short-answer questions with answers, as well as practice mid-term and final exams.

◎ Acknowledgements

We would like to acknowledge the following reviewers, along with those reviewers who wish to remain anonymous, whose thoughtful comments and suggestions have helped to shape *The Empowered Writer*.

Veronica Abbass, Seneca College
Trevor Arkell, Humber College
Paula Crooks, Conestoga College
Mark Feltham, Fanshawe College
Lynn Gresham, Conestoga College
Tom Gwin, Red Deer College
Chandra Hodgson, Humber College
Amanda Johnstone, Conestoga College
Louise Lloyd, Conestoga College
Roneen Marcoux, University College of the Fraser Valley

Preface

There are many books currently available that help students learn how to write at the college or university level. This particular text, while addressing the same material, differs by taking a more academic approach to the subject. For example, the student samples are genuine, coming from students who have taken courses with us or our colleagues. These samples are either actual essays, summaries, or excerpts, not pieces that follow a journalistic style. The professional essays that we have chosen to include in *The Empowered Writer* also follow the rules set out in this text. While a few of the samples use a journalistic style of writing, students generally are not asked to read about how to write an essay and then asked to analyze a piece that does not follow the same stylistic rules they have been learning.

Critical thinking is an essential skill for any successful writer at this level, and so the term is introduced and explained in detail from the outset, in Chapter 1. The application of critical thinking is then stressed throughout the following chapters. Students are also introduced to the differences between expository writing and argumentative writing, and clear examples, often with annotations, are provided so that the readers can see the differences. In addition, an extensive section about research and how to properly integrate and present sources in an essay outlines the most current practices used in APA and MLA documentation.

Writers at this level are typically required to use a more elaborate writing style than they have been accustomed to using. Unfortunately, many students take this to mean using more words, rather than choosing the most accurate words or phrases. The later chapters help students build on grammar rules they already know, so that their grammatical structures reflect a higher level of writing. A section about style will help students learn to write clearly and concisely, developing a skill that is valued in the workplace.

We have included a chapter to deal exclusively with summary writing, both as a stand-alone task and as a means to incorporate research material in an essay. Again, the student summaries that we have included to illustrate the concepts discussed are genuine, having come from students we have taught. Several of these summaries relate to the full-length essays found in *The Empowered Writer*, so learners can try their hand at summary writing before comparing their product with what other students have produced in the past.

Finally, the book includes chapter objectives, extensive exercises, and chapter summary questions. By involving the student and encouraging the completion of these exercises, we hope that students will apply what they have learned often enough that writing no longer seems an irksome task but a satisfying one.

Acknowledgements

I would like to thank Eric Henderson for allowing me to collaborate with him on *The Empowered Writer*. I would also like to thank Tim McCleary for his support and encouragement from the very beginning. My colleagues also provided invaluable feedback, for which I am grateful. Additionally, I am indebted to my family for the love and support shown through this project (especially when I lugged the computer along on vacations). Finally, I would like to thank my many students over the years. Their dedication to writing and learning has been a large part of the inspiration for this textbook.

K.M. Moran
January 2010

Kathleen Moran's keen sense of purpose initiated the process. I am indebted to many at Oxford University Press for their diligence and support throughout the book's development, including Eric Sinkins, Leslie Saffrey, Jacqueline Mason, and Arlene Miller.

Closer to home, the following individuals at the University of Victoria gave me their invaluable input and time, and I am very appreciative: Li-Shih Huang, Sandra Kirkham, Danielle Russell, and Joe Gibson.

Closest to home, the patience, support, and love of my family has been a vital and sustaining force in this project, as in every project I undertake.

Eric Henderson
January 2010

Basic Skills Development for Today's Student: Writing and Reading

In this chapter, you will

- learn about the differences between product and process approaches to writing

- learn about how reading, thinking, and writing are involved in the composition process

- learn reading strategies by asking important questions

- learn to understand the value of critical thinking

- learn how to read unfamiliar words in context and improve your vocabulary for writing at the college or university level

The writing process involves more than just putting pen to paper or entering thoughts in a word-processing program. This chapter will explain the importance of thinking, reading, and writing in the composing process. In addition, you will examine how to begin to organize an essay. Finally, the importance of critical thinking in the reading and writing process is discussed, along with guidelines for recognizing word meanings.

◎ Thinking, Writing, and Reading: An Integrated Approach

Student writers and professional writers have more in common than the fact they work with words and have to meet deadlines. They both know through experience that writing is hard work. It's often said that successful writers make writing look easy. But this cliché is countered by the well-known saying by Thomas Edison that genius is "1 per cent inspiration and 99 per cent perspiration." Certainly, "hard" does not mean hopeless. Composition textbooks, like this one, are designed to explain the task of writing by introducing you to practical methods and strategies to make the writing experience more rewarding throughout your college or university career. In addition, it's likely that your future jobs will involve at least some writing, so the writing skills you acquire will serve you well in the workplace. This is because good writing, no matter what the situation, involves organizing your thoughts logically, choosing your words carefully, and crafting documents that make sense to the reader.

In recent years, two approaches to essay writing—the product and process approaches—have received attention. The first stresses the goal, which is identified and kept in focus throughout. In the second approach, the process is emphasized; the final result is revealed as you work with your topic. Of course, these approaches are not mutually exclusive. Most writing you do is designed to meet a clear objective, and how you get there—your process—will affect the nature of the product itself. In other words, product usually assumes a process, while a process inevitably leads to something, such as a new skill, a new perspective, or a new awareness, brought about perhaps by your discovery of something you didn't know before.

The division between product and process is certainly not unique to essay writing. Most life skills and life experiences, including essay writing, combine these two approaches. Summaries of the two models, or "templates," for essay writing based on these two approaches start on page 4. Each offers an overview of writing—of the process and the product—and introduces you to concepts that will often arise as you write. But before we look at these models, it will be useful to examine how writing and thinking are related and how this relationship can challenge the writer. We will then briefly consider how reading fits into the equation.

> Good writing, no matter what the situation, involves organizing your thoughts logically, choosing your words carefully, and crafting documents that make sense to the reader.

◎ Writing and Thinking

What does it mean when a reader of an essay comments that the writer "didn't put much thought into it" or that the writer "put a lot of thought into it"? It might mean that, in the first case, the writer approached the task mechanically, doing what was required but no more. In the second case, perhaps the writer spent a long time thinking about the topic, planning the best approach and the ways that he or she might exceed the expectations of the instructor.

Exercise 1.1

Most people pursue the mastery of a skill or a hobby. Choose a skill or hobby of interest to you.

First, write down your spontaneous thoughts and feelings on this skill or hobby without stopping to edit yourself; give yourself 5 or 10 minutes for this. Then, in one or two paragraphs, answer the specific questions asked.

What is your ultimate goal in pursuing the skill or hobby? Is it always the same? Describe how you attain this goal. Are there different ways the goal could be approached? Which do you enjoy more: working towards a goal or achieving the goal? Why?

But simply stating that one "put thought" into an essay oversimplifies the relationship between thinking and writing. The first writer may, indeed, have spent as much time and thought on his or her essay as the second writer but, for one reason or another, the product did not appear as thoughtful or "finished" as the second essay. It can often be difficult or unfair to judge the writer's effort. For this reason, writing must be considered inseparable from thinking.

If you are like many writers, you may have found yourself "thinking out loud" as you contemplate your topic, or you may find yourself reading sentences aloud to get a better sense of your thought processes. Such natural responses underscore this complex relationship between thought and writing, which involves translating abstract ideas into concrete words. Furthermore, once you have set words down on paper or on a computer screen, you have to ask yourself whether these words reflect exactly what you meant to say. Although language takes a more concrete form than ideas, getting words onto the page is simply one important step in the process.

◎ Writing and Reading

Where does reading fit into this process? What actually happens when we read? Researchers are uncertain, but they do know that reading involves more than determining the meaning of each successive word. When we read, we look at larger units than the individual words, constantly anticipating content based on our familiarity with the reading experience and on the context of what we are currently reading. When you read, you are in effect processing or "translating" the thoughts of a writer, using both language and your understanding of the way it operates. Like writing, it is a complex process.

Some studies have shown that good readers tend to be good writers. Thus, studying the works of other writers can help you improve your own writing. This means you must first clearly understand the writer's language, both the individual words themselves and their combined meaning (see Thinking and Writing + Reading on page 7, and Word Meanings, page 25). "Active" reading usually involves more than simple comprehension, and most college- and university-level assignments will require you to do more than read for understanding. Studying the works of other writers can sharpen your critical thinking skills, as discussed below (Critical Thinking).

Most of what you read is in a finished form (exceptions include your rough drafts or those of your peers). In other words, you read a "product." Although the product is "finished" in this sense, it's usually possible to see how it was put together. For example, in every well-constructed piece of writing, you should be able to identify the main ideas. This is especially important if you are summarizing a work, perhaps in order to use it in your own essay. Also, there may be other features of the work that you can identify—for example, the writer's purpose in writing, whom it was written for, the writer's style, or specific strategies used to communicate meaning or tone. By analyzing any of these features, you can enlarge your own understanding and appreciation of the writing process to make you a more effective writer.

> By analyzing the features of a written work, you can enlarge your own understanding and appreciation of the writing process to make you a more effective writer.

◎ The Composing Process

Essay writing gives students the opportunity to exercise many kinds of thinking. To come up with a topic and develop it, you will probably begin with a concept. You will try to make connections in order to narrow the topic's scope and make it manageable. Most kinds of writing activate different skills at different times. In addition to linear or associative thinking, you might use analysis (breaking down) and synthesis (putting together). The various approaches to the thinking–writing process may stress one activity over another, but they all have one aim in common: to make you more conscious of how you write in order to make your writing more successful and, hopefully, more enjoyable.

The Traditional Linear Model

The **linear model** is one of the most common models of essay writing. It takes shape as a written "product," usually an essay or report, after clearly defining a goal (purpose), thinking about it (pre-writing), planning it (research and outlining), drafting it, and revising it. The five-paragraph essay is the most well-known example of such a written product. With an introduction containing a thesis statement, three body paragraphs with clear topic sentences and examples, and a conclusion that restates the thesis, the five-paragraph essay has proven adaptable to many different situations. However, it is important to remember that the five-paragraph essay is just a template and will not work for all situations. You will have to make choices about what information to include and how to best organize your thoughts so that your reader clearly understands your ideas. In order to do this, you may require more than five paragraphs, though in some writing assignments, you may need fewer than five paragraphs.

> It is important to remember that the five-paragraph essay is just a template and will not work for all situations.

Although essay writing is usually considered a linear, sequential process, that doesn't mean you will always follow a predictable order from start to finish. Sometimes no matter how much planning you do, you may find yourself looking for a stronger example, adding a detail, maybe even rethinking your organization. But even when you discover, say, in the first draft that the order of points isn't logical and you need to return to the outline and reorder these points, the process can still be considered linear—going backwards before going forwards again. Writing an essay is more like looking for a lost object or like a treasure hunt, in which you may have to double back or look twice in the same place. However, the traditional linear model recognizes that virtually all writing has a goal and distinct stages along the way, though the means used to get to the goal can vary.

The first of the traditional stages of essay writing is *inventing*, an explorative stage in which you may start with nothing more than a subject area, a topic, or perhaps something even less defined. This is where pre-writing strategies can help: systematic methods to generate ideas when you are otherwise faced with "writer's block." When you have enough ideas and have made connections among some of them, you may be ready to express your thesis (a statement about your topic). For a look at thesis statements, see pages 94–5.

As you continue expanding and exploring, you will soon find yourself able to construct an outline to clarify the relationships among the main points. The further you move along in the process in the traditional linear model, the less you will be *thinking about* a topic and the more you will be relying on specific methods and forms with measurable objectives. After constructing an outline, you will begin your rough draft, trying to create unified, coherent, and developed paragraphs. After you have completed the draft, you will revise it by paying particular attention to grammar, punctuation, sentence structure, and mechanics. One practical benefit of learning and using this traditional model is that it directly applies to a large number of school and workplace tasks, in which objectives are clearly defined and form is important—such as scientific experiments and business letters. This model can be adapted to a variety of specialized functions.

> Applied to format, mechanics include margin size, space between sentences, font size and type, and page numbers; applied to writing, they include abbreviations, capital letters, hyphenation, and numbers.

> The traditional linear method breaks down writing into successive stages, each of which involves characteristic activities.

Process-Reflective Writing

Typically, composing involves periods of intense activity balanced by periods of reflection, which may lead you to further develop an idea, to qualify it, or perhaps to abandon it in favour of another line of thought. You may stop to recall, to analyze, or to reconsider. Another characteristic activity is looking over what you have written.

As you write, your thinking is affected in two related ways: a choice, once made, excludes choices that may have existed before, but it also creates new options. In this way, what you *have written* serves to give direction to what you *will* write. By writing down your thoughts, you become conscious of them, and they become subject to your control. As a result, your thinking becomes clearer. Just as it is said that clear thinking produces clear writing, writing (especially clear writing) produces clearer and more directed thinking. In process-reflective writing, you *reflect on* your process in order to make your writing and your thinking clearer.

Process-reflective writing focuses on the necessary connection between writing and thinking, the back-and-forth nature of the composing process in which thinking alternates with writing, and rethinking with rewriting. In-class writing

> In process-reflective writing, you reflect on your process in order to make your writing and your thinking clearer.

and other kinds of timed writing require your immersion in the writing experience, during which you may ask yourself these kinds of questions: Where have I been going? Is my purpose the same as it was when I started? Where am I going now? How does what I have said determine what I need to say? What do I need to say (or do) to get me closer to my goal? How can my previous idea be expanded, illustrated, or linked to my next idea?

After you have provided the bridge to the next idea, you can consider the same set of questions to guide you to your next point. As the draft proceeds, you become more conscious of structure by building on what has come before. In this way, too, transitions provide the stepping stones for your reader to follow. Here are some tips for process-reflective writing:

- Look for appropriate transitions (word or phrase connectors; see Chapter 4), since they reveal shifts in thought.
- Ask if your transitions reflect the relationships between ideas that you want to convey.
- If you are uncertain that your words reflect your intended meaning, try rephrasing a previous point and choose the wording that best captures your meaning.
- Don't worry about grammatical or mechanical errors; the focus should be on clarity and the complete expression of your ideas.
- If you feel tentative about where a point is going, consider leaving an extra line and use a previous sentence or point as a new starting place.
- Keep your thesis in mind throughout, but don't be afraid to depart from it if necessary; it can be changed or reworded later.

Typical activities of process-reflective writing are questioning, clarifying, expanding, and emphasizing. Process-reflective drafts are often longer than final drafts, since the purpose of reflection is to generate clearer thinking, and a trial-and-error approach may be needed to achieve this clarity. The rough draft will probably not be a polished product. In addition to correcting grammar, word choice, and mechanics in later drafts, you also may need to rephrase your ideas to make them clearer. You may also eliminate what seems incompatible with the thesis or explain an idea further to bring it in line with your thesis.

In the process-reflective approach, you may not need a formal outline, but you should be clear on your purpose and thesis before writing. This can be done through intensive pre-writing activities. You may want to construct an outline after writing the rough draft, though an outline often is discovered within the draft itself. Instead of submitting outlines or rough drafts for written feedback, writers following this method can submit partial drafts: at least an introduction and first body paragraph. You and your peer editors can discuss potential further development of the paragraph, such as what links could be used to connect it to a hypothetical following paragraph. Reflecting on purpose, audience, thesis, and your main points with a peer is one way to clarify your thinking.

Table 1.1	The Two Approaches to the Composing Process	
	TRADITIONAL LINEAR	**PROCESS-REFLECTIVE**
Content	Focused on what you need to write	Focused on what you are writing
Typical activities	Following an outline, developing sub-points, giving detail, illustrating, completing	Clarifying, evaluating, reflecting, questioning, emphasizing, filling gaps, connecting
Typical questions	Are my points relevant? Do my sub-points develop my main points? Are they ordered logically?	How did I get here? Where am I going from here? How can I get there? What will make my thinking clearer?
Typical number of drafts	Two: a rough draft getting down ideas and a draft focused on the revision processes, including clarity	Two: a first draft focused on content and clarity and a second focused on revision, mechanics, and cutting repetition
Potential uses	Typical workplace writing tasks; some academic writing; business and science reports; research essays	Exam writing; some professional and academic writing

Table 1.1 compares the two approaches to the composing process. Although their distinct qualities are stressed here, in reality, writers often use different composing methods at different times without necessarily being conscious of using one or the other.

◎ Thinking and Writing + Reading

Most of us read for pleasure, at least sometimes. This reading can include novels, magazines, student newspapers, or web pages. Even when you read for pleasure, though, you are examining the text more than you may think. On one level, of course, you are reading words for meaning. While you are reading, you are continually interpreting the words—their meanings and associations—which combine to create an overarching pattern of meaning.

Reading to grasp content is essentially "passive" or "one-way" reading. But this one-way activity becomes two-way when you begin responding to the text. In a novel or short story, you may make personal associations—recollections, emotions, desires—or experience the simple pleasure of escaping into another world that is, in some way, like your own. Consider, for example, the beginning of the short story "Friend of My Youth," by Alice Munro:

I used to dream about my mother, and though the details in the dream varied, the surprise in it was always the same. . . . In the dream I would be the age I really was, living the life I was really living, and then I would discover that my mother was still alive. . . . Sometimes I would find myself in our old kitchen, where my mother would be rolling out piecrust on the table, or washing the dishes in the battered cream-colored dishpan with the red rim. But other times I would run into her on the street, in places where I would never have expected to see her.

—Munro, Alice. *Friend of My Youth.*
Toronto: Penguin, 1991 Print.

In theory, a person could read this passage merely by focusing on the meanings of the words and trying to grasp the literal meaning of the passage. But most readers will find themselves forming associations that reflect their experience and outlook.

Ask yourself the following questions about the passage:

1. What is a dream?
2. Where was her mother washing dishes?

These questions focus on the literal meaning of the words. Look at the next set of questions. These ideas are the ones that help you form associations and help you understand the meaning beyond the words. These associations are often what help us enjoy reading.

1. Have you ever dreamed about family members?
2. Do your dreams ever differ from reality?
3. Have you ever dreamed about someone you haven't seen in a long time?

Now, consider the beginning of another text, also about dreams, roughly the same length as the first:

Religion was the original field of dream study. The earliest writings we have on dreams are primarily texts on their religious and spiritual significance. Long before psychoanalysts, sleep laboratory researchers, and content analysts arrived on the scene, religious specialists were exploring dreams in a variety of ways: using dreams in initiation rituals, developing techniques to incubate revelatory dreams and ward off evil nightmares, expressing numerous dream images in different artistic forms, and elaborating sophisticated interpretive systems that related dreams to beliefs about the soul, death, morality, and fate.

—Doniger, W. & Bulkley, K. (1993). Why study dreams? A religious studies perspective. *Dreaming: Journal of the Association of Dreams, 3*(1), 69–73.

One difference between your responses to the two passages might have occurred at the literal level of the words. What do the following mean?

• "content analysts"
• "incubate revelatory dreams"

These phrases might have caused you to reach for a dictionary, while in the first passage, it is less likely the language would have been unfamiliar.

In reading the paragraph by Doniger and Bulkley, you no doubt went beyond one-way reading. Though you may have formed some personal associations, you probably reacted more critically: the writers were making general statements about the use of dreams in religious societies and cultures, and you were probably beginning to consider the use of dreams in this or a similar context. If you continued to read the article, you would have begun to make certain inferences and draw conclusions based on the writers' statements and the way they were presented. You would have, perhaps, begun to test the writers' points for logic and consistency as well as against your own experience. When testing this, we ask the following questions:

- Is the claim (statement) logical?
- Is it valid considering the circumstances?
- Is it truthful?
- Is it reliable?
- Is it consistent with previous claims?

When you engage in this process and ask these kinds of questions, you are responding *critically* to a work (see Critical Thinking, page 12).

A writer may say something directly or may present evidence from which the reader can draw a conclusion. For example, Doniger and Bulkley provide factual evidence that ancient societies developed highly sophisticated methods for studying dreams. The writers don't directly say that the ancient methods were as complex as those used in today's dream research, but readers could make that **inference**.

> Inference is a conclusion we make based on the evidence presented; the corresponding verb is *infer*.

The main point is that while both passages require you to react at some level beyond that of simple comprehension, the second passage calls forth a more critical response. In critical thinking, you use two-way reading to determine the validity of an author's statements, to test them by considering the logic and consistency behind them, and to decide whether the evidence supports the author's claims.

The main difference between what we usually call "reading" (that is, "two-way reading") and what's called "three-way reading" or *3-D* (Dimensional) *reading* is that in the latter you respond *consciously and analytically* to the text. Reading actively establishes the connection between the *what* and the *how* of an essay. Being fully engaged in the reading–thinking–writing process develops your writing skills, as well as your reading and thinking skills. A critical analysis of academic work involves both a critical *and* an analytical focus.

> 3-D reading at the college and university level means taking a three-step approach to the acts of reading/thinking/writing where you
>
> 1. focus on understanding
> 2. use critical thinking to test the validity of the statements
> 3. analyze and evaluate the work, considering the methods and strategies that the writer has employed to make it effective (or not).

As a homework assignment, you may be asked to write a response based on a 3-D reading of an essay you've studied. As you respond in writing following this method, you complete the cycle that incorporates reading–thinking–writing: you read a text; you think about it critically; you write about those thoughts, making them conscious and thereby closing the cycle of learning that started with reading. You can then go back and begin the cycle again by rereading the piece, rethinking it, and, perhaps, responding to your more developed perceptions by writing about them again. Responding to essays and thinking about the conscious choices

Responding to essays and thinking about the conscious choices that the writer made will lead you to reflect on your own writing processes and enable you to make sound and *conscious* choices in your own writing.

that the writer made will lead you to reflect on your own writing processes and enable you to make sound and *conscious* choices in your own writing.

Active Reading
Reading to Understand Meaning (Content) → *One-Way Reading*
Reading to Respond (Associative/Critical) → **Two-Way Reading**
Reading to Analyze Techniques (Analytical) → *3-D Reading*

The active-reading model above is not intended to illustrate levels of reading complexity. In a scholarly article, for example, it may be quite difficult just to grasp content, and understanding the precise meaning of certain terms might be the key to analyzing the article. What is usually true, though, is that these levels represent a "progressive" approach to reading where it is first necessary to understand content before proceeding to respond critically or analytically. Thus, active reading *at all three levels* is essential to your success in responding to the kinds of challenging texts you encounter at the college or university level.

Scanning Versus Focused Reading

The process of analyzing a work may sound intimidating, and you may think that a lot is being asked of you when asked to analyze. But remember that college- or university-level reading is not always detailed, microscopic reading. Rather, there are purposes for which scanning is useful just as there are purposes for which it is necessary to read for detail.

First, different kinds of reading may be needed depending on subject matter: for history, close reading dominates; poetry often requires intensive analysis at the level of letters in words; sociology necessitates seeking particular patterns of information, often of the kind that can be outlined; mathematics and chemistry may have to be read even more closely than poetry; and so on. But all you read will not require this level of precision. Thus, it is important to distinguish between different types of **selective reading**, such as scanning and focused reading, in which you have a clear purpose in mind.

Selective reading is a reading strategy designed to meet a specific objective, such as scanning for main points or reading for details.

When you **scan**, you read for the gist of an essay or its main points, or to identify another specific feature. To scan effectively, you often need to know where to look. For example, if you want to know the gist of a reading, you might scan the introduction; for main ideas, you might look at the first sentences of paragraphs (they are often topic sentences). You could also scan a table of contents or list of references for **keywords**. Note that scanning as defined above is not the same thing as idle browsing where you casually read to see what interests you. Like focused reading, scanning is reading with a purpose.

Scanning is a reading strategy in which you look for key words or sections of a text.

When you practise **focused reading**, you concentrate on smaller blocks of text. Sentences are read carefully for detail, and sometimes for tone or style. In this sense, focused reading is specialized reading—it asks you to become a specialist (historian, literary critic, sociologist, mathematician) in your reading of the text.

Focused reading is a close and detailed (i.e., word-by-word) reading of a specific, relevant passage.

In college- and university-level reading, scanning is often combined with focused reading. There are stages to follow that will help you conduct research thoroughly:

1. When you begin research, you need to be able to scan catalogue entries, journal indexes, book contents pages and indexes, reference books, and other types of sources in order to find materials to support your essay topic.

2. Once you have located most of your secondary sources, you will need to scan them to determine which are the most valuable for your purpose, so that you begin your focused reading with the most useful.

3. Then, you will scan individual articles, books, and websites to identify the main ideas.

4. After identifying the areas most relevant to your topic, you will then read closely to understand them and see how they fit with your thesis or with the ideas of other writers.

Scanning and focused reading are most effective when you employ them as deliberate strategies, asking specific questions in order to get as much from the reading as possible without wasting your valuable time by reading everything closely. Guidelines and strategies for selective reading are discussed in Responding Critically and Analytically through Questions, page 18. Some basic strategies for scanning and focused reading are outlined below.

Table 1.2   Basic Strategies for Scanning and Focused Reading

SCANNING	FOCUSED READING
Scanning begins when you know your purpose for reading and what you are looking for	Focused reading begins when you have identified important or relevant passages
Knowing *where* to look will help you scan efficiently	Breaking down the passage will help you access complex material—for example, separating main points from sub-points, and claims from supporting details and examples
In scanning, you will skip much of the text, isolating only the most relevant areas	Read the passage first for comprehension; then, apply active-reading skills
With practice, scanning can be done quickly	Although focused reading is a methodical process, frequent practice will enable you to read faster and at a greater depth
Activities associated with scanning include note taking and cross-referencing (see pages 178–9)	Activities associated with focused reading include summarizing, paraphrasing, and direct quotation (see pages 197–200)

> ### Exercise 1.2
>
> Book indexes are alphabetical listings of content found at or near the end of a book. Scan the index of one of your textbooks, or another book with an index, looking for a general topic that interests you (for example, in a sociology text, you could look for "sexuality" or "deviance"; in a psychology text, you could look for "depression" or "motivation"). Scan the entries under the category or topic you've chosen; then, scan the pages themselves. The purpose is to find a brief definition of the topic. (Introductory textbooks are probably your best choice because they often include definitions of both general and specialized terms.)

◎ Critical Thinking

What Is Critical Thinking?

One meaning of the adjective *critical* is to make a negative comment, or to criticize. However, the root of *critical* comes from a Greek word that means "to judge or discern", to weigh and evaluate evidence. When you apply critical thinking, you weigh the evidence and come to a conclusion. **Critical thinking** can be defined as "a series of logical mental processes that lead to a conclusion." Critical thinking may involve

> Critical thinking is a series of logical mental processes that lead to a conclusion.

- analyzing
- comparing
- evaluating
- questioning
- rethinking
- synthesizing (putting together), and other activities

Much of what we do today is done quickly. This is true not only of video games, text messages, and email but also in business where "instant" decisions are often valued (especially if they turn out to be good decisions!). However, because critical thinking involves many related activities, speed is not usually an asset. Leaders may need to make quick decisions, but more often, their decisions arise after carefully weighing an issue and receiving input from diverse sources. Since critical thinking is really a process, the best way to succeed at critical thinking is to slow down, to be more deliberate in your thinking so you can complete the stages of the process.

This section is not designed to *make* you think critically since you probably wouldn't be at college or university if you didn't use critical thinking daily. Rather, it is to *make you more conscious of the process,* especially when you read and analyze an essay or when you write one. Many of your assignments will require you to form conclusions about what you have read. Critical thinking skills are triggered whenever you read a work in order to comment on it, such as during a classroom discussion or debate, or to use it for support in your essay. The pages on Responding Critically and Analytically through Questions that follow this section focus on helping you become a careful reader who asks important, relevant questions.

Applying Critical Thinking

Critical thinking skills also apply to many everyday situations—from deciding what courses to take to what clothes to wear. Although choosing clothes might seem trivial, consider the importance of comparing, questioning, weighing, and rethinking if you were deciding on an outfit for an important job interview. What factors might affect your choice? They could range from the type of job you were applying for, the company that was hiring, the clothes you feel most confident in, or the weather on the day of the interview.

Critical thinking, then, involves making choices, but the most highly developed critical thinking is more than simple choice-making: it involves making the *best* choice given a range of possibilities. When you are reading an essay or book or evaluating a real-life situation, you are often not directly told what to think. A writer (or situation) might present the evidence and leave you to infer the meaning. When you **infer**, you arrive at a probable conclusion based on what you read (or see). The *best* inference is the *most probable* one after all the evidence is weighed.

Much research relies on inferences: astronomers, for example, study the phenomenon of black holes by observing the behaviour of matter that surrounds the black hole. They know that before gas is swallowed up by a black hole, it is heated to extreme temperatures and accelerates. In the process, X-rays are created, which escape the black hole and reveal its presence. Scientists cannot actually see black holes, but they can *infer* their existence through the emission of X-rays.

> Inference is a conclusion we make based on the evidence presented; the corresponding verb is *infer*.

Consider the following situation:

You invite a new friend for a coffee, but she does not show up. The next day, you meet her unexpectedly and ask her what happened. She pauses for a few seconds and then says matter-of-factly, "Well, actually, I was abducted by aliens, and they just released me." What do you make of her statement? What inferences are possible? Which are more likely? What could you say or do to ensure that your conclusion was the most probable one?

Possible inferences:

Probable inferences:

How to ensure that your inference is correct:

You use critical thinking as you read whenever you evaluate and draw conclusions about claims, and the evidence or sources of these claims. It is important to remember that **critical thinking** is a *process of engagement* with a text (or a situation) that may change as you read (or learn more about the situation).

Reading closely, then, means becoming more conscious of how you interact with an unfamiliar text, being open to challenges to your own ways of thinking, but not being swayed by other views unless they stand up to the tests of logic and consistency. The critical thinker questions assumptions, tests the evidence, and accepts (or rejects) conclusions after careful analysis. When questions arise, the critical thinker seeks for answers within the text itself, but may also consider relevant knowledge from personal experience or from outside sources. For example, in the situation described above, you might ask the woman's friends about her belief in aliens—or about her sense of humour.

In analyzing arguments, the critical thinker should carefully evaluate all claims made by the writer and look for failures in logic or misuse of emotion (see logical fallacies, pages 268–70). He or she should also consider points that the writer *doesn't* raise. Is the writer avoiding certain issues by not mentioning them? Expository (fact-based) writing can also produce disagreement and contradictory findings. For example, researchers determining the effectiveness of a new drug or investigating the connection between television viewing and violence may arrive at very different conclusions though their methods appear credible. What can account for the differing results? Attempting to answer this question involves critical thinking, too.

> Critical thinking is a *process of engagement* with a text (or situation) that may change as you read (or learn more about the situation).

Reading and Critical Thinking

As we read, we may not be aware that we are thinking critically. However, at times, critical thinking is clearly employed, such as when a writer makes a claim about a topic that experts have debated for years—for example, that cats are smarter than dogs. Making the best inference could involve weighing a number of factors:

- *The writer's credibility*. Is the writer considered an expert? What is the nature of his or her expertise? A researcher into animal behaviour? A veterinarian? An animal trainer? Someone who has owned dogs and cats? Someone who has owned dogs only? Could the writer have a bias? For example, does the author hate dogs? Are there any errors in logic, such as "Dogs smell; therefore, they are not smart?" Has fact been carefully separated from opinion?
- *Nature of the thesis or main points*. Specific points are stronger than general ones, and they are often easier to prove. Since there are many different dog breeds, it would be difficult to generalize about the intelligence of *all* dogs.

- *Basis of the statement.* Some claims are more straightforward than others. A claim may depend on an underlying assumption, such as a particular definition. There are various ways to define and measure intelligence: physiologically (e.g., the weight of the brain in proportion to the weight of the body) and behaviourally (e.g., trainability, adaptability, independence). Those who think a dog is more intelligent may point to trainability as the intelligence factor, while cat fanciers may point to adaptability or independence.

- *Method.* How does the writer attempt to prove his or her point? Since intelligence can be measured, a method that measured it scientifically would be more credible than one that relied on personal experience—especially since many pet-lovers are opinionated about their pets' intelligence and may not always distinguish between fact and opinion.

- *Support.* A credible writer would need to provide more than opinion to back up a claim, though research alone does not ensure a writer's credibility. In critical thinking, you must evaluate the nature of the evidence and the way the writer uses it. Typical questions might include the following: What kind of evidence did the writer use? Has the writer relied too much on one kind of evidence or one source? How many sources were used? Were they current sources (recent studies may be more credible than older ones)? Did the writer ignore some sources (e.g., those that found dogs more intelligent than cats)?

- *Conclusion.* While analysis and questioning are important when you read the work, as you complete your reading, you will be synthesizing (putting together) information in order to say something definitive about it and/or about the writer. *Your goal is to determine whether the weight of evidence supports the writer's claim.* You might consider how weaker points affect the validity of the findings. Were there any gaps or inconsistencies in the chain of reasoning? Was the writer's conclusion logically backed up?

Exercise 1.3

As discussed above, critical thinking and inferences are used in our everyday lives. The following scenarios call for critical thinking skills by asking us to make inferences.

A. What inferences could be made in each case?

B. Is there a best (i.e., most probable) inference? Justify your choice of the most probable inference. If you believe no inference can be made, explain what kind of information you would need to make an inference.

1. You arrive at your 8:30 class after missing yesterday's class because you overslept. You are surprised to see an empty classroom. As well, there is no one you recognize from class hanging around outside, and there is nothing posted on the wall or door to show that the instructor is ill.
   Inferences:
   a) You have mistaken either the time or the room
   b) The instructor cancelled class yesterday
   c) The instructor is ill, but no one put up a notice
   d) No inference is possible (what further information is needed?)

2. Matt suggested that he and Dee see a movie tonight. Shrugging, Dee said okay, but when Matt suggested they see a romantic comedy, Dee said she just wasn't in the mood. Matt suggested an action flick, but Dee replied, "You know I don't like them." Finally, Matt suggested a drama starring her favourite actress, but Dee said that she hadn't much enjoyed her last film.
   a) Matt is pressuring Dee too much
   b) Dee is finding it hard to decide on a movie
   c) Dee really doesn't want to go to a movie tonight
   d) No inference is possible (what further information is needed?)

3. It was Todd's roommate's turn to cook dinner, but when Todd got home, his roommate was glued to the TV and the kitchen looked untouched. "Wow! Something smells great," enthused Todd.
   a) Todd has a poor sense of smell
   b) Todd is sarcastically voicing his displeasure
   c) Todd is trying to give his roommate a hint that he should start dinner
   d) No inference is possible (what further information is needed?)

4. Brad was helping Kodi train for the 600-metre race by recording his time after every complete circuit of the track. For the first circuit, Kodi was timed at 60 seconds; he did the second circuit in 65 seconds.
   a) He will probably do the third circuit in about 55 seconds
   b) He will probably do the third circuit in about 65 seconds
   c) He will probably do the third circuit in about 70 seconds
   d) No inference is possible (what further information is needed?)

5. Lara works at the city's tourist centre, and she is often asked to recommend whale-watching tours. However, her boss has told her she should provide the relevant brochures and not make personal recommendations. She often tells tourists, "I've heard that Whales Galore is awesome, but I've heard a few good things about Spouting Off, too."
   a) Lara favours Whales Galore over Spouting Off
   b) Lara favours Spouting Off over Whales Galore
   c) Lara is careful to praise both companies equally in order to satisfy her boss
   d) No inference is possible (what further information is needed?)

Exercise 1.4

The writer of the following informal essay uses critical thinking to challenge the claim of a prominent American retailer. Read the essay and answer the questions that follow, using your critical thinking skills and ability to make logical inferences.

Amazon.con: How the Online Retail Giant Hoodwinks the Press
By Timothy Noah

I am the most successful writer in the United States. Based on what, you ask? You'll just have to take my word for it. Not good enough, you say? Then why is it good enough when Amazon claims to be the most successful retailer in the United States?

The day after Christmas, Amazon put out a press release declaring the 2008 holiday season "its best ever, with over 6.3 million items ordered worldwide on the peak day, Dec. 15." The story was eagerly snapped up by the Associated Press, Reuters, the *Washington Post*, the *Atlanta Journal Constitution*, and even the Web site for *Business Week*, which really ought to know better. Some, but not all, of these accounts went on to concede that Amazon would not provide revenue data for the entire shopping season, or even for its "peak day." Nor would Amazon confirm or deny that one or both of these revenue figures exceeded those for 2007. Without this information, we can't possibly know whether Amazon had a good year in comparison either to other retailers or to its own sales during the previous Christmas shopping season.

The same gullibility applies to coverage of the Kindle, Amazon's e-book reader. *The New York Times* reported on Dec. 23 that "the e-book has started to take hold." We "know" this "in part because of the popularity of Amazon.com's Kindle device," which is "out of stock and unavailable until February." The *Post* fronted essentially the same story in its business section on Dec. 27. But these newspapers were unable to report how many Kindles Amazon sold, much less how much revenue these sales generated, because Amazon won't release that information. We don't even know whether Amazon sold more Kindles this year than last. Amazon is famously stingy with financial numbers generally. This Christmas season, that's proving to be a winning strategy in dealing with a business press that, between layoffs and the usual holiday vacations, appears short-staffed to the point of utter witlessness.

—Noah, T. (2008, December 27.) Amazon.con:
How the retail giant hoodwinks the press. *Slate*.
Retrieved from http://www.slate.com/

1. Why does Noah say that *Business Week* "ought to know better"? In the third paragraph, why does he place quotation marks around "know"?

2. What reasons do you think a company might declare that an item is temporarily unavailable other than its being sold out?

3. Who exactly is Noah criticizing in his essay? Support your answer by referring specifically to the essay.

4. In analyzing the essay using your critical thinking skills, what weight (importance) would you give to a) Noah's credibility, b) the credibility of the magazine where this essay was published, c) Noah's support for his claim, d) your own experience with Amazon or friends' experiences? List as "most important" to "least important" and support your answer.

5. The following notice appears on *Slate*'s About Us web page: "*Slate* is part of the Amazon Associates program. When we mention books, CDs, and other products, we include links to their Amazon pages. If readers follow those links and buy products from Amazon, *Slate* receives a commission." Does this statement affect the writer's or the magazine's credibility in any way? Why or why not?

Responding Critically and Analytically through Questions

Active reading can also be triggered by asking questions about a written work. These can be asked before reading, while you read, after you have completed the first reading for content, or during later readings. Some of the questions can relate to content, such as those asking for a specific date of a historical event mentioned in the reading; others require you to read critically or analytically, such as questions asking about the causes of a historical event. Active reading typically involves each of these different responses at different times. Of course, your response to any of the questions can change at any point in the reading process as you gather more information.

Before Reading

If you wanted to go on a trip somewhere far away, you probably wouldn't just head for the nearest terminal and purchase your ticket, but rather first learn about that place before leaving. Pre-reading can give you valuable information to help plan your reading of a text; it can give you an agenda, just as planning a trip can give you an itinerary. When you select a book, ask yourself, "How much and what parts of it are useful to me?"

If you are researching a topic such as the changes in subsidized housing policy during the last 50 years in Toronto, you are going to need documents from the City of Toronto Archives, journal and newspaper articles, and books that may discuss the subject on a wider scale but bring Toronto policy into the discussion.

If you are researching an aspect of Aboriginal history in Saskatchewan during the 1900s, you may need to consult a range of texts, documents, newspaper archives, journal articles, and university archives to compile information on your subject. Some sources could provide you with methods and points of view for analyzing this kind of data. From some authors, you might need little more than their research plans.

Information about the writer could alert you to his or her qualifications, the intended readership, and possible writer biases. Sciences and social sciences articles may contain an "abstract," or a concise summary which precedes the article, giving an overview of the writer's hypothesis, method, and results. Abstracts direct readers to those articles most relevant to their own reading or research interests (see Chapter 9).

- **What information is given by the work's title?** A work's title can convey a lot of useful information about content, organization, tone, or rhetorical purpose. For example, consider the assumptions you would make about works with the following titles—both deal with the settlement of Canada's Prairies:

    Buckley, Helen. *From Wooden Ploughs to Welfare: Why Indian Policy Failed in the Prairie Provinces.*
    Owram, Doug. *Promise of Eden: The Canadian Expansionist Movement and the Idea of the West, 1856–1900.*

    Both titles contain words that inform their readers about rhetorical purpose, as well as time and place. The title of the first book suggests its author will analyze, and perhaps criticize, the causes for the failure of Indian policy. In the second title, the words *Promise of Eden* and *Idea* suggest Owram will focus on perception and ideology behind the movement during the specific years indicated. As opposed to the titles of literary works, the titles of non-fiction works—including many academic books and articles—need to inform readers about content. Of course, you should not decide whether a book will be useful to your research *solely* by its title, but it is often a good starting point.

> By reading each word of a work's title carefully, you can often determine whether it will be useful to your research.

Exercise 1.5

Many of your textbooks will include references to journal articles, books, and other media. These could be found in individual chapters, in a Notes section, in a Bibliography, or in a Suggestions for Further Reading section. Using a textbook in your favourite subject, choose two journal or book titles referred to and analyze them word for word. Describe what you think each work will be about.

Other pre-reading questions include the following:

- **How long is the text?** Few people begin an essay without leafing through the pages to find the ending; this impulse reveals how much reading time it will require. You should make sure you have the time to complete your first reading in one sitting to get a sense of the whole. With a longer essay or a book, you can follow the same procedures with relevant sections or chapters.
- **Who is the author?** Do you know anything about him or her? Has he or she been featured in your textbooks? Is this a person your instructor has mentioned?
- **What is his or her profession?** Nationality? Are any other important or defining characteristics apparent or notable, such as experience in the field?
- Does he or she belong to or **have affiliations** with a specific organization, group, or community? For example, is this person employed by the Government of Canada? Is he or she part of the minority being written about or studied?
- Does he or she seem to be **an expert** in the field? What shows you this? Has an academic institution or organization been listed that the author has an affiliation with? Has the author listed previous research that has been consulted?
- **Why was the book/essay written?** Has it been written to convince readers of a particular opinion or point of view? If so, how would this affect the way you use it?
- Is the essay/book **divided into parts**? Extra spacing between paragraphs could indicate divisions. Are there headings throughout the essay? Sub-headings? Do they tell you about content or organization? In a book, you would look for chapter titles and, perhaps, headings within individual chapters.
- **When was the essay/book written?** The date could be found in the beginning, in a footnote at the bottom of the first page, or after the essay. In a book, the publication date usually appears on the copyright page (the other side of the title page). The most recent date is not necessarily the relevant one for your purpose; for example, the book may be just a reprint of a much earlier edition. On the other hand, if the book is a second or revised edition, changes or updates may make it especially useful. Essays that appear in an edited collection will probably have earlier publication dates than the collection itself (though essays are sometimes commissioned for a volume and would then bear the same date).
- **To whom is the essay/book addressed?** Who was it written for? If an essay, what publication does it appear in or did it appear in, and what does this information tell you? If the publication is a journal, it could be a refereed scholarly journal or one that is not refereed. A refereed journal is one in which the articles have been evaluated by knowledgeable peers. You can usually assume that it is a reliable source if you are writing a research essay.
- If a book, **who is the publisher**? An academic or university press? Again, if you are writing a research essay, a scholarly publication might be a more reliable source than a trade publication since the latter are usually designed for a wide, non-specialized audience.

- What is the **level of language** used? Does it seem difficult, specialized? If the answer is "yes," you may have to do a little background reading or exploratory research—at the very least, you will need to read carefully, defining words by their contexts wherever possible and making sure you have your dictionary handy. (See Word Meanings below or pages 25–7)

- Is there **an abstract** that summarizes the entire essay? Usually, abstracts precede essays. In books, the Preface, Introduction, or Foreword might give you this information, saving you from unneeded reading. Editors of essay collections often summarize the specific essays in introductions or forewords.

First Reading

It's a good idea to first read the essay or chapter for content and general impressions. Some people like to underline or highlight what seem like important passages, but do not mark too much on your first reading. You will be better able to see what is more important and what is less important *after* you've read through the work once. As you read a text the second time, underline or highlight additional passages.

Other people prefer to make annotations, such as comments, thoughts, associations, criticisms, questions, or additions, in the margin of the text (assuming you own the text!). Still others prefer to respond to the text on a separate piece of paper or document, keeping their own notes and the source text apart. If you're not sure which method works best for you, experiment. Responding in some way to the text is the most natural way to make it relevant to you, even if that means you just write abbreviations or symbols such as ?, ??, !, N.B., or ★, ★★, or ★★★ in the margin to indicate levels of importance. Also see Chapter 10, Research Note-Taking.

When reading a text, remember to ask yourself questions, such as the following, that will help you read critically. As you begin reading texts at the college or university level, you are acquiring new critical thinking skills, so it is important to consciously think about these issues. Once you become more familiar with reading and critical thinking, the questions below will become second nature, and you will find that you answer them without even thinking about them.

> Your early written responses to a reading can be compared to your first explorative attempts to discover a topic or an approach to a topic during the inventing stage of writing. You may feel tentative about recording your thoughts, but simply giving them written form can be helpful; it will give you something to build on as you consider and reconsider the reading.

Exercise 1.6

Using the same material from Exercise 1.5, choose five of the questions on pages 20–21 and further analyze the book or journal. Write a short description (no more than one or two sentences) for each question you have chosen to analyze. Provide examples, if relevant. Would either of the two titles you have analyzed be appropriate for use in an essay? Be prepared to explain why.

- What are your impressions of the first few paragraphs? Did they draw you into the work?
- Is there a distinct introductory section?
- What is the **tone**? (i.e., the writer's attitude to the subject matter—for example, familiar, objective, detached, casual, humorous, ironic, formal, informal). Tone can vary greatly from discipline to discipline or even from journal to journal, with scientific writing typically sounding the most detached.
- What kinds of words are used? More specifically, what is the vocabulary level? (simple, sophisticated, general, specific, specialized?)
- Is jargon used? **Jargon** consists of words and expressions used among members of a group or in a particular discipline that its members would understand, but which people outside those groups would not necessarily understand. Sometimes jargon becomes part of everyday speech, such as ASAP (from the military) and STAT (from the medical community).
- What kind of essay is it? (persuasive, expository, personal, narrative, descriptive, combination of different kinds? See Chapter 3 for Kinds of Essays).
- What is the essay/chapter about? Do you know anything about the subject? Do you know of (or have you read) other works on the subject?
- Can you identify the thesis?
- Can you identify the essay's/chapter's main points? Are they in paragraph topic sentences, for example?
- Do the points seem well-supported? Is there always enough detail provided?
- Are secondary sources used? Does the writer use footnotes, endnotes, or parenthetical references?
- Is the text easy to follow? Are the points clearly expressed or is the meaning sometimes unclear? Note areas where the meaning is unclear to you. Underline unclear passages with a different-coloured pen or place question marks in the margin. If you are using an electronic copy, highlight the relevant passage. You may even choose to add comments in the white space at the side of the page, using the "New Comment" function in Microsoft Word. This will tell you that you need to come back to these passages and give them closer attention. If the passage is not clear, is it due to unfamiliar words? Can you determine word meanings from the context or should you use a dictionary?
- Does the author always seem confident and certain about what he or she is saying? Does he or she ever express reservations or doubt? Does he or she ever appear to contradict him- or herself?
- Does he or she seem to change his or her position at any point?
- Does the work shift its focus—if so, is there an apparent reason for this?
- Does the work seem to build? Does it get stronger or weaker? Where?
- Is there a distinct concluding section? Is it satisfying? Are questions raised in the introduction addressed in the conclusion?

Here is an excerpt from a reader's response to a first reading of an essay on the loss of knowledge in our society. Notice the use of underlining and annotation.

Sample Professional Essay (Excerpt)

HOW MORE INFORMATION LEADS TO LESS KNOWLEDGE

C. Thompson

Is global warming caused by humans? Is Barack Obama a Christian? Is evolution a well-supported theory?

> Author uses current issues to attract attention for American audience, but issues also relevant to larger audience

You might think these questions have been <u>incontrovertibly</u> answered in the affirmative, proven by settled facts. But for <u>a lot of Americans</u>, they haven't. <u>Among Republicans</u>, belief in anthropogenic global warming declined from 52 percent to 42 percent between 2003 and 2008. Just days before the election, nearly a quarter of respondents in one <u>Texas</u> poll were convinced that Obama is a Muslim. And the proportion of Americans who believe <u>God did not guide evolution? It's 14 percent today, a two-point decline since the '90s, according to Gallup</u>.

> incontrovertibly: not open to question or dispute
> Is it the same in Canada?

> Belief in evolution is decreasing?

<u>What's going on?</u> Normally, we expect society to progress, amassing deeper scientific understanding and basic facts every year. <u>Knowledge only increases, right?</u>

> Many questions used to involve the reader

Robert Proctor doesn't think so. A historian of science at Stanford, Proctor points out that when it comes to many <u>contentious</u> subjects, our usual relationship to information is reversed: Ignorance increases.

> Thesis supported by research: more information = more ignorance!!

He has developed a word inspired by this trend: *agnotology*. Derived from the <u>Greek root *agnosis*, it is "the study of culturally constructed ignorance</u>."

> Contentious: causing or involving argument – so do we prefer not to know?

As Proctor argues, when society doesn't know something, it's often because special interests work hard to create confusion. <u>Anti-Obama</u> <u>groups</u> likely spent millions insisting he's a Muslim; <u>church groups</u> have shelled out even more pushing creationism. The <u>oil and auto industries</u> carefully seed doubt about the causes of global warming. And when the dust settles, society knows less than it did before.

> New terminology developed to explain trend

> Only points to the right-wing —what about left-wing bias?

"People always assume that if someone doesn't know something, it's because they haven't paid attention or haven't yet figured it out," Proctor says. <u>"But ignorance also comes from people literally suppressing truth—or drowning it out—or trying to make it so confusing</u> that people stop caring about what's true and what's not."

> How can the truth be found?

After years of celebrating the information revolution, we need to focus on the countervailing force: The <u>disinformation revolution</u>. The ur-example of what Proctor calls an agnotological campaign is the funding of bogus studies by cigarette companies trying to link lung cancer to baldness, viruses—anything but their product.

> Clear examples to support thesis. Are there other examples where the truth has been manipulated to keep readers in the dark?

Think of the world of software today: Tech firms regularly sue geeks who reverse-engineer their code to look for flaws. They want their customers to be ignorant of how their apps work.

—Thompson, C. (2009, January 19). How more information leads to less knowledge. *Slate*. Retrieved from http://www.slate.com/

Exercise 1.7

Choose one of the articles that you used in Exercises 1.5 and 1.6. Using the strategies discussed in the section First Reading above, read through the article and make annotations based on the most relevant items in the bulleted list. Once you have completed this, examine the points that you have noted. Identify the strongest points in the essay. Are there particular arguments or statements that you feel are stronger than others? Are there any sections that you feel weaken the essay? Are there any words you do not understand based on the context? If so, do you need to look them up in a dictionary?

Second Reading

In your second reading and successive readings of a work, your ability to apply critical and analytical skills is very important. With practice, these skills will become active in all your reading. As well, these are the kinds of questions we will be asking in Chapter 4, Paragraph Essentials, and other places in this text that address specific writing skills.

An anecdote is an incident or event that is used because it is interesting or striking.

Narration relates a scene or incident and can even include some dialogue.

Description is the use of concrete information, primarily what can be seen, but it can also make use of other senses.

An analogy is a comparison between one object and a second object that is otherwise unlike the first one.

- Was the introduction effective? What made it effective or not?
- What specific strategies did the writer use to draw you into the work? (questions, quotation, **anecdote**, **narration**, **description**, **analogy**?)
- Was the author's purpose in writing clear from the start?
- What audience was the work written for? Was the choice of words always appropriate for this audience?
- Why did the writer use the tone that he or she did?
- Was the main thrust of the work argumentative (did it try to persuade you to change your mind about something?), or was the intent of the writer to explain or explore something? Or was it something different—to describe something or tell a story, for example?
- Was the main point of the work (the thesis statement) announced in the introduction? If so, what was the thesis statement? Can you put it in your own words?

- How, specifically, were the points backed up? What kinds of evidence were used? (examples, illustrations, facts, statistics, authorities, personal experience, analogies?)
- How did the writer organize the work? Was one method used more than any other? (compare/contrast, definition, cause and effect, narration, description, division, other?)
- Did the author appear reliable? Trustworthy? Fair?
- How were the main points arranged? Was the strongest point placed near the beginning, middle, or end? Was the most effective order of points used?
- Did the work depend more on logic or on emotion?
- Did the writer appeal to a set of values or standards?
- Did there appear to be any lapses in logic?
- If the points were not always clear, what were the reasons for this lack of clarity? (specialized language, insufficient background given, poorly constructed paragraphs, faulty or ineffective writing style, inconsistencies or contradictions in the argument?)
- Was the conclusion effective? What made it effective or not? Did it accurately wrap up the essay? Did it leave you feeling that something was missing?

◎ Word Meanings

Dictionaries are an indispensable part of writing, whether you are a professional writer or a student writer, whether you do your writing mostly by hand or use a word-processing program from start to finish. They are also an essential part of the reading life, and every student needs at least one good, recently published dictionary—two are preferable: one mid-sized dictionary for the longer, more complex writing you do at home and a portable one for when you are at school (you may also be able to access reliable online dictionaries through your library). But while a good dictionary is part of the key to understanding challenging texts, it is not the only one—often it is not even the best one.

The texts you read at the college and university level may be more challenging than you are used to. To look up every word whose meaning is unclear would require too much time. If you interrupt your reading too often, it will be hard to maintain continuity, reducing your understanding and retention of the material. Thankfully, you don't need to know the precise meaning of every word you read; you need to know the exact meanings of the most important words but only approximate meanings for many of the others.

We all have three vocabularies: a speaking vocabulary, a writing vocabulary, and a reading, or *recognition*, vocabulary. The speaking vocabulary is the smallest, and 2000 words can be considered sufficient for most of our conversational needs. Our recognition vocabulary is the largest, but it includes words we wouldn't use in our writing. If you're asked the meaning of a word from your recognition vocabulary, you might struggle to define it, though you might *think* you know what it means; however, you know it only within the contexts in which you have read it.

Since relying *only* on a dictionary is both inefficient and unreliable, you should cultivate reading practices that minimize—not maximize—the use of a dictionary. Use a dictionary when you have to or to confirm a word's meaning; otherwise, try to determine meanings through context clues or by noting similarities with words you *do* know.

Important nouns, verbs, adjectives, and adverbs are often revealed through context—the words around them. Writers may define difficult words, or may use **synonyms** or rephrasing to make their meanings easy to grasp; such strategies are used if the author thinks the typical reader will not know them. On the other hand, authors may use an unfamiliar word in such a way that the meanings of the surrounding words clarify the meaning and **connotation** of the unfamiliar word.

Context clues: Specialized words, such as words borrowed from another language or culture are defined for general audiences:

The hakapik (a spiked club) is an effective instrument. (Glavin, "An enviro's case for seal hunt.")

Particularly important concepts may be given an expanded definition:

Although there are "Big Men"—the best hunters and warriors of the wisest elders, for example—the influence of each is limited to their areas of expertise and, crucially, it is only granted with the approval of followers. (van Vugt, "The origins of leadership.")

Even in highly specialized writing, the writer may define terms the reader might not know:

Even though the Danish government has eliminated thimerosal (the preservative that anti-vaccination people believe causes autism) from its vaccines in 1992, rates of autism have continued to increase. (Thompson, "Science-fiction: why are so many radicals rejecting science as a right-wing conspiracy—and embracing irrationality?")

Rather than being stated directly in a clause or phrase that follows, a definition can be implied in a preceding sentence:

Ruttenbur and the soldier have a joint house and property in the game, even though the soldier is married in real life. Such in-game *polygamy* is common. (Thompson, "Game theories.")

When a writer doesn't define a word, you may be able to infer its meaning through context—by looking at the words around it and the idea the writer is trying to express. In the following example, a second statement (following the semicolon) helps to reveal the word's meaning:

Results from the emotions questionnaire indicated that the personality changes were *mediated* by the emotions experienced while reading; a person's emotional state is known to influence his or her scores on personality tests. (Oatley, "The science of fiction.")

In the next example, the author's use of the correlative conjunctions *either. . . or* shows us the contrastive relationship between two words that are close together. Since you probably know that *virtuous* means "morally good," you can infer that *insidious* must mean something bad ("deceptive" or "treacherous"):

We are blinded by cuteness, and the very traits that make a character either virtuous or *insidious* are lost on us. (Poplak, "Fear and loathing in Toontown.")

What follows a word may suggest its meaning, not by defining or rephrasing but by expansion or illustration through examples.

In the Nevada desert, an entire city, Las Vegas, has been turned into spectacle, a neon-lit 24-hour wonderland of *ersatz* experience, complete with fake Eiffel Tower, fake Venetian canals. (Posner, "Image world.")

Exercise 1.8

Using context clues, your knowledge of similar words, or a suitable dictionary, determine the meanings of italicized words in the short passages below. Then, write a one-sentence definition of the word. If you determine the meaning through context or other clues, look up the word in a dictionary and compare your definition with the "official" dictionary definition.

In *virtual* spaces, questions of moral behavior seem to have been passed over entirely, perhaps because, until recently, few games have been specifically designed to allow people to virtually participate in morally *reprehensible* behavior. The record-breaking sales of the Grand Theft Auto series guarantee that this will soon change. Such a huge market for the game has shown that there is a collective desire to *immerse* oneself in virtual *misbehavior*. (Andrew Tuplin, "Virtual Morality")

This is not to *disparage* political activism; the sheer *intractability* of injustice is why we have a moral *imperative* to fight it. But when I started writing about science, I felt, for the first time in a long while, an unusual emotion: *optimism*. The *dogged* focus on progress, on knowing a bit more about the world than we knew a few years ago, is insanely *infectious*. (Clive Thompson, "Science Fiction")

Sadly, *segregationist rhetoric* has consistently *hijacked* the debate over black-focused schools, overshadowing what's really at stake. *Proponents* of the concept say it bears no resemblance to segregation, and that they can't afford to worry about the political *optics* when they have the chance to do something—anything—to address the crisis in black education in not only Toronto but the country as a whole. (Andrew Wallace, "The Test")

In the sentence above, the use of the word *fake* implies that *ersatz* means something fake or artificial. If the author had not expanded on the phrase "wonderland of *ersatz* experience," it might have seemed that *ersatz* meant "spectacle."

Reading carefully to determine both the immediate context and the main idea of the sentence or passage can help you determine a word's meaning. Remember that the object is not necessarily to make the word part of your writing vocabulary but to enable you to know how the author is using it—to recognize its particular connotation. Of course, if you are still in doubt, you should look up the word. By examining a word's denotations (dictionary definitions) and at least one of its connotations (the way it is used by the author in a particular context) you are well on the way to making it part of your writing vocabulary.

Chapter Review Questions

1. What two approaches to essay writing are discussed in this chapter? How are they different? Are these two approaches used independently, or can they be combined?
2. Why is reading important in the writing process?
3. Explain how the traditional linear model of writing is different from process-reflective writing.
4. What role does critical thinking play in essay writing? In reading?
5. What are the different types of reading strategies you may use at college or university? What are the strengths of each?
6. Why is it important to develop vocabulary? What are some effective ways to build your vocabulary?

2

The Writing Situation

In this chapter, you will

- understand the importance of "purpose" in the writing process

- understand the importance of "audience" in the writing process

- learn the difference between a subject, a topic, and a thesis

- review the steps involved in the writing process

Having a clear understanding of why you are writing and to whom you are writing will help you create a strong essay that has your reader in mind. This chapter will help you assess your purpose and audience by introducing you to factors to consider before you begin writing. You will also be introduced to the important steps good writers use when drafting an essay for college or university.

◎ Writing Purpose

Before you begin writing, you need to consider all the factors that influence your writing task, including your purpose for writing and your audience. Purpose refers to more than your reason for writing. It could include many related areas, such as the skills that the assignment is intended to develop. Assessing purpose could involve any number of the questions below and address either broad concerns or more specific ones. If you are uncertain about writing purpose, seek clarification—either by asking your instructor or by utilizing techniques such as pre-writing designed to clarify purpose.

- Will you be choosing your own topic or have you been given a specific topic? If the latter, will you have to narrow the topic?
- What kind of writing will you be doing? What form will it take? (response, formal essay, research proposal, lab report?)
- What main activities are involved? (informing, explaining, arguing, narrating, describing, summarizing?)
- Does the assignment stress learning objectives or does it ask you to apply concepts and practices already taught?
- What specific skills will you need to demonstrate? How important is each to the overall assignment? For example, will you have to define, summarize, synthesize, analyze, compare and contrast, or classify? If the assignment includes a specifically worded question or statement, pay particular attention to verbs, such as *evaluate* or *assess*, *summarize*, *explore*, *explain*, *argue for or against*, *discuss*, *describe*. They all indicate a different purpose for the assignment.
- Will you be using your own ideas? Will you be basing these ideas on memory, observation, opinions, readings, class or group discussions?
- Where do your interests lie relative to the topic? How can you find out what they are and develop them further, if necessary?
- What level of knowledge does the assignment require? What level of specialization?
- Will the assignment test originality—new approaches to an old problem? (inventiveness, imagination, creativity?)
- Should your language be formal, like that of most academic disciplines? Will some informality be acceptable—the use of contractions and/or some informal diction?
- Will you be using other people's ideas? Will you get these from books and articles or other secondary sources? (interviews, surveys?)
- How much preparatory reading do you expect to do? What kind of reading?
- Will you be submitting work in progress, such as pre-writing assignments, a self-survey, a proposal, an outline, a plan, or a rough draft?
- Is there a specified length? Is it a word or page range? Will penalties, i.e., marks deducted, be applied if you write outside this range?
- How much time have you been given for the assignment? For example, an in-class exam would require a different assessment of purpose than that of an essay assigned weeks in advance.

Exercise 2.1

A good way to prepare for an assignment is to think about the questions discussed above so that you understand what is required of you. You can do this as a self-survey, as illustrated below. One way to set up the survey is to divide a page into three columns. In the first column, write abbreviated forms of the most relevant questions (these could vary, depending on the assignment); in the second column, write your responses; and in the third column, briefly state what you know and/or what you need to find out to satisfy the writing purpose.

After receiving guidelines for a research essay project, Simon Walter used some of the questions to clarify his understanding of the assignment, review his knowledge about the topic he wanted to write on—massively multiplayer online role-playing games MMORPGs—and assess his preparedness. For Walter's research proposal, see page 171. See also his outline, page 190, and his final draft, page 204.

Table 2.1   Self-Survey Table

QUESTION	RESPONSE	WHERE TO BEGIN/WHAT NEEDS TO BE DONE
Choice of topic?	Was given category (technology); need to narrow topic	I'm interested in writing about MMORPGs, but I need to make the topic more specific; brainstorming works best for me
Kind of writing	Formal research essay	I've done some online research in one of my courses but nothing on this scale before
Main activities	Informing and explaining, mainly, but I'll be summarizing the results of studies and relating statistics	I need to reread the sections in the text on exposition and summarizing
Specific skills	Many skills are relevant: analyzing, synthesizing, & summarizing; evaluating will be important because there are a lot of strong opinions out there about MMORPGs, including their pluses and minuses; I'll likely start by defining MMORPGs and divide RPGs into different categories	We're just starting to cover research, so obviously I need to become familiar with research methods and what's involved in synthesizing information from diverse sources
Interest and knowledge	My interest & knowledge levels are high, as I've been a gamer for most of my life, but I'm not very familiar with the academic studies done on RPGs	It might be hard to be objective all the time since I think that MMORPGs have been given a bad rap by many adults and educators due to recent studies; I need to be careful and not let opinion or bias creep in

(continued)

Table 2.1 (Continued)		
QUESTION	**RESPONSE**	**WHERE TO BEGIN/WHAT NEEDS TO BE DONE**
Language	Formal language, which means no contractions. I need to know if I can use gamer slang, though	I'm not always sure what is formal versus informal usage; I'll seek clarification from the instructor or the text
Sources	5 secondary sources are required; according to the handout, the "4 Re's of research sources" are reputable, reliable, relevant, & recent. We are also supposed to decide ASAP on what citation style we're using	I'm not sure how many studies have been done on the topic. Because the topic is current, I likely won't be using many books, but I may have to use some online sources, especially publisher's web pages. Will these be considered reliable sources? I'll have to check. As I'm a humanities student, I'm going to use MLA style
Preparatory reading	Not really, other than maybe some background on the gaming phenomenon	Look for encyclopedia entries, books on gaming; talk to friends who are gamers?
Work in progress	1) proposal; 2) outline; 3) 1st draft; 4) final draft; note dates for peer editing in the syllabus	I know that I will be asked to submit an informal proposal, explaining my interest and knowledge about the topic; by this point, I hope to have narrowed my topic
Length requirements	About 1500 words	Can I go over without penalty? How strict is the word count? Right now, it looks hard to do in 1500 words, which is why I need to work on narrowing the topic right away
Time requirements	We have 4 weeks before the final version is due with due dates for the stages of the project	I need to draw up a schedule to visit the library and begin preliminary research. I think I'll need to spend a lot of time on my outline since I find it easier to write a rough draft with a solid outline to work from

◎ "A" Is for Audience

Almost everything is written for an audience—readers with common interests, attitudes, reading habits, and expectations. There are many ways to test this statement. For instance, pick up a children's book with one hand and the closest textbook with the other. Note the many differences. The textbook will likely weigh more than the children's book; it will have more pages, and the print will be smaller. The cover of the children's book will be colourful; the cover of the textbook will be designed to give basic information in a pleasing form—no more.

Publishers have expectations about their readers: children's book publishers expect their readers will be looking for something to catch their interest. If the cover is appealing, a typical reader or parent might turn to the first page and begin reading. A typical textbook reader might read no further than the title, or might turn to the index or table of contents to get a general idea about content or to see how thoroughly a specific topic is covered. If the first few sentences of the children's book don't intrigue the reader, the book will be put back on the shelf; if the index of the textbook doesn't meet the reader's needs, the textbook will be put back.

Student writers need to "design" their essay for an audience or typical reader. Therefore, the kinds of questions that apply to publishers and book designers also apply to student writers.

When physicist Stephen Hawking set out to write his popular book on cosmology, *A Brief History of Time*, audience concerns were taken into account, as is evident in his first paragraph. Italics show where readers are specifically addressed:

> Where did the universe come from? How and why did it begin? Will it come to an end, and if so, how? These are questions that are of interest to *us all*. But modern science has become so technical that only a very small number of specialists are able to master the mathematics used to describe them. Yet the basic ideas about the origin and fate of the universe can be stated without mathematics in a form that *people without a scientific education* can understand.

How does Hawking tell you what kind of audience he is writing for? He begins with straightforward questions that he says interest us all, meaning curious people with no scientific training. He chooses direct language and simple sentence structure. If he were addressing his book to specialists, he probably would not have used the phrase "a very small number of specialists." Perhaps he would have said, "cosmologists, astrophysicists, and mathematical physicists," specifically addressing these readers.

The tone of the passage also shows his concern with audience. It is inviting and implies that a non-specialist reader can understand difficult concepts. Clearly, Hawking wrote the way he did because he wanted to meet the expectations of his target audience.

Reader-based Versus Writer-based Prose

Reader-based prose is focused on the reader. It makes clear communication a priority and acknowledges the active role of the reader in the communication process. Reader-based prose is geared towards the audience the essay was designed for. It is important that reader-based prose is not confused with pronoun use. As a writer of formal prose, you don't have to directly address the reader using the pronoun "you." However, you do need to consider who the audience is and where the reader's interests and values lie.

Audience refers to whom you are writing to and their expectations.

Reader-based prose is focused on the audience, not the writer.

Exercise 2.2

Writers want their message—their communication—to be received and to be accepted. Looking at the writer–reader relationship this way, you could consider it a kind of contract with responsibilities on both sides. What responsibilities would a writer have in this relationship to make it more likely the message will be received and accepted? What responsibilities, ideally, should a reader have in this relationship? Add to the list below, assigning additional responsibilities in this contract. When you've completed the list, share it with other class members.

Table 2.2	Responsibilities of Reader/Responsibilities of Writer	
RESPONSIBILITIES OF THE READER	**RESPONSIBILITIES OF THE WRITER**
1. to read attentively and closely	1. to use appropriate language and a clear, readable style
2. to test the writer's claims for logic and consistency	2. to reason fairly, logically, and with consistency
3.	3.
4.	4.
5.	5.

If your instructor asks you to write using informal prose, you can address the audience directly by using the pronoun *you*, as mentioned. You may also be able to discuss events in first person, using the pronoun *I*. However, in formal prose, pronouns such as *I* and *you* are usually replaced with *one* or nouns such as *reader*. In formal prose, the reader is often not addressed directly. Read the following sentences and determine whether they are formal or informal and then determine why you believe this. If the prose is informal, rewrite the sentence in formal prose. (For more on formal versus informal prose, see Chapter 17, pages 419–20.)

- Did you enjoy studying Shakespeare in high school?
- All high school students are required to complete at least one art credit in four years.
- When I chose a roommate, I was looking for someone who was responsible. I should have looked for someone who could pay the rent.
- When examining the requirements, one should pay close attention to what needs to be done first.

Writer-based prose, by contrast, is directed less towards its audience and the shared writer-reader role. Private journal writing is one example of a writing activity where there is no need to accommodate a reader.

Writer-based prose is focused on the writer, not the audience.

Exercise 2.3

Readings and student essays have been included in this textbook. Choose one of these and analyze whether the prose used is formal or informal. Are there places where the writer has changed from one type to the other? How does the style of writing affect the way you feel about the piece? Write a paragraph analyzing the reading you have chosen. Focus on whether the prose increases the writer's credibility, as discussed in Chapter 1, page 14. You may also want to use some of the questions posed in Chapter 1 about first and second readings, on pages 22–23 and 25.

Reader-based prose must be error-free and have a clear meaning. Ideas are to be expressed directly and concisely (see Chapter 17). In addition, there should be no obvious gaps in logic nor should you assume a reader knows something just because you know it. In some cases, you may have to define terms or clarify specific points. Even if the intended audience has specialized knowledge about a subject, it is safe to assume that *the reader knows a little less about the subject than you do.*

In the following example, the writer should have accommodated a general reader by giving additional information. A reader could legitimately ask what a "deer tag" is and how it is "filled." Readers should not have to fill in gaps.

In 1998, there were more than 1 million deer tags handed out in Pennsylvania; of these only 430,000 tags were actually filled.

Audience Factors

Although most writing assumes the existence of an audience, there are basic audience factors that should be kept in mind as you're writing. Consider the following criteria when you assess your work's purpose, when you choose what to

Exercise 2.4

Read the following sentences and rewrite them, adding detail for the audience, if necessary.

1. Of the 1500 students enrolled, only 750 actually completed the ECE course.
2. In order to improve the world economy, many governments are introducing stimulus packages.
3. More than 75 percent of PET bottles are being thrown into landfill sites.
4. Some people compare Canada's GST to Britain's VAT.
5. 3G networks have become a selling feature for Canada's wireless providers.

include or not to include, or when you consider what level of language and tone to use, how to develop your ideas, how much background to provide, what kind of support to use, and similar matters.

You can characterize an audience according to four criteria:

- *knowledge*: the background, expertise, or familiarity with the topic
- *interest level*: the extent of audience interest or potential interest
- *the reader–writer relationship*: the way an audience would be expected to respond to the writer
- *orientation*: the attitudes and emotional/ethical positions that define a typical reader.

By asking these questions and trying to find accurate answers, you will be better able to create reader-based prose.

Knowledge and Interest

There are three types of audiences you can address:

Audiences can vary in their knowledge and interest levels from a general audience to an explicit one, those who will be knowledgeable about and interested in the subject.

- **General audiences** have some interest in the subject but may not have any expertise. Some typical general audiences are students at your college or university, or readers of *The Globe and Mail* newspaper.
- **Implicit audiences** often have certain expectations and knowledge about a subject. They have both more knowledge about and interest in the subject than general audiences. Implicit audiences could include first-year science students at your college or university, or readers of the Entertainment section of *The Globe and Mail*.
- Finally, **explicit audiences** have specific assumptions and may have a more in-depth knowledge of and interest in the topic. When writing to this audience, you can use specialized terms and expect to be understood. Some typical explicit audiences are chemistry students at your college or university, or readers of the stock market reports of *The Globe and Mail*.

Meeting the expectations of an audience does not necessarily mean telling its members what they *want to hear*, but, rather, doing everything you can to make it more likely they *will hear* you and understand you. For example, if you don't meet their expectations by using familiar terms or explaining unfamiliar ones, they will be less likely to "hear" you and understand you; hence they may not pay attention to the points you make. It is more effective to write *to* your audience than *for* your audience.

Often, readers with some knowledge about a topic would also be interested in the topic, with an explicit audience being more interested than either general or implicit audiences; however, there is not always a direct link between knowledge and interest, and they can often be considered separate categories.

Knowledge and Interest Questions

1. How much do you know about your potential readers? How much do you need to know? What assumptions can you make about them? What might they value? What ambitions and goals might they possess? How could your writing appeal to their values and goals?

2. In what ways might the audience members differ from you? From one another? Consider such factors as where they live, their ages, gender, occupation, education, ethnic and/or cultural background, social status, politics, religion, hobbies, entertainment.

3. Is there a specific group of individuals you want to reach? (other students, scientists, people your age, people of varying ages?)

4. If your readers' knowledge about a subject is less than your own, what would help them better understand the topic? (background information, facts and figures, examples, analogies or comparisons, reference to experts?)

5. If your readers' interest in a subject is less than your own, what could help them better relate to the topic? (examples, questions, anecdotes or short narratives, personal experience?)

Writer–Reader Relationship

Many student writers assume that the only reader who *really* matters is the one marking the essay. But if you imagine you are writing a report for your boss, rather than an essay for your teacher, it may be easier to move away from this mindset. Your boss may have

Exercise 2.5

In terms of readers' knowledge and interest, what general or specific assumptions could you make about readers of a trendy e-zine; an academic journal; a book about recent discoveries in psychology; a book about Canadian television?

Exercise 2.6

Explore the databases your college or university subscribes to. The journals and trade publications found on these databases are written for explicit audiences. For example, the *International Journal of Clinical Practice* is written for people in the medical field, and most of the articles use terminology that these professionals are familiar with. Find an article that was written for an explicit audience. Then, using the databases, find an article about the same topic, but which is written for a general or implicit audience (you might try searching magazines or newspapers). Compare the prose and writing styles. How are different words used to convey the same information? How would you include some of the information if you were going to write for your professor who is an expert in the field? Which article would you cite more if you were writing to your peers in the classroom?

asked for the report and may be the one receiving it, but the report itself may be read and studied by many other people after your boss reads it. In such cases, you don't write for your superior but for many people you will not know. You would need to know the expectations of such individuals, as well as those of your boss. For any writing assignment, you should consider an audience comprising these kinds of hypothetical readers.

Of course, it's also important to acknowledge your instructor as a reader by following directions given for the assignment. For example, if you are required to include a title page with the instructor's name and course number on it, not including this information would be failing to meet his or her expectations. The presentation of your essay is one area that demands your careful attention since instructors vary in their requirements. For instance, one instructor may require you to use 12-point size type while another may say that a point size between 10 and 12 is acceptable. You will not make a favourable first impression with the first instructor if you use 10-point type.

Writer–Reader Relationship Questions

1. What is your relationship to the audience? Student to instructor? Student to student? Another kind of peer-based relationship, such as individual to professional associates or members of a group or community you are part of—for example, an organization of rock-climbers? Architects? Members of the union you belong to? Employee to employer? Employer to employee?
2. Do your readers expect you to conform to the conventions of a particular form or discipline? What are the specific formal requirements? (These questions are important when considering purpose as well.)

Audience Orientation

Audiences can have potential *positive, neutral,* or *negative* orientations towards the subject, the writer, or the writer's thesis.

- *Positive*: holds the same view as you or is more likely to agree than disagree
- *Neutral*: 1) has no particular view or 2) is divided between those who agree and those who disagree
- *Negative*: differs from your view or is more likely to disagree than agree

Assessing audience orientation to your thesis is especially vital in argument. Will most of your readers agree or disagree with your viewpoint, or will they have no opinion? As an arguer, part of your job is to convince those whose views differ from yours, or who have no particular opinion, that your view is worth supporting. Consider the subject of cloning. How might the opinions of members of a scientific community differ from those of a religious community? Would all scientific or religious communities have identical attitudes? What could affect differences? What about an audience of first-year philosophy students?

Although it is tempting to consider your instructor as your sole audience, there may be others, such as other faculty members or future employers, who will read your writing as well.

An audience can also vary in its attitudes towards the subject, the writer, or the thesis; these attitudes can range from very positive to very negative.

Audience Orientation Questions

1.   What is your audience's attitude towards your topic or viewpoint? If you're unsure, how could you find out? What preconceived opinions might its members hold? What has informed these opinions (any of the factors mentioned above, such as education or where they live?) Do you need to be sensitive to the audience's background? For example, are you a vegan writing to an audience of cattle farmers?

2.   If your readers are unsympathetic to your viewpoint, how could you make them more sympathetic? How could you bridge the gap between you and them? (See Chapter 13, Rebutting the Opposing View.)

Exercise 2.7

Five topics are given below followed by a group of potential readers. From what you know or can assume about the topic and audience, complete the third column indicating the probable orientation of the audience (positive, neutral, or negative) to the topic. Of course, categorizing a group this way isn't meant to suggest that individuals within the group could not hold differing views.

Table 2.3   Topic/Audience Table

TOPIC TO ARGUE	AUDIENCE	ORIENTATION
1. Mandatory physical education in school	History high school teachers gym teachers high school students	
2. Abolishing NHL hockey fights	NHL hockey fans referees' union NHL team owners	
3. Compulsory pet neutering	pet owners city council pet breeders	
4. Use of taser guns by the RCMP	a citizens' rights group RCMP officers dentists	
5. Laptops in the classroom	students who own laptops students who do not own laptops instructors who have taught for 20 years or more	

Finally, the following questions could be relevant to all the above areas: What kind of writing does your audience expect or appreciate—simple and direct? complex? subtle? original? Could you use humour? Would they understand or value irony? How could your knowledge of audience affect your writing style or your tone?

Exercise 2.8: Assessing the Writing Situation

Selecting one Purpose variable and one Audience variable from each category of column three (knowledge, interest, relationship, and orientation), discuss how you would approach writing an essay if you were given one of the 10 topics from column one. How could you ensure that your message is received and accepted? How could you meet audience expectations? Try to be as specific as you can about approach and strategy. Hint: Start with Purpose, follow with Topic, and then choose Audience variables, considering assumptions about that audience and the way they would affect your writing choices. You can use the questions above under Purpose and Audience as guidelines.

Table 2.4	Topic/Purpose/Audience Assessment	
TOPIC	**PURPOSE**	**AUDIENCE**
1. Smoking in public places	formal essay	general knowledge
2. Schizophrenia	in-class essay	implicit (moderate knowledge)
3. Abolishing final exams	tell something that happened to you (narration)	explicit (specialized knowledge)
4. Snowboarding	to explain (exposition)	low interest
5. Conservation	to persuade (argument)	moderate interest
6. Downloading music from the Internet	to summarize (put ideas in your own words)	high interest
7. The structure of DNA	to use research	superior–subordinate relationship
8. Age discrimination	to explore or discover	peer–peer relationship
9. Victims' rights	to describe	positive orientation
10. Blogs	to define	neutral orientation
		negative orientation

Exercise 2.9: Formulating an Audience Profile

Create an audience profile by considering the four criteria characterizing an audience. In groups of three, interview the other two members of your group, asking them questions that will enable you to assess your audience according to its knowledge, interest, and orientation (you can omit Writer–Reader Relationship, as it will likely be one of student-to-student). Assume your purpose is to persuade your audience. Therefore, if you follow the table in Exercise 2.8, you could use the following topics: smoking in public places, abolishing final exams, downloading music from the Internet, victims' rights, or blogs. You can also come up with a topic of your own that you feel strongly about and would like to argue for or against.

Write a four-paragraph profile based on the results of your interviews. Devote a paragraph to each variable of knowledge, interest, orientation, and strategies to consider in order to appeal to your specific audience. (You may also choose to create headings for each of the categories and then use bulleted lists to create an informal profile.) If you wish, you can pre-read about rebuttal strategies in Chapter 13.

In many cases, your instructor will inform you of the intended audience for your essay—perhaps a general audience or first-year students.

> Remember that you should consider not only what you know or need to know about your audience, but also your own attitude to them. Is it positive? neutral? cautious? mistrustful? What attitudes will the audience expect you to hold? What attitudes might disturb or offend its members, making them less likely to "hear" you?

◎ Stages in Essay-Writing

Once you have considered purpose and audience, you are ready to begin narrowing your topic. Whichever composing method works best for you, writing an essay inevitably means working steadily towards a goal. Although you may allot more time and energy to one stage or another, you will generally write an essay in five stages.

1. **Pre-writing (Inventing)**: thinking about and coming up with a topic
2. **Research**: finding background information and supporting evidence (This stage could involve intensive library resources or simply consist of examining your knowledge about a topic.)
3. **Organization**: determining the order of points; outlining
4. **Composing (first draft)**: getting down your ideas in paragraph form
5. **Revising (final draft)**: revising and editing to achieve the finished version

External factors could determine the time you devote to the pre-writing stage. If you are assigned a specific topic, you won't have to spend as much time on this stage as someone who is simply told to "write on a topic of your choosing." Similarly, if you have the option of not writing a formal outline, you may spend much less time on outlining—perhaps by writing only an informal scratch outline—than someone asked to complete a formal outline. However, when you revise your essay, you should always plan for enough time to ensure your writing is grammatical, mechanically correct, and clear.

Pre-writing

Subjects Versus Topics

A topic differs from a subject in being narrower or more focused. Similarly, a thesis is more focused than a topic because it makes a specific comment on the topic or tells the reader how you will approach the topic.

Like Simon Walter (see page 31), you may be given various subject areas and asked to narrow one down to a manageable topic. A subject is a broad category that contains many potential topics. Modern technology, global warming, and energy sources are examples of subject areas. A subject could also be more specific than these examples (the Internet, species extinction, and alternative energy sources could also be considered subjects). A topic differs from a subject in being narrower or more focused. Similarly, a thesis is more focused than a topic because it makes a specific comment on the topic or tells the reader how you will approach the topic.

Since thesis statements will be discussed further in Chapter 5, the focus here is on topics. Below we will consider using pre-writing strategies to come up with a topic. These strategies sometimes result in a thesis and even in some main points for your essay, but at other times, your thesis is not clear to you until after you've begun your research. However, your topic *should always* be clear before you begin your research.

Exercise 2.10

Read through the following list. Decide whether each item in the list is a subject, a topic, or a thesis.

1. The discrepancy between men's and women's basketball coverage is due to sexism.
2. Public transportation is influenced by many factors.
3. Studying abroad can provide valuable life experience.
4. Violence exists in sports.
5. Greed is responsible for the global economic difficulties.
6. Jazz is one of America's greatest musical genres.
7. Colleges and universities can change students' lives.
8. If one is illiterate, many career opportunities are lost.
9. Fish are great pets for those who cannot have cats or dogs.
10. Studying the classical languages in school is unnecessary today.

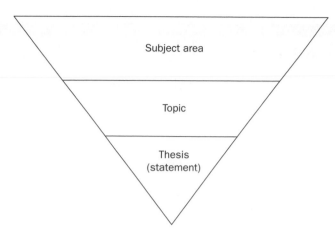

Figure 2.1   Subjects versus topics.

Topic Hunting

Your instructor may tell you to find your own topic or to narrow a subject to a manageable topic. In the first case, you will be beginning from scratch. Here are some questions you can consider if you need to come up with a topic from scratch:

- Where do your interests lie? (hobbies, leisure pursuits, reading interests, extracurricular activities?)
- What would you like to find out more about? Curiosity is a good motivator. Topics you are very familiar with don't always make good ones for a research essay as your knowledge could inhibit your ability to fully explore the topic.
- Are sufficient sources available? Consider not only research sources but also questionnaires, interviews, experts, statistics, etc.
- What topic do you think readers might like to learn about? Thinking of *other* people's interests can guide you to a worthwhile topic. What topic could benefit society or a specific group in society (for example, students at your college or university)?
- Can you think of a new angle on an old topic? Neglected areas of older topics can be new opportunities for exploration.

By using pre-writing techniques, you can narrow down a subject to a usable topic. However, not all topics can be turned into effective thesis statements. Some are too broad while others are too narrow. If the topic is too broad, it will be hard to do more than provide a general overview. Your essay may also be difficult to plan and write because there will be so much you could say about the topic. On the other hand, if your topic is too specific, you could feel yourself limited by the topic's scope; you may also have problems researching it if there's not much available.

Exercise 2.11

The following topics are arranged from broadest to narrowest. Place a check mark beside any topics you think could be turned into an effective thesis.

1. **species extinction**

   threatened species in Canada

   threatened species in Canada's Arctic

   threatened polar bear habitats in Canada's Arctic

   threatened polar bears living near Coats Island in Hudson Bay

2. **the Internet**

   online gaming

   MMORPGS

   popularity of World of Warcraft

   the contribution of quests to the popularity of World of Warcraft

3. **nutrition**

   dieting

   fad diets

   the Atkins diet

   loss of muscle mass while on the Atkins diet

Pre-writing Strategies

Pre-writing strategies should clarify your thoughts about the subject and enable you to generate useful ideas, some of which you will use in your essay; others can be discarded as you further clarify your topic. Pre-writing often brings you to the point where you can write a tentative thesis statement and, in many cases, determine your main points.

> Pre-writing involves clarifying your thoughts about a subject, enables you to generate useful ideas, helps you determine your thesis, and may determine your main points.

Kinds of pre-writing strategies include *asking questions* about the topic; **brainstorming**, by yourself or with others; **freewriting**, in which you write continuously for a specific time without editing yourself; and **clustering**, or **mapping**, in which you graphically represent your associations with a subject.

All these pre-writing techniques work by association—utilizing one or more of questioning, brainstorming, freewriting, or clustering will enable you to trigger associations, to tap into subconscious ideas and feelings. By employing these methods, you are taking a step towards writing your paper. Pre-writing is an especially worthwhile activity in the traditional linear model since it may help generate the ideas that could lead to an outline of your main points.

Although pre-writing techniques work similarly, they have unique differences and may be useful for particular kinds of writing:

- *Questioning* is often a good strategy for expository (or explanatory) essays in the sciences and social sciences where your thesis can be framed as a specific question or series of questions you will try to answer.
- *Freewriting* can be useful for beginning personal essays as it enables you to make unconscious or emotional connections.
- *Clustering* is often useful for starting argumentative essays, which rely heavily on logical connections. Unlike brainstorming, questioning, and freewriting, clustering is spatial and enables you to visualize the interrelations among your thoughts.
- *Brainstorming* can be useful for all kinds of essays, but because it can be done in groups, it's particularly useful in collaborative projects where all group members can give input.

The most important thing is that you learn to work with whatever method(s) serves you best.

Questions and Brainstorming

Asking questions and brainstorming are tried-and-true approaches for finding out more about a subject. Although you can pose any questions, asking the traditional journalistic questions *who?*, *what?*, *why?*, *when?*, *where?*, and *how?* can be helpful for almost any subject, such as "roommates":

Who?: Who make the best roommates? (worst?)
What?: What are the qualities of an ideal roommate?
Why?: Why are roommates necessary? (or not?)
When?: When is the best time to start looking for a roommate?
Where?: Where can you find a roommate? Where can you go for privacy when you have a roommate?
How?: How do you go about finding a good roommate? How do you get along with a roommate?

In brainstorming, you write down your associations—words, phrases, or sentences—with a subject. You can then begin looking for ways to connect some of the items by asking what they have in common. How can they be categorized? You can often combine brainstorming with one or more pre-writing methods. For example, if you began by asking the journalistic questions about the subject "roommates," you could brainstorm about the qualities of an ideal roommate, using the question *what?* to generate a list. You could continue to use these two methods by then asking *why* the most important qualities you listed through brainstorming contribute to a good roommate.

Although brainstorming can produce a list that looks something like an outline, the object is to come up with as many points as possible and then to connect them in some way. You don't need logical connections to begin with between any one item and the next.

> Brainstorming means writing down the words, phrases, or sentences that you associate with a subject.

In addition to listing random associations on one subject, you could set up the brainstorming session by applying different criteria to a topic. For example, using a topic like private and public health care, you could list your associations under *pro* and *con*. You could also list similarities and differences between two related items, such as two addictive substances, two movie directors, or two racquet sports; or you could divide a general category, such as contemporary music, into sub-categories and list your associations with each. For an example of a brainstorming list, see pages 101–2.

Freewriting and Clustering

Freewriting means writing without stopping. It is important to let your ideas flow without editing or censoring them.

In freewriting, you write for a span of time without stopping, usually five to ten minutes. You can freewrite without a topic in mind and see where your subconscious leads you, or you could begin with a specific subject or topic, though you may well stray from the topic and talk about something else. That is fine. You don't need to censor or edit yourself, or concern yourself with spelling or grammar. You are concerned with flow and process and should not worry about mechanics or content. In some freewriting, there is no need for any punctuation or capital letters: you just write without lifting your pencil from the page, or just continue typing without worrying about tabs. Many people, though, prefer to use punctuation occasionally and to write mostly in sentences. The important principle is that you don't stop. If you cannot think of anything to say, you write something anyway, such as "I can't think of anything to say," "what's the point in this?" or even "blah, blah, blah" until another idea or association comes to you.

In looping, you underline potentially useful words, phrases, or sentences; then, you choose the best one to focus on as the beginning point for more freewriting.

If you enjoy freewriting and find it beneficial, you can follow it with a looping exercise. In **looping**, you underline potentially useful words, phrases, or sentences; then, you choose the best one to focus on as the beginning point for more freewriting. You can also take the most useful phrase, sum it up in a sentence, and begin freewriting using that sentence as a starting point. Although freewriting is a popular pre-writing strategy, you can use it at any point in the composing process—if you get stuck on a particular point or experience writer's block when drafting your essay.

Freewriting has several functions:

- It can free you from writer's block. A typical problem in beginning to write is feeling you have nothing to say.
- It enables you to express undiscovered feelings and associations; in other words, it gives you access to thoughts or feelings you might not have known about.
- Included with looping, it can help you narrow down a topic and, sometimes, come up with a thesis and main points.

In the freewriting sample below, the writer discovers a potential thesis for an essay. After writing for five minutes, the student was asked to underline anything he thought was usable. In this case, five minutes of writing yielded an interesting topic that was complete enough to serve as a thesis statement (shown by heavy underlining):

Bureaucracy can be very disturbing you can get parking tickets even when there is <u>no parking left and you are forced to park by the yellow line</u> and you think you'll be gone early enough in the morning where was the bureaucracy when you needed them to make the decision in the first place and it can also lead to you having to take english 100 over again because you didn't get the B- required for the elementary post-degree program even though <u>you feel your writing should be at least a high B</u> or A average and the teacher says just be more clear and some comma errors and gives you a mediocre mark <u>who's to say that the best teachers are the ones who get the A average</u> because <u>I think the best teachers are the ones who know what it's like to struggle because they have learned hard work and they have also learned patience</u> these two things are the most important things being a teacher or they are up there anyway.

—Y.M.

Y.M., who chose to freewrite on "bureaucracy," began with a complaint about parking, which triggered another complaint, concerning his mark in a previous English course. He continued to follow this train of thought as he complained about how the teacher had marked his writing. This led him to consider the qualities of a good teacher, which, he discovered, have nothing to do with marking or education but with the idea of having to struggle and overcome obstacles. Y.M. could then proceed to test this claim by finding evidence to support it.

Clustering, or mapping, is an associative technique that is represented graphically rather than linearly. On a blank piece of paper, you circle your topic and then think of related words or phrases, which you record and circle, connecting each with the word or phrase that gave rise to it. Using the clustering method can help you develop your main points and provide a structure for your essay. Unlike questioning, brainstorming, and freewriting, clustering allows you to form distinct clusters of related words and phrases, which may be developed into main points. You can often see other relationships between circles in one cluster and those in another. In the example in Figure 2.2, dotted lines represent other possible connections.

> Clustering or mapping involves graphically linking your ideas or thoughts.

Figure 2.2 is the result of a group clustering exercise that began with the subject "vitamins," and produced this thesis statement: *Due to media hype and the promise of good health, more people than ever are taking vitamins before they really know the risks involved.* The statement needs further work, but it is a solid start.

> All the pre-writing methods could be considered meeting places between you and your topic. Because they are designed to "free up" your thoughts and feelings, don't hesitate to experiment with variants on these methods.

Research

If your essay is research-oriented, you will do most of your research in a library or in a similar environment where you have access to written and electronic material. However, not all research is library research because not all evidence comes from secondary sources; personal interviews and personal observation can be carried out elsewhere. Also, research may involve determining what you already know about a topic and considering how you will use this knowledge in your essay. Research is indispensable to college- and university-level reading, thinking, and writing. For a detailed analysis of research methods, see Chapter 10.

> Research can include both primary sources, such as personal interviews, and secondary sources, such as journal or newspaper articles.

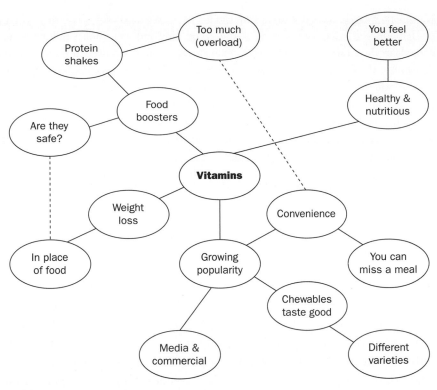

Figure 2.2 Clustering diagram about "vitamins."

Organization

Creating an outline is a crucial stage in essay writing, enabling you to see the arrangement of your ideas before you begin a rough draft.

Students rightly associate organization with outlines. Knowing how to construct an outline is a valuable skill that can save you time. Referring to an outline in the drafting stage can prevent you from getting off-track. As an outline gives you a specific plan, it can be reassuring, instilling confidence as you draft your essay. Three kinds of outlines are discussed below: scratch, formal, and graphic outlines.

Scratch (or Sketch) Outline

A scratch (or sketch) outline represents only your main points, usually indicated just by a word or phrase. Scratch outlines provide rough guidelines and give you flexibility in developing your points. They may be perfectly adequate for short essays and equally helpful for planning in-class essays where limited time can make formal outlines impractical.

Formal Outline

The formal outline includes sub-points as well as main points, revealing more of your essay's structure. In formal outlines, you can see at a glance how the parts interrelate—which is especially useful in longer essays and in those employing a

Exercise 2.12

Read through the student essay "The Virtual Life: An Overview of the Effects of MMORPGS on Individuals and Countries" in Chapter 11. While reading the essay, look at the outline for this essay on page 190, in Chapter 11. Do the paragraphs follow the outline? Are there instances where the essay does not match the outline? If yes, why do you think this is the case? How do you think the outline helped the writer?

complex structure, such as compare and contrast or research essays. Formal outlines are a good choice if you lack confidence in your organizational skills, since the outline can be used to remind you of the original plan. For examples of outlines, see chapters 5 and 11.

Graphic Outline

Graphic outlines show connections through spatial, rather than linear relationships. A flow chart is a kind of graphic outline that represents complex, multi-layered plans or procedures. For example, it can show the sequence in a scientific experiment or clarify the stages of a procedure, such as the steps in approving a loan or conducting a survey. Graphic outlines are especially useful for writers who work best with visual aids. One way to construct a graphic outline is to put your main points in rectangular boxes and use vertical arrows to show the order of the points. Horizontal or diagonal arrows can show sub-points or supporting points.

Graphic outlines typically look more like working outlines than formal outlines do. As needs are redefined, changes can be shown through arrows, parentheses, crossings-out, or additional boxes (or other shapes). You can think of graphic outlines as temporary road signs, aiding and guiding the traffic of your thoughts while construction is ongoing.

The example in Figure 2.3 applies a graphic outline to the topic "the stages of essay writing." Vertical arrows represent the sequence of stages (the main points), while diagonal arrows indicate sub-points—composing choices for writers. The two-pointed arrow shows the interrelationship between questioning and brainstorming discussed previously. The parentheses around *research* indicate that research may or may not be part of the composing process. Finally, the vertical arrows under *final draft* show that each activity in the circle is performed in the order indicated. The arrows, then, show sequence, while the use of ovals, rather than rectangles, calls attention to the fact that re-seeing, editing, and proofreading should not be treated as major stages like pre-writing, outlining, first draft, and final draft. Graphic outlines must be logical but, as mentioned, can be customized to reflect the writer's needs.

All outlines written before or during the first draft should be considered working outlines in the sense that they may change as your thinking changes or as you come across new evidence. Outlines should be considered organizational aids, which can be altered or adapted—not just as ends in themselves.

Although formal outlines can be followed closely, they should never impair spontaneity. Using outlines successfully is a matter of adopting a flexible attitude towards them and becoming familiar with your own unique composing processes.

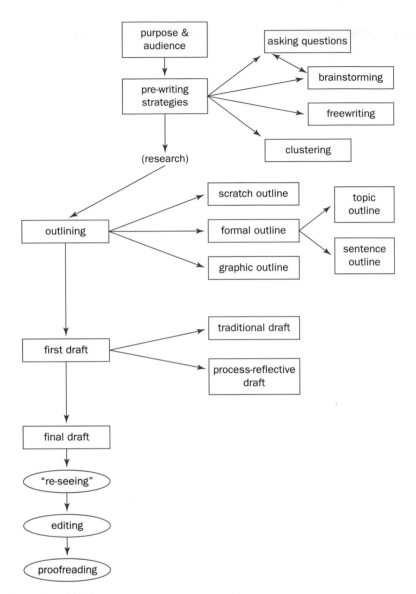

Figure 2.3 Graphic outline.

Composing: First Draft

Getting words on paper in sentence and paragraph form is the most challenging stage for most writers. The different approaches to composing have been discussed in Chapter 1. The traditional rough draft is based on the outline while the process-reflective draft is really an essay-in-progress that works towards a more finished form.

In first drafts, your focus should be on setting your ideas down. In the case of the essay-in-progress, though, you may sometimes find yourself reordering sentences, providing transitions, or working on other "road-clearing" activities to eliminate obstacles to clear thinking. If you find it difficult to paraphrase (put into

In first drafts, your focus should be on setting your ideas down.

your own words) something you've written, your thinking may not be clear about that point and you should consider revising it.

Composing on the Computer

Today, the computer is used for everyday tasks, such as sending email, going online, and composing documents. However, for many people educated prior to the personal computer revolution, composition meant starting drafts on a piece of paper, writing further drafts on paper, and finally, using a typewriter to prepare a final copy to be submitted. Therefore, for some, drafting an essay on a computer is a foreign idea. However, younger essay writers often find composing drafts on the computer is quite easy and natural, while writing drafts on paper seems cumbersome and an inefficient use of time.

There are advantages to both systems. When drafting on paper, even if only an outline, there is more room to add small notes. Some people write drafts on paper so that they can then draw circles and lines between similar ideas. Some feel that seeing an idea on paper helps give rise to creativity, as the blank page becomes a challenge to fill.

Drafting on a computer can save time, as you can often go back and add or revise ideas quickly. You can use different colours and fonts so that you can identify new thoughts or ideas that you want to add to the document. You can also cut whole sections and place them elsewhere to create a better sense of coherence in your paper. However, there are challenges to keep in mind when using computers to write documents: computers crash, files get lost, and printers run out of ink.

Keeping Copies

When you are composing your document, it is important to keep copies of previous drafts. At various stages of the writing process, save a clean copy and label it clearly so you can find it if you need to go back to it. For example, you will want to save a clean copy of your outline. Save a copy, label it clearly, such as ***ENG101_ HydeOutline1_09*** (using the course code, the essay title or topic, and the year). Create a system that works best for you.

Once you have created a clean file, copy the whole document and create a new file. Label this and then start to work from this document. Many students, once they have created an in-depth outline, will work from that by adding details and creating a draft of their essay. So, following our example above, you can label the new file ***ENG101_HydeDraft1_09***.

After saving this first draft, again copy the document, and create a new file. You now have a new document to work from as you revise and rework the essay draft. By creating new files as you progress in the drafting of your document, should you decide you don't like the changes you have made, or should you make a mistake and cut information you did not want to delete, you can revert to the older file and start again on a fresh document.

Alternatively, in most word-processing programs, there are track changes and comments functions you can use to make side notes or write reminders to yourself.

> When you are composing your document, it is important to keep copies of previous drafts.

These are especially useful in the editing stages of writing. For example, you can add a comment in the margin of your essay, such as "Find a better quote." One thing to keep in mind is that these comments and changes don't always transfer to the subsequent documents when you are saving new drafts.

While you are creating the new files and saving them, also make sure that you pause every 15–20 minutes and save your file to your hard drive on the computer. Also, make sure you save it to another source, such as a USB key. This will ensure that, even if your hard drive crashes, you have saved the document to another safe location. Most colleges and universities allow students access to the school network, so you can save documents there. (Make sure you know exactly where to save your document; saving it to the computer's desktop is generally not a safe location. Get help from the computing staff if you're unsure.) A final alternative is to pay for companies to store your data for you. There are many reputable firms that can be found on the Internet.

Finally, when using the computer, make sure you print out your final paper and read it carefully. Look carefully for typos, spelling errors, and grammar mistakes. Errors are often seen on paper that are missed when reading on the computer screen. Chapter 2, page 41 explains the stages of essay writing. Each of the stages discussed can be saved as a separate file on your computer.

Revising: Final Draft

The final draft probably is the most undervalued stage of the writing process. Many student writers think the final draft is the place to apply a few necessary touch-ups. They may have assumed they were supposed to "get it right the first time." However, professional writers almost never do, so why should this be expected of student writers?

> Remember that most first and even second drafts are essentially rough efforts to put your thinking into words.

Remember that most first and even second drafts are essentially rough efforts to put your thinking into words. To change the rough into final requires a new focus: the written document. When you revise, you want to build on its strengths as well as repair any weaknesses. This process could involve any or all of the following:

- **F**ine tuning
- **O**verview of purpose and audience
- **C**larifying meaning
- **U**nderscoring ideas
- **S**olidifying structure

The acronym FOCUS can serve as an aid to memory. It is important to remember that while there is no "right" order in revision, proofreading should always be the final stage.

Overview

Conduct an overview of purpose and audience. Ask yourself honestly whether the essay fulfils its purpose and whether it speaks to your intended audience. These questions seldom result in major changes, but you may decide you need to adjust your introduction or make minor changes in the body of the essay. For example, you might find a point that seemed relatively unimportant in your outline turned out to be very important. You might then need to rewrite a part of the introduction to be consistent with this new emphasis. On the other hand, you might find that you have over-developed a point that is only slightly related to your thesis. You might then decide to delete a part of a body paragraph. You might also now find that some of your words were too informal for your audience and you need to find new words to replace them.

Clarifying Meaning

Try reading complicated or unclear parts of the essay aloud. Will your audience understand your meaning? These unclear passages should receive your close attention. Wherever a sentence seems awkward or just overly long, consider rephrasing for directness and clarity.

It is hard to be objective when you look back at what you have written, especially if you have just written it. Allotting some time between completing the first draft and revising will help you see your essay more objectively. Also, getting someone else to read over your paper can give you valuable input, especially if he or she can point to unclear passages. Seeing the places where other people have difficulty will highlight those specific places for close attention. The problem may be as small as a word out of place or one that means something different from what you thought. Such seemingly small errors can obscure the meaning of an entire sentence and affect the impact of a paragraph. Work on these specific passages if you find them unclear or awkward.

> Getting someone else to read over your paper can give you valuable input, especially if he or she can point to unclear passages. Seeing the places where other people have difficulty will highlight those specific places for close attention.

Underscoring Ideas

In your body paragraphs, your main ideas are introduced and developed. These paragraphs should reinforce your thesis and support your points. Reviewing your body paragraphs might mean going back to your notes, outline, or early drafts to see if you can further support an idea that now strikes you as undeveloped. You might decide to include an example, illustration, or analogy to make an abstract or general point more concrete and understandable. Don't settle for "almost." The question to ask is if all your points are as strong as they *could* be.

What if you now see that a point is underdeveloped but you don't know how to go about developing it further at this stage? Remember that pre-writing strategies can be used at any point in the process; their main purpose is to generate ideas. Try a brief freewriting session (or whichever method works best for you) to help you expand on the undeveloped point.

Solidifying Structure

In order to solidify your structure, return to your outline. Does your essay's structure reflect your original plans for it? Do you see any weaknesses in the outline you didn't see before? Can the structure of the essay be made more logical or effective?

If the essay's structure seems strong, look at each paragraph as an essay in miniature with a topic sentence, a well-developed main idea, and a concluding thought. Not all paragraphs need to be constructed this way, but all do need to follow a logical sequence. Is the paragraph unified and coherent as well as adequately developed? Are paragraphs roughly the same length, or are some overly short or long?

When you revise, you want to make your essay stron*ger*, clear*er*, and *more* readable. When writers make changes to their drafts it is often because they discover better ways to say what they wanted to say. After all, you know much more about your topic now than you did at any other stage in the composing process.

Fine-Tuning

Working on the final draft could involve some large-scale adjustments, as described above, and it will almost certainly involve some small-scale ones. In the first stage of final drafting, focus on large, global concerns. Ask yourself whether you have addressed the audience and purpose for your essay. The crucial second stage—editing—shifts the focus to the sentence and to individual words. This means ensuring that each sentence is grammatical, that your expression is clear and concise, and that you have used appropriate transitions between sentences. You can also refine your style, asking, for example, if there is enough sentence variation. Can you combine sentences to produce more complex units, or can you use different sentence types to make your prose more interesting? Finally, the mechanics of presentation should be double-checked during the editing stage. The third stage is the final review—proofreading for mechanical errors and typos. For a full treatment of efficient writing and editing strategies, as well as proofreading guidelines, see Chapter 17.

> The final draft usually focuses on three important stages: (1) reviewing purpose and audience and/or essay restructuring; (2) checking for correct grammar and clear writing; (3) proofreading.

Chapter Review Questions

1. Why is it important to understand your audience?
2. How does formal prose differ from informal prose? Are there times when one is more appropriate than the other?
3. What are some questions you can ask to determine audience knowledge and interest?
4. What are the five stages in essay writing? Why are they all important?
5. What is the difference between "subject" and "topic"? Why is it important to have a topic that is not too narrow?
6. What acronym can you use when revising your final draft?
7. How can revising your draft improve your essay?

Kinds of Essays

In this chapter, you will learn

- about the different types of essays and when to use them

- how to write effective in-class essays

- how to write a critical response based on an essay you've read

Essays are written for a variety of reasons at college and university. You may be given a week or more to prepare an essay; yet on other occasions, you may be required to write an essay within a short period of time, such as during an in-class exam. It is always important to understand what kind of essay you are being asked to write. This chapter will introduce you to useful terms and guidelines for answering an essay prompt, and it will help you understand how to approach a topic, no matter what the time constraints.

◎ Rhetorical Modes of Discourse

Argument is persuading your audience to change its mind or to see your point of view.

Essays can be classified according to the traditional ways of organizing information for written or verbal communication. These are known as the rhetorical modes of discourse: **argument, exposition, narration,** and **description**. Because argumentative and expository essays are discussed in detail, they will be introduced here only briefly. Narration and description are discussed more fully in Chapter 6, Paragraph Development, as well as briefly below.

Exposition is informing, explaining, describing, or defining a topic for the audience.

Expository Versus Argumentative Essays

Narration is relating a scene or incident, perhaps even including some dialogue.

Often, expository writing is contrasted with persuasive or argumentative writing. Exposition explains or informs; argument persuades your audience to change its mind or see your point of view. Although these seem like basic differences, the dividing line between exposition and argument is not always a solid one, and many of the same skills and strategies apply to both kinds. Table 3.1 lists some ways that exposition differs from argument.

Here are some elements that exposition and argument share:

Description is used to add concrete detail, primarily what can be seen, but it can also make use of senses other than sight.

- Both can use factual information and reliable sources to support main points.
- Critical thinking is essential to successful expository and argumentative writing.
- In both, your voice should remain objective and your language neutral.

Table 3.1 Expository Versus Argumentative Writing	
IN EXPOSITORY WRITING	**IN ARGUMENTATIVE WRITING**
You use a fact-based thesis (see page 122)	You use a value- or policy-based thesis (see pages 122–3)
You begin with an open mind and see where your exploration takes you	You begin by considering where you stand on an issue and how you can support your position
In your body paragraphs, you look at the available evidence and rely on critical thinking for your conclusion	In your body paragraphs, you draw the reader's attention to supporting evidence but do not ignore or distort contradictory evidence
Research is usually an integral part of expository writing	Research is not always necessary in argumentative writing (although your instructor may ask you to include research to strengthen your argument)
If you are writing on a controversial topic, you do not take sides, though you may explain the position of both sides using objective language	You try to win your argument fairly, by using logic and making use of emotion where appropriate

Sample topic for an expository essay:

How the skeletal evolution of the penguin enabled it to adapt to an ocean environment.

In this case, the writer will inform and explain.
Sample topic for an expository essay that might use some argument:

What we can do to alleviate the impact of global warming on the emperor penguin habitat on Roosevelt Island.

How do you think argument might be involved—either directly or indirectly? What assumption is the writer making about the topic that the reader would be expected to agree with?
Sample topic for an argumentative essay:

Nations must act quickly and collectively to put an end to global warming, which is destroying penguin habitats in the Antarctic sub-continent.

Verbs like *must* and *should* usually signal an argumentative thesis.

Narration and Description

If you recall the excerpt by Alice Munro in Chapter 1, you will see that the writer is telling a story. That is what *narrative* does: it tells about something that has happened or is happening, relating incidents (usually, but not always, chronologically) and often revealing character. The narrative pattern is commonly used in fiction and in personal essays; it can be used occasionally in fact-based essays as well.

Description gives the reader concrete information, primarily about what is seen, but it can also make use of the other senses. If you use description in an expository essay, it is important to be as concrete as possible and avoid general, abstract words or phrases. Words such as "dank, dirty, and dreary," used in the third example below, help readers see details clearly in their mind. This helps them understand a detail as you meant it and not have to make assumptions that may be incorrect.

Narration and description are often used to convey immediacy. The selective use of either in factual writing can lend drama, directness, and impact to your essay. Consider the following as sample openings of fact-based expository essays.

Narrative:
Pali is five years old. She lives in sub-Saharan Africa in a small hut made of straw, mud, and cow manure. She lives with her two sisters, 13 and 15, and a brother, 2. She awakes at 2 a.m. Her older sister has returned home from her occupation—selling herself as a prostitute—in order to make enough to feed Pali and her siblings. She is now caring for Pali's brother who has severe diarrhoea. He has AIDS; he was born with it. Both of their parents are dead. Their

You can use narrative or description in an introduction to create a specific effect. In this narrative paragraph, the writer uses short, simple sentences with repetitive openings to suggest an endless cycle of suffering.

father died of AIDS two years ago; their mother was beaten to death one year ago after admitting that she, too, had AIDS. Such stories are not uncommon in sub-Saharan Africa today.

—Student writer James Pascoe

Description:

Today, Victoria's Parliament Building is the symbol of BC's government, and much of the interior is jammed with modern office equipment. However, visitors can stroll around the meticulously landscaped grounds during the daylight hours and, at night, view the building lit up with its geometric array of lights outlining one of the city's architectural wonders. Interior highlights include the giant rotunda, its walls adorned with historic murals. If you are lucky, you might discover a tiny spiral staircase that leads to the top of the main dome and end up in the stately legislative library which seems to retain the musty smell of BC's past.

—Student writer Stephanie Prizeman

The writer of this paragraph uses many adjectives and descriptive verbs to create a stereotypical city scene, then reverses the reader's expectations by the question at the end of the paragraph.

The alleyway is dank, dirty, and dreary. In its ill-lit past, it has harboured many of society's outcasts, providing temporary shelter to the homeless, out-of-the-way encounters for the prostitute and her customer, and, for the junkie, a convenient and anonymous place to shoot up. Tonight, it shrouds only four 16-year-olds, nervously sharing a brown-bagged bottle of vodka. The dinginess of the alley makes it hard to see that these teenagers are dressed in designer jeans and dark hoodies. What are respectable, middle-class young males doing in a place like this?

—Student writer Levi Newnham

Exercise 3.1

Read the above paragraphs. Underline specific words, phrases, or sections that illustrate the aspect of either narration or description. Are there any words or phrases that you think are not specific enough and could be improved? Once you have completed your analysis, work with a partner and discuss your findings.

Exercise 3.2

Narration, description, argument, and exposition are used in all types of writing. Look at some of your textbooks from other courses. Try to identify where the authors are using any of these methods. Why do you think they chose to use the method(s) they did? What other method(s), if any, could have been used?

The In-Class Essay or Examination Essay

You may have to do in-class writing, at least occasionally, during your academic career. Typically, you will be given a time in which to complete the assignment, which may add to your stress level. You will need to demonstrate both your knowledge of a subject and your writing skills. You may be able to use a text, notes, or a dictionary; or it may just be you, your pen, and some paper (or a computer).

Although in-class writing—especially exams—might be considered a necessary evil for many, it serves several practical purposes, demonstrating your ability to think, read, and write under pressure. Although these kinds of essays usually test recall, they also test other important qualities, such as organization and time management, discernment, and adaptability (see section on discernment and adaptability later in this chapter), as well as, possibly, creativity and imagination.

Recall

In-class or examination essays will require you to remember information from lectures, textbooks, and discussions; however, other factors may also be crucial. Being familiar with the *terminology* of your discipline is vital. This means that you need to be able to communicate effectively in the language of the discipline. For example, if you are writing an English literature exam, you will need to be able to understand and refer to terms used to analyze prose, poetry, and drama, such as metaphor or analogy.

You also need to be aware of *basic principles, procedures, and methods stressed throughout the year*. If you are asked to write one or more essays, you will need to know the basics of essay format and structure. If you are asked to write a summary of a text, you will need to know how to summarize; if you are asked to write a critical response to an essay, you will need to know how to analyze and think critically.

Nobody can remember everything that was taught, so you should allow enough time for a complete and leisurely review of your notes, highlighted sections of course texts, and instructor comments on term essays and tests. The goal is to distinguish the essential from the less-than-essential and enable you to focus on what you *need* to know. Although it's important to have a grasp of basic facts and details, essays more often test the *application* of facts than simple recall. For example, in psychology, you may need to know about B.F. Skinner and his theories of behaviourism, but the implications of his studies and the impact on the field of psychology may be more important than how he actually performed his tests. Use whatever methods you are comfortable with in committing these facts to memory. Writing out important material, reading critical points aloud, making personal associations, using verbal or visual aids, or using self-testing strategies all can be effective methods of study and reinforcement.

Organization and Time Management

It is important to spend a few minutes planning your approach to the questions. The advantages are two-fold: beginning the in-class assignment with a general plan ensures you will write a complete exam according to the exam instructions; second, planning the exam will give you a sense of control over circumstances that, otherwise, have been determined by someone else.

Once you have decided how the exam will be divided up and how much time to spend on the various parts, stick to your plan. It's common to spend too much

> Although in-class writing may test your ability to recall material, it also tests such important qualities as organization, time management, and adaptability.

> It is important to prepare for in-class writing with realistic expectations: the goal is to distinguish the essential from the less-than-essential and enable you to focus on what you *need* to know.

> Write It . . . Say It . . . Imagine It . . . Experience It . . . Picture It . . . Draw It . . . Test It . . . Repeat It . . . Understand It.

time on the first question. If you find yourself doing this, jot one or two points in the margin to follow up on, time permitting.

Do you begin with the longest question, the shortest question, the hardest or the easiest question, the one worth the most marks or ones worth fewer marks? It's probably safest to begin with the question you feel most comfortable with. Writing a confident answer can make you feel at ease when responding to the other questions.

Obviously, you should read the general exam instructions carefully before beginning. Resist the urge to dive right in. Read every word and underline key words or phrases to reinforce their importance and to keep them in mind as you write. Of course, the same applies to each question (see Discernment and Adaptability, below). Remember that writing skills are connected to reading and thinking skills. The student who misreads loses credibility as a writer because he or she has not followed directions. This is especially important when the question makes a distinction of some kind: "answer *three* of the following five questions"; "respond to *either* question one *or* question two." Also pay attention to the verb used to introduce or frame the question; *discuss*, *compare and contrast*, and *explain* give you three different instructions. Dictionaries are useful for interpreting questions and helping you find the right word. Ask your instructor if they are allowed. Once again, make sure your dictionary is suitable for college or university and that it is up-to-date.

Finally, plan for at least five minutes per question to look over the exam after you've finished writing to ensure that nothing has been omitted and that the marker will be able to follow your ideas. Final checks and careful proofreading are important—as are small additions, such as transitions to connect ideas. Instructors prefer to read a thoughtfully revised and carefully proofed essay, even one that has some deletions and, perhaps, even a couple of arrows, to one that is meticulous-looking but unclear in places. Neatness is important, but completeness and accuracy are more so.

> When writing an essay, pay close attention to the verb used to introduce the question. Words such as *discuss, compare and contrast,* and *explain* give you different instructions.

Discernment and Adaptability

Once you have done the necessary planning and are focusing on the individual question(s), you need to

1. distinguish what is important from what is less important, and
2. focus on strong, well-chosen points and supporting details, adapting the question, if necessary

In the sample essay question below, the writer has underlined the important parts of the question and has already begun to shape his answer by attempting to rephrase or elaborate on the question. At this stage, he is essentially looking for clues, hints, and suggestions for writing.

Before he can proceed from topic to thesis statement, he has to decide on his approach. The subject of discrimination is very large, and if he does not put some thought into limiting it, he may find himself becoming too vague. One of the common weaknesses of in-class essays is the tendency to generalize, or to be too broad. Therefore, first limiting the topic and finding a distinct area to make your own will result in a more manageable essay.

When you limit or refine a general topic, you want to achieve focus and intensity. Ask yourself the following questions to help limit the topic:

- What do you personally know about the topic?
- Have you or anyone you know had experience with it?
- How can you relate the topic to your own knowledge base or skills area?

Finding where you are knowledgeable is the key to refining the topic in order to use your demonstrable strengths to best effect.

All essays will benefit from examples and illustrations by giving you solid support for your points. Examples and illustrations will also turn the general and abstract into the concrete and specific. Details are essential. Consider using a pre-writing technique, such as questioning or brainstorming, to generate detail.

> Examples and illustrations will also turn the general and abstract into the concrete and specific.

The student who wrote the essay below was given 90 minutes, enough time to develop an approach to his topic and a thesis statement, and to prepare a scratch outline. Of course, you may not be given this much time to write an in-class essay; as a result, you might not be able to develop each point as thoroughly as this writer has done. Note that this student was very well-prepared and made use of a dictionary; as a result, he wrote an excellent paper.

Sample Student Essay

Exam question: Although Western cultures have striven to identify and eradicate many of the more obvious faces of discrimination today, subtle and covert forms of discrimination, particularly racism and sexism, exist in our lives, which can be activated by day-to-day circumstances. Discuss this form of discrimination as you believe it exists today.

Student's response: Although Western cultures have striven to identify and eradicate many of the more obvious faces of discrimination today, subtle and covert forms of discrimination, **(i.e., that are not acknowledged by society)** particularly racism and sexism, exist in our lives, which can be activated by day-to-day circumstances **(this makes them escape everyday notice)**. Discuss this form of discrimination **(i.e., hidden subtle forms)** as you believe it exists today **("believe" suggests that I can use opinion—as long as it is supported by facts and examples)**.

By Jon Zacks

(Continued)

Although racism is often not expressed overtly today, it is still very much alive. The fact that it often takes subtle forms makes it no less harmful; in fact, it could be considered more harmful. Our society has embraced a dominant ideology, which, while it accepts and tolerates "others," continues to affirm white, middle-class males as the power bloc. This is particularly obvious in the media, in politics, and in academia.

Discrimination in the media is perhaps the most difficult form to see, and thus to attack. However, an attentive viewer will realize just how pervasive it is. Perhaps the best examples can be found in film and television culture. Dominant cinema is one of the most powerful ideology mechanisms in contemporary North America. In film, no representation is ideologically neutral. Rather, mainstream cinema is laden with the hegemony that is encoded into the images we see. Films such as the *Die Hard* trilogy and *Indiana Jones* are examples of this. In these films, the white male hero saves the world from the disorder caused by the "others." Using binary oppositions, these "others" are set up as inferior and threatening to our comfortable existence.

Of course, it is not only the fictional in media that serves to promote this dominant ideology. Contemporary news media is rife with hegemonic treatment of public events. Never has this been more evident than after the terrorist attacks in New York City in September 2001. The media immediately set the terrorism up as the work of radical religious fanatics, Arab extremists, and anti-capitalist fundamentalists. By setting the terrorists up as others, retribution is justified. As well, national security is once again promoted by showing that these others live elsewhere and will be contained. The dominant ideology was thus served by "othering" the Islamic Arabs, and glorifying the (mostly white male) heroes at home. While there have been objections to the mistreatment of minorities in the US, the media has conveyed the message that these minorities must be accepted (superficially) because they are now American. The fact that the media is so successful with this hegemony also suggests that this latent racism is present not only in the powers that be but also in society itself.

In politics in general, this hegemony is promoted. The incidents since September 11 have shown American politicians trying to accommodate minorities while essentially serving the interests of the majority. Indeed, this is typical of politics in general. We can see regular occurrences of governments making changes to the system so that minorities will feel less oppressed. However, these changes are mere concessions. What is becoming obvious is that the entire system is built on discrimination, power, and patriarchy. This system must make concessions to accommodate the voices of opposition and avoid losing power. It is not until people realize that the system is indeed built on subjection and patriarchy that true changes can be made.

A final example of discrimination can be seen in academia. Areas such as art history, history, and cultural studies provide examples of discrimination within the educational and academic worlds. For example, History in Art has long been viewed as essentially a history of Western Art. Most of us are familiar with the works of great European artists of the Renaissance, etc. While almost everyone knows of the *Mona Lisa*, very few people are aware of any Aboriginal, African, Indian, Chinese, Japanese, Mesoamerican or Native art. Many see the *Mona Lisa* as the greatest painting created. By contrast, we often see Native American art as ugly or primitive. Not until these marginalized art forms are viewed as equal can they stand alongside dominant art. There are many people who would argue that Native arts, for example, have been accepted in Western culture. However, they have not been truly accepted. Rather, we buy Native arts because we see them as novel and feel good about having a Roy Henry Vickers (a Native-American hybrid) beside a Picasso or a Renoir.

Western culture continues to endorse the discriminatory hegemony that has plagued it since oppositional voices first began demanding acceptance. Our culture has heard these voices, and rather than changing the very structure upon which it has been built, it has made superficial concessions. As media and culture have shown, oppositional voices are tolerated, but they are still marginalized. It is not until we deconstruct our culture and realize that it is founded on discrimination that this discrimination can be eradicated. And, as always, the hardest thing to fight is complacency. If someone is not aware that the system is unjust, there is no reason that he or she would realize that it needs to change.

(Continued)

A.

1. How did the writer limit the topic? Do you think he has an area of expertise or specialization that he was able to use in order to adapt the topic to capitalize on his knowledge?

2. Identify the thesis statement and the main points (the latter take the form of topic sentences for the body paragraphs). Why do you think he used the order of points he did?

3. Some of the writer's statements could be challenged. Do you think that, within the constraints of the in-class essay form, the writer has adequately supported his points? How has he done this? Has he failed to do this anywhere?

4. Returning to the exam question, do you think the writer directly addressed what he was asked to address? Suggest other viable ways that a student writer could respond to the question.

B. Give yourself 90 minutes to write a 500-word response to the same question.

Exercise 3.3

Based on the information you collected for exercises 2.8 and 2.9 in Chapter 2 (pages 40 and 41), write an essay about the topic you chose. Address the audience you profiled for Exercise 2.9.

After you have written the essay, determine how you would change it if the audience were different. For example, what would you change if you were to write the essay for your professor or for someone in high school? Give specific examples of what you would change or how you would change it.

The Critical Response

Both in-class and out-of-class assignments often require you to analyze an essay you have never seen before. To do so, you need to exercise your active reading skills, beginning with comprehension of content. Responses should demonstrate effective critical thinking and your ability to analyze such elements as the writer's purpose, audience, and strategies. Depending on the nature of the assignment, you may be able to use your own perspective on and/or experience about an issue, as the writer of the in-class essay above has done. You may be asked to focus mainly on the essay itself or on the issue(s) the author raises. Critical responses can vary in length.

Because they provide a forum for opinion, critical responses can be considered argumentative: a strong response will convince readers that your thesis is valid and well-supported. Although critical responses often clarify your thoughts about an issue or reveal your feelings about it, you should not force your opinions on the text. The main function of critical responses is to engage with the text and through this engagement to share your views with others.

Below are some of the objectives and conventions of response writing. Remember, though, to pay careful attention to the guidelines you're given, as they can vary greatly from instructor to instructor and from assignment to assignment.

> The main function of critical responses is to engage with the text and through this engagement to share your views with others.

- Your first sentences could include an overview or generalization about the text or the central issue(s) it raises.
- If your reader is unfamiliar with the text, you will need to briefly summarize its main ideas (or plot, if the text is a literary work or a movie).
- Include a thesis statement in which you succinctly state your approach to the essay, topic, or issue.
- Don't lose sight of the fact that you are primarily reacting to *a text* and that the text should remain front and centre in your analysis. If you use personal experience or observation, it should never *replace* analysis but should help support a point.
- You don't need to research the topic, unless your instructor requires this.
- The length of critical responses can vary considerably from a couple of well-developed paragraphs to 500 words or more, depending on the nature of the assignment and length of the work you are responding to.
- In some critical responses, you may be required to respond to more than just the text—for example, to another student's response to the text. In that case, you will need to filter your perspective through that of another reader, considering the validity of his or her views and your agreement or disagreement. Sometimes, instructors will help get you started by posing specific questions about the text.
- In addition to analyzing what is in the essay, you can consider what is *not* in the essay. What has the writer left unsaid?

The following questions are often relevant to critical responses. (For a more complete list of questions applicable to a wide range of readings, see Responding Critically and Analytically through Questions, page 18).

- Does the author appear reasonable? Has he or she used reason effectively, establishing a chain of logic throughout? Are there failures in logic?
- Does the author succeed in making the issue relevant to the reader? Does he or she appeal to the reader's concerns and values? How does he or she do this? (or not?)

- Is the tone inviting? (openly challenging, neutral?)
- Is the order of points appropriate? Are all points well supported?
- What, specifically, would strengthen the writer's argument?
- Does the essay appear free of bias? Is the voice as objective as possible given the argumentative stance? Authors sometimes openly declare their opinions. If this is the case, do you think this was a good strategy?
- Has the author acknowledged the other side? How has he or she responded to the opposing viewpoint? (fairly, effectively?)
- Does the author make emotional appeals? Are any extreme or manipulative?

Sample Professional Essay

AN ENVIRO'S CASE FOR SEAL HUNT
By Terry Glavin

I saw something the other day that made me sick to my stomach. It was in the February edition of The Grocer, a British retail-food magazine.

There was an article about a campaign that a group called Respect for Animals is waging to convince consumers to boycott Canadian seafood products. The magazine also carried two huge advertisements from the same outfit.

One of the ads consisted of a photograph of a masked man on an ice floe, and a seal lying prone at his feet. The man was brandishing a club with a spike on the end of it. The words You Can Stop This were superimposed upon the picture. The other advertisement proclaimed "Boycott Canadian Seafood & Save the Seals," with a picture of a can of Canadian salmon.

The Canadian fishing industry exports more than $100 million worth of products into Britain every year. The point of the campaign is to squeeze those sales until the industry begs our government to end the seal hunt.

5   Here's what makes me sick.

The Newfoundland seal hunt is transparently and demonstrably sustainable and humane. There are roughly half a million people in Newfoundland and Labrador, and nearly six million harp seals, which is almost three times as many seals as when I was a kid.

Roughly 6,000 fishermen, mostly Newfoundlanders, but some are from Quebec and the Maritimes, take slightly more than 300,000 harp seals annually. The fishermen share more than $16 million from the hunt at a critical time of year when there's little in the way of fishing income to be had. The seals are harvested for their pelts and their fat, for a range of products, mostly for clothing and for Omega-3 vitamins.

The killing is as about as clean as anything you're likely to find in an abattoir. Seals don't spend their lives cooped up in paddocks or feedlots. They live free, and in all but the rarest cases, the ones that die at the hands of a swiler (a sealer) die instantly. The hakapik (a spiked club) is an effective instrument.

Even so, most seals are first shot with rifles. The killing of nursing white-coats was banned 20 years ago.

Exploiting empathy

10 Here's one of those obligatory disclosures: over the years, several environmental organizations—the Sierra Club, the David Suzuki Foundation, Greenpeace, etc.—have subsidized my preoccupation with things that move in the water by having me do research projects for them and so on. With that out of the way, I can now say, if it isn't obvious already, that it's the seal hunt's opponents who turn my stomach.

It's not just that anti-hunt crusades like this are especially foul in the way they dishonestly misrepresent facts. It's also that they dishonestly manipulate one of the most redeeming traits the human species has inherited from hundreds of thousands of years of natural selection and cultural evolution—our capacity to expand the embrace of our empathy to include other forms of life.

But far worse than all that, boycott campaigns like this muddy the important distinction between sustainability and sentiment, and between broadly co-ordinated acts of social responsibility and mere lifestyle choices. When we fail to make these distinctions we undermine everything worthwhile that environmentalism has accomplished since it emerged in the early 1970s.

As citizens and consumers in free societies, we are burdened with the duty to make important decisions at the ballot box, in the work we do, and also in the marketplace. Boycotting Canadian seafood to try and stop the seal hunt is the consumer-choice equivalent of deciding to buy a tie-died shirt, move into a Volkswagen van and subsist solely on lentils and tofu.

Serious stakes

Just as the excesses of postmodernist relativism have enfeebled the left over the past quarter-century or so, a corrosive strain of fact-distorting, science-hating, Gaia-bothering obscurantism has enfeebled environmentalism.

15 It was there from the beginning, and it persists most noticeably in animal-rights crusades. It is the environmentalist equivalent of anti-evolution, rapture-seeking Christian zealotry. It has to be attacked wherever it rears its head. There's too much at stake to pretend we can be innocent bystanders here. This is a fight we all have to join.

Here's why.

The last time the planet was in the throes of an extinction spasm this cataclysmic was when the dinosaurs disappeared 65 million years ago. One in every four mammal species, one in eight bird species, one in nine plants, a third of all amphibians and half of all the surveyed fish species on earth are threatened with extinction.

When Greenpeace was born in Vancouver in 1971, the single greatest cause of species extinction was understood to be habitat loss. Now, the greatest threat to biological diversity is global warming. The last time the atmosphere was accumulating greenhouse gases this fast was 650,000 years ago. The prospects look exceedingly grim—broad-scale ecological disruption, crop failure and famine, desertification and the mass disloca-tion of some of the most heavily-populated regions of the world.

A key reason environmentalists found themselves so ill-prepared to con-vince the world to take global warming seriously was that their move-ment had been corrupted by precisely the same trippy sentiment-mon-gering that has animated the holy war against the Newfoundland seal hunt, which now turns its sights on Canadian fisheries products.

Where was Greenpeace?

20   When the founders of Greenpeace were being born, back in the 1950s, the world's fishing fleets were taking roughly 40 million tonnes of marine biomass from the world's oceans every year. By the 1980s, it was 80 mil-lion tonnes. Then the seas just stopped giving. Fully 90 per cent of all the big fish in the sea—the tunas, the marlins, the sharks, the swordfish—are now gone.

Of the many fisheries collapses that have occurred around the world in recent years, it is sadly ironic that the greatest single collapse occurred in the seas around Newfoundland, where the bulk of Canada's Atlantic seal hunt takes place. The Grand Banks cod fishery was the largest and oldest pelagic fishery in the history of the human experience.

The cod were mined from the sea by the same big-boat offshore fleets that had caused such devastation everywhere else. A way of life disappeared, and by the early 1990s, tens of thousands of workers were reduced to welfare. While all this was happening, what were environmentalists doing on the Newfoundland coast, in the country where Greenpeace was born, at a time when Greenpeace was at the height of its powers?

They were out cavorting with rich hippies and snuggling up to harp seal pups on the ice floes. They were meditating cross-legged in the snow and posing for the television cameras and demonizing the good people of Newfoundland, while the seas around them were being emptied of cod . . . .

The whole point of sustainability is to ensure that people can exercise the rights and accept the responsibilities that come with sustainably harvest-ing the natural resources of the ecosystems within which they live. The harp seal hunt is a living embodiment of that principle. That's why envi-ronmentalists should not just give the boycott a pass, or stay neutral, but should actively support and defend the seal hunt.

The one consolation we can take from the recent hullabaloo is that it's faltering. Last year, when animal-rightists in the United States boasted that they'd convinced more than 200 restaurants and seafood retailers to boycott Canadian products to protest the hunt, it turned out that only a small minority were doing so. Most of them didn't even know they'd been listed as boycott-compliant.

Also, the European Commission, citing the absence of evidence to support contentions that the hunt is inhumane, has refused, for now, to enforce the European Parliament's proposed ban on seal products.

Contested Council

30 But the consumer boycott campaign that's just begun in Britain is particularly insidious. Its aim is all Canadian fisheries products, and its targets are Tesco, Sainsbury's, Somerfield and other major retail chains that have already made a commitment to eventually carrying only those seafood products that have been certified by the Marine Stewardship Council (MSC).

The MSC standard remains hotly contested by responsible environmentalists, but its coveted "eco-label" holds out the hope of forcing improvements to fisheries-management policies around the world. In Canada, those improvements are increasingly driven by the fishermen themselves, because they want the MSC label on their product.

British Columbia's halibut fishery was turned down once, and has since re-applied, because groundfish management has significantly improved—thanks in no small part to halibut fishermen. Other fishermen are now lobbying federal fisheries officials to improve stock-assessment research to give B.C.'s dogfish fishery a shot at the MSC label. British Columbia's sockeye salmon fisheries have just undergone an arduous certification examination, and a decision is imminent.

If the cuddliness of a particular species harvested in a particular country is allowed to become the factor that determines whether that country's products are considered environmentally acceptable, then everything we won at CITES [Convention on the International Trade in Endangered Species] and in the Brundtland Commission is lost. If those are the kinds of choices we present to everyone from major retailers down to ordinary seafood consumers, then we'll have wasted all our efforts to marshal consumer power to force the sustainable use of the oceans.

It's long past time for conservationists to make a clean, clear, open and unequivocal break with crystal-gazing animal-rights eccentrics and all their camp followers. For them, the conservation of wild resources was always just a flag of convenience. They're dead ballast, so over the side with them.

35 On the question of the Atlantic harp seal harvest, there's only one defensible and honest position for a conservation-minded citizen to take:

Support the swilers.

—Glavin, T. (2007, March 7). An enviro's case for seal hunt. *TheTyee.ca.*
Retrieved from http://thetyee.ca/Views/2007/03/07/SealHunt/

Remember that the essay you respond to may be written more informally than your critical response to it. For example, the writer may not have cited sources or may have used slang or colloquial language. You should check with your instructor before using an informal style.

Below, student Bryan Smith has written a 500-word critical response to Glavin's essay. After you have read the essay and the response, discuss with a partner whether it satisfies the requirements of the response essay. Then, write a 350–500 word response to Glavin's essay. If your instructor wishes, you may refer to Smith's response (as he refers to responses of other students in his class).

Sample Student Essay

Response to "An Enviro's Case for Seal Hunt"
By Bryan Smith

Glavin provides a strong argument for the seal hunt in his article, a rare and unexpected standpoint. Though his argument takes on a fire and brimstone tone that gets more offensive as he proceeds, Glavin has me convinced: the seal hunt is wrongly accused. While I feel much of what Glavin says must be taken with a grain of salt, a number of his points make a convincing argument. First, the boycott of Canadian seafood against the seal hunt is doing more damage than good. As proven by the whale and cod crises, boycotts result in over fishing because fishermen have to take more to make profit. Canadian seafood is an entirely different problem; with increasing international fish exploitation off the shores of Canada, the boycott only steps on the toes of activists trying to fight for sustainable local fisheries. Is it any wonder Glavin is calling for responsible activism?

What makes the seal hunt so awful? Indigenous hunters and fishers have been practicing their traditional methods off Canada's coasts for thousands of years with proven moderation and sustainability. Hunting is not everyone's cup of tea, but that doesn't mean it is bad. The seal hunt has gone on for thousands of years as a means of subsistence and economic support in a climate where little else can. It is not only a means of life but also a way of life for many people. If Canada truly is a country that celebrates diversity, condemning hunters and fishers for their traditional means of subsistence and economy is just a little hypocritical.

Simply because Glavin is "ill-tempered" is not a good reason to take the other side of the argument, as some of my classmates have done. Glavin is understandably frustrated—with so much that needs to change in the world, the anti-seal hunt is just another distraction that divides a population that needs to act quickly and in unison. Glavin has clearly put a lifetime into conservationism only to have his work ignored while far-away people denounce what is perhaps the only example of sustainable fishing left. What did you expect Glavin to be? He has every reason to be ill-tempered: change needs to happen now, and it needs to be led by people who are in possession of all the facts, the power to lead, and the experience to do so. Yet distractions bar this from happening.

That said, perhaps Glavin goes too far. The seal hunt has a number of benefits, it seems sustainable, and according to Glavin, it is responsibly carried out. But that doesn't mean some preventative measures should not be taken. Why not put some preventative restrictions on the hunt? With a full and thriving population, we have the time to analyse the effects of maximum kills and season restrictions before such measures have no worth. Thus, perhaps "support the responsible, moderated, and sustainable swilers" might be a better slogan.

1. Has the student written a good response? Give specific examples to support your thoughts.

2. What specific points has he chosen to address from the original essay?

3. Are there any important points that you feel he missed and should have included?

4. Are there points that you feel the student writer should not have included?

5. Do you agree with the student's point of view? Do you feel that he could have added more information to strengthen his position?

6. Are there any areas in this response essay that are unclear, or did the student judge his audience appropriately?

Chapter Review Questions

1. What is the difference between an expository and an argumentative essay?

2. What is the purpose of writing an argumentative essay?

3. What are some characteristics of narrative essays?

4. Why are descriptive essays written?

5. What are some important factors to remember when writing an in-class or an examination essay?

6. What is a critical response and how does its purpose differ from expository and argumentative essays discussed at the beginning of this chapter?

Paragraph Essentials

In this chapter you will

- learn how to construct an effective paragraph

- understand why it is important to write coherently

- learn techniques to improve paragraphs

- understand how effective paragraph structure reflects effective essay structure

Like essays, all paragraphs need to have a beginning, middle, and end. If any of these elements are missing, such as the topic sentence at the beginning, the paragraph could lack unity and coherence, and you could lose the reader's attention. In addition, paragraphs need to be connected to each other to help the reader follow the essay's points. This chapter will help you create unified and coherent paragraphs so you will write an essay that keeps the reader's interest.

◎ Introducing the Paragraph

Like essays themselves, paragraphs must be organized to serve specific functions:

- to introduce an important point
- to develop that point
- to convey both the important point and its development clearly to the reader

Paragraphs and essays both have beginnings, middles, and ends. The beginning announces what is to follow, usually in the **topic sentence** of the paragraph or the *thesis statement* of the essay. Without a clear topic sentence, the points will lack force and the paragraph will not be unified.

The middle of the paragraph develops the main point, while the ending provides a satisfying conclusion. The concluding sentence may act as a **wrap** by summarizing the main idea in the paragraph, in this way functioning much like the conclusion of an essay.

In high school, you may have been taught to end a paragraph by leading into the next one. This, in practice, can be very difficult, and it can become tedious for the reader if you end each paragraph this way. Instead, try to focus on wrapping up the topic in your paragraph effectively before introducing the next topic. Above all, do not try to end a paragraph with one sentence that both concludes your main idea *and* introduces the next one as this would likely confuse a reader.

Topic Sentences

Topic sentences introduce the main idea in the paragraph. Therefore, the topic sentence is usually the most general sentence while the other sentences in the paragraph illustrate or expand on the main idea in some way. The topic sentence is usually the first sentence in the paragraph for the same reason that the thesis statement usually occurs in the introduction (first paragraph) of the essay: it provides a logical starting point and makes the paragraph easy to follow.

Paragraph Wraps as Conclusions

Using a paragraph wrap is a satisfying way to conclude a paragraph as it reminds the reader what the paragraph was about. However, the wrap doesn't just repeat the topic sentence; it reinforces its importance using different words. In the following paragraph, student writer Jordan Van Horne successfully wraps the main idea, which is introduced in the first (topic) sentence (both sentences are italicized):

If speed limits were abolished on highways, the necessity for law enforcement officers to patrol the highway for speeders would be curtailed. As a result, police chiefs might have more officers to assign to special community projects, such as MADD or drug awareness projects in elementary schools.

These officers could spend their time on a variety of social and community projects that would benefit a large number of youths precisely at the time when they need this guidance. In addition, more officers could be allotted to other important areas that are typically understaffed today, such as surveillance and patrol duty to prevent drug smuggling. *Surely the presence of police in the community or their dedication to large-scale projects such as drug-smuggling would be more beneficial to public safety than having them patrol the highways.*

Wraps are especially effective in longer paragraphs (five to eight sentences) where the reader might lose track of the main idea.

Connecting Paragraphs by Using Transitions

Whether or not the paragraph contains a wrap, it is important that the reader can connect it to what follows. Well-constructed paragraphs not only state the main point, develop it, and reinforce it, but also lead the reader smoothly to the next

Exercise 4.1

In each set of sentences, choose which one would make the best topic sentence for the paragraph. Remember that the topic sentence states the main (most general) point.

1. essay topic: the 100-mile diet

    a) In small communities, stores often use local products to produce their own wares.

    b) Eating locally is one way to sustain the local economy and farming community.

    c) For example, on Vancouver Island, most grocery stores sell dairy products from Island Farms and other regional dairies.

2. essay topic: cell phones

    a) Recent studies have found that the brain cannot handle all the multitasking we try to do.

    b) We interrupt our meals, leave conversations, and forget to concentrate on our driving in order to answer our cell phones.

    c) Cell phones dominate the lives of many people in society today.

3. essay topic: physical education classes

    a) Physical education classes teach skills and knowledge not usually stressed in other classes.

    b) Skills like physical coordination and teamwork are developed in PE classes.

    c) PE classes allow more opportunities for social interaction, which is an essential skill in building future relationships and careers.

point (paragraph), like a well-oiled hinge connecting two solid objects. This is can be done through transitions: words, phrases, or clauses that link ideas. Theoretically, transitions can occur at the end of one paragraph as a form of a wrap or at the beginning of the next paragraph as part of the topic sentence. Your instructor may prefer one position or the other or leave it up to you. Remember, though, that you must complete the paragraph so that the reader understands that you are finished discussing that particular topic or aspect of it.

The question to ask yourself is if the reader can follow your train of thought from one paragraph to the next. Most readers expect a new paragraph to introduce a new topic. However, the precise relationship between the two topics may not always be clear. If not, consider using a transition to clarify it. In the following student essay, Marissa Miles began her new paragraph with a dependent clause transition (underlined) before introducing the topic for the paragraph (italicized). From the transition, you can see that the previous paragraph focused on the fostering of independence through home schooling.

> <u>Although the qualities of independence and self-motivation are important in a home-schooled education</u>, *its flexibility enables the child to learn at his or her own pace, matching progress to the child's natural learning processes.*

The writer of the following paragraph has combined an indirect reference to the preceding paragraph with the topic sentence of the current one:

> Another crucial function of genetic engineering is its application to the pharmaceutical industry.
>
> —Student writer Neil Weatherall

> When making connections between paragraphs, avoid brief one-word transitions. They usually aren't strong enough to link two main points, though they can be useful *within paragraphs* to link two sub-points.

In general, avoid the kinds of transitions used to connect sentences *within* paragraphs, such as *for example, consequently, moreover,* and similar words and phrases (see Transitions, below). They are not usually strong enough to connect a main idea in one paragraph to a main idea in the next one.

Good paragraphs are unified, coherent, and well-developed. Paragraph unity and coherence are discussed below. Because there are many different ways that main points can be developed in a paragraph or throughout an essay, Paragraph Development is discussed separately in Chapter 6.

> All paragraphs in formal writing should possess unity, coherence, and development.

Paragraph Unity

> Each paragraph should focus on *one* central idea announced in the topic sentence.

As mentioned, each paragraph should focus on *one* central idea announced in the topic sentence. Although it is usually best to place your topic sentence at the beginning, *the topic sentence anchors thought in the paragraph*, so this anchoring *could* occur in the beginning, middle, or end. In a unified paragraph, all sentences in the paragraph relate to the main idea wherever that idea occurs.

Paragraphing, however, is not a mechanical process. Although the principle of one idea per paragraph is sound and logical, it may sometimes be difficult to tell where one idea ends and the next one begins. This is especially true in rough drafts where you are trying to get your ideas down and may not always be attentive to paragraph structure. Therefore, when you revise your essay, an important question to ask is whether each paragraph contains one main idea.

Also, in revising, you may see that one paragraph is much longer than the others. In such cases, you can determine a logical place to divide the paragraph into two smaller paragraphs. In the case of short paragraphs, you should consider combining them, as short paragraphs may come across as simplistic and underdeveloped. When combining short paragraphs ensure that logical transitions are used between connecting sentences.

> Although there is no "perfect" paragraph length, some instructors will give students an ideal range—such as between four and six or seven sentences—to ensure each paragraph is sufficiently developed but not so long that it becomes complicated and hard to read.

Exercise 4.2 Paragraph Exercise: Unity

The lengthy paragraph below needs to be broken up into several smaller unified paragraphs. Determine the natural paragraph breaks and mark where the new paragraphs should start. Remember to avoid a succession of very short paragraphs; occasionally, short paragraphs may be acceptable, but too many of them make for choppy and disconnected writing.

In argumentative essays, defining something is often the first stage of an argument in which you go on to develop your thesis statement through means *other than* definition. On the other hand, definition essays can expand and elaborate on a subject, using a variety of organizational methods. Definition often provides a necessary starting point for an argument. The success you have in getting your reader to agree with your definition will help establish your credibility as a writer, strengthening your argument. Defining something also enables you to set the terms on which you want your argument to rest: successful definition enables you to take control of a controversial or abstract topic. Definition is often an essential part of expository essays. Essays in the humanities, natural sciences, and social sciences often begin by defining terms that the writer will employ throughout the essay. It may be crucial for the writer to establish the sense or connotation of one or more terms that have been subject to a variety of definitions in the writer's discipline. Many academic texts—above all, introductory textbooks—include a glossary or index of common terms that is designed to make it easier to apply terms correctly. It is important to provide an accurate definition in your essay, as definitions sometimes change over time and according to place, as well as according to cultural, national, social, and other factors. For example, the way you would define *privacy* today would likely be different from the way it would have been defined 25 years ago, due partly to technologies that have made it easier for others to access personal information. If you fail to provide the correct definition as it applies to your essay topic, you fail to prove your credibility, which in turn affects the reader's reaction to your essay.

When you have decided on logical paragraphing, look at the way the paragraph was divided in this text (the revised paragraphs are in Chapter 8, pages 141–42).

Exercise 4.3

In the following paragraphs, one sentence is off-topic, affecting the paragraph's unity. Identify the sentence that doesn't belong and explain why it is off-topic.

1. The requirement to display the N (new driver) sign on your vehicle is a reasonable one. It allows other drivers to recognize that the driver may be inexperienced. These drivers may drive more cautiously around the novice driver. It also alerts law enforcement officials to the fact that the driver is learning how to cope in traffic. However, officers have been known to pull over an N driver even if they have no legitimate reason to do so. Since alcohol consumption is often high in teenagers, the N sign in the rear window enables police to monitor for drunk driving more effectively. The requirement is therefore beneficial for both other drivers and the police.

2. The ability to concentrate during classes can easily be affected by a student's lack of activity. Most students find it difficult to sit around for six hours each day with only a lunch break, during which they might also do nothing but sit and eat. Exercise gives students relief from simply passively taking in information hour after hour. It especially helps children with high energy levels who find it hard to sit still. In addition, exercise is a solution to the ever-growing problem of obesity. By breaking up the day by at least one compulsory period of activity, students will be able to retain more information and perform better academically.

Paragraph Coherence

> In a coherent paragraph, the writer has used strategies to connect one sentence to the next one.

It is often easy to identify a paragraph that contains more than one idea or an off-topic sentence, but identifying a paragraph that lacks coherence may be more difficult. The word *cohere* means "stick together." Someone who is incoherent doesn't make sense; his or her words or ideas don't stick together. By contrast, someone who is coherent is easy to follow. It is the same with a paragraph: one that lacks coherence is hard to follow. The words and the ideas might be jumbled or disconnected. They do not stick in the reader's mind.

Here is the opening of an essay about the need for a nutritional diet. Although the ideas are quite simple, the passage isn't easy to follow. Try to determine why this is the case.

Most children throughout Canada depend on their parents to provide them with the proper nutrients each day. There are many contributing factors that make this ideal unachievable, and this lack can cause children to cultivate a serious disease known as obesity.

Now consider a rewritten version of this passage. Do you find it easier to follow? Why?

Most Canadian children depend on their parents for adequate daily nutrition. However, many factors can prevent them from achieving their nutritional ideal, which may result in obesity, a serious medical disorder.

Part of the problem lies in the words themselves: *cultivate* and *disease* are not the best words in this context. However, what also helps the words and ideas stick together is the careful use of repetition and transitions. In the rewritten version, the writer has replaced *this ideal* by *their nutritional ideal*, linking the *ideal* to *nutrition* in the first sentence. By adding the transition *however* and replacing *and* by *which*, the relationship between the ideas becomes clearer.

Most Canadian children depend on their parents for adequate daily *nutrition*. *However*, many factors can prevent them from achieving their *nutritional ideal*, *which* may result in obesity, a serious medical disorder.

In this example, student writer Walter Jordan evokes the new awareness of his friend during a camping trip after the death of his friend's grandfather. Coherence here is achieved largely through the use of repetition, rhythm, and balanced structures, all of which are discussed below.

On previous trips, we had noticed the smell of nature when we woke and filled our lungs with fresh air, but this time he noticed the smell of the water and of the rain-sprinkled flowers. We had often looked at the stars on a clear night, but this time he spoke of the deep darkness of the sky; we had always seen the ground we stepped on, but this time he saw the footsteps left behind us.

There are specific strategies you can use to ensure your paragraphs are coherent, or easy to follow.

Word Choice

When you consider what words to use, remember that it is not always a case of the right word versus the wrong word. Often, more than one word can convey your intended meaning, so it may be a question of choosing the best word for the given context. Whenever you use a word that is not part of your everyday vocabulary, you should confirm its meaning by looking it up in a dictionary. For written assignments, it's helpful to exchange your writing with someone else and pay attention to any passages that strike your reader as unclear. You will probably know words that he or she will not know and vice versa.

Patterns of Development

Coherent paragraphs often follow a distinct pattern. Paragraphs can be given a spatial, chronological, cause and effect, division, compare and contrast, or other pattern. Organizational patterns are discussed in detail in Chapter 6.

Understanding the meaning of words is important for both reading and writing. If you do not understand a word when you are reading, this can affect *your* understanding of the essay. If you do not understand the meaning of a word when writing, this can affect *your reader's* understanding of your essay. Strategies for learning word meanings are discussed in Chapter 1, p. 25.

Logical Sentence Order

Recall that your writing is closely connected to your thinking and that you need to make your thought process clear to your reader. If one idea does not logically proceed from the previous one, then the paragraph will not be coherent. Similarly, there may be one or more gaps in a paragraph that need to be filled in, perhaps by inserting a sentence.

Repetition and Synonyms

By repeating key words or phrases, you can help the reader follow the main idea in the paragraph. While repetition enables the writer to reinforce the core idea in the paragraph, think of alternative words and expressions, such as **synonyms**. Experienced writers also consider the rhythm of the sentence, often placing the repeated words, or key words, at strategic points in the paragraph.

Using selective repetition is not the same as being repetitious, which can occur when you *needlessly* repeat a word or idea.

> Synonyms are words that mean the same thing as, and can therefore replace, other words.

Parallel Structures

Experienced writers also use parallel and/or balanced structures to achieve coherence. One of the reasons why so many readers can remember the beginnings and endings of Charles Dickens's novels is that Dickens often employed balanced structures: "It was the best of times; it was the worst of times" (*A Tale of Two Cities*). (See Chapter 16, page 389 for more information about parallelism.)

Transitions

Transitional words and phrases guide the reader from one sentence to the next, signalling the exact relationship between them. Often, just adding the right transitional words will give the paragraph the coherence that is needed. However, if you fail to use a transition to connect two ideas, the reader may find it hard to follow the paragraph's development. Some of the most useful transitions are listed below:

> Note the way that the word *However* in the third line of the paragraph opposite tells the reader that the idea in the third sentence contrasts with the idea in the first two. *However* is a transition of contrast.

- **Transitions of Limit or Concession:** admittedly, although, it is true that, naturally, of course, though
- **Transitions of Cause and Effect:** accordingly, as a result, because, consequently, for this reason, if, otherwise, since, so, then, therefore, thus
- **Transitions of Illustration:** after all, even, for example, for instance, indeed, in fact, in other words, of course, specifically, such as
- **Transitions of Emphasis:** above all, assuredly, certainly, especially, indeed, in effect, in fact, particularly, that is, then, undoubtedly
- **Transitions of Sequence and Addition:** after, again, also, and, as well, and then, besides, eventually, finally, first . . . second . . . third, furthermore, in addition, likewise, next, moreover, or, similarly, too, while

- **Transitions of Contrast or Qualification:** after all, although, but, by contrast, conversely, despite, even so, however, in spite of, instead, nevertheless, nonetheless, on the contrary, on the one hand. . .on the other hand, otherwise, rather (than), regardless, still, though, whereas, while, yet
- **Transitions of Summary or Conclusion:** finally, in conclusion, in effect, in short, in sum (summary), so, subsequently, that is, therefore, thus, to summarize

In spite of their helpfulness, transitional words and phrases can be overused. Too many can clutter the paragraph and the essay. In addition, try to avoid wordy transitions as they, too, produce clutter (examples include *in spite of the fact that, due to the fact that, first and foremost, finally in conclusion, in the final analysis*). See Chapter 17, page 411, for further information about this topic.

Remember, too, that a transitional word or phrase, by itself, does not provide a link in thought—it cannot be a substitute for that link; it can only assist the reader to move from one idea to the next. As mentioned in the section above about logical sentence order, writers need to be careful that there are no gaps in thought and that they have written with the reader in mind. The reader needs to be able to follow the writer's logic every step of the way. In the following passage, the writer has left something out, and no transitional word alone could bridge the gap:

> Society relies on an unbiased newscast in order to gain a true perspective on current events. Front-line employees are entering the TV news field underage and under-educated, thus often producing ill-informed reporting.

The writer has quickly moved from a generalization about the need for "unbiased" reporting to an example of one of the causes of "ill-informed reporting" but has not linked the generalization and the example. One logical link would be that newscasts today are sometimes biased or ill-informed. Then the writer can proceed to give examples of or solutions to this problem. As it is, the problem has not been stated clearly.

> Society relies on an unbiased newscast in order to gain a true perspective on current events. However, newscasts today are sometimes biased or ill-informed. This may be because front-line employees are entering the TV news field underage and under-educated, thus often producing ill-informed reporting.

Unified paragraphs, then, refer to one central idea; in coherent paragraphs, one sentence leads logically to the next sentence. Here are two diagrams that illustrate unity and coherence in which the sentences are represented by arrows:

S1 = sentence 1
S2 = sentence 2
S3 = sentence 3
S4 = sentence 4

When you use words or phrases to connect one idea to the next, be careful to punctuate correctly. In some cases, a comma may be correct, but in many other instances, you should begin a new sentence or use a semicolon before the transitional word or phrase. See Chapter 15 for punctuation rules governing transitional phrases.

Do not begin a sentence with the transitions "and," "but," "or," "so," or "yet." They should be used to connect two main ideas *within* a sentence.

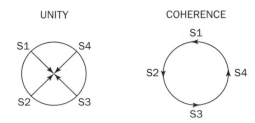

Figure 4.1   Unity and coherence.

Exercise 4.4 Paragraph Exercise: Coherence

The following passage contains a gap. Provide a logical link to make it coherent.

> The surprise attack on Pearl Harbor forced the US to be more aggressive in world politics. This interventionist policy has recently evolved into a policy of pre-emptive strikes on those perceived as a threat to US security.

Exercise 4.5 Paragraph Exercises: Coherence

I. Coherence through paragraph organization

You can use different ways to organize paragraphs: by chronology (time order), by spatial order (to describe a person, object, or scene), by comparing and contrasting, by division (dividing a general category into specific ones), and other methods (see Chapter 6).

A.   How are the ideas organized in these paragraphs? (See the methods in the paragraph above.)

B.   Besides the main organizational method(s), find other ways that the writer has achieved coherence.

> They came over the land bridge connecting Asia with Alaska, those first men of the Western Hemisphere. The date was between 20,000 and 30,000 years ago. They were hunters, dressed in the skins of the animals they hunted. Their weapons were stone-tipped spears. All this was long before Homer, before the dynasties of Egypt, before Sumer and the Land of the Two Rivers, and, of course, long before the Christian Bible was written. At that time, the glaciers that covered Canada and parts of the northeastern United States during the last ice age were melting. They melted first along river valleys, which turned into great misty, fog-haunted corridors between receding walls of ice.
>
> The hunters roamed south along those corridors, pursuing animals for food and clothing. They died eventually, as all people do, and their children came after them in

the long stammering repetition of humanity everywhere. The animals they hunted were principally caribou, bear, and mammoth—the latter long since extinct in North America. Camps of those early men have been discovered recently. They are the ghostly forbears of modern Indians and Eskimos.

—Al Purdy, *Aklavik on the Mackenzie River*

C.   What do you think the writer might have written about in the next paragraph?

II. Coherence through sentence order

Combine the sentences below in the most logical order to form a coherent paragraph; one sentence is not relevant to the topic of this paragraph and should be discarded. Supply any necessary links between one sentence and the next. More than one order may be possible. Be prepared to justify the particular order you used to achieve coherence.

1.   The disaster was caused by several safety procedures not being followed.

2.   Nuclear energy power plants, although very potent and about 50 to 80 times more efficient than coal-burning plants, produce wastes that are more hazardous than those of coal-burning plants.

3.   The explosion at Chernobyl not only contaminated the immediate surroundings but also contaminated areas several hundred miles away.

4.   The effects of radioactive wastes are long-lasting and may affect the environment for thousands of years.

5.   The disaster at the Chernobyl power plant in the Ukraine occurred in the summer of 1986.

6.   A lack of respect for potential disaster led to one of the biggest human-made disasters our planet has known.

7.   Nuclear energy will be able to meet the energy requirements of our society.

8.   This contamination was due to the nuclear fallout.

9.   Because of this disaster, a large area will no longer be habitable to human life for thousands of years.

10. Radioactive wastes are very damaging to the environment.

11. As is the case with everything on this planet, with great power comes an even greater responsibility.

III. Coherence through transitions

Using transitions can help sentences cohere, or stick together. The following paragraph lacks transitions. Provide logical connections between the sentences by choosing the appropriate transitions from the list below, filling in the blanks. Note: One transition has been given to you, and one transition should not be used in the paragraph.

Massive energy consumption is having a negative impact on the planet. ___, in the summer of 2006, western Europe experienced some of the hottest weather on record. *Moreover*, this temperature increase is not an isolated occurrence. ___, almost every credible scientist today believes that the earth is experiencing climate change due to the emissions of greenhouse gases from cars and coal-burning power plants. Ninety percent of the energy used in the US comes from fossil fuels: oil, coal, and natural gas (Borowitz 43), ___ problems arise from other sources, too. ___, nuclear power plants leave radioactive by-products, making storage difficult. ___, dams are not much better as nearby populations must be relocated, and the surrounding habitat is destroyed.

~~Moreover~~

But

Above all

For example

In fact

Unfortunately

For example

Exercise 4.6

Coherence through use of repetition, parallel structures, and transitions

Even though a writer uses a specific organizational method and carefully orders his or her points, a paragraph may not be coherent if there are not enough transitional words and phrases to link these points. In addition, such devices as repetition and even rhythm can help achieve coherence. In the following paragraph, the writer uses transitional words and phrases, repetition, and balanced constructions—all of which make the paragraphs more coherent. If these words and phrases were taken away, much of the paragraph would be unclear. Transitions are in **boldface** type, repetitions are in *italic*, and balanced constructions are underlined.

In contrast to allopathy, in Traditional Chinese Medicine (TCM) organs are viewed as "networks"—**that is**, functional physiological and psychological domains—**rather than** discrete anatomical structures. All our organs are related; **in fact**, *our* body, [our] behavior, and the environment we are in are also interconnected. **In other words**, TCM focuses more on the *context* where the disease exists than on the disease itself. Such emphasis on *context* implies that the way people get sick and can be treated are highly personalized.

People with different *symptoms* may have the same underlying problem, requiring similar treatments; yet people with the same *symptom* may need completely different remedies. While we are equally endowed with our basic parts, our lungs, heart, kidneys, liver, and so on, our way of co-ordinating these parts is individualized. **For example**, if arthritis is due to an invasion of "heat" (inflammation), it is different from the same condition with a different cause—**for example**, "cold" (reduced circulation) or "dampness" (accumulation of fluids). **In the first case**, practitioners would administer <u>cooling</u> herbs; **in the others**, <u>warming</u> or diuretic herbs would be used.

—Student writer Grace Chau

1. Read the paragraph below to determine how the writer has used transitions and repetition to achieve coherence. Underline transitions and repetitive devices. Identify the topic sentence. One of the ways to achieve coherence is to number your points, though unnecessary numbering can add to clutter. Do you think that it was a good choice for the writer of the passage below to number his points? If so, why?

Critics of the World Trade Organization (WTO) argue that its approach to globalization causes more harm than good because it undermines democracy. The WTO is undemocratic in several respects. First, ambassadors from member nations are appointed, not elected. Second, the coalition known as the "Quad," comprised of the European Union, the United States, Japan, and Canada, holds almost all the real power. In theory, at least, such decisions as new membership, rule changes, and rule interpretations of WTO rules should be voted for with a three-quarters majority. In practice, however, the Quad determines the WTO agenda. Third, WTO trade talks are held in secret to avoid public criticism and scrutiny. Furthermore, an organization that is not elected controls trade so effectively that it possesses the power to supersede the power of elected communities, states, and even nations on any issue, however ambiguous, related to trade.

—Student writer Tao Eastham

2. Read the paragraph below to determine how the writer has used transitions and repetition to achieve coherence. Underline transitions and repetitive devices. Identify the topic sentence. This paragraph is an introductory paragraph to a chapter of a book. What topic do you think will be developed in the next paragraph? Why?

The news media's power to trivialize anything that comes to their attention is almost magical. News service advertisements talk about providing a "window on the world" or a report on "history in the making." But the nightly television newscast and the daily newspaper fall far short of these ideals. Instead, we get a fast-paced smorgasbord of unconnected and disembodied news stories where meaning and context are lost in the rapid-fire delivery of colourful prose and dramatic pictures. As a result, much of what passes for news is instead isolated, unconnected, and almost meaningless bits of information—in effect, the news is trivialized. This trivialization operates at both the structural level of news gathering and dissemination, and at the level of individual news stories. We have termed this style "the trivialization effect."

—adapted from R.A. Rutland, *The Newsmongers*

Chapter Review Questions

1. Why is it important to create a coherent paragraph?
2. What are some advantages in using transitions in writing paragraphs?
3. How are topic sentences and paragraph wraps different?
4. Why is paragraph unity important?
5. How can you effectively repeat an idea?
6. What are some types of transitions that you can use in your writing? How are these types different? How do they change the meaning of your thoughts? Create some sentences and try switching transitions.
7. Create a paragraph about a topic you are interested in. Use specific ideas presented in this chapter. Then switch with a partner and see if he or she has any suggestions, also based on this chapter.

5

Essay Basics

In this chapter, you will

- learn different ways to introduce an essay

- learn how to create an effective thesis statement

- understand the importance of creating and using an outline

- learn how to write a conclusion that wraps up your essay

You will have probably written many essays by the time you begin your college or university education; however, the requirements for essays at this level are more advanced than those at the high school level. In this chapter, you will examine how to effectively draw your audience into your essay and keep them engaged through to your conclusion. You will also be introduced to detailed outlining, which is an essential part of essay writing.

◎ Introductions

Almost everything you read will begin with an introduction. Even if it is not called the "introduction," it will act as one by giving a preview of what follows. It will do that by presenting the main idea and, probably, the organizational pattern of the document—whether it is a book, an article in a scholarly journal, a class essay, a sales proposal, or a résumé. The kinds of introductions students are asked to write are made up of one or more paragraphs that fulfill specific functions, and should, like all paragraphs, be unified, coherent, and well-developed.

It is useful to compare the preparations for writing the essay's introduction with the care you take when meeting someone for the first time. Just as there are people you do not notice because they do not present themselves well, or you notice them for the wrong reasons, there are introductory paragraphs that are not noticed or are noticed for the wrong reasons. As it is one of the most important parts of your essay, take the time to write an introduction that meets the requirements below. It will draw the reader into your essay and provide necessary information, satisfying the expectations of your audience.

◎ Functions of Introductions

Reader Interest: Logical, Dramatic, and Mixed Approaches

Introductions should create **reader interest.** Although most of your essay's "substance"—your main points and sub-points, the supporting details—will be placed in the middle (body) paragraphs, an ineffective introduction could mean that these details are wasted as the rest of the essay may not be read. Reader interest can be created through two different methods with variations on each.

Logical Introductions

The **logical** approach is the most common and traditional way to create interest. You begin with the general and proceed to the specific; the most specific is your thesis statement. This is also called the **inverted pyramid** structure.

A logical opening helps you establish the topic's relevance and shows where it fits in as you progressively become more specific. Your thesis statement is usually the last sentence of the introduction. You will use the first part of the introduction

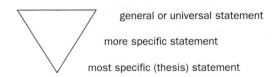

Figure 5.1   Structure of paragraph introduction.

to build your emphasis. In the following introduction, the writer begins with a general claim and gradually brings the subject into sharp focus—Laos's dependence on hydroelectric power. The pyramidal development is important for general readers who may not know much about Laos and the topic.

> Rivers have always been a central part of civilization. From the banks of the Tigris and Euphrates was born the idea of civilization, and almost all subsequent peoples have relied on rivers for trade, transportation, irrigation, fishing, and drinking water. The Lao of Southeast Asia are one such people, living for thousands of years in villages by the many rivers of that country. They have depended on their waterways for clean drinking water, irrigation for their crops, and fishing. The heart of the Lao river system lies in the Mekong River, the longest river in Southeast Asia. Laos is a landlocked country and is therefore doubly reliant on its rivers as a source of trade. Impoverished by war and political turmoil, Laos has turned to its rivers to provide a new, modern resource: electricity.
>
> —Student writer Ian Stock

Sentences 1–2: Rivers have always been a central part of civilization. From the banks of the Tigris and Euphrates was born the idea of civilization, and almost all subsequent peoples have relied on rivers for trade, transportation, irrigation, fishing, and drinking water.

> The paragraph begins with a general statement before making specific connections between rivers and their uses by civilizations.

S 3–4: The Lao of Southeast Asia are one such people, living for thousands of years in villages by the many rivers of that country. They have depended on their waterways for clean drinking water, irrigation for their crops, and fishing.

S 5–6: The heart of the Lao river system lies in the Mekong River, the longest river in Southeast Asia. Laos is a landlocked country and is therefore doubly reliant on its rivers as a source of trade.

> The writer focuses on a specific country and discusses how Laos has used its rivers in the past.

S 7: Impoverished by war and political turmoil, Laos has turned to its rivers to provide a new, modern resource: electricity.

In another kind of logical approach, you begin by mentioning something *familiar* to the reader and proceed to the *unfamiliar*. The following opening illustrates this approach:

> The writer further narrows the topic by mentioning a specific river system and stressing its importance to Laos.

> While the intelligence quotient (IQ) has long been a useful tool to determine one's intelligence, a development in the study of human intellectual experience has expanded to include one's emotional state. It is called Emotional Intelligence, or EQ.
>
> —Student writer Chin-Ju Chiang

> In the thesis statement, the writer announces the essay's main point, the most specific sentence.

Dramatic Introductions

The **dramatic** approach can be used in various ways: you could begin with an interesting quotation (citing from a dictionary is *not* a good example of the dramatic approach), a thought-provoking question, a personal experience, an illuminating statistic, a description of a scene, or a brief narrative, like an anecdote.

Unlike the logical approach, here you begin with something quite specific. The object is to surprise or intrigue your reader. Advertisers and marketing specialists often use this approach to catch the attention of the reader or viewer in order to try to sell their product. Remember, though, that the object is to gently

> An anecdote is an incident or event that is used because it is interesting or striking.

Expository is the term used to describe an essay that is written to inform, explain, or define a topic.

surprise, not to shock or startle. Although it is used more often in argument than in exposition, it can prove effective in some expository essays as well, as the example below illustrates. In the following paragraph, the student writer creates a scenario that enables the reader to experience an unfamiliar martial art first-hand, just as she experienced it.

> Imagine a circle of adults and children dressed in white pants with different coloured cords around their waists. Everybody is clapping and singing in an unfamiliar language—entranced by what is unfolding within the circle. Musicians are playing drums, tambourines, and an instrument that looks like a stringed bow with a gourd attached. There is an inescapable feeling of communal energy within the circle. Uncontrollable curiosity lures the unknowing spectator; peering into the circle exposes two people engaged in an intense physical dialogue. Kicks and movements are exchanged with precision and fluidity, which create a dance-like choreography. What is being witnessed is called a *roda* (pronounced ho-da, it means "circle" in Portuguese). A person's first encounter with this intriguing display of physicality and grace is an experience not easily forgotten. I did not forget my first *roda*, and, consequently, I later began training in this Brazilian form of martial arts—*capoeira* (pronounced cap-where-a).
>
> —Student writer Kerry Hinds

The writer evokes a scene in order to interest the reader, using both descriptive detail and narration (telling a story).

S 1–4: Imagine a circle of adults and children dressed in white pants with different coloured cords around their waists. Everybody is clapping and singing in an unfamiliar language—entranced by what is unfolding within the circle. Musicians are playing drums, tambourines, and an instrument that looks like a stringed bow with a gourd attached. There is an inescapable feeling of communal energy within the circle.

Putting the reader in the place of "the unknowing spectator," the writer continues to evoke the scene, arousing the reader's curiosity and suspense.

S 5–7: Uncontrollable curiosity lures the unknowing spectator; peering into the circle exposes two people engaged in an intense physical dialogue. Kicks and movements are exchanged with precision and fluidity, which create a dance-like choreography. What is being witnessed is called a *roda* (pronounced ho-da, it means "circle" in Portuguese).

S 8–9: A person's first encounter with this intriguing display of physicality and grace is an experience not easily forgotten. I did not forget my first *roda*, and, consequently, I later began training in this Brazilian form of martial arts—*capoeira* (pronounced cap-where-a).

The writer concisely defines capoeira in her thesis statement. Note that her use of personal experience is a strategy designed to create reader interest. Her essay will probably make minimal or no use of personal experience but will explain significant aspects of this martial art form.

Mixed Approaches

An introduction could use more than one method to attract interest. This is called the **mixed approach**.

Exercise 5.1

Rewrite the paragraph above using the logical approach. (In order to do so, you might have to do some research into capoeira.)

- *Dramatic-logical:* The writer could begin with a question and then proceed to develop the rest of the paragraph through the logical approach.
- *Logical-dramatic:* The writer could use a "reversal" strategy, beginning with a general statement before dramatically turning the tables and arguing the opposite. The writer employs this strategy in an essay that criticizes the use of fur in today's society.

Since the beginning of time, people have depended on fur. Cavemen wore animal skins as clothing; furthermore, after killing an animal, such as a buffalo, the flesh would be eaten and the bones would be used in tool-making. They used as much of the animal as possible due to their spiritual beliefs and because with few other resources, it made sense to waste as little as possible. Wearing fur in that age was a necessity: it was warm, practical, and readily available. Today, it is a far different story. Fur is part of the upscale fashion industry, but killing wild animals for their skin extends beyond fur fanciers; it is a luxury product for more many different consumers today, such as car owners with leather upholstery. There are more than 40 different animal species that are killed for their skin, and not a single one needs to be.

—Student writer Grace Beal

[Margin notes:]

general statement

Using the logical method, the writer adds detail, becoming more specific.

The writer reiterates her main point before contrasting the cavemen's needs with those of society today.

In her thesis statement, she forcefully announces her argumentative claim: killing animals for their fur today is wrong.

You may notice that some academic articles do not use any of the kinds of introductions referred to above. They may begin with a direct and concise statement of the problem or purpose and may even include the study's findings in the introduction. This is often the case with scientific articles designed for those with specialized knowledge of the subject.

Introductions in Academic Writing

Writers in the academic disciplines often use a slightly different approach in their introductions since their essays, typically, are much longer and more complex than those you will write. For example, their research might consist of dozens of relevant sources. They might begin by giving necessary background, such as an overview of the major works in the field or the various positions relevant to the topic. Following this background information, the writer explains his or her own approach, usually in the form of a thesis statement. For an example of an academic introduction, see the academic essay at the end of chapter 12 (page 253).

Whatever approach you use, the way that you choose to create interest should be relevant to your topic, your purpose in writing, and your audience. For example, if you were trying to argue in favour of euthanasia, or another issue with a built-in emotional aspect, and you knew your audience opposed it, a strongly emotional opening might not be a good approach because you could run the risk of alienating your readers.

Other Features of Introductions

Introductions serve three other important functions:

- To announce your topic and the main point. The **thesis statement**, occurring near or at the end of the introduction, gives the main point of the essay and must have two parts: the topic itself plus a comment on the topic (see Thesis Statements, below).
- To introduce the *writer*. The introduction is the place where the reader first comes to know that he or she is in competent hands. The introduction is

the writer's first chance to establish **credibility**, presenting himself or herself as knowledgeable about the topic as well as reliable and trustworthy. One of the ways this comes across is through good writing; another way is by appearing rational, fair, and in control.

- To indicate *how* the writer plans to develop the main points. What organizing method will be used? Examples of organizational patterns include description, narration, definition (saying what something is), chronology (using time order), compare and contrast, and cause–effect, along with several other patterns discussed in Chapter 6, Paragraph Development.

Introduction Length

In the introduction you should not *develop* your main points, but that does not mean that skimpy is better. The length of the introduction will depend partly on the length of the essay itself; it may also depend on your decision whether to include the main points of your essay (expanded thesis) or background information. In general, an introduction should not be more than about 15 per cent the length of the essay, but you should check with your instructor for specific guidelines.

Although the introduction should never overbalance the rest of the essay, there is no reason to shy away from including your main points and expressing them fully if the introduction seems to call for this. See Kinds of Thesis Statements, page 94.

Starting at the Beginning

You could consider most introductions as gradual build-ups to the last sentence of the introduction, your thesis statement. However, you should not focus all of your energy on the last sentence at the expense of the first sentence. Your opening sentence needs to be carefully crafted too. Ineffective openings may be too general, obvious, too abrupt, overstated (making a false universal claim), or irrelevant. If you start your essay with any of these types of openings, the reader may be put off and then read your essay much more critically than if you had opened with an effective sentence. Using the analogy of meeting someone for the first time, you could say that ineffective openings are the equivalent of a weak handshake or an averted glance rather than a firm handshake or direct eye contact.

Too general or broad:

> In the twentieth century, many historic events have occurred around the globe, especially in Europe, Asia, and America.

Why is this too broad? Does the phrase beginning with *especially* help to make it more specific? How can the statement be made more effective?

Obvious:

> As population continues to rise around the world, the need for transportation will also increase.

Exercise 5.2

In a group, consider the following opening statements and what makes them ineffective, whether one of the reasons above or something else. How could you revise them to make them more effective and interesting?

1. Franz Anton Mesmer discovered hypnosis in the 1770s.

2. Although email is a modern communications miracle, it is also the biggest nuisance ever invented.

3. It is said that ignorance is bliss.

4. I guess we would all like to look like Kate Moss if we could.

5. There are many issues surrounding end-of-life treatment of terminally ill individuals.

6. Leprosy is, without doubt, the most brutal disease known to humanity.

7. Why not buy the best-made sports car the world has to offer?

8. The movement of people away from the Catholic Church today is mostly due to its teachings on issues like abortion, women's equality, and homosexuality.

9. Sports are something we all watch.

10. In all American literature, no character ever gave more thought to moral decisions than Huckleberry Finn does.

11. Most people in our society today dream of growing up, marrying, and getting a good job so they can start a family.

12. Desperate times call for desperate measures.

13. The importance of education has been reiterated many times.

14. Who was Roger Bannister?

15. Fighting is a part of hockey—no ifs, ands, or buts.

What makes this statement too obvious? Is there a way it can be rewritten to make it more appropriate as an opening?

Too abrupt:

> Changes need to be made to the current regulations involving the Class 7 driver's licence in British Columbia.

Why is this statement too abrupt? Would it be less abrupt if it were placed somewhere else in the introduction?

> First Nations' self-determination and self-government must come from within.

The previous example suggests a strongly partisan point of view that might be quite acceptable if audience members clearly supported this kind of self-government; but it could alienate members of a general or neutral audience. It might be considered overstated. Is there a way it can be adapted to be less abrupt or overstated?

Overstated—False universal claim:

Everyone these days has used a computer at one time or another.

Many people in the world, even in Canada, have not used a computer. There are few situations satisfied by the "everyone" claim. Knowing this, how can the statement be revised?

Irrelevant, or "So what?"

Few people know that sea otters can live to the age of 15 years.

This could be an effective opening if the statement really fell into the category of "believe it or not"—but it doesn't. How could it be revised so that it is appropriate for a college- or university-level essay?

Writing an introduction requires time and patience. You should not feel discouraged if, after having produced an outline, you cannot quickly come up with a strong introduction. It may be best to return to your introduction *after* you've written the rest of the essay. In fact, some instructors believe that the introduction should be the last part of the essay you write.

> Be wary of making "everyone" claims unless your statement truly applies to everyone.

> Don't feel discouraged if, after having produced an outline, you cannot quickly come up with a strong introduction. It may be best to return to your introduction *after* you've written the rest of the essay.

◎ Thesis Statements

Nearly all essays need a thesis statement, which is the main point of your essay or what you will be attempting to prove. A thesis statement has two parts: the *topic* and *the comment*. It does not just state a topic. For example, "My essay will be about life in residence at the University of the South Pole" states a topic and does not comment on it. By contrast, the thesis "Life in residence at the University of the South Pole helps prepare one for life after university" makes a comment about the topic. "Life in residence at the University of the South Pole" is the topic; "helps prepare one for life after university" is the comment. It tells the reader how you will be addressing the topic, what your focus will be. See Chapter 2, page 42, for more information on subjects, topics, and theses.

Kinds of Thesis Statements

Simple Versus Expanded

Simple thesis statements have the two necessary parts and no more. **Expanded thesis statements** give more detail, usually by including your main points.

Life in residence at the University of the South Pole helps prepare one for life after university.

Just as a simple thesis statement goes further than a topic, so an expanded thesis statement goes further than a simple thesis statement by answering questions like "how?" or "why?," by accounting for or justifying the main idea. *How* does life in residence prepare one for life after university?

Life in residence at the University of the South Pole helps prepare one for life after university by making a student independent, by reinforcing basic life skills, and by teaching one how to get along with other penguins.

Here's an example of a topic, followed by a simple thesis statement and an expanded one that answers the question "why":

Topic: School uniforms

Simple thesis statement: Making school uniforms mandatory has many advantages for students.

Expanded thesis statement: Making school uniforms mandatory has many advantages for students as they eliminate distractions, encourage a focus on academics, and reduce competition based on appearances.

Should you use a simple or expanded thesis statement in your essay? There is no easy answer, but simple thesis statements may be sufficient for short essays, such as those of fewer than 500 words. Simple thesis statements are sometimes used in fact-based (expository) essays in which you attempt to answer a question or solve a problem. In argumentative essays, you try to convince your reader of something. An expanded thesis that announces all your points in the introduction gets you off to a forceful start. Check with your instructor for specific guidelines about simple versus expanded thesis statements.

◎ Effective Thesis Statements

Effective thesis statements should be interesting, specific, and manageable.

- **Interesting**: the thesis is likely to attract the reader, especially the general reader, to the topic and the essay.
- **Specific**: the thesis isn't so general, broad, or obvious that it lacks relevance; it informs the reader about what will follow.
- **Manageable**: the thesis sounds as if it can be reasonably explored in the space of the essay; the writer is going to be able to successfully carry out what is promised in the thesis.

◎ Ineffective Thesis Statements

Although thesis statements may be ineffective because they are not interesting, specific, or manageable, they may have other problems. Unclear thesis statements may confuse, not inform. For example, the following thesis statement doesn't clearly express the main points of the essay. In this case, the writer needs to be more detailed and precise.

> Pets are important in that they can unify and heal, and are an inevitable part of human nature.

Do we know what the writer means by these items? As an expanded thesis statement that includes the main points of the essay, it is inadequate because it will likely baffle readers, not inform them.

> *Revised:* Pets are important in bringing people together, helping them recover from an illness or depression, and enabling them to express important human values, such as love.

Some thesis statements are unclear because they seem to straddle two topics rather than centre on one. This could be the result of the writer's early uncertainty: he or she may not know the essay's major focus. In revising your essay, you should always ensure that your thesis accurately reflects the essay's main point. In this example, we don't know whether this essay will be about excessive dieting or body image:

> *Ineffective:* Many youths are obsessed by dieting today due to the prominence our society places on body image.

To successfully revise this thesis, the writer needs to narrow the topic to one specific area, such as the following:

- unhealthy diets and the problems they create
- the effects of body image on youths
- the relationship between body image and dieting

The last topic would likely involve extensive research and might not be manageable within the scope of a medium-length essay.

Avoid stiff and self-conscious thesis statements that refer directly to the writer or to the essay's purpose:

> *Ineffective:* I (or, This essay) will examine the phenomenon of online gambling and argue in favour of strict government regulation of this growing industry.
> *Revised:* Online gambling is of increasing concern to governments today and should be subject to strict regulations.

Thesis statements can be difficult to write. Most clear theses begin with the writer's clear thoughts. As is the case with all writing, clear thinking produces clear expression.

Exercise 5.3

A. Look at the following statement of a topic:

My essay will be on aliens.

Consider the three following thesis statements and evaluate their effectiveness using the three criteria for effective thesis statements on page 95:

1. It is probable that aliens exist somewhere in outer space.

2. It is clear that aliens have infiltrated the highest levels of the Canadian government.

3. Everyone is curious about the possible existence of aliens.

B. If you were asked to write an essay on the way that the computer influences people, which of the simple thesis statements below would be the best one(s) to use? Rate each according to whether it is interesting, specific, and manageable. Be prepared to explain your decisions.

1. Computers are one of the most entertaining pastimes we have today.

2. Violence found in computer games is affecting children these days by increasing the number of shootings in schools.

3. The computer has helped change the way we live today compared to the way our grandparents lived 50 years ago.

4. Computers take away our free time by creating a dependency that is very hard to escape from once we are hooked.

5. TV is losing its influence today thanks to the increasing popularity of computers.

6. Computers are a great babysitter for pre-school–age children.

C. Write an effective thesis statement on the topic of the computer's influence, using any pre-writing technique you feel comfortable with and making sure that you include the three requirements of a good thesis statement.

D. The following thesis statements are either simple or expanded. Identify the type. If they are simple thesis statements, add detail, turning them into expanded thesis statements.

1. Regular, moderate doses of stress not only are inevitable in today's world but also can be good for you.

2. As consumers, we must keep ourselves informed about the activities of the industries we support.

3. Although poor waste management has already had a significant impact on the planet, through recycling, waste reduction programs, and public education, future damage can be minimized.

4. Education is viewed as a benefit to individuals, but too much education can have negative results.

5. Many people today misunderstand the meaning of success.

Exercise 5.4

In groups, use a pre-writing technique to formulate a simple thesis statement that has all three criteria discussed above. Begin with a choice of broad subjects, such as the ones below. When each group has come up with a thesis statement and written it on a piece of paper, exchange it with another group's and have that group evaluate it according to the three criteria. One mark should be given for an interesting thesis statement; another mark should be awarded for being specific; and a third mark should be given if it seems manageable (half marks are possible). When each group has completed the evaluation process, discuss the ratings and the reasons behind them.

After each group has received feedback on its thesis statement and revised it accordingly, use another pre-writing technique to come up with three main points. Then reword the simple thesis statement so that it is an expanded thesis statement. The thesis statements can again be marked. Expanded thesis statements can be given three marks by awarding a mark for points 4, 5, and 6 in the Thesis Statement Checklist beginning on page 100.

Possible topics: aliens, backpacking, clothes, diet, energy, Facebook, ghosts, humour, indie rock, justice, karma, laughter, malls, nature, organic food, pets, Quebec, relationships, science, taboos, (the) unconscious, virtual reality, waste, xenophobia, youth, Zen Buddhism.

Exercise 5.5

Evaluate the following introductory paragraphs according to the criteria discussed in the previous pages. Do they function as effective introductions? Specifically consider the following:

a) Which method(s) did the writer use to create reader interest? (logical, dramatic, mixed?)

b) Is the opening effective? What makes it effective? (or not?)

c) Identify the thesis statement. Is it interesting, specific, and manageable? Simple or expanded?

d) Has the writer established credibility? (shows knowledge, seems reliable or trustworthy?)

e) Is the essay's main organizational pattern apparent (e.g., chronology, compare and contrast, cause–effect, problem–solution, cost–benefit)? If you wish, you can look ahead to Chapter 6, which discusses organizational patterns.

f) Does the paragraph length seem appropriate?

    1.   Clothing has always reflected the times, and a prime example is the bathing suit. From their most cumbersome and unattractive beginnings to the array of styles we see today, bathing suits have always reflected the lives of the

women who wore them and the society in which they lived. In the last hundred years, roles of the sexes, improvements in women's rights, changes in the economy, and perceptions of body image have all played a part in bathing suit design. —Student writer Stephanie Keenlyside

2. What is it about the Italian Mafia that fascinates millions of people? Could part of the answer lie in Hollywood's depiction of a 5' 9", 275-pound Italian named Bruno Francessi who drives a black Cadillac, wears $3,000 silk suits, and claims to have "two" families; or is it the way the media creates celebrity status for Mafiosi people and events? The media and film industry portray a mobster's lucrative lifestyle as the result of thoughtless killings, a regimen of violence and corruption. But to fully understand the mob lifestyle, one must understand how mobsters operate—not what they appear to be on the surface, but the structure, conduct, and economic realities that created their power and enable them to maintain it. As someone who lived close to this power, I know that behind the media perception lies a fundamental belief in and adherence to a system. —Student writer Dino Pascoli

3. The sport of bodybuilding has evolved considerably through the ages. Starting with muscle man competitions, it has now turned into what some would call a "freak show." Bodybuilding is a sport that requires its athletes to display their best aesthetically pleasing physiques on stage; they are judged according to specific criteria. Many factors leading up to the judging itself contribute to the outcome of the competition; for example, nutrition from whole foods and supplements, and low body fat percentage from proper diet and cardiovascular training all contribute to the success of the competitors. Steroids, too, are a major factor in professional events like the International Federation of Bodybuilders (IFBB) competitions, where athletes are not tested for drug use. Anabolic steroid abuse plays a large role in bodybuilding, often resulting in adverse health effects. —Student writer Mike Allison

4. Two 20-year-old Vancouver men were street racing three years ago when one of the cars, a Camaro, struck and killed Irene Thorpe as she crossed the street. The car was going so fast that Thorpe was thrown 30 metres into the air. Both men were convicted of criminal negligence causing death. They were given a two-year conditional sentence to be served at home, put on probation for three years, and had their drivers' licenses revoked for five years. Like most street-racing tragedies, this one was preventable. Though the street-racing phenomenon has been around for decades, it is growing exponentially. Recent movies have glorified this activity, enticing young, inexperienced drivers. The increase in street racing has led to an increase in the injuries to racers, spectators, and innocent bystanders. In addition, racing often results in property damage and is associated with assault, weapons offences, and drug and alcohol abuse. To help combat this growing problem, anti-racing legislation needs to be introduced and strictly enforced. Furthermore, an education program needs to be implemented and legal racing venues created. —Student writer Maureen Brown

5. Why does my cell phone not work? Why do I get radiation poisoning when I travel by plane? Why is the light switch not working? These are the kinds of questions we ask ourselves when solar flares are striking the earth. Solar

flares originate from the sun. Every eleven years, the sun switches its magnetic poles, causing the magnetic fields to twist and turn in the atmosphere above sunspots, which are eruptions on the sun's surface. The magnetic field seems to snap like a rubber band stretched too tightly. When one of these fields breaks, it can create energy equal to a billion megatons of TNT exploding. The magnetic fields seem to flip and reconnect after they break. Solar flares occasionally head towards the earth, and even though we are 1.5 million kilometres from the sun, these flares can reach us in fewer than two days. While the earth is experiencing a solar flare, multiple problems can occur—from malfunctions of orbiting objects to disruption in power systems and radio signals. While the flares can produce these problems, they can also create the most beautiful and unusual auroras seen around the world. —Student writer Nicholas Fodor

Exercise 5.6

Evaluate the following introduction according to the criteria discussed in the sections above. For example, you could consider whether the opening is successful, whether the writer creates interest and appears credible, and whether the thesis statement is effective. Then, rewrite it, correcting any weaknesses you find. You can add your own material or ideas, but try not to increase the length of the paragraph (approximately 130 words).

Something drastic needs to be done about obesity among teenagers today! Over the last decade, there has been a disturbing trend toward teenage obesity. Teenagers today would rather lodge themselves in front of the TV or play video games for hours on end than get some form of physical exercise. This problem becomes pronounced in high school because physical education is not compulsory in most schools. However, PE classes have a lot to offer. Participation can reduce the risk of heart failure, improve overall fitness, promote good health habits, improve self-discipline and skill development, boost self-confidence, increase academic performance, and enhance communication and co-operative skills. Obesity is an alarming trend among high school students today and should be a concern to both students and their parents.

When you use an expanded thesis statement, you need to express your main points in parallel structure; otherwise, it could be hard to follow (see Chapter 16, pp. 391–2).

Like outlines, discussed in the next section, the thesis you start with shouldn't be considered fixed. As you write your outline or rough draft and uncover areas about your topic you weren't aware of before, you may want to go back and revise your thesis.

A Thesis Statement Checklist

1. Have you written a complete thesis statement, not just a topic?
2. Does it have two parts? (simple thesis statement)

3.   Have you included your main points in the order they will appear in your essay? (expanded thesis statement)
4.   Is there enough detail to enable the reader to understand your main points (i.e., is it clearly phrased and not confusing?)
5.   Is it clear what *one topic* the thesis will focus on (i.e., it does not appear vague or appear to straddle two topics)?
6.   Is it worded objectively and not self-consciously (i.e., by mentioning the writer or the essay itself)?
7.   In arranging your main points, have you applied parallel structure?

Outlines

The Value of Outlines

Three kinds of outlines were introduced in Chapter 2. Not all writing requires an outline, but the more complex the writing task, the greater the need for an outline. Even in simpler tasks they are useful: they help clarify and order your thoughts; they also save you time, preventing you from getting off topic.

Using outlines effectively is really a matter of timing. You would not put together even a rough outline without having thought about your thesis and main points. For formal outlines, you need more detail, including paragraph development. The outline is the skeleton from which the fleshy contours of your essay will take shape. Your audience will notice these contours and will not likely stop to think about the planning that went into the essay. However, in any organized and coherent piece of writing, the outline will always be apparent, implied by the arrangement of main and sub-points in the essay.

Organizing an Outline

An outline is a vertical pattern of ideas and their support. General and introductory points are like headings; under them, you will place ideas connecting to the main points (related, less important points, expansions of the main point, examples, evidence). These can be considered sub-headings. See Chapters 11 and 13 for detailed discussions of outlines for particular types of essays. See Chapter 11, page 190, for a developed outline.

Although outlines typically proceed from the general (main) points to the specific (sub)points, another ordering principle is involved: *emphasis.* You can order the points in the body of your essay according to a logical method, such as the strength of the argument presented in each (this is particularly important in argumentative essays). There are several ways to order your points logically:

• *Climax order:* You begin with your weakest, or least important point and proceed to the strongest, most important point.

- *Inverted climax (dramatic) order:* You begin with your strongest point and end with your weakest.
- *Mixed order:* You begin with a moderately strong point and follow with the weakest argument, before concluding with the strongest.

The number of main points and the strength of the opposing argument are factors that can help you determine which method is best for your topic.

General Guidelines for Outlines

1. Decide on your topic and the main point you want to make about your topic; you can use brainstorming, question–answer, clustering, or freewriting to develop ideas.
2. Divide outlines into Introduction, paragraphs for development, and Conclusion.
3. Plan for a *minimum* of five paragraphs altogether unless told otherwise or unless your essay is very short.
4. Ensure you have one main idea per paragraph.
5. Divide your main ideas (points) into sub-points (at least two per paragraph) that develop the main idea.
6. Represent the relationship between main ideas and their points of development (or sub-points) graphically by indenting sub-points or, more formally, alternate letters and numbers to show the level of development (e.g., I, A, 1, a; see the sample outline below).
7. Ensure that the main points themselves are ordered logically and effectively.

An outline can be created by using a template similar to the one discussed in Chapter 8, page 134.

Developing an Outline with Thesis Statement

Topic: using cars versus bicycles for transportation
Brainstorming List: check marks indicate items from the brainstorming list that were used to create the outline

Cars
cars faster and more convenient ✓
status of having a car
  − you can drive friends
  − car pooling
people who work on their cars as hobby

expensive ✓
- gas
- upkeep to keep running

bad on environment ✓
- greenhouse effect
- global warming
- use of valuable resources

traffic jams
- frustration (road rage)
- rush hour delays (time)

Bicycles

takes longer to get anywhere
- but maybe not during rush hour
- what if you have to bike a big distance every day? ✓

nice to take a car in bad weather
- but park far away at the college

healthy
- healthy lifestyle ✓
- fitness, you'll live longer ✓
- good for heart
- reduce stress ✓
- helps with mental health

save money
- gas and upkeep ✓

elderly/handicapped can't use

most cities encourage bikes
- build bicycle lanes
- good for the environment ✓
- fewer vehicles

Outline

Paragraph 1: Introduction

I.   Scenario: Describe traffic at 5 p.m. leaving Toronto.

II. Concession: Cars are faster and more convenient.

III. Thesis statement: People who drive a short distance to work or school should bicycle instead. Although a car is faster and more convenient, riding a bike is cheaper, easier on the environment, and improves your health.

Paragraph 2: The expense factor

I.   Bikes save money compared to cars (topic sentence).

  A. There are gas and routine costs.

  B. There may be expensive breakdowns.

   1. Car parts are costly; for example, a timing belt is about $100.

   2. Money saved for car repairs can be put toward bike accessories.

Paragraph 3: The environment factor

I.   Using bikes reduces the number of cars, which is good for the environment (topic sentence).
A.   Cars contribute to greenhouse effect.
B.   We feel good because we are helping the planet.

Paragraph 4: The health factor

I.   A person's health will be improved by biking (topic sentence).
A.   There are many physical health benefits.
1.   Biking helps strengthen the cardiovascular system.
2.   Biking can help a person lose weight or maintain a healthy weight.
B.   Biking will not only help a person live longer but also live *better* (mental benefits).
1.   Stress will be reduced.
2.   People will feel better about themselves and gain confidence.

Paragraph 5: Conclusion

I.   Concession: Bikes are not going to replace cars completely.
II. Reinforce thesis: Because it is cheaper, better for the environment and for us as individuals, the number of those using bicycles is increasing; this is a healthy trend all around and should continue into the future.

◯ Conclusions

Functions of Conclusions

Unlike the surprise ending of some short stories, the conclusion of an essay should have been prepared for every step of the way—both by the introduction and by the points that have been developed within the essay itself. So, if an essay contains a surprise ending, it indicates serious structural problems in the body as well.

A conclusion should be predictable because you have prepared the reader for it, but it should *not* be boring or merely repetitive. A conclusion that simply repeats the thesis statement will be boring. It will leave the reader with the impression of a static, undeveloped argument.

In your conclusion, you need to find a way to bring the reader back to reconsider the thesis statement in light of how the thesis has been developed through

Introduction

Conclusion

Figure 5.2   Introduction-conclusion inverted pyramid.

your main points. The conclusion *recalls* the thesis statement and what has been discussed in the body paragraphs. It is also a good idea to end with a clincher statement—an idea to remain with the reader.

Two Kinds of Conclusions

Introductions and conclusions are not like identical bookends with the books (body paragraphs) in between, though their main function is to remind the reader of the thesis. Conclusions can underscore the importance of the thesis in two ways: (1) they can reiterate the thesis using different words that stress its importance, perhaps by a call to action if you are arguing for a practical change of some kind; (2) they can suggest a specific way that the thesis could be applied, ask further questions, or propose other ways of looking at the problem. These two strategies for concluding essays suggest two fundamental patterns:

1. a *circular* conclusion: reminds and reinforces the thesis
2. a *spiral* conclusion: refers to the thesis but also leads suggestively beyond it

A **circular conclusion** "closes the circle" by bringing the reader back to the starting point. It is particularly important in circular conclusions not to simply repeat the thesis statement word for word but to show how it has been proven. A **spiral conclusion** might point to results of the thesis or suggest follow-up research. Sometimes, conclusions can include personal reflection, such as considering the way your thesis has affected you or people you know. This kind of conclusion, however, is more acceptable in personal and some argumentative essays than in expository ones. If you have not used personal experience in the essay, it might be jarring to do so in the conclusion.

Conclusions often work from the specific to the general, whereas the introduction often starts with the general and works towards the specific (the thesis statement)—the inverted pyramid structure.

There are specific things to avoid in conclusions:

- restating the thesis statement word for word
- mentioning a new point; conclusions should reword the old in an interesting way, not introduce something new
- giving an example or illustration to support your thesis; examples belong in your body paragraphs
- writing a conclusion that is very much longer than your introduction. Exceptions sometimes occur—especially in the sciences and social sciences where essays may end with a lengthy Discussion section.

Set your conclusion beside your introduction to check that it fulfills all the above functions of a conclusion and relates to your introduction in a satisfactory way.

Exercise 5.7

Consider these sets of paragraphs, which form the introduction and the conclusion for three essays. Is it clear from the introduction what the writer will be discussing? What kind of introduction did the writer use? Is it clear from the conclusion what the writer has discussed? What kind of conclusion is each writer using?

Write a brief analysis of how the two parts of the essays intersect yet, at the same time, operate independently. Consider strengths and possible weaknesses. Remember that the paragraphs should not only function as effective specialized paragraphs but also display unity, coherence, and development.

A. An expository essay

Topic: A racial incident in Canada's past

Introduction:

> One of Canada's most important features, which figures prominently in its self-presentation to the world, is as a peaceful nation that respects the individual and celebrates multiculturalism. The country is known for its cultural and ethnic diversity. Often, however, Canadians idealize their image and push inequality out of their presentation of their country. However, if we look carefully at the history of Canada, there have been many occasions when the clean image of national tolerance has been seriously undermined, such as in the Komagata Maru incident in Vancouver in 1914.

Conclusion:

> Although much has changed for the better since the beginning of the twentieth century and Canada is justifiably proud of its diversity today, people sometimes ignore past incidents of racial discrimination. Since the Komagata Maru incident is not well-known, it is important that people hear about it so they can be aware that even in a democratic country like Canada injustice and intolerance have occurred in the past and will continue to occur unless people learn from the past and guard against such incidents. —Student writer Ruth Wax

B. An argumentative essay

Topic: Government-funded screening

Introduction:

> Last month, the colour pink sprang up in store windows of retailers nationwide as part of the annual campaign to fund breast cancer research. Breast cancer takes the lives of 44,000 women in the US every year. As a potential carrier of a gene predisposing me to breast cancer, I face the perpetual fear that one day I or my sister could become its victim. It would be almost unthinkable if the mammogram, the screening test for breast cancer, were not covered by our health-care plan. However, for men with a predisposition to prostate cancer, which has been linked to the gene associated with breast cancer, the cost of a blood test to screen for prostate cancer is not covered by the plan. Prevention and early intervention are critical for successful health care, and government-funded coverage for the $35 prostate cancer screening test is essential for men aged 45 and older.

Conclusion:

Today the best hope for a cure to prostate cancer lies in early intervention through the PSA screening test. Although the benefit of screening may be controversial, the evidence is hard to dispute: 80 per cent of patients with elevated PSA levels have prostate cancer. Surgical procedures are rapidly improving, and new options exist to treat complications of surgery or radiation therapy. Until proper medical coverage exists for early detection of prostate cancer, it will continue to cause the largest number of cancer-related deaths in men. Gender bias in government-funded cancer screening tests is unacceptable, and public pressure should be exerted for universal access to cancer screening. —Student writer Heather Dyble

C. An argumentative essay

Topic: Smoking and organ transplantation

Introduction:

The atmosphere grew tense in the cramped hospital room as eight-year-old Marla looked up through frightened eyes, trying to be strong for her mother. Everyone was trying to be hopeful, but Marla instinctively knew that she would not be getting a heart transplant in time; the waitlist was long, and an organ match was unlikely. Although Marla was an otherwise healthy girl, there were others on the transplant list who were ahead of her, though not all of them had as good a prognosis. Due to the scarcity of organ donations in comparison to many in need, serious debates have arisen concerning the suitability of some potential heart and lung recipients. Some feel that everyone should have equal right to a transplant and that there should be no pre-conditions relating to what they see as lifestyle choices, such as smoking. Others advocate that smokers should be refused transplants on medical or moral considerations since smokers are more likely to experience complications after surgery. Given the current crisis of long waitlists and variable success rates, lung and heart transplant candidates should be required to quit smoking at least six months prior to surgery in order to reduce smoking-related complications and maximize transplant success.

Conclusion:

The scarcity of organ donations and the length of waitlists have placed an increasing obligation on the part of health-care professionals to ensure the best outcome for their patients. Denying transplants to those who refuse to quit smoking may appear to discriminate against smokers and their lifestyle choice. However, doing so would result in better odds for post-transplant success and would involve the most efficient use of limited health-care services and resources. In short, health authorities should move to institute clear guidelines on pre-surgery smoking restrictions for the benefit of both individuals and the health-care system. —Student writer Annie Gentry

Exercise 5.8

Choose one of the topics below and create an expanded thesis statement, an introduction, and a conclusion. Begin by brainstorming and creating an outline. Note that the topics are very general to allow you to choose the focus.

a) Voting

b) Funding for the arts

c) Canada's role on the world stage

d) Travel as education

e) Volunteerism

f) The effects of events around the world on Canadians

g) Funding for intervention programs

h) Reality TV shows

i) Exercise and health

j) The role of education

Chapter Review Questions

1. Why is a clear thesis important?
2. What is the difference between a simple thesis statement and an expanded thesis statement?
3. Are simple thesis statements appropriate for all essays?
4. How can an effective expanded thesis statement be evaluated?
5. What is meant by a logical approach to organizing an introduction?
6. When can you use a dramatic approach when writing an introduction?
7. Why should you never start an introduction with an overly broad or obvious statement?
8. How can you create and develop an outline?
9. Why does an essay need a conclusion?
10. What are two types of conclusions and when would you use each?

Paragraph Development

In this chapter, you will learn how to

- identify different rhetorical writing patterns

- develop your essay through substantial paragraphs

- combine organizational patterns within an essay

A well-written essay requires you, the writer, to consider many outside factors, such as audience, so your essay is interesting and informative. However, you also need to decide how to organize your essay to make it logical and easy to follow. You may decide to use one main pattern for your essay, but different patterns for individual paragraphs. This chapter will introduce you to various rhetorical writing patterns and help you determine how to organize your paragraphs into a unified, coherent, and well-developed whole.

Developing Your Essay through Substantial Paragraphs

As discussed in Chapter 4, effective paragraphs are unified, coherent, and well-developed. Unified paragraphs focus on one topic. Coherent paragraphs make sense and provide logical connections so the reader can follow the writer's train of thought.

Well-developed paragraphs contain supporting information organized by consistent patterns. A well-developed paragraph, then, will not only thoroughly expand on a point, but also increase the paragraph's coherence, contributing to the essay as a whole.

The paragraph below, from the student essay about safe injection sites (page 289), clearly illustrates these concepts. The author connects drug use and disease, showing unity. Coherence is provided by repeating words, such as *problem*, and by using synonyms, such as *situation*. Finally, the paragraph is well-developed, as it illustrates the drug problem in Victoria before the writer discusses the solution to the problem, which is the main focus of the essay.

> Victoria is an urban centre with a heroin and drug-related disease problem. This situation is easy to see when one is walking through the downtown core. The problem may not be as severe as Vancouver's, but it is necessary to take proactive actions to prevent the spread of AIDS and hepatitis. Having been involved with The Youth Empowerment Society downtown and working with street youth in Victoria, I see the need for such a program in Victoria; the personal health of users, old and young, is at stake.

In many essays, the writer chooses to use one main method of development but uses other methods in supporting roles. An essay may set out to examine a cause–effect relationship, for example, but may use different methods from paragraph to paragraph to introduce, clarify, illustrate, or expand the main points.

Choosing the appropriate development pattern is one of the keys to writing a complete and interesting essay. Which patterns should you use for your essay? This will depend on the kind of essay, your purpose in writing, your topic, your audience, your essay's primary organizational method, your main points and their order (climax, reverse climax, or some other), along with a host of other factors.

Methods for Developing Paragraphs

A topic alone may lend itself to a particular method of development. In fact, in some cases, your main organizational method is given to you by the topic itself, so from that you will know how your points should be developed. For example, for the topic "Which is more important at college or university: acquiring skills or getting good grades?" you might guess that the essay should be organized by compare and contrast. For the topic "Solutions to the problem of homeless people," you would know that the essay should be organized as problem–solution where you briefly describe the problem and then suggest ways to solve it. On the other hand, if the question to

Unified paragraphs focus on one topic.

Coherent paragraphs make sense and provide logical connections so the reader can follow the writer's train of thought.

Well-developed paragraphs contain supporting information organized by consistent patterns.

answer was "Do you believe that homeless people today are a problem?" you might develop your essay in a similar way, but the *problem* of homelessness would be much more important than the solutions, which you might mention only briefly, or not at all. Even if the topic determines the *main* way that the essay should be developed, there will likely be opportunities to consider different methods for developing individual paragraphs. These methods, which are often referred to as **rhetorical patterns**, are discussed below and are followed by examples.

> The topic of the essay may determine the main way you will organize your essay, but each paragraph may be organized using different rhetorical patterns.

Analysis and Paragraph Development

Analysis, meaning "loosen" or "dissolve," as well as "separate" or "break up," is sometimes considered a distinct method of development. When you analyze, you are really loosening, then separating something in order to look at it closely. Many development methods involve this process. Thus, you analyze when you divide and classify, compare and contrast, and consider problems and solutions, costs and benefits, and the like. Not all methods truly involve analysis—description, narration, and examples do not—but many of them do. Analysis is one of the keys to critical thinking.

> You analyze when you divide and classify, compare and contrast, and consider problems and solutions, costs and benefits, and the like.

One way to generate methods of development is to ask questions about the topic:

> Analysis is one of the keys to critical thinking.

Table 6.1   Question/Method of Development

QUESTION	METHOD OF DEVELOPMENT
What is it?	definition
When did it occur?	chronology
What does it look like?	description
How can it be told?	narration
How do you do it? or How does it work?	process/"how to"
Why should/does it affect me?	personal
What kinds/categories are there?	division/classification
What causes/accounts for it?	cause–effect
What is the result/effect?	cause–effect
What is the answer?	question–answer
How can it be shown?	example/illustration
How can it be (re)solved?	problem–solution
What are the advantages/disadvantages?	cost–benefit
How is it like something else?	analogy
How is it like and/or unlike something else?	compare and contrast

Each of these questions leads to a particular method for developing a paragraph. If, for example, your topic is "fast foods," it would be possible to use any of the methods below to develop an essay on this topic.

Definition—What Is It?

Define something in an essay in order to tell the reader precisely what you will be talking about. Defining a subject, such as an abstract concept, can also help you understand your topic better and, perhaps, help you organize your main points. By "fast foods," do you mean something like a "Big Mac?" Do you mean food that you can buy at a store that is quickly heated and eaten? Both could be considered "fast foods," but they are not the same. Below, the writer concisely defines "peer-to-peer file sharing" for his general audience and then uses the division pattern to expand the definition. (For an example of a definition essay, see Chapter 8, page 142.)

> Peer-to-peer file sharing (P2P) is a technology that enables users to share files among themselves without the use of a central host of the files (traditionally called the client–server model). In P2P, each client acts as a "mini server" and can both send and receive files. The information regarding the files on each client usually is distributed in one of three ways. The first involves the use of a central server to store this information and the use of a protocol for clients to update the central server with file information whenever they connect or disconnect from the network. A more modern method for distributing information about files on different hosts, "hybrid P2P," involves the use of certain hosts on the network to maintain the information and distribute it. The third approach, called "decentralized P2P," is similar to hybrid P2P, but differs because it uses each individual host on the network to store and share file information.
>
> —Student writer Mik Nuotio

Chronology—When Did It Occur?

In the chronological method, you do more than simply look back to a specific time: you trace the topic's *development over time*. (If you looked back to a specific time and compared an aspect of the subject to that aspect today, you would be *comparing and contrasting*.) When did fast foods begin, and when did they truly begin to affect people and society? Tracing the evolution of fast foods in the last 15 years might provide evidence that many fast-food restaurants have been forced to expand their choices and reduce their portion sizes to counter the perception that these foods are unhealthy. Applying this method of development, then, could also involve a cause–effect or problem–solution approach; see below.

> The earth shook as father and son wrestled high above the clouds; Kronos, the dreaded father who ate his children, battled his powerful son to rule the Earth. However, Zeus, whom the Fates had protected as a child from Kronos' mighty jaws, triumphed once again, becoming, in the words of Homer, "father of gods and men"; his children would honour his victory as a celebration known as Olympia. From 776 BCE the Olympic Games occurred every

four years to celebrate Zeus' success. By 260 CE the Games' importance had deteriorated so much that they were held only occasionally, until the Roman Emperor Theodosius outlawed them completely in 394 CE. The Olympic Games were founded on a profound religious significance, specific ideals about athletes, and strict rules that enabled the Games' long existence and prohibited the inclusion of women. As Olympia changed, the founding principles that had originally made Olympia so significant were disregarded, eventually leading to the end of the ancient Games.

—Student writer Courtenay O'Brien

Description—What Does It Look Like?

You can use description at any point in your essay to add concrete, physical detail, but description should play a limited role. You could describe something by using the spatial method of organization, a particular kind of descriptive method. In the spatial method, you describe something in a systematic manner—for example, from left to right, or as you approach the object. You could describe a fast-food burger from the sesame-seed top bun with its assorted condiments and extras to the plain lower bun.

> Description adds concrete, physical detail to an essay.

The Parc Guell, constructed between 1900 and 1914, was originally intended as the setting for a garden city. The park is fairy tale-like in appearance: the first building one sees on entering the site resembles a gingerbread house. The rounded corners on the brown façade and colourful decoration of the window sills give the building a magical, playful appearance. Other structures that stand out within the park include a giant fountain shaped like a lizard and a mile-long bench that winds along one path in the park. The most remarkable feature, though, is Gaudí's use of beautiful, multi-coloured tile work throughout.

—Collins, George R. *Antonio Gaudí and the Catalan Movement 1870–1930*.
Charlottesville: American Association of Architectural Bibliographers/University
Press of Virginia, 1973. Print.

Narration—How Can It Be Told?

A story can lend drama to an argument or be used to illustrate a point. To narrate an incident, or even include some dialogue, can be an effective way to introduce or reinforce your topic. Through observation and a little imagination, a visit to a fast-food restaurant could produce interesting stories about those who eat or work there. Narration is a natural method in personal essays but can also be used in argumentative essays, and even in expository essays, as the example below shows about the legendary origins of coffee. Because description and narration are generally considered more informal, you should ask your instructor before using them extensively in formal essays.

> Narration can be an effective way to introduce or reinforce your topic.

Legend has it that one day, Kaldi, an Ethiopian goat-herder, noticed his goats were so frisky when they returned from grazing that they "danced." Curious about the source of their excitement, Kaldi followed them the next day and observed the animals eating the berries of a nearby tree. Kaldi grabbed some berries himself and soon experienced a slow tingle that spread throughout his body. According to the legend, Kaldi was soon "dancing" alongside his goats.

—Pendergrast, Mark, *Uncommon Grounds: The History of Coffee and How It Transformed Our World*. New York: Basic Books, 1999. Print.

Process—How Does It Work?

> Relating a process focuses specifically on the steps in a sequence.

Although process analysis essays are usually fact-based essays that relate the chronological, step-by-step stages of a process, this method of development can also be used in argumentative essays—for example, if you wanted to convince a reader that one games system was easier to operate than another. This method can also be used for less technical subjects—for example, "How to Impress Your Boss, or Professor, in Ten Easy Steps." Remember that relating a process focuses specifically on the successive steps in a *sequence*. Since the production of fast-food burgers is often a regimented process, you could describe this process from the time a customer places an order to the time it is handed to him or her. (For an example of a process essay, see Chapter 8, page 139.)

> The traditional method of painting icons is a long process, requiring a skilled and experienced painter. The artist takes a wooden panel, one with the least amount of resin, knots, and risk of splitting, and covers it with cheesecloth. A gesso is then made from rabbit-skin glue and calcium carbonate (chalk). It is applied to the panel seven to ten times and then polished by hand until it is mirror-like. The original is traced to perfection and then transferred onto the gessoed surface. After this, gold leaf is laid on everywhere it is required (backgrounds and halos, for example). Egg tempera paint is freshly made from powdered pigment and egg yolk and is applied from the darkest dark to the lightest light with an egg-white glaze spread on between each coat.
>
> —Student writer Magda Smith

Personal—Why Should It Affect Me?/ How Does or Did It Affect Me?

> Personal essays focus on an aspect of the writer's life or a relevant experience.

Personal essays are focused on the writer—an aspect of his or her life or a relevant experience. Personal experience in an essay contributes immediacy and, sometimes, drama. But don't use personal experience extensively, unless you are writing a personal essay. In successful personal paragraphs and essays, the writer is able to make personal experience seem relevant to the reader.

To apply your personal experience to fast-food restaurants, you might consider your visits to such restaurants as a child when the busy and exciting atmosphere itself was more important to you than the food. Below, the writer began his expository essay on college binge drinking by citing a recent personal experience; such an approach would be particularly appropriate if his audience were composed mostly of college or university students.

> Exam time is approaching at my college, and stress levels are at an annual high. For this reason, when Friday night arrives, I know I will be drinking—and I definitely will not be alone. Last weekend, my friends and I went to a typical residence party. If I can remember correctly, there were about 15 people noisily crowded into a room the size of a large closet, and many more were herded in the hallways. According to a study in the *American Journal of Public Health*, today's

North American college students have the highest binge drinking rate of any group, even when compared to their peers who do not go to school; furthermore, alcohol is associated with many social problems on college campuses and is the most widespread and preventable health issue for the more than six million students in America (Wechsler et al., 1995, p. 921).

—Student writer Brian Gregg

Classification/Division—What Kinds Are There?

Humans, apparently by nature, tend to classify things. In classification, you begin with a large number of items—for example, commonly known members of the animal kingdom—which you organize into more manageable groups: mammals, birds, fish, reptiles, and amphibians. Each of the categories, such as mammals, could in turn be organized into still smaller units, such as rodents, primates, and carnivores. Fast-food burgers can easily be classified according to their different kinds: hamburgers, chicken burgers, fish burgers, veggie burgers. In the example below, the writer uses classification to break down movies into five designations; the differences could then be analyzed by applying the same criteria to each category.

> Classification focuses on a large number of items that can be organized into more manageable groups.

Ontario has five categories for rating movies: general, parental guidance, 14A (those under 14 must be accompanied by an adult), 18A (those under 18 must be accompanied by an adult), and restricted. In the "general" category, the language must be inoffensive, though words like "damn" and "hell" can occur occasionally. Violence must be limited and permissible; sexual activity includes only embracing and kissing "in a loving context"; horror is defined by genre—for example, fantasy giants, ogres, and dragons are acceptable.

—Ontario Film Review Board, http://www.ofrb.gov.on.ca/english/page6.htm

In division, you are more concerned with the whole than with the individual parts. You break a subject down into parts in order better to understand or explain the whole (the subject). For example, to illustrate how essay structure works, you can divide the essay into introduction, body paragraphs, and conclusion. Under Definition—What Is It? above, the writer divides peer-to-peer file sharing into three different kinds.

> Division breaks the subject down into parts in order to better understand the whole.

Cause–Effect—What Is the Cause?

You can use the cause–effect method to organize an entire essay, or you can use it in one or more paragraphs to analyze a main point. When you deal with causes, you consider the reasons for an occurrence. Cause–effect essays or paragraphs might focus on one effect, which would be accounted for by one or more causes. Or, you could focus on one cause and consider one or more effects or results arising from this cause. Since fast food has often been blamed for obesity, you could look at studies that link obesity (effect) to unhealthy diets (cause). Cause–effect studies are particularly common in the sciences. The **antecedent–consequent** organizational method uses time–order relationships in a similar way to cause–effect relationships. (Think of "before and after" photographs.) The following essay excerpt discusses one cause for stress in first-year students.

> Cause–effect essays or paragraphs might focus on one effect, which would be accounted for by one or more causes. Or, you could focus on one cause and consider one or more effects or results arising from this cause.

An antecedent is a preceding event, condition, or cause.

Consequent means following an event (or antecedent) as a natural effect, result, or conclusion.

A major cause of stress in first-year students is the need to establish a new social base. Students not only find themselves among strangers, but also often have to rely on these strangers for moral support. Consequently, friendships tend to be forged rapidly but superficially. When students inevitably find themselves dealing with mid-terms, assignments, and an increasingly heavy course load, they need close friends and family for support but are forced to turn to these new acquaintances instead. Intense friendships may be formed during such times, but often the stress is insurmountable, leading students to give up and head home.

—Student writer Alexis Parker

Question–Answer—What Is the Answer?

Questions—including the journalistic questions *who?, what?, when?, where?, why?,* and *how?*—can be applied to almost any topic.

This method is effective when you ask the question in the topic sentence and then answer it in the paragraph. Questions—including the journalistic questions *who?, what?, when?, where?, why?,* and *how?*—can be applied to almost any topic, including fast foods. Posing a relevant question is a good way to engage the reader since it directly invites his or her answer to the question. Below, the writer began his essay by asking two questions, suggesting that his essay will focus on two related areas of foreign policy:

> In the post-Cold War era, do military solutions still have a place or is diplomacy able to solve all our foreign policy questions? Does the United Nations still have a useful purpose or will military coalitions like NATO usurp its role entirely? With increasing world tensions and the current American-led wars in Iraq and Afghanistan, many people around the world are asking these questions.
>
> —Student writer Robert Tyre

Example/Illustration—How Can It Be Shown?

Using concrete examples is one of the best ways of supporting a point and clarifying an abstract idea.

Using concrete examples is one of the best ways of supporting a point and clarifying an abstract idea. This method of development can often be combined with other methods, such as cause–effect, cost–benefit, or compare and contrast. If you were using the cause–effect method and you wanted to develop the point that fast foods save valuable time (an effect), you might talk about the convenience of drive-through lanes at fast-food restaurants as one example; another example might be the use of assembly-line workers. Examples are indispensible in most writing and may consist of brief expansions of a point or more fully developed explanations.

> *Brief expansion*: Graffiti art can be seen as a political message on a sidewalk, a limerick on a bathroom wall, a doodle on a desktop, or even a digital image on the Internet.
>
> *Fully-developed explanation*: During the 2002 Commonwealth Games, Kelly Guest was suspended from participating in the triathlon by the International Olympic Committee (IOC). Guest tested positive for nandrolone, a substance banned by the IOC. Guest argued that he had never intended to use nandrolone to enhance his performance, but had ingested the banned substance through the natural supplements he was taking.
>
> —Student writer Tim Dewailly (from his introduction to an essay on the use of natural supplements by elite athletes)

Problem–Solution—How Can It Be (Re)Solved?

The problem–solution method of development could focus on a problem, a solution to a problem, or both a problem and solutions. A problem with fast foods is their dubious nutritional value. After this problem is stated, you could propose ways that fast foods could be made healthier or perhaps give examples of how this is being done today; in this case, you would be combining problem–solution with example/illustration. Studies focusing on problem–solution and cost–benefit (see below) are particularly common in the social sciences where human behaviour is the focus. In the following essay conclusion, the author restates his thesis that Canada's Confederation in 1867 was not so much an effect, or consequence, of various causes, but the best solution to unanticipated problems.

> Politicians were not entertaining the idea of uniting the British North American colonies until numerous problems arose. Political alliances, foreign raids, railway expansion, industrial booms, and the termination of long-standing agreements would have been significant events on their own, but their convergence before 1867 helped push Canada towards Confederation. The most logical solution to these problems was union. Macdonald, Brown, and other nineteenth-century politicians did not strategically plan Confederation, but rather Confederation offered itself as a solution to the problems imposed on them.
>
> —Student writer Chris Hoffart

Cost–Benefit—What Are the Advantages and Disadvantages?

Analyzing something often involves weighing the advantages and disadvantages, the pros and cons. Cost–benefit analysis can be applied to almost any topic since few things in life come without some costs or negative consequences. You could apply cost–benefit analysis to fast foods by focusing on the individual, community, or perhaps even global costs or benefits. In expository essays, cost–benefit analysis involves the objective weighing of pluses and minuses. However, if you were *arguing* that the benefits were more important than the costs, you might well consider the costs first and *then* the benefits, leaving the strongest argument for the last. If you took the opposing position, you might begin with benefits, as the writer does below in her argumentative essay on genetically modified organisms.

> Some scientists believe that releasing GMOs into the environment could reduce pesticide use since crops could be genetically modified to produce a toxin against the pests. Unfortunately, such a toxin could have adverse effects on other organisms, such as the pollinator species of the plant. Some believe that genetic engineering could reduce hunger in third-world countries by allowing more food production. However, after growing genetically modified crops, the farmer would be unable to sow the seeds to grow more crops because GMO seeds are sterile, forcing the farmer to buy new seeds every year—an unrealistic expense. Furthermore, introducing GMOs in third-world countries would

The problem–solution method of development could focus on a problem, a solution to a problem, or both a problem and solutions.

Cost–benefit analysis involves studying the pros and cons of the topic.

The organizational pattern used for a cost–benefit essay depends on whether the essay is expository or argumentative.

be risky as most countries have limited resources and few safety measures in place for controlling GMOs.

—Student writer Jutta Kolhi

Analogy—How Is It Like Something Else?

An analogy is a comparison between one object and a second object that is otherwise unlike the first one. Analogies enable the reader to better understand the original object. You could compare fast foods to the fast pace of society itself. Below, the author began his essay on water resource management by using the analogy of a desert to stress the importance of water management in North America.

> Imagine a hot, torturously dry desert. Throughout this arid wasteland, no life exists—not a tree, shrub, or animal alive. Though to many residents of Europe and North America this scenario may seem highly abstract and incomprehensible, it is the reality faced by many equatorial nations, such as China, Africa, Saudi Arabia, and parts of India. Residents of these nations have developed a keen understanding of the importance of water, and how best to manage it to enable a basic level of existence. However, residents of nations more endowed with water, such as Canada, seem largely indifferent to such a reality.
>
> —Student writer François Beaudet

Comparison and Contrast—How Is It Like and/or Unlike Something Else?

To compare and contrast is a method of systematically drawing similarities and differences between two things. When you compare and contrast, you begin by finding logical bases of comparison and then analyze their similarities and differences. In arguing that one hamburger restaurant is better than another, you could use as bases of comparison their prices, their food quality, their hygienic values, and the friendliness of their staff. Early in her comparison and contrast essay, the writer contrasts two different environmental philosophies by defining each, according to the beliefs of an influential philosopher.

> Conservation is a "shallow ecology" approach to viewing the environment and the role of humans within it. Conceived by Norwegian philosopher and linguist Arne Naess in the early 1970s, "shallow ecology" begins with "an assumption, often unexamined, that human beings are [the] central species in the Earth's ecosystem, and that other beings, as parts of systems, are of less importance or value." Preservation, on the other hand, is based on Arne Naess's "deep ecology" movement, which places humans within ecosystems and holds that humans are different from, but not more valuable than, other species.
>
> —Student writer Bree Stutt

For an example of a comparison and contrast essay, see Chapter 8, page 145.

Sidebar: Analogies are comparisons that enable the reader to better understand the original object.

Sidebar: When you compare and contrast, you begin by finding logical bases of comparison and then analyze their similarities and differences.

Exercise 6.1

On page 120 are 15 general topics. Using at least three different organizational methods per topic, come up with at least three different topic sentences for each topic. Here are some examples using the topic "rap music":

1. **Cause–Effect:** Rap music, with its reliance on ever-changing slang, has expanded people's vocabulary; for instance, one's boyfriend is now called one's "boo."

2. **Definition:** Rap music is defined by some as being no more than talking over someone else's music.

3. **Description or Narration:** The lights were dim, and the crowd, writhing to the rhythm of the bass, was pressing forward to the stage.

4. **Chronology:** The style of rap music has evolved considerably since it first gained popularity with North American youth in the early 1990s.

5. **Question–Answer:** How does rap music manage to offend a broad demographic group while maintaining a strong fan base?

6. **Problem–Solution:** It may seem somewhat ironic, but it is possible that many of the problems addressed in rap lyrics could be solved through this very same medium.

7. **Compare and Contrast:** Rap and hip hop music of the late 1980s and early 1990s, with their offensive lyrics and radical counter-cultural appeal, can be compared in terms of their sociological implications to the rock-and-roll revolution of the late 1960s and early 1970s.

8. **Personal:** When I first heard rap music I found the lyrics offensive and sexist.

9. **Cause–Effect:** Living in the ghetto, surrounded by "booty" and the "brothers," can sometimes cause young men to chant words to a particular rhythm that has no melody.

10. **Cause–Effect:** Rap music has been used as a vehicle for an oppressed minority to get its voice heard.

11. **Process:** To create rap music you need a DJ to provide the beats by mixing records and an MC who takes the beats and contributes the vocals to make the finished product.

12. **Classification:** There are many different forms of rap; these include hip-hop, hard core, and R&B.

13. **Definition and Division:** Rap is a unique form of music that is built around heavy bass beats mixed with sharp, quick lyrics. There is a whole spectrum of rap music, ranging from slow love ballads to fast-paced dance songs.

14. **Cost–Benefit:** Though rap may lead young people to openly and healthily question authority and the status quo, it can lead some adolescents to commit acts of violence against society.

15. **Analogy:** Rap can be compared to the insistent and repetitive chants of an evangelist preacher.

Topics:

1. Alternative schooling
2. Animal rights
3. Eating disorders
4. Email
5. Evolution
6. Exercise
7. Gas prices
8. Global warming
9. Internet piracy
10. Organ transplants
11. Privacy
12. Public speaking
13. Same-sex marriages
14. Sports violence
15. Stress

Exercise 6.2

Find an essay in this textbook and choose a body paragraph. (Do not use an introduction or conclusion.) Read through the paragraph and identify how the author has created a unified, coherent, and well-developed paragraph. Identify where the author connects the paragraph to the next paragraph and to the essay as a whole. Look for transitional words or phrases, identify the main ideas of the paragraph and the development of these ideas, making sure that you can follow the author's train of thought. Also identify any areas that you feel can be improved. Be prepared to explain your answer with a partner. Your instructor may also ask you to analyze the paragraph and submit it to him or her.

Chapter Review Questions

1. What are some of the characteristics of effective paragraphs?
2. Why is supporting information important in paragraphs?
3. What are the different types of development patterns?
4. Explain when it is appropriate to use the different development patterns.

7

The Design of An Essay

In this chapter, you will

- be introduced to a generic model of the essay

- discover the differences between three types of claims and where they are used

- learn what kinds of evidence can be used to support your claim

- learn how to increase your credibility with your readers

No matter what type of essay you are writing, your thesis needs to be supported by solid evidence so that the reader can clearly follow your logic. In this chapter, you will learn how to present a claim and then prove it by using appropriate kinds of evidence. By choosing your support carefully, you increase your credibility with the audience, which is another important aspect of essay writing.

The Essay: An Analytical Model

Successful essays can be analyzed, or "broken down," in different ways. For example, you can divide an essay's structure into introduction, body paragraphs, and conclusion, or you can divide essay writing into five chronological stages. When you are asked to write a critical analysis, you may discuss such areas as the writer's use of logic and reason, the number and reliability of sources, the tone or style of writing, the writer's background or bias, and the like.

Examining a generic model for the essay will help you know what to look for when you analyze other essays. It will also help with your own writing since the elements discussed below are common to most essays—from scholarly studies for specialized readers to the kinds of essays you will write. But whether you are reading an essay or writing one, you will often begin by identifying the claim, a general assertion about the topic on which the essay is based.

When you analyze, you break something down in order to look closely at its parts or to see how the parts connect to make a whole.

Kinds of Claims: Fact, Value, and Policy

Most essays make some kind of **claim** and then proceed to prove the claim by various means of support. Thus, there are two main parts to an essay, whether it is argumentative or expository: the *claim* and the *support*. Generally, the claim is made in the thesis statement. The essay writer may use a claim of fact, value, or policy.

A claim is an assertion about your topic that appears in your introduction. It usually takes the form of a thesis statement.

Most topics can be explored through any of these three claims, depending on the way the claim is presented. In expository essays, the claim will be presented as factual. In argumentative essays, the claim will typically be presented as one of value or policy. If you were asked to write an essay on the topic of homelessness, for example, your claim could take a similar form to one of the following:

Factual claim: Due to the unsettled economic climate, the prevalence of homelessness is increasing in most Canadian provinces.

Value claim: In a society of excess, our indifference to the problem of the homeless on our doorsteps is an indictment of our way of life.

Policy claim: To solve the problem of homelessness in our city, council needs to increase the number of permanent shelters, erect temporary shelters in downtown parks, and educate the public about this escalating social problem.

A factual claim is proven by facts and figures or through the findings of relevant studies.

Claims of Fact

A claim of fact is usually an **empirical** claim that uses the evidence-gathering methods of observation and measurement, a claim that can be proven by facts and figures or through the findings of relevant studies. Claims of fact are used in most expository essays.

Empirical means observing and measuring data under controlled conditions in order to reach a conclusion about a phenomenon.

Claims of Value

A claim of value is an ethical claim and appeals to one's sense of values or a moral system; such values could be inherent in a religious, philosophical, social, cultural, or other system. Claims of value are supported through a process of **reasoning** where certain standards of good or bad, right or wrong, fair or unfair, are accepted as **premises**.

Claims of Policy

A claim of policy is usually a call for some kind of action to fix a problem or improve a situation. Although claims of policy do not have to be based on claims of value, they often are. For example, a proposed change to a law or regulation that gives people more control over something in their lives may be rooted in a claim of value and could involve the argument that the change will produce a more democratic society in which people have greater freedom to assert their rights.

Tentative and Conclusive Claims

Although readers expect your claim early in your essay, usually at the end of the introduction, you may find yourself rewriting your claim *after* you have written your body paragraphs. This is because claims are generalizations based on specific evidence or careful reasoning. You are often better able to make a generalization after you've thoroughly explored your topic, gathered detail, and analyzed all the evidence.

Thus, claims can take two forms. **Tentative** (temporary) claims are generalizations that seem true or applicable to your topic but which could change as you become aware of new information. Claims made in research proposals and outlines—even sometimes in rough drafts—can be considered tentative. **Conclusive** claims act as conclusions: you can express them with confidence in your introduction because the evidence you've uncovered has pointed to them. (See Thesis Statements, Chapter 5, page 94.)

◎ Support: Evidence and Credibility

Claims will not be accepted without **support**—in other words, without **evidence** to back them up. But evidence alone is not enough. To convince your reader that your claim is justified, you need to demonstrate your **credibility**. Although many student writers believe that evidence is more important than credibility, the effort of evidence-gathering and arranging may be wasted if you do not present yourself as credible. When you produce support in your body paragraphs, you then need to present ample evidence and do so in a credible way.

Organization of Evidence

You support your claim through your main points and sub-points. These points function effectively when appropriate organizational methods are used and when the points are ordered logically (climax, inverted climax, or mixed order).

> A value claim is an ethical claim and appeals to the reader's sense of values or moral system.

> A premise is a statement assumed to be true.

> A claim of policy is usually a call for some kind of action to fix a problem or improve a situation.

> Tentative (temporary) claims are generalizations that seem true or applicable to your topic but which could change as you become aware of new information.

> Conclusive claims act as conclusions.

> Support in your body paragraphs is provided by the use of ample and credible evidence.

Organizational methods include definition, division/classification, cause–effect, compare and contrast, problem–solution, and chronology. (They are discussed in detail in Chapter 6, Paragraph Development.)

Kinds of Evidence

Literary texts include novels, short stories, poetry, or even newspapers and letters. Original sources are known as "primary" sources.

Depending on your topic, the instructions for the assignment, and the discipline in which you are writing, you may use some kinds of evidence more than others in your essay. Writing in the humanities often relies on primary, or original, sources. If you write an English essay, for instance, you will probably use many quotations from literary works. The primary sources commonly used in historical research are biographies, newspapers, letters, and records from the era being studied.

Social sciences writing tends to focus on facts and figures, statistics and other numerical data, case studies, interviews, questionnaires, and personal observation. Scientific studies may use similar kinds of evidence but frequently rely on direct methods that involve experimentation. Examples are important in just about every discipline.

Using a variety of evidence will likely produce a stronger essay than relying solely on one kind of evidence. However, it is important, especially if you are using research, to find **hard evidence** to support your key points. Hard evidence includes facts, statistics, and authorities (experts). Soft evidence alone might make your essay readable and understandable, but it will likely not be as convincing as it would have been if you used at least some hard evidence. Hard evidence is essential in factual claims. It is also effective in policy claims because these claims advocate specific actions. It may be less important in value claims in which appeals to reason, emotion, and ethics, along with examples, analogies, brief narratives, description, or personal experience in themselves could produce an effective argument.

Facts and Statistics

When you use research sources, you should check to see that the conclusions are based on factual data tested under controlled conditions.

It is hard to argue with facts. For this reason, factual information is the strongest kind of evidence in an essay. Its effective use will also enhance your credibility by making you appear knowledgeable. Although facts from reliable sources are always relevant to research essays, they can provide support in essays not involving research if you are arguing a topic you know a lot about. The student writer of the essay in Chapter 3, pages 62–3, uses several facts, including references to the September 2001 tragedy in New York City, as well as to works of art, artists, and art periods. When you use research sources, you should check to see that the conclusions are based on factual data tested under controlled conditions. Reliable findings from research can be treated as factual.

You probably are familiar with the saying that statistics lie or that numbers can be twisted to say whatever you want them to say. It's important that you take statistics from reliable sources. Although a statistic may not be an outright falsehood, you should pay attention to the wording of the passage from which a statistic is drawn in order to assess possible bias or distortion. Use caution with statistics cited by people or organizations promoting a particular cause or viewpoint. For example, surveys conducted by special interest groups can be deceptive.

Consider the case of a union that wants to put pressure on the government by making its case public. The group's executive pays for a full-page ad in major newspapers, claiming 93.7 per cent support among the public. The questions to ask are, "Who were the survey's respondents?" "How many were surveyed?" "How was the survey conducted?" Perhaps in this situation a small number of people who happened to be walking by the picket lines were stopped and surveyed. Reliable sources reveal their information-gathering methods, which you can evaluate.

It will often be apparent whether the source is trustworthy or not. For example, although People for the Ethical Treatment of Animals (PETA) strongly opposes practices like animal testing, many statistics they publish can be considered reliable because they are obtained from reliable sources. In a PETA factsheet criticizing animal research, for instance, the writer cites a 1988 study that appeared in the refereed journal *Nature*, which "reports that 520 of 800 chemicals (65 per cent) tested on rats and mice caused cancer in the animals but not in humans" (Lave et al. 631). In sources like this, however, remember that statistics and factual data are being used for a specific purpose; evaluate them on an individual basis and with this purpose in mind. Also bear in mind that sources like PETA may report only on those studies that agree with the organization's mission or viewpoint, ignoring contrary findings.

All the essays in Chapters 12 and 13 make effective use of facts and statistics.

Authorities and Experts

When you apply for a job, you may be asked for letters of reference. Unless your prospective employer asks specifically for a character reference, you would normally submit letters from knowledgeable experts—perhaps from your former bosses or those you have worked with. They would be considered authorities who could support your claim of competence and testify that you are a good candidate for the job.

Authorities can be used for support if they have direct knowledge of your subject. Authorities who are not experts will have less authority. For example, in an essay that argues a scientific or mathematical point, citing Albert Einstein would be an example of hard evidence. In an essay about vegetarianism, citing Einstein would provide soft evidence as he is not considered an expert on the topic. You will usually locate experts as you research your topic. However, it's also possible to conduct an interview with an expert, asking questions pertinent to your claim. See page 187.

Examples, Illustrations, Case Studies, Precedents

While hard evidence provides direct support, **soft evidence** indirectly supports your points and makes them more understandable to the reader. Kinds of indirect support

When using facts or statistics that special interest groups and similar organizations have cited in their papers, remember that the data is being used for a specific purpose. Evaluate the facts and statistics with this purpose in mind.

Authorities can be used for support if they have direct knowledge of your subject. Authorities who are not experts will have less authority.

While hard evidence provides direct support, soft evidence indirectly supports your points and makes them more understandable to the reader.

include examples, illustrations, case studies, and precedents. Analogies, description, and personal experience may also be used if your instructor approves.

We use **examples** in both speech and writing. To support his argument, the teenager arguing for his independence might give several examples of friends who live on their own. Examples should always be relevant and representative. The teenager's parents might refute the examples by pointing out that they are not representative—for example, that one friend, Shawn, has a full-time job and that another one, Giovanna, spent the summer travelling throughout Europe before moving out of her parents' house.

In most writing, examples bring a point home to the reader by making it specific and concrete. Examples are especially useful if you are writing for a non-specialist reader, as they make it easier to grasp a difficult or an abstract point. Illustrations, case studies, and precedents are extended examples that can be used to explain or reinforce important points.

Illustrations are detailed examples that often take the form of anecdotes or other brief narratives. In this example, the writer uses an illustration to support his point that logic can be used to draw different conclusions from the same premise (a statement assumed to be true):

> Consider the example of the hydroelectric dam that the Urra company constructed in Colombia. The dam provides electricity to industry and profit to the companies and people who invest in it. The area flooded by the dam was inhabited by indigenous peoples. The river was a source of fresh water and fish, and on the river's now flooded banks were food plants that sustained them. . . . If an analysis of this situation were based on the premise that all people should be treated equally and with respect, then through reason, the conclusion would be that this was a bad thing for the indigenous peoples living along the river. If, however, the basic premise was that business interests are primary, then the logical conclusion would be that the hydroelectric dam was a good thing.
>
> —Student writer Graeme Verhulst

Case studies are often used as support, particularly in the social sciences, education, and business; they can also be the focus of research studies. A case study is a carefully selected example that is closely analyzed in order to provide a testing ground for the claim the writer is making. Because case studies are practical, real-life examples, they can be used to support a **hypothesis**. For example, to ask if youth involvement in decision-making could produce a safer school environment, a Vancouver school planned a series of student-led initiatives and activities. When the results were analyzed, it was found that the students felt safer and had improved their pro-social and conflict resolution skills. The outcome supported the hypothesis concerning the effectiveness of youth involvement in decisions of self-governance.

Precedents are examples that refer to the way that a particular situation was dealt with in the past. Judgments in courts of law establish precedents that influence future court decisions. Once you have established some course of action as a

---

Examples are especially useful if you are writing for a non-specialist reader, as they make it easier to grasp a difficult or abstract point.

Illustrations are detailed examples that often take the form of anecdotes or other brief narratives.

A case study is a carefully selected example that is closely analyzed in order to provide a testing ground for the claim the writer is making.

A hypothesis is a prediction or expected result of an experiment or other research investigation.

Precedents are examples that refer to the way that a particular situation was dealt with in the past.

precedent, you then apply it to your argument. The success in using precedents as evidence depends on your ability to convince the reader that

1. similar conditions apply to your topic today, and
2. following the precedent will produce a desirable result.

For example, if you were arguing that Canada should offer free post-secondary studies to all academically qualified individuals, you could refer to the precedent of Denmark, one of the first countries to provide universal access to post-secondary schooling. Then you must make it clear that

1. the situation in Denmark is comparable to the situation in Canada, and
2. Denmark has profited from this system, so Canada will also likely benefit from a similar course of action.

Analogies, Description, Personal Experience

These kinds of evidence are suggestive and indirect; they cannot in themselves prove a claim.

Analogy, a kind of comparison, and **description** can be used to make a point easier for the reader to understand and relate to. Like narration, description may also play a limited role in argument, perhaps to attract interest in the essay's introduction or to set up a main point. (For examples, see Chapter 6, pages 113 and 118.)

Personal experience could take the form of direct experiences or observation. It can help the reader relate to your topic. You should keep your voice objective when using personal experience; any bias will undermine your credibility. Personal experience can be effective in supporting a value claim. For example, if you had witnessed a dog fight, your observations on dog fighting could be effective in supporting the claim that dog fighting is cruel. Similarly, if you have had personal experience with homeless people by working in a food bank, you could use your experience to help support a related policy claim. Student writer Kerry Hinds uses personal experience to support her thesis (see Chapter 13, page 290).

> Personal experience can often be effective in supporting a value claim.

Credibility

Demonstrating credibility as a writer will strengthen your claim. Three factors contribute to credibility: knowledge of the topic, reliability/trustworthiness, and fairness. Showing your knowledge by itself doesn't make you credible. Consider again the analogy of job-hunting: when you send out your résumé, you want to impress prospective employers with your experience and knowledge; however, during the interview, the employer will likely ask questions that pertain more to your reliability as an employee than to your knowledge—for example, *Why do you want to work for*

> Three factors contribute to credibility: knowledge of the topic, reliability/ trustworthiness, and fairness.

us? Where do you see yourself in five years? Why did you quit your last job? Furthermore, when employers check your references, questions of your reliability are bound to arise. Similarly with essay writing, once you have conveyed your knowledge, you must convince the reader that you also are reliable.

You demonstrate **knowledge** through the points made in the essay and the kinds of evidence you use to support them. But you can present yourself as knowledgeable without being thought reliable. You instill confidence in your **reliability** or trustworthiness by being able to answer "yes" to questions like the following:

- Is your essay well-structured?
- Are your paragraphs unified, coherent, and well-developed?
- Is your writing clear? Is your grammar correct? Is your style effective?
- Have you used the rules and procedures of your discipline (if applicable)?
- Have you used critical thinking skills effectively? Are your conclusions logical and well-founded?

You must demonstrate **fairness** in an argumentative essay, though fairness can also arise in expository essays if you are not objective in your use of the evidence. In many argumentative essays, it is important to consider opposing views. While presenting a strong case for yourself, it will help if you pinpoint the shortcomings and limitations of these views. A writer who is fair comes across as objective in addressing the other side, avoiding slanted language that reveals bias. While you can demonstrate reliability by avoiding misuse of reason, you can demonstrate fairness by using emotional appeals fairly and selectively (discussed in more detail in Chapter 13).

In the essay model diagram in Figure 7.1 on page 129, each part coexists with the other parts; none is an isolated entity that you can simply inject into an essay mechanically or without considering where it fits in. This inter-relatedness is evident in many places in a successful essay. In your own essays, you can ask questions like, *Am I using the kinds of evidence favoured by my discipline? Am I organizing this evidence logically? Have I used enough sources? Is my essay well-structured and is my writing clear and grammatical? Have I used evidence fairly?*

When reading an essay in order to analyze it, you can ask similar questions of the writer and the essay. When you analyze, you *break something down* into parts so you can look closely at each part. The interdependence of the various parts of the essay can be clearly seen. For example, grammatical errors will affect the writer's reliability, which will reduce credibility and weaken support for the claim. Being aware of the relatedness of the different parts should enable you to approach your own writing critically as well as give you the tools to analyze other writing.

Student writers sometimes have the impression that an effective essay comprises parts that function in isolation. But the opposite is true: it is really one entity with many interdependent parts.

Breaking down the essay into its essential parts enables you to analyze your own writing processes and those of other writers. It can show you how different parts of an essay contribute to the whole.

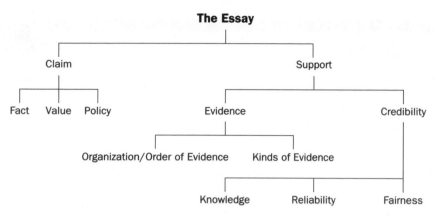

Figure 7.1 The essay: an analytical model.

Exercise 7.1

It is important to be able to distinguish between a factual claim and a value or policy claim. Although there may not always be a firm line between exposition and argument, you may be asked to write an essay that is either one or the other; and, of course, your reader should recognize what kind of essay he or she is reading. Determine whether the statements below are most suited to argument or exposition by putting an "A" or "E" beside them.

1. British Columbia's environmental policy is better than Alberta's policy.

2. Legislators should impose an outright ban on smoking in indoor public establishments and places of business.

3. Diplomacy and militarism are the two main approaches to foreign policy which, though sometimes used independently, are much more effective when used in combination.

4. 3M's tradition, strategy, and corporate image have helped it maintain its top-ten ranking in *Fortune* magazine year after year.

5. Organic farming has many costs, but the benefits seem much greater as this farming method is becoming more popular.

6. Hip-hop today acts as a cultural bridge for widely diverse groups of young people to communicate across racial, class, religious, linguistic, and national divisions.

7. In spite of ethical concerns, can the human race really afford to ignore the tremendous potential benefits of embryonic stem cell research to find cures for many diseases?

8. The government should take steps to regulate the monopolistic practices of airlines today.

9. Probably nobody in the history of psychology has been as controversial—sometimes revered, sometimes despised—as Sigmund Freud.

10. What are the physical effects of artificial and natural tanning? What are the risks involved, and what can be done to educate the public about both?

Exercise 7.2

The 15 simple thesis statements below contain claims of fact, value, or policy. Identify the kind of claim and then write two sentences under the original one in which you turn the original claim into the two other kinds of claims. You may make any changes in wording you wish as long as the topic remains the same.

Example:

Thesis Statement: Cellphones are a wonderful modern convenience, but they can be dangerous in cars because they often distract the driver.

Kind of Claim: Claim of value: the statement asserts that cellphones can be dangerous (a bad thing).

A. The recent use of cellphones in cars has increased the number of accidents in many urban centres—especially during rush hour.

Kind of Claim: Claim of fact: the statement asserts that the number of accidents has increased.

B. Cellphones in cars should be prohibited as they are dangerous both for the user and for other drivers.

Kind of Claim: Claim of policy: the statement advocates an action, though this action is based on a value, i.e., that cellphones in cars are dangerous (bad).

1. It is increasingly necessary to be bilingual in Canada today.

2. The lyrics of rap music are inherently anti-social and encourage violence.

3. Women should not be allowed to serve in the military in anything but administrative roles.

4. Whatever one may think of same-sex marriages, it is evident that they are here to stay.

5. After completing high school, one should travel for at least a year before proceeding to college or university.

6. It is necessary to provide more funding for technology in today's classroom and to spend less on teachers' salaries.

7. The current practice of appointing Supreme Court judges in Canada is undemocratic.

8. With the number of sports teams, clubs, and cultural groups on campus, students who do not participate in extra-curricular activities are not getting good value for their education.

9. School uniforms provide many benefits to students and their parents.

10. The government should subsidize organically grown food.

11. Recreational use of steroids can cause physical and psychological damage to the user.

12. Before committing more resources to space exploration, we should work to solve global problems, such as poverty, that affect people everyday.

13. The growing popularity of Eastern medicine today shows that society is tending towards a more natural approach to health care.

14. Parents should have the right, within reason, to discipline their child as they see fit.

15. While advocates of a shorter work week believe that this measure will help our troubled economy, opponents say it will only weaken it and create social problems.

Exercise 7.3

Taking one of the claims for each statement in Exercise 7.2, determine how you would most effectively support it in the body of an essay. This exercise could take the form of a group discussion, or your group could write out a strategic approach, referring as specifically as possible to those parts under Support in Figure 7.1 on page 129.

Strategies to Consider

Organization of Evidence: Which patterns of organization/development would you likely use? Which could be used? (See Chapter 6).

Kinds of Evidence: Which kinds of evidence would most effectively back up your claim? (See pages 124–7.)

Which of the three categories of credibility seem the most important (knowledge, reliability, fairness)? Why? What general or specific strategies could you use to ensure your support was credible?

Chapter Review Questions

1. What are the two main parts of an essay?
2. Are there advantages to using certain claims? When would these advantages occur?
3. What kinds of evidence can be used in an essay? What is the difference between hard and soft evidence?
4. Why is credibility important?
5. How can you establish your credibility?

The Expository Essay

In this chapter, you will

- learn how to write expository essays

- be introduced to a template to help you structure expository essays

- learn how to write process, definition, and comparison and contrast essays

An expository essay seeks to inform readers. Expository essays often require research, although personal observation or background knowledge can also be used to support a writer's points. Expository essays can follow many different patterns and you, the writer, need to choose those best suited for your audience and purpose. Among the most common expository essays not requiring research are process, definition, and comparison and contrast essays.

Expository Writing

The main difference between an argumentative essay and an expository essay is that the former seeks to convince the reader, to change his or her mind about a subject. The expository essay doesn't seek to change the reader's view, but it does seek to convince the reader that the thesis is valid by using facts, observation, and clear thinking for support. In this sense, argument is involved in expository writing. Expository essays may also use statistics and the findings of research to support the thesis. (Note that the examples of expository essays used in this chapter do not use research; however, your instructor may require it. Always pay attention to instructor requirements, as discussed in Chapter 2.) Expository essays that use research are discussed in depth in Chapters 11 and 12. Effectively integrating research is discussed in Chapter 11.

Exposition means "put forth" and is an inclusive term for writing concerned with *explaining* or *informing*—distinct from arguing or persuading. Much of the reading you do every day is in the form of expository writing. From the time you wake up and turn on your TV or computer to get the latest news to your review of a textbook chapter at the end of the day, you will have been exposed to many examples of exposition.

Types of Expository Essays

There are many types of expository essays. They can

- show the reader the steps in a process
- use definition to help the reader understand the various ways something can be understood
- use comparison and contrast to point out similarities and differences
- use examples to help the reader understand the main points
- classify or divide a subject
- show cause and effect

The expository essay is often the first type of essay to which students are introduced. You may have seen an essay template such as the one in Table 8.1 on page 134, which has been designed with this type of essay in mind.

Templates can help you organize your thoughts in a coherent way, making the writing process easier. They can also be expanded or contracted to fit the length required for your essay. For example, if you need more than five paragraphs (three for the body plus an introduction and conclusion), you can continue using this pattern to expand your essay. Also, not all paragraphs will require three sub-points. Some may need only two, while others may include four or more. In addition, each box may contain more than one sentence or illustration. Chapter 4 explains paragraph composition in more detail, so remember to refer to that when you begin composing after creating your outline.

Table 8.1 Expository Essay Template

Thesis Statement		
	Supporting idea	1.
		2.
		3.
Paragraph 1	Topic sentence	
	Sub-point 1	
	Illustration	(quotation, personal observation, etc.)
	Sub-point 2	
	Illustration	
	Sub-point 3	
	Illustration	
	Conclusion	
Paragraph 2	Topic sentence	
	Sub-point 1	
	Illustration	
	Sub-point 2	
	Illustration	
	Sub-point 3	
	Illustration	
	Conclusion	
Paragraph 3	Topic sentence	
	Sub-point 1	
	Illustration	
	Sub-point 2	
	Illustration	
	Sub-point 3	
	Illustration	
	Conclusion	
Concluding paragraph	Main ideas to summarize	
	Clincher	Idea to leave reader with

The sample in Table 8.2 uses the topic "eating disorders" to illustrate this template. The thesis statement is included as well as the first body paragraph. As you can see, the first paragraph uses definition to give the reader the necessary background in order to understand the rest of the essay. It also has

Table 8.2   Expository Essay Template: Eating Disorders

Thesis Statement	Eating Disorders are a problem for society	
	Supporting idea	1. explanation of different types 2. why they are on the rise, or at least seem to be 3. medical and psychological impact
Paragraph 1	**Topic sentence**	**When people think of eating disorders, they often think of teenage girls or runway models who starve themselves, but that is only one of the many disorders.**
	Sub-point 1	Anorexia nervosa—most well-known
	Illustration	Find medical definition from journals and explain whom it affects and side effects
	Sub-point 2	Bulimia (binge and purge)
	Illustration	Find medical definition from journals and explain whom it affects and side effects
	Sub-point 3	Compulsive overeating
	Illustration	Find medical definition from journals and explain whom it affects and side effects
	Sub-point 4	Selective eating
	Illustration	Find medical definition from journals and explain whom it affects and side effects
	Conclusion	Many different types of eating disorders, but they all have the same outcome.

more than three sub-points. The next paragraph, as indicated in the template, will possibly use chronology to establish an increase in eating disorders over a certain time period. The final paragraph may use a cause–effect pattern. Remember that this is just like an outline. Full sentences do not have to be used, nor do your ideas have to be fully developed at this stage. Ideas introduced here can also be modified later if you find they are not strong enough or if they overlap. At this point, it is important to write your ideas down and organize them. You may find that, as you compose your essay, some paragraphs seem much longer than others. If this is the case, you can divide paragraphs to make them shorter and more manageable.

Three common kinds of expository essays that do not always require research are process analysis, definition, and comparison and contrast essays. Each is discussed below and is followed by an example of this type by a student writer. Each writer used a variant of the essay template discussed above.

Exercise 8.1

Look through the following essay topics and create a template for one of them.

1. Narrate the experience of a first-year student during orientation
2. Causes of tuition increases
3. Effects of tuition increases
4. How to alleviate stress during the first year of college or university
5. Explain how Millennials are different from Boomers

◎ The Process Analysis Essay

When you explain or inform, you must be familiar with your topic in order to communicate it to your reader. Like most people, you've probably experienced the awkward situation of trying to explain something you weren't completely sure about—or, perhaps, you've over-explained, and your listener has become impatient or even broken in with "I know that!" These examples underscore the importance of both topic and audience in expository writing.

One way to become an expert is to read what other people have written—in other words, to research the topic. (The research process is discussed in chapters 10 and 11.) On the other hand, you can also become an authority through your personal experience, by doing something over a period of months or even years. Many professional and recreational skills are acquired this way and may be good topics for process essays.

If you wanted to explain these skills to someone, you would first have to consider how much he or she knew about the topic—you would have to consider your audience. You would not write for readers who knew as much as you did, unless you wanted to alert them to a special area they might not know about. For example, you might write an essay on the steps for surviving in the extreme cold for a general audience of winter sports enthusiasts or for the more specific one of out-of-bounds skiers.

The kind of essay that explains the stages of a process is called **process analysis**. In process analysis, you break down a process by describing the activities involved step by step. In writing process analysis essays, as with all essays, you need to consider your topic, audience, and purpose before beginning to write. There are two main reasons to write a process analysis essay:

1. to stimulate reader interest, or
2. to make readers familiar with a process so they can do it themselves.

In both cases, you need to establish your credibility.

The following is a step-by-step breakdown in the planning and writing of a process analysis essay. It is followed by a sample student process essay of about

Analysis is a common rhetorical pattern in which you break something down to look at its parts individually or to see how they fit together as a whole. Most methods of essay development involve some kind of analysis. In a process analysis, you break an activity into its *chronological* stages, showing how it is done.

500 words. A longer essay might go into more detail in the body paragraphs. Process analysis can also be used as a method of paragraph development within a longer essay not mainly concerned with describing the stages of a process. (See Chapter 6, Paragraph Development, page 114.)

Planning Process Essays

- After you've decided on a topic, determine your audience's knowledge and interest levels. This will also help you decide on your purpose for writing (i.e., to stimulate your reader's interest or to enable him or her to duplicate the steps in the process).

- Consider the level of detail that is needed. Again, if your main purpose is to stimulate interest, you will need less detail than if you are guiding the reader carefully through each stage. But that doesn't necessarily mean your essay will be shorter. One way to stimulate interest is to use strategies designed to arouse the reader's curiosity (see next point).

- Consider the way you want to come across to your reader. For example, you may want to show your enthusiasm for an activity if your essay is interest-focused. However, you need to do this subtly—not, for example, by using lots of exclamation points! Although process essays are usually expository, not argumentative, one way to stimulate interest is to mention the practical benefits of the activity/process you're describing (if you stress both benefits and costs, you will be writing a cost-benefit analysis, a different kind of expository essay).

- Before beginning to draft your essay, you need to decide how you're going to address your reader. If your purpose is to enable the reader to duplicate the steps in a process, it might be natural to use the subject "you." Remember, though, that your essay should not read like an instruction booklet. Process analysis essays are designed to be *used*, but their practical function shouldn't override other considerations. Notice in the following set of instructions that each stage is structured as a command; the writer uses a series of **imperative clauses**. This impersonality may be appropriate for a mechanical set of instructions, but not for your essay.
  - Disengage the paper clamp by pushing the wire clamp on the side of the sanding pad towards the sander's body.
  - Line up the edge of the sandpaper with the edge of the sanding pad.
  - Insert the sandpaper tightly over the foam pad. . . .

Your instructor may want you to avoid the informal *you*, in which case you must use nouns, like *a person*, or *the user*, or third-person pronouns, like *one*. See the sample essay below.

Writing Process Essays

- Although outlines are useful in structuring all essays, they are not always essential in process essays, which are arranged by the order of the stages in the process.

As you do with any essay, before you write a process analysis, you need to consider the topic itself, your audience, and your purpose in writing. From the beginning, you need to establish your credibility.

You demonstrate your credibility by showing you are knowledgeable, reliable, and fair. See Chapter 7, p. 127.

An imperative clause or sentence issues a command. Its subject, "you," is always understood even though it is not expressed. See Chapter 14, pp. 311–2.

Using templates like the ones in Tables 8.1 and 8.2, pp. 134–5, can help you structure process analysis essays.

- Introductions vary depending on audience and purpose. However, they are usually brief and direct. They may provide background information or include preparations, such as equipment or tools needed for the activity. As with your other essays, you should end the introduction with a clear thesis statement.

- Arrange each stage in chronological order (you can number them to make them clear in your own mind, but in your final draft, remove the numbers unless leaving them in makes the essay easier to follow). Ensure each step is discussed in an exact sequence—don't consider step 2 until you have covered step 1. If any stage is out of order, it will confuse the reader.

- If the process you're describing is broken into many short stages, don't allot one paragraph per stage. Combine two or more stages in the same paragraph, using appropriate transitions to connect one stage to the next. Closely related stages can be placed in the same paragraph. For example, if you were writing on race walking, in one paragraph you might discuss the walker's body position from when the heel touches the ground to when the leg is vertical, during which the body's position undergoes several minor changes, before beginning a new paragraph.

- Keep focused on the key details of the process in each paragraph. These may include instructions on what *not* to do or warnings about mistakes people often make. You also may need to briefly define unfamiliar terms. If the term applies to the entire process, however, the best place to do this would be the introduction.

- Restrict the use of personal experience and description, though these methods of development may sometimes be used in the introduction or conclusion.

- In your conclusion, you may focus on the importance or the benefits of the activity, or on mistakes people often make, reinforcing the value of having the proper equipment, of taking safety precautions, and the like.

The following list of 10 topics suggests the range of options for writers of process essays. If you are assigned to write a process essay, the most important factors in choosing would be your expertise and interest in the topic.

1. Choosing an ideal apartment or roommate
2. Creating a web page or your Facebook home page
3. Deciding on an iPod or other media player
4. Giving a presentation using PowerPoint
5. Grooming or bathing a pet
6. Organizing a social or educational event for a group you are involved with
7. Preparing for a job interview
8. Successful rock climbing, skydiving, or snowboarding
9. Travelling abroad on less than $20 a day
10. Writing an email to your professor or boss

Sample Process Essay

The following is an essay by a student writer that uses process to describe the stages of Bikram Yoga. Read the essay and respond to the questions below.

Sample Student Essay

Where Hot Is "Cool": The Stages of Bikram Yoga
By Vanessa Tilson

Stepping into a Bikram Yoga class can be a shock to the system: the room is 40°C and is lined with mirrors. The intense heat is not the only shock: half of what you hear will be in Sanskrit, one of the sacred languages of Hinduism and Buddhism. Bikram Yoga, or "hot Yoga," was started in Los Angeles by Yogiraj Bikram Choudhury. Originally from India, Choudhury travelled to North America to open yoga studios that would use the form of yoga he designed after a weightlifting injury. Bikram Yoga consists of twenty-six postures and two breathing exercises that take the body through a cycle that works every muscle and organ.

> General information about the origins of Bikram Yoga would be common knowledge for anyone trained in this form of yoga. In addition, it is easily obtainable information; thus, no citation is given. However, if the writer had included more specific detail, such as the date and place of Choudhury's birth, a citation would have been needed.

The standing and floor postures consist of a warm-up series, standing series, spine strengthening series, and floor series; each posture has medical benefits. Bikram Yoga begins with Pranayama breathing, a method of deep breathing that opens the lungs and prepares the mind for class. Next, Bikram Yoga moves into warm-up, which consists of three postures: Half Moon Pose with Hands to Feet Pose, Awkward Pose, and Eagle Pose. Awkward Pose , as its name suggests, can be a challenge to newcomers as it involves bending the knees as if one is sitting down in an imaginary chair. After ten seconds in which the arms are held out straight in front, one comes up slowly to stand on the tips of the toes, again holding this position for ten seconds. All the while, the focus is on slow, deep breathing.

> In this introduction, background information is given. There is no need to discuss preparations or equipment since none are needed for yoga. In the simple thesis statement, the writer announces her topic, its stages, and its main benefits.

> Note that the writer expands on only one of the poses, deliberately choosing "awkward pose," which is not as self-explanatory as Half Moon Pose with Hands to Feet Pose or Standing Head to Knee Pose.

Standing series starts with Standing Head to Knee Pose and finishes with Toe Stand Pose. All the poses help increase circulation to the heart and lungs. The floor section follows, starting with Savasana, or Dead Body Pose, in which the mind rests and the body rejuvenates. Every floor posture ends with Savasana to achieve deep relaxation after the Asana

> The writer begins a new paragraph after completing the stages of the warm-up series.

(Continued)

The meanings of two Sanskrit words are briefly defined in this paragraph.

The writer includes a warning about a common problem during one stage of the process.

(active poses). Those unfamiliar with yoga may find it hard to stay awake during this stage, a real problem because one needs to complete this stage consciously.

In spine strengthening, the two processes of extension and compression are stressed. The entire spine, along with the nervous system and many muscle groups, is worked on with the goal of increased strength and flexibility. This is especially true in the last two poses in this series, the Camel Pose and the Rabbit Pose. The final floor series has only three postures. The last is the Spine Twisting Pose, carefully prepared for by the previous poses to ensure it is performed correctly and without injury. The class ends with Khapalbhati breathing, a method used to expel all the air left in the lungs.

In her conclusion, the writer discusses some of the benefits of Bikram Yoga.

Yoga is said to be a healing process. Although Bikram Yoga may feel like an intense workout, it actually gives one energy while the postures themselves build mental and physical strength, balance, and flexibility. To these benefits, the heated room adds one important one: it allows the muscles to stay warm, helping to prevent injuries. The heat also induces sweating, helping to eliminate toxins through the skin. For the beginner or the seasoned yogi, hot yoga is a "cool" experience.

1. What kind of reader do you think this essay was written to? Very knowledgeable, moderately knowledgeable, or not knowledgeable?

2. Do you think the main purpose of the essay was to stimulate interest or to enable the reader to perform the stages of the activity?

3. Is there anything the writer could have done to further stimulate interest?

4. Is there anything she could have done to ensure that each stage could be duplicated?

◎ The Definition Essay

In argumentative essays, defining something is often the first stage of an argument in which you go on to develop your thesis through means *other than* definition. On the other hand, definition essays can expand and elaborate on a subject, using a variety of organizational methods.

Definition often provides a necessary starting point for an argument. The success you have in getting your reader to agree with your definition will help establish your credibility as a writer, strengthening your argument. Defining something also enables you to set the terms on which you want your argument to rest: successful definition enables you to take control of a controversial or abstract topic.

Definition is often an essential part of expository essays. Essays in the humanities, natural sciences, and social sciences often begin by defining terms that the writer will employ throughout the essay. It may be crucial for the writer to establish the sense or **connotation** of one or more terms that have been subject to a variety of definitions in the writer's discipline. Many academic texts—above all, introductory textbooks—include a glossary or index of common terms that is designed to make it easier to apply terms correctly.

> Connotation is the meaning that words can have besides their literal dictionary meanings.

It is important to provide an accurate definition in your essay, as definitions sometimes change over time and according to place, as well as according to cultural, national, social, and other factors. For example, the way you would define *privacy* today would likely be different from the way it would have been defined 25 years ago, due partly to

---

Exercise 8.2

As well as definition, the following paragraph includes other methods of development as discussed in Chapter 6. Identify two such methods in the paragraph.

Vegetarianism, derived from a Latin word meaning "to enliven," was practiced in ancient Greece as early as the sixth century BCE by the Pythagoreans, and its reputation has spread to many other countries since then. It is a way of life in China, India, Japan, Pakistan, and even in North America with more than 14 million vegetarians. Since its beginnings, many well-known people have been non-meat eaters, including Socrates, Plato, Leonardo da Vinci, Charles Darwin, Thomas Edison, Albert Einstein, and Isaac Newton. The term *vegetarian* refers to someone who does not eat any flesh; however, there are many varieties of vegetarianism. If one eats no flesh (red meat, poultry, fish), but consumes dairy and egg products, one is said to be a lacto-ovo vegetarian (the most popular type in North America). Pesco-vegetarians eat seafood but avoid red meat and poultry. Vegans are "strict vegetarians," who not only avoid consuming any type of animal but also avoid anything manufactured from animals (soap, leather, wool, honey, gelatine). Any form of vegetarianism is a healthy way of living, which not only benefits humans but also benefits animals and the planet itself.

—Student writer Jessica Charbonneau

technologies that have made it easier for others to access personal information. If you fail to provide the correct definition as it applies to your essay topic, you fail to prove your credibility, which in turn affects the reader's reaction to your essay.

◎ Sample Definition Essay

The following is a student exam essay that uses definition to address the topic of leadership. Read the essay and respond to the exercises below.

Sample Student Essay

What Is Leadership?
By Andrew Fodor

An unconscious car accident victim enters the emergency room of a local hospital. Nurses, technicians, doctors and other health care providers swarm around the patient and begin administering tests and procedures. The attending physician stands back to assess, monitor, and give orders to the emergency team. The life of the patient depends on the leadership skills of the attending physician.

Leadership is a skill that actively encourages, directs, co-ordinates, and guides one or more individuals towards the completion of a goal. Leadership is a valuable attribute in nearly all areas of society, such as the military, government, business, education, as well as in families. Although a power structure is often developed to identify or assign an individual, groups of individuals, or organizations to a leadership role, this is not a prerequisite of leadership. For example, the child of a mother undergoing chemotherapy may provide hope, encouragement, and inspiration to his or her family.

A classic example of leadership is a project manager (PM). He or she has a responsibility to complete a project on time, within budget, and to the requirements of the client, usually a third party or company department. The PM must provide direction (a project plan) for his or her team; delegate responsibility to team members (sub-projects); monitor team progress; communicate between management, the project team and the client, as well as manage a number of other tasks (for example, team morale).

There are numerous ways to improve an individual's leadership skills; these can often be accomplished by education (such as workshops) and on the job experience.

Leadership is the co-ordination of people, resources, and tasks towards the completion of a goal. Leadership can be demonstrated in many situations, from a doctor trying to save a life in the ER to a university teacher to a military commander. Although leadership is often provided by qualified, educated persons, it may sometimes arise from unlikely sources. Regardless, leadership is a skill that can be developed through experience and education.

Exercise 8.3

Leadership is an abstract topic; therefore, the writer has tried hard in the limited time allotted to put it in more concrete and immediate terms. He begins the essay by narrating a scenario (an emergency room of a hospital) where leadership is urgently needed. He gives examples of other situations that evoke leadership qualities. He also gives a specific example, which is thoroughly developed as a "case study" in paragraph three. Is there anything in the essay that doesn't seem to belong or that detracts from its effectiveness?

Exercise 8.4

Write a 300–400-word essay (about the length of the essay on leadership) on one of the following general topics:

1. Censorship
2. Consumerism
3. Freedom
4. Human rights
5. Justice
6. Multiculturalism
7. Nationalism
8. Self-expression
9. Success
10. Tradition

◎ The Comparison and Contrast Essay

Comparison and contrast can be used as the primary organizational method in both argumentative and expository essays. As writing these kinds of essays can be more challenging than other kinds, consider using the three-step approach:

1. Ensure that the topics you want to compare are, indeed, comparable. It is not possible to compare the health-care system in the United States to the educational system in Canada. While it might be possible to compare the health-care systems of the two countries, such a topic would be too broad and complex for anything much less than a book. However, it might be manageable to compare the health-care systems of two Canadian provinces.

2. After you have determined that the topics are comparable and that the essay is manageable, carefully choose at least three bases of comparison for the main points of your essay, ensuring that each basis of comparison is logical and manageable.

3. Organizing comparison and contrast essays is especially crucial. To ensure the essay is clearly laid out with the points easy to follow, you can choose between the **block** and the **point-by-point** methods.

Block and Point-by-Point Methods

In the block method, you consider all the points that relate to your first subject of comparison (which becomes your first block of material). When you have finished, you consider all the points as they apply to the second subject of comparison (your second block). When you are comparing the second subject, you use the same order as you did with the first.

In the more commonly used point-by-point method, you consider one basis of comparison as it applies to each subject and continue until you have considered all the bases of comparison. In the following outline, "A" and "B" represent your subjects, or what you are comparing, and the numbers represent your points, or bases of comparison:

Block Method

A: SUBJECT OF COMPARISON
    1. Basis of comparison
    2. Basis of comparison
    3. Basis of comparison

B: SUBJECT OF COMPARISON
    1. Basis of comparison
    2. Basis of comparison
    3. Basis of comparison

Point-by-Point Method

1. BASIS OF COMPARISON
    A: Subject of comparison
    B: Subject of comparison

2. BASIS OF COMPARISON
    A: Subject of comparison
    B: Subject of comparison

3. BASIS OF COMPARISON
    A: Subject of comparison
    B: Subject of comparison

Below, the two methods are applied to the identical topic and bases of comparison.

Topic: **Compare and contrast benefits of walking to benefits of cycling.**

Block Method

A: CYCLING
1. transportation
2. exercise
3. health
4. cost

B: WALKING
1. transportation
2. exercise
3. health
4. cost

Point-by-Point Method

1. TRANSPORTATION
   A: Cycling
   B: Walking

3. HEALTH
   A: Cycling
   B: Walking

2. EXERCISE
   A: Cycling
   B: Walking

4. COST
   A: Cycling
   B: Walking

○ Sample Comparison and Contrast Essay

After reading this essay, complete the exercises that follow.

Sample Student Essay

Tail of Opposites
By Barclay Katt

Meow, meow, or woof, woof?

For most people, it is an easy choice. In fact, it is not really a "choice" at all: it is simply the way it is. There are "cat people" and "dog people" in the world, and neither group speaks the language of the other. They are as separate as curds and whey, and when a cat person meets a dog person on neutral turf, the result is a war of words in which the fur is sure to fly. It seems that each group disdains the other; in many other ways, each doggedly or cattily proclaims its separate identity.

Just by walking into a house, you can tell whether the owner is a feline fancier or a canine connoisseur. (The fact that you have made it to the front door tells you something; have you ever heard of a watchcat?) The cat owner will show you to

(Continued)

the elegant living room. Elegant? Cat owners possess the most costly furniture, but it is invariably armoured by ugly plastic coverings with perhaps a swath of towels wrapped around sofa ends. The dog owner will conduct you swiftly to the humble kitchen table. En route, you will notice the unmistakable "odeur du chien." But in the kitchen, cooking odours will mingle with those of dog, disguising the latter, though not erasing them completely.

Talk to these two different groups of people, and you will again notice a difference. It is not that cat people are snobbish or that they believe themselves superior; the tilt of their noses has nothing to do with it. But there is one thing that they will expect of you: unremitting absorption in the object of their affection—Kitty. You had better be prepared to spend much of your time gazing in adoration at the magnificent specimen. You must also suffer the fastidious attentions of the cat, if it deigns to give them—even if the tribute takes the form of the kneading of its knife-like claws on your thigh.

It is not that dog people are crude or that they have no concern for social graces. But there is one thing that they will expect of you: conviviality, even to the point of garrulousness. Be careful not to turn away from your host too often (resist the temptation to find out where that annoying series of yips is coming from). Dog owners are famous back-slappers, jabbers, and unapologetic probers of your person. But they will never ask you to share the virtues of their pet and will suddenly lose their warmth if you show too much interest. They are possessive of the bond and discourage interlopers.

Most people have been struck, at one time or another, by the way pet owners come to resemble their pets. It is strange why this is so, and never the other way around—that pets come to look more like their owners. For some reason, the face of the cat or dog is more transferable to the human face than the human face is to that of the dog or cat. Here, it must be admitted that the dog owner is at an advantage. As there are far more breeds of dogs than of cats, the observer cannot help but be impressed by the infinite variety of possible faces of dog owners—from pushed-in pug to the full-blown majesty of Irish wolfhound.

Perhaps it is due to these differences that dog owners and cat owners do not seem able to abide one another; they just never can see eye to eye on anything—or whisker to whisker, for that matter—especially where it concerns the superiority of their own pet. Certainly, the day that cat people and dog people do agree on something will be the day that world peace is finally possible.

Exercise 8.5

Identify the thesis statement, the method used for comparing, and the bases for comparison in the above essay. You can use the appropriate diagram in the section above as a guide to show method and bases for comparison.

Exercise 8.6

Part of effective essay writing involves being able to identify your audience. Identify the audience characteristics for the above essay. What are some of the clues that help you determine this? How would you change this essay if the requirements were for a more formal essay? (See Chapter 17, Achieving Clarity and Depth in Your Writing.)

◎ Points to Remember

Expository essays, like argumentative essays, may require research, which is discussed in depth in Chapter 10. If no research is required, it is important to remember that essays at this level are best written with an objective tone. Therefore, good writers do not use phrases like "I think . . .", or "I believe . . .", or "I feel. . . ." Your writing, if strong enough, will convey these ideas to the reader.

Also, remember that you are not trying to convince the reader of a particular point of view. You are informing the audience about a particular subject. Once you have provided the readers with information, they may choose to agree or disagree, but your job is to help them understand a certain topic.

Exercise 8.7

1. Using your school's database, look for articles that address an issue you are interested in. Determine whether it is an expository or argumentative essay. If it is expository, determine what type of essay it is. (Definition, classification or division, process, compare and contrast, narration, description?)

2. If you were going to use this particular article in your essay, would it be better in an expository or argumentative essay? Why?

3. Try to find another article about the same topic that uses a different method for elaborating on the content. Is one article more effective than another? Why?

While reading the following essay, consider the questions below.

1. What type of organizational pattern did the writer use?
2. How is it similar to, and different from, the essay on leadership on page 142? Does it give the reader a better idea of what leadership is? Does van Vugt use any methods for development that Fodor does not?
3. How could this piece be turned into an argumentative essay?

Sample Professional Essay

Reading Tip: The title of the essay suggests that the author will be explaining the concept of leadership by looking at its origins—i.e., by tracing its development over time. However, to be certain about his thesis, it is necessary to read the first few paragraphs of the essay.

The writer begins by asking the kinds of questions that might occur to a reader. What does this tell you about the intended audience? (You can compare and contrast this first paragraph with the first paragraph of "Institutional 'Incompletedness': The Challenges in Meeting the Needs of Canada's Urban Aboriginal Population," Chapter 12, p. 253.)

In this paragraph, the writer universalizes his topic, stressing the importance of the issue in our daily lives, not just the lives of Americans.

In the topic sentence of paragraph 3, van Vugt states how his approach differs from previous approaches to the topic. He mentions three specific areas to be investigated. Can you identify the specific paragraphs in which he follows up on these points?

Before reading this essay, consider the pre-reading questions discussed in Chapter 1, pages 18–21. For example, you could do a brief online search to determine the author's qualifications. You could try to determine the type of magazine in which the work was published and the essay's intended audience. You could also consider essay length and the information contained in the work's title.

THE ORIGINS OF LEADERSHIP
By Mark van Vugt

What makes a good leader? Do different political, economic, and social situations demand leaders with particular styles? How should we judge who is right for the job? Why are we so often disappointed with those in charge?

In the run-up to the US elections Americans will doubtless be asking such questions. They are not alone. Leadership is an issue that pervades almost every aspect of our lives, from the family and the office to our local community, national politics, and beyond. No wonder the subject attracts so much attention.

Despite the seeming glut of information, however, one aspect has been sorely missing—the historical perspective. Until recently, very few people have considered the origins of leadership. Yet to understand how our ancestors acquired the psychological biases upon which leadership is based is to see the concept in a whole new light. In particular, the evolutionary perspective highlights the importance of those who follow and the reasons why leaders and followers may not see eye to eye. It can also indicate what sort of leader is best suited to take charge in a particular situation. It can explain some of our seemingly arbitrary preferences—for tall leaders, for example—and it even suggests why there is a bias towards men as leaders.

The author's thesis appears in this paragraph.

In essence, leadership is a response to the need for collective action. How do members of a group decide what to do and how and when to do it? An obvious solution is for one individual to take the initiative and provide guidance while the rest agree to follow. If this strategy promotes survival, then psychological adaptations for both leadership and 'followership' are likely to evolve. In humans these would have included specialised mental mechanisms for planning, communication, group decision-making, competence recognition, social learning, and conflict management. Although such traits are generally associated with higher reasoning, cognitive pre-adaptations for leadership probably evolved long before modern humans ever appeared on the scene.

> van Vugt gives a brief definition of leadership. You could compare this definition with that of Andrew Fodor, the author of the essay "What Is Leadership?" (p. 142).

> Specific examples expand on his point connecting leadership to survival.

The foraging patterns of many insects, the schooling of fish and the flying patterns of birds all suggest that species lacking complex cognitive capacities can nevertheless display leadership and followership—perhaps using the simple rule 'follow the one who moves first.' Our closest animal relatives, chimpanzees, also use leadership to coordinate group movement and to keep the peace or wage war.

The animal evidence supports the idea that adaptations for leadership and followership tend to evolve in social species. In humans, they were probably further shaped by our unique evolutionary history. There were three distinct stages in human development where the nature of leadership altered to reflect cultural and social changes (*American Psychologist*, vol 63, p 182).

The first and by far the longest phase extended from the emergence of the genus Homo, around 2.5 million years ago, until the end of the last ice age about 13,000 years ago. Natural selection for certain successful strategies of leadership and followership during this long era is likely to have shaped the distinctly human leadership psychology we still have to this day. Throughout this time, our ancestors probably lived in semi-nomadic, hunter-gatherer bands of between 50 and 150 mostly related individuals. Their lifestyle is widely thought to have resembled that of today's hunter-gatherer societies such as the Kung San of the Kalahari desert and the Amazonian Yanomamo. These groups are fundamentally egalitarian, with no formal leader. Although there are 'Big Men'—the best hunters and warriors or wisest elders, for example—the influence of each is limited to their areas of expertise and, crucially, it is only granted with the approval of followers. This suggests that collaboration among subordinates allowed early humans to move beyond the dominance hierarchies found in other primates, towards a much flatter prestige-based hierarchy with a more democratic style of leadership.

> Notice the way that this paragraph, focusing on the first "stage" of leadership development, is set up by the last sentence of the previous paragraph. van Vugt then allots one paragraph for each stage. Doing so contributes to coherence.

> **Reading/Writing Tip:** The writer doesn't cite all his sources, unlike the writer of an article in a scholarly journal. When you use research sources in your essay, you *must* carefully cite all your sources just as the author of "Institutional 'Incompletedness'" (p. 253) does.

With the development of agriculture some 13,000 years ago, groups settled, populations grew rapidly and, for the first time in human history, communities accumulated surplus resources. They needed leaders to redistribute this surplus and to deal with increasing conflict both within and between groups. The power of leaders grew accordingly, and with it the potential to abuse this power. Leaders could now siphon off resources and use them to create cultural elites, while disgruntled followers were less free to move away from exploitative rulers. The result of such changes was a more formalised, authoritarian leadership style and the emergence of the first chiefs and kings, as well as warlords bent on extracting resources through force.

> This paragraph is developed through cause and effect. van Vugt discusses the main effect, or result, of having "surplus resources": the emergence of an "authoritarian leadership style."

The industrial revolution, some 250 years ago, paved the way for the final phase of leadership—the one to which academic discussions of leadership, which tend to focus on business and politics, almost exclusively refer. At the beginning of this era followers were little more than slaves, but as citizens and employees acquired more freedom to defect from overbearing leaders, the balance of power shifted away from authoritarian leaders and back to something more like the egalitarian approach of ancestral times.

> Having traced the origins of leadership, van Vugt asks a question that is relevant to leadership today, answering it by using academic studies and examples throughout the paragraph.

So, what can evolution tell us about modern leadership? The ancestral environment may have equipped us with innate preferences for certain characteristics in our leaders. For a start, we want them to be both competent and benevolent, because these sorts of people will be better at acquiring resources and more willing to share them. We also tend to choose leaders with certain physical characteristics.

> The author reinforces his thesis that leadership preferences are related to "an evolutionary [i.e., historical] perspective."

Other theories of leadership have failed to account for the importance of seemingly arbitrary attributes such as height, age, weight, and health, but these make sense from an evolutionary perspective. For example, ancestral Big Men were probably quite literally that: by dint of their imposing physique, all people would have been more effective peacekeepers and more intimidating foes. Even today we have a bias towards taller leaders (*Journal of Applied Psychology*, vol 89, p 428). In ancestral times elders were likely to have acquired specialist knowledge, and in the modern world older leaders are preferred in situations where knowledge is crucial, such as in running public corporations (*Leadership and Governance from the Inside Out*, edited by Robert Gandossy and Jeffrey Sonnenfeld, Wiley, 2004). Followers may also have evolved a preference for fit and healthy leaders in situations where strength and stamina mattered. That could be why modern voters prefer physically fit and energetic political candidates (*Personality and Social Psychology Review,* vol 10, p 354).

More controversially, evolution might explain our bias towards male leaders in most circumstances. When men and women work together, men are quicker to claim leadership roles even when women are better qualified (*Psychological Bulletin*, vol 130, p 711). Moreover, a recent experiment by myself and Brian Spisak, also at the University of Kent (to be published in Psychological Science later this year), revealed that groups tend to look to men for leadership when faced with a threat from another group, possibly because inter-group conflict would have been resolved by force throughout most of human history. However, we also found that in situations where there is internal conflict in a group, women are the preferred and most effective leaders. This is confirmed by a recent mock election study which found that people tended to vote for a male president when their country was at war, but a female during peacetime (*Evolution and Human Behavior*, vol 28, p 18).

> **Reading Tip:** Notice the way van Vugt conveys the speculative nature of his statement. Verbs like "might have predisposed" and "could be" (in the next sentence) suggest uncertainty. Presumably, no studies exist to confirm or refute his statements.

A history of inter-group conflict might have predisposed men to adopt a hierarchical leadership style, while a need for social unity might have equipped women with a more egalitarian, personalised, and communal style. If the predominance of male leaders in many sectors of modern life is a vestige of our past, it could be a costly one in an interconnected world in which the emphasis is on interpersonal skills and network-building.

This raises another important aspect of leadership that is often overlooked—that what constitutes good leadership varies according to the situation. The different leadership styles adopted by various organisations, nations, and cultures can be understood in part by considering the specific challenges posed by their particular physical and social environment. In the Netherlands and Australia, for example, where harsh natural conditions force the authorities to collaborate closely with citizens, there is a strong egalitarian ethos. In emergencies such as wars or natural disasters, followers readily defer to the decisions of a single autocratic individual. Indeed, US voters tend to choose hawkish presidents when threatened by war.

All this suggests that leadership and followership are flexible strategies shaped by the interplay between ancient evolutionary pressures and modern environmental and cultural demands. However, there are major differences between modern leadership roles and the kind of leadership for which our psychology is adapted, and this mismatch can be problematic. For a start, our hunter-gatherer ancestors would have deferred to different leaders depending on the nature of the problem at hand. Yet today a single individual is often responsible for managing all aspects of an enterprise. Few leaders have the range of skills required, which may account for the high failure rate of senior managers—in corporate America it runs at 50 per cent (*Review of General Psychology*, vol 9, p 169). Surveys routinely show that between 60 and 70 per cent of employees find the most stressful part of their job is dealing with their immediate boss. This may be partly because ancestral leaders only acquired power with the approval of followers, whereas in modern organisations leaders are usually appointed by and accountable to their superiors, while subordinates are rarely allowed to sanction their bosses. What's more, our psychology equips us to thrive in smallish groups of closely related individuals, which may explain why many people feel indifferent to large organisations and their leaders. Finally, in ancestral societies there would have been minimal differences in status between leaders and followers. In the US, average salaries for CEOs are 179 times those of their workers.

The upside is that insights from evolution also suggest more effective leadership strategies. In recent years there has been increasing interest in the idea of shared or distributed leadership. Some organisations are finding that executives are more likely to succeed if subordinates are included in the selection process. Meanwhile, effective businesses—including Toyota and Virgin—are designing and structuring their organisations to more closely resemble hunter-gatherer bands. For instance, they delegate decision-making to managers far down the chain of command, creating functional groups of between 50 and 150 members.

By emphasising interdependence and shared interests, values, and goals, a truly transformational leader can change followers from self-interested individuals to committed collectivists. Unfortunately, such people are thin on the ground. Instead, we are often required to defer to leaders whose remit and behaviour is inconsistent with our evolved expectations of leadership. That can be alienating, but at least followers can sometimes do something about it. That is exactly what millions of US citizens will be doing when they exercise their power to vote for a new president.

* * *

Considering leadership from the evolutionary perspective throws a spotlight on followers. The psychology of followership is usually neglected, but it is more interesting than that of leadership. Most of us are destined to be followers, yet we are only starting to understand what makes a good follower and how

---

Reading Tip: *Egalitarian* and *ethos* may be unfamiliar terms. If they cannot be determined by context, you must use a dictionary. (Hint: If you know what the phrase "collaborate closely" means, you may be able to determine the meaning of *egalitarian*; then you can confirm the meaning by using a dictionary.)

van Vugt uses the first sentence to summarize previous paragraphs. In the second sentence, he indicates his developmental method for the paragraph: compare and contrast with the focus on differences (contrast).

Writing Tip: Transitions are used effectively to connect ideas in this lengthy paragraph: "However," "For a start," "Yet." Can you identify two other transitions in this paragraph?

The next paragraphs suggest how we can learn from the evolutionary approach to leadership.

In his conclusion, van Vugt discusses the "psychology of followership," which he explains is a "neglected" area of research. His speculations are probably intended to give his readers, most of whom are followers, something to think about.

they influence leaders. A key puzzle is what motivates followers. Why would individuals agree to subordinate themselves when this puts them at a disadvantage compared with leaders in terms of power, status, and resources?

The decision to follow may simply be a rational one: if the costs of competing for higher status outweigh the benefits, then following frees up time and energy that can be used more effectively elsewhere. Besides, followers can improve their position relative to leaders by engaging in collective action. Another idea is that complying with and observing leaders may allow followers to prepare themselves for future leadership. Finally, the disadvantages of following are partly offset by the benefits of belonging to a well-led group. So natural selection at the group level might account for leadership.

The relationship between followers and leaders is inherently ambivalent because there is always a risk that leaders will try to coerce or exploit their followers, and that followers will plot to depose their leaders. This tension probably created an evolutionary arms race in terms of the strategies used to gain control. Nevertheless, research shows that people readily adopt leadership/followership behaviour in circumstances that mirror adaptive problems, such as when there are internal group conflicts or external threats (*Journal of Personality and Social Psychology*, vol 76, p 587).

However, there are situations in which leadership is not necessary, and is even resented by followers. Experiments show that unnecessary leadership can actually undermine team performance (*Group Dynamics*, vol 2, p 168). The lesson for businesses and politicians here is that when faced with relatively simple or routine coordination problems, people usually perform better if left alone.

—van Vugt, M. (2008). Follow me: The origins of leadership.
New Scientist, 2660, 20–21.

Chapter Review Questions

1. What is the difference between expository and argumentative writing?
2. What are the different kinds of expository essays?
3. Should expository essays try to convince the reader of a certain point of view?
4. How can templates help when writing an essay?
5. What are some important points to keep in mind when writing a process essay?
6. What are some important points to keep in mind when writing a definition essay?
7. What are the two ways to structure a comparison and contrast essay? Why is it important to stick to one method?

9

Summaries

In this chapter, you will learn

- the difference between summary, paraphrase, abstract, and annotated bibliography

- the steps used in writing a summary

- how to paraphrase

- how to create an annotated bibliography

In college and university classes, students are often asked to summarize or to paraphrase another author's work. This material can then be integrated into your essay, which can add variety and credibility to your writing, as you will not just be inserting quotations. This chapter will help you learn how to write effective summaries and paraphrases. In addition, abstracts and annotated bibliographies are discussed, with information about how to use them and write your own, should you be asked.

What Is a Summary?

When writing essays in the past, you may have concluded by summarizing your thesis and main points. Therefore, you already have experience writing summaries.

In the student essay "What is Leadership?" in Chapter 8, the author uses the concluding paragraph to summarize his definition of leadership.

> Leadership is the co-ordination of people, resources, and tasks towards the completion of a goal.
>
> Leadership can be demonstrated in many situations, from a doctor trying to save a life in the ER to a university teacher to a military commander.
>
> Although leadership is often provided by qualified, educated persons, it may sometimes arise from unlikely sources.
>
> Regardless, leadership is a skill that can be developed through experience and education.

Summary writing skills are used both in essays and for stand-alone exercises. Your instructor may ask you to summarize an essay you have read. You may also be asked to complete various summaries and construct an annotated bibliography as part of the required steps in writing a research paper. In addition, well-written essays often include paragraph summaries rather than direct quotations, as discussed in Chapter 11. All of these activities have one thing in common: you are presenting your audience with someone else's ideas. However, you are doing this in your own words, so you must first clearly understand the material you are summarizing.

Before you examine how to write a summary, it is important that you understand terminology used at the college and university level. While some of the ideas presented below may seem to overlap, you need to recognize the differences between paraphrase and summary so that you provide your instructor with what he or she wants.

The sidebar notes aligned with the above passage read:

Although you may have experience summarizing your thesis and main points in your own essays, an important college or university writing skill is learning the steps in summarizing the ideas of *other* writers.

The author restates his definition using wording that is different from that used earlier in the essay.

The author gives relevant examples referred to in the essay to illustrate his thesis.

The author reinforces yet another aspect of his thesis, again using different words.

After an appropriate transition, the author concludes with his belief, which has been stated earlier.

Terms Related to Summarizing

Summary is a general term for the rephrasing of somebody else's ideas. Summaries are always shorter than the original and must be mostly or completely in your own words.

Paraphrase is a term for the rephrasing of someone else's ideas completely in your own words; however, when paraphrasing, you do not shorten the original.

An **abstract** is an overview of your purpose, methods, and results. An abstract is often found at the beginning of journal articles, such as those found on the databases in your school library.

An **annotated bibliography** is an *expanded* bibliography (annotate = to + note). It concisely summarizes similar works in the field of study.

Paraphrases, abstracts, and the annotated bibliographies are discussed in more detail beginning on page 164.

How to Write Summaries

Summaries can be of sentences, paragraphs, entire essays, or long reports. Throughout your time at college or university, instructors will often ask you to write extended summaries of articles or passages from textbooks to ensure you understand the writers' ideas. This type of exercise is also beneficial because it can help you develop both reading and writing skills.

When writing an essay, draft a short summary if you want to use a source's main idea(s) to provide background information, to set up a point of your own (to show similarity or difference, for example), or to explain one or various positions relevant to your thesis. Examples below and on pages 165–6 will illustrate different summary lengths.

Summary Length

A summary is shorter than the original work. Summary length can range from one sentence to several paragraphs or even pages. It will depend on the use you have for the summary. For example, you may want to summarize an entire paragraph in one sentence because including the longer passage with irrelevant material may distort your purpose and distract your reader. At other times, you may be asked by your instructor (or your boss) to summarize an entire report or lengthy essay in a one-page document to be shared with others. In the examples found in this chapter, you will see summaries of various lengths, accompanied by related exercises.

> Summary length is dictated by the intended use. A summary can be as brief as a sentence or two, but extended summaries need to be longer.

Main Features of a Summary

The summary

1. is accurate
2. includes the main idea(s)
3. does not add anything that wasn't in the original
4. is in your own words

Sample Sentence Summaries

The following summaries show how to condense a paragraph into a sentence or two. This type of summary is useful when you want to include key ideas in your essay but do not want to quote extensively. Bear in mind that your instructor may require more detail.

Sample 1:

Helen Thompson was one of the first women to obtain a Ph.D. from the University of Chicago. Her thesis, *The Mental Traits of Sex* (1903), illustrates the main arguments in the similarities tradition. These include the importance of overlap between genders, the requirement of highest methodological standards to demonstrate difference, the search for social explanations of difference, and the demonstration of the specificity of difference.

—Kimball, M.M. (1994). The worlds we live in: Gender similarities and differences. *Canadian Psychology/Psychologie canadienne, 35*(4), 388–404.

Summary

Helen Thompson's 1903 thesis, *The Mental Traits of Sex,* shows the importance of scientific and social study of the similarities and differences between men and women.

Sample 2:

It is time for some perspective. With the growing urgency of climate change, we cannot have it both ways. We cannot shout from the rooftops about the dangers of global warming and then turn around and shout even louder about the "dangers" of windmills. Climate change is one of the greatest challenges humanity will face this century. It cannot be solved through good intentions. It will take a radical change in the way we produce and consume energy—another industrial revolution, this time for clean energy, conservation and efficiency.

—Suzuki, D. (2005). The beauty of wind farms. *New Scientist, 186*(2495), 20.

Summary

In order to fight global warming, people have to choose to become actively involved and not complain about the changes that will be necessary.

Exercise 9.1

Examine the following summary sample below, taken from "The Worlds We Live In: Gender Similarities and Differences," by Meredith M. Kimball. It is not a strong summary. First, consider how it fails to meet the criteria discussed above. Then, write a summary that does meet these criteria.

Original passage:

> Throughout the history of feminism, from Wollstonecraft to the present, two views of gender differences have been advocated (Cott, 1986). In one, similarities between the sexes have been emphasized, whereas in the other, women's special characteristics that differ from men's have been emphasized.

Summary:

> The history of feminism, from Wollstonecraft to the present, shows two different views of gender differences (Cott, 1986). Similarities between the sexes are highlighted in one, but women's special characteristics have been spotlighted in the other.

Exercise 9.2

Choose a paragraph from one of the readings included in this textbook. Summarize it in one or two sentences.

Main Features of an Extended Summary

The extended summary

1. is factually accurate
2. retains the essence of the original piece
3. includes the main idea(s); includes sub-points if it is a longer summary
4. omits examples and illustrations, unless very important
5. uses the same order as the original
6. does not add anything that wasn't in the original
7. keeps weighting of ideas the same as the original (if the writer gives less space to one particular idea, do not expand this idea so that it takes as much space as other more important thoughts that the writer has)
8. uses concise prose
9. is mostly your own words, but you may use some words from the original (though no more than you strictly have to). You *must place quotation marks* around any phrases that you cite directly. If you cite more than *three* consecutive words, you should place them in quotation marks.
10. is approximately 10–30 per cent the length of the original. However, if the work you are summarizing requires more expertise than your audience has, you may occasionally need to write a summary that is longer than 30 per cent. In addition, you may have to add a few transitions to make the summary easy to follow. Add no more than necessary for clarity, however.

> Extended summaries apply the rules for summarizing to an entire work or a main part of it. Although these summaries are too long to use in your essays, they show your ability to identify key ideas and put them in your own words.

> When writing an extended summary, you'll have to decide whether to include all the main ideas or just the most important ones. However, if you are using the summary in an essay, only use the parts relevant to your thesis.

Extended Summary Writing Steps

Summaries contain the main ideas of the source, so can be thought of as miniaturized versions of their longer, more detailed originals. Writing such summaries sharpens your reading and analytical skills. As you read a work for summarization, you will first be concerned with understanding its meaning. You must not only understand and synthesize the information—as you need to do any time you read for content— but also separate the most important ideas from the less important ones.

You can summarize using four steps.

1. Read the work for the first time to learn its purpose, thesis statement, intended audience, purpose, etc.
2. When you reread it, note its major points, along with the most important sub-points and/or key examples, and from these points write an outline. Use your own words for this.
3. Following your outline closely, write a summary that includes the thesis statement and all the main points (if you're summarizing the entire piece). If you are writing a summary of a specific length and have room for more than the main points, pick the most important sub-points or developments of ideas to reach the required word range.
4. Create the title for your extended summary (if required) using the format shown below on page 163 for the summary of the article "Fighting hockey violence will give you a concussion." Avoid repeating the title and author's name as much as possible.

When you summarize, it is best to leave time between each step. Sit down and read the original all the way through one time. Make sure you have few distractions, as you want to make sure you understand the writer's meaning. If the work is short, and you feel you can concentrate well, reread it, highlighting the main ideas and writing them in your own words. As with all major writing assignments, at this point, take a break. If you have enough time, leave a few hours, or even a day, between this step and the next.

After you have left some time, go back and

*   reread the article and your points to make sure you have not missed any of the main points.
*   check your wording against the original. Have you unconsciously used any of the original writer's wording? Have you accurately reworded the points?

Go on to the next step once you are satisfied with your work thus far. When you have completed your summary, do not forget to go back to edit and proofread.

A summary, at its minimum, should contain the work's thesis statement and, depending on the length, the main ideas. The thesis statement should appear at the end of the introduction of the original, and the main ideas are often the topic sentences of major paragraphs. Remember, though, that not all topic sentences are the first sentences of paragraphs—indeed, not all paragraphs in all writing have topic sentences. Furthermore, not every paragraph will contain a main idea, so there will not necessarily be a predictable relation between the original's number of paragraphs and the number of points in your outline. When you have written the summary, check it over to ensure that it is essentially in your own words and that you have put quotation marks around words and phrases taken directly from the source.

Summarizing Your Sources

When you summarize from a secondary source, you take the important parts of somebody else's work to use in your own essay. Always ensure that you give credit to your source. During the research stage, it is a good idea to write out the summaries from all the main sources you plan to use, as well as to carefully record significant direct quotations. It is a great nuisance to try to find again books and pages (or webpages) and lines once you have returned them to library shelves (or not bookmarked webpages). Summarizing a book, article, or Internet source puts the main points before you when you come to write your essay, enabling you to *demonstrate your understanding of the source and its applicability to your thesis statement*. Summarizing the content of a source also avoids the practice of *too much* direct quotation.

When summarizing, the writer is acting partly on behalf of the original writer. Careful representation of these ideas is a sign of a good summary.

Summaries and Argument

If the purpose of the essay is to persuade its reader, rather than present factual information, you may need to carefully distinguish between fact and opinion. For example, this is the way that one professional writer began an essay:

> In the course of two years' research for a book on how we think about pain, I've spoken to neurologists, doctors, artists, therapists of every stripe, as well as psychologists—the frontline workers. And frankly, I preferred the people selling healing magnets to most of the psychologists. They were bad communicators. They couldn't make eye contact. They seemed more interested in certain folds in the brain than in helping human beings cope with pain.
> —Jackson, Marni, "Every Breath You Take: A Former Hospital Pain Specialist Puts His Faith in the Powers of Meditation." *Maclean's* 16 August 1999 Print.

If, in such a case, you did not acknowledge the writer's words as opinion, you would seriously misrepresent her:

A distorted summary: Psychologists generally communicate badly and are shifty-eyed.

However, you could acknowledge the author's argument this way:

Correct: Marni Jackson preferred "the people selling healing magnets" to the majority of psychologists she spoke to.

Using Signal Phrases

Signal phrases can be used to clearly attribute a statement to one or more people. Carefully choose a signal verb that reveals whether the writer is explaining or arguing—verbs like *prefer*, *believe*, *claimed*, and *argued* all suggest opinion, whereas *says*, *states*, *described*, and *found* do not. (Signal phrases are discussed in more detail in Chapter 11.) In using appropriate verbs or phrases like *according to*, you are showing the writer's attitude towards the subject. But do not characterize the writer's stance as negative or make assumptions from what you know about the writer's background that refer to his or her possible bias. Summaries should *represent*, not judge. The writer may be opinionated; when representing those opinions, you should not express your *own* opinions.

> When you summarize, be especially careful *not* to
> • become too general or vague; be *specific* but *not detailed*;
> • distort the writer's meaning in any way; use *your words* but *the writer's ideas*.

Extended Summary Samples

In the first summary, based on the essay "Fighting hockey violence will give you a concussion," the main ideas are presented in the form of an outline, and then a summary was written from these ideas. In the second summary, based on the student essay about multiculturalism (page 245), the outline stage was omitted.

When you write an extended summary, the title of the summary should include the title of the document you are summarizing, as well as the original author's name. The preferred method is Summary of "Title of Essay," by "Name of Author," as illustrated in the summaries below.

After identifying these elements in the title, you may not need to include them again in the summary itself.

Sample Professional Essay

FIGHTING HOCKEY VIOLENCE WILL GIVE YOU A CONCUSSION

By Jeffrey Simpson

Specialists in diagnosing and treating concussions should know about the perils of bashing heads against a brick wall. But, nonetheless, bravo to those who know about concussions for having recently recommended an end to fighting in hockey.

Medical experts, minor hockey executives and former National Hockey League players who suffered from concussions recently gathered in London, Ont., to try to improve safety in the game. They made many suggestions about better head protection, but they also said: Stop the fighting.

Concussions can be caused by many aspects of hockey, and by numerous rules that leave heads inadequately protected. Shots to the head are endemic in hockey, and the NHL has always been fitfully attentive, at best, in trying to protect against them. But some damage to the head, even the occasional death, occurs from fighting as a player's head is struck, either by a fist or when he falls against the ice.

The medical experts were right: An end to fighting would reduce head injuries. But just as threatened legal cases against on-ice thuggery have come to naught, so medical advice won't change the cultivated culture of violence in professional hockey.

Fighting, however, is to professional hockey as hearts are to Valentine's Day. People just love it. Those noble souls who wish to ban it will give themselves concussions trying to end it, although the case against fighting, rationally speaking, is overwhelming.

Those who gathered at the concussion conference were bashing their heads against not just one wall but many. There's the wall of tradition; fighting has always been there. There's the wall of the NHL Players' Association, some of whose members are fighters, lacking any other skill that would give them a job in professional hockey. There's the wall of the owners, who know—and rightly so—that fighting means excitement, and excitement means money. There's the wall of commissioner Gary Bettman, who knows that fighting puts bums in seats. And, sad to say, there's the wall of the fans.

Attend an NHL game in any arena. When a fight starts, fans throughout the building rise, shout and gesticulate as vigorously as when a goal is scored. A few Canadians like to insist that fighting really only appeals to Americans. Fighting exists in hockey to sell the game in U.S. markets where people carry guns, watch football players smash each other and where television is overrun with violence.

Alas, such an argument merely reflects Canadian conceit about Americans in general, and American hockey fans in particular. Watch a fight in any Canadian city with a professional team, or attend a junior hockey game where fights break out even more frequently than in the NHL. Canadian fans eat up fighting.

It's in Canada, don't forget, where the highest media priests who defend fighting reside. And not only in Canada, but on the CBC. As if Don Cherry were not already the country's leading cheerleader for fisticuffs, the CBC went out and hired the worst general manager of the past 20 years, Mike Milbury, as an "analyst." He quickly joined Mr. Cherry in trotting out the old cliches about the indispensability of fighting as an outlet for aggression. He then added his own denunciation of "pansification" in hockey, for which he had his knuckles rapped.

Fortunately for literate hockey fans, there is TSN, where the quality of hockey commentary vastly outstrips anything on the CBC. On that hockey-savvy network, there are some defenders of fighting in hockey, but the brilliant Pierre McGuire opposes it and, of course, he is right. Even on TSN, however, the highlight package each night usually features a brawl or two, rather than some extraordinary defensive play or slick passing move.

Fighting is not endemic to hockey, except for the evident fact that the sport allows it. Fighting could be eliminated with the snap of a finger if owners and players didn't believe that the fans want fighting. It is, after all, the only professional sport that allows fighting. Hockey is no rougher than football or Australian-rules football or rugby, where to fight is to be expelled from play. The argument that fighting is a necessary outlet for aggression is wholly bogus.

Go to the Hockey Hall of Fame, or watch films of classic encounters of yesteryear. You won't remember the fighters, but rather the skilled players. Today, the NHL markets the Sydney Crosbies and Alexander Ovechkins for national and international purposes. But the owners also watch us, the fans, and our reaction to fighting. We, or at least most fans, like it.

It used to be that North American players fought and Europeans did not. True, most of the fighters remain North American, but we have passed on bad habits to a handful of Europeans, too. The Cherryfication of hockey that glorifies fighting has spread, and will not be stopped, notwithstanding the excellent advice of the concussion experts. (815 words)

—Simpson, Jeffrey. "Fighting hockey violence will give you a concussion." *The Globe and Mail* 14 February 2009: A19. Print.

When you decide on the main points of the source you are summarizing, paraphrase them as you construct an outline. Remember that the final summarized version must be essentially in your own words and that words and phrases quoted directly must be placed in quotation marks.

Outline:
- A conference was held in London, Ontario, about player concussions in hockey.
- Concussions occur because of fights or falls, and the NHL is not consistent in protecting players.
- Medical professionals think ending fighting in hockey would help prevent head injuries.
- However, many do not want to see an end to fighting—the players, especially those whose only skill seems to be fighting, the owners, who know fighting draws the fans, and many of the fans themselves.

- While Canadians like to think that fighting in hockey is something Americans like, this is untrue because you see fighting at all levels of hockey in Canada, from the junior leagues to the professionals.
- Broadcasters, like CBC, hire people like Don Cherry, who are advocates for fighting in hockey.
- Other networks try to focus more on the game itself, but in the end, even they provide the fight highlights of games.
- Hockey is the sport that allows fighting. In other sports, players are kicked out of the game if they fight.
- Unfortunately, fighting in hockey has spread from North America to Europe and this fighting trend does not seem about to stop.

Note that in the original piece, there are many illustrations, such as the passage that discusses Don Cherry and Mike Milbury. Much of the information in this passage is used to support the writer's thesis and does not need to be included in the summary. Also, some of the passages in the article just elaborate on the main points, so the writer summarizing the piece chose to leave those out.

Summary of "Fighting hockey violence will give you a concussion," by Jeffrey Simpson.

The medical dangers of hockey fights are well-documented, yet these fights continue to occur. The danger of concussions from fights and falls in hockey has become severe enough that medical professionals, hockey executives, and former players attended a conference to discuss this issue in London, Ontario. These people all feel that fighting should be eliminated from the game because it is so dangerous. However, there are many others, such as owners, players themselves, and fans, who want to see fighting remain in hockey. Some Canadians argue that Americans are the ones who like the fighting, but this is not true, as fighting is seen in all levels of hockey in Canada, and Canadian broadcasters often show game highlights that focus on the fighting. While fighting is not necessary in sports (in many sports, players are penalized for fighting), hockey seems to encourage violence. This violence is spreading from North America to Europe, and no one seems able to stop it. (173 words)

—Student writer Krystal Noonan

The following sample is a summary of the essay about multiculturalism, which is found in Chapter 12, page 245.

Summary of "Multiculturalism in Canada: Controversial Consequences of the Multicultural Act," by Renée MacKillop.

The uncertainty of the Act from the view of both sides, the supporters and the detractors, is addressed. The Multiculturalism Act recognizes both heritage and culture differences and promotes diversity and tolerance among all Canadians. The emphasis on multicultural diversity has raised questions concerning the lack of national unity and Canadian identity. Those who support the Multiculturalism Act believe the government's involvement in cultural affairs is essential to prevent racism and discrimination. Those opposing the

Multiculturalism Act feel the government should not have jurisdiction over this matter. Both sides agree, however, that the validity of the government's involvement in the cultures of Canadians is unclear. Although the focus of multiculturalism was primarily on nation building, policy makers are being accused of establishing the Act for the purpose of national competitiveness and economic gain. Instead of immigrant integration, critics believe there is excessive accommodation for immigrants. Some cultural practices are viewed by western society as unacceptable. Whether or not this is considered judgmental or discriminatory is debatable. It is difficult to establish a national identity among Canadians when multiculturalism forces Canadians to be different. The Multiculturalism Act needs to be revised to bring national unity to all Canadians. (196 words)

—Student writer Penny Gaston

Paraphrase and Other Types of Summaries

Paraphrase

> Summaries are shorter than the original, but when paraphrasing, the length remains the same.

A **paraphrase** is usually about the length of the original. You would normally paraphrase an important part of a text, perhaps as much as one paragraph or even, occasionally, more. A strict paraphrase is entirely in your own words and in a different order from the original. Because paraphrases don't omit anything of substance from the source, they are unlike summaries whose main purpose is to condense the original, retaining its essence.

> A paraphrase restates the source's meaning using only your own words. Paraphrase when you want to cite a small amount of material that is directly relevant to your point. When you paraphrase, you include *all* of the original thought, but rephrase it.

Below is an example illustrating the differences between summarizing and paraphrasing an original paragraph taken from Katt's essay, "Tail of Opposites" (in Chapter 8).

Most people have been struck, at one time or another, by the way pet owners come to resemble their pets. It is strange why this is so, and never the other way around—that pets come to look more like their owners. For some reason, the face of the cat or dog is more transferable to the human face than the human face is to that of the dog or cat. Here, it must be admitted that the dog owner is at an advantage. As there are far more breeds of dogs than of cats, the observer cannot help but be impressed by the infinite variety of possible faces of dog owners—from pushed-in pug to the full-blown majesty of Irish wolfhound.

Summary:

Many have noticed that people who own pets often look like their animals, but this comparison is found more often with dog owners than cat owners.

Paraphrase:

It has often been observed that those who own pets look like their animals. However, pets seldom resemble the people who own them. Perhaps this is because people see animals in human faces, but not humans in animal faces. People who own dogs are compared most often to their pets because there are more kinds of dogs than cats. Therefore, people can see many types of breeds in human faces, such as a pug or an Irish wolfhound.

As with summaries, to paraphrase, you must use your own words. Unlike summaries, though, paraphrases are the same length as the original work.

Exercise 9.3

Take the paragraph from one of the readings of the text you summarized above in Exercise 9.2 and paraphrase it.

Abstract

An **abstract** is an overview of your purpose, methods, and results. You write it *after* you have finished your essay, or, at least, after you have arrived at your conclusions. However, abstracts physically precede the essay; they are placed after the title and author notation and before the introduction, enabling readers to decide whether they wish to read the full work that follows.

An essay abstract is generally 75–100 words. The abstracts for scientific papers are typically at least twice as long (150–250 words); some are even longer. Many abstract writers incorporate key phrases or even complete sentences from the full work into the abstract. You will often find abstracts at the beginning of papers in peer-reviewed journals. When you search databases, you can look at the abstracts to determine whether an article may be of some use to you for your own essay; however, do not use the abstract alone for your research. Scan the whole article to ensure that what you have chosen does, in fact, relate to your topic.

An abstract is an overview of your purpose, methods, and results. It can include key phrases or even whole sentences from the full work. Not all the material needs to be reworded.

Articles in peer-reviewed journals have been evaluated by experts before publication.

Exercise 9.4

Step 1: Using your school's databases, find articles that have abstracts. Choose two articles that you find easy to understand by scanning the contents.

Step 2: Read the abstract for one article and then read the complete article.

Step 3: Read the second article without looking at the abstract first.

Step 4: Compare your understanding of the two articles. Was it easier understanding the first or the second article?

Step 5: Finally, without looking at the abstract for the second article, try writing a one-paragraph summary (i.e., an abstract) of the article and then compare it to the actual abstract. How different are the two?

Annotated Bibliography

An **annotated bibliography** is an *expanded* bibliography. Annotated bibliographies often accompany large research projects, such as books, dissertations, or other major studies. They can take the form of critical surveys, demonstrating the variety of approaches that other writers or researchers have taken to the subject. While abstracts concisely summarize your own work for potential readers, annotated bibliographies concisely summarize similar works in the field of study—they tell readers where the writer's particular piece of the puzzle fits into the whole.

Because the number of entries in an annotated bibliography may be in the hundreds for a widely researched field, each entry must be brief. Generally, the entry provides a concise summary of content, focusing on the thesis statement and major points and findings. If the entry refers to a book-length study, the main points may take the form of major section or chapter headings. Sometimes, annotated bibliographies contain an appraisal of the study's usefulness or contribution to the field of study.

Following is a sample annotated bibliography entry of the essay "The Imperfection of Perfectionism: Perfectionism as a Maladaptive Personality Trait," by Erin A. Walker (from Chapter 12).

> An annotated bibliography summarizes similar works in a field of study. It includes a concise summary of the content, focusing on the thesis statement and major points or findings. It can also include an appraisal of the study's usefulness.

The author discusses perfectionism and its negative implications from a social psychological viewpoint. She separates perfectionism into "normal" and "neurotic" types, and then discusses the characteristics and suspected causes of perfectionism. Walker cites studies that demonstrate its negative effects, such as its connections to depression and difficulties in intimate relations. Information from psychological studies is effectively integrated into the paper to support the author's points. She uses logically ordered subtopics to present a successful overview of current social psychological findings concerning perfectionism. (82 words)

Exercise 9.5

Create an annotated bibliography using the articles from Exercise 9.4 above.

◎ Summarizing at the Workplace

Preparing a summary is not only a classroom activity. While working at a job, you may also be asked to summarize information for colleagues or your boss. You may be asked to attend a seminar or conference and come back and report what you learned. You obviously will not give people a very detailed account of the event. Nor will you give your opinion about how beneficial it was. Instead, you will need to apply the same rules you learned here and provide a summary of the important information you learned.

Exercise 9.6

Look at the following memo and write a summary to present to your instructor. Try to keep the summary length at 10 per cent of the original.

MEMO

TO: Juan Alexandros, District Supervisor

FROM: Gail Fromme, Human Resources Manager

DATE: November 12, 2010

SUBJECT: CHANGES TO WORKPLACE ASSESSMENTS

As of January 1, we will be implementing a new system to evaluate the managers in each district. This new evaluation includes the latest in psychological testing, which we feel will better predict who will succeed as a manager and whom we need to eliminate.

I will be sending out the new forms within the next few days, once our legal team has vetted them. Please do not share these forms with the staff, as District Supervisors will be the only ones using them.

The company would like you to inform the managers that changes will be made to the yearly evaluations. Please notify them that the new evaluations will

1.   include feedback from the staff they manage.

2.   include a minimum of 15 hours on-site supervision by the District Supervisor.

3.   require a self-evaluation, which will be compared to the staff feedback.

4.   include a visit to the head office to meet with an evaluation team.

Once you receive the new evaluation package, which will include all the necessary new forms, as well as detailed instructions, please take the time to read everything carefully. Any questions you have will be answered at the training session we will be having in mid-December. In the meantime, feel free to call me at ext. 267 between 8:30–4:00, Monday to Thursday.

Chapter Review Questions

1. What are the key characteristics of a summary?
2. Can you use the original author's words when writing a summary?
3. What is an "extended summary"?
4. What steps can be used in writing an extended summary?
5. What is the difference between summarizing and paraphrasing?
6. What is an abstract?
7. What is an annotated bibliography and when is it used?
8. How can summarizing be useful in the workplace?

10

Research

In this chapter, you will learn

- how to conduct research for your essay topic

- how to determine whether your sources are reliable

- how to use the Internet for research

- what other types of resources are available for researching your topic

At college and university, you will be required to write essays with a strong thesis that is supported by research. By adding relevant, reliable outside information, you demonstrate to the reader that you are familiar with the topic, and if you research well, you show that you are becoming an expert in that field. This chapter explains how to begin a research essay by exploring what you know about a topic. It then addresses how to conduct research and where to find reliable and credible sources.

Developing Research Skills

This chapter is designed to help you develop your research skills so that you can support your thesis using what other people, such as scientists and other researchers, have discovered about your topic. You may decide to summarize or paraphrase parts of published works, as discussed in Chapter 9, or to use direct quotations (discussed in Chapter 11). Much of this chapter addresses expository essay writing, but can be applied to argumentative essays as well. For further details about argumentative essays, see Chapter 13.

Research, which comes from the French *rechercher*, meaning "to seek again," is an important part of most expository essays and some argumentative essays. In order to use research effectively in papers, you need to *look again*—explore, check, and recheck. Once you have all your information, you need to synthesize it. (**Synthesis** means "put together.") You put together the evidence provided by your primary and secondary sources to create your essay.

In expository research essays, claims of fact are generally used, so you need to find reliable information and analyze what various researchers have discovered about a topic and, on the basis of their conclusions, come to a reasoned conclusion of your own.

While a successful argumentative essay relies on the *effectiveness* of your *argument*, the *presentation* of your *information* is vital in an expository essay. You should find ways to make the essay interesting and appealing to the reader. Don't just assemble the facts and add transitions between ideas. You need to find out what someone else says or thinks about something, and then rewrite it in your own words. This means that, at the college or university level, exposition usually involves research.

It is often said that great thinkers stand on the shoulders of giants. This means that they build on the knowledge of the researchers and thinkers of previous generations. The Wright brothers did not just wake up one day and decide to build an airplane. They studied previous designs and ideas, such as Samuel Langley's aerodrome. Langley himself had no doubt studied gliders and so on back in time. This is what we call "progress" in the sciences, the social sciences, and the humanities. The most knowledgeable experts depend on the findings of others to help in their own explorations; the research they do, in turn, adds to their store of knowledge, enabling them to contribute to their chosen field.

Part of the training you are undertaking in your field of specialization at college or university will involve research: exploring topics and finding out what conclusions other researchers have come to. However, you have to be able to *apply* your knowledge, which means being able to synthesize, or integrate, your new-found learning. Thus, while exposition implies research, research implies synthesis—putting together what you have learned.

Writing a research essay involves drafting an outline, adding and checking citations, and assembling the information you have found so that your essay presents the information in the most effective way. When you are drafting the essay, you may begin linearly with an outline, but you will probably then go back and add research and check citations. You will also need to go back and make sure your research is

Primary sources include literary texts, historical documents, surveys, questionnaires, and interviews. Secondary sources include authoritative written sources such as books and journal articles, but can also include oral presentations and conference papers. Primary sources are original sources; secondary sources comment on those sources.

When you write an essay for college or university, your instructor judges it not only on grammar and mechanics but also on your critical thinking. Therefore, your essay is not just a rewrite of what others have said, but a combination of your thoughts and theirs.

While exposition implies research, research implies synthesis—putting together what you have learned.

accurately represented and that you have focused on the most relevant and important aspects. The following section will help you proceed with greater confidence.

Research—Finding and Exploring

Your first step in writing a research paper often involves choosing a topic (unless your instructor has provided it for you). This step involves determining your topic and possible sources. At this early stage, it is helpful to write a summary of your purpose as well as a tentative list of source material. Your instructor may even ask for a brief proposal or a few paragraphs asking you to explain your topic, the focus, and the reason you have chosen to write about it. The paragraphs below were submitted by student writer Simon Walter to explain why he chose to write about Massively Multiplayer Online Role-Playing Games (MMORPGs) for his research paper, "The Virtual Life: An Overview of the Effects of MMORPGs on Individuals and Countries," in Chapter 11. Also, see Walter's self-survey in Chapter 2, page 31

When choosing my topic, I immediately drew upon video games as a topic I was both interested in and motivated to write about, most likely because I have been involved in gaming for most of my life.

My interest in MMORPGs specifically is not from personal experience, however. In fact, it is mostly because of my graduating year in high school; I found a large portion of my friends' circle sucked into the vortex which is the world of MMORPGs such as Everquest and World of Warcraft. I was a fairly active kid both academically and athletically in high school, and though I considered myself a gamer, I could never understand how so many people could almost completely disappear from their real lives to make synthetic ones online. Mostly, it was frustration with losing a lot of friends to a video game and the fact that I had too many commitments going on to join them, even if I wanted to.

Of course, that period of my life is past, but curiosity about the nature of those games remained; I wanted to know how a video game could have such an allure. I knew why I was attracted to certain video games, but I wanted to know why others could spend so much time with these MMORPGs. Then I starting noticing new "research" coming out concerning them and an overall dislike for them in the circles of other gaming genres.

All this contributed to my choosing MMORPGs as a topic: I wanted to learn what traits exactly defined an MMORPGs, why it consumes so much time, and, finally, the reasons for an increasingly negative media bias on the subject.

I don't consider myself an authority on video game culture, but I believe I'm a well-informed participant. I like the idea of gaming as both a technological and social movement. As my thinking on the topic progresses, I am starting to study the politics behind MMORPGs more than simply the positive and negative effects. My essay will be less comparative and more analytical in its approach. I have come across many articles studying the effects on long-term gaming in a country and am fascinated by many journalists' attempts to incorporate not just the game, but the gamers themselves, into the economics of a country. My essay began as an interest derived from a basement hobby, but I ended up choosing a particular facet of the issue which I find fascinating and current: the economic component.

> By asking yourself key questions about the topic, you will discover what you already know and what you need to find out.

Proposals like the one above help you in the "finding and exploring" stage of essay writing. Even if you are not asked to submit a proposal, you will have to think about the topic and use the pre-writing strategies you find the most effective. There are some key questions to ask to help you get started.

Questions to ask:
- What am I interested in?
- Do I know enough to explore a topic thoroughly?
- If I don't know very much, how can I obtain background information?
- What am I hoping to contribute to this subject area?
- Who is my audience?
- What kind of sources would be appropriate given my topic and my audience?
- Where will I find my source material?
- Do I know of the major authors in the field, or how can I find these authors?
- Have I given myself sufficient time to research, synthesize, organize, compose, document, and revise?

Synthesis I—Integration

After you have found your sources, you begin to **assimilate** the information. By taking notes and summarizing where appropriate, you demonstrate that you can accurately represent another person's ideas and integrate them with your own ideas. This vital stage of the research essay is discussed in this chapter and in Chapters 9 and 11. When you have finished taking notes and understand the information, you are ready to begin organizing your essay.

Questions to ask:
- Is my research geared towards supporting my points?
- Have I understood the results of the studies I've looked at and/or the positions of the experts whose works I have read?
- Are all my sources credible? Are there many recent ones?
- Have I summarized adequately and/or quoted accurately all sources I might use?
- Which sources are the most important?
- How do the different experts' views or conclusions fit together?
- Are there opposing positions? Do some findings challenge other ones, for example?

- How do they help me in my exploration of the topic?
- Has my research changed my view of my topic? If so, how? Do I need to change my thesis?

Organization—Arranging

Every essay needs a structure; usually this will take the form of an outline, a kind of blueprint for the writing stage. Outlines for expository essays are discussed in Chapters 2 and 5. It could also take the form of a template like the kind discussed in Chapter 8. See Chapter 11 for an example of a student outline.

> Successful writers create outlines to help them organize their thoughts early in the writing process.

Questions to ask:
- Do I have enough support to begin an outline? If so, what kind of outline template should I use?
- Is there a natural organizational method I should use? (chronology, cause–effect, problem–solution?)
- Do my points thoroughly explore the topic?
- Are some points inadequately developed to produce substantial paragraphs?
- Are all areas of my research relevant to the points I want to make?
- What points are most essential and what sources are most relevant?
- Am I off topic anywhere?
- Does the structure I chose reflect my purpose? Does it reflect my audience? Is it logical?

Synthesis II—Composing

During the first-draft stage—as you are now concerned with integrating your sources into your essay—synthesis takes place at the level of language. Thus, how you use direct quotations, summary, and paraphrase will be important (see Chapters 9 and 11).

Questions to ask:
- Am I overusing my sources? Underusing them?
- Which sources should be summarized, which paraphrased, and which quoted directly? (This will depend on various factors including length, importance, and phrasing of the source.)
- Am I using my sources effectively?
- Can I use ellipses (see Chapter 11) to omit less important parts of the source?
- Am I providing smooth transitions between my sources and my own writing?
- Is the language level roughly the same throughout? Is it appropriate for my audience?
- Are direct quotations grammatically integrated and easy to read?
- Have I double-checked them for accuracy?
- Is my own writing clear, grammatical, and effective? (See Chapters 14–17.)

Documenting—Following Rules

With APA and MLA, you can include a source on the References page or Works Cited page only if you have used it in your essay.

In this final stage of the research essay, you must document sources using an appropriate format. The two main scholarly formats for referencing are those of The Modern Language Association (MLA) and the American Psychological Association (APA) style. These resources should be available in your college or university library or bookstore, or online. See Chapter 12 for specific documentation formats for both APA and MLA styles.

Questions to ask:

- What documentation style is expected for this essay?
- Where is information on documenting to be found?
- If I am using electronic sources, am I clear on acceptable methods for documenting them? (Has my instructor given me guidance or directed me to specific sites or sources?)
- Do I know what needs to be documented and what does not?
- Is it possible that the reader could confuse my own ideas or observations with information taken from another source?
- Have I carefully documented other people's words and ideas but without cluttering the essay with unnecessary citations?

◎ What Is Research?

You have been conducting research informally for some time now. Chances are you did not just randomly choose the school you are now attending or the program you are enrolled in. You probably read brochures, talked to people—perhaps to current students, graduates, or school counsellors. This information was no doubt helpful, but you probably also relied on *factual evidence*: programs, prerequisites, tuition fees, housing, and campus size. You may have consulted objective experts, such as people who have researched the different schools, ranking them according to various criteria.

Formal research requires you to analyze, compare, assess, and/or synthesize the scholarship of experts in your subject area, generally by discussing multiple approaches to a problem.

This process of decision-making based on research is a life skill, and the critical skills of analysis, judgment, and evaluation are involved in the decision-making process. Research assignments in college or university are similar to this, but involve formal research that requires you to analyze, compare, assess, and/or synthesize the scholarship of experts in your subject area, generally by discussing multiple approaches to a problem. Simply rephrasing these sources is not necessarily research, nor is a summary of your own opinions or experiences.

One common approach to organizing a research paper is to compare and contrast the similarities and differences between two or more ideas. Another method is to evaluate the strengths and/or weaknesses of a point of view based on criteria that you create or borrow from experts. The following example involves both comparison and contrast, and evaluation.

1. Identifying a problem:

   Scientists report that holes have appeared in the earth's ozone layer in the past two decades.

2. Stating a claim or the thesis about this problem (what the writer will explore or prove):

   Acid rain is causing holes in the earth's ozone layer.

3. Describing the points made by one or more "experts" concerning the claim:

   Scientist one claims his research demonstrates that ozone holes did not exist before 1983. He presents information gathered from weather balloons that shows acidic particles in the air over North America in the same time period.

   Scientist two asserts that ozone layer holes are not new phenomena, and should not be attributed to acid rain. Since she began viewing ozone holes by telescope in 1983, she has measured ozone holes as they have increased in size.

4. Reaching a decision on the merits of these experts' approaches to the thesis:

   Scientist one's arguments are more convincing than those of scientist two. Scientist one claims to have information that shows that the holes in the atmosphere appeared at a particular time. Scientist two is able to demonstrate an increase in size, but cannot pinpoint the onset of these holes in the earth's ozone layer.

5. Concluding with your judgment on the thesis, either by rating the experts' approaches or by suggesting a new way of thinking about the problem:

   Scientist one has convinced you that there is a relationship between acid rain and holes in the ozone layer. His experiments began before such holes were identified, and he has data that show their existence in 1983. However, scientist two's work should not be completely discounted, as these ozone holes may have existed much longer but were not recognized until the mid-1980s.

◎ Who Are These Experts . . . And Where Can You Find Them?

Experts are people who are experienced or well-educated, who have published or produced significant work about a subject. A documentary filmmaker may be an expert; watching his or her film will enable you to gather information for your essay. A writer for a magazine or newspaper may also be an expert; so, too, could a person interviewed on radio or television be very familiar with a topic, either through his or her research, knowledge, or personal experience. The shelves of libraries are filled with the publications of experts, and the Internet may be another source of expertise. Since the number of these experts may be enormous, you need standards for screening the quality

> Experts are people who are experienced or well-educated, who have published or produced significant work about a subject.

of their information. In the case of the filmmaker, you could consider the following criteria for credibility:

- An important part of research is to select sources whose work has been scrutinized by their colleagues. Anyone who can run a camera can make a documentary film. Are there any reviews in journals or other comments you can read about the film? This will help you know what the filmmaker's colleagues think about this film.
- Is the film part of your institution's collection or available through a reputable organization like the National Film Board?
- Since you are writing a research paper in an educational context, you may wish to consider the filmmaker's academic credentials.

Another criterion used to measure the usefulness of research material is *publication date*. Since attitudes and analyses change over time, more recent information allows you to consider the latest developments in your field. A further advantage in beginning with recent material is that the source often will refer to previous studies that might be useful. Sometimes just scanning the Works Cited or References section at the end of a recent work will suggest other potential sources.

> When conducting research, ask your instructor about publication dates. Is there a limit to how far you can go back? Does the article have to be published after a certain year? Depending on the research area, research conducted 10 years ago can be extremely dated, or it can be relatively new.

◎ A Note about the Internet

When assessing the credibility of a secondary source, especially an Internet source, you could consider the following quotation from George Orwell's *Animal Farm*: "[S]ome animals are more equal than others." Anyone with basic computer skills can publish online, which has created both new opportunities and new challenges for researchers. For instance, if you enter the phrase "essay writing blogs" in a search engine, you will no doubt discover numerous blogs related to this topic; however, is the author an expert? Is he or she credible?

Searching the Internet for iPod prices and using it for academic research require different criteria; research is focused on the trustworthiness of the author(s). The Internet has countless sites created by individuals, companies, and institutions with very few controls to guarantee the accuracy or fairness of the information placed online. To retrieve quality information, you must assess the reputation of a site's creator(s) and double-check the information in other sources. Many thoughtful and well-respected authors use the Internet to reach others who share their interests; however, it is important to judge a website author's motivation carefully.

Some of the information available on the Internet promotes the author's point of view or contains inaccurate information. Therefore, its usefulness is limited. Ask yourself, "Is the author I'm reading providing a reasoned argument or just an opinion about the subject being discussed?" Be aware that personal blogs and listservs are, by and large, designed for conversation and opinion rather than the promotion of academic research.

College or university library websites provide a wealth of accurate scholarly information, so an excellent strategy for beginning researchers is to use them to guide you towards appropriate online material. The final part of a website's Universal Resource Locator (URL) directs you to these websites. The addresses of degree-granting American educational institutions always end with the domain ".edu." Canadian schools' websites generally contain a shortened version of their name, followed by ".ca."

Researching Your Topic

Exploring

The first stage in researching a topic is to determine the major authors in your subject area and what they say about your topic. As well, you need to know where they provide this information so that you can quote or paraphrase what these experts have to say and document them in your essay.

Finding important authors and works in your area may be easier if your instructor can recommend them. However, in most cases, especially if you are free to choose your own topic, beginning and narrowing the search will be something you do yourself. Looking for a general work, such as a textbook, in your subject area is a useful first step. General works frequently include extensive bibliographies (alphabetical listings of works used or consulted), which you can scan for relevant titles and authors. Consult works in the library's Reference section, such as indexes, encyclopedias, dictionaries, and comprehensive guides in your area. Most books in a library's reference section can't be taken out of the library, but they can direct you to more specific sources that can be taken out. However, some of these reference sources may also be available electronically through the library, so check with the librarians.

> A useful first step when conducting research is to use a general work, such as a textbook.

> Writing or underlining in library books themselves is both destructive and inefficient as a note-taking method because you should be able to refer to your notes without rereading the entire text again.

Internet search engines and subject directories can also provide excellent starting points, providing you with general topics that you can narrow down. If you are having trouble finding information about your topic, use the glossary section of your textbook, which contains keywords relevant to your chosen topic.

When you find potentially useful sources, you can add them to your **working bibliography**, a list of books and articles you plan to look at. When you find a book on the list, scan the index and the table of contents to determine how helpful it will be. If it looks promising, read the writer's Introduction, Preface, or Foreword. The author often summarizes his or her approach and, sometimes, provides chapter-by-chapter summaries in the introductory section. Chapter 1 explains useful reading strategies, such as scanning, that can be used when conducting research. With articles, read the **abstract**.

> An abstract is a short summary that precedes journal articles in the sciences and social sciences.

Your working bibliography may not look much like the final list of works you actually use, but it often leads you to the most relevant sources. Remember to note the date of the work's publication on the copyright page of books (the other side of the title page). If possible, use more recent works not only because they will be up-to-date but also because they may draw on relevant previously published works and provide you with other useful sources.

Research Note-Taking

Keeping clear records during the research phase of the essay-writing process will allow you to read material efficiently as well as save time (and your sanity) when you write your paper. You should make notes as you research your sources, ensuring that you record the following information:

1. A direct quotation, a summary, or a paraphrase of the writer's idea; if it is a direct quotation, make sure you put quotation marks around it
2. The complete name(s) of the author(s)
3. The name(s) of editor(s) or translator(s), if applicable
4. The name of the book, journal, magazine, newspaper, or website affiliation or sponsor
5. The name of the specific article, chapter, section, or website
6. Full publication details, including date, edition, or translation; for a journal article, this could be the volume and issue number; for Internet sites, this could be the date the site was started or updated
7. The name of the publisher and the company's location (including province or state) for books
8. In the case of Internet sites, the day you viewed the page and either the URL or the **digital object identifier** (DOI)
9. The call number of a library book or bound journal for later reference, if needed
10. The page numbers you consulted, both those from which specific ideas came and the full page range (or some other marker for unnumbered online documents, such as paragraph numbers or section heading)

Organizing Research Notes

There are many ways to organize your notes, but this is an extremely important aspect of research. There is nothing worse than trying to complete a research paper and not being able to find one key piece of information. One method is to write these notes on index cards (remember to number them). You can also record notes in a journal and use tabs to section the book into particular headings. If using a computer, you can create a record-keeping system, either by using a database program like Access or by simply creating multiple document files in a folder. In addition, there are a number of software programs available that can assist you in organizing your research. Programs such as Scribe (http://www.scribes.com) imitate the card file system. Others, like EndNote (http://www.endnote.com), Bibliographix (http://www.bibliographix.com), and Nota Bene (http://www.notabene.com), are databases.

Another program you can use to keep track of material is called RefWorks (http://www.refworks.com). You can enter the bibliographic information

When you are taking down information, don't forget to record your observations, comments, and queries. You will need bibliographic details, of course, but you will also need to synthesize the ideas of the source with your own ideas as your essay develops; you will have to relate it to other sources and to your own thesis statement.

It's important to keep source material separate from your own comments—by writing your responses on another piece of paper or by writing your comments in pencil or a different coloured pen. *Always give clear directions to yourself when you take down this information.*

Digital object identifier (DOI) is a number-alphabet sequence that begins with the number 10 and is often found on documents obtained electronically through databases. It forms the last element in your citation sequence just like a Uniform Resource Locator (URL).

into the systems and it will create a References or Works Cited page (depending on whether you specify APA or MLA style, which is discussed in Chapter 12). Creating such a document can help you retrieve information if you lose or misplace it. Before submitting a final essay, review all the entries to ensure you have eliminated any sources you decided not to use.

Learning programs such as these take time, but they generally offer beneficial extra features like the automatic formatting of citations and references or bibliographies. If you choose to record your notes electronically, you should back up your work regularly in case of technical failure.

Cross-Referencing

Cross-referencing your notes can increase the ease with which you retrieve your information when you are writing your essay. You can create a list of central or keywords, names, or themes, and record where in your notes these occur. You can cross-reference by writing notes in a margin or by using either index cards or computer files. Some students draw themselves a visual aid like a mind map (graphic organizer) on a large sheet of paper to connect their keywords. Some word-processing programs include a cross-referencing feature for single documents (in Word 2007, for example, this is found under Insert, then Links, in the drop-down menu). The computer programs mentioned previously often have built-in, keyword-based cross-referencing systems.

> It is important to keep your research notes organized so that you can retrieve information quickly at a later date without having to go back and reread material.

Some Useful Research Strategies

Assimilating

- Begin the research by gathering definitions of the keywords in your thesis statement.
- Read or view everything with the thesis statement always in mind. Resist getting sidetracked by reading unconnected material, however interesting it might seem.
- Judge whether or not a book will be worth your time by looking up your cross-referencing keywords in the index at the back of the book. Read the abstracts of journal articles to similarly determine their usefulness.
- Consider how the information you take from your sources can be connected using transitional words and phrases like *because*, *as a result of*, *on the other hand*, or *in contrast*. This will help you select points that flow logically.
- Try to find an example to support every major statement you wish to make. An example can be a quotation, a paraphrase, or a larger concept like an author's comment on or solution to your thesis statement.

Arranging

- When you've finished your first round of research, write an outline that lays out the structure of your paper by creating primary and secondary headings corresponding to the major elements of your thesis statement. Under the headings, list the lines of reasoning that support these points and the examples that support each of them. You can also use the template provided in Chapter 8.

- Decide how many pages you will allot for each section of the paper, taking the instructor's requirements for paper length into serious account.
- Look over your outline. Do you have sufficient examples to support all your major statements? Review the assigned word count. Do you have enough material in your study notes to fill the pages? If neither of these things appears to be true, perhaps you need to do more research. On the other hand, if you have too many key points and several examples for each one, now is the time to choose the strongest ones in order to meet length requirements.
- Consider laying out your paper in a word-processing program according to the suggested page number count. If you use the manual "page break" option (under "Insert" in most programs) to create document sections that follow your outline, you'll easily be able to judge whether you're writing too much or too little for any portion of the paper.
- Design a timeline for each of the steps in your paper if you haven't done so in a research proposal. This will help ensure that you don't spend too much time on any segment of the paper.

Using Contradictory Evidence

In the initial research stage, you will need to find sources relevant to your topic; however, not all studies on a given topic come to the same conclusion. If your primary purpose is to explain or investigate a problem, you will have to assess the different findings, trying to discover why the findings are different, perhaps by analyzing their respective strengths and weaknesses. This process of assessing, a critical thinking skill, is a fundamental part of the research process.

In the humanities, your thesis is often based on your interpretation of the findings, so you must carefully show how the interpretations of other academics differ from your own. An excellent strategy when discussing conflicting results is to acknowledge another interpretation and use it as a springboard into your own interpretation. Contradictory interpretations should not simply be dismissed without explanation; it is better to acknowledge them and qualify them, possibly by briefly discussing their limitations. If you do not address contradictory studies, the reader may assume that you do not know enough about the topic, reducing your credibility. For example, there have been many recent studies that attempt to show the health benefits of vitamins. If you are investigating the benefits of vitamin E in preventing heart disease and have found that credible evidence exists, you still need to acknowledge contradictory studies and explain how these findings fit into your claim about the value of vitamin E.

Researching a topic can be a challenging process—possibly a trial run for the kind of work you will do later in your academic or professional career. If

Chapter 8, p. 134, has a template that you can use for arranging the information from research sources. You can either use this one or create your own electronically. Having a few copies on hand will make it easier if you rearrange material. Use a clean copy and record changes there, rather than erasing or crossing out information. This way you can make sure nothing gets left out by mistake.

At the college and university level, in order to write a well-researched paper, you need to acknowledge a different point of view if there is one. If you ignore contradictory findings, your instructor may tell you that you have not researched the topic adequately.

you experience doubts or uncertainties at any stage of the process, talk to your instructor as soon as possible. Don't wait until the day before your paper is due!

Sources of Research Material

There are many different kinds of source materials available; most of the important ones are discussed below.

Primary and Secondary Sources

The distinction between **primary** and **secondary sources** is crucial as essay assignments frequently include a requirement that both primary and secondary sources be identified and referenced. Primary sources are the original compositions of authors. Personal documents, such as letters and other material created at the same time as an event, and initial scientific articles reporting on a work are also considered primary sources. A secondary source is another writer's analysis and commentary about a primary source. An article that cites someone else's research or a textbook that explains others' theories are both secondary sources. An encyclopedia entry is also considered a secondary source.

> Primary sources are the original compositions of authors, but secondary sources cite someone else's research or theories.

Start Your Research by Looking at Secondary Sources

An efficient way to construct a general framework of research from your thesis statement is to access reference sources such as indexes, almanacs, encyclopedias, dictionaries, and yearbooks. These can provide you with concise summaries of statistics, definitions, and biographies, and they also generally provide a reading list of the principal primary and secondary sources. As mentioned, the paper copies of these books are found in the Reference section of a library and usually can't be taken home. However, this type of information is widely available on the Internet. For instance, a Google search of "black hole" and "encyclopedia" returns results that include the *Encyclopaedia Britannica*, the *Columbia Encyclopedia*, *Encarta Encyclopedia*, and numerous online library-based sites offering further links to information on the subject. The *Britannica* entry includes a listing of relevant books, articles, websites, magazine articles, and videos on black holes.

> When using texts accessed online, it is important to remember that multiple translations/editions often are available, and the online version may not be the most accurate or accepted one. Check with your instructor before you go ahead and use Internet material as a primary source.

Books

Once you've developed a basic understanding of your topic, you can look for books and journal articles that refer specifically to your thesis statement. Continue your research by locating either books or periodicals mentioned in your preliminary search of reference materials. A book can be written on a single topic; a compilation of articles, essays, or chapters by a number of authors around a topic; or a collection of pieces by a particular author that have already been published individually. Books that are available to you can be located by searching a library's catalogue, or sometimes can be found online by doing an author or title search, or by using a database. For instance, Project Gutenberg (http://gutenberg.org) has digitally republished more than 30,000 e-books, ranging from the contemporary *Human Genome Project, Y Chromosome,* by The Human Genome Project, to the nineteenth-century novel *The Hunchback of Notre Dame*, by Victor Hugo.

Periodicals

Periodicals are newspapers, magazines, journals, and yearbooks; a yearbook is a book of facts or statistics published every year.

Periodicals are published regularly—for instance, monthly, yearly, or daily. Examples include newspapers, magazines, journals, and yearbooks. Unless you are writing about an extremely current aspect of contemporary culture, you will probably be concentrating on periodicals called **journals**, which publish articles written by academics, scientists, and researchers. The most respected journals are **peer-reviewed**, which means that other experts in that field have assessed the work prior to its being published.

If an article appears in a peer-reviewed journal, it has been assessed by experts in the field before it is published.

Locating Journal Articles

The articles published in scholarly journals are the places where researchers publish their findings in order to share their ideas—and advance their careers. As a result, there are thousands of scholarly journals publishing a wealth of research on just about any topic you can imagine. However, finding these articles online can be a challenge because the journals generally are distributed only through expensive subscriptions. College and university libraries subscribe to some of the journals that they consider most valuable and then allow students, faculty, and staff access to them either in paper editions or online.

Locating a hard copy (paper copy) of a journal article generally begins with a library's catalogue search. Let's say you have located an article from the bibliography of a well-known textbook on your topic. In order to find the article, you'll need some detailed information that makes up what is called a **citation**, which includes much more than the author's name and the name of the journal. The following components of a citation illustrate what you will need:

Author(s) Name(s): Zigler, E.F. & Gilman, E.
Publication Year: 1993
Article Title: Day care in America: What is needed?
Journal Name: *Pediatrics*
Volume and Issue Number: 91, 1 (an issue number is not always required in your citation, but you should record it in case it is needed)
Page Numbers: 175–178

The complete citation written in APA style (see Chapter 12) looks like this:
Zigler, E.F. & Gilman, E. (1993). Day care in America: What is needed? *Pediatrics, 91*(1), 175–178.

Most library catalogues are designed so you can select "journals only" in the search options and then search for the journal name (as opposed to the article title or author name). You will be given a call number that will direct you to a location in the library where you will find either unbound or bound (into a book) journals. Look up the volume month or issue, and then follow the page numbers to the article. If you are unsure how to do this, ask for help. The librarians or library technicians have received training (and usually have lots of personal experience), so they can show you how to search quickly and efficiently.

Internet Searches

College and university libraries also subscribe to databases and indexes that contain the full texts of journal articles, which you can save directly onto your computer's hard drive. Supplied by private companies, these services are called **aggregator databases** since they collect or aggregate many different journals together in searchable interfaces that give you access to many more journals than any individual library could ever afford to subscribe to or find the space to store.

Databases also may house a blend of scholarly and non-scholarly information, including popular magazines, newspapers, and non-peer-reviewed journals, along

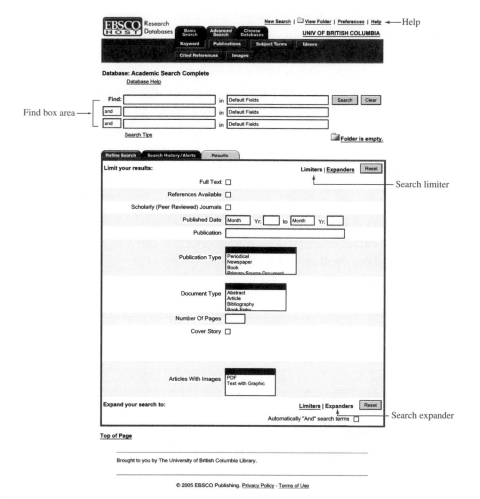

Figure 10.1   Screenshot capture of EBSCOhost research database page.

This database screen shows how databases typically organize research information. By entering a word or phrase in the **find** box, you can retrieve any article that contains your keywords in either the title or the body of all of the thousands of periodicals available through EBSCOhost. Needless to say, this list can be enormous and somewhat overwhelming. For this reason, EBSCOhost allows you to select **limiters** on your search, including a time period of publication and the option to search only peer-reviewed journals. There is also an advanced search window, which permits you to define various combinations of key words and **search limiters** or **expanders**. Each academic discipline has specialized databases and indexes that concentrate on publications that are particularly relevant to that field. You can ask your instructor to direct you to the most appropriate databases or search your library's website for discipline-related listings. All databases have a link to online help. When you need help in your search, use the **help** button.

with government-produced documents. In addition, databases supply links to the growing number of journals that don't publish a paper version at all, and are available only online: electronic journals, or e-journals. When conducting research using these databases, if possible, indicate that you want full-text articles, as searches can produce articles for which only the abstract is available. When you are using journal articles, never cite from an abstract and only use full-text articles.

Although database interfaces can vary, most function on the principle of keywords (including authors' names). For instance, the database EBSCOhost provides links to several thousand journals and millions of articles by using a combination of keywords and search options.

Boolean operators are used to customize your search. Search limiters include the words "AND" and "NOT." If you type the word "AND" between two or more search terms, your results will include both search terms; if you type the word "NOT" between search terms, your results will omit what follows "NOT." If you use "OR" as a search expander, your results will include *at least one* of the terms.

Let's say you were undecided about the topic you wanted to explore but were seriously considering either caffeine or alcohol. A database search on "caffeine OR alcohol" using EBSCOhost turns up 27,388 entries. This is far too many to be useful, so you then enter only one search term, "caffeine"; this yields 1658 entries. Thinking that you might want to compare caffeine and alcohol, you use the limiter "AND," which produces 116 results. In order to exclude "tobacco" from your search, you add a second limiter, "NOT tobacco" and hit Search. Using the two limiters (caffeine AND alcohol NOT tobacco) produces 93 results—a more manageable start.

Some Popular Databases

BioMed Central indexes hundreds of journals offering peer-reviewed research about biology and medicine.

Business Source Elite is a database assembled for business schools and libraries, which incorporates 2804 scholarly journals and business periodicals relating to marketing, economics, and accounting.

CANSIM (Canadian Socio-economic Information Management) Database (Statistics Canada) is a comprehensive database from Statistics Canada containing nearly 18 million government documents.

EBSCOhost is a comprehensive "gateway" database service for more than 9500 journals on a vast range of discipline areas, with an Internet style (Boolean logic) search interface. EBSCOhost is the inclusive academic database operating at this time. It is widely available through college or university library sites; see your institution's library site for login directions.

Boolean operators, such as "AND," "OR," and "NOT," are used to customize your search.

Depending on your search engine, you can narrow or expand your search by using specific symbols. For example, putting words between double quotation marks will restrict the search to text in which the words appear in the order you place them; for example, typing in "fair trade coffee" (using quotation marks) will greatly reduce the number of entries you will get because they will exclude results that contained the three words in a different order or separated by one or more words.

ERIC (Educational Resources Information Center): This large database pertains to education and is best known for its short synopses on pertinent topics (ERIC Digest Records) written by educational experts. The ERIC Social Sciences Citation Index provides a multi-disciplinary directory of more than 1725 social and behavioural sciences journals published after 1995.

Health Source Nursing/Academic Edition offers full-text articles from more than 500 health and medical journals and indexes the abstracts of more than 850 publications.

IEL (IEEE/IEE Electronic Library) makes available full-text access to more than 125 technical journals and 600 conference proceedings in engineering, physics, computer science, and materials sciences.

InfoTrac describes itself as a source for "research in academic disciplines as well as current news and general interest articles." It provides indexing and abstracts for 1550 journals, along with full-text articles from more than 500 social sciences, technology, and humanities journals.

Ingenta is an excellent source for journals in the humanities, sciences, social sciences, and education. It features full texts of millions of articles from some 30,000 publications.

Lexis-Nexis Academic Universe contains full-text articles from nearly 2000 sources such as company reports, newspapers, transcripts of broadcasts, wire services, newsletters, journals, legal case law, government documents, as well as some valuable reference texts.

Newspaper Source allows access to a range of full-text articles from 18 international newspapers, including *The Christian Science Monitor*, 6 newswires, and 139 regional American newspapers.

Project Muse offers full-text articles from more than 100 scholarly journals in the humanities, the social sciences, and mathematics. Articles are available from 1995.

ProQuest describes itself as an "online information service" that provides access to thousands of current periodicals and newspapers that are updated daily; it contains full-text articles from as early as 1986.

Psyc INFO is operated by the American Psychological Association and offers citations (not full-text articles) for reports, articles, dissertations, and book chapters relating to psychology in fields such as education, business, medicine/nursing, and sociology.

WorldCat, operated by a consortium of more than 9000 universities, libraries and colleges, allows users to view or borrow audiovisual materials, books, films, government documents, computer files, and research reports in 400 languages. This "database of databases" has thousands of full-text articles and an interlibrary loan service for non-digitalized items.

Notes on Library Research

Reference librarians and library technicians have been specially trained and often know of unique ways to retrieve information. Help desks are staffed with these people specifically to help students find information.

With the wealth of research information available electronically, it may seem unnecessary to go to a college or university library in person. In reality, libraries continue to be valuable resources for researchers at all levels of expertise, partly because they have books not available online and they are staffed by professionals who understand how information is organized and interrelated. Most libraries have reference librarians who can save you time and direct you to sources you might never come across on your own. Reference librarians and library technicians have been specially trained and often know of unique ways to retrieve information. Help desks are staffed with these people specifically to help students find information.

Libraries often run courses to familiarize students with the specific systems the college or university uses, so it is a good idea to find out when these are being held and sign up for a session or two. Participating in the same session more than once is often beneficial, as the information can be overwhelming, and you can learn things you missed the first time. Furthermore, libraries hold many important records, including the following:

- Indexes for many periodicals, images, films, microfiche files, and videos
- Theses and dissertations (book-length documents written by university students as part of their advanced degree requirements)
- Historical documents, including maps and public records
- Collections of textual and graphic material on special subjects, sometimes including original documents
- Clipping files from newspapers and magazines
- Bound volumes of journals
- Collections of audio and film or video recordings

When searching for information, do not leave it to the last minute or you will be competing for help with other students who have the same deadline.

In addition, libraries store print information that has been gathered, sometimes over centuries, that is too expensive or fragile to digitize. Even for documents that are considered essential, the gradual transition to electronic record-keeping means that many important compilations of information made before 1985 are available only in paper form at a library. If your college or university library is small, or you are attending a newer school, ask about borrowing privileges at other schools close by. You may be able to access those libraries using only your student card, or you may be able to get special permission to use another school's library if they have information your own does not. Another option that may be available is the interlibrary loan. If your college or university has this service, you may be able to borrow documents from other libraries without having to go there yourself. The documents will be delivered to your school library where you can then pick them up. However, you do need to plan ahead, as it can take several days to a week or more to get the document.

Using electronic sources to access journals that publish paper versions has another wrinkle that can frustrate inexperienced researchers: these publications often hold their latest year's editions from databases in order to maintain their sub-scription lists. This means that it is still necessary to view the most current issues in person; and remember, accessing recent studies is vital, especially if your subject is a topical one.

Although the nature of research has changed dramatically with the increasing availability of online resources, the best way to think of the cyber–paper relationship is as a complementary one. Relying *only* on the Internet is inadvisable, and some instructors may specify how much electronic research is allowable.

Alternative Information Sources

Although this section has emphasized research information that is written, many disciplines accept support for your thesis from visual or audio media, such as television, film, video, works of art, performances, surveys or questionnaires, interviews, and observations. Using these alternative sources of information requires the same attention to detail in note taking as when using traditional materials, and most citation styles provide instructions for citing and referencing non-textual research information. As these approaches to research are more acceptable by some disciplines than by others, it is wise early in the writing process to review with your instructor an essay outline that emphasizes alternative information sources.

Interviewing

If you have direct access to a noted authority in your field, interviewing can be an effective form of research. The principle advantage of an interview, whether face-to-face, by telephone, or by email, is that you can ask questions specific to your research rather than having to search many potential sources for this particular information. Interview subjects can be treated the same way as other expert sources of knowledge; that is, their words can be summarized, paraphrased, or quoted directly. There are also specific methods for documenting interviewees. The college or university community—including, perhaps, one of your professors—is an ideal place to look for experts.

Chapter Review Questions

1. What is the difference between primary and secondary sources?
2. Why is it important to know the experts in the field you are researching?
3. What is the difference between a database and the Internet?

4. What sources, other than books, can you find at a college or university library?
5. What is a Boolean operator?
6. What is the difference between a popular magazine and a journal or periodical?
7. What does it mean if an article is peer-reviewed?

11

Using Your Research

In this chapter, you will learn

- the importance of creating outlines for research essays

- about plagiarism and how to avoid it

- how to use direct quotations in your research essays

- how to integrate summaries and paraphrases into your essays

- how to use a mixture of direct quotation and paraphrase to effectively integrate sources

- how to use signal phrases

When you are writing a research paper, you need to use outside sources (primary, secondary, or both), as discussed in Chapter 10. However, good writers do not mechanically insert the material: they integrate it seamlessly into their work, increasing the essay's readability. Several ways to integrate sources are discussed in this chapter. When using primary or secondary sources to support your thesis, you must make sure that you use these sources correctly so that you do not plagiarize, a serious academic offence. This chapter explains plagiarism and outlines the steps to take to ensure you acknowledge the work of others properly.

◎ Outlines for Research Essays

How do you know when you have enough support for your points and can begin an outline? The answer may depend on the assignment itself, as your instructor may be expecting a specific or minimum number of sources. Otherwise, you should probably have at least one source (direct quotation, paraphrase, or idea) to support each main point. Whereas an argumentative essay depends on effective reasoning and various kinds of evidence—including examples, illustrations, analogies, anecdotes, and *perhaps* the findings of secondary sources—many expository essays rely heavily on outside support. Therefore, it may be a good idea to include such sources in your outline, as Simon Walter does in the outline below. Being specific in your outline will make it easier to write your first draft where a main concern will be integrating the sources with your own words.

Below is the outline for the student essay on page 204. However, not all outlines need to be this detailed; for example, many essays you write will be shorter and not require as many points. The outline below shows the detail that Walter felt he needed before beginning to draft his essay. He includes much of the relevant research that is found in the final version of his essay; however, other research points were eventually discarded as he wrote his rough draft and between the rough draft and his final draft. Note that this outline closely follows the template found in Chapter 8.

The Virtual Life: An Overview of the Effects of MMORPGs on Individuals and Countries
By Simon Walter

Introduction

I. Thesis: In the modern world, the effects of online gaming are a relatively new area of study; some countries are beginning to criticize the MMORPG genre specifically as an unhealthy pastime for psychological and physical reasons, but this opinion is not held by all and illustrates the world's continued division on the issue: what will be the long-term effects of massive online gaming on individuals and the world?

A. The presence of MMORPGs in mainstream gaming is barely more than a decade old, which means its effect on the world is only just beginning, and the current generation of youth is the first to suffer or benefit from its effects.

B. The reception received by the genre varies by the country, and research into the topic is growing rapidly.

> The writer wanted to also cover these points and so included them in the introduction.

II. Paragraph 1: Background of the MMORPG

> Walter does not include a clear topic sentence, but uses a short heading instead. This will later be expanded in the essay into a topic sentence.

A. The development of MMORPGs in video gaming is both recent and relatively unstudied.

  1. The first modern MMORPG (Massively Multiplayer Online Role-Playing Game) was released in 1996 by a South Korean company; games like *Everquest* are popular today.

  2. The popularity of these games rapidly increased and revenues have surpassed other gaming genres.

B. The presence of MMORPGS in mainstream gaming is barely more than a decade old, which means its effect on the world is only just beginning.

  1. The current generation of youth has been a part of the birth of MMORPGS; thus, they are the first to suffer or benefit from its effects.

  2. Many criticize the MMORPGS saying they are unhealthy, but the criticism is not based on research.

C. Paragraph conclusion

> While Walter does not have a concluding statement yet, the word *conclusion* was added to remind him that he needs to end each paragraph clearly.

III. Paragraph 2: Time Commitments and Social Aspect

A. Unlike first-person shooters or real-time strategy games, MMORPGS are a "persistent state world."

  1. The game does not stop when the player does. Like the real world, life goes on (Day 111).

> Note that the writer indicates relevant research that he wants to include in the essay.

  2. Success depends on how much time a gamer can invest in the game.

> After further research, Walter will uncover a useful source, Yee, enabling him to expand on this point and include a direct quotation later in this paragraph.

B. The tasks associated with improving a character in an MMORPG are often repetitive and simple, demanding large quantities of time for improvement.

C. The most powerful items to be found in the game are often rare and available as a treasure from the most powerful creatures. This makes

(Continued)

"hunts" and "raids"—large gatherings of online characters—an intrinsic part of the MMORPG genre and constitutes part of its appeal. Yet again, it demands a large amount of time.

1. The social aspect of the game is a defining characteristic of the genre.

2. "Guilds" and "clans" are formed. Many quests *require* a player to fight with friends, encouraging cooperation and teamwork to accomplish tasks no single player ever could.

D. Paragraph conclusion

IV. Paragraph 3: The Controversy Surrounding the MMORPG

A. MMORPGS demand an incredible amount of time, which many sources argue conflicts with other time commitments necessary for the proper development of youth.

1. One journal reports an average MMORPG player is online for 22 hours a week.

2. Competitive gaming is starting to replace sports, offline friends, and even parental guardians, all of which can be garnered, in a way, from the virtual landscape.

B. The media and increasing amounts of research link MMORPGS and prolonged periods of play to increased aggression, asocial behaviour, and symptoms similar to substance addiction.

C. Paragraph conclusion

V. Paragraph 4: The Current State of Affairs in North America

A. North America is concerned primarily with the physical health of gamers, and the MMORPGS represent a major threat to the already sedentary lives of many youth.

B. In the United States, there exists a popular anti–video game movement criticizing not only the physical effects of gaming but also the psychological effects.

In his final draft, Walter did not create a separate paragraph containing this information. Instead, he used some of the information here in paragraphs 4–6. Because this paragraph was deleted, the paragraph numbers that follow do not correspond to the paragraphs in his final draft.

Based on further research and Walter's discovery of a relevant and reliable source, Yee, he changed this point in his final draft.

C. Research shows that as other pastimes decline in popularity, such as bowling and arcades, online gaming's popularity is rising. (Williams 15)

> Walter again includes the name of a source, along with the page number to ensure that he will be able to find the exact page later.

D. Paragraph conclusion

VI. Paragraph 5: The Current State of Affairs in China

> In this and the next body paragraph, Walter contrasts the attitudes of China and South Korea to MMORPGs. His in-depth comparisons will be an important part of his essay.

A. The Chinese government is particularly concerned with the effect of MMORPGs on the socioeconomics of their country.

1. Chinese officials view the MMORPG as a "third place," outside of work and home, which the government believes is creating a sphere of development in their country they cannot control.

2. Players converse and exchange information outside of government control and across borders. (Golub and Lingley 63–69)

> Walter identifies a major source to help him develop this paragraph. In his draft, he will use information in these pages for support.

B. "Gaming addiction is likened to addictive drugs, not only at the level of the individual; it is also regarded as a social problem." (63)

> The writer's use of quotation marks will remind him that he has used the exact words of the source.

C. An entire generation of Chinese youth is using its money to subscribe to a (most likely) foreign business. With the One-Child Policy already contracting the urban population in China, MMORPGs could have a detrimental effect on the working class.

D. Paragraph conclusion

VII. Paragraph 6: The Current State of Affairs in South Korea

A. South Korea displays a more positive embracing of video game culture in general. Gamers in South Korea, though not necessarily MMORPG players, are worshipped like North American sports stars, and they can make a living playing games.

B. The first graphic MMORPG, *The Kingdom of the Winds,* originated from Nexon, a South Korean company, and as the creators of the modern MMORPG, South Korea would arguably be the first country to show problems with the genre. However, media coverage and high profile research have not led to as negative a response as in other countries. (Jin and Chee)

> As in the previous paragraph, Walter identifies a major source of information. However, in contrast to the previous paragraph, he does not include much supporting detail here, as he has not fully investigated the source.

(Continued)

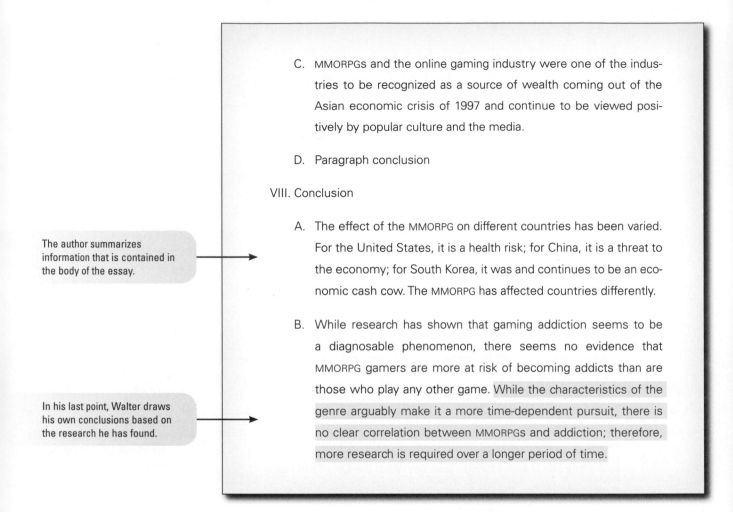

C. MMORPGs and the online gaming industry were one of the industries to be recognized as a source of wealth coming out of the Asian economic crisis of 1997 and continue to be viewed positively by popular culture and the media.

D. Paragraph conclusion

VIII. Conclusion

A. The effect of the MMORPG on different countries has been varied. For the United States, it is a health risk; for China, it is a threat to the economy; for South Korea, it was and continues to be an economic cash cow. The MMORPG has affected countries differently.

B. While research has shown that gaming addiction seems to be a diagnosable phenomenon, there seems no evidence that MMORPG gamers are more at risk of becoming addicts than are those who play any other game. While the characteristics of the genre arguably make it a more time-dependent pursuit, there is no clear correlation between MMORPGs and addiction; therefore, more research is required over a longer period of time.

The author summarizes information that is contained in the body of the essay.

In his last point, Walter draws his own conclusions based on the research he has found.

◎ Plagiarism

What Is Plagiarism?

Plagiarism is an issue that you will hear about over and over again. You will probably hear it so often that you will become tired of it, perhaps even before the first week of classes is over. Your college or university library may have handouts or online resources about plagiarism. If your school has a writing centre, tutors there can explain it or provide a handout. Finally, your composition instructor (and this text) will address it. Why is it so important to understand plagiarism?

Much has been written recently about society's disregard for copyright laws. Millions of people download music or movies. Studies have shown a rise in student cheating, and some say more than half of high school students have cheated on tests. File sharing is common, with sites such as YouTube making it possible to post videos directly from its site to your Facebook or MySpace account. Lines have blurred between personally owned material and that which is protected by copyright.

However, in academia, this sort of "sharing" is not acceptable. Borrowing someone else's words or ideas without acknowledging the source is plagiarism.

Intentional plagiarizing is a serious academic crime with equally serious consequences. Intentional plagiarizing includes using, without acknowledging, sections, sentences, or even just phrases from a website, a book, a newspaper article, a magazine, etc. It also includes using a friend's essay and turning it in as your own or buying one from the Internet. Another example is reusing a paper you have written for another class. Unintentional or inadvertent plagiarizing usually leads to the same consequences, even if the reason for the plagiarism was careless note taking, improper documentation, or a lack of knowledge about plagiarism itself. Therefore, it is important to cite information that is taken from other sources, either primary or secondary.

The consequences for plagiarizing can range from a zero for that particular paper to failing the course or being expelled from your school. It is often easy for an instructor to detect plagiarism because there may be a shift in tone or word use. When an obvious clue like this shows up, many instructors will then type the questionable phrase into a search engine and see if the exact wording matches anything on the Internet. Many colleges and universities now subscribe to services such as "Turnitin." You may be required to provide an electronic copy to such a service before submitting your essay. Such sites maintain an electronic copy of your essay and compare it to thousands of documents. If any matches are found, the results will be posted electronically for you and your instructor to see, along with the sources that match.

Plagiarism occurs when you

- fail to cite an idea, a paraphrase, or a summary
- use the exact language of the source without putting it in quotation marks
- use the identical structure of the original

In the section below, examples of plagiarism are shown. In Chapter 12, you will find complete information for citing the most common sources used in research essays. In addition, some colleges and universities subscribe to services like RefWorks. These programs allow you to enter all the bibliographic information from your sources; they then create a Works Cited or References page for you. Such services help ensure you do not plagiarize unintentionally.

To Cite or Not to Cite?

Fortunately, you may not need to cite *everything* you include in your essay. Anything that falls under the category of "general knowledge," even if you obtained the information from a specific source, does not need to be cited. If in doubt about what constitutes general knowledge, refer to the sunrise–sunset rule of thumb: you do not need to cite the fact that the sun rises in the east and sets in the west; it is general knowledge. If you were writing an essay about Amelia Earhart, you would not

---

All secondary sources require parenthetical citations and an alphabetical listing in the Works Cited section at the end of your essay (MLA) or the References section (APA). You must cite secondary sources—whether you quote from them directly, summarize them, paraphrase them, or just refer to them in passing—by using the appropriate style of your discipline.

Remember that plagiarism does not apply just to the words of the source, but also to any idea you obtain from a source. You are plagiarizing if you use the language of the source without enclosing it in quotation marks or if you closely imitate the structure of the material cited—even if you changed the words.

Plagiarism, whether intentional or unintentional, usually leads to the same harsh consequences, which may even be a zero in the course or expulsion from your school.

have to cite a source when discussing her disappearance while attempting to fly around the world: it is a well-known fact. You would, however, have to cite a source that includes conjecture about where she vanished, as this has not yet been determined, and many theories exist about where her remains might be.

If there is a reasonable presumption that a typical reader would not know it, then cite the source. If, however, a fact would be *easily obtainable* by a reader from a number of different sources (even if a typical reader would not know it), it may not be necessary to cite it. Your instructor may be able to tell you how many sources constitute "easily obtainable" information; a minimum number often given is three.

General knowledge can vary according to audience. If you are writing for an audience with a scientific or medical background, for example, you may not need to cite the fact that the active ingredient in marijuana is tetrahydro-cannabinol; if you are writing a paper for historians or political scientists, you may not need to cite the fact that British Columbia became a Canadian province in 1871 because your readers could easily obtain this information. If the general knowledge or the easily obtainable standards do not apply, make the citation.

Plagiarism Sample 1:
Original:

Anybody who will look at the thing candidly will see that the evolutionary explanation of morals is meaningless, and presupposes the existence of the very thing it ought to prove. It starts from a misconception of the biological doctrine. Biology has nothing to say as to what ought to survive and what ought not to survive; it merely speaks of what does survive.

—Stephen Leacock, "The Devil and the Deep Sea:
A Discussion of Modern Morality"

Language of the source unchanged:

A person willing to see *the thing candidly* would realize that morals cannot be accounted for through evolution.

Sentence structure unchanged:

Biology does not distinguish between what should and should not survive; it simply tells us "what does survive."

Acceptable paraphrase:

An honest appraisal can tell a person that morals cannot be accounted for through evolution.... Biology tells us only "what does survive," not what should and should not survive (Leacock 57).

When trying to determine whether to cite information in your essay, remember these two principles: if the fact is *easily obtainable* by the reader or if it is *general knowledge* for your audience, you do not need to provide a citation.

Plagiarism Sample 2:
Original:

Previous studies by the American Psychological Association show cheating is relatively in-frequent in elementary school, but increases as children become adolescents and progress through grade levels. The increasing incidence of cheating correlates almost perfectly with increasing pressure from teachers to get good grades.

> Minsky, A. (2009, 9 August). Cheating stats getting out of control: Researcher. *CanWest News*. Retrieved from CBCA Current Events.

Language of the source unchanged:

As students progress to higher grades, cheating correlates almost perfectly with increasing pressure.

Language changed, but **sentence structure unchanged**:

Students cheat more because of mounting pressure to achieve high marks.

Acceptable paraphrase:

As students advance from one grade to the next at school, they often feel that they need to perform well, and this pressure seems tied to the frequency of cheating.

> A good strategy for avoiding plagiarism (and consciously integrating the information) is to carefully study the passage you want to use; then, close the text and write the passage from memory completely in your own words. Finally, look at the passage again, ensuring that it is different in its structure as well as in its language—and that you have accurately restated the thought behind it.

◎ Integrating Secondary Sources

Using secondary sources enables you to support your argument and demonstrate your familiarity with source material. Your essay, interwoven with citations in the correct format, reveals your skills as a reader, researcher, and writer.

You can treat secondary sources in three major ways:

1. You can summarize the source, or the section of the source that is most directly relevant to your point.
2. You can paraphrase the source.
3. You can cite from the source directly.

Summary, Paraphrase, Direct Quotation, Mixed Format

One of the choices you will have in using secondary sources is the way you decide to integrate the information with your own ideas. Using a variety of methods is usually best. However, there are general guidelines to help you make choices. In all cases, remember that the source must be identified either in a signal phrase (see below) or in a parenthetical citation if you do not use a signal phrase.

Summarize

Summarize if you want to use a source's main idea(s) to provide background information, to set up a point of your own (to show similarity or difference, for example), or to explain one or various positions relevant to your discussion. You can summarize passages of just about any length—from one sentence to several pages. For more about summaries, see Chapter 9.

Paraphrase

A paraphrase restates the source's meaning using only your own words. Paraphrase when you want to cite a relatively small amount of material that is directly relevant to the point you wish to make. When you paraphrase, you include *all* of the original thought, but rephrase it. For more about paraphrases, see Chapter 9, pages 164–5.

Direct Quotation

Direct quotation is used when the source itself *and* the exact wording are important. This could be due to specialized vocabulary in the cited passage or the unique way that the source uses language or expresses the idea. You can use direct quotations for small amounts of text or for larger ones. If you choose to quote four or more consecutive lines, use the block format in which you indent one-half inch from the left margin. You double-space the text, *but do not use quotation marks*. The usual procedure is to introduce the block quotation by a complete sentence followed by a colon. For examples of block format, see the student essay on page 227. See also Mixed Format.

Use single quotation marks to indicate a word or passage in your source that is in quotation marks:

> "In a number of narratives, the (usually female) character finds herself at a significant crossroad between home and a problematic 'elsewhere'" (Rubenstein 9).

The single quotation marks around 'elsewhere' inform the reader that quotation marks were used in the original.

Avoid direct quotations if there is no compelling reason to use them; use summary or paraphrase instead. Direct quotations are most effective when used for one of the reasons stated above. You demonstrate your ability to understand and synthesize sources when you summarize and paraphrase.

Avoid using direct quotes if

- the idea in the passage is obvious, well-known, or could be easily accessed
- the material is essentially factual and does not involve a particular *interpretation* of the facts
- it can be easily paraphrased

Direct quotation is used when the source itself *and* the exact wording are important. This could be due to specialized vocabulary or the way that the source uses language or expresses the idea.

Use single quotation marks to indicate a word or passage in your source that is in quotation marks.

Avoid large blocks of quoted material. Some instructors discourage this practice by not including direct quotations in your total word count. Direct quotations used *selectively*, however, are an essential part of most essays.

The following are examples of direct quotations that are unnecessary or ineffective. The preferable alternatives are given after them.

"About one-third of infants are breast-fed for three months or longer."

Paraphrase: Approximately 33 per cent of infants receive breast-feeding for at least three months (Statistics Canada).

"The greenhouse effect is the result of gases like carbon dioxide, nitrous oxide, and methane being trapped in earth's atmosphere."

Paraphrase: The accumulation of such gases as carbon dioxide, nitrous oxide, and methane in the atmosphere has led to the greenhouse effect.

The following are examples of direct quotations that are effective.

Albert Einstein once said, "It always seems to me that man was not born to be a carnivore."

> Many facts can be paraphrased rather than quoted directly. Avoid the practice of quoting long or successive passages of statistical information. They can easily distract the reader. Paraphrasing the material is usually better.

The fact that you are quoting as well-known a personality as Einstein, even though he is speaking from personal opinion, would make direct quotation a good choice—though not an essential one. However, in the following instance, precise wording matters and gives authority to the passage:

"Neither capital punishment nor life imprisonment without possibility of release shall be imposed for offenses committed by persons below 18 years of age"— UN Convention on the Rights of the Child.

Mixed Format

Using a mixture of paraphrase and direct quotation can be an effective means of showing your familiarity with a source and confidence in your ability to integrate words and ideas smoothly into your essay.

Although in his tribute to Pierre Elliott Trudeau in *The Globe and Mail*, Mark Kingwell recalls the former prime minister as "the fusion of reason and passion, the virility and playfulness, the daunting arrogance and wit, the politician as rock star," behind this he finds "the good citizen."

Compare with the original text below. The text crossed out shows what was not used.

~~It's hard to say anything about Trudeau now that has not been said a thousand times before:~~ the fusion of reason and passion, the virility and playfulness, the daunting arrogance and wit, the politician as rock star. ~~All true; all banal.~~ But underneath all that I find ~~a more resonant identity, one which is at once simpler and more profound:~~ the good citizen.

When you use direct quotations, you must ensure that the quoted material is integrated grammatically, clearly, and gracefully. See below for examples. For information on how to use ellipses or brackets to integrate quotations, see the section below on signal phrases, ellipses, and brackets.

Examples:

Ungrammatical:
Charles E. Taylor discusses the efforts of scientists "are defining a new area of research termed artificial life" (172).
Grammatical:
Charles E. Taylor discusses the efforts of scientists to "[define] a new area of research termed artificial life" (172).

Unclear:
Art critic John Ruskin believes that the highest art arises from "sensations occurring to *them* only at particular times" (112).
Clear:
Art critic John Ruskin believes that *artists* produce the highest art from "sensations occurring to *them* only at particular times" (112).

Signal Phrases, Ellipses, and Brackets

Signal Phrases

The examples above under Mixed Format use **signal phrases** to introduce direct quotations. Signal phrases contain the source's **name** (Taylor, Ruskin) and a **signal verb**, such as recalls, discusses, or believes. Signal phrases alert the reader to exactly where the reference begins. They can also guide the reader through the complexities of an issue that involves different findings or interpretations. The following paragraph contains two citation formats: the first reference contains a signal phrase; the second one does not.

MLA style:

Richard Goldbloom states that a surveillance video taken in Toronto showed that in more than 20 per cent of incidents where bullying was involved, peers actively became part of the bullying (2). Furthermore, recent statistics show not only the pervasiveness of the problem but that outsiders perceive bullying as a problem in schools today (Clifford 4).

The reader of this paragraph would easily be able to separate the two sources, so a second signal phrase is unnecessary, though not incorrect. In fact, it is often helpful to "signal" your intentions.

When you integrate a direct quotation using mixed format, you can remove the quotation marks and just look at the portion of the quoted text as words, phrases, or sentences that, like all sentences, must be written grammatically. Don't forget to put the quotation marks back in when you've integrated it grammatically, and also ensure that any changes you made to the original are indicated through brackets or ellipses.

Signal phrases include the source's name and a signal verb; they "signal" an upcoming reference.

The example above uses MLA citation style. If you are using APA style, the signal phrase will include the year of the work's publication after the author's name. A citation without a signal phrase will use commas between the name and year, as well as between year and page number (preceded by the abbreviation "p." if a page number is required). See The Major Documentation Styles, Chapter 12.

APA style:

Asch and Wishart (2004) state that the Slavey communities had grade schools by the 1960s, and people left their homes to live in communities so as to retain social benefits (p. 186). As children and parents were reminded, a half-dozen absences from school could result in fines and jail for the parents and the loss of family allowance payments (*The Catholic Voice*, 2000, p. 5).

Ellipses

In direct quotations, you can use points of ellipsis (…) to indicate that you have omitted one or more words from a direct quotation. Three spaced dots (periods) show an ellipsis (omission). Four dots with a space at the beginning of the sequence (childhood requires….) indicate that the omitted text includes all the remaining words up to the period at the end of the sentence. The fourth dot is also used if you omit one or more complete sentences.

If a parenthetical citation follows an ellipsis, the fourth dot (i.e., the period) will follow the citation:

"Going green might cost a lot, but refusing to act now will cost us the Earth . . ." (*BBC News* par. 5).

You can use points of ellipsis before or after the original punctuation to show exactly where you have dropped material:

But some damage to the head occurs from fighting as a player's head is struck, . . . either by a fist or when he falls against the ice.

Use an ellipsis to omit unnecessary words. If only part of the quotation is relevant to your essay, you can omit what precedes or follows it. For example, if you find a quotation that discusses two points and you want to discuss only one, you can leave out the section that is not relevant. In fact, keeping it in might confuse the reader. However, if the information is important and relates to your topic, make sure that leaving it out would not be misleading. You may hear people say that they have been quoted "out of context." This could mean that the writer has left out relevant information, perhaps to deliberately create a bias that did not exist in the original.

> You can use points of ellipsis (…) to indicate the omission of one or more words within a direct quotation. You add a fourth dot if you omit all the words up to and including the final period.

> As a general rule, do not use an ellipsis (…) *before* the beginning of a direct quotation.

Brackets

Square brackets (or just *brackets*) are used to indicate a change or addition to a direct quotation. Brackets can indicate a stylistic change (e.g., upper case to lower case), a grammatical change (e.g., the tense of a verb), or a change for clarity's sake (e.g., adding a word to make the context clearer). The following illustrates these kinds of changes, though you would probably paraphrase a passage that contained as many brackets and ellipses as this:

> The text states that "[a]ll secondary sources require parenthetical citations and an alphabetical listing ... at the end of [the] essay.... [Students] must cite secondary sources, whether [they] quote from them directly, summarize them, paraphrase them, or just refer to them in passing by using the [MLA or APA] style...."

The original text:

> All secondary sources require parenthetical citations and an alphabetical listing in the Works Cited section at the end of your essay (MLA) or the References section (APA). You must cite secondary sources, whether you quote from them directly, summarize them, paraphrase them, or just refer to them in passing by using the style preferred by your discipline.

You may occasionally use brackets to explain an unfamiliar term within a direct quotation:

> Emergency room nurse Judith McAllen said, "we triage [prioritize by severity of injury] patients if it's a non-emergency, and don't treat them on the basis of their arrival time."

Avoid the use of brackets any more than is strictly necessary.

Inserting "sic" (which means "thus") between square brackets tells the reader that what immediately precedes [sic] occurs in the original exactly the way it appears in your quotation. One use of [sic] is to call attention to an error in the original:

> As people often say, "Vive le différence!" [sic].

[Sic] here calls attention to the article error: "le" should be "la." In APA documentation style, italicize "*sic*" within brackets: [*sic*].

Punctuate a direct quotation exactly as it is punctuated in the original, but do not include any punctuation in the original that comes *after* the quoted material. Note the omission of the original comma after "recklessness."

Parentheses would be incorrect in the passages to the right. Parentheses, like dashes, are a form of punctuation (or may explain or expand on something, as these parentheses do); square brackets (usually just called "brackets") tell the reader that a change has been made to the original passage or that something has been inserted.

Original:

"Any accounting of male-female differences must include the male's superior recklessness, a drive, not, I think, towards death. . . ."

Directly Quoted:

In his essay "The Disposable Rocket," John Updike states that "[a]ny accounting of male-female differences must include the male's superior recklessness."

◎ Documentation: Citations

Necessary versus Unnecessary Citations

You now know *what* needs to be documented; basic APA and MLA guidelines for *how* to document follow in Chapter 12. However, understanding *where* and *when* to document can also be confusing. If you document too much, your paper will not flow well. However, if you do not properly document your in-text sources, you will be plagiarizing.

Parenthetical citations (the parentheses you see after a quotation, paraphrase, or summary that contain bibliographic information) are intended to convey as *much* information as possible about the source while interfering as *little* as possible with the essay's content and readability. The general rule is that you cite enough to give the reader the information needed, while avoiding unneeded citations. If it is clear what specific source is being referred to without a citation, do not give one.

Do not cite every statement or fact from a source if you use that one source for consecutive references. In fact, you can sometimes combine a few references from the same source in one citation. For example, let's say you used three pages from your source, Jackson. When you were finished drawing from that source, you could refer to a page range: "(Jackson 87–89)." This citation would tell the reader that you used that one source continuously for three of her pages—perhaps one idea came from page 87, two facts from page 88, and a paraphrased passage from page 89. However, if your own or another source's information intervened, you would need to cite Jackson more than once.

> Parenthetical citations are intended to convey as *much* information as possible about the source while interfering as *little* as possible with the essay's content and readability.

◎ Sample Student Research Essay

In the following essay, the writer, Simon Walter, uses some of the different methods discussed above to integrate sources. He has used the MLA style for citation, which will be explained in further detail in Chapter 12. The outline of this essay is on pages 190–4. Post-reading questions follow the essay. Note that due to space restrictions, the essay does not follow standard essay format, which you will find in Chapter 17.

The Virtual Life: An Overview of the Effects of MMORPGs on Individuals and Countries
By Simon Walter

In the *South Park* episode "Make Love, Not Warcraft," Stan's father says, "you've been on your computer all weekend. Shouldn't you go out and socialize with your friends?" Stan, from his computer, angrily replies "I *am* socializing! I'm logged on to an MMORPG with people from all over the world getting EXP with my party using Teamspeak." Though sometimes crude in its contemporary satire, *South Park* tackles serious issues, and their ridicule of *World of Warcraft*, the most popular online game to date, is one such issue. The increasing popularity of online gaming today begs the question: when worlds are created online, what befalls the offline one?

MMORPGs (Massively Multiplayer Online Role-Playing Games) are recent developments; the first modern MMORPG was released by a South Korean Company in 1996 (Jin and Chee 38). Thus, the current generation of gamers has received the first exposure to these massive online worlds and, consequently, will be the first to feel their effects. Consumer reception has been astounding; the popular MMORPG *Everquest* makes more than $5 million per month in subscription fees—revenue unheard of in any other gaming genre (Day 111). With the realization that incredible profits can be made, researchers are finally receiving enough company funding to regain ground against the anti-videogame movements of China, the United States, and other developed countries (Golub and Lingley 66; Anderson and Dill 774). In the modern world, the effects of online gaming are a relatively new area of study; some countries are beginning to criticize the MMORPG genre as an unhealthy pastime for socioeconomic reasons, but this criticism is often the product of rumour rather than research. As of now, countries are ambivalent about the MMORPG issue, and this indicates the need for objective research to find reliable results in lieu of international speculation.

Unlike first-person shooters or real-time strategy games, MMORPGs are "persistent state worlds." The game does not stop when the player does; the world continues whether one is logged in or not (Day 111). Success becomes time-dependent. Players, in order to be better than others, must log more game-time than other players. As Yee notes, the game is functioning twenty-four hours a day; server operating costs are exorbitant, and "pay to play" monthly subscriptions are typical of the genre

("The Labor of Fun" 70). Gamers are in control of a character with various skillsets. The tasks associated with improving a character in an MMORPG are often repetitive and simple, demanding large quantities of time for improvement. Attributes, equipment, and wealth are gained through trading, hunting creatures, and producing goods. This often demands hours of a player's time before his or her character is competitive with others on the server. The most powerful items in the game are often rare and exclusively available as treasure from the most powerful creatures. This makes "raids" and "quests"—parties of players hunting together—an intrinsic part of the MMORPG genre. According to Putnam (qtd. in Williams), "time spent in front of [the computer] is time spent away from human contact" (14). However, the social aspect of the game is a defining characteristic of the genre: massive intersections of humanity trade, fight, and socialize in MMORPGs. Most feature complex, player-driven economies as important to the game as the stock exchange to the real world, including the sale of rare weapons, staple items, and unique skills; this can lead one to question the asocial stigmata associated with gaming. *Star Wars Galaxies*, an older MMORPG, permits users to produce pharmaceuticals:

> Everything that is bought or sold has to be bought or sold by another player.... Manufacturers must decide how broad or narrow their product line should be, how to price and brand their products... whether to start a price war with competitors or form a cartel with them.... It takes about 3 to 6 weeks of normal game play to acquire the abilities and schematics to be competitive in the market, and the business operation thereafter requires daily time commitment. (Yee, "The Labour of Fun" 69)

This large amount of time dedicated to life-like endeavours (amassing wealth, developing skills, conversing and journeying with friends) sets MMORPGs apart from any other game genre. The virtual world of an MMORPG never ends, and one's success is measured against other players' wealth, skill, and experience—all attributes that are achieved through time and dedicated play.

This staggering time demand has prompted the United States to oppose MMORPGs. Gaming as a whole is interpreted as an impediment to normal youth development both socially and physically. The anti–video games movement links gaming to poverty, increased aggression, obesity, and even physical addiction (Anderson and Dill 788). However, Nicholas Yee argues that, according to his findings, "there is no one discrete point where a player becomes suddenly addicted.... The claims that MMORPGs are completely healthy or completely addictive are both extreme to the point of absurdity, and are not supported by the empirical data provided"

(Continued)

("Ariadne—Understanding MMORPG Addiction" 7). Yee has headed the Daedalus Project, a continuing study of the psychological effects of MMORPGs on gamers, which has spanned six years and involved 40,000 MMORPG players (*The Daedalus Project*). Though gaming is undoubtedly a sedentary practice, MMORPG players are no more at risk of physical problems than gamers of another genre. Earlier research indicated gaming takes an individual's time away from family and friends; from this, researchers extrapolated the theory that simply *because* they consume more time, MMORPGs are more threatening to the American family. New findings, however, suggest that the decline of arcades, bowling, and other offline activities has encouraged online gaming's rise to popularity in America (Williams 15). It is evident that the United States is only just beginning to see the benefit of legitimate research into online gaming.

Unlike the US, which believes MMORPGs hazardous to the individual, China sees MMORPGs as a threat to national stability. Social venues—bars, coffeehouses, community halls, cybercafés, and even churches—constitute "third places" (Williams 14), social areas that are not home or work. The People's Republic of China fears that MMORPGs will become the next "third place" (Golub and Lingley 66). In a government like China's, the existence of a "social sphere" outside of government censorship that ignores international borders could constitute a threat to national sovereignty and state control (66). China is, therefore, in the process of actively demonizing the practice of online gaming and stigmatizing its players: "Gaming addiction is likened to addictive drugs, not only at the level of the individual; it is also regarded as a social problem.... [T]he Internet is therefore linked not simply to addictive drugs in general but to opium and opium's long association with a wide range of social problems in China" (63). In short, China views online gaming as a new breed of opium: a substance that made the Chinese and their culture subservient to both Europeans and the Japanese in the 19th century during the Qing Dynasty (64). With the number of individuals online increasing exponentially, the Chinese fear that the next generation of youth will define themselves through online means that require independence from parents, the traditional wellspring of Chinese values (69). With the One Child Policy already creating a contracting population, it is easy to see why the last thing China needs is the MMORPG. Their youth may develop under reduced national influence in the face of a transnational world inside MMORPGs and the Internet; their diminished working class may end up spending valuable time and money on a foreign game company—money and time consequently exported out of the Chinese economy. The MMORPG and the virtual medium it provides are thought to undermine Chinese sovereignty.

Though China and the US both oppose MMORPGS, one country has embraced online gaming fully: South Korea. First, gamers have not been marginalized; they are adored like North American sports stars, and it is possible to live opulently as a professional cyber-athlete there.[1] As of March 2007, 89.4 percent of South Korean households were connected to broadband Internet. Of those, 74.6 percent confirmed the connection had been used for online games (Jin and Chee 46). Second, South Korea was the home of the first modern MMORPG, *Kingdom of the Winds*, in 1996 (38). Therefore, one would assume South Korea would be the first to suffer its effects, yet the negative response of China and the US has not occurred in South Korea. This could be because South Korea's online game industry has allowed foreign investment through the "transnationalization" of its domestic online game industry (45). It was one of the first industries to be recognized as a means of stimulating the economy during the Asian economic crisis of 1997, continues to be subsidized by the South Korean government, and is hailed by popular culture as an economic saviour (47). Whether the same physical and psychological negatives that have been widely publicized in other countries are present in Korean youth is hard to determine because research has been superficial with a more "celebratory emphasis [on] positive business... due primarily to the accelerated pace of development" (39). In short, South Korea partly owes its developed status, stable economy, and next-generation identity to the development of its online gaming industry; why bite the hand that feeds you? South Korea provides compelling evidence that MMORPGS are not all negative. In fact, for a country that needed to break out of an economic crisis and join the technology movement of the 21st century, they were a godsend.

To find controversy concerning MMORPGS, one merely has to compare countries. Reception of the new genre is not evenly spread worldwide. Panic in North America over obesity, sedentary lifestyles, and socially isolated youth has increased with the introduction of a more time-consuming videogame. On the other side of the world, China views the international nature of MMORPGS and the Internet as a political and socioeconomic threat. Meanwhile, South Korea continues to enjoy a cultural revolution and an economic boom in the 21st century. While research has shown

---

[1] South Korea is particularly fond of the real-time strategy game *Starcraft* and televises matches between the most skilled players.

(Continued)

that perceived health hazards during gaming are a diagnosable phenomenon, more recent research suggests MMORPGs are no more dangerous than any other genre. While their characteristics make them a more time-dependent hobby, no substantial evidence suggests that MMORPGs are more or less harmful than another type of game. Furthermore, negative traits expressed by individual players associated with the genre are minimal and open to interpretation. Thankfully, the presence of more in-depth research on the horizon may clarify the costs and benefits of MMORPG use, perhaps even putting current controversy to rest.

Works Cited

Anderson, Craig A., and Karen E. Dill. "Videogames and Aggressive Thoughts, Feelings, and Behaviour in the Laboratory and in Life." *Journal of Personality and Social Psychology* 78.4 (2000): 772–90. Print.

Day, Grantley. "Online Games: Crafting Persistent-State Worlds." *Entertainment Computing* 34.10 (2001): 111–12. Web. 1 Mar. 2009.

Golub, Alex, and Kate Lingley. "'Just Like the Qing Empire': Internet Addiction, MMORPGs, and Moral Crisis in Contemporary China." *Games and Culture* 3.1 (2008): 59–75. Web. 4 March 2009.

Jin, Dal Y., and Florence Chee. "Age of New Media Empires: A Critical Interpretation of the Korean Online Game Industry." *Games and Culture* 3.1 (2008): 38–58. Web. 4 Mar. 2009.

"Make Love, Not Warcraft." Writ. Trey Parker and Matt Stone. *South Park*. Comedy Central. 4 Oct. 2006. Television.

Williams, Dmitri. "Why Game Studies Now? Gamers Don't Bowl Alone." *Games and Culture* 1.1 (2006): 13–16. Web. 1 Mar. 2009.

Yee, Nick. "Ariadne—Understanding MMORPG Addiction." 2002. Web. 1 Mar. 2009. <http://www.nickyee.com/hub/addiction/home.html>.

— — —. *The Daedalus Project*. Palo Alto Research Center. 2007. Web. 4 Mar. 2009. <http://www.nickyee.com/index-daedalus.html>.

— — —. "The Labor of Fun: How Videogames Blur the Boundaries of Work and Play." *Games and Culture* 1.1 (2006): 68–71. Web. 1 Mar. 2009.

Post-reading Questions

1. Go through the essay and identify the different ways the writer incorporated his sources. Find two examples each of direct quotation, paraphrase, summary, and mixed format.

2. Did the writer rely too much on one particular method for integrating his sources? Explain why you think he did or did not, pointing to specific instances.

3. Find at least two examples each of ellipses, indicating material omitted from a direct quotation, and brackets, indicating changes to a direct quotation.

4. How effective was the essay's introductory paragraph? Why do you think the writer chose to quote from a popular television program?

5. How much background information does Walter give about his topic? What does this tell you about his intended audience?

6. Do you think the writer presented both sides of the debate fairly and reliably?

7. Look at the Works Cited list. Do you feel that Walter has included enough sources? Do they seem reliable? Be specific.

Exercise 11.1

Look through a textbook from one of the courses you enjoy. Find a section that you think you could write an essay about. Choose five or six passages that you could use for this essay. Then, using the techniques for integrating sources discussed in this chapter, create direct quotations, summaries, paraphrases, and examples of mixed format for these passages.

Exercise 11.2

Using the sources from Exercise 11.1, create an outline for a research essay.

Chapter Review Questions

1. Why is outlining an important part of essay writing?
2. Why is it crucial to cite your sources?
3. What kind of information does not require a citation?
4. Summarize in two or three sentences the paragraphs under the heading "What Is Plagiarism?" on pages 194–5.
5. What are the three main ways of integrating information from a source? What are their differences?
6. When should you avoid direct quotations in essays? When should you use them?
7. What are signal phrases and why are they important?
8. What is the "mixed format" method of source integration?
9. How could you indicate a grammatical change to a direct quotation in order to integrate it smoothly with your own writing?
10. What are ellipses and when should you use them?

12

APA and MLA Documentation Styles

In this chapter, you will

- learn how to cite sources according to APA and MLA styles

- learn how to create a References page and a Works Cited page

- see examples of writing using APA and MLA styles

As you saw in Chapters 10 and 11, when you write a research essay, you need to add information from outside sources to help support your points. While the previous chapter dealt with how to integrate these sources into your essay, this chapter will introduce you to the two major citation methods, the APA and MLA styles, enabling you to give proper credit to your sources. Common formats, including electronic ones, are shown with examples of each. APA and MLA sample essays are included to illustrate how to correctly use these styles in your own essays.

◎ Choosing Your Citation Style

The purposes of citations and references are

- To give appropriate credit to the work of others.
- To establish your own credibility as a researcher.
- To show where your own work fits into other work in the field.
- To avoid plagiarism, a form of theft, and certainly one of the most serious academic crimes with severe penalties for anyone who knowingly or unknowingly plagiarizes.
- To enable readers (such as markers) to trace or verify your sources.
- To find the reference again if you need it for further research.
- To enlarge on a matter (in a footnote or endnote) that would be disruptive if placed in the text.

Handbooks are published for both APA and MLA citation styles (as well as many other styles) and contain extensive guidelines for use. However, usage rules are updated every five years or so. This is done for a variety of reasons. For example, in the 1980s, the Internet did not exist as the research tool we have today. Therefore, rules had to be adapted to fit the changing technology and the ways people retrieved information. Even the change to Web 2.0 has created new procedures, as websites are no longer static and contain a broader range of materials that can be used as sources for essays.

College and university libraries provide a range of current style manuals. When using the manuals, ensure that you have the most up-to-date edition. If you want to purchase your own book, be aware that older editions and second-hand copies may not provide accurate rules.

Different areas of academia favour distinct styles. Below is a list of some of the more common areas. However, your department or your instructor should be the final guide in your choice of citation style.

APA (American Psychological Association)

- Business
- Education
- Psychology
- Social sciences and some sciences

MLA (Modern Language Association)

- English literature
- Philosophy
- Religion

CSE (Council of Science Editors)

- Science

In addition to the major styles, some subject areas have their own style specifications:

- Chemistry
- Engineering
- History
- Mathematics
- Medicine
- Music
- Sociology

Although there are many subtle differences among the various styles, the main elements of a citation usually include

1. the name(s) of the author(s)
2. the page number or a similar locator of the information cited
3. the year of publication
4. other publication details

Most styles require an abbreviated citation in the sentence where the reference appears. In parenthetical styles, the information is enclosed in parentheses. Further details are given in an alphabetized list at the end of the essay under a heading such as References, Works Cited, or Bibliography. The following references have been styled according to the rules of each handbook or manual.

Humanities: The Modern Language Association. *MLA Handbook for Writers of Research Papers.* 7th ed. New York: The Modern Language Association, 2009. Print.

Social Sciences: American Psychological Association. (2010). *Publication Manual of the American Psychological Association* (6th ed.). Washington, D.C.: Author.

◎ The Major Documentation Styles

In the following APA and MLA sections, the basic standards for documenting sources are shown with examples to illustrate format. For examples not given below, you can check updates on the APA and MLA websites. As well, you can consult a college or university reference librarian or your instructor for hard-to-find formats.

However, if you use an online site for help, always double-check the information with one or more other sites, taking note of when the website was updated, if possible. If you have run out of resources, or simply do not have more time to spend on the citations chase, common sense suggests you adapt the rule closest to your particular case.

> APA and MLA are both parenthetical styles, meaning that parentheses are used to enclose brief bibliographical information about the source.

APA Citation Style

In the social sciences, the principal documentation style has been developed by the American Psychological Association (APA). It is sometimes used in the sciences as well. The APA publishes a manual (*Publication Manual of the American Psychological*

Association, 6th ed.) and maintains a website (http://www. apastyle.org) that offers updates, FAQs, and specific information on Internet citations.

APA style is parenthetical, meaning that whenever you directly quote or paraphrase an author in your essay, or use an author's idea, you include the author's last name and the year of the work in parentheses; you will usually include page number(s) as well. Then, you will provide a more complete description of all the sources on the final page(s) of your essay, titled "References."

APA In-text Citations

Guidelines

> APA in-text style includes author's last name, year of publication, and, usually, page number(s).

- APA in-text formats include author(s) and year. If the author is named in a signal phrase (e.g., "Ashton found that. . .";" . . . according to Hoffman"), the year follows the author's name and precedes the verb: "Ashton (2008) found that. . .";" . . . according to Hoffman (1998)." Otherwise, the publication year follows the author's name in the end parentheses: "(Ashton, 2008)."
- A specific reference, such as a direct quotation or paraphrase, requires a page number. Use the abbreviation "p." for "page" and "pp." for "pages."
- Use commas to separate items in the citation.

Specifics

Citation after a direct quotation. Give the last name of author(s), a comma, year of publication, a comma, and page number(s) all in parentheses:

No signal phrase:

> During World Wars I and II, the Canadian government often employed masseuses because surgery and medical care were insufficient "to restore severely wounded men" (Cleather, 1995, p. ix).

The author, Cleather, is not named in a signal phrase, so the parenthetical citation includes the author's name.

You can use a signal phrase to set up your reference (see page 200). After the author is named in the signal phrase, follow with the year. The page number is placed at the end of the reference.

Signal phrase:

> According to Stambouli and Traversa (2002), "each gallon of gasoline produced and used in an internal combustion engine releases roughly 12 kg of CO_2" (p. 299).

Stambouli and Traversa are named in the signal phrase "According to Stambouli and Traversa (2002)," so the parenthetical citation consists only of the page number. Note that the year follows the authors' names.

Block quotation. A quotation that is at least 40 words is placed on a new line and indented one half-inch from the left margin. Quotation marks are not used, and the quotation is double-spaced. The author's name, the year of publication, and the page number appear in parentheses at the end of the quotation *after* the final period.

. (Ellis & Bochner, 2000, pp. 81–82)

Citation for a specific reference (such as a paraphrase). State the last name of author(s), year of publication, and the page number(s) in parentheses:

> Most of the profits from BC's aquaculture industry go to Norwegians, who control 92 percent of the industry (Macdonald, 2009, pp. 148–149).

A paraphrase includes all the content of the source put entirely in your own words. When you paraphrase material, your citation must include the page number.

Citation for a non-specific reference. An example of a non-specific reference might be an author's thesis statement or the main findings of a study. It will apply to the essay as a whole rather than to a specific page in the work. Give the last name of author(s) and the year of publication in parentheses.

> Conservation biologists agree that protecting habitats is the most effective way to conserve biological diversity (Primack, 2000).

You do not include a page number in a citation that refers to the work as a whole rather than to specific page(s).

The information does not come from a specific page.

Citation referring to an indirect source. If it is necessary to refer to a source found in another work, include the original author in the sentence, along with the name(s) in parentheses of the source of the information. This is followed by the phrase "as cited in" and year of publication. In the References section, list the details for the indirect source.

> Francis Bacon (as cited in Lindemann, 2001) observed that language affects our thinking when he said that "words react on the understanding" (p. 93).

An indirect source is one that is cited in another source. Always prefer original sources, but if you have to cite information from an indirect source, make sure you use the phrase "as cited in" followed by the place where you got the information.

Personal communication, including interviews. Give the author's name, including first initial(s), the phrase "personal communication," and a date all in parentheses:

> (J. Derrida, personal communication, September 20, 2000).

Note that personal communications are cited only in the text of your essay; they are not listed in the References section.

Multiple sources in one citation. You may cite more than one relevant source in a single citation if the point you are making applies to both. Order the sources alphabetically by last name and separate them by a semicolon.

You may include more than one source in a single citation. Separate sources by semicolons.

> The practices of teaching composition in college have not radically changed in the last few decades (Bishop, 2005; Williams, 2007).

APA In-text Citations by Format

Kinds of Authors

Work by one author (book or article). In parentheses, give the author's last name, a comma, year of publication, a comma, and page number(s) (if required). Note that a book with an author and an editor will usually be cited by author.

(Bloom, 2002, p. xviii).

Work by two authors. State the last names of both authors with an ampersand (&) between them, a comma, a date, a comma, and a page number in parentheses:

(Higgins & Wilson-Baptist, 1999, p. 44).

When naming the authors *in the text* of your essay, as in a signal phrase, use the word "and" instead of an ampersand:

Higgins and Wilson-Baptist (1999) argue that "a tourist exists outside of experience. A traveller, though, submerges herself in the new" (p. 44).

Works by three, four, or five authors. List the last names of all authors in parentheses for the first citation. Later citations need the last name of the first author followed by the abbreviation "et al." with the publication year in parentheses. If the authors are mentioned more than once in a paragraph, the year of publication is not included after the first reference.

> When you refer to a work with more than one author in a citation, use an ampersand (&) to separate the last author's name from the preceding name.

(Higgins, Wilson-Baptist, & Krasny, 2001)
second citation in the paragraph: (Higgins et al.)

Work by six or more authors. State the last name of the first author followed by the abbreviation "et al.", a comma, and the publication year in parentheses:

> To cite six or more authors, give the name of the first author followed by "et al."

(Terracciano et al., 2005)

Two or more works by the same author in the same year. Add an alphabetical letter in lower case (a, b, c) to distinguish works chronologically in that year:

. . . self enforced discipline (Foucault, 1980a, p. 37)

The "a" after the year, above, indicates that you have used at least two works by the same author in 1980 and that this is the first published work.

Two authors with the same last name. Include the authors' first initial(s) separated from the last names by commas:

(Sinkinson, S. & Sinkinson, B., 2001, pp. 225–237)

Group or organization as author (corporate author). Documents published by companies and government departments may not list an author. If the group title is long or is well known by an acronym or abbreviation of the name (for example, The United Nations Children's Fund is commonly known as UNICEF), for the first citation include, in parentheses, the entire title where the author's name would appear; follow with the acronym in square brackets, a comma, and the year of publication. Use the abbreviation with the year of publication throughout the rest of the paper. If the group name is not well-known, use the full name with publication year each time.

> (American Educational Research Association [AERA], 2001)
> later citations: (AERA, 2001)

Work with an unknown author (including many dictionary and encyclopedia articles). Put the first few words of the title of an article or chapter in quotation marks and follow with a comma, and the year of publication.

> ("Plea to City Hall," 2003)

Author designated as "Anonymous." Cited in the same way as a named author:

> (Anonymous, 1887, p. 12)

APA In-text Citations: Electronic Sources

The most challenging aspect of citing online documents is that they often lack page numbers. If paragraph numbers are given, cite by paragraph number preceded by the abbreviation "para." If neither page nor paragraph numbers are available but the document includes section headings, cite the heading title in quotation marks and include the paragraph number(s) in which the material occurs.

Sample in-text Internet citation. Include author's last name, a comma, the year the site was mounted or updated, a comma, a heading title (if applicable), a comma, and page or paragraph number in parentheses:

> (Gregoire, 2000, "Bones and Teeth," para. 5)

Internet site without an author or without a date. Use the title or an abbreviated form of the title in quotation marks, a comma, the year the site was mounted or updated, a comma, and a page or paragraph reference. Use the abbreviation "n.d." if the date that the site was created is absent.

> ("Muchinfo's Poll," 2002, para. 16)
> (Hannak, n.d., para. 2)

Sidebar notes:

If no author is given, use the name of the group or organization in place of the author's name.

Many articles retrieved from a database are viewed as Portable Document Format (PDF) files. In such cases, use the page numbers in the document. They are usually the same as the page numbers of the print version if one exists.

If you cannot locate page or paragraph numbers in an electronic document, give the section heading in quotation marks and count by paragraphs from the heading to the paragraph(s) that the information is from.

APA In-text Citations: Non-textual Sources

Film, video, audio, TV broadcasts, and musical recordings. Use the most senior production person's name, a comma, and the year of public release or broadcast in parentheses:

(Coppola, 1979)

Installation, event, performance, or work of art. Use the format followed by other non-textual resources, such as name of artist(s), a comma, and a date of showing or creation:

(Byrdmore, 2006)

APA Citations in the References Section

In APA style, the References page(s) containing complete retrieval information appears at the end of your essay and begins on a new page that continues the numbers of your essay. The References list is double-spaced, with a one-inch margin. Omit redundant words like "Publishers," "Inc.," and "Co." after publisher name, but write out complete names of associations, corporations, and university presses. Some of the most common abbreviations include

- ed. (edition)
- Ed. (Editor), Eds. (Editors)
- No. (Number)
- p. (page), pp. (pages)
- para. (paragraph)
- Pt. (Part)
- Rev. ed. (Revised edition)
- Trans. (Translator[s])
- Vol. (Volume), Vols. (Volumes)

Guidelines

- The title is centred an inch from the top of the page.
- The list is alphabetized by author's last name; each entry begins flush left with the margin; subsequent lines are indented half an inch from the margin. Items are not numbered.
- The standard APA citation begins with the author's last name followed by initial(s), not given name(s). Titles of full-length works are italicized.
- Capitalize the following elements of work titles: the first word, the first word after a colon, all proper nouns, and acronyms like NFB or CBC, regardless of how the original is capitalized. Titles of *journals* do not follow the capitalization rules for book and article titles.

Sample book entry. List book and report data in the following sequence: author, date of publication, title of book, place of publication, publisher:

Fries, C. C. (1962). *Linguistics and reading*. New York, NY: Holt, Rinehart & Winston.

Sample journal entry. List journal article data in the following sequence: author, date of publication, title of article, title of journal (italicized), volume number (italicized), issue number (if required), page range, and DOI or URL:

Valkenburg, P. M. & Jochen, P. (2007). Who visits online dating sites? Exploring some characteristics of online daters. *CyberPsychology and Behavior, 10*, 849–852. doi:10.1089/cpb.2007.9941

A "DOI" (digital object identifier) is included in many journal articles whether in print or electronic format. It enables readers to locate documents throughout the Internet. See page 223.

Kinds of Authors

Work by one author. See above, "Sample book entry."

Work by two authors. Use an ampersand (&) to separate the authors, and invert the names of both authors with commas between last name and initial and before the ampersand to separate both names. Conclude with a period:

Luckner, J., & Nadler, R. (1992). *Processing the experience*. Dubuque, IA: Kendall/Hunt Publishing.

Work by three to seven authors. List all the authors:

Festial, L., Ian, H., & Gomez, S. (1956). *When economics fails*. Minneapolis, MN: University of Minnesota Press.

Work by eight or more authors. List the first six authors and the last author with three points of ellipses (. . .) between the sixth and the final author:

Terracciano, A., Abdel-Khalek, A. M., Ádám, N., Adamovová, L., Ahn, C.-K., Ahn, H.-N., . . . McCrae, R. R. (2005). National character does not reflect mean personality trait levels in 49 cultures. *Science, 310*, 96–100. doi:10.1126/science.1117199

Two or more works by the same author. Works by the same author are arranged chronologically, earliest to latest. Works with the same publication year are arranged alphabetically by first major word of the title. Below, the earliest article is listed first; the "h" in "history" precedes the "P" in "Power," justifying the order of the second and third items.

The order for most final-page citations is author's last name and initial(s); publication date; title of work; and publication details, which vary depending on whether the work is a book, journal article, or electronic document.

With two to seven authors, invert all authors' names and use an ampersand (&) between the last and the second-last name.

Unless there are more than seven authors of the article, include all authors' names in the citation.

Foucault, M. (1977). *Discipline and punish: The birth of the prison.* A. Sheridan (Trans.). New York, NY: Random House.

Foucault, M. (1980). *The history of sexuality,* (Vol. 1). R. Hurley (Trans.). New York, NY: Random House.

Foucault, M. (1980). *Power/Knowledge: Selected interviews and other writings 1972–1977.* C. Gordon (Ed.). Brighton, England: Harvester Press.

Work by two authors with the same last name. Alphabetical order of initials determines sequence. If two works have the same first authors, the order is determined by the last name of the second author.

Jason, L. A., & Klich, M. M. (1982). Use of feedback in reducing television watching. *Psychological Reports, 51,* 812–814.

Jason, L. A., & Rooney-Rebeck, P. (1984). Reducing excessive television viewing. *Child & Family Behavior Therapy, 6,* 61–69.

Group or organization as author (corporate author). Use the full group name in place of the author's name. If the organization name begins with an article (e.g., "The"), omit it.

> When a work has a group author, rather than an individual author, the group name takes the place of the author's name.

Education International. (2008). *Guide to universities & colleges in Canada.* Victoria, BC: EI Education International.

Work with an unknown author (non-electronic source), such as an entry in a reference book. List alphabetically by the first major word in the title. When an author is listed as "Anonymous," alphabetize by the letter "A."

> When there is no author in a non-electronic source, the entry is listed alphabetically by the first major word in the title. (This does not include words such as "The.")

Interveners. (1993). In *Canadian Encyclopedia* (Vol. 11, pp. 344–348). Ottawa. ON: Smith Press.

No date: Replace date in parentheses by "n.d."

Source Type

Work with an editor. Begin with the editor(s) name followed by "Ed." (one editor) or "Eds." (more than one editor) in parentheses:

Corcoran, B., Hayhoe, M., & Pradl, G. M. (Eds.). (1994). *Knowledge in the making: Challenging the text in the classroom.* Portsmouth, NH: Boynton/Cook.

Chapter or other type of selection, such as an essay, in edited volume. Begin with author name, year, and chapter (or essay) title. Follow with name(s) of book editor(s), not inverted and preceded by "In." The abbreviation "Ed.(s.)" follows, and the citation concludes with book title, page range (in parentheses), and publication information.

> The usual order for an essay or other selection in an edited book is author name, year, essay title, book editor's name preceded by "In," the abbreviation "Ed.," book title and page range, and other publication details.

Sanders, D. E. (1984). Some current issues affecting Indian government. In L. Little Bear, M. Boldt, & J. A. Long (Eds.), *Pathways to self-determination: Canadian Indians and the Indian state* (pp. 113–21). Toronto, ON: University of Toronto Press.

Translated work. The translator's name is placed in parentheses after the work's title and is followed by "Trans."

Lacan, J. (1977). *Écrits: A selection*. (A. Sheridan, Trans.). New York, NY: W. W. Norton. (Original work published 1966)

To cite a republished book in the text of your essay, use both original and current publication dates:

(Lacan, 1966/1977)

Volume in multivolume work. Include the volume number after the title:

Bosworth, A. B. (Ed.). (1995). *A historical commentary on Arrian's history of Alexander* (Vol. 1). London, England: Oxford University Press.

If referring to more than one volume, give the specific volumes or range (e.g., Vols. 1–3).

Second or subsequent edition of a work. Include the edition number after the title:

Suzuki, D. T., Griffiths, A. J., & Lewontin, R. C. (1989). *An introduction to genetic analysis* (4th ed.). New York, NY: W. H. Freeman.

> If there is a new edition of the work, include the edition number in parentheses after the title.

Article in a journal with continuous pagination. If the numbering continues from the previous issue, include the volume but not the issue number. Page numbers in journals are not preceded by "p." or "pp."

Garner, R. (2003). Political ideologies and the moral status of animals. *Journal of Political Ideologies, 8*, 233–246.

> Whether you include the issue number in a citation depends on whether each issue is numbered separately (include issue number) or the numbering continues from the previous issue (do not include issue number).

Article in a journal that is paginated by issue. If every issue begins with the number "1," include both volume (italicized) and issue number (in parentheses and not italicized).

Trew, J. D. (2002). Conflicting visions: Don Messier, Liberal nationalism, and the Canadian unity debate. *International Journal of Canadian Studies, 26*(2), 41–57.

Article in a magazine. Cite the complete date beginning with the year; follow with a comma and the month or month and day. Include the volume and issue number if available.

> Knapp, L. (2007, September/October). Licensing music to the film and television industries. *Canadian Musician, 29*(5), 49–56.

Article in a newspaper. List the author if given; if no author, begin with the title. The abbreviation "p." or "pp." is used for newspapers. If the article breaks off and continues later in the work, give all page numbers, separated by commas, or the page range. A letter to the editor or editorial follows the same format and includes specific information in square brackets after the title: e.g., "[Letter to the editor]."

> Lawyer seeks mistrial for client accused of illegal midwifery. (2003, April 20). *National Post*, p. A8.

Unlike journal and magazine articles, newspaper articles require the abbreviation "p." (page) or "pp." (pages) with all page numbers included. The exact publication date is given (i.e., year, month day).

Book/movie review. Follow article format but include in brackets the title of the book and the reviewer's name preceded by "Review of" and the medium: e.g., "[Review of the DVD...]".

> Mihm, S. (2009). Swindled: The dark history of food fraud, from poisoned candy to counterfeit coffee [Review of the book *Swindled: The dark history of food fraud, from poisoned candy to counterfeit coffee*, by B. Wilson]. *Business History Review, 83*(2), 379–381.

Government document. If the author is unknown, begin with the name of the government followed by the agency (e.g., ministry, department, crown corporation) and the document name:

> British Columbia. Office of the Auditor General. 2005. *Salmon forever: An assessment of the provincial role in sustaining wild salmon*. Victoria, BC: Author.

Because the publisher is the same as the author (i.e., Office of the Auditor General of British Columbia), "Author" replaces the publisher's name in the example above.

In cases or reports, such as government documents, the report number can be placed after the work's title: (e.g., "Research Report No. 09.171").

Indirect source. List the work the citation comes from, not the original text. See page 215.

Because they cannot be reproduced or verified, personal communications (including emails, phone calls, interviews, and conversations) are not included in the list of references.

Personal communication. Because they cannot be reproduced or verified, personal communications (including emails, phone calls, interviews, and conversations) are not included in the list of references.

APA Internet Citations in the References Section

The 6th edition of the APA manual recommends that online sources include the elements of print sources in the same order with exact location information added as needed. If available, include the DOI, which is found with other publication information, such as journal title and volume number, and/or on the first page of the article. The DOI is a number–alphabet sequence that begins with "10." It forms the last element in your citation sequence and, like a Uniform Resource Locator (URL), is *not* followed by a period.

Since not all publishers use this system, cite the URL using the home page of the journal or book publisher if the DOI is unavailable or if your instructor tells you to do so. If the document would be hard to locate from the home page, provide the exact URL or as much as is needed for retrieval. APA does not usually require your date of access for Internet sources, but you should confirm electronic links before including them in your paper. More information on electronic reference formats recommended by the APA is available at http://www.apastyle.org/elecref. html.

Sample electronic reference. Citation formats follow those of print sources with the title of the website replacing the journal title.

> Czekaj, L. (2009, February 7). Promises fulfilled: Looking at the legacy of thousands of black slaves who fled to Canada in the 1800s. *InnovationCanada.ca.* Retrieved from http://www. innovationcanada.ca/en/

Note the absence of a period after the URL. If it is necessary to break the URL from one line to the next, break *before punctuation*, such as the period before "innovationcanada" above; never use a hyphen to break a URL unless it is part of the URL.

Group or organization (e.g., corporate or government) **website**. If there is no author, list by the organization's name:

> Environment Canada. (August 12, 2009). 10 things you should know about climate change. Retrieved from http://www.ec.gc.ca/cc/default.asp?lang = En&n = 2F049262–1

The complete URL is given because it would be hard to locate the document from the organization's home page.

Article in online-only journal:

> Rye, B. J., Elmslie, P., & Chalmers, A. (2007). Meeting a transsexual person: Experience within a classroom setting. *Canadian On-Line Journal of Queer Studies in Education, 3*(1). Retrieved from http://jps.library.utoronto.ca/index.php/jqstudies/index

The home page of the journal has been used for retrieval information.

Sidebar notes:

APA encourages the use of a DOI (digital object identifier) where available instead of a URL.

Always remove the hyperlink from the URL before printing your essay.

If you use a URL in your citation, make sure you enter it exactly as it appears in the window of your search engine. An inaccurate URL could prevent a reader from locating your source. If you need to break a long URL between one line and the next, break before a mark of punctuation and do not use a hyphen to separate the URL.

If there is a DOI or if there is no DOI and you include the journal home page, the name of the database can be omitted.

Article from a database (with a DOI). The name of the database is not usually required:

> Martel, M. (2009). "They smell bad, have diseases, and are lazy": RCMP officers reporting on hippies in the late sixties. *Canadian Historical Review, 90*, 215–245. doi:10.3138/chr.90.2.215

In the example, above, the first part of the article is in quotation marks, indicating that a direct quotation is part of the title.

Article from a database (no DOI). The home page of the journal is used; the name of the database is not usually required:

> Barton, S. S. (2008). Discovering the literature on aboriginal diabetes in Canada: A focus on holistic methodologies. *Canadian Journal of Nursing Research, 40*(4), 26–54. Retrieved from http://cjnr.mcgill.ca/

No author or date. Place "n.d." in parentheses:

> Hegemony. (n.d.). In *Merriam-Webster online dictionary*. Retrieved from http://www.merriam-webster.com/dictionary/hegemony

Electronic-only book:

> Radford, B. (n.d.). *Soil to social*. Retrieved from http://on-line-books.ora.com/mod-bin/books.mod/javaref/javanut/index.htm

Electronic version of print book. Do not include publication details of the print version but include reader version, if applicable, and either the DOI or URL:

> Douglass, F. (1881). My escape from slavery [MS Reader version]. Retrieved from http://etext.lib.virginia.edu/ebooks/

Message posted to online forum, discussion group, or blog post:

> Koolvedge. (2009, August 8). Reply to massacre in Peru [Web log message]. Retrieved from https://www.adbusters.org/blogs/dispatches/massacre-peru.html#comments

If you use a video blog post, indicate this in square brackets: [Video file].

APA Citations for Non-textual Sources

Lecture or other oral presentation. Include the name of the lecturer, the date (in the order year, month day), the title (or topic) of the lecture, followed by "Lecture presented at" and location detail, such as the sponsoring agency (or department if at a college or university) and/or building name, name of the school, and location of the school:

> Armstrong, M. (2009, April 2). *Darwin's paradox*. Lecture presented at David Strong Building, University of Victoria, Victoria, BC.

Film, video. Use the following order: producer, director, year, and title of film followed by "Motion picture" in square brackets. Conclude by giving the country of origin and studio.

> Coppola, F. F. (Producer & Director). (1979). *Apocalypse now* [Motion picture]. USA: Zoetrope Studios.

Episode from a television series. Use the following order: writer, director, year, and title of episode followed by "Television series episode" in brackets. Conclude by giving the city and broadcasting company.

> Lindelof, D. (Writer), & Bender, J. (Director). (2005). Man of science, man of faith [Television series episode]. In J. J. Abrams (Executive producer), *Lost*. New York, NY: American Broadcasting.

Music. Use the following order: writer, copyright year, and title of song followed by the recording artist in brackets (if different from the writer). Conclude by giving the album title preceded by "On," the medium of recording in brackets, the country of origin, and the label. If the recording date is different from the copyright year, provide this information in parentheses.

> Morrison, V. (1993). Gloria. On *Too long in exile* [CD]. UK. Polydor.

Sample Student Research Essay (APA)

In the following student essay, Erin Walker uses extensive research to investigate a problem in her field of study, social psychology. She cites her sources using APA style.

To conserve space, the essays in this chapter are not double-spaced and the References, Works Cited, and Notes are not on separate pages; in addition, the essay does not follow standard essay format requirements for title pages or identification information (see Chapter 17, Essay Presentation).

The Imperfection of Perfectionism:
Perfectionism as a Maladaptive Personality Trait
By Erin A. Walker

After addressing the common perception of perfectionism, the writer gives one **definition** of the term, explaining, however, that its **connotation** is misleading. Her thesis, like her title, makes it plain she will use research to investigate the problems of one type of perfectionism, "maladaptive perfectionism."

APA Note: Walker refers to an indirect source here. The page reference follows the direct quotation.

In this paragraph, the author uses **compare and contrast**, outlining the kinds of behaviours that separate the two types of perfectionists.

Writing Tip: Walker uses strategies for **coherence** in this paragraph, including **transitions** ("on the other hand," "clearly") and **parallel structures** ("whereas...whereas").

APA Note: When two or more authors are named in the text of your essay, you don't use the ampersand (&) symbol. Notice that the previous citation is only a general one, so no page number is needed. Below, Walker uses a specific reference, so the page number is included.

What does it mean to say that one is a perfectionist? Does it mean that one does everything perfectly? As it is commonly understood, the term "perfectionist" carries the connotation that the perfectionist does everything perfectly, but this is not the case. According to perfectionism experts in social psychology, the term refers to a mentality, or set of cognitions, that are characteristic of certain people. According to Hollender (as cited in Slade & Owens, 1998), perfectionism refers to "the practice of demanding of oneself or others a higher quality of performance than is required by the situation" (p. 384). Although the term might suggest that perfectionism would be a desirable trait, this quality is, in fact, underappreciated and often unrecognized for its harmful effects on the lives of people who are maladaptive perfectionists. Perfectionism not only is associated with mental illness but also can contribute to problems in areas of life such as academic success and intimate relationships.

When research on perfectionism first began, perfectionism as a social psychological construct was conceptualized as two dimensional: there was "normal" perfectionism and "neurotic" perfectionism. Normal perfectionism was characterized by setting realistic standards for oneself, taking pleasure in hard work, and having the capacity to be less selective when necessary. Neurotic perfectionists, on the other hand, set unrealistically high demands for personal achievement, feel chronically dissatisfied with their efforts, and have inflexible personal standards (Hamacheck, 1978). Clearly, normal perfectionism can, at times, be highly adaptive, whereas neurotic perfectionism is typically maladaptive. Normal perfectionism can be an adaptive quality insofar as it propels a person toward excellence and meeting important goals, whereas neurotic perfectionism is maladaptive in that it can foster self-defeating behaviours, concerns over how others view the self, and excessive worry over mistakes (Slade & Owens, 1998). Slade and Owens summarized the similarity and differences between adaptive and maladaptive perfectionism when they wrote,

[f]or both types of perfectionists, the setting of high standards is a common feature. The crucial difference is that the normal perfectionist, when achieving these standards, feels pleased and satisfied, whereas the neurotic perfectionist can never do enough to feel satisfied with his or her performance. (p. 374)

Finally, research by Hewitt and Flett (1991) suggests that there are three dimensions to perfectionism, termed self-oriented perfectionism, other-oriented perfectionism, and socially-prescribed perfectionism. Self-oriented perfectionism, "is not simply the tendency to have high standards for oneself; it also includes the intrinsic need to be perfect and compulsive striving for perfection and self-improvement" (p. 468). Not surprisingly, other-oriented perfectionism is the opposite, with outward-directed perfectionistic expectations. Other-oriented perfectionism, then, is characterized by one "hav[ing] unrealistic standards for significant others, plac[ing] importance on other people being perfect, and stringently evaluat[ing] others' performance" (p. 457). Finally, socially-prescribed perfectionism involves "the perception of other people's imposed expectations... [and] a perceived incontingency between one's own behaviour and the unrealistic standards prescribed by others" (p. 468). Considering the two-dimensional concept of perfectionism described above, other-oriented perfectionism is a new concept, while self-prescribed perfectionism would map on to normal or adaptive perfectionism, and socially-prescribed perfectionism would coincide with neurotic or maladaptive perfectionism (Slade & Owens, 1998, p. 377).

Research on theories of perfectionism has not been as prolific as investigations into the types of perfectionism. However, one conceptualization by Slade and Owens (1998) suggests that perfectionism may have three roots: social contingency, avoidance, and rule-governing. With social contingency, perfectionism may develop upon repeated reinforcement of skilled (or unskilled) behaviour. Otherwise, perfectionism may be an avoidance behaviour, whereby children will over-perform in response to inconsistent parenting, so that they will not have to learn what punishment would result from imperfect achievement. Finally, perfectionism may be a form of rule-governed behaviour, in that a child may infer correctly or incorrectly, through implicit or explicit cues, that only perfectionistic behaviour will be rewarded; as a result, the child will become perfectionistic.

Long direct quotations are set up in **block format**. They are indented and do not include quotation marks. Because a signal phrase was used ("Slade and Owens summarized"), the parenthetical citation includes only the page number.

Writing Tip: In order to deal with complex material, Walker uses the **classification pattern**, discussing three "dimensions," or categories, of perfectionism. She then discusses them in the order they are listed in the **topic sentence**.

APA Note: APA style, often used in the social sciences, particularly psychology, includes the **publication year** in most references; however, when you use a source more than once in the same paragraph, you do not need to repeat the year. Because the same source is used consecutively in this paragraph, only the page numbers are required after the first reference.

Walker uses two sources in this paragraph, integrating them effectively through **summary** and **mixed format**. She uses **brackets** to make necessary grammatical changes. Note that she provides a page reference here as she has paraphrased specific content.

In contrast to the previous paragraph where the specific wording seems important, Walker uses only **summary** here, putting the main ideas in her own words.

(Continued)

Reading Tip: Try to determine the meanings of specialized words like *etiology* and *longitudinal* (in the last sentence of this paragraph) by context. The meanings of other challenging words, like *avert* and *propensity*, can be determined the same way.

APA Note: Multiple sources can be combined in a single citation; semicolons separate the sources.

Reading Tip: Essays using APA style can be hard to read because of the number of multi-authored studies in the social sciences and sciences. A good strategy is to ignore parenthetical citations when you read an article for the first time, returning to them later if you need more information.

Writing Tip: Walker numbers some of her points in this paragraph to make the ideas easier to follow.

After summarizing the research, Walker concludes that one theory is more "plausible" than another.

Notice that all the sources in this paragraph are current ones (in contrast to the previous paragraph, which discussed theories of perfectionism). By looking at the topics of both paragraphs, can you infer the reason for this?

While Slade and Owens (1998) have taken a behaviourist perspective as to the etiology of perfectionism, other researchers have proposed the common psychoanalytic theory of perfectionism arising from faulty parenting. That is, perfectionism results from overly critical (Flett, Hewitt, & Singer, 1995; Frost, Lahart, & Rosenblate, 1991; Rice, Ashby, & Preusser, 1996, as cited in Kawamura, Frost, & Harmatz, 2002), demanding (Rice, Ashby, & Preusser, 1996), and authoritarian (Flett, Hewitt, & Singer, 1995) parenting. Recently, Kawamura, Frost and Harmatz (2002) found that maladaptive perfectionism is associated with authoritarian parenting, and suggested four reasons for this. First, parental approval often determines a child's sense of self-worth, and the child may develop an obsession with perfection as one way to avert parental criticism (Burns, 1980; Driscoll, 1982; as cited in Kawamura, et al., p. 325). Second, it was proposed that after a while, authoritarian parenting may instil in a child a similar propensity for self-criticism. Third, it is possible that authoritarian parenting is merely a mistaken perception on behalf of independently perfectionistic children. Finally, Kawamura et al. proposed that perfectionism may develop as "perfectionists are constantly focused on their own mistakes, [and] can more easily recall instances in which their parents were also harsh and critical in their evaluation of them" (p. 325). Since research on perfectionism only began in earnest approximately 25–30 years ago (Slade & Owens, 1998), there has not yet been longitudinal research that can provide solid evidence for particular types of parenting leading to perfectionism, although logically, a psychoanalytic theory seems most plausible.

Given the nature of perfectionism and its pervasiveness, it is not surprising that recent research has shown associations between perfectionism and mental illness. Research by Rice, Vergara, and Aldea (2006) has found that "[s]elf-critically perfectionistic evaluations were associated with poorer self-regulation capacities and worse adjustment" (p. 469). Furthermore, maladaptive perfectionists were found to hold more inflexibly dichotomous perceptions of people and issues, as well as themselves, and to report greater amounts of stress in their lives (Rice et al.). It was proposed that these problems result due to perfectionists' problematic coping styles and stress-management efforts (Dunkley, Zuroff, & Blankstein, as cited in Rice et al.), attributional style (Chang & Sanna, 2001, as cited in Rice et al.), and social problem-solving (Chang, 2003, as cited in

Rice et al.). In addition, a study by Kawamura, Hunt, Frost and DiBartolo (2001) found that anxiety—in the form of social anxiety, trait anxiety, and worry—was associated with maladaptive perfectionism. This study also revealed an association between adaptive as well as maladaptive perfectionism, and Post-Traumatic Stress Disorder (PTSD) (Kawamura et al., 2001). Surprisingly, the authors found that depression is related to adaptive perfectionism, although this correlation is not as strong as the association between depression and maladaptive perfectionism (Kawamura et al.). Therefore, it is clear that perfectionism, regardless of type, is associated with facets of mental illness, although maladaptive perfectionists appear to be more seriously afflicted than are adaptive perfectionists.

A logically related correlate of the association between perfectionism—as a personality problem—and mental illness is academic success. Rice and Dellwo (2002) found that maladaptive perfectionists reported less emotional, academic, and social well-being compared to adaptive perfectionists and non-perfectionists. Adaptive perfectionists, on the other hand, reported greater self-esteem, academic integration, and social integration—although, consistent with Kawamura, Hunt, Frost and DiBartolo's (2001) finding, this group did evidence higher levels of depression than did non-perfectionists. There was no difference found in GPA, however, in the three groups. The authors concluded that

> [t]he emotional and interpersonal correlates of maladaptive perfectionism suggest that this comparable level of academic achievement comes with decided costs to well being . . . . [Maladaptive perfectionists] feel considerably worse and do not consider themselves to be as academically well-integrated as the other students. (Rice & Dellwo, 2002, p. 194)

Finally, it is likely that, due to its permeating nature, perfectionism would affect one's intimate relationships. Considering more specifically what effect perfectionism might have on intimate relationships, Martin and Ashby (2004) proposed that, due to their fear of revealing personal inadequacies and tendency to perceive their efforts as unsuccessful, or not achieving their personal standards, maladaptive perfectionists would have a fear of intimacy in close relationships. This research was deemed necessary due to the overwhelming evidence that intimacy, an element of social support, has been shown to buffer effects associated with maladaptive perfectionism, such as anxiety and depression (Martin & Ashby). As suspected, the authors found that compared to non-perfectionists, maladaptive

APA Note: Walker uses one source, Rice et al. often in this paragraph. In her first reference, she names all authors; for later references she uses the abbreviation "Rice et al." Can you identify one other source in this paragraph where she uses the same formats?

Writing Tip: Walker has used two appositives in this sentence, surrounding them by commas. An example of non-essential information, appositives can be taken out of the sentence without changing its meaning.

Writing Tip: This paragraph is **unified** by its focus on one significant study, Martin and Ashby (2004), which was conducted to test the findings of previous studies. Walker then explains the result of the Martin and Ashby study: their prediction was confirmed. She summarizes the authors' explanation for their findings and concludes with a **paragraph wrap**.

(Continued)

perfectionists show an increased fear of intimacy. Martin and Ashby proposed that the reason for this is that maladaptive perfectionists, feeling personally inadequate, feel exposed and vulnerable in close relationships, therefore leading to a fear of intimacy. They will "fear the honest self-disclosure necessary for the development of intimacy in family relationships and romantic partnerships" (Martin & Ashby, p. 372) due to their need to disguise personal flaws that they perceive as unacceptable and a tendency to overcompensate in response to their perception of inferiority to intimate others. Clearly, maladaptive perfectionism has important, negative repercussions on an individual's intimate relationships.

As a personality characteristic, perfectionism is often a psychologically harmful quality. Although adaptive perfectionism has been associated with positive elements such as the pursuit of excellence, it has also been associated with increased levels of depression as compared to non-perfectionists. Maladaptive perfectionism is that much more detrimental to an individual's life in that it is associated with more elements of mental illness and with difficulty in academics and intimate relationships. Since, as Costa and McCrae (1986) point out, personality is relatively stable, research on perfectionism is needed to better understand and help people suffering from this trait.

Walker briefly summarizes her thesis and main points in her **circular conclusion**, focusing on both types of perfectionism, but mostly the maladaptive type. In her last sentence, she makes a brief appeal for further research.

APA Note: Under the heading "**References**," the writer alphabetically lists all her sources. APA replaces author's first names by initials, and the first letters of most words in article titles are not capitalized. Walker has used journal articles in her research, ensuring that her information is current.

APA Note: APA encourages the use of a DOI (digital object identifier) for both print and online journal sources where it is available.

References

Bieling, P. J., Israeli, A. L., & Antony, M. M. (2004). Is perfectionism good, bad, or both? Examining models of the perfectionism construct. *Personality and Individual Differences, 36*, 1373–1385. doi:10.1016/S0191-8869(03)00235-6

Costa, P. T., & McCrae, R. R. (1986). Personal stability and its implications for clinical psychology. *Clinical Psychology Review, 6*, 401–423. doi:10.1016/0272-7358(86)90029-2

Hamachek, D. E. (1978). Psychodynamics of normal and neurotic perfectionism. *Psychology: A Journal of Human Behaviour, 15*(1), 27–33.

Hewitt, P. L., & Flett, G. L (1991). Perfectionism in the self and social contexts: Conceptualization, assessment, and association with psychopathology. *Journal of Personality and Social Psychology, 60*, 456–470. doi:10.1037/0022–3514.60.3.456

Kawamura, K. Y., Frost, R. O., & Harmatz, M. G. (2002). The relationship of perceived parenting styles to perfectionism. *Personality and Individual Differences, 32*, 317–327. doi:10.1016/S0191-8869(01)00026-5

Kawamura, K. Y., Hunt, S. L., Frost, R. O., & DiBartolo, P. M. (2001). Perfectionism, anxiety, and depression: Are the relationships independent? *Cognitive Therapy and Research, 25*(3), 291–301.

Martin, J. L., & Ashby, J. S. (2004). Perfectionism and fear of intimacy: Implications for relationships. *The Family Journal: Counseling and Therapy for Couples and Families, 12*(4), 368–374.

Rice, K. G., Ashby, J. S., & Preusser, K. J. (1996). Perfectionism, relationships with parents, and self-esteem. *Individual Psychology: Journal of Adlerian Theory, 52*(3), 246–260.

Rice, K. G., & Dellwo, J. P. (2002). Perfectionism and self-development: Implications for college adjustment. *Journal of Counseling and Development, 80*, 188–196.

Rice, K. G., Vergara, D. T., & Aldea, M. A. (2006). Cognitive-affective mediators of perfectionism and college student adjustment. *Personality and Individual Differences, 40*, 463–473. doi:10.1016/j.paid.2005.05.011

Slade, P. D., & Owens, R. G. (1998). A dual process model of perfectionism based on reinforcement theory. *Behaviour Modification, 22*(3), 372–390.

APA Note: If each journal issue is numbered separately (i.e., begins with page 1), you must include the issue number after the volume number; the issue number is put in parentheses with no spacing after volume number; it is not italicized. Contrast this example with the one above it that does not include issue number.

APA Note: Where consecutive entries begin with the same last name and author initials, order is determined by the last name of the second author.

MLA Citation Style

In the humanities, the principal documentation style has been developed by The Modern Language Association of America (MLA). The MLA publishes two manuals that define its style. The *MLA Style Manual and Guide to Scholarly Publishing* is designed for publishing academics. The *MLA Handbook for Writers of Research Papers*, 7th edition (2009), is compiled specifically for student researchers in such disciplines as cultural studies, English, and modern languages. The Association also maintains a website (http://www.mla.org) that offers guidelines on Internet citations and updates. If you use an online source for documentation, ensure it is reliable and follows the guidelines of the *Handbook*'s 7th edition.

MLA style is parenthetical, meaning that whenever you directly quote or paraphrase an author in your essay, or use an author's idea, you include the author's last name and the location of the reference (usually a page or paragraph number) in parentheses. Then, you provide a more complete description of all the sources on the final page(s) of your paper, titled "Works Cited."

MLA In-text Citations

Guidelines

MLA in-text formats include author(s) and page number(s) (e.g., "Ashton 17"). If the author is named in a signal phrase (e.g., "Ashton found that. . . ." ; "according to Hoffman"), only the page number will be in parentheses: "(17)."

- Do not use page abbreviations ("p," "pp"); in page ranges, drop the redundant hundreds digit in the second page number (e.g., "212–47," *not* "212–247"), but use both tens digits (e.g., "34–37").
- Leave one space between the author's last name and the page number. Do not use commas to separate items unless you need to include both an author and title in the citation or if you need to separate author from paragraph number in an electronic source.
- Readability and efficiency are key principles in the MLA system: parenthetical references should not intrude in the text, but clearly indicate the cited source(s).

Specifics

Citation for a direct quotation, paraphrase, or summary. Give the last name of the author and the page number in parentheses:

No signal phrase:

During World Wars I and II, the Canadian government often employed masseuses because surgery and medical care were insufficient "to restore severely wounded men" (Cleather ix).

Signal phrase:

You can use a signal phrase to set up your reference (see page 200). Since a signal phrase names the author, the citation requires only the page number.

According to Stambouli and Traversa, "each gallon of gasoline produced and used in an internal combustion engine releases roughly 12 kg of CO_2" (299).

Block quotation. In MLA style, a quotation that is longer than four typed lines is indented one inch from the left margin. Quotation marks are not used, and the quotation should be double-spaced. The author's name and page number appear in parentheses at the end of the quotation and *after* the final period.

. (Ellis and Bochner 81–82)

Citation referring to an indirect source. If it is necessary to refer to a source found in another work, include the original author in the sentence, along with the name(s) in parentheses of the source of the information. This is preceded by the abbreviation "qtd. in" and followed by page number(s). In Works Cited, list details for the indirect source:

> Francis Bacon observed that language affects our thinking when he said "words react on the understanding" (qtd. in Lindemann 93).

Personal communication, including interviews. These kinds of communication need the interviewee's last name only, in parentheses:

> (McWhirter)

Multiple sources in one citation. You may cite more than one relevant source in a single citation if the point you are making applies to both. Order the sources alphabetically by last name and separate them by a semicolon.

> The practices of teaching composition in college have not radically changed in the last few decades (Bishop 65; Williams 6).

However, if the citation is lengthy, consider moving the entire citation to a note (see MLA Notes, page 244).

MLA In-text Citations by Format

Kinds of Authors

Work by one author (book or article). Give the author's last name and page number in parentheses. Note that a book with an author and an editor will typically be cited by author.

> (Bloom 112)

Work by two authors. Give the last names of both authors with the word "and" between them, in addition to a page number all in parentheses:

> (Higgins and Wilson-Baptist 44)

Work by three and by more than three authors. Include the last names of all authors with commas between them. When following this format for citing three authors, the word "and" is placed between the second and third names in the list in addition to page number(s) in parentheses. For more than three authors, include all names as above or give only the last name of the first author with the abbreviation "et al.," and page number(s) in parentheses.

> (Higgins, Wilson-Baptist, and Krasny 102); (Terracciano et al. 96)

If you cite two sources in the same sentence, placing the citation after each source may help with clarity: e.g., "One study looked for correlations between GPA and listening to music (Cox and Stevens 757) while another study related academic performance to three types of music (Roy 6)."

Two or more works by the same author. Give the author's last name, along with a shortened version of the work's title separated by a comma, and a page number:

> "self-enforced discipline" (Foucault, *Power/Knowledge* 37)

Two authors with the same last name. Include the authors' first initials along with page number(s):

> (S. Sinkinson and B. Sinkinson 225–37)

Group or organization as author (corporate author). Documents published by companies and other groups may not list an author. MLA style recommends including the entire name of the organization in the sentence itself, if possible, in order to avoid overly long citations. For example, the organization commonly known as UNICEF would appear as The United Nations Children's Fund (along with a page number in parentheses). However, it is also acceptable to shorten the organization's name and place it in parentheses, accompanied by the page number in the same manner as a standard author citation.

> The United Nations Children's Fund reports that indigenous children are at exceptional risk of becoming refugees (204).

> Some child protection advocates suggest that indigenous children are at exceptional risk of becoming refugees (UNICEF 204).

Work with an unknown author (including many dictionary and encyclopedia entries). Begin with the title, if it is short, followed by the page number, in parentheses. When the title is lengthy, a condensed version can be used. Distinguish articles from complete works by placing article titles in quotation marks.

> ("Plea to City Hall" 22).

MLA In-text Citations: Electronic Sources

The most challenging aspect of citing online documents is that they often lack page numbers. If your source is the entire website, place the author's name within the sentence without a citation. If you are citing a specific quotation or paraphrasing and the document uses paragraph numbers, use these (preceded by the abbreviation "par." [one paragraph] or "pars." [more than one] with a comma and space between author's name and "par."). If sections are numbered, you may use these numbers (preceded by the abbreviation "sec."). If the reference is specific but the document has neither numbered pages nor paragraphs or section headings, the work must be cited without a page, paragraph, or section reference.

Sidebar notes:

If no author is given, use the name of the group or organization in place of the author's name—in the sentence itself, if possible.

For specific references from electronic documents without page numbers, use paragraph number(s) if visible, separated by a comma from the author's name; the abbreviation for "paragraph(s)" is "par(s)." If sections are numbered, use these, preceded by a comma and the abbreviation "sec."

Many articles retrieved from a database are viewed as Portable Document Format (PDF) files. In such cases, use the page numbers in the document. They are usually the same as the page numbers of the print version if one exists.

Citation of entire website. Give the author's last name within the sentence:

> In his article, Dillon compares reading practices for print media to those for electronic media.

Citation from specific passage. The specific location is given in the parenthetical citation:

> One firmly entrenched belief is that reading screens will never replace reading books and other print media (Dillon, sec. 1).

Internet site without an author. A site without an author's name follows the guidelines for a print document without an author and uses the site title to direct readers to the source of any information.

> ("LHC Machine Outreach")

If you are referring to a website itself, rather than a specific part, include the author's name within the sentence and do not use any numbering.

MLA In-text Citations: Non-textual Sources

Film, video, audio, TV broadcasts, musical recordings, and other non-textual media. Place the name of the individual(s) most relevant to your discussion in the text. In the case of a film, this could be the director, performer, screenwriter, or other contributor. If your focus is on the whole work, use the title.

> Francis Ford Coppola's film *The Conversation* explores the psychology of surveillance.

In the Works Cited section, the entry would be alphabetized under "C" for Coppola, the film's producer.

MLA Citations in the Works Cited Section

In MLA style, the Works Cited page(s) containing complete retrieval information appears at the end of your essay and on a new page that continues the numbers of your essay. The Works Cited list is double-spaced, with a one-inch margin. Omit words like "Press," "Inc.," and "Co." after publisher name (but university presses should be abbreviated "UP" for "University Press"). Some of the most common abbreviations used in MLA style include

- assn. (association)
- ch. (chapter)
- ed. (editor[s], edition)
- fwd. (foreword)
- introd. (introduction)
- P (Press)

- par. (paragraph), pars. (paragraphs)
- pt. (part)
- rev. (revised)
- rpt. (reprint)
- sec. (section)
- trans. (translator)
- U (University)
- vol. (volume)

Guidelines

- The title is centred an inch from the top of the page without underlining or bolding.
- The list is alphabetized by author's last name; each entry begins flush with the margin with subsequent lines indented half an inch.
- The standard MLA citation begins with the author's last name, followed by a complete first name (unless the author has published only initial[s]). Italicize book titles and titles of other complete works, such as plays, films, and artistic performances—along with journal titles and websites; place quotation marks around titles of articles, essays, book chapters, short stories, poems, web pages, and TV episodes.
- All first letters of major words in the title are capitalized, even if the source did not do so.
- Medium of publication or similar descriptor is included, usually as the last element.

Sample book entry

List book (pamphlet or brochure) data in the following sequence: author; title (italicized); place of publication; shortened version of the publisher's name created by removing articles like "A" or "The" and abbreviations; year of publication; publication medium:

> Fries, Charles, C. *Linguistics and Reading*. New York: Holt, Rinehart and Winston, 1962. Print.

Sample journal entry

List journal article data in this sequence: author; title of article (in quotation marks); title of journal (italicized); volume number; issue number; year of publication; inclusive pages; publication medium:

> Valkenburg, Patti M., and Peter Jochen. "Who Visits Online Dating Sites? Exploring Some Characteristics of Online Daters." *CyberPsychology and Behavior* 10.6 (2007): 849–52. Print.

Kinds of Authors

Work by one author (book). See above, "Sample book entry."

> The order for most Works Cited entries is author's last name and first name; title of work; publication details, which vary depending on whether the work is a book, journal article, or electronic document; and medium of publication.

Work by two or three authors. Only the first author's complete name is inverted with a comma before "and":

> Luckner, John, and Reldan Nadler. *Processing the Experience*. Dubuque: Kendall/Hunt, 1992. Print.

Work by more than three authors. MLA style provides two possibilities: 1) the complete names of all authors, reversing the name of the first author only and including a comma between the authors' names, or 2) the complete name of just the first author plus the abbreviation "et al." ("and others"):

> Festial, Lawrence, Harold Inch, Susan Gomez, and Komiko Smith. *When Economics Fails*. Minneapolis: U of Minnesota P, 1956. Print.

or

> Festial, Lawrence, et al. *When Economics Fails*. Minneapolis: U of Minnesota P, 1956. Print.

Two or more works by the same author. Works by the same author are arranged chronologically from earliest to most recent publication. The author's name appears in the first listing only, with three dashes substituted for it in the additional citation(s).

> Foucault, Michel. *Discipline and Punish: The Birth of the Prison*. Trans. Alan Sheridan. New York: Random, 1977. Print.
> ———. *The History of Sexuality*. Trans. Robert Hurley. 3 vols. New York: Random, 1978. Print.

Work by two authors with the same last name. Alphabetical order of first names determines sequence. If two works have the same first authors, the order is determined by the last name of the second author:

> Srivastava, Sarita, and Margot Francis. "The Problem of 'Authentic Experience.'" *Critical Sociology* 32.2–3 (2006): 275–307. Print
> Srivastava, Sarita, and Mary-Jo Nadeau. "From the Inside: Anti-Racism in Social Movements." *New Socialist* 42 (2003): n. pag. 18 May 2006. Web. 8 Dec. 2009.

The order in the example, above, is determined by the last name of the second author, "Nadeau."

Group or organization as author (corporate author). Use the full group name in place of the author's name. If the organization name begins with an article (e.g., "The"), omit it.

> Education International. *Guide to Universities & Colleges in Canada*. 2000 ed. Victoria: EI Education International, 2000. Print.

In a work by two or three authors, all authors are listed with only the first author's name inverted. Use a comma between the first author's first name and the word "and." With more than three authors, you may name all authors or only the first and use the abbreviation "et al." to indicate that there are at least three more authors.

When a work has a group, rather than an individual, author, the group name takes the place of the author's name.

Work without an author, publisher, or publication location (non-electronic).
If the work being cited does not provide an author's name, it is preferable to list it
alphabetically by the title. For missing publication details, use the following abbreviations: "N.p." means "no place" if inserted before colon and "no publisher" if inserted
after; "N.d." means "no date." Use square brackets to identify any information that
isn't from the source; if the information may be unreliable, add a question mark.

No author name (unsigned encyclopedia entry):

"Interveners." *Canadian Encyclopedia*. 1985 ed. Print.

No publisher:

Webb, Noah. *The Great Haileybury Forest Fire*. [Ontario?]: n.p. 1971. Print.

The entry above has no known publisher; the place of publication is tentatively
identified as Ontario.
The entry below has neither a place nor a date of publication.

No publishing place or date:

Case, Michael. *Opus Dei*. N.p.: Slipshod P, n.d. Print.

Source Type

Work by author with an editor or translator. Begin with the author's name
unless you refer primarily to the work of the editor (for example, his or her introduction or notes); original publication date can be included after the title. Follow
the same format for a translated work. "Ed." is used for one or more editors.

Referring primarily to the text:

Hawthorne, Nathaniel. *The Scarlet Letter*. 1850. Ed. John Stephen Martin. Peterborough:
Broadview, 1995. Print.

The first date indicates the year the book was originally published.

Referring primarily to editor's work:

Martin, John Stephen, ed. *The Scarlet Letter*. By Nathaniel Hawthorne. 1850. Peterborough:
Broadview, 1995. Print.

Translated work. The abbreviation "Trans." precedes the translator's name after
the work's title:

Calvino, Italo. *Why Read the Classics?* Trans. Martin McLaughlin. New York: Pantheon,
1999. Print.

Chapter or other type of selection, such as an essay, in edited volume. Begin with the author's name and chapter (or essay) title. Follow with the book title and book editor(s) names, not inverted and preceded by "Ed." The citation concludes with publication information, the complete page range, and publication medium:

> Sanders, Douglas E. "Some Current Issues Affecting Indian Government." *Pathways to Self-Determination: Canadian Indians and the Indian State*. Ed. Leroy Little Bear, Menno Boldt, and J. Anthony Long. Toronto: U of Toronto P, 1984. 113–21. Print.

If you use more than one work from the same collection, you can economize by creating one entry for the work as a whole and abbreviated entries for specific works.

Main entry:

> Little Bear, Leroy, Menno Boldt, and J. Anthony Long, eds. *Pathways to Self-Determination: Canadian Indians and the Indian State*. Toronto: U of Toronto P, 1984. Print.

Specific entry using Sanders, above (other works would be set up the same):

> Sanders, Douglas E. "Some Current Issues Affecting Indian Government." Little Bear, Boldt, and Long. 113–21.

Introduction, preface, foreword, or afterword. Begin with the author of the introduction, etc. followed by the section name (not in quotation marks). The title of the complete work comes next, then the work's author preceded by "By."

> Scholes, Robert. Foreword. *The Fantastic: A Structural Approach to a Literary Genre*. By Tzvetan Todorov. Trans. Richard Howard. Ithaca: Cornell UP, 1975. v–xi. Print.

Volume in multivolume work. State volume number if you use one work; if you use more than one, give the number of volumes used in place of the specific volume number:

> Bosworth, A. B., ed. *A Historical Commentary on Arrian's History of Alexander*. Vol. 1. London: Oxford UP, 1980. Print.

If you used 2 volumes, "2 vols." would replace "Vol. 1," above. In your essay, the parenthetical reference would include author's name, volume number followed by a colon; after a space, include the page number(s).

Second or subsequent edition of a work. Include the edition number after the title (or editor, translator, etc.):

> Suzuki, David, Aaron Griffiths, and Rebecca Lewontin. *An Introduction to Genetic Analysis*. 4th ed. New York: Freeman, 1989. Print.

The usual order for an essay or other selection in an edited book is author's name, essay title, book title, book editor's name preceded by "Ed," and publication details. Page range and publication medium then follow.

Book published before 1900. The publisher's name can be omitted; between the place of publication and year, insert only a comma.

> Baring Gould, S. *Old Country Life*. 5th ed. London, 1895. Print.

Article in a journal that uses continuous pagination or is paginated by issue. Whether the numbering of the journal continues with each succeeding issue (continuous pagination) or begins with the number "1" for every issue, you should include both volume and issue number. Of course, if the journal does not use both volume and issue in its numbering, one of these will be missing.

> Trew, Johanne Devlin. "Conflicting Visions: Don Messier, Liberal Nationalism, and the Canadian Unity Debate." *International Journal of Canadian Studies* 26.2 (2002): 41–57. Print.

> Always include the volume *and* issue number of the journal in your citation.

Article in a magazine. Cite complete date (day, month, year) if the magazine is issued every week or every two weeks; if issued monthly or every two months, include month and year. If the article breaks off and continues later in the work, cite the first page number followed by a plus sign—not the page range (e.g., "12 +" indicates the article begins on page 12 and continues somewhere after page 12).

> Knapp, Lonny. "Licensing Music to the Film and Television Industries." *Canadian Musician* Sept./Oct. 2007: 49–56. Print.

Article in a newspaper. Cite the author if given; if no author, begin with the title. Give the day, month, and year; give page number preceded by section number or letter if more than one section. If the article breaks off and continues later in the work, cite first page number followed by a plus sign—not the page range. A letter to the editor follows the same format and includes "Letter" after the title.

> "Lawyer seeks mistrial for client accused of illegal midwifery." *National Post* 20 April 2003: A8. Print.

Book/Movie review. Follow reviewer's name by title of review; if there is no title, continue with "Rev. of" and book/movie title followed by "by" and the author's (director's) name. Conclude with publication information.

> Mihm, Stephen. Rev. of *Swindled: The Dark History of Food Fraud, from Poisoned Candy to Counterfeit Coffee*, by Bee Wilson. *Business History Review* 83.2 (2006): 379–81. Print.

Government document. If author is unknown, begin with the name of the government followed by the agency (e.g., ministry, department, crown corporation) and document name:

> British Columbia. Office of the Auditor General. *Salmon Forever: An Assessment of the Provincial Role in Sustaining Wild Salmon*. Victoria: Office of the Auditor General of British Columbia, 2005. Print.

Indirect source. Cite the work where you found the citation rather than the original text:

> Lindemann, Erika. *A Rhetoric for Writing Teachers*. 4th ed. New York: Oxford UP, 2001. Print.

> (See MLA In-text Citations, "A citation referring to an indirect source," for the in-text format.)

Personal communication, including interview. Include a description of the communication. "TS," below, stands for "typescript":

> Carr, Emily. Letter to Lawren Harris. 12 December 1940. TS.

MLA Web Publication Citations

As online sources often change or even disappear, the MLA recommends that you download or print research material that may become inaccessible later. In cases where some relevant information is unavailable (such as page or paragraph numbers), cite what you can to enable the reader to access the source. Note that a URL surrounded by angle brackets is used only if the source would be otherwise hard to locate. (If you need to divide the URL between two lines, break it after single or double slashes.) The date of access, however, is a basic part of web citations.

Sample electronic citation. Title of the website follows work's title, which is then followed by the site's publisher or sponsor; if unavailable, use "N.p." The first date is that of the website or the latest update. The date that follows publication medium (Web) is the date of your latest access:

> Czekaj, Laura. "Promises Fulfilled: Looking at the Legacy of Thousands of Black Slaves Who Fled to Canada in the 1800s." *InnovationCanada.ca*. Canada Foundation for Innovation, 7 Feb. 2009. Web. 19 Apr. 2009.

Group, organization (e.g., corporate or government) **website**. If there is no author, list by the organization's name:

> Environment Canada. "10 Things You Should Know About Climate Change." 12 Aug. 2009. Web. 15 Aug. 2009. <http://www.ec.gc.ca/cc/default.asp?lang=En&n=2F049262–1>.

When you type in a URL, most word processing programs automatically flag it as a hyperlink. This means that the URLs are underlined and usually show up in blue. If you are reading the document electronically and click on the hyperlink (and if you are connected to the Internet), you will automatically be taken to that URL. However, in print documents, you must delete the hyperlink. Therefore, before printing your essay, make sure all URLs show up as plain text and not as hyperlinks.

The first date in a web entry is the date of the site itself or most recent update; the second is the date you last accessed the site.

The URL is included because the page would be hard to locate otherwise.

Article in online-only journal. Online-only journals may not include page numbers, in which case use the abbreviation "n. pag." (no pagination) after the website date:

> Rye, B. J., Pamela Elmslie, and Amanda Chalmers. "Meeting a Transsexual Person: Experience within a Classroom Setting." *Canadian On-Line Journal of Queer Studies in Education* 3.1 (2007): n. pag. Web. 21 Oct. 2008.

Internet article based on a print source and retrieved from a database. In addition to the information required for the print version of a journal article, the name of the database and date of access are included:

> Barton, Sylvia S. "Discovering the Literature on Aboriginal Diabetes in Canada: A Focus on Holistic Methodologies." *Canadian Journal of Nursing Research* 40.4 (2008): 26–54. *Ingenta*. Web. 11 May 2009.

Work online that appeared in print. Include details of the print source and follow with the title of the website, publication medium, and date of access:

> Douglass, Frederick. "My Escape from Slavery." *The Century Illustrated Magazine* Nov. 1881: 125–31. *Electronic Text Center, University of Virginia Library*. Web. 14 Jan. 2010.

Letter or email. If the letter is published, cite it as you would a work in an edited volume, adding the date of the letter. If it is a personal letter or email, include a description, such as "Message to the author" (if you received it) and date. If the message is a typed letter, use "TS" (typescript) as publication medium.

> Barrett, Anthony. "Re: *Lives of the Caesars*." Message to the author. 15 Aug. 2008. Email.

Message posted to online forum, discussion group, or blog post. Follow the guidelines for "Sample electronic citation," above. If no title is given, the entry should include a generic label after the author's name.

> Koolvedge. Online posting. *Adbusters.org*. Adbusters Media Foundation, 8 Aug. 2009. Web. 30 Aug. 2009. <https://www.adbusters.org/blogs/dispatches/massacre-peru. html#comments>.

The author, above, did not include a first name, so this information cannot be given.

MLA Citations for Non-textual Sources

MLA style has been updated to include specific citation formats for a variety of non-textual information sources. As a general rule of thumb, the person(s) most relevant

---

In addition to the information included in the print version, journal articles retrieved from a database require database name and date of access, which follows medium of publication.

to your discussion should be featured in your citation, along with an abbreviated description of their role. For example, if your paper is about actors, you can cite their contribution in a film either alongside or instead of naming the director.

Lecture or other oral presentation. Begin with the name of the speaker, the title of the presentation, the meeting and/or sponsor (if applicable), location detail, and date. Conclude with the equivalent of publication medium (e.g., "Lecture," "Reading").

> Armstrong, Nancy. "Darwin's Paradox." Department of English. David Strong Building, University of Victoria, Victoria. 2 April 2009. Lecture.

Film or video. Begin with the work's title unless you are referring mainly to one person's contribution (for example, a performer or writer). Follow with the name(s) of the most relevant individuals and conclude with the distributor's name and year of release.

> Citing the film: *Apocalypse Now*. Dir. Francis Ford Coppola. United Artists, 1979. Film.
>
> Citing a specific individual: Brando, Marlon, perf. *Apocalypse Now*. Dir. Francis Ford Coppola. United Artists, 1979. Film.

The abbreviation "perf." stands for "performer."

Performance (e.g., play, concert). Begin with title of performance and follow with relevant information, usually the writer, director, and main performers. Conclude with company name, theatre, city, date of performance, and the word "Performance."

> *Macbeth*. By William Shakespeare. Dir. Des McAnuff. Perf. Colm Feore and Yanna McIntosh. Stratford Shakespeare Festival Company. Festival Theatre, Stratford, ON. 1 June 2009. Performance.

If you are citing one individual's contribution, begin with that person's name (see "Film or video," above).

Episode from a television or radio series. Use the following order: title of episode (in quotation marks), title of program (italicized), network, call letters of local station, and city, if relevant. Conclude by giving the broadcast date and medium of reception.

> "Man of Science, Man of Faith." *Lost*. Dir. Jack Bender. CTV. CFTO, Toronto, 21 Sept. 2005. Television.

Information relevant to the episode (e.g., the writer or director) follows episode title; information relevant to the series follows series title.

If you are citing one individual's contribution, begin with that person's name (see "Film or video," above).

Music. Use the following order: performer (or other most relevant individual), recording title, label, year of issue, and medium (e.g., CD, LP):

> Morrison, Van. *Too Long in Exile*. Polydor, 1993. CD.

If you are citing a specific song, place its name in quotation marks after the performer's name; use a period before and after song's name.

Work of visual art. Use the following order: artist, title (italicized), date of composition (or "n.d." if this is unavailable), medium of composition, name of institution that contains the work, and city:

> Escher, M. C. *Drawing Hands*. 1948. Lithograph. Cornelius Collection, National Gallery of Art, Washington.

Interview. Begin with the name of the interviewee and follow with the interviewer's name preceded by "Interview by." Conclude with publication details.

> Murakami, Haruki. Interview by Maik Grossekathöfer. *Spiegel Online International* 20 Feb. 2008. Web. 8 Dec. 2009.

If you are the interviewer, begin with the interviewee followed by the type of interview (e.g., Telephone Interview) and date of interview.

MLA Notes

MLA permits either footnotes (at the bottom of the page) or endnotes (at the end of the document) as a way of including information you feel is valuable but does not fit well within the text. You may footnote in order to further explain a point, to cite multiple sources, to suggest additional reading, or to cite related points of interest. These notes are indicated by a superscript (raised) number directly to the right and above the word most related to the note, or at the end of a phrase; they run consecutively through your paper. Format the notes to match the rest of the document by double-spacing and indenting each note. For examples of student essays that include notes, see pages 207 and 295.

Sample Student Essay Using MLA Style

In the following student essay, the writer analyzes the arguments on both sides of an important issue. By using critical thinking and keeping her voice objective, she is able to write an effective expository essay on an arguable topic. She cites her sources using MLA style. A student summary of this essay is found in Chapter 9, page 163.

Multiculturalism in Canada: Controversial Consequences of the Multiculturalism Act
By Reneé MacKillop

What does it mean to be Canadian? The act for "the preservation and enhancement of Multiculturalism in Canada" declares recognition and promotion of understanding racial and cultural diversity as important parts of the Canadian identity (Bissoondath 36–37). The Multiculturalism Act allows all Canadians to freely safeguard and develop their cultural heritage (36). This act, however, has evoked questions concerning its validity, acceptance, and limits as well as questions of national unity and identity. According to supporters of multiculturalism, being Canadian means being a part of a cultural mosaic in a pluralistic society; according to critics of the Act, there is no conclusive answer to what it means to be Canadian because multiculturalism hinders the national quest for unity and identity. The Multiculturalism Act has required government involvement in cultural affairs and has extended accommodations to immigrants. The absence of restrictions on multiculturalism has blurred lines between what is acceptable and what is not. The ambiguity of the Act has forced questions about what unites Canadians as a national community and what makes this country Canadian.

The validity of government involvement in the cultural affairs of Canadians is a debatable issue. Opponents of the Multiculturalism Act believe that, similar to religion, culture should be a private matter left to individuals and families (Bissoondath 112). They argue that the state has no jurisdiction in the cultures of Canadians. Opponents refer to Canada's past foundation based on "white supremacy" and on the shift from Canada as an "ethnic nation" to a "civic nation" (Kymlicka 25). After World War II, individuals became included in the national community by becoming legal citizens as opposed to past inclusion based on ethnicity; the Citizenship Act of 1946 provided a new way to be Canadian (James). Therefore, in the declaration that Canada is a "civic nation," ethnic and cultural neutrality in the government is implied. Supporters believe that government involvement, namely the Multiculturalism Act, is vital to ending racism and discrimination. They

---

The author uses **mixed format**, combining important wording of the Multicultural Act with her own phrasing.

Writing Tip: MacKillop uses a semicolon to connect two closely related, contrastive main ideas.

After summarizing the two sides, in her **simple thesis statement**, MacKillop states that the Act's ambiguity raises questions about Canadian identity. Her essay will explore this issue by looking at two opposing interpretations of the Multiculturalism Act.

Most of the information in this paragraph is paraphrased; however, specific terms are left in quotation marks.

MLA Note: There is no page number to include after the name as this is a **non-textual source**. More information is given in Works Cited.

(Continued)

The writer represents opposing views in the same paragraph but ends on a note of agreement, reinforcing a key point: both sides agree that the Act raises many unresolved issues.

MLA Note: In this citation, MacKillop uses an indirect source: the quotation by Gwyn appeared in Bissoondath. The citation in Works Cited is from the indirect source, Bissoondath.

MLA Note: The second reference in this paragraph is a summary of four pages of the source. Because MacKillop has previously cited the source, the citation in the following sentence requires only the page number.

Writing Note: In her **topic sentence**, the writer introduces the topic for the paragraph that follows and, as she does in most paragraphs, then summarizes and paraphrases opposing views.

MLA Note: The writer names Kymlicka again because another source (Bissoondath) intervenes.

feel that it is the Canadian government's duty to redress past wrongs by ensuring equality to present-day ethnic minorities. However, both opponents and supporters agree that the true motives behind government involvement in the cultural affairs of the nation are unclear.

Although the policy of multiculturalism was established with the equality of all Canadian citizens in mind, Richard Gwyn has accused policy-makers of creating a "slush fund to buy ethnic votes" (as cited in Bissoondath 25). Moreover, due to "internal globalization" and the neo-liberal shift in Canadian society, emphasis is diverted from the original intentions of the policy to national competitiveness and economic gain (Abu-Laban and Christian 119–23). Ethnic entrepreneurs provide valuable trading and investment connections to the global community (111). The government issued an evaluation of the Multiculturalism Act, the Brighton Report, in 1996, which reviewed the program through literature, media coverage, and interviews, along with providing a statistical analysis of funding for the policy. The Brighton Report stated that past funding reinforced attendance to special interests and not to all Canadians (113). However, the Report did not mention ulterior motives for government funding of multiculturalism. Nonetheless, some Canadians question whether the support and funds for multiculturalism are government strategies for attaining an international competitive advantage and not primarily for nation-building.

The Multiculturalism Act is a renegotiation of immigrant integration (Kymlicka 37). Critics feel that the policy has created excessive accommodations for immigrants, instead of integration, while advocates feel that accommodations are necessary. Critics hold the opinion that immigrants expect integration and that newcomers are responsible to learn an official language, abide by Canadian laws, and accept Canadian society (Bissoondath 23). However, advocates believe that multiculturalism is not intended to create new nations within Canada for individual cultures (Kymlicka 37). Proponents of multiculturalism feel that in response to problems of social marginalization and historically stigmatized communities' political inequality, it is necessary to redress past injustices and ensure a better and more equal future; the Multiculturalism Act encourages victims of stigmatization to seek redress (Dyck 117). After progress recognizing ethnic minorities, providing funding, and confronting past wrongs (wrongs frequently authorized by the government) ethnic minorities had endured in Canada, critical opposition surfaced in the 1990s (120–21). Critics of multiculturalism believe that immigrants are threatening job security. They cite as an example the "instant Liberals" who were welcomed into the party based solely on their ethnicity, which undermined hard-working members who had been active in the party for considerable lengths of time (121). Opposition has grown as Canada continues to increase accommodations for ethnic minorities. Political and legal protections of cultural expression allow the open-ended policy constantly to be stretched (Bissoondath 134). Some critics fear the direction that multiculturalism is taking in Canada by legitimizing all forms of cultural expression.

The official recognition of minority contribution, personal freedom, and diversity, namely pluralism, has declared that society is best served by the ◄— contribution of varied components (Bibby 2). Tolerance and respect are enforced, and coexistence has become a national objective. Canadian critics do not consider pluralism beneficial, however, because it entrenches relativism, "the inclination to see the merits of behaviour and ideas as universal or absolute, but as varying with individuals and their environments, and, in the end, as being equally valid because they are chosen" (Bibby vi). According to the critic, "pluralism establishes choices; relativism declares the choice valid" (10). The essential concern is the lack of restrictions limiting what is socially acceptable in Canada.

Reading Tip: The writer assists the reader by defining *pluralism*. Two sentences later, she uses a direct quotation to define *relativism*. It is important that both terms are clearly defined as they are significant concepts and are discussed in the following paragraphs. Can you identify another term in the next paragraph that she defines?

The thorny question of restrictions is difficult because relativism has validated all viewpoints, eliminating cultural expectations (Bibby 10). Hopeful advocates of multiculturalism believe that boundaries would enable the multiculturalism policy to be successful. However, critics continue to caution that the "slippery slope" of relativism is leading towards acceptance ◄— of all forms of cultural expression and away from civic and political integration, regardless of the impact on Canada (Kymlicka 60). They believe that "rights [are] outstanding rules" and "relativism has slain moral consensus" because there are no authoritative instruments capable of measuring Canadian social life (Bibby 10–11). On the contrary, a pluralistic nation, which entails relativism and individualism (the tendency to stress the individual over the group), is notably rewarding because Canadians are free to live out their lives as they see fit, resulting in high standards of living,

MacKillop refers here to a **logical fallacy**, or error in reasoning. This fallacy is defined on p. 269.

(Continued)

Writing Tip: Notice that MacKillop uses no **signal phrases** in her essay (signal phrases announce the source before the reference is made). Therefore, she must place her citations carefully, so the source is always known. In this paragraph, there is no doubt where her information has come from. For an example of an essay that uses many signal phrases, see "The Imperfection of Perfectionism," p. 226.

To illustrate a key objection of the Act's opponents, MacKillop uses the **example** of female circumcision.

Writing Tip: To avoid overusing words like *supporters* and *opponents*, MacKillop uses **synonyms**, like *advocates* and *proponents*, and *critics* and *detractors*.

Writing Tip: Although the writer uses **paraphrase** and **summary** throughout this paragraph, significant phrases are placed in quotation marks. The memorable phrasing of the last sentence makes **direct quotation** a good choice.

peaceful existence, and, ultimately, freedom (90). However, what is best for Canada is no longer relevant because everything is equal and, therefore, no particular way can be better than another, according to opponents (14). A clear example of the feared results of relativism is the continued practice of female circumcision by some African minorities in Canada. In spite of western society's view of female circumcision as a form of mutilation and a health risk, it is a vital, traditional rite of passage to womanhood for some African women (Bissoondath 134–35). The questions are whether this practice should be acceptable in Canadian society and how far, in the Canadian context, should Canada go in accommodating these kinds of cultural expressions? Detractors of the Multiculturalism Act believe that the policy ends where notions of human rights and dignity commence (135). Critics fear that Canadians are "not differentiating between being judgemental and showing sound judgement and between exhibiting discrimination and being discriminatory" (Bibby 101).

Despite the concerns over relativism and individualism in a pluralistic society, supporters of multiculturalism claim that the policy provides external protection to minorities, possibility for redress, access to mainstream institutions, and protection from discriminatory and prejudiced conduct (Kymlicka 65). These advocates believe that, despite the lack of explicit restrictions limiting the policy, the preamble to the Act emphasizes human and individual rights and sexual equality (66–67).

Multiculturalism encourages accepting the rights of others to be different and, consequently, national togetherness (Bibby 90). However, critics pose the following question: "If what we have in common is our diversity, do we really have anything in common at all?" (92). There is freedom for the individual, but how are people brought together into the national community? This implicit criticism suggests that a group needs an identity because individualism brings freedom and equality, but it also removes persons from the guidance of the group and the security of tradition. Thus, the identity of merely being an autonomous Canadian is forced upon citizens (96). Whereas proponents advocate the policy's ability to instil pride in Canadians and a sense of belonging to a mosaic of cultures, opponents call the policy a "song and dance" affair that encourages stereotyping and national divisiveness (96–98). Proponents acknowledge multiculturalism as officially recognizing the reality that Canada has never been unicultural; opponents see it as extenuating national minorities. Aboriginal and Francophone Canadians, two national minorities, are offended by being categorized with other minorities and not being recognized as founding peoples (James). René Lévesque called multiculturalism "folklore" and named the policy a "'red-herring' . . . devised to obscure the 'Quebec business', to give an impression that we are all ethnics and do not have to worry about special status for Quebec" (Bissoondath 37). Some Canadians propose officially declaring Canada multinational along with multicultural as a solution to the problem of national unity. The problematic criticism remains, however, that multiculturalism is divisive and prevents Canadians from establishing a national identity.

The Multiculturalism Act, like all political policies, is not above criticism, and the concept of multiculturalism has both supporters and detractors. It is essential that a democratic state be constantly analyzed, critiqued, and questioned. Diversity is a reality in Canada; however, government involvement in immigration integration is controversial. The outcomes of a pluralistic society, officially recognized as being polyethnic, are uncertain as Canada diverges from the melting pot standard. Not surprisingly, there have been unexpected consequences of The Multiculturalism Act, such as relativism, individualism, and division. In the words of the Brighton Report, critics "misunderstand and misrepresent Canada's multiculturalism policy." However, the report concluded that the policy is in need of amendments (Abu-Laban and Christian 113). In summary, the Multiculturalism Act is progressive, yet in need of revision to allow Canada to flourish as a unified country with a strong national identity.

Works Cited

Abu-Laban, Yasmeen, and Gabriel Christian. *Selling Diversity: Immigration, Multiculturalism, Employment Equity, and Globalization.* Peterborough: Broadview, 2002. Print.

Bibby, Reginald. *Mosaic Madness: The Poverty and Potential of Life in Canada.* Toronto: Stoddart, 1990. Print.

Bissoondath, Neil. *Selling Illusions: The Cult of Multiculturalism in Canada.* Toronto: Penguin, 1990. Print.

Reading Tip: The use of **single quotation marks** around "red-herring" and "Quebec business" indicates that they were in quotation marks in the original. **Ellipses** (three spaced dots) indicate one or more words were omitted from the sentence.

MacKillop uses **synthesis** in this paragraph, bringing together several opposing viewpoints. Thus, she prepares the reader for her last sentence concerning the "divisive" nature of the multiculturalism debate. In her **conclusion,** however, she stresses the potential for unity.

MLA Note: When two authors are used, the names of the second author are not inverted. Note the comma before "and."

MLA Note: The writer has used the fourth edition of this book, preferring a recent source to an older one.

Dyck, Rand. *Canadian Politics: Critical Approaches.* 4th ed. Toronto: Thomson Nelson, 2004. Print.

James, Matt. Political Science 101. Department of Political Science. Elliott Building, University of Victoria, Victoria. 25 Nov. 2004. Lecture.

MLA Note: One of MacKillop's sources is a lecture in an introductory course. Such sources need to be cited along with the print sources.

Kymlicka, Will. *Finding Our Way: Rethinking Ethnocultural Relations in Canada.* Don Mills: Oxford UP, 1998. Print.

Questions to consider in a critical and analytical reading of "Multiculturalism in Canada: Controversial Consequences of the Multiculturalism Act":

1. Summarize the arguments of the two sides as they are presented in the first body paragraph (paragraph 2).

2. MacKillop uses direct quotation and mixed format to support her points, along with some paraphrase and summary. Why does she choose to use a variety of methods? What is the role and importance of direct quotation in an essay that presents two opposing views of a topic?

3. Explore the writer's credibility. Does her essay demonstrate knowledge, reliability, and fairness?

4. Explain her use of secondary sources. Do you think she uses them well (for example, is there an over-reliance on any source)? Do the sources themselves appear reliable?

5. MacKillop's essay compares and contrasts two positions on multiculturalism and the Multiculturalism Act. Which of the two methods for organizing compare and contrast essays, block or point-by-point, does she use (see Chapter 8)? Are the two positions always clearly separated from one another? Give specific examples.

6. Does the first paragraph function as an effective introduction? Does the last paragraph provide a satisfactory conclusion? What kind of introduction does the writer use? What kind of conclusion? Do they work well together? (See Chapter 5, page 105.)

Exercise 12.1

The following exercises ask you to apply information from Chapters 9, 11, and 12. They test your ability to use summary, paraphrase, direct quotation, mixed format, block format, signal phrases, ellipses, brackets, and APA and MLA in-text citations.

Part I

Following the instructions given in this text, complete A, B, and C, creating sentences that show your understanding of how to use sources.

The excerpts for Part I are from the website article "Comets May Have Led to Birth and Death of Dinosaur Era," by Hillary Mayell. It was published in *National Geographic News* on 16 May 2002. The information for part A is taken from paragraphs 1 and 2 of the source; part B is taken from paragraph 4; part C is taken from paragraph 3.

A. Paraphrase the following in one or two sentences. Do not use a signal phrase or any direct quotations. Use MLA style for the parenthetical citation.

> Comets slamming into the Earth may be responsible for both the birth and the death of the dinosaur era, an international group of researchers report. There is a considerable amount of evidence that a bolide [a comet or asteroid] collision with Earth triggered the end of the dinosaur era 65 million years ago.

B. Paraphrase the following sentence, but include one direct quotation that is no more than eight words (choose the most appropriate words for the quotation). Use a signal phrase to set up the paraphrase (i.e., source's name and signal verb).

> "We have been able to show for the first time that the transition between Triassic life-forms to Jurassic life-forms occurred in a geological blink of an eye," said Paul Olsen, a geologist at the Lamont-Doherty Earth Observatory of Columbia University.

C. Using brackets, grammatically integrate the direct quotation into the complete sentence. Do not use a signal phrase.

> The cause of the end of the dinosaur age might have been "a giant ball of ice, rock, and gases smashed into the supercontinent Pangaea."

Part II

Integrate the passage below as if you planned to use it in your essay, following the instructions. Use a signal phrase and APA style, which includes source's name, year, and signal verb, followed by a direct quotation of the passage. In sentence three, omit (1) "oral contraceptives, transoceanic phone calls" and (2) "just to mention a few," indicating to the reader that material is omitted. Format the quotation in the most appropriate way—i.e., either as part of the text or in block format.

(The author is David Suzuki; the name of article is "Saving the Earth"; the date of publication is June 14, 1999; the quotation is from page 43 of *Maclean's*.)

> In this century, our species has undergone explosive change. Not only are we adding a quarter of a million people to our numbers every day, we have vastly

amplified our technological muscle power. When I was born, there were no computers, televisions, jet planes, oral contraceptives, transoceanic phone calls, satellites, transistors or xerography, just to mention a few. Children today look at typewriters, vinyl records and black-and-white televisions as ancient curiosities.

PART III

A. Paraphrase the passage below, which is from page 45 of the same Suzuki essay as in Part II, and cite using APA style. Include one direct quotation no longer than three words as part of your paraphrase. Do not use a signal phrase.

B. Summarize the passage in one sentence of no more than 20 words (there are 54 words in the original); begin with a signal phrase and use APA style. Do not use any direct quotations.

In biological terms, the globe is experiencing an eco-holocaust, as more than 50,000 species vanish annually, and air, water and soil are poisoned with civilization's effluents. The great challenge to the millennium is recognizing the reality of impending ecological collapse, and the urgent need to get on with taking the steps to avoid it.

Sample Academic Essay

The following academic article is annotated to show some of the similarities and differences between academic essays and the kind of essays you will write. Academic essays, which usually appear in academic journals and can be accessed electronically through your school's databases, are longer and more complex than most student essays. Many of the challenges they present, however, can be overcome by knowing where to look for information. Following the steps below will make the reading process easier:

1. Read the title and abstract to get an idea of the essay's purpose, topic, and results or findings. If the essay includes specific headings, they may also give useful information.
2. Read the introduction, especially the last paragraphs, where important information is placed.
3. Read the Conclusion or Discussion section (or, if it is not labeled as such, the last few paragraphs) in which the findings are summarized and made relevant, applying the strategies discussed in Chapter 1, Scanning Versus Focused Reading.
4. If you know the essay will be crucial to your own research, you can now go back and read the other sections closely.

Before reading this essay, you can review the questions discussed in Chapter 1, Responding Critically and Analytically through Questions, page 18.

Sample Academic Essay

INSTITUTIONAL "INCOMPLETEDNESS": THE CHALLENGES IN MEETING THE NEEDS OF CANADA'S URBAN ABORIGINAL POPULATION

By Jack Jedwab

Reading Tip: Closely reading the title of an academic essay can be a useful pre-reading activity. Before the colon, the author has used a significant phrase. Notice that he puts "incompletedness" in quotation marks, showing his specific use of this word. What follows the colon tells you that the article will focus on possible solutions to a problem among the members of a specific group.

Abstract

A substantial share of Canada's Aboriginal people live in cities where the provision of services is often rendered complex owing to a wide variety of residential patterns. The institutional response to addressing the needs of the growing urban aboriginal population is the Aboriginal Friendship Centre. First established by Aboriginal people in the 1950's the ACFs are today the largest off-reserve Aboriginal network of institutions in the country and provide an extensive range of programs and services. On the basis of an analysis of a national survey of aboriginal opinion around the effectiveness of the ACFs, it is contended here that while these institutions are seen as generally successful in responding to the cultural needs of their constituents, ACFs will need to better define roles and relationships with the broader institutional network when it comes to addressing the economic condition of aboriginal peoples.

Reading Tip: Like many academic articles in the social sciences, this one includes an **abstract**, a summary written by the author (see p. 165). It gives background information, briefly explains how the research was carried out, and, in the last four lines, gives the results.

Introduction

In his widely acclaimed work on the institutional completeness of ethnic communities, sociologist Raymond Breton (1964) maintained that the greater the degree of a community's organizational capacity, the stronger its sense of group consciousness. Institutional completeness is characterized by the degree to which a given group possesses a network of institutions that can respond to the needs of those who identify with the community. Breton contended that the wider the range of services the community could deliver, the greater the opportunity for the preservation of the group's identity. Over time, supporters and detractors of the idea have respectively contributed to refining the concept. Among the issues raised was the source of funds for community institutions and the conditions set out by organizational stakeholders with regards to the priority in the delivery of services. This further raised the issue of a group's institutional autonomy, notably where government is the principal source of funding.

Reading Tip Academic writers often begin by summarizing work done by other scholars in the field.

The author defines this important term as it applies to group identity.

Like many definitions, "institutional completeness" has changed over time.

In Canada, the role of preserving Aboriginal identities is undoubtedly influenced by the extent to which the communities are institutionally complete. Among the indicators for assessing whether community institutions contribute to the Wellness of their constituents are such things as the degree of awareness of the institutions, the extent to which the services are being employed by constituents, and the perceived impact of the program in attaining prescribed

Reading Tip: This paragraph, like many in academic essays, includes some challenging words. If words like *stakeholder* or *autonomy* cannot be determined by context, you will need to look them up in a dictionary.

The author gives three criteria for measuring institutional completeness.

Like most essays, this one includes important information near the end of the Introduction. This paragraph begins with a direct statement about the topic and the author's approach; although it looks different from the kinds of theses you write, it fulfils the same purpose of informing its audience about what will follow.

Authors of academic essays in the sciences and social sciences often give a detailed explanation of their research methods. This is necessary so that other researchers can set up a similar experiment. In this case, research data was gathered through a questionnaire.

In this paragraph the author mentions two "sub-groups" who were studied closely. You can infer that the findings relevant to these groups will be compared and contrasted later in the essay.

Writing Tip: Like **definition**, **chronology** is an organizational pattern often used near the beginning of essays. The decision whether to include background information often relates to audience: readers of the journal that this essay appeared in would not necessarily be familiar with ACFs.

Academic journals often publish entire issues that deal with a specific problem. Because the author is making a very general reference to an article in the same issue, there is no full citation.

objectives. How and by whom such issues are evaluated has an important bearing on community governance, which in turn has an impact on the establishment of priorities.

This paper examines the role of Aboriginal Friendship Centre(s) (hereafter ACFs) and the extent to which they meet the criteria for contributing to institutional completeness. The findings will be based in large part on an evaluation of ACFs done by the department of Canadian Heritage in 2003 and, in particular, a survey commissioned by the firm EOKS to provide a more detailed assessment. The survey involved 606 completed interviews with Aboriginal people (16 years of age or older) living in urban communities where ACFs are located (the margin of error is +/–4.0% for the entire sample and –vl–1 to +/–12% for most sub-groups).

In analyzing the extent to which Aboriginal people perceive ACFs to be effective, particular attention will be directed at two sub-groups: those who have lived on a reserve or First Nations community for at least six months; and, those who have not. We will also consider the issue of whether the ACFs strengthen ties between Aboriginal people and, if so, whether this occurs at the expense of building bridges with Non-Aboriginal people.

Background

Established by Aboriginal peoples in the 1950's, ACFs were the principal institutional response to addressing the needs of the growing urban Aboriginal population. The first ACFs were intended to be "drop-in centres" where social interaction and networking took place often in Aboriginal languages. By 1968, there were over 25 ACFs across Canada, and they took on greater responsibilities by providing referral or direct access to various services. Today, ACFs are the largest off-reserve Aboriginal service infrastructure in Canada. They provide services in such areas as housing, education, human resource development and employment, youth and family, health, recreation and culture to off-reserve First Nations, Non-Status Indian, Métis and Inuit people.

ACFs initially relied on volunteers, fundraising events, private donations, grants from foundations, and project funding from provincial and federal governments. In 1972, federal funding was extended under the Aboriginal Friendship Centre Program (AFCP) to support the activities that encourage equal access and participation in Canadian society of urban Aboriginal people while fostering and strengthening Aboriginal cultural distinctiveness. To effectively deliver programs, ACFs have developed a diverse network of community and government linkages.

The effectiveness of ACFs is of considerable importance to its stakeholders – perhaps more so today than ever. As has been documented extensively elsewhere, including in this journal (see paper by Guimond), the urban

Aboriginal population continues to grow in both size and complexity. In this context, the relevance of programming designed to support urban Aboriginal people is clear—as is the importance of ensuring that this programming responds to the needs and concerns of urban Aboriginal communities.

Knowledge and Use of the ACFs

As noted above, among the criteria for determining the degree of completeness is the level of awareness of the institutions on the part of community membership. Aboriginal residents were asked to rate their own level of knowledge and understanding of Aboriginal Friendship Centres and what they do. The EKOS survey asked two questions of Aboriginal residents living in areas where ACFs are located to test their awareness. On the basis of an unprompted question, some one quarter of respondents referred to ACFs when asked whether they were able to identify any organizations offering services for Aboriginal people in their community. Some 53% were able to identify organizations other than ACFs. Approximately one in three were unable to identify such organizations. When asked, however, in a follow up question whether they had heard of ACFs, an important majority (82%) responded positively. Probing yet further about how knowledgeable they were about ACFs, some 14% rated themselves as very knowledgeable, another 43% as somewhat knowledgeable, and 42% saying they were not very knowledgeable. Not surprisingly, there is a link between knowledge and use of ACFs: those who have visited an ACF are far more inclined to rate themselves as very knowledgeable than those who have not visited a centre.

As to the use of ACFs, overall 58% of Aboriginal residents have visited a Centre, whereas 42% have not. Some two-thirds who are aware of the Centres (67%) indicated that they have visited them. A majority of that group had been to a Centre within the past two years. Hence, one-third of Aboriginal residents who are aware of ACFs have never been to one. Although they provide a variety of services to Aboriginal people, a social visit is the most common reason for visiting an ACF (this accounts for half of all responses for those visiting a local ACF in the previous two years). Others services most frequently sought in visiting ACFs are education and culture (39% each), programs for youth (36%) and employment (34%). Health and child-related programs and information are sought approximately one-quarter of the time (28 and 25 per cent, respectively). One in five visitors to ACFs said that they have not used a program or service.

The table below provides figures for the actual number of programs in each area and the number of participants. As to program expenditure during the year 2003–2004, most funds were directed at health programming (37%), youth programming (21%) and housing (9%), justice (6.5%) and housing (6.5%).

Reading Tip: The three headings following the background section focus on the three criteria mentioned in the introduction. The author has organized the information for easy access.

The author reminds the reader of one of the criteria discussed above before giving the statistical findings about the awareness criterion.

Reading Tip: Research studies in the sciences and social sciences often rely on figures, tables, graphs, and charts to summarize their findings. Both experienced and inexperienced readers can access complex information quickly this way.

Table 1 Participants in AFC Programs (2003–2004)

TYPE OF PROGRAMMING	# OF PROGRAMS	# OF PARTICIPANTS
Health	302	110,205
Justice	78	29,526
Education	62	8,147
Employment	75	32,721
Language	8	1,435
Youth	197	92,771
Sports (not recreational)	12	10,647
Cultural	55	98,258
Housing	25	35,115
Economic Development	7	28,442
Other	81	58,193
Total	902	

Satisfaction and Purpose of Friendship Centres

When asked about satisfaction with programs and services used, between 81 and 84 per cent of program users said that they are satisfied. There is no one program or service that engenders more (or less) satisfaction than the others. Virtually everyone who attends a program or uses a service is satisfied with it (at least four in five are), with little difference in satisfaction levels between the different programs. About half of the visitors obtain referrals to a program or service and satisfaction levels are equally high on this front.

Close to three-quarters of Aboriginal people surveyed by EKOS agree that AFCs are a place to participate in activities in their language and relate to their culture. A similar percentage agree that they help Aboriginal people to feel connected to their community. Two-thirds remark that AFCs provide a safe haven for urban Aboriginal people. Agreement with the view that AFCs offer a place to participate in activities in their language and to relate to their culture declines with age (from 81% of those under 35 to 68 per cent of those 55 and older) because they tend to not know about them.

The impact of AFCs appears to be viewed as moderate when rated by Aboriginal respondents with some awareness of them. As illustrated in the table below, six in ten respondents agree that AFCs have a positive impact on the sense of Aboriginal community as well as on the sense of personal well-being. Just less than six in ten agree that AFCs have a positive impact in the community on the level of social support. About one in two agree that AFCs have a positive impact on the level and quality of education (53%), the health of Aboriginal people, and preservation of Aboriginal languages and culture (51%). Respondents felt

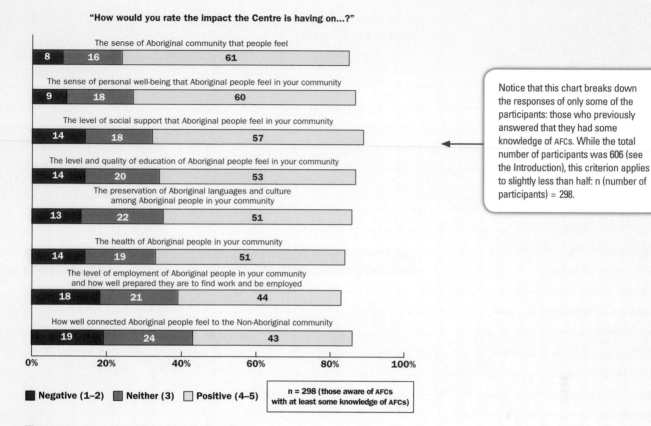

"How would you rate the impact the Centre is having on...?"

The sense of Aboriginal community that people feel
8 | 16 | 61

The sense of personal well-being that Aboriginal people feel in your community
9 | 18 | 60

The level of social support that Aboriginal people feel in your community
14 | 18 | 57

The level and quality of education of Aboriginal people feel in your community
14 | 20 | 53

The preservation of Aboriginal languages and culture
among Aboriginal people in your community
13 | 22 | 51

The health of Aboriginal people in your community
14 | 19 | 51

The level of employment of Aboriginal people in your community
and how well prepared they are to find work and be employed
18 | 21 | 44

How well connected Aboriginal people feel to the Non-Aboriginal community
19 | 24 | 43

0%   20%   40%   60%   80%   100%

■ Negative (1–2)   ■ Neither (3)   □ Positive (4–5)

n = 298 (those aware of AFCs
with at least some knowledge of AFCs)

> Notice that this chart breaks down the responses of only some of the participants: those who previously answered that they had some knowledge of AFCs. While the total number of participants was 606 (see the Introduction), this criterion applies to slightly less than half: n (number of participants) = 298.

Figure 1   Impact of Friendship Centres.

that the AFCs had a lesser impact on the level of employment of Aboriginal people to the non-Aboriginal community (43%).

In the next section, we will examine the degree to which those respondents who have lived on a reserve or in a First Nation community for at least six months and those who did not differ on the extent to which they perceive AFCs to be effective. We focus on those persons who have heard of AFCs. Whether or not one reported living on a First Nation community, the percentage contending that friendship centres provide a safe haven for urban Aboriginal people is roughly similar, with two in three in agreement with this view. While the majority agree that the sense of connection to the Aboriginal community created by AFCs is good, those who lived on a reserve (68%) are less likely than those who did not (78%) to give a positive assessment in this regard.

As to the impact of the AFCs on a variety of factors (see Table 2), one observes that the most important difference between the two groups is with respect to the preservation of Aboriginal languages and culture among Aboriginal people in your community. Those who have lived on a reserve for more than six months are less likely to rate the impact as positive compared to those who have not lived on-reserve for an extended period of time. Those who have lived on-reserve or in a First Nation community are less likely to favorably rate the AFCs on issues of employment but are more likely to positively evaluate the level of social support.

Are AFCs Bridging and/or Bonding?

A concern around institutional completeness of groups with a shared identity is that they risk becoming insular when they target raising group consciousness in the extension of services. Hence, they do bonding as opposed to bridging between groups as characterized by the respected American scholar Robert Putnam in his discussion of social capital in his seminal work entitled *Bowling Alone*. One of the goals of the funding provided by the government of Canada

> Referring to a significant book on the subject of communities and identity, the author acknowledges an area of debate about AFCs.

Table 2 Perceived effectiveness of AFCs		
	I HAVE HEARD OF ABORIGINAL FRIENDSHIP CENTRES	
VERY AND SOMEWHAT POSITIVE IMPACT COMBINED	Lived on a reserve or in a first nation community for at least six months of the year	Did not live on a reserve or in a first nation community for at least six months of the year
The level of employment of Aboriginal people in your community, and how well prepared they are to find work and be employed	32.8	40.7
The preservation of Aboriginal languages and culture among Aboriginal people in your community	37.0	52.8
The sense of Aboriginal community that people feel in your community	48.1	54.6
The sense of personal well-being that Aboriginal people feel in your community	55.5	56.4
The level of social support that Aboriginal people feel in your community	58.2	51.8
The health of Aboriginal people in your community	43.6	44.4

to the AFCs is to ensure the creation of "…a bridge for urban Aboriginal peoples, enabling them to derive strength from their peers as a means of relating to the rest of the urban population." Indeed, in the formal evaluation of the AFCs conducted by the Department of Canadian Heritage, several AFC leaders pointed to the "individual and collective role played in expressing, and at times representing, the views of urban Aboriginal peoples…." Half (52%) agree that Friendship Centres help Aboriginal people to feel connected to the non-Aboriginal community. Some 57% of those who have lived on a reserve or in a First Nations community for more than six months (versus 44% who have not done so) feel that AFCs help make such connections. As to whether they feel more connected to their own community, some 70% agree that AFCs do so with two in three who have lived on a reserve for more than six months sharing that view and three in four feeling as such amongst the group who have not lived on-reserve for more than six months.

While survey respondents feel that AFCs are more effective in bridging than bonding, it would be wrong to conclude that bonding represents an obstacle to bridging. As observed in the Table above, those who strongly agree that AFCs help Aboriginal people feel connected to their own community are more likely to also strongly agree that AFCs help Aboriginal people in their community to feel connected to the non-Aboriginal community.

> Researchers and other academic writers do more than report their findings: they often interpret them for their readers. In this case, Jedwab cautions against making an invalid inference.

Conclusion

We have attempted to determine whether, from the perspective of Aboriginal peoples, AFCs could be described as offering a complete range of services to the community.

But the idea is not to limit assessment to whether the services exist; rather, this study has sought to determine the perceived level of effectiveness of each of the services provided. Indeed, simply identifying whether a given group has services to extend in several areas makes for an inadequate evaluation of institutional completeness if the services are not sufficiently effective in strengthening group consciousness. Moreover, a proper analysis of institutional completeness will also consider whether, after review, a community is best positioned to deliver the service and, if not, should the service be offered outside the community or is some partnership called for? These questions are somewhat outside the scope of the discussion above.

But in this preliminary research, it is fair to contend that the AFCs get a positive review from most Aboriginal people around the preservation of culture and identities. When it comes to matters related to wellness (i.e. social support), the ratings are also favorable. When it comes to employment, however, the AFCs get a somewhat weaker rating. It is not clear, however, from our analysis to what extent AFCs want to invest resources in employment services, and we assume that this varies across the cities where they are located. Still, the question emerges as to whether the mix of offering employment assistance and cultural programming represents the best practice for AFCs. The means to provide services may exist; however, if the

> At the beginning of this paragraph, the author summarizes his findings. However, he uses **analysis** later in the paragraph. One of the functions of conclusions in academic essays is to analyze and interpret the results, applying them to real-life situations. This is a major difference between academic essays and student essays, in which conclusions are usually concerned with reminding and reinforcing the thesis.

AGREEMENT WITH: FRIENDSHIP CENTRES HELP ABORIGINAL PEOPLE IN MY COMMUNITY TO FEEL CONNECTED TO THE NON-ABORIGINAL COMMUNITY	FRIENDSHIP CENTRES HELP ABORIGINAL PEOPLE TO FEEL CONNECTED TO THEIR OWN COMMUNITY				
	Strongly disagree	Somewhat disagree	Neither agree nor disagree	Somewhat agree	Strongly agree
Strongly disagree	45.8%	25.9%	15.6%	8.9%	4.4%
Somewhat disagree	8.3%	25.9%	15.6%	14.0%	3.1%
Neither agree nor disagree	12.5%	3.7%	50.0%	17.8%	16.2%
Somewhat agree	20.8%	29.6%	14.1%	38.9%	31.6%
Strongly agree	8.3%	7.4%	3.1%	12.7%	37.7%

AFC in a particular community is not best positioned to deliver said services, it may detract from broader efforts to meaningfully reinforce group identities. These questions need further examination.

Finally, the data presented here refute the argument advanced in some quarters that the reinforcement of the bonds between Aboriginal people and building of bridges between Aboriginal and non-Aboriginal peoples are mutually exclusive goals. While not necessarily a surprising finding, it is nevertheless worth highlighting. Recall the definition of "institutional completedness" provided above: to the extent that both strong bonds among Aboriginal people and healthy relationships between Aboriginal and non-Aboriginal people may be viewed by urban Aboriginal people as "needs"; it is exciting to be able to report that AFCs are making important contributions to both the well-being and the institutional completedness of Canada's urban Aboriginal community.

> At the end of his conclusion, the author refers again to the key definition of "institutional completedness" from the Introduction.

References

Breton, Raymond. (1964). "Institutional Completeness of Ethnic Communities and the Personal Relations of Immigrants." *American Journal of Sociology*, 70:2, pp. 193–205.

Department of Canadian Heritage, Corporate Review Branch, (2004, February 25). Report on the Audit of the Aboriginal Friendship Centres Program (AFCP).

EKOS Research Associates. (2004). Aboriginal Friendship Centre Survey. Final Report submitted to: Richard LaRue, Department of Canadian Heritage.

Putnam, Robert D. *Bowling Alone: The Collapse and Revival of American Community.* New York: Simon & Schuster, 2000.

Chapter Review Questions

1. Why are citations needed in an essay?
2. What are some of the different citation styles?
3. Can you combine different citation styles?
4. Why is it important to use the most current style guide when documenting your sources?
5. What is the difference between an in-text citation and a References/Works Cited page?
6. What order is used on the References/Works cited page to list the sources used in your essay?
7. What are the basic elements of APA in-text citations? How does the use of a signal phrase affect this?
8. What are the basic elements of MLA in-text citations? How does the use of a signal phrase affect this?

13

The Argumentative Essay

In this chapter, you will

- learn the difference between an emotional argument and a logical argument

- learn to identify and avoid common errors of logic

- learn what kinds of evidence can be used in an argumentative essay

- learn why it is important to include the opposing point of view

- learn how to build a credible argument using specific strategies

- review outlining and learn techniques for creating an outline for an argumentative essay

Argument requires the use of careful planning and critical thinking skills. Argumentative essays written at college and university rely on logic and reason supported by convincing evidence. Importantly, errors in logic need to be avoided, as these can destroy your credibility with your reader. This chapter will introduce you to some of the most common errors in logic, discuss effective argumentative strategies, and include examples of well-argued essays.

Emotional Versus Logical Arguments

People argue every day, and many think they do it well. However, often these arguments are emotionally based, such as when parents argue with a teenager about the use of the family car. Arguments can also be based on reason and moral standards. When you read a letter to the editor or a proposal for change, often those with the most impact use a combination of argumentative strategies and make appeals to reason, emotion, and ethics.

Even résumé writing involves argument, as you are convincing the employer to hire you rather than someone else applying for the same position. An argumentative essay requires the same logical and critical thinking skills that you use every day. Appeals to reason, emotion, and ethics all can be used in argument, as the following real-life scenario suggests:

You are disappointed by an essay grade and arrange to meet your instructor in her office. By your effective use of reason, you try to convince her to change your mark, conceding the validity of some of her criticisms (concessions are used in many arguments). Going through the paper systematically, you focus on points that seem arguable, asking clarification or elaboration and presenting your counterclaims. As you do, you begin to come across as a responsible, conscientious student: you make an ethical appeal.

You appeal to her as fair-minded, reiterating her helpfulness, your interest in the course, and your desire to do well. In this way, you succeed in establishing common ground, as you would try to do with the reader of your essay. If you argue with integrity, you will leave a good impression. Emotional appeals, such as tearfully bemoaning your stressful life, are apt to be less successful, but subtle appeals may have influence.

In most argumentative essays, the most important appeal is to a reader's reason and logic. Ethical appeals play a vital secondary role, often depending on your topic, but *always* in establishing your credibility as an arguer. Emotional appeals can also be useful, depending on your topic, your audience, and their placement in the essay.

> Successful arguments at the college and university level make appeals to reason, ethics, and emotion. Of these, appeals to reason are usually the most important.

Although good writers build their credibility by using valid arguments and arguing fairly and ethically, some writers do not argue well because they use faulty logic, or they rely solely on emotional appeals. At the college and university level, when you are writing an argumentative essay, you need to avoid these errors, as they affect your credibility, and ultimately, your grades.

Sample Argument

In the scenario below, Ivannia Herrera argued with her roommate over what might seem a trivial issue, a "Tempest in a Teapot"; however, the underlying issues are not trivial. In the course of the argument, some values are seen as more important than others. Although this is an informal argument, it contains many of the features of a formal argument—for example, a claim and supporting evidence. Rebuttals and concessions also are involved. (See pages 278–80.)

Read the argument carefully to find the appeals to reason, emotion, and ethics.

Tempest in a Teapot

Background: My roommate and I share a kitchen and utensils. Each day I make tea in a small stainless steel pot, which has a glass cover and a pouring spout with tiny holes that serve as a strainer. I pour two cups of water into the pot, let it boil, then add the leaves. When the tea is ready, I strain the tea water from the pot, leaving the tea leaves behind. I leave the pot on the counter until the next time I make tea.

The reason for the argument: My roommate has made it plain she does not enjoy seeing the pot with drenched tea leaves in the bottom.

Which points in the argument seem the most convincing to you? Why? Do you think there are any irrelevant points? Are points missing that might have been made?

Table 13.1 My Side/Roommate's Side

MY SIDE	ROOMMATE'S SIDE
If I leave the pot with the tea leaves on the counter, I can reuse them three times. Since I make the same type of tea several times a day, it makes sense that I reuse the leaves rather than throw them out, which will cost me more money in the long run.	The pot is left on the counter for many hours. Though it's okay to reuse the leaves, the kitchen looks messy. I don't like the kitchen looking dirty with an unclean pot sitting there every day. Furthermore, I can't use this pot because it is always filled with tea leaves that I can't throw away.
I bought all the pots and pans in this household, and I am happy to share them; however, if you need a pot like this to use regularly, you should consider buying one yourself.	I also bought utensils for the household—and even the computer. I share these things and understand the concept of sharing. I think that having roommates means having to compromise.
I think of myself as a clean person, and I contribute greatly to the cleanliness of the household. I think that your having to look at a small pot is a small "defect," considering.... Drinking tea is part of my daily life, and I enjoy it. As well, it costs me $6 per month; if I were to discard the tea each time, I would be spending $18 per month, and I can think of better ways to spend those extra $12!	I am not saying that you should throw away the tea leaves, but just find a better way to use them so they are not in sight and taking over the pot. I think that the cleanliness of my living space is a reflection on me, which is why I want a clean environment. I do not like seeing a messy pot, and that is my "defect." I also think I should be able to use the pot if I like, and I can't with the leaves in it.
We both agree on the need to compromise. I'm willing to compromise and buy a ball strainer that can hold the tea leaves inside for as long as need be. It is a small ball attached to a chain; the ball divides in half, the tea leaves are put in one half, the ball is closed, and it is placed inside a cup filled with boiling water. I suggest we compromise and each pay half for the ball strainer.	I'm happy to pay for half of it, as long as you keep the ball with the tea leaves in a cup in your own room. That way, you can bring it out anytime you want tea, but it will be out of my sight.

Argument, Opinion, and Facts

Although the discussion above illustrates an ordinary occurrence, it contains the necessary elements of argument. However, the sample paragraph below is based solely on opinion and cannot be considered an argument. Although her topic can be argued, the writer oversimplifies and uses generalizations that are not backed up by evidence.

> Sports Utility Vehicles, commonly called SUVs, can also be called Stupid Useless Vehicles.
>
> They were designed for people who wanted to travel over different types of terrain in all kinds of weather. A Jeep is a perfect example of this type of vehicle.
>
> If SUVs were used for their intended purpose, then they would be beneficial.
>
> However, most people who purchase them seem to live in towns and cities, and the SUVs never seem to be dirty, which shows they are not used off-road.
>
> Many of these vehicles are driven on highways with rarely more than one passenger, and these overly large vehicles use precious resources and pollute the environment.
>
> Unless people can prove that the SUV is going to be used for the purpose for which it was designed, they should not be allowed to purchase one.

The writer starts by abruptly stating an opinion that not all readers will share.

The writer uses a fact and an example, but also introduces opinion with the adjective "perfect," weakening the statement.

The writer fails to support this point, which is based simply on moral high ground—she also uses flawed reasoning in assuming there is one "intended purpose" for these vehicles.

The writer makes a broad generalization that cannot be argued against. Facts or statistics are more effective in convincing the reader that a claim is valid.

Again, the writer uses a generalization and provides no support.

The writer ends using opinion only, which is ineffective.

As the example above demonstrates, opinion is not the same thing as argument. Many arguments are based on opinion, but in order to be persuasive, shouldn't come across as *opinionated*. Everyone has opinions, but not everyone argues well. Consider the following passage in which the writer makes it clear to the reader that he is opinionated; in doing so, however, he shows poor argumentative skills. In being overwhelmed by opinion, the reader may well miss his points:

> Institutions of higher learning are meant for people hoping to broaden their interests and knowledge in order to contribute to society. I, myself, agree with this principle, and I also

Many arguments are based on opinion, but in order to be persuasive, they shouldn't come across as *opinionated*. Argument at the college or university level is not just writing with an "attitude"; in fact, in effective arguments, writers express themselves objectively, using neutral language.

agree that a degree can help me acquire a job and be good at it. Along with this, I do not doubt that these institutions facilitate higher cognitive functioning. What I do not agree with is the approach that these institutions have towards the sciences. In fact, I categorically oppose the favouritism that is always shown to the sciences whenever financial matters are considered.

Exercise 13.1

Rewrite the paragraph, eliminating the references to opinion and changing pronouns from "I," "me," etc., to "one" or a suitable noun. Does the revised paragraph sound more forceful? How is the writer's credibility enhanced?

> In your own argumentative essays, always clearly separate fact from opinion. When you use opinion, it should be supported—by logic and/or reliable evidence, such as facts.

Opinions are also not the same as facts, which can be verified by observation or research. Opinions can be challenged. As you will see, you cannot argue a position on a topic that has no opposing view—in other words, that cannot be challenged. On the other hand, facts can be interpreted differently and used for different purposes. Facts, therefore, can be used to support the thesis of an argumentative essay. However, effective arguers are always clear about when they are using facts and when they are using opinion. In reading, use your critical thinking skills to ask if the writer always clearly separates facts from opinion. If not, he or she might be guilty of faulty reasoning. See below.

Fact (not challengeable):

- The moon is 378,000 kilometers from earth's equator.

Fact:

- According to moon landing conspiracy theories, the 1969 Apollo moon landing was faked.

Opinion (challengeable):

- The Apollo moon landing didn't actually take place; it was all a hoax.

Fact:

- On November 13, 2009, NASA announced that water had been found on the moon.

Opinion:

- Now that water has been found on the moon, humans should set up colonies at the moon's poles by 2050.

Exercise 13.2

Consider the two pairs of statements above on the topic of humans on the moon. Discuss the ways that fact differs from opinion in each case. Come up with other topics and write two statements for each, one of which represents a fact and the other of which represents an opinion.

Exercise 13.3

Recall a recent argument. Begin by briefly describing the circumstances that led to it. Then, divide a page in half vertically and summarize each point raised by "your side" and "the other side" (see Table 13.1). Simply report what was said (do not embellish with interpretations of what was said)—each side's point of view and the counter-argument, if there was one. When a new point begins, draw a horizontal line to separate it from the next point. Then analyze the strengths and weaknesses of each point. Did the point make an appeal to reason? Did it make an emotional appeal? An ethical one? Was an opinion supported? Were facts used to support an opinion? Were the points logically related to one another? Was the argument resolved? If so, how? Write a paragraph response to the argument, analyzing flaws, such as simplifications and generalizations. In your analysis, try to be as objective as possible to *both* sides.

Faulty Reasoning

Because it is so easy to make mistakes when first trying to write an argumentative essay, it is important to understand what *not* to do before learning how to argue well. Besides, when you argue, you will be in a better position to point out flaws in your opponent's argument if you understand where arguments can go wrong. Once you have become familiar with some of the common problems that affect argumentative essays, you will be shown how to create arguable claims and support these claims by well-reasoned points and specific argumentative strategies.

> A fallacy is a misleading or unsound argument.

Logical, Emotional, and Ethical Fallacies

Ineffective arguments that use logical, emotional, or ethical **fallacies** detract from the writer's credibility: we do not trust someone who misuses logic or reason. For example, we might well mistrust a person who argued that because some students are underage, all college and university campus pubs should be closed.

> Misuse of emotional or ethical appeals shows unfairness to the other side: emotional fallacies *exploit* emotions so are very different from valid appeals to emotion.

Misuse of emotional or ethical appeals shows unfairness to the other side: emotional fallacies *exploit* emotions so are very different from valid appeals to emotion. People frequently misuse emotion. We have all been told that the emissions from vehicles affect the environment and that larger vehicles are more harmful than smaller ones. But that fact alone does not mean that all drivers of pick-up trucks or SUVs in the city should be condemned, as the writer of the paragraph on page 265 stated. The vehicles have several uses within a city. The owner of an SUV might be a landscaper and need the vehicle for work. By stating that *all* people driving large vehicles in the city do not care about the environment, one is guilty of misusing emotional or ethical appeals.

Some fallacies are based on faulty inductive reasoning, for example, cause–effect fallacies, such as if I wash my car, it will rain. Others are based on the faulty use of deductive reasoning where general or universal statements are made that may not be true, such as all people who ride bicycles are environmentalists. (Inductive and deductive reasoning are discussed below, pages 276–8.)

Avoid faulty reasoning in your own writing and look for examples in the argument of your opponent. Avoiding them in your own writing and analyzing

> Writers should be careful in making generalizations. When you make a generalization, something that is applicable to all people in a large category, make sure it does truly apply to *all people* in the category.

Table 13.2   Fallacy Terms

TERM	DEFINITION	EXAMPLE
Treadmill logic	An argument that does not move forward or that continues in a circle. The main point is just repeated, but not expanded.	Applied degrees are now available at some community colleges in Canada. They are only offered there because community colleges teach applied skills.
Guilt by association	An argument that uses the fact that some supposedly disreputable person or group supports a view as an argument against it or opposes it as an argument in its favour.	How bad can whale hunting be when an extremist group like Greenpeace opposes it?
Red herring	A fallacy of irrelevance that attempts to distract or sidetrack the reader, often by using an ethical fallacy. In the first example, there may be some validity to the point, but it should not form the basis of an argument.	My honourable opponent's business went bankrupt. How can we trust him to run the country? I know that particular business supports the arts, but it made $1.5 billion last year.
Straw man	Another fallacy of irrelevance; it misrepresents an opponent's main argument by substituting a false or minor argument in its place. The point is to get the audience to agree with the minor argument, making it easier to criticize the opponent's overall argument. The "straw man," then, is a flimsily constructed argument that is substituted for a valid one.	Thaddeus Tuttle points out that while women have not achieved wage parity with men, they often take maternity leaves, which means they don't work as much as men. Among its flaws, this argument ignores the basic principle of equal pay for equal work.

(continued)

Table 13.2   (Continued)

Bandwagon	An emotional fallacy; it argues in favour of something because it has become popular.	Everyone has seen the movie. We have to see it tonight.
Doubtful causes	Insists that a result is inevitable and cites too few causes to support that result; it bases an argument on a relationship that may not exist.	He looked unhappy after the exam; he must have failed miserably. (This assumes there was only one cause for his unhappiness—if, indeed, he was unhappy; making this assumption is also an example of a cause–effect fallacy.)
False cause	Another cause–effect fallacy; asserts that simply because one event preceded another one, there must be a cause–effect relationship between them.	Neesha wears her favourite socks to class the day she fails a test; consequently, she throws the socks away. Superstitions can arise when people assume a causal relationship between two events. Of course, there are causal relationships between many events; for example, if Neesha walked in front of a car and was hit, then obviously her action resulted in her injury. A false cause assumes a connection without valid evidence.
Hasty generalization	Forms a conclusion based on little or no evidence.	I talked to two people, both of whom said the text was useless, so I will not buy it. (Perhaps many people bought the text, so two people may not be a good sample.)
Certain consequences (slippery slope)	A common fallacy with many other names. It insists that a result will be inevitable based on an oversimplified cause–effect relationship.	If we legalize marijuana, other more dangerous drugs are going to end up being legalized as well.
Either/or (false dilemma)	Suggests that there are only two available options.	Either I borrow the car tonight or my life is over. Consider that notorious cry "you're either with me or against me," which takes the logical either/or fallacy and gives it a strong emotional thrust.
Middle ground fallacy	In contrast to either/or above, this fallacy assumes that in the face of two seemingly irreconcilable options, a third option, such as a position midway between extremes, is the only one.	Since Donnie wants the family pet to be a dog and Ronnie wants a cat, we'll get a bird.
"It does not follow"	This suggests that there is a logical connection (such as cause–effect) between two unrelated areas.	If we hadn't built planes to conquer gravity, the NY tragedy of September 11 wouldn't have happened. I worked hard on this essay; I deserve at least a B+. (Unfortunately, working hard at something does not guarantee success, even if it does make it more likely.)
False analogy	Compares two things that are, in fact, not alike. While true analogies can provide support for a point, to draw a true analogy you need to have a real basis for comparison, which does not exist in the example.	How can people complain about circuses that use wild animals in their acts; we keep animals, such as cats, that were once wild in small spaces in our homes.

(continued)

Table 13.2	(Continued)	
TERM	**DEFINITION**	**EXAMPLE**
Fortune-telling	Denies an effect as arising from a cause on the basis that it hasn't happened yet—therefore, it's not going to. In this distorted cause-effect fallacy, the arguer projects into the future without considering probability or other evidence.	Uncle Harry has smoked two packs of cigarettes a day for 20 years, and he hasn't died yet, so smoking obviously is not that dangerous.
Finite categories	Asserts that something belongs in a certain category on the basis of only one characteristic.	I am sixteen now, so where are the keys to the car? (The illogical assumption here is that legality alone determines the right to drive a car.)
Desk-thumping (dogmatism)	This common type of argument asserts without supporting evidence on the basis of what you firmly, perhaps passionately, believe.	It is everyone's moral obligation to oppose the new tax. (In argumentative essays, it's best to avoid the self-conscious reference to your opinion; instead, you should let your points talk for you.)
Tradition (or, that is the way we have always done it)	Argues for a course of action because it has been followed before, even if the same conditions no longer apply.	You shouldn't ask if you can go to Toronto for the Thanksgiving weekend. This is a time you always spend with your family.

the flaws in others' arguments will enhance your credibility. Although these categories may enable you to identify the misuse of reason, emotion, or ethics, the categories are not all-inclusive; in some instances, more than one type of fallacy may be involved.

There are certainly many occasions when, for example, you will be able to successfully argue that the ends do justify the means, where there may be only two alternatives to consider (either/or), or where a point can be explained using an analogy. For example, as discussed below (page 273), analogies and other comparisons are often used in argument, but if the basis for comparing two things is faulty, the writer's credibility will be affected.

When writing an argumentative essay, remember that all lines of argument work most effectively when they are combined with other arguments. However, using fallacies oversimplifies the point being discussed. The writer using them weakens his or her argument, as a reader could easily think, "Wait a minute; that doesn't make sense." When you use argument, you want your statements to be forceful and effective—not to arouse suspicion.

Writers need to look closely and objectively at the *way* they argue and ensure that their arguments are always based on logic and that their appeals to emotion are always moderate, not extreme or exaggerated. Watching out for the first will make the writer appear reliable and trustworthy; watching out for the last will make the writer appear fair.

Writers need to look closely and objectively at the *way* they argue and ensure that their arguments are based on logic and that their appeals to emotion are moderate.

Exercise 13.4

Silencing

Writers sometimes resort to logical or emotional fallacies because they can silence the listener or reader. They do so because there is no logical response possible since their reasoning is flawed. Each of the following statements is based on faulty reasoning. Try to determine why it fails the test of reason and why it would not be effective in an argumentative essay. If it seems an example of one of the fallacies listed in Table 13.2, decide which one; in some cases, more than one fallacy might be involved.

1. In our family, males have always been named "Harold" and females "Gertrude"; therefore, you should name your twins "Harry" and "Gerty."

2. If you don't get a degree in law, medicine, or business these days, you're never going to make any money.

3. When I serve you dinner, it's terrible not to eat all of it when you consider that one-third of the world's population goes to bed hungry.

4. The teacher hasn't called on me to answer a question for three consecutive days; it looks like I don't need to do the reading for tomorrow.

5. I know I went through the red light, officer, but the car in front of me did, too.

Using Slanted Language

In addition to the misuse of logic and emotion, writers can show their lack of objectivity by using **slanted** or **loaded language**. Such language shows that the writer is not objective and detracts from his or her credibility. Slanted language can take many forms from extreme statements to qualifiers (adjectives or adverbs) that convey, sometimes subtly, a bias. When slanted language is direct and offensive, it is easy to spot. For example, if you dismissed the other side as "evil" or their argument as "horrible" or "disgusting," you would reveal your bias. When you use slanted language, readers could easily take offence and question your fairness.

> Slanted language reveals the writer's bias, affecting his or her credibility. It can take direct forms, such as accusatory language, or be more indirect.

However, slanted language can be less obvious, for example, when words play unfairly on the **connotations**, rather than the denotations, of language—in other words, on the negative implications of particular words, rather than on their literal meanings. A writer's careful and conscious use of a word's connotations can be effective in an argument, but if the purpose is to distort the truth, then the writer's credibility will be at stake. For example, in the passage below, "removed from office," in place of "voted out of office," plays unfairly on the connotations of the first phrase. The italicized words in the following reveal slanted language:

> A connotation is the implied meaning of a word in addition to its literal (dictionary) meaning.

In the recent election, the *reigning* political *regime was removed from office* as a result of the *atrocities they had committed* against the people of the province. The voters believed the new government would improve things, but when you achieve such easy victory there is a tendency to overlook the reason for your victory: the people who elected you. Today, the government is ignoring the middle class, *betraying* the very people who *naively* voted them into office.

Exercise 13.5

The following paragraphs suffer from faulty logic and/or emotional appeals, as well as examples of slanted language. In groups, analyze the arguments, determine what fallacies and inconsistencies make them ineffective, and suggest improvements to make the argument stronger. More important than being able to identify the precise fallacy is being able to see that the statements are illogical or make unfair appeals to emotion.

1. Genetically engineered foods are being sold in most supermarkets without anyone knowing that we are being used as guinea pigs for the corporations developing this technology. The general public is being kept in the dark entirely, and the way that this food is being sold is through one-sided advertising. The public is being told that genetically engineered foods are a safe and effective way to grow a lot of food faster by inserting genetic material of one species into another. Though the proponents of genetically engineered foods attempt to convince the public that this technology will save lives, the reality is that major biotechnology companies are developing genetically engineered food crops to maximize their profits. Corporations would have us believe that the reason why 19,000 children starve to death daily is because of inefficient agricultural practices, but the world currently produces enough food today to provide a decent diet for every person on this planet. In spite of this fact, genetically engineered foods are being sold as the cure for Third World starvation. This, however, is simply not true. The motives of the companies selling genetically engineered foods are not to save the lives of starving people, but to line their own pockets by profiting from the biotechnological industry. As a society, we should move to force governments to ban the development of genetically engineered foods before it is too late.

2. The legalization of marijuana would destroy society as we know it today. The typical Canadian would be exposed to many harsh drugs, such as coke, crack and heroin, due to the increased acceptance of drugs within the community. Rehabilitation clinics for chronic drug users would be a huge drain on the economy. There would have to be new laws and screenings implemented to prevent people from working with heavy machinery or operating a motor vehicle while impaired by marijuana. Canadian business owners would be dissatisfied with many of their employees, and then discrimination would rear its ugly head. Firing someone for smoking marijuana and not being productive at work is not discrimination; however, the point would be made that it is. Clearly, our society would sink to a despicable level if this drug were legalized.

Creating Your Argument by Claims and Support

In order for your argument to be effective, you can use a variety of general strategies, including

- making a claim of value (something is right or wrong)
- making a claim of policy (a policy or practice needs to be changed)
- interpreting facts, such as statistics, to support your claim
- providing evidence from the experts
- supporting your points with credible examples, such as case studies
- supporting your points using soft evidence, such as analogies, description, or personal experience
- defining a term or concept, especially if the term could be misunderstood
- comparing your ideas to other ideas that the audience understands

Considering these points while avoiding fallacies will help create a paper that builds your credibility as an arguer.

One way to help make a point easier for a reader to understand or relate to is to use an analogy (comparison) or description. For example, author Elizabeth Bowen used the following analogy in her book *The House in Paris:*

"Memory is to love what the saucer is to the cup."

Analogy can often help the reader visualize your argument, making a point easier to understand. However, you need to make sure you use an analogy that the audience can relate to.

Description may also play a limited role in argument, perhaps to attract interest in the essay's introduction or to set up a main point. Student writer Leslie Nelson began her essay on adolescent depression this way:

Imagine a deep, dark hole that stretches forever without end. There is no light at either end of this hole; there is nobody else in this hole except you. Imagine living in this hole for hours, days, weeks, years. Imagine believing that you will never escape. Most teenagers find themselves in this hole—depression—at least once in their adolescent life, a time when nothing seems to go right.

If you use **personal experience**, it is important to keep your tone objective. See Chapter 7, page 128. Check with your instructor before you use personal experience.

Definition can also help your readers understand how you are using a concept or term. For example, in writing a paper about the value of post-secondary education, you might want to define what this concept means to you. Does it include university, community college, and private degree-granting institutions (such as the ones you see commercials for on television), or does it include only university and community college?

An analogy is a comparison between two objects that are not usually associated in order to explain or clarify one of the objects.

Description gives sensuous detail to enable a reader to visualize a scene or situation.

The limited use of personal experience is often effective in argument. However, simply using the pronoun *I* or *my*, as in "I believe…", "my opinion is…" is not the same thing as using personal experience as evidence.

Comparison and contrast can help a reader visualize something by setting it alongside what he or she knows. A student writer was trying to explain how housing in Japan can be more sanitary than that in North America because people do not wear their shoes in the house. She described tatami flooring, but wanted to make sure her audience could visualize the flooring. (This example also uses description.)

Tatami, or rice mat, flooring is common in Japan. Tatami is similar to the rice mats that one can buy for use on the beach; however, tatami does not fold up. The rice matting is placed on large wooden frames and fastened securely to these frames. One mat is difficult for most adults to pick up alone. An average room can have six or eight mats on the floor.

Any of these strategies can be used to support your argumentative thesis. However, the beginning point for argument, as in most college and university writing, is in the introduction where you state your major claim, your thesis.

Arguable Claims

As mentioned, arguments relying solely on opinions have no place in a reason-based argument. What is needed for a valid argument? First, you need an *arguable topic*. If you and a friend start debating whether a homemade hamburger tastes better than one from the frozen food aisle, who is right? How can you determine this? If you are using only subjective standards (such as what you *think* tastes better), obviously neither you nor your friend is "right" because the topic is not arguable. On the other hand, you could base your argument on the respective nutritional values, comparing the fat content or the additives and preservatives.

> A topic that can be argued is (1) based on objective, not just subjective, standards, and (2) has an opposing viewpoint.

There are other kinds of claims that are not arguable. You could not easily write an argumentative essay on the virtues of good health, as there is no opposing view. Similarly unarguable are obvious claims, such as "computers have changed a great deal in the last decade." A controversial subject does not always translate into an arguable one. For example, an argument that justifies computer hacking or the writing of viruses likely is not valid.

Specific, Interesting, and Manageable Claims

You also need to ensure that the claim, like all thesis statements, is **specific**, **interesting**, and **manageable**. Below, we focus on a sample argumentative claim, showing the kinds of questions you can ask to help you develop a strong and effective thesis for an argumentative essay. To review claims and thesis statements, see Chapters 5 and 7.

Specific Claims

A **specific claim** states clearly what you will be arguing. The reader should know whether the claim is one of fact, value, or policy. In addition, a specific claim is worded precisely.

> A specific claim states clearly what you will be arguing and is worded precisely, not vaguely.

Vague claim: Parents of children who play hockey would like to see fighting eliminated from the game at all levels.

Is this claim specific? Although it technically satisfies the two conditions for an arguable topic, it is not specific enough to suggest the kind of argument to follow or even if the essay will be focused on argument rather than exposition: "parents," "would like to see," and "at all levels" are vague. Also, the phrase "eliminated from the game at all levels" does not seem connected to the rest of the claim. What has this got to do with the parents who presumably don't like seeing their children fight? Expanded thesis statements can be useful in arguments (see Chapter 5), as the reader will see at a glance that you have supported your claim. In the following revised thesis statement, the claim is expressed more clearly due to the choice of specific words as well as the inclusion of main points. As well, "should" clearly reveals a policy claim.

> *More specific argumentative claim*: Fighting should be prohibited in hockey, since violence gives young hockey players a negative model and reinforces a "win at all costs" mentality.

Although a claim may be specific if it is precisely worded, it is often a good idea, as mentioned above, to follow the claim by defining concepts central to your argument. In the claim above, the writer might define what is meant by "fighting." Does the dropping of hockey gloves constitute the beginning of a fight? Does overly physical contact? Does a fight begin when there is a third player involved? Definition enables the writer to narrow the topic, to make it more specific.

An "all or none" kind of claim is also non-specific. Where your claim is too broad, you should either use qualifiers to restrict its scope or reword it to make it more realistic. Examples of qualifiers include *usually*, *often*, *sometimes*, *in part*, *many*, *some*, *several*, *a few*, and many others. In addition, you can use verbs and verb phrases that qualify and limit, such as *may*, *seems*, *contribute to*, and *play a role in*.

Interesting Claims

Is this claim interesting? To help ensure your claim is interesting, it should be drafted with a specific audience in mind. In the claim about fighting in hockey, the intended audience is hockey parents as well as coaches, managers, and other hockey executives, people who can make changes. Many die-hard fans of professional hockey would not be interested in the main point of the argument, as it applies mostly to children. Those who never watch hockey or don't have children playing hockey probably would be even less interested. Similarly, an argument concerning the best measures to prevent eutrophication and growth of single-celled algae in China's lakes and reservoirs might be interesting to marine biologists, but probably not to the average reader.

Along with audience interest, an important consideration is the viewpoint of your audience. Are most people to whom the argument is addressed likely to agree with you? Disagree? Be neutral? Will they possess general knowledge of the topic? Is the topic a current one that most will have heard of? These kinds of questions will be even more relevant when you come to structure your essay

> To help ensure the claim is interesting (as well as specific), it should be drafted with a specific audience in mind. Whom do you think might be interested in the topic but not share your viewpoint?

and support your claim. For example, if your audience will include many opponents, it may be important to establish common ground and to convince them that you have similar values and goals. See "Rebutting the Opposing View," on page 278, for specific audience strategies.

Manageable Claims

Although the manageability of a claim will be determined partly by whether it is specific and interesting, it will also depend on essay length, availability of support, and the complexity of the issues raised by the claim.

Policy-based claims, which try to persuade people to take action, go beyond simply proving something is bad or unfair. Often needed are realistic solutions or at least suggestions that these kinds of solutions exist. Is the proposal realistic? To say that a government should increase funding to post-secondary education by 25 per cent is probably not realistic given the current economy. If the change you propose isn't realistic, it may be best to change your claim to one of value or else reword it. Your supporting points may be complex, but the thesis statement itself must be workable and clear to the reader.

The claim about hockey violence was found to be arguable, specific, and interesting (to its intended audience), but is it *manageable*?

> Fighting should be prohibited in hockey, since violence gives young hockey players a negative model and reinforces a "win at all costs" mentality.

The issue of banning fighting throughout hockey, especially at the professional level, seems too complex to be manageable if the issues relating to young hockey players are also to be addressed. Realistically, would the fact that many hockey players act as role models for younger players motivate those who manage the game to ban fighting? To make the statement manageable, the writer could focus *either* on the way that fights in professional hockey undermine hockey players as role models *or* on the consequences of fighting in minor hockey.

> *Value claim*: Fighting in professional hockey gives young hockey players a negative model since violence reinforces a "win at all costs" mentality.
> *Reworded policy claim*: Fighting should be prohibited in minor hockey at below the midget level since violence reinforces a "win at all costs" mentality.

A Closer Look at Reason

Two main kinds of reasoning are used in arguments: **inductive** and **deductive** reasoning. In inductive reasoning, you arrive at a conclusion based on occurrences that are observed and recorded. Deductive reasoning arrives at a conclusion by stating a general principle, the **major premise**, and applying it to a specific case, the **minor premise**, as explained below.

Sidebar 1: Factors in manageable claims include essay length, support available, complexity of the topic, and practicality of the claim.

Sidebar 2: Remember that all claims need to focus on one main topic, not to straddle two related topics. In addition to specific, interesting, and manageable claims, all claims must be focused and clear.

Inductive Reasoning in Practice   Inductive reasoning is called *scientific reasoning* because scientific research frequently relies on the collection and analyzing of specific data to arrive at a conclusion. We also use inductive reasoning daily to draw conclusions. Consider the following example:

Recorded observations:
on June 5 the sun set at 9:16
on June 6 it set at 9:16
on June 7 it set at 9:17
on June 8 it set at 9:17
on June 9 it set at 9:18
Prediction/Claim:
on June 10, the sun will set at 9:18

It is possible to make this prediction because we have observed specific data about the setting sun. (Of course, knowledge of the motion of the earth around the sun would also be needed to ensure the accuracy of the predictions.)

If we had simply recorded the times that the sun set on June 5 and 6, we might conclude that the sun would set at 9:16 on June 7, which would be incorrect: we would be drawing a conclusion without enough evidence. On the other hand, if we made our first set of observations in Edmonton, Alberta, on June 5 and 6 and the second set in Regina, Saskatchewan, on June 7 and 8, the conclusions would also be incorrect because the method for evidence-gathering would be flawed.

Most research studies focusing on causes and effects, such as clinical trials to confirm the causes of a disease or to test a new drug, work by induction to discover a probable cause or effect.

Logical fallacies in inductive reasoning can develop where

- there is not enough evidence to make a generalization
- the means for gathering the evidence are flawed or biased

Again, a fallacy of this type in an essay can affect your credibility, so it important to always use sound reasoning and consider the validity of every statement you make when you argue.

Deductive Reasoning in Practice   The deductive reasoning process can be broken down into two parts, each of which can be represented by two statements, one general and the other specific, a major premise and a minor premise. The third step involves combining the two to reach a conclusion. Below is an example of a logical argument based on the deductive method.

Major premise: It is wrong not to treat all people with respect.
Minor premise: In building the dam, the Urra company did not treat the indigenous peoples with respect.
Conclusion: The Urra company was wrong to build the dam.

Inductive reasoning is sometimes called *scientific reasoning* because scientists and other researchers use it to answer questions about the natural world and make predications about natural phenomena.

Two questions to ask yourself when using inductive reasoning are (1) Have I provided enough support for each statement I make? and (2) Have I been logical and consistent in the way I have used reason (my reasoning method)? Several examples of flawed inductive reasoning are illustrated in the table on logical fallacies, p. 268—for example, "hasty generalization" and "doubtful causes."

Two questions to ask yourself when using deductive reasoning are (1) Does the major premise (general statement) apply to the people or situation described? and (2) Is it a valid generalization? Faulty logic, like that used in the example above, weakens your credibility. Several examples of faulty deductive reasoning are illustrated in the table on logical fallacies, p. 268—for example, "finite categories" and the "tradition" fallacy.

Examples of faulty reasoning can be observed daily, and, unfortunately, can have negative consequences. Many forms of stereotyping are based on faulty deductive reasoning.

Major premise: People who spend more than two hours a day at their computers are geeks.
Minor premise: Brandon spends more than two hours a day at his computer.
Conclusion: Brandon is a geek.

Most logical arguments combine inductive and deductive reasoning. Arguing successfully is a challenge; to be successful, you need to test the logic of your own reasoning as you proceed from one point to the next.

Rebutting the Opposing View

> The rebuttal is that part of your argument in which you raise the points on the other side, usually in order to strengthen your argument and to appear fair.

When you write an argumentative essay, you should present the opposing viewpoint. In the past, you may have been told not to introduce the opposing side, as this could weaken your argument. However, by including the other side, you are showing the reader that you are aware of it and that your own points are strong enough to counter your opponent's. The rebuttal is that part of your argument in which you raise the points on the other side in order to strengthen your own argument. Your rebuttal may be determined by

Exercise 13.6

Detective Work: Read the following short scenarios and analyze how the police reached their decision (i.e., analyze their reasoning methods) or why the investigation failed. How might *inductive* methods have been involved? If inductive methods were flawed, was the problem related to a lack of evidence or faulty methods of evidence gathering? How might *deductive* methods have been involved? If deductive methods were involved, what generalization was used as a major premise?

1. *Scenario*: After a robbery at an expensive and seemingly burglar-proof home, the police investigation settled on two possible suspects. One suspect had been seen near the house near the time of the robbery, but had never previously been arrested. The second suspect had not been seen near the house but was unable to account for his movements that night; furthermore, he had two prior robbery convictions. *Result:* Police brought the second man in for questioning.

2. *Scenario*: Police believed they would easily be able to determine the suspect of an assault when they discovered blood samples on the floor and wall of the crime scene. But the crime scene officer, who was working on his first case, neglected to prepare the samples correctly, and they deteriorated. *Result:* Police were unable to come up with a suspect.

- the topic itself
- your audience
- your purpose in arguing

Topic If the reader is likely familiar with the topic and the major points of debate (such as arguments about legalizing marijuana), it is a good strategy to raise each point and rebut it; see Strategy B below. If a topic is likely to be less familiar to a reader, it may be best to acknowledge only the major counter-argument(s), while ensuring that your points are stronger and more numerous. If the main arguments on the other side are obvious, however, there may be little point in giving space to them in your essay.

Audience If your audience is made up of mild opponents and the undecided, it may be wise simply to acknowledge the other side and counter it by a strong argument, employing Strategy A, Acknowledgement. If, however, you are addressing strong opponents, acknowledging their side and perhaps even making concessions would be advisable (see below). An important aspect of rebuttal is to anticipate your opponents' objections. Analyzing the views of your opponent should show that, having considered them, you find them inadequate. Consider using Strategy B, Point-by-Point Rebuttal, then, if your audience opposes you.

Being sensitive to your audience might mean stressing ways readers can benefit—either personally or as members of a community—from considering your view. In her essay on safe injection sites (Sample Student Argumentative Essay, page 289), Kerry Hinds addresses mild opponents by pointing to the disadvantages drug users must overcome; when she argues that these sites would reduce health care costs, she is addressing a stronger opponent, one, perhaps, motivated more by practical than human concerns.

Whether the reader is undecided, mildly opposed, or strongly opposed, you should work to establish **common ground**. This can be done by showing that you share basic values with your readers, though you may disagree with the action to be taken. Making **concessions**, agreeing in part to their argument, shows your reasonableness and desire to compromise.

Purpose The primary goal of an argumentative essay is not always to win the argument, and an argument should not be judged successful just because it silences the opposition. An argument may be an opportunity to engage in dialogue with others who share your concern about the topic, to enable your reader to see another side of a problem or another dimension to an issue in order to view it with greater tolerance. Long-lasting change is often a result of an attitude of openness and flexibility on the arguer's part, while a "pin the opponent" approach may result in nothing more than a fleeting victory. The open approach to arguing can be particularly effective with value-based claims.

> Showing how opponents can benefit by agreeing with your thesis is a common argumentative strategy.

> When you establish common ground, you show that you and your opponent share basic values; using this strategy may make opponents believe your side and theirs are not far apart.

> When you make a concession or concede a point, you acknowledge its validity. Doing so enables you to come across as fair and reasonable. Arguers often concede a point in order to follow with a strong point of their own.

Two Strategies for Rebuttal

Strategy A: Acknowledgement   Acknowledging the other side is important in most arguments. In cases where you need only acknowledge the opposition, you will have to decide how much space to devote to this. In the following example, student writer Laura Benard briefly characterizes the opposing viewpoint using only a prepositional phrase ("Despite their aesthetic value") ahead of her thesis statement. She presents no real rebuttal, but treats the opposing argument, that people use pesticides to make their lawn look attractive, as obvious:

> Despite their aesthetic value, the negative impacts of maintaining lawns by means of pesticide, lawn mower, and water use are so great that lawn owners should adopt less intensive maintenance practices or consider lawn alternatives.

Writers often put the acknowledgement in the form of a dependent clause that contains the less important (opposing) information, followed by their own claim expressed in an independent clause. "Although some may argue . . . [major point of opposition argument], the fact is/I believe that . . . [your thesis]."

It is often necessary to provide background for the reader or a brief summary of the opposing view. In such cases, the writer can begin with this view, then follow with his or her own argument. Deciding how much space you spend on the opposing view requires striking a balance between the desire to demonstrate your willingness to be objective and the desire to present a strong argument of your own.

Strategy B: Point-by-Point Rebuttal   You should consider responding thoroughly to the other side if it has strong support or if your purpose is to arrive at a compromise; in the latter case, you will be trying to find a meeting place. In both cases, you would raise individual points, usually beginning with the opponent's point, and respond to the weaknesses in the opponent's position. If your purpose is to win the argument, you will stress the opponent's inadequacies and inconsistencies, and draw attention to any fallacies. If your purpose is to find common ground, you will point out the inadequacies of the opposing viewpoint but assume the role of a constructive critic more than that of a strong opponent. In both cases, though, your voice should be unbiased and objective.

In the excerpt below, student writer Spencer Cleave addresses a common argument supporting the US embargo against Cuba. After a concession (italicized below), he introduces two counter-claims, developed in the succeeding paragraph, that attempt to undercut the original claim:

> Many supporters of the maintenance of the trade embargo against Cuba contend that the Cuban government fails to uphold the human rights of its population. *It is true that Cuba has had a number of human rights violations in its past. Thus, it is conceded that Cuba is also morally at fault on certain issues.* However, many reforms have recently been made by the government in an attempt to remedy its human rights problems. These efforts show that the government has a desire to improve the conditions within its own nation. Furthermore, it

A concise method of acknowledging your opponent is to summarize the argument in a phrase or dependent clause and follow with your own summarized thesis in an independent clause.

When you give background information or summarize the opposing view, make sure you use an objective tone and neutral language. It is a good idea to summarize as concisely as possible while stating that side's points clearly and fairly.

would be in the best interest of the US to applaud the Cuban government in any human rights improvements, thus giving the image of a co-operative partner.

Because the opponents of legalized marijuana have a strong and often–debated case, student writer Stewart Lord chooses to address the main points of their argument systematically, summarizing these points and refuting them with facts and statistics (Sample Student Argumentative Essay, page 292). Similarly, because some environmentalists have been vocal in their public opposition to wind farms, David Suzuki responds to their claims systematically throughout his essay. Suzuki also uses emotional appeals, concessions, and appeals to common ground (see page 285).

The section on the argumentative essay began by noting the importance of argument in all aspects of our lives. What follows is adapted from an information campaign of a medical service company in response to a government decision to restructure the company's services. Although the form of the argument is very different from that of an essay, notice that the necessary parts of an argument are included and that in other respects, too, it conforms to the basic argumentative model discussed above. Numbers and letters have been added in order to make it comparable to body paragraphs in an outline.

> If you use a point-by-point rebuttal, you do not have to respond to *all* your opponent's points. In shorter essays, you may not have the space to rebut any more than one point. As well, the opposing side might have only one strong argument, in which case it would be counterproductive to mention other points.

"Please Sign Our Petition": A Case Study

WE NEED YOUR SUPPORT! PLEASE SIGN OUR PETITION

The government plans to fundamentally change how laboratory services are delivered. These plans jeopardize the lab services you depend on.

These plans could also compromise one of the best lab systems there is—one that has been serving patients in communities across our province for more than 45 years.

I. WHAT THE GOVERNMENT IS PLANNING:

A.	B.	C.
It has already announced a 20% cut in the fees it pays to community labs for the testing services we provide.	It is planning to dismantle the existing province-wide system and create six independent lab delivery systems—one within each of the health authorities.	It is planning to establish a bidding process that would see each health authority going to tender for all outpatient lab services.

> As with most arguments, the claim is announced early. It is a policy claim, as the reader is asked to take an action—sign a petition. However, it is based on a value claim, that government plans could "compromise one of the best lab systems." To support this, the company cites facts and statistics in the bulleted list, showing that the labs provide essential services.

(Continued)

The argument begins by summarizing three points of the opposing position. Systematically, the points are refuted in the next two sections. For example, point A above is countered by two points under "What this means to patient care" (point A below). The argument is developed through cause and effect: a 20% cut (cause) will affect patients and patient care.

II. WHAT THIS MEANS TO PATIENT CARE:

A.	B.	C.
1. Alone, the magnitude of the fee cuts will affect patients and patient care.	The government's plans will result in six fragmented systems—potentially providing six levels of service and access—and six new bureaucracies to manage them.	Applying a competitive bidding process to laboratory medicine comes at a very high risk. Price is always a major factor in any competitive bidding process, and lowest bids come with reduced access service levels.
2. The government's other plans will bring a period of complete instability, turning today's system upside down.		

III. OUR CONCERNS:

A.	B.	C.
The government based its plans on flawed, faulty, and unsubstantiated data.	We don't understand why the government chose to dismantle a system that works well, instead of building on its strengths.	We fully support the government's goals. However, we don't agree with the way it is trying to achieve these goals.

In addition to countering the major points of the government's argument, the company is concerned with establishing its credibility. Topic II addresses "patient care," focusing concern directly on the reader. Topic III Point C attempts to find common ground in an effort to show fairness to the government side: "We fully support the government's goals."

IV. WHAT WE'VE DONE

A.

1. We've told the government repeatedly that we support its goals and can help them achieve them. We've told the government to put its plans on hold so that we can talk to them about less disruptive alternatives.

2. We've told patients and physicians about the government's plans and how they could affect lab services and service levels.

WHAT WE'RE DOING NOW

B.

1. We're asking people who value the services we provide to show their support by signing our petition.

2. If you want to know more about the government's plans and our concerns, please visit our website.

C. **If you care about protecting the lab services you rely on — please sign our petition.**

IV. serves as a conclusion to the argument. The information in Points A, B, and C, in effect, summarize the claim by rewording it: in the claim/thesis, the phrase "jeopardize the lab services you depend on" is used; compare — "affect lab services and service levels," "value the services we provide," and "protecting the lab services you rely on." Point C makes an emotional appeal with its deliberate choice of the words "care" and "protect."

Community Lab Facts (statistical evidence to back the claim):

- For more than 45 years, physicians and their patients have relied on the quality cost-effective diagnostic testing and information services community labs provide.
- The testing and information services we provide help doctors diagnose, treat, and monitor their patients.
- Every day, the 1600 people working in community labs
  - provide a selection of several hundred different tests, from routine to specialty diagnostics.
  - support early discharge hospital programs by providing access to lab testing at home and in the community.
  - perform more than 55,000 tests on the 16,000 patients who visit one of our labs.

- ○ visit more than 700 patients in their homes and in long-term care facilities, at no charge to the patient or health-care system.
- ○ deliver more than 5000 specimens to public testing agencies at no cost to the patient, agency, or health care system.
- ○ transmit lab results electronically via PathNET to more than 3000 physicians.
- ○ support our services through an extensive collection and transportation network, information technology, and analytical expertise that's taken years to develop.

Exercise 13.7

In collaborative groups or individually, analyze the argument presented above and evaluate its effectiveness, using the questions below as guidelines.

1. Consider your own position towards the issues. Do you have any knowledge about this or similar issues relating to government decisions about health care (or education)? How do government decisions affect you and/ or other consumers of these kinds of services? What are the sides of the debate? Which side do you support? How might your prior knowledge and opinions affect your response to this argument or others like it?

2. Is there anything that would have made the argument more effective? Be as specific as possible.

3. Are there any questionable appeals to emotion or ethics? Are there any logical fallacies? Why do you think the company does not give specific information in main point III sub-point A: "The government based its plans on flawed, faulty, and unsubstantiated data"?

4. Analyze the refutation, bearing in mind topic, audience, and purpose. Why do the authors employ Strategy B to refute the three points mentioned in the first main point (I), which gives background about the government's position?

5. What specific changes would you make if you were writing this argument as a formal essay? In what ways does it differ from a formal essay? (See Chapter 17 for some of the characteristics of informal writing.)

6. Imagine that one year has passed. The government is proceeding with its plans; some lab employees have lost their jobs, and there are dire predictions in newspaper editorials that our health care will be directly affected. How do you think the company's argument will change in response? Write a revised claim that reflects the new current conditions. Choose one specific form: informal brochure for distribution, letter to the editor/editorial, or argumentative essay.

Sample Professional Argumentative Essay

In the following essay, noted scientist and environmentalist David Suzuki argues for wind turbines. Note his use of point-by-point rebuttal and many other rebuttal strategies discussed in this chapter.

Sample Professional Argumentative Essay

THE BEAUTY OF WIND FARMS
By David Suzuki

Off the coast of British Columbia in Canada is an island called Quadra, where I have a cabin that is as close to my heart as you can imagine. From my porch on a good day you can see clear across the waters of Georgia Strait to the snowy peaks of the rugged Coast Mountains. It is one of the most beautiful views I have seen. And I would gladly share it with a wind farm.

> Suzuki makes an **emotional appeal** in his introduction, describing an idyllic scene; however, in the last sentence, he uses an unexpected statement to get the reader's attention.

But sometimes it seems like I'm in the minority. All across Europe and North America, environmentalists are locking horns with the wind industry over the location of wind farms. In Alberta, one group is opposing a planned wind farm near Cypress Hills Provincial Park, claiming it would destroy views of the park and disturb some of the last remaining native prairie in the province. In the UK, more than 100 national and local groups, led by some of the country's most prominent environmentalists, have argued that wind power is inefficient, destroys the ambience of the countryside and makes little difference to carbon emissions. And in the US, the Cape Wind Project, which would site 130 wind turbines off the coast of affluent Cape Cod, Massachusetts, has come under fire from famous liberals, including Senator Edward Kennedy and Walter Cronkite.

> Here Suzuki discusses the opposition to wind farms, and in the next paragraph he offers his rebuttal.

It is time for some perspective. With the growing urgency of climate change, we cannot have it both ways. We cannot shout from the rooftops about the dangers of global warming and then turn around and shout even louder about the "dangers" of windmills. Climate change is one of the greatest challenges humanity will face this century. It cannot be solved through good intentions. It will take a radical change in the way we produce and consume energy—another industrial revolution, this time for clean energy, conservation and efficiency.

> In this paragraph, the writer introduces the logic behind his argument.

> Here Suzuki uses an appeal to **common ground.**

We have undergone such transformations before, and we can do it again. But first we must accept that all forms of energy have associated costs. Fossil fuels are limited in quantity and create vast amounts of pollution. Large-scale hydroelectric power floods valleys and destroys animal habitat. Nuclear power is terribly expensive and creates radioactive waste.

> In this paragraph, Suzuki offers factual summaries to bolster his argument.

Wind power also has its downsides. It is highly visible and can kill birds. The fact is, though, that any man-made structure can kill birds—houses, radio

> Suzuki begins the paragraph by offering a **concession** (wind farms kill birds), following it with a **rebuttal** (other structures kill *more* birds). In the next paragraph, he acknowledges that the opposition does have valid points by making another concession. He shows his understanding that not all his audience agrees with him.

towers, skyscrapers. In Toronto alone, it is estimated that 10,000 birds collide with the city's tallest buildings every year. Compared with this, the risk to birds from well-sited wind farms is very low.

> Here Suzuki uses statistics to show that his opponents' argument is not as strong as his.

Even at Altamont Pass in California, where 7000 turbines were erected on a migratory route, only 0.2 birds per turbine per year have been killed. Indeed, the real risk to birds comes not from windmills but from a changing climate, which threatens the very existence of bird species and their habitats. This is not to say that wind farms should be allowed to spring up anywhere. They should always be subject to environmental impact assessments. But a blanket "not in my backyard" approach is hypocritical and counterproductive.

> Now that the writer has acknowledged the opposition, he moves on to support his argument by facts and statistics.

Pursuing wind power as part of our move towards clean energy makes sense. It is the fastest-growing source of energy in the world—a $6 billion industry last year. Its cost has dropped dramatically over the past two decades because of larger turbines and greater knowledge of how to build, install and operate turbines more effectively. Prices will likely decrease further as the technology improves.

> In these two paragraphs, Suzuki uses **comparison** to convince the reader of the validity of his viewpoint.

Are windmills ugly? I remember when Mostafa Tolba, executive director of the United Nations Environment Programme from 1976 to 1992, told me how when he was growing up in Egypt, smokestacks belching out smoke were considered signs of progress. Even as an adult concerned about pollution, it took him a long time to get over the instinctive pride he felt when he saw a tower pouring out clouds of smoke.

We see beauty through filters shaped by our values and beliefs. Some people think wind turbines are ugly. I think smokestacks, smog, acid rain, coal-fired power plants and climate change are ugly. I think windmills are beautiful. They harness the power of the wind to supply us with heat and light. They provide local jobs. They help clean our air and reduce climate change.

> Suzuki's conclusion returns us to his first paragraph, playing on the hypocritical saying "not in my backyard."

And if one day I look out from my cabin's porch and see a row of windmills spinning in the distance, I won't curse them. I will praise them. It will mean we are finally getting somewhere.

David Suzuki is a scientist, environmentalist, broadcaster, author and chair of the David Suzuki Foundation (www.davidsuzuki.org).

Suzuki, D. (2005). The beauty of wind farms. *New Scientist, 186* (2495), 20–21.

Organizing an Outline for Argument

When outlining and drafting argumentative essays you should pay attention to the order of your main points. Ensure that they are ordered logically—i.e., from least to most important point—**climax order**—or from most important point to least important—**inverted climax**—whichever is most relevant for your argument; other orders are possible. You do not have to include all the elements listed below nor follow the same order of parts; for example, it may not be necessary to include background if the issue is well known to most readers. The rebuttal may not require a lot of space. Depending on the topic and other factors, you might choose to place it before your main points. If you use Strategy A to acknowledge the other side, you could place the acknowledgement in either the Introduction or the Background section. In Strategy B, you could begin a point-by-point rebuttal in body paragraphs 1 or 2.

The following pattern is based on the classical five-part argumentative model used from the time of the orators of the ancient world to the present day. Other patterns are possible, including **holding back the claim**, which can be useful if you expect strong opposition or if your opening is dramatic or memorable in another way. In this pattern, you do not announce your claim until you have

> The order of your points is often vital to argument. In the climax order, you begin with your weakest point, saving the strongest point for your final body paragraph. In the often-used mixed order, you begin with a moderately strong point, follow with a weaker one, and conclude with the strongest.

Table 13.3	Argumentative Essay Template
Introduction	• gain reader's attention and interest • include your claim • suggest the primary developmental method (if there is one) • establish your credibility (knowledge, reliability, and fairness)
Body Paragraph 1: Background	• present background information, if relevant
Body Paragraph 2: Lines of Argument	• present good reasons (logical, emotional, and ethical appeals) in support of thesis • use all relevant evidence—facts, statistics, examples, views of experts/authorities • present reasons in specific order related to argument
Body Paragraph 3: Rebuttal	• consider opposing points of view • note both advantages and disadvantages of opposing views; may use concessions or common ground • argue that your thesis is stronger than opposing view and more beneficial to the reader
Conclusion	• summarize argument • expand or elaborate on the implication of your thesis • make clear what you want reader to think or do • possibly make final strong ethical or emotional appeal

Exercise 13.8: Practice exercise

Look at the following topics. Choose one for which you can prepare an outline using the organizational pattern above, narrowing the topic down if necessary. Make sure you choose a position that you can argue and that you use a value or policy claim; do not create an expository essay with a factual claim. If possible, conduct some research before creating the outline and include relevant quotations or paraphrases in your outline.

1. Bullying
2. Communication
3. Physical activity among teens
4. Recycling programs
5. Social networking sites
6. Technology in schools
7. Civics courses
8. Space exploration
9. Salaries of sports celebrities or CEOs
10. Nuclear weapons

provided the evidence, so your claim, in effect, would act as a conclusion. The most common pattern in formal writing, however, is the classical model (or variants on this model). This model has been placed in the template similar to the one introduced in Chapter 8. Of course, in your own essay, you may allot more than one paragraph for any of these areas, especially for "lines of argument."

Sample Argumentative Essays

The first of the following argumentative student essays uses minimal research. For examples of argumentative essays that use little or no cited research, see pages 61, 66, and 285. The second essay (page 292) uses extensive research.

Annotations are given for the first essay, and a series of questions follows the second. To conserve space, the essays are not double spaced and References and Works Cited sections are not on separate pages. The essays do not follow correct essay format requirements for title pages or identification information. For the correct ways of dealing with these issues, see Chapter 17, Essay Presentation, page 431.

Sample Student Argumentative Essay (APA style)

A Case for Safe Injection Sites in Victoria
By Kerry Hinds

The 12 October 2004 edition of *The Globe and Mail* had the following headline on its front page: "107 'Safe' Overdoses at Gallery a Success." It is rare that heroin users and reports of overdoses reach the front page of a newspaper; most citizens usually forget these people. Due to the city's high number of heroin users, however, Vancouver is the home to North America's only legal "shooting gallery." Recently there has been investigation into the need for and viability of a safe injection clinic in Victoria, B.C. Programs such as these raise the question of whether or not British Columbians' health care dollars should be spent on a clinic for citizens living in poverty who are not paying taxes. However, looking beyond the personal safety and health of addicts and directing our gaze towards the health of non-using citizens, it is apparent that Victoria is in need of a safe injection house. It is also important to look at this problem with foresight to avoid unneeded spending on health care for chronic disease. Opposition to spending for this and similar social programs stems from the perpetuation and misunderstanding of drug addiction and behaviour.

The author uses a headline to gain the reader's attention.

In the opening paragraph, following her thesis, the author acknowledges the opposition and shows how she will offer rebuttal.

The clinic in Vancouver is open 18 hours a day and is a safe location for heroin users to shoot up: clean needles are distributed, needles are properly disposed of, and the area is a police-free zone. There are also counseling and medically trained professionals on site. The goal of this three-year $3.7 million project is to reduce deaths by overdose and slow the spread of drug-related diseases, mainly AIDS and hepatitis. Over six months in the Vancouver clinic, there were 107 overdoses out of more than 108,000 visitors; none of these people died (Armstrong, 2004, p. A1).

The author uses statistics to support her argument that the clinic is successful.

Victoria is an urban centre with a heroin and drug-related disease problem. This situation is easy to see when one is walking through the down

*Here the author uses Vancouver's safe injection site as a **precedent**, arguing that Victoria is similar to Vancouver and, therefore, needs a similar clinic.*

(Continued)

town core. The problem may not be as severe as Vancouver's, but it is necessary to take proactive actions to prevent the spread of AIDS and hepatitis. Having been involved with The Youth Empowerment Society downtown and working with street youth in Victoria, I see the need for such a program in Victoria; the personal health of users, old and young, is at stake.

Lack of support for shooting galleries comes from a prevalent conservative attitude of people believing that their tax dollars should not be spent to support people who have lived their lives in poverty and as drug addicts. Unfortunately, these people are not looking beyond their tax dollars; they do not see that safe injection clinics are also protecting their own health. Having recently met people who have been pricked by needles while cleaning their storefronts and others who have contracted hepatitis from disposing of crack pipes, I can see that safe houses are necessary for the safety of public health. Also, reducing the spread of AIDS is beneficial for everybody, not just the users who are sharing needles. If we wish to control the spread of AIDS, we cannot look at AIDS as strictly a drug-user's disease; many non-users get infected also. If money is not put into programs such as these, our health care system will be further burdened with the care of chronically ill patients, costing the tax payers even more money than the cost of opening a clinic. Without foresight and action, the health of non-users will be further compromised, and our health care system will be further debilitated.

A lack of understanding of drug addiction and behaviour perpetuates a negative attitude in the general public, who may blame the addicts for their lack of self-control and motivation to get themselves out of their situations. Society should be educated in the behaviours of drug addicts; brain functioning is impaired even while a drug addict is straight; as well, many addicts justifiably see recovery as blocked by many barriers. The social, psychological, and biological barriers involved in getting straight can outweigh the benefits of being straight: weeks of withdrawal and intense introspection into their life histories

Here the author uses her personal experience as evidence.

Hinds makes an **ethical appeal**.

Writing Tip: In her last body paragraph, the writer provides support for the last sentence of her introduction. She has laid out her essay logically, following the order of points in her introduction.

Writing Tip: In this sentence, Hinds uses punctuation effectively to guide her reader through complex material. Note the use of commas and semicolons for items in a series, and the colon to set up one of the lists.

and circumstances; a prolonged process of rebuilding their self-esteem and self-worth; and the rejection of a life that is known for an unknown life of poverty and new social groups. It is important to remember that these are still people with different stories and life experiences. There are many reasons why people end up being users. For instance, people who start life in a low socio-economic family have fewer opportunities for success and lack education and self-worth. Also, people who are children of young and addicted parents are more likely to exhibit generational patterns of drug abuse. It is uncharitable to not look beyond the drug problem—we must realize that poverty and drug use are largely a social problem.

> Ethical appeals are an important strategy in Hinds's essay; she ends this paragraph by making another ethical appeal.

Victoria needs a safe injection clinic, not only for the health of users but also for the safety of public health. Without proactive programs such as this one, many lives will be unnecessarily lost or drastically affected, and British Columbians will be burdened with the future health costs of chronic disease. With education about drug addiction and behaviour, perhaps the stereotypes associated with drugs addicts will be eliminated and public support will increase for safe injection clinics.

> In her **circular conclusion**, the author restates her argument, briefly summarizing her main points in the order of the introduction.

Reference

Armstrong, J. (2004, October 14) 107 "safe" overdoses at gallery a success, backers say. *The Globe and Mail*, pp. A1, A8.

Exercise 13.9

In the following essay, the author, Stewart Lord, discusses marijuana use. Read through the essay and try to determine how Lord has supported his argument based on what you have learned in this chapter. A series of questions follows the essay.

Numbered footnotes
are permitted in MLA,
but they should provide
additional information,
suggested reading, and
similar functions—not just
bibliographical information. For
another example of an essay
using MLA style, see p. 245.

Sample Student Argumentative Essay (MLA style)

The Prohibition of Marijuana: A Legacy of Moral Entrepreneurship
By Stewart Lord

How many times have you, your friends or family enjoyed a cold beer on a hot day, a glass of cabernet sauvignon with dinner, or a nightcap of single malt scotch? Whether or not you regularly consume alcohol, imagine if it were illegal to do so. Consider for a moment the implications of this and the value of being able to make your own decisions about alcohol. Unfortunately, this freedom does not extend to marijuana. Its use has long been a subject of dispute; the arguments on both sides of this issue are long and complex. What is true of this debate, however, is the tendency to avoid the real subject of ethics and to introduce less important discussions. Opponents of marijuana's legalization generally focus on its negative health effects or addictive and gateway tendencies, while proponents herald its medicinal and practical applications. Although these digressions have their place, in this vein of the debate they only serve to draw away our attention from the fundamental injustice of its prohibition. The criminalization of this substance robs us of our innate liberty, the freedom to choose. The recreational use of marijuana is shrouded in disrepute due to the unfounded and arbitrary imposition of moral entrepreneurship.

Moral entrepreneurship can best be defined in sociological terms from a conflict theorist's perspective. It is the legislation of subjective moral standards by those in a position of considerable power or influence over society. In Canada, our drug laws concerning marijuana have a particularly dubious origin. The Opium Act of 1908, which itself was formed with the racist agenda of curbing the freedoms of Asian-Canadians, set the precedent for all laws concerning illicit drug use that would follow (Dion).[1] By outlawing substances not typically favoured by European cultures, minority groups were effectively targeted for harassment and deportation. This basis of racism played a significant role in the eventual criminalization of cannabis. It was Emily Murphy, Canada's first female judge, who, under the pen name of Janey Canuck, wrote exposés on the drug trade that helped to swing public opinion against marijuana. These articles depicted hemp smokers as "the lowest class of yellow and black men" and found such strong support from many of Canada's white Christians that they were later published in a book titled *The Black Candle*. In this form, they served as powerful government propaganda, spreading fears and lies. In 1927, on the heels of similar decisions south of the border, Canada passed laws banning the use and trafficking of cannabis (Bruce B2). Numerous extensive and well-funded studies concerning the effects of marijuana, such as the La Guardia report and Le Dain Commission report, have found no link between its use and crime or violence.[2] Despite these results and the urging of lobby groups, welfare agencies, and medical associations to decriminalize the substance, its consumption still constitutes a criminal act. Although the deceptions spread through media such as *The Black Candle* and *Reefer Madness* have subsided, current programs continue to proliferate unsubstantiated fears.[3] In the impressionable minds of many, this misinformation, coupled with the illegal nature of recreational marijuana use, only serves to reinforce the stigma that surrounds it.

There is little that justifies the legal distinction between this drug and other "soft" narcotics such as alcohol, tobacco, and coffee. Tetrahydro-cannabinol, the active ingredient in *cannabis sativa*, is a unique substance and, as such, may pose distinct health concerns. That said, alcohol, tobacco, and coffee are equally dubious and, in some cases, considerably more dangerous. Statistics on the consequences of abusing these socially accepted agents bring the issue into sharp focus. An estimated 6,507 Canadians died in 1995 due to alcohol consumption, while another 82,014 were admitted to hospital. During the same year, the percentage of vehicle accidents attributed to drinking was 43 per cent (MADD 3).

Even more alarming is that tobacco is the number one preventable cause of death in Canada with 45,214 recognized fatalities in 1996. That amounts to roughly three times more victims than car accidents, suicides, drug abuse, murder, and AIDS combined. Statistics regarding marijuana-related fatalities, reliable or otherwise, are hard to obtain. Health Canada does, however, report that an estimated 804 Canadians died in 1995 due to drug abuse (Health Canada). What fraction of these deaths is attributable to marijuana is speculation, but many contend that the reason no mortality

(Continued)

statistics are available is because use of the substance does not constitute a direct health threat. Clearly, any responsible user should acknowledge not only the obvious consequences of smoke inhalation but also the possibility of unknown long-term effects. There is a fine line between the use and abuse of any substance; therefore, conscientious habits are essential. Whatever the circumstance, neither "potheads" nor casual smokers should commit any direct or indirect offence against any other person. Beyond that, we must all recognize the right of each individual to define his or her own ethical and moral boundaries.

When faced with this argument, many react in moral panic and rhetorically ask, "why don't we legalize all drug use?" This question of where to draw the line is difficult to answer, yet, specific criteria could be established and each drug evaluated according to these merits. Concerns such as short-term effects, user dependence, long-term consequences, and correlations with crime and violence would need to be addressed, but eventually a consensus should emerge. As a result, we may find softer legal substances at one end of a scale with legal, yet controlled ones in the middle, and hard drugs that bring strict criminal sentences at the other. Whatever form such a system might take, it is clear that direct comparisons with currently legal substances would place cannabis on the non-criminal side of the scale. By nearly all accounts, it is a milder substance than alcohol or nicotine, particularly in addictiveness. It is true that marijuana users can become psychologically addicted, but they do not form the physical dependencies that accompany excessive alcohol and tobacco consumption.[4]

This point commonly spurs opponents of legalization to ask, "why not prohibit drinking and smoking as well?" By reversing the short-sighted "all or nothing" argument, the circular nature of the argument becomes apparent. Furthermore, this approach has been tried in the past and notoriously failed. In 1920, the United States introduced prohibition. The lifting of the ban in 1933 coincided with the height of the Depression (Thornton). Although it is unlikely that this decision had much to do with the economic upturn of the mid-1930s, it does raise a strong point. In 1998–9, the taxation of alcohol amounted to $3.6 million in proceeds for the Canadian government (CCSA). Through upholding the outdated legislation regarding recreational marijuana, our government has forced the industry underground and is therefore missing out on significant revenue.

In addition to the positive direct impact that this industry could have on our economy, legalization would indirectly alleviate stress on our judicial system. An estimated 2,000 Canadians are jailed for marijuana possession every year. At an average cost of $150 per inmate per day (not taking into account legal expenses or the cost of finding and apprehending these individuals), it is clear that fighting the use of marijuana constitutes a heavy burden (CCSA). The funds obtained from legalization would be more than just profit-taking. This money would be needed to fund research initiatives, establish strict production standards, and restructure existing organizations to accommodate and control the sale of cannabis. Users would no longer need to associate with a criminal element of society to obtain the drug. They could either grow it themselves or purchase it from a licensed retailer. This would bring a level of safety and security not present in the current black market. Buyers could be confident of a product's purity, quality, and potency.

The main reason why marijuana is still illegal and socially marginalized today is the haunting legacy of racial and ethnic snobbery that founded its prohibition. There is no rationale or validation for outlawing the recreational use of cannabis while condoning alcohol, tobacco, or even coffee. We must all push for the legalization of this substance both for the benefits of our economy and judicial system, and most fundamentally to protect the rights and ensure the safety of those who use it.

Notes

1. See Dion for further analysis of this relationship with racism.

2. Refer to the "Crime" subsection in "The Mental Attitude of the Marihuana Smoker chapter of La Guardia report and "Cannabis" (166) under "A Review of Selected Drugs" in the Le Dain Commission report.

3. *Reefer Madness* (1938) is possibly the most famous exploitation film ever, depicting marijuana smokers as murderous villains.

4. See "Cannabis" (179) under "A Review of Selected Drugs" in the Le Dain Commission report.

(Continued)

Works Cited

Bruce, Harry. "The Real Janey Canuck." *The National Post* 15 April 2000: B2. Print.

Canadian Centre on Substance Abuse. *Cannabis Control in Canada: Options Regarding Possession*. Ottawa: CCSA, May 1998. Print.

Canada. Le Dain Committee. *The Commission of Inquiry into the Non-Medical Use of Drugs*. Ottawa, 1970. Print.

City of New York. La Guardia Committee. *The Marihuana Problem in the City of New York*. New York: City of New York, 1944. Print.

Dion, Guy. "The Structure of Drug Prohibition in International Law and in Canadian Law." *Parliament of Canada*. Special Committee on Illegal Drugs. August 1999. Web. 31 October 2002.

Canada. Health Canada. *Deaths in Canada Due to Smoking*. Ottawa: Health Canada, January 1999. Print.

Mothers Against Drunk Driving. *The Real Facts on Alcohol Use, Injuries and Deaths*. MADD Canada, 22 August 2002. Print.

Thornton, Mark. "Alcohol Prohibition Was a Failure." Policy Analysis No. 157. *CATO Institute*. The CATO Institute. 17 July 1991. Web. Oct. 2002.

Questions to consider in a critical and analytical reading of "The Prohibition of Marijuana: A Legacy of Moral Entrepreneurship":

1. In his introduction, how does Lord attempt to distinguish his essay and his argument on legalizing marijuana from the many others on this topic?

2. What two methods of development does the writer use in his first body paragraph (paragraph 2)? Identify two different methods used in paragraphs 3 and 4.

3. Do you believe that Lord successfully demonstrates his credibility? (Is he knowledgeable, reliable, fair?) In what ways does he succeed (or fail to do this)?

4. Of the two strategies for handling opposing views discussed on pages 280–1, which did Lord choose to use? Do you think he adequately considered his topic, audience, and purpose in arguing in his approach? Specifically, what shows you he did this (or failed to do this)?

5. What kinds of appeals does Lord use? Logical, emotional, ethical?

6. In the paragraph preceding his conclusion, Lord discusses some advantages of legalizing marijuana. Do you believe this paragraph fits well with the rest of the paper? Why or why not? What order of points do you think he used in the essay (see page 287)?

Chapter Review Questions

1. What are the three kinds of appeals often used in argument and when is it appropriate to use each?
2. What is the difference between opinion and argument? Between opinion and fact?
3. Why is it important to use an objective voice when arguing?
4. Why is definition often important in an argument?
5. What are some examples of faulty logic?
6. Give some examples of language that shows a bias.
7. Think of arguments you have heard lately. Can you think of any that illustrate the categories listed in the section about faulty reasoning, page 260? Could those arguments be improved?
8. Why should you acknowledge the opposing side in argumentative essays?
9. Name three specific argumentative strategies that depend on your audience.
10. Why is the classical five-part model a good pattern to use for argumentative essays?

14

Sentence Essentials

In this chapter, you will

- review the importance of using correct grammar

- be introduced to the parts of speech: what they are and why they are important

- be introduced to sentence structure

- learn the four errors of sentence incompletion and how to avoid them

- be introduced to phrases and clauses and their roles in the sentence

- learn the errors of sentence combining and how to join sentences correctly

In this chapter and the two that follow, you will be introduced to the basic concepts for understanding and using English grammar and punctuation. First, you will study the parts of speech, phrases and clauses, and then the sentence itself. In Chapter 15, you will find guidelines for using commas, semicolons, colons, and apostrophes. In Chapter 16, you will refine your skills by learning how to craft grammatically correct sentences.

◎ Grammatical Groundwork

For some, grammar is simply a set of rules to be learned; for others, it is a way to improve their writing and further their understanding of how the English language works. What correct grammar will *always* help do is help create a channel of clear communication between writer and reader.

In general, the rules of grammar apply to all writing across the academic disciplines. That means you will need to follow rules that define acceptable academic writing. Academic writing is formal writing, so the rules of formal usage and correct grammar need to be applied. In this chapter and the next two, we approach grammar formally, but without excess terminology.

Although formal grammatical rules are stressed throughout, not all your writing at college or university will be formal. For example, when you take notes on a lecture, you may be concerned solely with content, using point form or even just key phrases. You might correspond with classmates by email, in which case you will probably write more informally, using colloquialisms or other "casual," everyday language.

Informal writing may also apply to certain kinds of business, technical, or journalistic writing. Some of the readings in this book are designed for a wider reading

> Academic writing is formal writing, and that means that the rules of formal usage and correct grammar need to be applied.

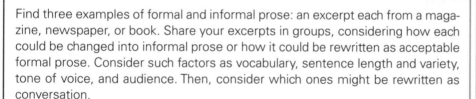

Exercise 14.1

Find three examples of formal and informal prose: an excerpt each from a magazine, newspaper, or book. Share your excerpts in groups, considering how each could be changed into informal prose or how it could be rewritten as acceptable formal prose. Consider such factors as vocabulary, sentence length and variety, tone of voice, and audience. Then, consider which ones might be rewritten as conversation.

To help you identify these three writing styles, think in terms of different kinds of audiences, but particularize—you can think of a specific person or persons whom you are writing for: e.g., a friend, for informal prose or conversation; a workplace acquaintance, such as your boss, for semi-formal prose; and the chairperson of the English or Communications Department for formal prose.

Exercise 14.2

Listen to the speakers around you. Find samples that illustrate how the rules governing speech can be different from those governing semi-formal and formal writing. Again, consider factors such as vocabulary, sentence completion, tone of voice, and audience.

Guidelines for usage determine what words are suitable for a typical reader or listener. The typical reader of academic prose is different from the typical reader of a popular book, an office memo, a blog, or an email. Therefore, the level of usage is usually different.

public than are academic papers and may employ more informal language and looser sentence structure. In all your writing assignments, you should consider your instructor the final judge on the level of formality required. For more information on the differences between formal and informal writing, see Chapter 17, page 419.

◎ The Grammar of Reading and Writing

As a reader, your comprehension depends on your ability to recognize grammatical and other linguistic "signposts" that are part of the English language. The processing of grammar and syntax is, therefore, inherent in the act of reading. To illustrate this point, read this stanza from Lewis Carroll's poem "Jabberwocky":

"Beware the Jabberwock, my son!
The jaws that bite, the claws that catch!
Beware the Jubjub bird, and shun
The frumious Bandersnatch!"

Do you understand what a "Jabberwock" is? The grammar clues tell us it is a concrete noun, and probably alive. The meaning of "frumious" is not found in a dictionary, but again, the reader sees that it is modifying the proper noun "Bandersnatch," which again is a concrete noun and probably a person or thing.

As a writer, you are responsible for ensuring that readers can understand your message, so you need to become familiar with grammatical rules if you are to write effectively. Knowing and applying these rules will help open up the channel of communication from you, the writer, to your reader.

In addition to ensuring the reader's clear understanding of your message, the proper use of grammar makes a good impression. Just as dressing for the occasion increases your standing in the group you are interacting with, the proper use of language creates a positive image. If your document contains errors, the reader's assumption is that you, as the writer, are either careless or are uneducated, and therefore your opinion and research are not worthy of attention.

The fastest, least complicated way to learn English grammar is to start with the basic *concepts* that underlie the rules of grammar. The pages that follow teach a concept-based grammar, beginning with the smallest word-units in the sentence: the parts of speech. From there, we look at what a simple sentence is, how to recognize phrases and clauses, and how to join clauses to form more complex sentence types.

◎ Introducing . . . the Parts of Speech

Before considering the sentence, the basic unit of written communication in English, you need to be able to identify what makes up a sentence. The sentence can be divided into individual words, which, in turn, can be categorized as different parts of speech. Phrases and clauses are larger units than individual words.

Being able to identify the forms and functions of the parts of speech will help you understand these larger units, too. The seven major **parts of speech** are nouns, pronouns, adjectives, verbs, adverbs, prepositions, and conjunctions.

Articles, such as *a*, *an*, and *the*, and determiners, such as *this* and *her*, may precede nouns and can be considered to function as adjectives. *Interjections*, such as *oh!* and *hey*, are not grammatically related to the rest of the sentence. They express surprise or emotion, and should not be used in formal writing unless they form part of a quotation. Many words can be used as more than one part of speech. For example, the word *fish* is a noun (a thing), but *fish* also is a verb (to perform the act of fishing). When *fish* as a noun is placed in front of another noun, as in a "fish market," it functions as an adjective (modifying the concept "market").

The Parts of Speech at Work

When you are hired by an organization and given a job title along with a detailed job description, the job title is what you will be called; but the full job description explains your responsibilities, duties, or functions within the organization. The parts of speech, too, have specific, assigned roles within their organizational structure, the sentence.

As mentioned, words may have many meanings and may even serve as different parts of speech. *Cause* may be a noun and used as the subject of a sentence, such as "The *cause* was worthy of support." *Cause* may also be a verb and used as the predicate of a sentence, such as "The accident on the highway *caused* me to miss my flight." When one meaning of a part of speech is assigned to a function in a sentence, *that meaning* cannot be applied to a different part of speech in the same clause. For example, when a noun is the subject of the verb in a clause, it cannot also be object of the verb in the same clause. This is clear in the following: "Frasier has gone to see Frasier." Evidently the second *Frasier* must refer to a different person of the same name, or, perhaps, to a television program or a town, or some other thing.

The tables that follow identify the parts of speech, along with their major functions. Moving from the ability to identify the categories of the parts of speech to being aware of their functions within the sentence (their job description) will enable you to apply the rules of grammar.

Nouns and Pronouns

Nouns and pronouns are the *significant* words in a sentence because they name people, places, things, and ideas.

> The subject of a clause or sentence usually performs the action of the verb.

1. Subject. The subject noun usually performs the action (but see Chapter 17, page 411 for examples of the passive construction, which changes this).

In the following examples, the subject is in bold; the action word, the verb, is italicized.

Table 14.1   Nouns and Pronouns

IDENTIFICATION	FUNCTIONS
Noun (*nomen*: "name"): name of a person, place, thing, or idea. *proper* nouns refer to names and begin with a capital letter *common* nouns refer to class or a general group and are not capitalized *concrete* nouns refer to physical objects and things experienced through the senses *abstract* nouns refer to concepts, ideas, and abstractions *count* nouns name things that can be counted *non-count* nouns refer to things that can't be counted *collective* nouns refer to groups comprised of individual members	1. **Subject:** performs the action of the verb (the *doer* of the action); sometimes called the simple subject to distinguish it from the complete subject that includes the simple subject plus its modifiers 2. **Object** (also called the **direct object**): receives the action of the verb 3. **Object of a preposition** (also called the **indirect object**): is usually preceded by a preposition (such as *in*, *between*, *with*) 4. **Subject Complement** (also called the **predicate noun**): follows a linking verb (often a form of *to be* such as *is, are, was, were*) and can be linked to the subject 5. **Appositive:** is grammatically parallel to the previous noun or noun phrase
Pronoun (*pro + nomen*: "in place of the noun"): usually takes the place of a noun in a sentence. For a list of kinds of pronouns, see below.	Since pronouns generally replace nouns, they share the functions of nouns (see "nouns" *above*).

Dan *stood* at the front of the line-up; **She** *awoke* before dawn; The **rain** in Spain *falls* mainly on the plain.

The subject usually comes before the verb but sometimes follows it, as, for example, with some questions: *Was* the final **exam** difficult?

> The object of the verb is the receiver of the action of the verb.

2. Object (of the verb) is also called the **direct object.** It is the receiver of the action of the verb.

In the following examples, the object is in bold; the verb is italicized.

James *beat* **Dan** into the movie theatre. Erin *let* **him** into the house.
They *chopped* the **logs** for firewood.

> When nouns or pronouns act as objects of prepositions, they are usually preceded by a preposition.

3. Object of the preposition (also called **indirect object**). The noun/pronoun is usually preceded by a preposition.

In the following examples, the object is in bold; its preposition is italicized.

She awoke *before* **dawn**. The rain *in* **Spain** falls mainly *on* the **plain**.
I never heard *of* **it** before.

4. Subject complement (completion). The noun or pronoun that "completes" the subject after a linking verb.

In the following example, the subject complement is in bold; the linking verb is italicized; the subject is underlined.

<u>Rayna</u> *was* the first **person** to get a job after graduation.

5. Appositive. A noun, noun phrase, or pronoun that is grammatically parallel to a preceding noun/pronoun and that rephrases or (re)names the preceding noun.

In the following example, the appositive is in bold; the preceding noun is italicized.

Madeline's *cats*, **Evie and Nanny**, have very different personalities.

The subject of the sentence is "cats"; the names of the cats are **in apposition to the subject** (the names are not part of the simple subject).

Kinds of Pronouns

Personal pronouns refer to people and things; in the possessive case, they can function as adjectives.

He ran all the way to the sea. *She* sat down because *her* feet were blistered.

Relative pronouns introduce dependent clauses that *relate* the clause to the rest of the sentence; these clauses usually function adjectivally. *That, which, who.*

The book, *which* I lost on the bus, was about Greek history. The student *who* found it returned it to me.

Interrogative pronouns introduce questions. *How, what, which, when, why, who, where.*

Where is the book I lost on the bus? *How* can I thank you enough for returning it?

Demonstrative pronouns point to nouns; they can function as adjectives. *This, that, these, those.*

This is the *day* of reckoning.
This *day* will be long remembered.

Indefinite pronouns refer to unspecified individuals or groups; many do not require an antecedent and form their possessives in the same way as nouns. E.g., *Any, some, whoever.*

It is *anyone's* guess when the boat will arrive.

> A noun appositive names the previous noun.

> Personal pronouns refer to people and things and replace the corresponding nouns in a sentence.

> Relative pronouns introduce dependent clauses that *relate* the clause to the rest of the sentence.

> Interrogative pronouns introduce questions.

Reflexive pronouns have the form of personal pronouns with the *-self* suffix; they refer back to the subject as the receiver of an action. In the following example, the subject is italicized and the reflexive pronoun is in boldface.

> *Ben* congratulated **himself** on his successful election.

Intensive pronouns also have the form of personal pronouns with the *-self* suffix; they serve to reinforce their antecedents.

> The *teacher herself* was often late for class.

Reciprocal pronouns refer to the separate parts of a plural antecedent. In the following example, the reciprocal pronoun is in bold and the antecedent is italicized.

> *People* need to accept and tolerate **one another**.

Verbs

Verbs convey an action, state, or condition. There are three different kinds of verbs, each having different functions.

The various tenses of English verbs are illustrated in Appendix A.

1. Main verbs express action, condition, or a state of being. Some kinds of action are not necessarily visible—*think*, *imagine*, and *suggest* are examples of action verbs in which the "action" is interior or mental. Verbs may be modified by adverbs or adverbial phrases.

Table 14.2 Verbs	
IDENTIFICATION	**FUNCTIONS**
Verb (*verbum*: "word"): conveys an action, state, or condition, or precedes another (main) verb. The different kinds of verbs have different functions.	1. **Main verbs** may be transitive (take a direct object) or intransitive (do not take a direct object) and usually convey an *action*, not necessarily physical, in the predicate. 2. **Helping or auxiliary verbs** precede a *main verb* to form more complex *tenses* (indications of the time, continuance, or completeness of the action); to express a *mood* such as obligation, necessity, probability, or possibility; or to show *voice*, i.e., whether the relation of verb to subject is active or passive. 3. **Linking verbs** are followed by a predicate noun or adjective that refers back to the subject.

2. **Helping verbs (**also called **auxiliary verbs)** combine with main verbs. The two most common helping verbs are *to be (am, are, is, was, were, will be,* etc.) and *to have (have, has, had,* etc.) Forms of *to be* are used in the *progressive* tenses; forms of *to have* are used in the *perfect* tenses (see Appendix A).

Helping verbs combine with main verbs to form different tenses.

Modals are verb forms placed before the main verb to express necessity, obligation, possibility, probability, and similar conditions: *can, could, will, would, shall, should, may, might, must,* and *ought to* are modals.

3. **Linking verbs** like *to be* are used to connect subject and predicate in one of six ways:

A linking verb joins (links) a subject to a noun or adjective that follows it.

1. expressing identity: Today *is* Saturday.
2. expressing condition: I *am* upset.
3. expressing state: These *are* my colleagues.
4. expressing opinion: We *are* for freedom of speech.
5. expressing total: One and one *are* two.
6. expressing cost: The fundraiser *is* $200 a plate.

Verbs that imply "to be" also may function as linking verbs:

Mildred becomes [begins to be] faint as the night grows [continues to become] cold.

Compare: "He **acted** the part of Hamlet *splendidly*." "He **acted** *sick* by staying home from school."

In the first sentence, "acted" is a main verb used transitively (takes the object "part"); it is modified by the adverb "splendidly." In the second sentence, "acted" is a linking verb—he acted [behaved as one who *is*] sick—the verb implies "to be"—and thus is followed by a subject complement, the predicate adjective "sick" (see "Subject complement" in Table 14.3).

Modifiers: Adjectives and Adverbs

Adjectives and adverbs modify, or give more information about, the major parts of speech—nouns and verbs.

Adjectives modify nouns and usually precede them. Adjectives follow linking verbs, where they *modify the subject* as *predicate adjectives*. In the following examples, the adjective is in bold and the modified noun is italicized.

Adjectives modify nouns and usually precede them. Adjectives follow linking verbs, where they modify the subject as predicate adjectives.

They attended the **delightful** *party*.

In the following example, the predicate adjective is in bold, the linking verb is italicized, and the subject is underlined.

Table 14.3 Modifiers: Adjectives and Adverbs	
IDENTIFICATION	**FUNCTIONS**
Adjective (*ad + jectum*: "put near to"): a word that modifies and precedes a noun or follows a linking verb; it answers the questions *which, what kind,* or *how many?*	1. **Adjectival modifiers** describe or particularize a noun and precede it. 2. **Subject complement** (also called the *predicate adjective*) follows a linking verb (see "nouns" above) and modifies the subject.
Adverb (*ad + verb*: "to the verb"): a word that modifies a verb, adjective, adverb, or even an entire sentence; it often ends in *-ly* and answers the questions *when, where, why, how, to what degree,* or *how much?*	1. **Adverbial modifiers** describe or particularize a verb and may precede or follow it; an adverb may also modify an adjective or another adverb; a *sentence* adverb may be the first word of the sentence and modify the entire sentence. 2. **Conjunctive adverbs** are a specific group of adverbs that may be used to connect two independent clauses.

The party *was* **delightful**.

Adverbs modify verbs, adjectives, and adverbs.

> Adverbs modify verbs, adjectives, and adverbs.

1. **In this example**, the adverb, in bold, modifies the verb, italicized.

    Jake *turned* **suddenly**.

2. **In this example,** the adverb, in bold, modifies the adjective, italicized.

    That looks like a **very** *contented* cow.

3. **In this example**, the adverb, in bold, modifies another adverb, italicized.

    They lived **quite** *happily* together.

Some adverbs can also act as **conjunctions** to connect two independent clauses:

> Richard was hired by the publicity firm on Monday; *however*, he was fired on Tuesday.

Note the semicolon separating the clauses and the comma after "however."

Joiners: Prepositions and Conjunctions

Prepositions and conjunctions are classed together here as they connect different parts of a sentence.

Table 14.4   Joiners: Prepositions and Conjunctions

IDENTIFICATION	FUNCTIONS
Preposition (*pre + ponere*: "to put before"): a small word/short phrase that often refers to place or time.	1. **Prepositions** join the noun or pronoun that follows to the rest of the sentence.
Conjunction (*con + junction*: "join together"): a word/phrase that connects words, phrases, and clauses of equal or unequal weight or importance. For a list of common subordinating conjunctions, see page 316.	1. **Coordinating conjunctions** join *equal* units, including independent clauses; there are seven coordinating conjunctions. 2. **Subordinating conjunctions** join *unequal* units, including independent and dependent clauses. 3. **Correlative conjunctions** join *parallel* units; they join in pairs.

Prepositions join nouns and pronouns to the rest of the sentence and help add information to the subject or predicate. Where there is a preposition, you will usually find an object of the preposition (noun or pronoun) following. Prepositions introduce prepositional phrases, which function as *adjectives* or *adverbs* depending on what part of speech they are modifying. In the following examples, the preposition is in bold, the object of the preposition is italicized, and the prepositional phrase is underlined.

> You will find the letters **in** the *attic*. She worked **during** the summer *vacation*. They laughed **at** *him*.

The noun or pronoun that follows a preposition will usually function as the object of the preposition. Many prepositional phrases, such as *as well as, in spite of, on account of*, are not listed as prepositions (see right margin), but can often be recognized by the fact that a noun or pronoun follows.

Conjunctions have two main joining functions: they can join equal or unequal units.

1. Coordinating conjunctions join *equal* units—words to words, phrases to phrases, clauses to clauses. An important use of coordinating conjunctions is to join *independent clauses* in compound sentences. In the following example, the coordinating conjunction is in bold:

> Tanya objected to their new roommate, **but** Bronwyn liked her.

Note the comma before the conjunction.

Coordinating conjunctions are often referred to as the FANBOYS (For, And, Nor, But, Or, Yet, So).

Prepositions join nouns and pronouns to the rest of the sentence, adding information to the subject or predicate.

Commonly used prepositions:
about, above, across, after, against, along, among, around, as, at, before, behind, below, between, beside(s), beyond, by, despite, down, during, except, for, from, in, inside, into, like, near, next (to), of, off, on, onto, out, outside (of), opposite, over, past, regarding, since, than, through, throughout, to, toward(s), under, until, up, upon, with, within, without

Coordinating conjunctions join equal units.

Subordinating conjunctions join dependent clauses, which contain less important information, to independent clauses, which contain more important information.

2. Subordinating conjunctions join *unequal* units, usually a *dependent* clause, which it begins and is part of, to an *independent* clause. In the following examples, the subordinating conjunction is in bold. Note the comma in the second sentence.

He plans to exercise his option **once** the season is over.
Once the season is over, he plans to exercise his option.

3. Correlative conjunctions occur in pairs and require parallel structure. In the following examples, the correlative conjunctions are in bold:

Either you will support me, **or** you will not be able to borrow my car.
Both Ali **and** his father work at the community centre on Saturdays.

Exercise 14.3

Each group is to come up with a list of five to ten examples of **one** of the following parts of speech (nouns, verbs, adjectives, or adverbs). When deciding on the list, try to avoid common words in favour of unusual or funny ones (e.g., nouns: *gelatin, dumpster*; verbs: *ooze, pout*; adjectives: *crinkly, repulsive*; adverbs: *tritely, gluttonously*). After the sentence skeletons below are written on the board, each group decides on an "appropriate" word from the list for each blank, and one member writes it on the board in the order indicated in each sentence. For example, in sentence 1, one of the verb groups would decide on the first word, followed by one of the adjective groups until the sentence is complete. Remember: the idea isn't to try to "make sense" but to provide a strange (grammatical) sentence!

1. If you do not ____ your ____ ____, someone might ____ ____ your ____.
              verb   adj noun   adv verb   noun

2. We all occasionally ____ ____, but some ____ ____ ____their ____
                         verb adv   noun (pl) adv verb   noun
    every day.

3. The ____ ____ looked ready to ____ ____ into the ____ ____.
        adj noun   verb adv   adj noun

4. Before you ____ your ____ ____, it's best to ____ your ____ ____.
               verb   adj noun   verb   noun adv

5. The ____ ____ that ____ on the ____ ____ ____.
        adj noun   verb   noun verb adv.

Exercise 14.4

Read the following paragraph and identify the following:

5 nouns

2 pronouns

6 verbs

3 adjectives

2 adverbs

4 prepositions

2 conjunctions

> Once we left the main road and turned down a narrow side street, we were in nothing more than an extended slum. The car came to a stop in front of a house that was far better than any of the others around it. Set back a little from the street, it was a well-kept bungalow. The cemented front garden had a garish marble fountain in the middle, with an arrangement of plastic flamingoes and penguins around it. The windows had heavy bars across them, and even the front door had an extra door of iron bars in front of it. My grandmother did not get out; instead she had the driver toot his horn imperiously. A woman stepped out of the front door, and when she saw the car, she immediately nodded and smiled and went back inside. (Selvadurai, Shyam. "The Demoness Kali." *Short Fiction & Critical Contexts*. Ed. Eric Henderson and Geoff Hancock. Don Mills: Oxford UP, 2010. 384. Print.)

◎ Introducing . . . the Sentence

Because the sentence is the basic unit of written (though not of spoken) communication, you need to know how to identify incomplete sentences in your writing so you can make them complete in formal writing. In order to know what an incomplete sentence is, you need to first consider the concept of the sentence.

What Is a Sentence?

It's not always easy to identify a complete sentence. Which of the following is a sentence?

Write!
Right!

Now, consider this pair:

Seeing As Believing.
Seeing Is Believing.

Although you may have been able to correctly identify "Write!" and "Seeing Is Believing" as complete sentences, the examples show that just the appearance of a word or group of words isn't a reliable guide to identifying a sentence. In commands, the subject "you" is implied (see below, page 312); therefore, "Write!" means "You write!" and is a complete sentence. A **sentence fragment** is the term for a less-than-complete sentence. "Right!" and "Seeing As Believing" are examples of fragments. "Right!" is missing both subject and predicate: "You are right!" is complete. "Seeing As Believing" is a noun phrase; there is no predicate.

Some textbooks define a sentence as a complete thought. Most complete sentences express a completed thought or idea, but if we define a sentence simply as a complete *thought,* we need to know what a thought is. As well, sentences certainly can contain more than one "thought."

Which of these word groups is a sentence?

Rules of grammar.
Grammar rules!

If we accept "rules" in the second example as a colloquialism (an informal expression) that means "helps students get high grades," then the second word group would form a sentence. The first, however, is not a sentence because nothing is happening and no comment *about* the rules of grammar is being made. Some groups of words can be recognized as sentences because a word or words suggest something is happening or a relationship is being observed.

The word "rules" in the second sentence tells us something the writer is observing about "Grammar." The first word also is necessary to make the sentence complete; it indicates *what* "rules." So, you can say that complete sentences need two things:

> Although verbs often convey an action, some verbs do not express what a subject is doing but express a condition or state of being. The most common of these verbs are forms of *to be*: *is, are, was, were, has been, have been, will be,* etc. Because you will use these verbs often, you need to become familiar with them and recognize them as examples of a particular category of verb (see linking verbs, p. 305).

1. A *subject* that answers the reader's question "What or who is this about?"
2. A *predicate* that tells us something the subject is doing or what is being observed about it.

A sentence, then, is *a word or group of words that expresses a complete thought.*

More important, it can be defined grammatically: *a sentence is a group of words that contains at least one subject and one predicate and needs nothing else to complete its thought.*

> A sentence is a group of words that contains at least one subject and one predicate and needs nothing else to complete it.

One question to ask to determine the subject of a sentence is "Who or what is doing the action in the sentence?" When you ask this question, you are attempting to connect a verb, the main part of the predicate, to a noun or pronoun, the main part of a subject. Consider a very simple sentence:

Dogs bark.

The answer to the question "Who or what is doing the action in the sentence?" is "Dogs." So, "Dogs," a noun, is the subject.

To determine the predicate of a sentence, you can ask the question, "What does the subject do?" The answer is "bark." A predicate will always include a *verb*. The line in the sentence below divides the subject from the predicate.

Dogs | bark.

The sentence "Dogs bark" is very brief. How can we make this sentence longer and more interesting? Adding words or phrases to the subject make it more informative, but it doesn't usually change its basic structure. The line between subject and predicate will remain; the difference will be that a reader will know more about the dogs. Similarly, we could add words or phrases to the predicate so we would know more about their barking.

Dirty, dangerous dogs | bark balefully behind the barn.

The reader has been told that the dogs are "dirty" and "dangerous." The predicate also has more information: the reader has been told *how* the dogs barked ("balefully") and *where* they barked ("behind the barn"). The longer sentence illustrates that more interesting statements can be made by adding words or phrases, *modifiers*, to the subject and to the predicate. The subject together with its adjectival modifiers is called the **complete subject**; the main noun or pronoun alone is sometimes called the **simple subject** to distinguish it from the complete subject.

> The subject together with its adjectival modifiers is called the complete subject; the main noun or pronoun alone is sometimes called the simple subject to distinguish it from the complete subject.

Another way you can give more information in a sentence is to add more subjects and predicates. When you add one or more subject–predicate units, the sentence is no longer simple. While simple sentences convey one complete thought, more complex sentences can convey more than one complete thought.

The first thing to check in your writing is that you are writing in complete sentences, which means you must make sure that the sentence you write has two parts, a subject and a predicate.

When you look to see whether the word group has a subject, make sure you don't mistake a noun or pronoun in a prepositional phrase for a subject. (See Fragment 2, Add-on Fragments, page. 313.) In this sentence, there are two nouns in the complete subject, "end" and "troubles." The first noun is the true subject; "troubles" is preceded by the preposition "of" and cannot be linked with the verb "is."

> A prepositional phrase consists of a preposition and a noun or pronoun; it modifies a noun or a verb. The noun or pronoun that immediately follows the preposition will not be the subject.

The *end* of our troubles | *is* in sight.

The Invisible-Subject Sentence

The need for a subject and a predicate in every complete sentence suggests that the minimum English sentence must contain at least two words. There is one

Exercise 14.5

Which of the following are complete sentences? Draw a line between the subject and the predicate. Mark with an "S" those that contain only a subject and a "P" those that contain only a predicate. Indicate an "N" if there is neither subject nor predicate.

1. The cat on the window ledge.

2. Wanted to bury his treasure where it would never be found.

3. A door in the wall.

4. Dropped the ball with only ten yards to go.

5. A sweet-smelling fragrance.

6. Opportunity knocks.

7. Is willing to give a presentation.

8. The high levels of stress of today's students.

9. Can schizophrenia be cured?

10. Hundreds of geese in the field.

11. Send in the clowns!

12. An enemy of the people.

13. Pay attention to the number of times that you end a sentence with a preposition.

14. All dressed up with no place to go.

15. This term will be my most successful one ever.

exception: an **imperative sentence**, which is a command, may consist only of a predicate (verb). The subject, which is always implied, is the pronoun *you*, although it is invisible. For example, in the imperative sentence, "Listen!" "you" is understood to be the subject: "[You] listen!" In the command, "Go to the store!" "you" is understood to be the subject: "[You] go to the store." Notice that "you" could be plural, i.e., the command could be to more than one individual; indeed, all readers of the sentence could be implied.

Four Errors of Incompletion

The first step to ensure that all your sentences are complete is to check that there is a noun or pronoun subject to connect with a verb in the predicate. However, checking for fragments can be a little more complicated than this. To help you recognize *all* kinds of fragments in your writing, they are divided into four types below.

Fragment 1—lacks subject or predicate. In this type of fragment, discussed above, either a subject or a predicate is missing.

In sentence 10 above, "Hundreds of geese in a field," something essential is missing. What about geese in a field? Do they exist? Are the geese doing something? What did they look like? Who saw them?

To answer any of these questions is to complete a thought—and the sentence. For example,

> Hundreds of geese in a field | were resting before the next stage of their long journey.
> Mr. Elford | imagined hundreds of geese in a field.

In the first example, a predicate has been supplied. In the second example, a subject, "Mr. Elford," and a verb, "imagined," have been introduced, and the "hundreds of geese in a field" have become part of the predicate, the direct object of the verb "imagined."

The following sentence, like the one above, is incomplete because it consists only of a subject. In this case, the noun "instructor" is followed by a word group that expands on the subject. The subject is not doing anything.

> An instructor who never gives an "A."

"Who never gives an 'A'" tells us what kind of instructor he or she is but goes no further. To turn this into a complete sentence, you would need to complete the thought by adding a predicate.

> An instructor who never gives an "A" *marks too hard*!
> An instructor who never gives an "A" *sets very high standards*.

Exercise 14.6

Come up with two other ways to complete the fragment above; then, complete the following fragments, all of which lack a predicate.

1. The cell phone that I lost yesterday.
2. The brilliant idea that came to me in the middle of the night.
3. A leader who is capable of motivating others.
4. The kind of doughnut that doesn't have a hole in the middle.
5. The baseball bat that was put in the museum.

Fragment 2—add-on fragment. Add-on fragments contain neither complete subject *nor* predicate. Writers can mistake them for complete sentences because in speech a pause is usual between them and the preceding sentence; you may

One kind of fragment is missing a subject *or* a predicate.

mistakenly associate a pause or drawn breath with a new sentence. The easiest way to fix these kinds of fragments is to make them part of the previous sentence or to supply missing essentials, such as subject and predicate. Punctuation may not be needed; at other times, you can use a comma or a dash.

Add-on fragments may begin with transitional words and phrases: *such as, like, for example, including, also, as well as, except (for), besides, especially,* and similar words. They may also begin with prepositions like *on, in,* and *to.*

Fragment:
Exaggerated images of fitness are everywhere. Especially in teen-oriented magazines.

Corrections:
Exaggerated images of fitness are everywhere, especially in teen-oriented magazines.
Exaggerated images of fitness are everywhere—especially in teen-oriented magazines.

Fragment:
Sewage contains more than 200 toxic chemicals that are flushed down sinks or toilets. Not to mention the runoff from roads.

Correction:
Sewage contains more than 200 toxic chemicals that are flushed down sinks or toilets, not to mention the runoff from roads.

When you begin a sentence with a word like *in, to,* or *at* (i.e., a preposition), check to see that the sentence expresses a complete thought and includes both a subject and a predicate.

Fragment:
On a mountaintop in the remotest region of the Yukon.

Who or what is there and what is taking place?

Corrections:
A confused goat | stood *on a mountaintop in the remotest region of the Yukon.*
On a mountaintop in the remotest region of the Yukon, the climbers | *unfurled a flag.*

Fragment 3—"–ing" fragment. A third kind of fragment occurs when an incomplete verb form ending in *–ing* or *–ed/en*, or a base verb form, is mistaken for a complete verb. To avoid sentence fragments, always ensure you write a *complete* verb form.

Here are some examples of incomplete verb forms:

- listening, studying, thinking, being (present participle form of verb)
- given, thought, written, taken (past participle form of verb)
- to begin, to tell, to be, to look (infinitive form of verb)

While *complete* verb forms can be joined to a subject by adding a helping verb, incomplete verb forms can't:

Incomplete: She listening, they given. . .
Complete: She *was listening,* they *are given.* . .

A common sentence error is mistaking the –*ing* part of a verb form for a complete verb form. The following are examples of fragments with incomplete verb forms:

Holiday crowds *milling* around shopping malls.

What are the crowds doing? If you said "they are milling," you have changed the fragment into a complete sentence by adding the helping verb *are*:

Holiday crowds │ *are milling* around shopping malls.

Fragment:
As a new doctor fascinated by innovative surgery procedures.

Correction:
As a new doctor, he │ *was fascinated* by innovative surgery procedures.

The three incomplete forms mentioned above can act as nouns, adjectives, and adverbs in a sentence—but not as verbs.

Incomplete verb form as noun: Eating sensibly │ is the best way to lose weight.

"Eating" is the noun subject of this sentence.

Incomplete verb form as adjective: My growling stomach │ told me it was time to eat.

"Growling" is an adjective modifying "stomach," the noun subject. Note that there is another incomplete verb form in this sentence, "to eat," which is acting as an adjective, modifying "time."

> Learn how to recognize incomplete verb forms in your writing. Doing so will help you avoid this kind of sentence fragment. See also Appendix A (verb tenses).

Exercise 14.7

To the remaining fragments in Exercise 14.5, add a subject and/or predicate to create grammatically complete sentences.

Fragment 4—dependent clause fragment. A dependent clause fragment is the most common type of fragment. That is because, at first glance, a dependent clause looks a lot like a grammatical sentence.

Independent clauses are equivalent to simple sentences: they have a subject and a predicate and need nothing else to complete them. *Dependent* clauses also contain a subject and a predicate, but they express incomplete thoughts because the information they contain is *dependent on* information in the independent clause. That is one way you can tell a dependent from an independent clause. (Recall that one definition for a complete sentence is that it expresses a complete thought.)

> Independent clauses are equivalent to simple sentences: they have a subject and a predicate and need nothing else to complete them.

> Dependent clauses contain a subject and a predicate, but they express incomplete thoughts because the information they contain is dependent on information in the independent clause. By themselves, they cannot form complete sentences.

Common subordinating conjunctions and relative pronouns:

after, although, as, as if, as long as, as soon as, as though, because, before, even though, ever since, if, if only, in case, in order that, once, since, so that, that, though, unless, until, what, whatever, when, whenever, where, whereas, wherever, whether, which, whichever, while, who, whoever, whom, whose, why

Another way that dependent clauses can be identified is by the word they begin with—a subordinating conjunction or a relative pronoun. Common subordinating conjunctions and relative pronouns appear in the margin.

Dependent clause fragments sound incomplete and leave us wondering about the missing part.

Consider this fragment:

Because his car wouldn't start this morning.

You can think of dependent clauses as searching for an answer to something—in this case, *what happened because his car wouldn't start?* When you provide that information in an independent clause, you will have a complete sentence. You can also test a sentence for completeness by asking whether the word group is true or false. "Because his car wouldn't start this morning" can be neither true nor false due to missing information.

Because his car wouldn't start this morning, he was late for his first day of work.

The subordinating conjunction that introduces the dependent clause indicates the relationship of that clause to the independent clause, such as one of cause–effect (*as, because*), time (*before, since, when, while*), or contrast (*although, though, whereas*). (For more information about subordinating conjunctions as joiners, see pages 233–4.) If you take away the subordinating conjunction, you are left with a subject and a predicate and a sentence that expresses a complete thought. Another way to fix a dependent clause fragment, then, is to take away the subordinating conjunction; you will have a simple sentence expressing one idea. However, it may not be the idea you intended to convey:

His car wouldn't start this morning.

This is a complete sentence, but it does not explain the consequences of his car not starting.

Note that a dependent clause could precede or follow the independent clause. The placement of the dependent clause often determines whether you use a comma to separate it from the main idea (see pages 334–5).

To test whether you have written a dependent clause fragment: (1) does the idea sound complete? (2) can you answer "true" or "false" to it? If the answer to (1) or (2) is no, it is probably a fragment. (3) does it begin with one of the words in the margin box above?

Exercise 14.8

The following may or may not be sentences. If they are not, identify what kind of fragment they illustrate (lacks subject or predicate, add-on fragment, *–ing* fragment, dependent clause fragment). If they are fragments, make them into complete sentences with a subject and a predicate and needing nothing else to complete them.

1. Ensuring that you write in complete sentences.

2. Huge tears rolled down his cheeks.

3. Being that she was insured as the principal driver.

4. Whenever they called her into work.

5. He promised to call on her tomorrow. To see if she was still all right.

6. He must be guilty. Since he's already confessed.

7. I won't vote tomorrow. Unless I hear something that makes me change my mind.

8. Introducing our next prime minister.

9. A row of stately elms interspersed with sprightly cedars.

10. Swimming on her back.

After you've checked your answers (see Appendix D), complete the exercise by doing questions 11–25.

11. Walking beside the tracks, he eventually reached the town.

12. Because spiritual values are more enduring than material ones.

13. Stress can make us victims of illnesses. Including mild to life-threatening ones.

14. The student sauntered into class. After he opened the door and cautiously peeked inside.

15. Which leads to another popular argument for lowering the drinking age.

16. For example, the famous TV show *American Idol*.

17. This is the information age. When ideas are literally at your fingertips.

18. The opposition to vaccinations is a manifestation of fear. That the side effects will be more harmful than the disease itself.

19. Learning about people from different ethnic groups.

20. Stress can have devastating effects on many groups of people. Such as depression in those who fail to meet their own expectations.

21. Golf courses always include obstacles. These being water hazards and sand traps.

22. More than half of depressed adolescents are given antidepressants. Which raises the question of whether they are the best long-term solution.

23. Although there are options in today's schools for Aboriginal students to learn about their culture.

24. Sounds and textures are common features of dreams. While smell and taste are usually absent.

25. On 4 November 2008, millions of viewers tuned in to see one of America's most historic elections. If not the most historic ever.

Exercise 14.9

Each of the following passages contains four sentence fragments. Underline them. Then, correct them by joining them to complete sentences or by adding information. Each passage contains three *kinds* of fragment error, as discussed above. Which kind of fragment error is *not* present in each passage?

1. Although it is known that the people who inhabited the island were of Polynesian descent. In 1994, DNA was extracted from 12 skeletons found on the island, and it was proven to be from people of Polynesian descent. Furthermore, it was suggested that these Polynesians came from Southeast Asia. From the fact that the crops grown by the indigenous people were native to Southeast Asia. For example, bananas, sugarcane, taro, and sweet potato. For more than 30,000 years prior to human settlement of the island, the area was a subtropical forest of trees and woody bushes. Towering over a ground layer of shrubs, herbs, and grasses.

2. International concern has grown in recent years over the proliferation of weapons of mass destruction, but weapons used to exterminate enemy forces are nothing new. In the First World War, artillery was used. In addition to gas, machine guns, grenades, and bombs. The 1940s brought more powerful weaponry. As well as the first nuclear weapon. A weapon capable of killing hundreds of thousands of people. After the Second World War, the Cold War began, as Russia and the US became involved in an arms race. Building hundreds of nuclear weapons more potent than those used in the Second World War.

◎ Introducing . . . Phrases and Clauses

Phrases and **clauses** are grammatical units within the sentence that are larger than one of the parts of speech by itself but usually smaller than a complete grammatical sentence. (The exception is an independent clause, which is equivalent to a simple sentence.)

Prepositions join nouns and pronouns to the rest of the sentence, while conjunctions handle the other joining functions. **Coordinating** conjunctions join two or more independent clauses while **subordinating** conjunctions and relative pronouns join dependent and independent clauses. By joining clauses, you can form different sentence types.

Phrases

Phrases function as nouns, verbs, adjectives, and adverbs. When they act as these parts of speech, it is important to remember that they do so as a unit, though each word *within* the unit may be made up of a different part of speech and have a function distinct from that of the unit itself.

Phrases | function (*as a unit*) (*within the sentence*).

A phrase is a group of grammatically linked words that lacks a subject or a predicate or both and functions as a single part of speech.

"As a unit" and "within the sentence" are functioning as adverbs, modifying the verb "function." (Recall that adverbs modify verbs.) The first phrase answers the question "*how?*" while the second answers the question "*where?*" of the verb. But though each phrase is acting adverbially, the individual words within the unit have distinct functions, none of which is adverbial.

as = preposition

within = preposition

a = indefinite article

the = definite article

unit = noun (object of preposition "as")

sentence = noun (object of preposition "within")

Prepositional Phrases

Prepositional phrase units will act as either adverbs or adjectives. As you've seen above, a group of words that includes more than one part of speech can, as a unit, modify a verb. If it does, it is said to be functioning **adverbially** (as an adverb) within the sentence.

She drove me (*into town*) so I could do my laundry.

The prepositional phrase "into town" begins with the preposition "into" and is followed by the noun "town," the object of the preposition. But if you look at the phrase as a unit, you can see that "into town" is functioning as an adverb modifying the verb "drove" by explaining where the action took place: drove *where? Into town.*

Similarly, a group of words can modify a noun or pronoun, in which case it is functioning **adjectivally** (as an adjective).

Consider the prepositional phrases (indicated by parentheses) in these sentences:

An obsession (*with Star Wars*) | led to her career (*as an astronomer*).

> Adjectival phrases usually *follow* the noun or pronoun they modify. This order is different from that of one-word adjectives, which usually *precede* the noun they modify.

"With *Star Wars*" is a prepositional phrase that gives us more information about (i.e., modifies) the noun "obsession." It is functioning as an adjective.

with = preposition
Star Wars = proper noun (object of preposition *with*)

The second phrase, "as an astronomer," modifies the noun "career," functioning as an adjective.

as = preposition
astronomer = noun (object of preposition *as*)

Prepositional phrases do not contain the actual subject of a sentence. In the following sentence, "At the beginning of class" does not contain the actual subject even though it begins the sentence.

At the beginning of class, students in Japan bow to their teacher.

The subject here is "students," and "at the beginning of class" is a prepositional phrase answering *when* they bow. Since it answers *when?* of the verb "bow," you know it is acting adverbially in the sentence.

Noun and Verb Phrases

In this example, the indefinite pronoun "Some" combined with its modifier, "of the injured," makes up a **noun phrase**. The entire phrase, "Some of the injured passengers," functions as the subject in this sentence because it tells us *who* "had to be hospitalized."

Some of the injured passengers | had to be hospitalized.

Phrases, then, can function as noun subjects or objects.

Finally, consider the following sentence, in which a **verb phrase** acts as a unit in the sentence, conveying the action of the subject "We":

We *will be looking* carefully for the person with a red flag on her backpack.

Verb phrases are very common since you will often need to use helping verbs with main verbs to create different tenses beyond the one-word simple tenses (verb phrases are italicized):

Simple present: I think, you say, she takes....
Simple past: I thought, you said, she took....
Present progressive: I *am thinking*, you *are saying*, she *is taking*....
Past perfect: I *had thought*, you *had said*, she *had taken*....

For more information about the tenses, see Appendix A.

Exercise 14.10

First, identify the word groups in parentheses as adverbial, adjectival, noun, or verb phrases. Then, identify the subject of the sentence.

1. Yesterday, (the price of food) was the main item (in the news).

2. (Some of my favourite books) (have gone) out of print.

3. The room (with the two computers) (has been locked) (from the inside).

4. A search (of the abandoned house) (turned up) several cartons (of stolen goods).

5. The best player (on our paintball team) broke his arm and (will be lost) (for the season).

In addition to forms of *to be* and *to have*, verb phrases occur when modals, a special kind of helping verb, combine with main verbs to convey ability (*can, could*), possibility (*may, might*) necessity (*must, have*), and other meanings.

Clauses

A word group larger than a phrase that can be broken down into two grammatical units, a subject and a predicate, is called a **clause**. In the following sentence, the subjects are in bold, the verbs are italicized, and the conjunction is underlined. Clauses can be combined to create longer sentences than simple sentences.

> **Frances** never *answers* questions in class <u>unless</u> the **teacher** *calls* on her.
> *First clause*: Frances never answers questions in class
> *Second clause*: unless the teacher calls on her.

The first part of this sentence could stand alone as a sentence, as it has a subject, "Frances," a predicate verb, "answers," and needs nothing else to complete its thought. The second part could not stand alone as a sentence—the word "unless" makes it a dependent clause fragment.

Thus, this sentence illustrates two different kinds of clauses: (1) an **independent clause**, which can stand alone as a sentence, and (2) a **dependent clause**, which cannot stand alone as a sentence. It is especially important to be able to distinguish an independent clause from a dependent clause in order to avoid writing a sentence fragment. As discussed under Fragment—dependent clause fragment 4 (page 315), a dependent clause contains an idea subordinate to (dependent on) the idea of the main clause.

Using Conjunctions to Join Clauses

An independent clause by itself is equivalent to a *simple sentence*. "Frances never answers questions in class" is a simple sentence consisting of an independent clause. Clauses are used as building blocks to construct more complex sentences. The function of **coordinating conjunctions** is to connect *equal* units, such as two independent clauses. The function of **subordinating conjunctions** is to connect *unequal* units, such as an independent clause and a dependent clause. Different rules for punctuation apply to independent and dependent clauses connected this way.

Sentence Patterns

Compound sentence: Sentences formed by two or more independent clauses joined by a coordinating conjunction are called **compound sentences**. We can see these kinds of conjunctions (italicized) operating as joiners in the following examples:

A clause is a group of words containing both a subject and a predicate.

An independent clause can stand alone as a complete sentence; a dependent clause cannot stand alone as a complete sentence.

Coordinating conjunctions connect *coordinate* or *equal* units, such as two independent clauses; subordinating conjunctions connect clauses of *unequal weight*, an independent clause and a dependent clause.

The seven coordinating conjunctions are *for, and, nor, but, or, yet,* and *so*. The coordinating conjunctions spell out the acronym FANBOYS.

Exercise 14.11

Identify all independent and dependent clauses in the following sentences by underlining independent clauses and placing parentheses around any dependent clauses. To help, you can refer to the list of subordinating conjunctions below, page 323; these kinds of conjunctions introduce dependent clauses. Remember that pronouns, such as *I* or *it*, can act as subjects.

1. While drug testing has become more common, athletes are still taking drugs.
2. Although I think winter is here, the temperature is not cold enough for snow.
3. I became hooked on reality shows when I began watching them with my roommate.
4. In most parts of North America, Daylight Saving Time begins in March.
5. The battle against cancer will continue until a cure is found.
6. While it is important that students volunteer, mandatory volunteerism does not instill a sense of civic duty.
7. The folk music of the 60s and 70s often encouraged peace; however, the message was not always received.
8. Studying grammar does not guarantee good grades, but it certainly helps.
9. Despite her good intentions, the governor general has not been able to satisfy many Canadian politicians.
10. Plastic water bottles have become the focus of public scorn, though more pressing moral concerns need attention.

The woodwinds warbled, *and* the strings sang sweetly.

Our profits in the first quarter showed a ten per cent increase, *but* in the second quarter, they dropped again.

I discovered there was a great deal written on my topic, *so* I knew I would have to narrow my search.

A sentence can have two subjects or two verbs and still be a simple sentence (but not two subjects *and* two verbs). Coordinating conjunctions join equal units, so as well as joining two independent clauses, they can join two nouns that are the subject of one verb or two verbs governed by one subject. Such compound-subject and compound-predicate constructions can occur in simple sentences. However, a compound *sentence* contains two independent clauses, *each* with its own subject and verb.

Here is an example of a simple sentence with compound predicate:

Jason *awoke* before dawn *and listened* happily to the sounds of the new day.

One noun with two verbs makes up a simple sentence.

Note that there is no comma before the conjunction "and" because the two verbs it connects are parts of the same clause. The sentence below contains two subjects and two predicates:

Jason awoke before dawn, *and* **he** *listened* happily to the sounds of the new day.

Don't use a coordinating conjunction to begin a sentence. Words like "and," "but," and "or" should occur only *within* a sentence where they join two equal units, such as two independent clauses.

Incorrect: The popularity of Facebook is undeniable. And it shows no sign of abating.
Corrected: The popularity of Facebook is undeniable, and it shows no sign of abating.

Complex sentence: A sentence formed by one independent clause joined by a subordinating conjunction to a dependent clause is called a **complex sentence**. In a complex sentence, two or more subordinating conjunctions may connect two or more dependent clauses to an independent clause. We can see these kinds of conjunctions operating as joiners in the following examples:

Plagiarism is a problem at many universities *where* much research these days is conducted through the Internet.
Although much work has gone into developing artificial organs, the results, to date, have been disappointing.

In the first sentence, "where" is the subordinating conjunction that begins a dependent clause and joins it to the preceding independent clause. In the second sentence, the dependent clause comes first, but the subordinating conjunction "although" nevertheless joins the dependent to the independent clause. (You can just as easily start a sentence with a dependent clause as an independent one.)

In the sentence below, an independent clause is followed by two dependent clauses; "after" and "that" are the subordinating conjunctions that join them:

Ena began taking night classes *after* her company announced *that* there would be layoffs in the near future.

You need to carefully distinguish clauses in order to punctuate them correctly. For example, in this sentence, a dependent clause intervenes between the subordinating conjunction "that" and the rest of the dependent clause. The dependent clause that interrupts is italicized:

The students felt it was unfair that, *because the instructor was late*, they weren't given enough time for the test.

Common subordinating conjunctions and relative pronouns:
after, although, as, as if, as long as, as soon as, as though, because, before, even though, ever since, if, if only, in case, in order that, once, since, so that, that, though, unless, until, what, whatever, when, whenever, where, whereas, wherever, whether, which, whichever, while, who, whoever, whom, whose, why

Compound-complex sentence: The last sentence type, a **compound-complex sentence**, combines a compound sentence (independent clause + coordinating conjunction + independent clause) with a complex sentence. It will contain two independent clauses along with one or more dependent clauses. For example,

The woodwinds warbled, the brass bellowed, *and* the strings sang sweetly, *though* the timpani thundered, almost drowning out the other instruments.

Exercise 14.12

Examples of the simple, compound, and complex sentence types appear below. For compound and complex sentences, underline independent clauses, circle conjunctions, and put parentheses around dependent clauses. Identify each sentence type.

1. The class average was low in the first semester, but it has gone up this semester.
2. Since the beginning of time, people have worn fur for warmth.
3. The mosquitoes are biting again, and the BBQs are being fired up.
4. She ran the race in record time but collapsed at the finish line.
5. Salmon oil is a supplement that lowers cholesterol.
6. Expository writing explains or informs the reader about something.
7. Snowboarding began in the early 70s, and it has grown in popularity ever since.
8. His library privileges have been suspended until he pays his fines.
9. The committee began its search in September and has not yet found a suitable candidate.
10. She is convinced that she will get an "A" in the course.

Exercise 14.13

To demonstrate your familiarity with the different kinds of clauses and joiners, construct compound, complex, and compound-complex sentences from the independent clauses (simple sentences) below. After you have joined the clauses in the most logical way, identify the sentence type: compound, complex, or compound-complex. Ensure that you have at least one example of each type of sentence. Small changes can be made so that it is easier to make up complex sentences, and sentence order may be changed.

1. They intended to eat at Benny's Bistro.

   They saw a long line-up outside Benny's.

   They went to Kenny's Kitchen instead.

2. There may be nearly two million kinds of plants in the world.

   There are likely at least as many different kinds of animals.

   No one can know how many species have evolved, flourished, and become extinct.

3. Timothy Findley's story "Stones" takes place in Toronto.

   Norman Levine's "Something Happened Here" takes place in northern France.

   Both stories describe the tragic assault by Canadian troops on Dieppe during the Second World War.

4. We may suspect that earth is not unique as a life-bearing planet.

   We do not as yet have any compelling evidence that life exists anywhere else.

   We must restrict our discussion of the presence of life to our own planet.

5. Drug-testing procedures for Olympic athletes are becoming more and more elaborate.

   Athletes often feel they have to boost their performance.

   They want to compete at the same level as their competition.

Errors of Combining

A fragment in formal writing suggests the writer does not fully understand what a sentence is, but sometimes writers run one sentence into another, suggesting they don't know where to end the sentence. The two major errors in ending a sentence are the **run-on sentence** (sometimes called "the fused sentence") and the **comma splice**, or the comma fault.

The Run-On Sentence

Writers of run-on sentences join two sentences without stopping. Doing this is like running a stop sign without changing speed. The writers charge through the end of the first complete thought and into the second one without separating their statements. These writers do not place a period at the end of the first sentence and so do not capitalize the first letter of the word that should begin the second sentence.

A sentence may contain one, two, or more subject–predicate units, and these units (independent clauses) must be either separated by a period or joined correctly so the reader can distinguish one main idea from another.

Incorrect:

The cruise to Alaska was full Yumi decided to fly to Jamaica instead.
The Dene peoples live in Northern Canada they speak different languages.

Once you determine where the first clause ends and the second one begins, make them into two simple sentences or use a comma and the appropriate coordinating conjunction to join them.

Corrected:

The cruise to Alaska was full. Yumi decided to fly to Jamaica instead.
The cruise to Alaska was full, *so* Tom and Yumi decided to fly to Jamaica instead.

The Dene peoples live in Northern Canada. They speak different languages.
The Dene peoples live in Northern Canada, *and* they speak different languages.

The run-on sentences below contain two complete thoughts, or two main ideas. Lines indicate the division between subject and predicate; diagonal lines show where the first sentence ends and the second begins, and where a period or a comma and coordinating conjunction should be placed.

> A run-on sentence isn't just a long sentence: it's a major grammatical error in which two subject–predicate units (two "sentences") are not properly separated.

Incorrect:

Few Koreans | have animals in their homes // pets | are not a large part of Korean culture.
Toxic chemicals and pollutants | do not disappear // they | accumulate in our natural resources.

Corrected:

Few Koreans have animals in their home. Pets are not a large part of Korean culture.
Few Koreans have animals in their homes, *for* pets are not a large part of Korean culture.

Toxic chemicals and pollutants do not disappear. They accumulate in our natural resources.
Toxic chemicals and pollutants do not disappear, *but* they accumulate in our natural resources.

> A comma splice isn't just a problem in comma usage; it's a major grammatical error in which a comma alone is used to separate two complete thoughts.

The Comma Splice

An error more common than the run-on sentence is the comma splice—the joining of two complete sentences by only a comma. This error is like slowing down at a stop sign without coming to a full stop, then charging through. The comma has many uses *within* the sentence, but, by itself, a comma cannot be used to connect two sentences.

The simplest way to avoid comma splices is to think about where one complete thought (independent clause) ends and the next begins and to place a period there or use a comma and a coordinating conjunction. Comma splices sometimes occur when two clauses are very closely related or the second clause seems a continuation of the first one. In formal writing, it's important to be able to separate two independent clauses.

Incorrect:

Fights in hockey are more than pointless, they are often dangerous.

Legalizing marijuana is not just the better choice, it is the right choice.

Although the second clauses in these sentences are closely related in meaning to the preceding clauses, they are not part of those clauses and must be separated from them by something stronger than just a comma. As you will see in Chapter 15, a "stop" form of punctuation, such as a semicolon or colon, may be a good choice in these cases:

Corrected:

Fights in hockey are more than pointless. They are often dangerous.

Fights in hockey are more than pointless; they are often dangerous.

Legalizing marijuana is not just the better choice. It is the right choice.

Legalizing marijuana is not just the better choice; it is the right choice.

Remember that pronouns generally replace nouns that precede them in a sentence. Like nouns, pronouns can act as subjects of a clause. In the following sentences, a pronoun is the subject of the second clause. Lines indicate the division between subject and predicate; diagonal lines show where the first sentence ends and the second begins, and where a period or the comma and coordinating conjunction should be placed.

Incorrect:

Working in a busy office environment | was completely new to her, //she | had always worked at home.

Censorship | does not just mean getting rid of swearing and nudity, //it | can also mean blocking an idea or viewpoint.

Corrected:

Working in a busy office environment was completely new to her. She had always worked at home.

Working in a busy office environment was completely new to her, *for* she had always worked at home.

Censorship does not just mean getting rid of swearing and nudity. It can also mean blocking an idea or viewpoint.

Censorship does not just mean getting rid of swearing and nudity, *but* it can also mean blocking an idea or viewpoint.

Remember that if you wish to use a comma to connect two independent clauses, you must also use one of the seven coordinating conjunctions. You cannot use a comma before words like *however, therefore,* or *thus* to join two independent clauses. That would also produce a comma splice. For the correct form of punctuation with these and similar words and phrases, see page 343.

Exercise 14.14

Fix the sentences by using a period to make two separate sentences, or if you already know the rules for using other forms of punctuation to join independent clauses, you can use them. Also, identify whether the sentence is a run-on or a comma splice.

1. I took two buses to get downtown it was a long way.

2. Our neighbour's dog howled all last night, it was just impossible to get a night's sleep.

3. I was frightened during my first driving lesson the instructor yelled at me.

4. It's easy to punctuate sentences, just put a comma whenever you pause.

5. Janne ate as quickly as he could then he went upstairs to finish his homework.

6. The incidence of breast cancer has increased, it takes the lives of many women today.

7. Homelessness has existed for centuries, literature on the subject dates back to the feudal period in Europe.

8. Humans are imitators, conforming is something they are good at.

9. Mozart composed his first minuet at the age of five he wrote his first symphony before he turned nine.

10. Asthma is a common problem among Canadians, exposure to second-hand smoke in public places can intensify this condition.

Exercise 14.15

Determine what is wrong in the following sentences. It could be a fragment, a run-on sentence, or a comma splice; then, make the correction.

1. He managed to pass the year though he seldom did his homework, what will happen to him next year is anyone's guess.

2. The opening ceremonies were delayed. On account of rain.

3. She went to France for the summer. It being a fine opportunity to learn another language.

4. Though they both liked to read, they usually read different books, she read adventure stories while he liked detective stories.

5. While books are still the main source for acquiring knowledge.

6. The only way a person can learn. To pay attention to what is going on in class.

7. He was too tall and thin to excel at sports. Except basketball, of course.

8. The concept that "bigger is better" is part of our culture, it is promoted by both advertisers and the media these days.

9. Understanding the theory of relativity and its impact on our daily lives.

10. Martin Luther King led protests during the civil rights movement, his enthusiasm and his will to end discrimination made him a leader.

After you've checked your answers, complete the exercise by doing questions 11–25.

11. The Romans were willing to change their religious beliefs quite easily, the Greeks, however, were less willing to do this.

12. Although TV can corrupt the minds of innocent children if it is not monitored closely.

13. The computer is not the only way to access email today, telephones and palm pads may come equipped with email capability.

14. It seems that the North American mass media prescribes two roles for women, they can be sex objects or passive housewives.

15. Martial arts are attracting more people than ever before. Especially those who want to gain self-control and self-awareness.

16. We can no longer turn our backs to what is happening in the north it is time to take action.

17. Nintendo held a launch party in Times Square, New York, it was hosted by a local VJ.

18. Racism in Canada exceeded just social and personal racism, it was institutional racism.

19. A story of an Indo-Canadian woman who rejected her arranged marriage.

20. Carpal Tunnel Syndrome has many causes, the most common is from repetitive wrist movements.

21. The tobacco in cigarettes is not the only problem, they contain many dangerous chemicals as well.

22. One of the most tragic events of the twentieth century. The detonation of the atomic bomb over Hiroshima.

23. Podcasts are current, up-to-date and appear automatically, thus they can be enjoyed anywhere at any time.

24. In the final book of the series, Harry visits his parents' grave and sees two inscriptions on their graves the inscriptions refer to passages from the Bible.

25. Many factors contribute to poverty. Including geographic factors, disease, and lack of education or health care.

Exercise 14.16

Identify the sentence errors in the following paragraph; they may include fragments, run-on sentences, and comma splices. Then, correct them.

In recent decades, our society has become obsessed with body image through fitness and weight loss this infatuation can be seen in the popularity of fad diets. Such as the Atkins diet and its many variants. Fitness routines popular today include yoga and Pilates, there has also been a marked increase in the number of women having plastic surgery. In general, the obsession with body image is a greater concern for females than for males. Since many women are socialized to equate self-worth with physical appearance. One of the causes of this socialization is the popular media. Which often portrays unrealistic standards of the ideal body type.

Chapter Review Questions

1. What is a noun? A noun phrase?
2. What is a verb? A verb phrase?
3. What is an adjective?
4. What is an adverb?
5. What is a preposition? Prepositional phrase?
6. What is the difference between a coordinating and subordinating conjunction?
7. What are the different types of sentence patterns?
8. What are the two essential parts of a sentence?
9. What are the different types of sentence fragments?
10. What is the difference between a run-on sentence and a comma splice?

15

Commas and Other Forms of Punctuation

In this chapter, you will learn how to

- use commas

- use semicolons

- use colons

- use dashes and parentheses

- use apostrophes

- avoid common punctuation errors

While some punctuation rules change slowly over time, not all the uses you see every day are correct. Therefore, this chapter will introduce you to the current standards for properly using punctuation. Once you have studied the rules, you may even begin to notice other people's erroneous use of commas, semicolons, colons, dashes, parentheses, and apostrophes. Later in the chapter, you will be shown how to avoid some of the common punctuation errors that writers make. Various exercises will help reinforce the punctuation rules you need to know in order to write error-free documents.

Do Commas Matter?

Does the precise placement of those visually challenged marks on paper *really* matter? The short answer is "yes" because readers look for commas in specific places to help them read. When a comma is missing or where it shouldn't be, the reader might have to reread the sentence, looking for another cue to its meaning. Furthermore, if you make comma errors, your reliability will be affected. Missing commas in the short sentences below could confuse a reader:

1. The year before a deadly virus ravaged much of the countryside.
2. Although dating services may ask you for a photo appearance is less important than personality.

Applying rule (2b) for independent clauses outlined below means correctly placing commas after "before" in sentence (1) and after "photo" in sentence (2).

As a student, you will be writing essays or reports for many of your classes. As a future working professional, you may write letters, email, reports, summaries, memoranda, or other documents that need to be punctuated. Correct comma use guides the reader through the sentence, clarifying the relationships among its parts.

Myths about comma use abound, such as the "one breath rule," which states that wherever you naturally stop to pause, you should insert a comma. However, commas are there to assist the average silent reader more than the one who reads aloud. If you are coaching yourself to read a speech, you may want to place commas where you plan to pause for breath, but in formal writing, the "one breath rule" is simply too vague to be of use; it can even lead you astray.

The word *comma* comes from the Greek word *komma*, meaning "cut" or "segment." In general, commas separate (segment) the smaller or less important units in a sentence. Working with coordinating conjunctions, however, they are also used to separate large units, independent clauses. Commas separate the following in a sentence:

- items in a series
- independent clauses
- parenthetical (types of non-essential) information
- adjectives, dates, addresses, titles, and the like.

> Commas separate the smaller or less important units in a sentence. Working with coordinating conjunctions, they are also used to separate large units, independent clauses.

Rule Category 1: Use Commas to Separate Items in a Series

This rule category applies to three or more grammatically parallel items whether single words—such as nouns, verbs, or adjectives—phrases, or clauses. For example:

> Commas separate three or more items in a series: words, phrases, and clauses.

A series of three nouns:

It doesn't matter whether the items in the series are words, phrases, or clauses.

A series of three predicates:

> Every Saturday, Davina gets up, drowns herself with coffee, and stumbles to the door before she realizes what day it is.

A series of three clauses:

> Come to the Broadmead Art Tour tomorrow: view artworks in a variety of media, add to your collection, and meet with talented artists on their doorstep.

A series or list is *three* or more of something. When you refer to *two* of something with a joiner in between like *and*, you do *not* usually use a comma unless *and* is joining two independent clauses. The grammatical name for a group of words consisting of two of something (such as two nouns or two verbs) is a **compound**.

The comma before the last item in a series of three or more items, referred to as the *serial comma*, is often omitted in informal writing.

> My three favourite months are May, June and September. (Informal)

However, there are places where using the serial comma makes a sentence much easier to follow. It should *not* be omitted if the last element or the one that precedes it is a compound (contains two items). In this example, the last item in the list is a compound, a single thing, "toast and jam," consisting of two elements: "toast" and "jam."

> She ordered orange juice, an omelette with cheese, and toast and jam.

The serial comma is especially helpful to the reader where the second-last or the last item is significantly longer than the other items.

> The two-year specialization includes 10 half-courses, two full courses that involve internships in health care facilities, and a research paper.

Rule Category 2: Use Commas to Separate Independent Clauses

This rule category applies to three related situations: (a) two independent clauses joined by a coordinating conjunction, (b) introductory words, phrases, or clauses when an independent clause follows, and (c) some conclusions when an independent clause precedes the conclusion.

a) Use a comma after an independent clause when that clause is followed by another independent clause with a coordinating conjunction in between.

> A list or series contains *three* items; commas separate the items. A compound contains *two* items; a comma is not used unless the items are two independent clauses with a word like *and, or,* or *but* in between.

> Always include the serial comma, the comma preceding the conjunction joining the last and second-last items in a list, unless your instructor tells you otherwise.

> Use a comma before the coordinating conjunction in a compound sentence.

In other words, use a comma before the coordinating conjunction in a compound sentence.

> The course was supposed to be offered in the fall, *but* it was cancelled.
> The grocery store is two kilometres away, *so* he never walks.
> Dyana was the best dancer on the cruise ship, *and* she won an award to prove it.

Remember that the comma goes *before*, not after, the coordinating conjunction.

Short Independent Clauses: Exceptions to this rule may be made if the second clause is very short or if the clauses are so closely related that they could be considered compounds (i.e., the ideas are hard to separate). For example, the comma may be omitted between "dress" and "and" because the clauses are short:

> "She wore the dress and I stayed home," sang Danny Kaye in the movie *White Christmas*.

b) Use a comma after an introductory word, phrase, or clause when an independent clause follows it.

> After six years as committee chair, it was time for her to retire.
> In order to get the maximum enjoyment from his stereo equipment, Curtis put it in a room where the acoustics were excellent.

In the following example, the introduction is one word, a **sentence adverb**, an adverb that modifies the independent clause that follows it:

> Unfortunately, we have run out of mineral water.

Introductory dependent clause: When you begin the sentence with a dependent clause that is followed by an independent clause, a comma follows the dependent clause introduction (italicized below).

> *While the drinking age is 19 in most provinces*, it is only 18 in Alberta.
> *When she first encountered the Canadian educational system*, she was surprised by the many differences between the North American and Japanese systems.

Compare with rule (c), below.

c) In general, use a comma before a concluding word or phrase when an independent clause precedes it.

Sidebar notes:

Use a comma after an introductory word, phrase, or clause when an independent clause follows it.

Combining rules: In the following sentence, independent clause rules (2a) and (2b) are illustrated:
   In America, (2b) 20 per cent of homeless children repeat a grade in school, (2a) *and* another 16 per cent of these children are enrolled in special education classes.

In general, use a comma before a concluding word or phrase when an independent clause precedes it.

W.J. Prince wrote to his client Larry Drucker, asking direction in the case.

Rule (c) will apply when a statement is followed by a reference to the person or group that made the statement:

> "We still think of a powerful man as a born leader and a powerful woman as an anomaly," Margaret Atwood once said.
> Students who participate in sports or social activities at school are more likely to consider themselves satisfied with their lives compared to those who do not, according to a recent study.

Concluding dependent clause: Rule (c) does not usually apply when an independent clause is followed by a dependent clause. So, if you begin with a dependent clause and follow with an independent clause, you use a comma to separate the clauses, as rule (2b) above states. However, if you *begin with an independent clause and conclude with a dependent clause*, you do *not* generally use a comma. However, a dependent clause that begins with *although*, *though*, *even though*, or *whereas* suggests a contrast with the independent clause and *should* usually be preceded by a comma.

> The sleek Siamese cat lay on the sofa *where it was sunny*. (no comma; general rule)
> The sleek Siamese cat lay on the sofa, *whereas the old Labrador retriever curled up by the fire*. (clause begins with "whereas," suggests contrast)

Rule Category 3: Use Two Commas to Separate Parenthetical Information

When you place something in parentheses, you signal to the reader that this information is less important than what is not in parentheses. Commas operate similarly to separate less important from more important information in the sentence. The three rules below will help you decide whether the information is non-essential (additional) or essential; then, you can punctuate accordingly.

a) Use commas before and after non-restrictive (non-essential) phrases or clauses. Restrictive and non-restrictive clauses often begin with the relative pronouns *who*, *whom*, *which*, or *that*. They follow nouns, which they modify.

Although the information in non-restrictive clauses may be important, it *can* be left out without changing the essence of the sentence. By contrast, a restrictive clause is *essential* to the meaning of the sentence. If you left it out, the sentence would mean something different or would be ungrammatical.

It is important to look closely at clauses that begin with *who*, *which*, and *that* in order to punctuate them correctly. When the clause gives additional (non-essential) information, separate the clause from the rest of the sentence by commas. If it gives essential information, do not use a comma. Consider these sentences:

1. Tony, who often wears a leather jacket, was identified as one of the rescue team.
2. A man who wore a leather jacket was identified as one of the rescue team.

Combining rules: In the following sentence, independent clause rules (2b) and (2c) are illustrated:
By banning the use of cell phones, (2b) Newfoundland encouraged its drivers to focus on the road, (2c) reducing the number of collisions.

In general, use a comma when you begin a sentence with a dependent clause and follow with an independent clause, but do not use a comma if you begin with an independent clause and follow with a dependent clause.

Relative pronouns introduce dependent (adjectival) clauses.

The main idea in sentence 1 is that Tony was identified as part of the rescue team. Tony's leather jacket may be important elsewhere in a larger narrative, but in this sentence it is not part of the main idea; therefore, the information about his jacket is enclosed by commas. Note that *two* commas are required, just as two parentheses would be required.

In sentence 2, the information about the jacket is essential to the identification of this person on the team. If you were to leave out the clause "who wore a leather jacket," the sentence would mean simply that a man, not a woman, was on the rescue team. That's the way you can test whether information in clauses beginning with *who*, *which*, or *that* is essential: if you omit the clause and the sentence says something different, you've proven that the information is essential. Try omitting the "who" clause in the following:

> *Incorrectly punctuated:* Many students, *who take out loans*, have a heavy debt burden on graduation.

If you take out what is in italics, you are left with a sentence that says simply "Many students have a heavy debt burden on graduation." That's different from the more specific statement about those students *who take out loans*. No commas should be used because "who take out loans" is essential information in this sentence.

Note: Use *who* to refer to people in restrictive and non-restrictive clauses. Use *which* to refer to non-humans in non-restrictive clauses and *that* to refer to non-humans in restrictive clauses.

> The actor *who* [not "that"] appeared in the movie *Outbreak* also appeared in *Sweet Home Alabama*.

b) Use commas to set off appositives. These are nouns—words or phrases—that are grammatically parallel to a preceding noun or phrase. They name, rephrase, specify, or explain the noun or noun phrase that comes just before. Appositives are underlined below.

> Her first work, <u>a short story collection called *Drying the Bones*</u>, was given outstanding reviews.
> Seal hunting, <u>a traditional means of livelihood among Inuit</u>, has been criticized by some environmentalists.

Use commas for true appositives. Sometimes the second noun completes the first noun, giving essential information. In such cases, you do not set off the second noun by a comma. If in doubt, take the second noun or noun phrase out of the sentence and see if the sentence is complete without it and makes grammatical sense.

Can you explain why commas are placed around "king of the beasts" in the following sentence but not before "Aesop," the name of the Greek writer? Which

---

In clauses beginning with who, which, *or* that, *use two commas around the clause if it can be omitted without changing the meaning of the sentence.*

Use who *to refer to people in restrictive and non-restrictive clauses. Use* which *to refer to non-humans in non-restrictive (inessential) clauses and* that *to refer to non-humans in restrictive (essential) clauses.*

Use commas around nouns that (re)name the previous noun and with which they are grammatically parallel.

is the true appositive? Hint: try taking "king of the beasts" and "Aesop" out of the sentence to test for essential versus non-essential (additional) information.

Correct:
The lion, king of the beasts, is the subject of many fables by the Ancient Greek writer Aesop.

Although they are not strictly appositives, you can use the appositive rule for words and phrases that can be considered "subsets" of a larger set—this would include examples in phrases beginning with *such as* and *including*.

The celebration of certain holidays, such as Christmas and Halloween, have been banned by several local school boards.

c) Use commas to set off adverbs and adverbial phrases that interrupt the flow of the sentence from subject to predicate and from verb to object or subject complement. Such words or phrases often emphasize or qualify a thought. See page 343 for a list that includes *indeed, after all, for example, however, in fact, indeed, needless to say, therefore,* and many more.

Use commas to set off the name of the person you are addressing directly:

"I must say, Frank, that your performance on the aptitude test demonstrates, beyond a doubt, that you would make an excellent engineer."

There are times, especially in informal or semi-formal writing, when using two commas around a small word that interrupts the sentence may produce clutter. Except in the most formal writing, commas around adverbial interruptions can be omitted if they directly follow a coordinating conjunction, such as *but,* to avoid three commas in close proximity.

Commas can be omitted: Leslie worried about her driver's test, but in fact she aced it.
Not incorrect, but cluttered: Leslie worried about her driver's test, but, in fact, she aced it.

Rule Category 4: Conventional and "Comma Sense" Uses

Stylistic convention more than grammar dictates that you use commas between coordinate adjectives before a noun, with dates, addresses, titles, and before and after direct quotations.

a) Adjectives modify nouns and usually precede them. When the adjectives are *coordinate,* or equal and interchangeable, you separate them by a comma. When the adjectives are *non-coordinate,* or unequal and not interchangeable, you do not use a comma.

Coordinate adjectives: big, friendly dog; tall, white tower; proud, condescending man
Non-coordinate adjectives: white bull terrier; welcome second opinion; incredible lucky break

Combining rules: In the following sentence, the appositive rule (3b) and independent clause rule (2a) are illustrated:
His first purchase, (3b) the painting of the Northern Ontario Landscape by Tom Thompson, (3b) is now worth thousands of dollars, (2a) but he says he will never sell it.

Use commas around words and phrases that interrupt the flow of the sentence.

Use a comma between two coordinate (equal and interchangeable) adjectives.

One way to confirm that coordinate adjectives are being used is to mentally place the word *and* between the adjectives, such as *big (and) friendly dog*. If this makes sense, then coordinate adjectives are being used and commas are required. You will note that applying this test to *white (and) bull terrier* does not work, as the phrase contains non-coordinate adjectives; therefore, commas are not used.

b) To separate quotations from the rest of the sentence, as in attributions (i.e., where a source is named):

> The sign says, "trespassers will be prosecuted."
> "I am not a crook," said Richard Nixon.

c) To distinguish names and locations in addresses:

> The Prime Minister of Canada, 24 Sussex Drive, Ottawa, Ontario, Canada

Convention also dictates that you place a comma *after* the name of the province or state if the sentence continues:

> I lived in Calgary, Alberta, until I moved back to Ontario.

d) Dates:

> October 7, 1951 but 7 October 1951 and October 1951

A comma is not used if you begin with the day and follow with the month and year, nor is it used with the month and year alone.

e) Degrees, titles, and similar designations:

> Sabrina Yao, M.D., Ph.D., F.R.C.P.S.

f) Numbers:
Under the metric system, there is a space rather than a comma between every three digits in a number of more than four digits (the space is optional with four-digit numbers). You will sometimes see the non-metric format where a comma separates every three digits starting from the right.

> The output of chemical wastes was 13 890 457 kilolitres per day for that factory.

> In 2006, the population of Nunavut was 29 474, according to Statistics Canada.

> The US Defence Department listed 2356 casualties earlier in the year.

Commas are used between some elements in addresses, dates, degrees, and numbers, and between quotations and their source.

g) The convention in North America is to place commas and periods *inside* quotation marks. Other marks of punctuation are placed *outside* quotation marks.

> The new topic, "Where Ecological Ends Meet," has been posted.
> We have been told that our meals "are not gratis"; however, the company has paid for our transportation.

h) In some cases, you will have to apply "comma sense." If a sentence sounds confusing when you read it over, it may be necessary to insert a comma. Commas in the following sentences ensure the sense intended.

> In 1971, 773 people were killed in an earthquake in Peru.
> He told the student to come now, and again the following week.

> The convention in North America is to place commas and periods *inside* quotation marks. Other marks of punctuation are placed *outside* quotation marks.

> *Combining rules:* In the following sentence, the rule for comma use with quotations (above) and the independent clause rule (2c) are illustrated:
>   "You should always put periods and commas inside quotation marks," (4b) said Professor LeGuin, (2c) though this system only applies to North America.

Exercise 15.1

Add commas to the following sentences, if and where required. Also, name the rule category discussed above. There is one comma rule to apply in each sentence.

1. After her inaugural speech several members of the house rose to congratulate her.
2. The optional package includes bucket seats dual speakers and air-conditioning.
3. We have collected more than $20,000 and there is a week remaining in our campaign.
4. Metaphors similes and personification all are examples of figurative language.
5. As one can see the tower is leaning four-and-one-half metres to the south.
6. Hardly daring to breathe Nelson took a quick look at the valley far below him.
7. Although many are called few are chosen.
8. The magnificent country estate is hidden behind a long elegant row of silver birches.
9. "We can't achieve peace in our time if we assume war is inevitable" he said.
10. Her house was a newer one with dark wood trim and large open rooms.
11. As well as the Irish many Africans were forced to leave their families behind during times of famine.
12. Because of the humidity levels it feels hotter than the actual temperature.
13. Joe Clark the former prime minister has a famous wife.
14. Even though many people are aware of global warming and climate change fewer are aware of the term "carbon footprint."

15. James Earl Jones who is the voice of Darth Vader in *Star Wars* is a well-known actor.

16. *The Globe and Mail* is a popular paper across Canada whereas the *Toronto Star* was created for the Toronto and area market.

17. Trust is important in any relationship and it always takes time to develop.

18. The types of RNA required for protein synthesis are messenger RNA transfer RNA and ribosomal RNA.

19. People have immigrated to Canada from countries in Asia Europe the Middle East and Central and South America.

20. The committee studying the proposal is a mixture of health officials journalists and politicians.

21. Caffeine a stimulant is unregulated and completely legal.

22. Since climate change is a global problem it requires global solutions.

23. Diesel-powered cars have long been on the North American market yet they have never been widely accepted by the typical motorist.

24. The aggression effect of a video game depends on the type of game the way it is played and the person playing it.

25. Now a widely accepted theory evolution was discounted when Charles Darwin published *On the Origin of Species* in 1859.

Exercise 15.2

Add commas to the following sentences, if and where required. There is more than one comma rule to apply in most sentences.

1. I had planned to go to Calgary but my bus was delayed for more than four hours so I decided to go back home.

2. Juliet studied medicine at The University of Western Ontario in London Ontario before becoming a doctor near Prince Albert Saskatchewan.

3. Like Jane Austen's character Emma the heroine of *Clueless* Cher is less superficial than she first appears.

4. Nick and Nicole were married on April 20 1995 but they separated two years later.

5. Jessica Julep the mayor of Nowhere Nova Scotia provided inspirational leadership.

6. The simple sentence as we've seen is easily mastered by students but compound sentences necessitate an understanding of various forms of punctuation.

7. The waste of our resources including the most precious resource water is the major environmental problem that Canada is facing today.

8. British general Sir Frederick Morgan established an American-British headquarters which was known as COSSAC.

9. The book with the fine red binding on the highest shelf is the particular one I want.

10. Agnes Campbell Macphail the first woman elected to Canadian Parliament served for 19 years beginning her career in 1921.

11. The first steam-powered motorcycle known as the "bone-shaker" led to the bikes we use today.

12. Following successful completion of the English test another skills test is taken which is in a written format.

13. He combed through directories of professional associations business and trade associations and unions looking for possible contributors to his campaign.

14. Oliver Wendell Holmes an American was known as a master essayist but Canadian Barry Callaghan is also internationally respected as an essayist.

15. After visiting her ancestral homeland China and meeting her sisters from her mother's first marriage Amy Tan wrote the novel *The Joy Luck Club*.

16. The soldier with the red coat in the picture fought on the side of our enemies the Americans.

17. In 1885 the Canadian government introduced a racist bill the Chinese "head tax" which forced every Chinese person entering the country to pay a $50 fee.

18. Currently ranked fourth behind heart disease stroke and respiratory infections AIDS is set to become No. 3 say researchers in a new report.

19. Leslie Hornby known as "Twiggy" became a supermodel overnight and was identified by her skinny 90-pound body.

20. Jeff Deffenbacher PhD a specialist in anger management thinks that some people have a low tolerance for everyday annoyances.

Exercise 15.3

Add commas in the paragraphs below, following the rule categories as discussed above and avoiding comma splices. A few commas have been included to help with comprehension, but they may be incorrect.

1. If you asked people to name the most gruelling and challenging race in the world most of them would probably say that it was an auto race such as the Indianapolis 500, few people would name the Tour de France which is a bicycle race. Thousands of cyclists however vie for an elite position in this annual event. Even with the modern advances in bicycle technology cyclists still find the course very challenging, it offers a variety of climbs including slight inclines hills and steep grades. The Tour de France has a history that dates back about one hundred years, in the years to come the race will continue to challenge inspire and glorify new riders.

2. Autism is a much misunderstood problem, often children with autism are viewed as a "handful" and "hyperactive." Very little is known of its causes and characteristics can vary making a diagnosis difficult. In children it is even harder because normal children can exhibit some of the characteristics associated

with autism. Although autism can cause many behavioural difficulties autistic children can still live near-normal lives if they are surrounded by understanding caregivers. Working with autistic children can change a person and make one realize the need for better understanding and education. Treating autism can be difficult because often there is no feedback from the patient. Over the years there have been many ideas of how to treat autism but not all were correct and have at times made treatment problematic.

Other Forms of Punctuation

The careful use of semicolons, colons, dashes, and parentheses gives your writing polish and precision. The colon and semicolon are stronger, more emphatic marks of punctuation than the comparatively mild-mannered comma. For stronger breaks, longer pauses, and to show emphasis, learn where to use these marks in your writing.

Semicolons

As discussed, one of the major functions of commas is to separate independent clauses in a compound sentence. Two rules for semicolons also involve independent clauses; the third rule is to separate items in a series that contains commas.

> Use a semicolon to replace a comma + a coordinating conjunction in closely related independent clauses.

1. To join independent clauses. You may use a semicolon rather than a comma and a coordinating conjunction to join independent clauses if there *is a close relationship between the clauses*. Using a semicolon to join two independent clauses, rather than a comma + a coordinating conjunction, signals to the reader the close connection between the ideas in the two clauses. Consider the following examples:

1. Strong economies usually have strong school systems, and investment in education is inevitably an investment in a country's economic future.
2. Strong economies usually have strong school systems; weak economies generally have weak school systems.

In sentence 1, the second clause is logically related to the preceding one; however, they have different subjects and are not so closely related that a semicolon would be called for. In sentence 2, however, both clauses are concerned primarily with the relationship between economic strength and school systems. That focus in each clause justifies the use of a semicolon. A semicolon is often used if you want to stress a contrast between two independent clauses as in the examples below:

1. Scott was impatient to get married; Salome wanted to wait until they were financially secure.
2. Japanese food is generally good for you; fast food is not healthy.

Note that the semicolons in both sentences could be replaced by a comma and the coordinating conjunction *but*—they could *not* be replaced by a comma alone.

Here are other examples where a semicolon would be a good choice to stress the close relationship between independent clauses:

Gymnastics is not just any sport; it's one of the most challenging and physically taxing of all sports.

Some children may have lost a parent due to illness or divorce; others may have been cared for by grandparents or other relatives.

> Do *not* use a semicolon to separate an independent clause from a *dependent* clause. The rules for punctuating independent and dependent clauses are given on pp. 334–5.

2. To join independent clauses using a conjunctive adverb. To review, the rules for independent clauses we have looked at so far demonstrate many options for connecting important ideas.

1. You can begin a new sentence after you have expressed your first idea. This is particularly useful if you are conveying a lot of information that makes it hard for a reader to follow or if the sentence is just too long.
2. You can join the two clauses by using a comma + a coordinating conjunction.
3. You can use a semicolon in place of a period and a new sentence or in place of a comma + a coordinating conjunction if you want to stress the closeness of the ideas in the independent clauses.

> Use a semicolon before words like *however* and *therefore* if they are joining independent clauses. Follow the joining word/phrase by a comma.

A fourth option is **the use of a semicolon with a conjunctive adverb/ transitional phrase followed by an independent clause**. Conjunctive adverbs and transitional phrases are too numerous to list, but all can be used to connect two independent clauses.

1. My roommate lacks charm, friendliness, and humour; *still*, he is an excellent cook.
2. A recent study has found a surprising correlation between a rare form of sleeping disorder and those with telephone numbers that include the number six; *however*, the conclusion is being challenged by several researchers.

A common error is to miss the distinction between adverbs like *however* and *therefore* acting as ordinary adverbs (interrupters) and these same words acting as conjunctive adverbs (joiners), as described above. The following sentence pair illustrates this distinction. In sentence 1, commas are required because the adverb

> **Here are some of the most common conjunctive adverbs and transitional phrases:** accordingly, afterward, also, as a result, besides, certainly, consequently, finally, for example, if not, in addition, in fact, in the meantime, further(more), hence, however, indeed, instead, later, likewise, meanwhile, moreover, namely, nevertheless, next, nonetheless, otherwise, on the contrary, on the other hand, similarly, still, subsequently, that is, then, therefore, thus, undoubtedly

occurs in the midst of the clause as an interruption between the subject "he" and most of its predicate. In sentence 2, a semicolon is required before the conjunctive adverb because "however" is joining two independent clauses:

1. Dr. Suzuki will not be in his office this week; he will, *however*, be making his rounds at the hospital.
2. Dr. Suzuki will not be in his office this week; *however*, he will be making his rounds at the hospital.

In the following sentences, the word that changes its function from interrupter to joiner is "therefore":

1. The CEO has been called away for an emergency briefing; her secretary, *therefore*, will have to cancel her appointments.
2. The CEO has been called away for an emergency briefing; *therefore*, her secretary will have to cancel her appointments.

The only apparent difference between these sentences is word order: in sentence 1, "therefore" is the third word of the clause, whereas in sentence 2, it begins the second clause. If you look closely, though, you can see that changing where words like "however" and "therefore" occur can change their function. In sentence 2, an independent clause precedes and follows "therefore, " necessitating the semicolon before and the comma after. (The comma is required since "therefore" acts as an introduction preceding an independent clause.)

Be careful not to confuse the words and phrases discussed above with another large group of joiners, subordinating conjunctions, which join dependent to independent clauses (see page 323). *Although* and *whereas* are sometimes mistaken for conjunctive adverbs, but they are subordinating conjunctions and cannot be used to join two independent clauses.

3. To separate items in a series: the serial semicolon. A semicolon can be used *between items in a series if one or more of the elements contain commas*. Without semicolons, these sentences would be confusing:

> Her company included Alex Duffy, president; Marie Tremble, vice-president; John van der Wart, secretary; and Chris Denfield, treasurer.
>
> Bus number 1614 makes scheduled stops in Kamloops, BC; Valemont, BC; Jasper, Alta.; and Drayton Valley, Alta., before arriving in Edmonton.

You may also use semicolons to separate *items in a list* where each item is a long phrase or clause, especially if there is internal punctuation. Using semicolons to separate the items makes this sentence easier to read:

> The role of the vice-president will be to enhance the school's external relations; strengthen its relationship with alumni, donors, and business and community leaders; implement a fundraising program; and increase the school's involvement in the community.

Don't put a semicolon before words like although *or* whereas*; don't put a comma after these words. They do not join independent clauses but introduce* dependent *clauses.*

A semicolon can be used between items in a series if one or more of the elements contain commas, or if one of the elements is much longer than the others.

Exercise 15.4

The following sentences are punctuated correctly. The italicized word or phrase is either an ordinary adverb acting as an interrupter or a conjunctive adverb (joiner). Rewrite the sentence by moving this word/phrase to another place in the second clause in which its function will be different. Punctuate accordingly.

Example: The weather this summer was very wet; *however*, it did not make up for the drought we have experienced.

The weather this summer was very wet. It did not, *however*, make up for the drought we have experienced. *OR*

The weather this summer was very wet; it did not, *however*, make up for the drought we have experienced.

1. One of my roommates rode her bicycle to school most of the time; she was more physically fit, *as a result*, than my other roommate, who didn't even own a bicycle.

2. SPCA officers work for but are not paid by the government. It is donations, *in fact*, that provide their salary.

3. If homelessness continues to increase, it will be costly for taxpayers; *moreover*, homelessness affects downtown businesses.

4. Many professional golfers have used the same caddy for years; *for example*, Steve Williams has caddied for Tiger Woods since 1999.

5. Scientists tend to strongly support stem-cell research. Most evangelical Christians, *however*, just as strongly oppose it.

Note that this is the only rule for using semicolons that does not involve independent clauses. You can use semicolons to join independent clauses in one of the two ways discussed above or to separate items in a series where, otherwise, confusion might result.

Colons

It is often said that while a semicolon brings the reader to a brief stop, the colon leads the reader on. The colon has three main uses: (1) to introduce quoted material, (2) to set up or introduce a list or series, and (3) to answer, complete, or expand on what is asked or implied in the preceding independent clause.

1. To set up a quotation. When you use direct quotations in your essays, you can set them up formally with a colon:

The *Oxford English Dictionary* defines the word "rhetoric" this way: "The art of using language so as to persuade or influence others."

You may use a colon to set up a direct quotation if the thought is complete and fully expressed before the colon.

Health Canada has made the following recommendation for dentists: "Non-mercury filling materials should be considered for restoring the primary teeth of children where the mechanical properties of the material are safe."

Direct quotations can also be set up less formally. In such cases, a comma may be required or no punctuation at all. To determine which, treat the complete sentence as if it contained no quotation and see if one of the rules for using commas applies:

According to the American Academy of Dermatology, "a tan is the skin's response to an injury, and every time you tan, you accumulate damage to the skin. "

The most general definition of evolution is "any non-miraculous process by which new forms of life are produced" (Bowler 2).

In the first sentence, a comma rule dictates the use of a comma before the quotation; in the second sentence, there is no rule that would necessitate a comma before the quotation. A comma after "is" would be incorrect.

2. To set up or introduce a list or series. The most formal way to set up a list or series is to make a complete statement and follow with a colon and the list of items:

In 1998, the CBC outlined three challenges for the future: to attract more viewers to Canadian programming, to increase the availability of "under-represented" categories, and to direct its resources towards this kind of programming.

Avoid the temptation to insert a colon just before you start the list unless what precedes it is completely expressed. Normally, you would *not* use a colon after *including* or *such as*, or right after a linking verb like *is* or *are*, though these words are often used to set up a list or series.

Incorrect uses of the colon:
Caffeine withdrawal can have many negative effects, such as: severe headaches, drowsiness, irritability, and poor concentration.
One of the questions the committee will attempt to answer is: Does our current public health system work?

A comma is also incorrect after *such as* or *including*.

3. To separate an independent clause from a word, phrase, or clause that answers or completes what precedes it. What follows a colon may answer, complete, or expand on what is asked or implied in the preceding independent clause. This could be as little as a word or as much as an independent clause. Like the comma and semicolon, then, the colon can be used to separate independent clauses; however, what follows the colon must answer a question asked in the previous clause:

> There is only one quality you omitted from the list of my most endearing characteristics: my modesty. (answers WHAT quality)

> David's driving test was a memorable experience: he backed over a curb, sailed through two stop signs, and forgot to signal a left turn. (answers WHY the test was memorable)

> The New Testament of the Holy Bible gives the ultimate rule for Christians: to treat others the way you want them to treat you. (answers WHAT rule)

If what follows the colon is at least the equivalent of an independent clause, you may begin with a capital letter. It is perfectly acceptable to begin with a small letter, however, as in the examples above.

Dashes and Parentheses

Although some people use dashes and parentheses interchangeably, their functions are different. Imagining this scenario might help: you are in a crowded room where everyone is talking. Somebody takes you aside and begins speaking in an unnaturally loud voice about the latest rumour. You look around. People are listening, which is the design of the person talking. A couple of minutes later, somebody else approaches and very discreetly begins whispering the same information in your ear.

Using dashes is like giving information that is meant to be overheard, to be stressed. But parentheses are more like asides. They convey additional information which is not important enough to be included in the main part of the sentence.

Dashes, then, set something off and can convey a break in thought. You can use dashes sparingly to emphasize a word or phrase; two dashes (one dash if the material comes at the end of a sentence) will draw the reader's attention to what is between the dashes.

You can type two hyphens to indicate a dash—if you don't leave a space after the second hyphen, your computer may automatically convert the hyphens to an *em*-dash like this: —.

> Don't use one hyphen if you want to set off a word or phrase. Hyphens are a mark of spelling—not punctuation.

Use parentheses sparingly to include a word or phrase, even occasionally a sentence, that isn't important enough to be included as part of the main text; where dashes emphasize, parentheses de-emphasize.

> "Crayolas plus imagination (the ability to create images) make for happiness if you are a child" (Robert Fulghum).

You may use a colon to separate an independent clause from a word, phrase, or clause that answers or completes what precedes it.

Remember that unless you are using semicolons to separate items in a series, what *precedes and follows a semicolon* should be an independent clause.

What *precedes a colon* should be an independent clause that makes a complete statement.

You may also use parentheses to refer to a source in a research essay. This parenthetical use is illustrated in the example above to refer to the source of the quotation about Crayolas. For information about parenthetical documentation methods, see Chapter 12.

Punctuating parenthetical insertions depends on whether the statement in parentheses is 1) complete in itself or 2) part of the larger sentence. If the parentheses enclose *a complete sentence*, the period should be placed *inside* the second parenthesis, as the information pertains only to what is between parentheses. The following sentence illustrates this rule. (The period in this sentence goes inside the second parenthesis.)

In the second case, punctuate the sentence just as you would if there were no parentheses there. The sentence below illustrates punctuation that has nothing to do with the parenthetical insertion but is required to separate independent clauses. Notice the absence of the capital letter beginning "both":

> Cassandra wanted to be an actor (both her parents were actors), but she always trembled violently as soon as she stepped on a stage.

Use dashes and parentheses sparingly in your writing.

Exercise 15.5

Using the rule categories discussed above, replace commas in the sentences below with the most appropriate form of punctuation (semicolon, colon, dash, parentheses). In some cases, the commas are correct and should not be replaced.

1. April showers bring May flowers, May flowers bring on my asthma.

2. A developing salmon goes through four stages, the alevin, the fry, the smolt, and the adult.

3. Every essay needs three parts, an introduction, a body, and a conclusion.

4. He paused to admire the splendid sight before his eyes, the ruins of Montgomery Castle.

5. Mayumi tended to look on the good side of things, Glenn usually saw the bad side.

6. The following is not a rule for comma use, put a comma wherever you pause.

7. It is probable, though not certain, that she will be promoted to the rank of corporal next year.

8. It was the best of times, it was the worst of times.

9. Marselina has a fine ear for music, unfortunately she can't sing a note.

10. In my health sciences class, we studied the four main food groups, dairy products, meats, carbohydrates, and fruits and vegetables.

11. Whenever I order designer clothing for my boutique, I shop in Toronto, Canada, Buffalo, New York, and London, England.

12. The Online Dictionary defines animal cruelty this way, "treatment or standards of care that cause unwarranted or unnecessary suffering or harm to animals. "

13. The tuition increase has affected many lower income families, therefore, there is an even greater demand for student loans.

14. Brian never tired of misquoting Shakespeare, "the quality of mercy is not stained."

15. Virginia Woolf had this to say about the essay, "Of all forms of literature it is the one which least calls for the use of long words."

After you've checked your answers, complete the exercise by doing questions 16–30.

16. First advice to those about to write a novel is the same as Punch's to those about to wed, don't (Victor Jones).

17. The Romans were willing to change their religious beliefs quite easily, however, the Greeks were less willing to do this.

18. In compound sentences, use a comma to join independent clauses where there is a coordinating conjunction, use a semi-colon where two such clauses are not joined by a coordinating conjunction.

19. His plans for the new development included the following, an apartment complex, single-family residences, a 60-store mall, and a multi-use recreation centre.

20. Oil, electricity, and solar power are popular sources for heating homes in Ontario, however, the most popular is natural gas.

21. The tour includes visits to the following museums, the Prado in Madrid, Spain, the Louvre in Paris, France, and the Rijksmuseum in Amsterdam, the Netherlands.

22. It was the ideal summer job, you were outdoors in lovely weather, you were active, and the pay was more than reasonable.

23. School cafeterias often offer unhealthy options, such as hot dogs, which have virtually no nutritional value, hamburgers, which have a high fat content, and poutine, known as "heart attack in a bowl. "

24. The zero emissions of a battery-electric vehicle come with a drawback, the emissions are only as clean as the means used to generate the power.

25. This year's conference on the environment is intended to focus concern on three main areas, global warming, pollution, and the destruction of natural habitat.

26. The art of writing the news lead is to answer as many of the following five questions as possible, Who?, What?, Where?, When?, and How?

27. The current figures of mercury absorption have been announced by the ADA, however, the group's review has been criticized as misleading.

28. A lack of essential nutrients can result in deficiencies, for example, a vegetarian may have iron deficiency.

29. As rainwater travels downwards through the soil, it may collect a number of pollutants, furthermore, an extended period of time may elapse before this pollution is discovered.

30. Freewriting can be a useful means of overcoming blocks, it can help you write when you're not in the mood, it can generate ideas, even if you are the kind of writer who has a hard time coming up with main points, and it can energize your writing.

Exercise 15.6

The poem that follows is Edward Lear's nonsense poem "The New Vestments." Write it in paragraph form, making sense out of nonsense by punctuating it for correctness and effectiveness. Most of the original end-of-line punctuation has been taken out, and some internal punctuation also has been omitted; some of the nineteenth-century spellings have been changed.

There lived an old man in the kingdom of Tess

Who invented a purely original dress

And when it was perfectly made and complete

He opened the door and walked into the street

By way of a hat he'd a loaf of Brown Bread

In the middle of which he inserted his head

His Shirt was made up of no end of dead Mice

The warmth of whose skins was quite fluffy and nice

His Drawers were of Rabbit-skins but it is not known whose

His Waistcoat and Trousers were made of Pork Chops

His Buttons were Jujubes and Chocolate Drops

His Coat was all Pancakes with Jam for a border

And a girdle of Biscuits to keep it in order

And he wore over all as a screen from bad weather

A Cloak of green Cabbage leaves stitched all together.

He had walked a short way when he heard a great noise

Of all sorts of Beasticles Birdlings and Boys

And from every long street and dark lane in the town

Beasts Birdles and Boys in a tumult rushed down

Two Cows and a half ate his Cabbage-leaf Cloak

Four Apes seized his Girdle which vanished like smoke

Three Kids ate up half of his Pancaky Coat

And the tails were devoured by an ancient He Goat

An army of Dogs in a twinkling tore up his

Pork Waistcoat and Trousers to give to their Puppies

And while they were growling and mumbling the Chops

Ten boys prigged the Jujubes and Chocolate Drops

He tried to run back to his house but in vain

Four Scores of fat Pigs came again and again

They rushed out of stables and hovels and doors

They tore off his stockings his shoes and his drawers

And now from the housetops with screechings descend

Striped spotted white black and gray Cats without end

They jumped on his shoulders and knocked off his hat

When Crows Ducks and Hens made a mincemeat of that

They speedily flew at his sleeves in a trice

And utterly tore up his Shirt of dead Mice

They swallowed the last of his Shirt with a squall

Whereon he ran home with no clothes on at all

And he said to himself as he bolted the door

"I will not wear a similar dress any more"

"Any more any more any more never more!"

Exercise 15.7

Correct or add commas in the following passages. Among your changes and additions, include *at least* one semicolon and one colon in each passage. Some commas have been included to help with reading; however, they may not be correct.

1. Cocaine an alkaloid obtained from coco leaves is a stimulant to the nervous system, unfortunately it is one of the most addictive drugs and it is possible to overdose and die on first use. Among the 3 million users today 500,000 are highly addicted. Cocaine users describe the high as a euphoric feeling, they feel energetic and mentally alert, however this feeling wears off in as little as 20 minutes. User responses to the drug vary but may include the following, hyperactivity elevated blood pressure and heart rate and increased sexual interest. Large amounts of cocaine such as more than 100 milligrams can cause bizarre erratic and violent behaviours.

2. Labour shortages during the late nineteenth century in Canada became an impediment to progress and something had to be done to fix this problem. For white politicians and business owners the solution seemed obvious, exploit cheap labour. Chinese immigrants provided exactly what was needed to boost the labour scene, they were male unskilled and cheap. Between 1881 and 1885 approximately 17,000 Chinese immigrants arrived in Canada, Chinese men were employed in masses, their jobs included those in mining forestry canning and above all railroad construction. Sir Matthew Begbie the Chief Justice of BC said "Chinese labourers do well what white women cannot do and what white men will not do."

◎ Punctuation Prohibitions

Several common errors in punctuation are summarized below. Learning the rules for punctuation and being aware of these common errors will greatly enhance your writing skills.

No-Comma Rules

Do *not* use a comma to separate simple compounds (two of something with a word like *and* between). Writers sometimes generalize this non-rule from the items in a series rule: recall that a series consists of *three or more* items. A separate rule applies to compound sentences where a comma is required before the coordinating conjunction.

> *Incorrect*:
> Some of the heaviest damage from steroid use occurs to the heart, and the liver. (two nouns)
> Logging reduces the number of old-growth forests, and destroys these habitats. (two predicates: "reduces. . . destroys")

Do *not* use a comma to separate the subject and the predicate. This non-rule is probably the result of writers mistakenly applying the "pause" non-rule.

> *Incorrect*:
> The only way our society is going to be fixed, is if we change our laws.
> One advantage in using helicopters to fight fires, is the accuracy of their drops over the scene of the fire.

It is easy to be distracted by parentheses and mistakenly insert a comma between a subject and a predicate. In the example below, another option would be to add a comma after "Medicine" and remove the parentheses:

Incorrect:

The American College of Sports Medicine (a body that advances research into exercise and sports), considers all physically active females at risk for developing eating disorders.

Do *not* use a comma alone to join independent clauses or with a word other than a coordinating conjunction. This produces a comma splice, a serious grammatical error.

Incorrect:

Football is one of the most popular sports in North America, it is also one of the most brutal of all sports.

You must use the buttons provided at the bottom of the pages to navigate through the application, otherwise, you could lose your connection. (*from an online application form*)

No-Semicolon Rules

Do *not* use a semicolon if what follows the semicolon is a fragment. In the first two examples, below, what follows the semicolon is an incomplete verb form (an "–ing"). In the third sentence, what follows is a prepositional phrase: "such as" and two nouns. An independent clause should follow a semicolon unless semicolons are being used to separate items in a series. In all the sentences, a comma should replace the incorrect semicolon to separate the independent clause from the concluding phrase.

> An independent clause should precede and follow a semicolon unless semicolons are being used to separate items in a series.

Incorrect:

When the media portrays minorities, it often stereotypes them; leading audiences to reinforce the stereotype through their behaviour.

Valuable land is destroyed when it is cleared for grazing; reducing habitats for other animals.

For many years, Canada has been a leader in multiculturalism, along with a few other countries; such as the United States and England.

Do *not* use a semicolon to introduce a list or series; a *colon* is correct.

Incorrect:

Shakespeare's last plays are sometimes called romances and include the following; *Cymbeline*, *A Winter's Tale*, and *The Tempest*.

Apostrophes

Technically, the apostrophe isn't a mark of punctuation; it is an internal change that indicates the possessive case of nouns and some indefinite pronouns. It is also used to show the omission of one or more letters. The apostrophe, then, has two main uses: (1) to indicate the possessive and (2) to show where letters have been omitted, as in contractions.

1. Apostrophes for possession in nouns. The possessive case in nouns and pronouns indicates ownership and similar relationships, such as association, authorship, duration, description, and source of origin, between two nouns. The possessive is a short form indicating that the second noun belongs to or is associated with the first noun. When a noun adds an apostrophe to show the possessive, it is functioning adjectivally and can be replaced by the corresponding possessive adjective. Most pronouns, however, do not show the possessive through an apostrophe.

> the hard drive of the computer = the computer's hard drive (*its* hard drive)
> the landlady's apartment (ownership) (*her* apartment)
> the tenants' rights (association) (*their* rights)
> Dvorak's *New World Symphony* (authorship) (*his* symphony)

Singular nouns. The usual rule with *singular* nouns, including proper nouns (nouns that begin with a capital letter) ending in *s*, *ss,* or the *s* sound, is to add *'s* to make them possessive.

> the attorney's portfolio, Mr. Price's car, the week's lesson

A few plural nouns do not end in *s*. They are treated as singular nouns because of their ending: *children, women, men, people*:

> the popular children's book, the women's group

Plural nouns. With plural nouns, an apostrophe after the *s* is added to make them possessive.

> the islands' inhabitants, the Hansons' children, the Gibbses' marriage certificate, two weeks' lessons, the readers' perceptions

Make sure you carefully distinguish between singular and plural nouns when applying the rules for possessives:

> "company" is singular + *'s* ⟶ the company's profits (one company)
> "companies" is plural + *'* ⟶ the companies' profits (more than one company)
>
> "society" is singular + *'s* ⟶ our society's attitude toward war (one society)
> "societies" is plural + *'* ⟶ past societies' attitudes toward war (many societies)

Proper nouns ending in *s*. Because it may look and sound awkward to add an apostrophe + *s* to a proper noun ending in *s*, some authorities would write "Tracy Jarvis' book," meaning "the book of Tracy Jarvis." Others would follow the rule for singular nouns by adding an apostrophe + *s*: Tracy Jarvis's book. Whichever rule you follow, it's important to be consistent in applying it.

> Singular nouns add an apostrophe + *s* to indicate the possessive; plural nouns that end in *s* add an apostrophe.

Joint ownership. In the case of *joint ownership*, where both nouns share or are equal parties in something, only the last noun should show the possessive. Ensure from the context that both nouns reflect a truly equal, shared relationship. In the following sentences, the assumption is that Salem and Sheena shared duties as hosts at one party but that the general manager and the district manager were paid separate wages.

> I attended Salem and Sheena's party.
> Morana raised the general manager's and the district manager's wages.

The following would be *incorrect* as these educators do *not* share the same belief or theory:

> Piaget and Montessori's beliefs about how children learn were similar in many ways.
> *Correct*:
> Piaget's and Montessori's beliefs . . . .

Apostrophes are sometimes misused with plural nouns. Avoid the following incorrect uses:

> *Incorrect*:
> • I have 6 CD's.
> • The 1990's were a decade of extravagant spending.
> • The lemon's are on sale this week.

Exception: Apostrophes can be used for clarity with numbers, letters, or symbols to indicate the plural:

> Adrian got two A's and three B's on his transcript.

Apostrophes with indefinite pronouns. Like nouns, but unlike other kinds of pronouns, many indefinite pronouns add an apostrophe + *s* to show the possessive:

> In times of stress, it is not in *one's* best interest to act quickly or reflexively (i.e., the best interest of one).

Indefinite pronouns, unlike personal pronouns, add an apostrophe + *s* to indicate the possessive: e.g., "one's beliefs."

2. Contractions. The second main use of the apostrophe is to show missing letters. People often confuse the contraction *it's (it is)* with the possessive form of the pronoun *its* (as in *I gave the dog its bone*). The contraction *who's (who is)* is sometimes confused with the possessive form of *who (the man whose house I'm renting)*. Contractions are not generally used in formal writing. You should check with your instructor to see if they are acceptable in your assignment.

The apostrophe is *not* used to indicate the possessive of *pronouns* (except for indefinite pronouns, as discussed above).

Don't confuse *its*, the possessive pronoun, with *it's*, the contraction for *it is*.

Exercise 15.8

Decide which nouns in the following sentences require the possessive; then add apostrophes and make any other necessary changes.

1. In South Africa, the current crime rate is using up much of the countrys GDP.

2. Parents and teachers often complain about televisions influence in todays society.

3. The Crosses house is up for sale, and its list price is $179,000. (The last name is Cross.)

4. Ones education should not depend on the financial resources of ones parents.

5. The schools biggest draw for new students was the brand new recreation complex.

6. The course I took required two hours homework a day.

7. The mayors biggest asset is her commitment to the citys future growth.

8. In anorexia nervosa, a patients fingernails and teeth may be damaged due to a lack of calcium.

9. Ryans and Jessicas birthday is on the same day.

10. Apples, oranges, mangoes, and tomatoes are the stores specials today.

After you've checked your answers, complete the exercise by doing questions 11–25.

11. Its a shame that Lennys parents werent able to attend their sons graduation ceremonies. (Lenny is an only child.)

12. I dont know whether this etching is his or hers, but theres no doubt its worth a lot in todays market.

13. Its true there are four *ss* and four *is* in the word "Mississippi," but there are only two *ps*.

14. This weeks classifieds had several jobs for legal secretaries, all requiring three years experience in solicitors work.

15. Zebra stripes always make me homesick for my Uncle Filbert, whos in jail for stealing his brothers life savings. (one brother)

16. The instructor found Bens copy of Shakespeares play *The Winters Tale* in the recycle bin after the last class.

17. As a child whose parents were relatively well off, I thought all my relatives lives were as easy as mine.

18. Our societys fascination with celebrities lives is a product of the medias daily obsession.

19. Books, music, and DVDs can be found on Amazon.com, one of the Internets most popular sites.

20. The young man stated his churchs mission is to spread Jesus message to people throughout the world.

21. Drugs called immunosuppressants can interfere with the bodys ability to fight infection.

22. Nowadays, rap is used to express a persons experiences, feelings, and opinions.

23. Climate change is caused by harmful chemicals that trap the suns energy in the earths atmosphere.

24. The Smiths and the O'Neils won the trip to see the Seattle Mariners play the Blue Jays in the Mariners home town.

25. The introductory paragraph should capture the readers interest while developing the writers credibility.

Exercise 15.9

Punctuate for correctness and effectiveness, using commas and other forms of punctuation as appropriate. Minimal punctuation has been provided in places to aid in understanding; however, some punctuation may be incorrect. Correct all errors in apostrophe use. The passage concerns the response to an investigative article entitled "Spin Doctors," posted on the Canadian news and information website *Canoe*.

Reader reaction was swift and impassioned. The sites traffic which averages 65 to 70 million views each month experienced an additional 50,000 page views within the first 10 days of the posting. The investigation drew more than 400 letters to the editor hundred's of emails to the message boards and more than 16,000 responses to an online poll.

The intensity of the response surprised veteran investigative journalist Wayne MacPhail the articles author. Although the sheer volume of letters was unexpected it proved to him that there was an audience for online journalism in Canada. MacPhail has experimented with hypertext reporting since the late 1980s but outside of "Spin Doctors" he believes that by and large newspapers have done a "woeful job" of building an audience for Web-based investigative reporting . . . .

Unlike it's media rivals Canoe has never made journalism it's only or even its most important focus. A headline announcing the top story of the day appears underneath the Canoe banner but there are so many other things to do, shopping email contests Web utilities and lifestyle tips all compete with the news.

The CNEWS section isnt necessarily the first place people are expected to go on the network though it is usually at the top of the highlighted sections. It is also part of the site that changes the most during daylight hours. In other words when CNEWS changes the entire home page changes. A "This Just In" feature was recently added but theres no set schedule for posting stories. Despite this expansion of the news section Canoes promotional material drives home the message that the site is about much more than current events. One recent ad reads, "shop chat email read, in that order."

Chapter Review Questions

1. What are the comma rules?
2. When should you not use a comma?
3. Identify at least one comma use that you did not know or that you learned incorrectly.
4. When do you use semicolons?
5. When should you not use a semicolon?
6. When do you use colons?
7. When should you not use a colon?
8. Why do you use dashes or parentheses?
9. What are the rules for apostrophe use?
10. Provide examples of incorrect apostrophe use that you have seen outside the classroom.

16

Agreement, Pronoun, and Sentence Structure Errors

In this chapter, you will

- learn about subject–verb agreement

- learn how to fix different kinds of pronoun errors

- understand how the incorrect use of pronouns can show gender bias

- understand how modifiers can affect clarity

- learn how to use parallelism to create clear sentences

The grammar rules discussed in this chapter are ones that are easily missed when you write your rough draft. Mastering these rules will increase your credibility as a writer and help you create documents that are easy to understand.

◎ Agreement

A verb must agree in number with its subject; similarly, *a pronoun must agree in number, person, and gender with its antecedent.* These forms of agreement reinforce the close connection between a subject and the verb it governs, along with the close connection between a noun and the pronoun that replaces it.

Subject–Verb Agreement

A verb must agree with (i.e., match) its subject in number—that is, a singular subject requires a singular verb, and a plural subject requires a plural verb.

You will not usually have to stop and think about whether a verb agrees in number with its subject, especially if English is your first language. However, determining whether a subject is singular or plural is not always straightforward. In the specific instances explained below, the rules help the writer apply the important principle of subject–verb agreement.

Finding the Subject

Usually, the subject of a sentence or clause is the noun or pronoun that performs the action of the verb (or that exists in the state or condition expressed by the subject complement). In most cases, the subject precedes the verb and is easy to find.

> *Kevin and Nigel* are happy that they passed the exam.

Sometimes the subject is harder to spot for one of the following reasons:

a) The sentence begins with *Here is/are, There is/are, There has/have been*, etc. The subject follows the verb, not precedes it, and you will have to look ahead in the sentence to the first noun/pronoun to determine whether the subject is singular or plural.

> There *are* many *reasons* for supporting the legalizing of marijuana.
> Here *is* one *person* who supports raising the drinking age.

b) The sentence is phrased as a question. You may need to look ahead to determine the number of the subject.

> What *is* the main *reason* for legalizing marijuana?
> Where *are* all of the *people* who are in favour of raising the drinking age?

Look ahead in the sentence to find the subject if the sentence begins with *Here/There is...,* is set up as a question, or uses a delayed subject construction.

c) The subject is delayed. Because the sentence begins with a prepositional phrase, the noun(s) in the phrase may *seem* to form the subject, but the subject will be found later in the sentence. You can always rearrange these kinds of sentences to confirm that you have, in fact, used a delayed subject construction.

With the dependence on caffeine *come withdrawal symptoms.*

Sentence rearranged with subject first:
Withdrawal symptoms come with the dependence on caffeine.

Among Graham's favourites *was the recent album* by Green Day.
Sentence rearranged: The recent album by Green Day *was* among Graham's favourites.

d) The subject is governed by a linking verb that has a plural complement. Don't be distracted by what follows the verb; the subject alone determines whether the verb is singular or plural.

Tanning *salons are* not the safest way to get a tan these days.
The *topic* for discussion tomorrow *is* the pros and cons of indoor tanning.

e) The subject is followed by one or more prepositional phrases that contain nouns and/or pronouns that are *not* the subject. People sometimes forget that the common word *of* is a preposition and that the following noun or pronoun will be the object of the preposition, not the subject. If there are several nouns before the verb, backtrack carefully to find the noun or pronoun that can be connected to the verb. You can put parentheses around the distracting words.

A long *list* (of items, including vegetables, fruits, meats, and several kinds of bread,) *was* handed to Tao.
The *roots* (of his dissatisfaction with the course) *go* very deep.

> If several nouns precede the verb, make sure you identify the true noun/pronoun subject before deciding whether the verb should be singular or plural.

Mistaking the Subject

In the (c) examples, above, the nouns *dependence* or *caffeine* in the first sentence and *favourites* in the second sentence could be mistaken for the subjects of *come* and *was,* respectively; however, they are preceded by prepositions. A noun or pronoun that directly follows a preposition cannot act as a subject; it will be the object of the preposition.

A related problem occurs when a writer mistakes a prepositional phrase or even a dependent clause for a subject. The sentences below can be fixed by omitting the preposition and beginning the sentence with the noun subject:

Incorrect:
By choosing to take a few correspondence courses may afford a student athlete greater flexibility in meeting academic requirements.
"By choosing" has been mistaken for the subject.
Correct:
Choosing to take a few correspondence courses may afford a student athlete greater flexibility.

Incorrect:
With the development of the computer led to automated robots on the production line.
"With the development of the computer" has been mistaken for the subject.

Correct:

The development of the computer led to automated robots on the production line.

Incorrect:

Although Edna thinks of her children at the last moment before her death does not change the fact she is still willing to leave them.

"Although Edna thinks of her children at the last moment before her death," a dependent clause, has been mistaken for the subject. Dependent clauses contain their own subjects.

Correct:

Although Edna thinks of her children at the last moment before her death, she is still willing to leave them.

Edna thinks of her children at the last moment before her death, though this does not change the fact she is willing to leave them.

See also *false predication* (page 421).

Rules for Subject–Verb Agreement

1. Compound subjects joined by the conjunction *and* usually require a plural verb form.

> Thanh *and* his friend *are* visiting Ottawa.

Occasionally, a compound subject expresses a single idea.

> *Rhythm and blues was* always popular with younger audiences.
> *To compare and contrast* the roles of setting in the novels *is* sure to be a question on the exam.

In both examples, the compound subject can be treated as a singular subject since both elements are so closely connected that they can't be separated or their meaning would change.

> A compound subject consists of two nouns, two pronouns, or a noun and a pronoun acting as the subject.

2. When the compound subjects are linked by the conjunctions *or* or *nor,* along with the correlative (or paired) conjunctions *either . . . or* or *neither . . . nor,* the verb form is determined by the noun or pronoun nearest the verb. These conjunctions suggest a choice between one thing or the other much more than *and,* which clearly suggests two or more of something, requiring the plural verb.

> The chairs *or the table is* going to auction.
> Neither famine nor *floods are* going to force the people to leave their homes.

If you changed the order of the nouns making up the compound subject in the above sentences, you would need also to change the number of the verb.

3. Prepositional phrases can also be used to join two nouns in a compound subject. *As well as, along with, in addition to, together with,* and *combined with* are examples of such phrases. These phrases do not have the strength of the conjunction *and.*

When you use these joiners, you stress the first element more than the second one. Logically, then, the verb is *singular* if the first element of the compound is *singular*. If the writer of the following sentence wanted to stress equality, the sentence should read "The instructor *and* her students *are* . . . ."

> The *instructor, as well as* her students, *is* going to be attending the symposium on the environment.
>
> The Australian *prime minister, along with* his ministers for education and foreign affairs, *is* set to arrive tomorrow.

4. Collective nouns refer to groups. They are singular in form but may be either singular or plural in meaning, depending on context. If the context suggests singular, then the verb form is singular; the same applies, of course, for plural. Examples of collective nouns include *band, class, family, audience, committee, jury, team, gang, group, congregation, staff,* and similar nouns.

Whenever the context suggests the members of the group are to be thought of as *one unit*, all doing the same thing or acting together, the verb form is *singular;* when the members are considered as *individuals,* the corresponding verb form is *plural.*

> The jury *is* out to consider the evidence before it.
> After the lecture, the class *are* going to be able to ask questions of the guest speaker.

Most often, collective nouns are considered singular, so, if in doubt, choose the singular form. If a plural verb with a collective noun sounds odd, you can rephrase the subject so that the collective noun functions adjectivally before an appropriate plural noun.

> After the lecture, *class members are* going to be able to ask questions of the guest speaker.

5. In the following phrases, the verb form will be singular, even though the noun or pronoun that follows will be plural: *one of, each of, either/neither of, every one of,* and *which one of.* The verb form following *the only one who* also will be singular.

> *One of* our 115 students *has* written an A+ essay.
> Alec is *the only one of* those attending who *has* difficulty speaking before a large group.

6. Indefinite pronouns refer to nonspecific individuals or objects. Most indefinite pronouns are considered singular and take a singular form in agreement. *Each, either, neither, one, no one, everyone, someone, anyone, nobody, everybody, somebody, anybody, anything, everything,* and *nothing* are singular indefinite pronouns. Unlike other pronouns, many indefinite pronouns use the apostrophe to express the possessive: *Everybody's* opinion is welcome. Compare with: *His or her* opinion is welcome; *their* opinions are welcome.

When using a compound subject, look at the word(s) doing the joining to determine whether the subject is singular or plural.

Collective nouns may be singular or plural depending on context. If in doubt, consider them singular.

Most indefinite pronouns are considered singular even though they may refer broadly to many people, objects, etc.

Some authorities believe that when context clearly warrants the use of plural agreement with the antecedents *everyone* and *everybody*, as in the second sentence below, you may use the plural pronoun.

> *Everyone is* going to stand when the opening ceremonies begin.
> When the pepper was spilled, *everyone* rubbed *their* noses.

7. There is a separate rule for phrases involving portions and fractions + *of*, such as *any, none, some, part, much, all, more, most, plenty, the majority/minority, a lot, a variety, a number*, and *(one-) half*. The form of the verb depends on whether the noun or pronoun following *of* is singular or plural.

> *None of the missing* **pieces** *have* been found yet.
> *Some of the* **losses** incurred with the companies' merger *are* being absorbed by the shareholders.
> *Half of the* **pie** *is* gone.
> *One-third of the* **employees** *are* out on strike.

When the subject is *a number of*, the verb will be singular or plural depending on whether the noun/pronoun following *of* is singular or plural; when the subject is *the number of*, the verb will be singular.

8. Subjects referring to distance, time, money, weight, or mass will usually be *singular*; also, when the subject is **the** *number of*, the verb is *singular* (in contrast with rule 7).

> *Twelve miles is* not a great distance to an experienced hiker.
> *The number of* people attending the courses *has dropped* in the last two years.

9. Some nouns end in *s*, but because they usually refer to a singular concept or subject, they require the singular form of the verb. Examples include *politics, economics, mathematics, statistics, physics, billiards, darts, athletics, gymnastics, measles, mumps*, and *news*.

> *Statistics is* an inexact science; no *news is* good news

Depending on their context, many of these nouns can be considered plural and should then take a plural verb form. For example, *statistics* could refer to a set of facts, rather than to one subject:

> The *statistics* on global warming *are* alerting politicians to the need for worldwide action.

Whether the titles of artistic works or the names of companies are singular or plural in form will not affect the verb. A singular verb will be needed to agree with the subject.

> *Montreal Stories is* a collection of Mavis Gallant's fiction; McClelland & Stewart *is* the publisher.

10. The following will be plural and will require the plural form of the verb: *both, few, many, several, parts of.*

> A well-educated *few seem* to care about correct grammar and punctuation these days, but *both are* essential parts of the writing process.

Most errors in subject–verb agreement are due to one of these three situations:

- use of a compound subject
- use of an indefinite pronoun as the subject
- intervening words between the subject and the verb

> *Most errors in subject–verb agreement are due to one of these three situations:*
> - *use of a compound subject*
> - *use of an indefinite pronoun as the subject*
> - *intervening words between the subject and the verb*

Pronouns at Work

Pronoun–Antecedent Agreement

Most problems in pronoun–antecedent agreement apply to **personal pronouns**, such as *she, he, they,* and *them,* as well as the possessive form of pronouns, *its* and *their.* The **antecedent** of a pronoun is the noun it replaces, and a pronoun must agree with its antecedent noun in number. If you have difficulty finding the antecedent, see if it, or an equivalent form, can be substituted for the pronoun in the sentence:

Testing for the antecedent:

> The first thing that usually strikes us about *a person* is his or her (*a person's*) physical appearance.
> *The dieter* should realize that diets will only work when he or she (*the dieter*) restricts his or her (*the dieter's*) caloric intake.

> *Personal pronouns refer to persons. The first person refers to the one doing the speaking or writing; second person refers to the one spoken to; third person refers to the one spoken about.*

Most of the rules for subject–verb agreement also apply to pronoun–antecedent agreement. For example, compound antecedents require the plural form of the pronoun and adjectives formed from pronouns (possessive pronouns).

> *The antecedent of a pronoun is the noun it replaces, and a pronoun must agree with its antecedent noun in number.*

> Connie *and* Steve *have* invited me to *their* cottage.

If the compound subject includes the words *each* or *every,* the singular form should be used.

> *Their is an adjectival form of the pronoun they. The rule for pronoun–antecedent agreement also applies to possessive adjectives, such as their, which are formed from pronouns.*

> *Each* book and magazine in the library *has its* own entry.

When two antecedents are joined by *or* or *nor,* the pronoun agrees with the closest antecedent (see rule 2, subject-verb agreement).

> Neither the prime minister *nor his advisors were* certain how to implement *their* proposal.

As with subject–verb agreement, collective noun antecedents require the singular pronoun form if they are thought of in the collective sense, as a unit; if the context suggests that individuals are being referred to, the pronoun will take a plural form (see rule 4, subject–verb agreement).

> Our hockey team will play *its* final game against *its* archrivals. (The team will be playing as a unit.)
> The team will be receiving *their* new jerseys Friday. (Individual team members each will be given a jersey.)

With pronouns referring to portions and fractions, agreement depends on whether the noun following *of* is singular or plural (see rule 7, subject–verb agreement).

> Studies show that *a* large *number of college and university students are* cheating on *their* exams and essays; however, a much larger number are not.

If the pronoun has an indefinite pronoun antecedent such as *one, anybody* or *someone*, the singular form will apply, as it does with subject–verb agreement (see rule 6, subject–verb agreement).

> *One* should be careful about pronoun agreement, or *one's* teacher will certainly point out the error to *one*.

Although grammatically correct, the sentence above could be improved by using a personal pronoun to replace the indefinite pronoun "one." However, you must be careful to use a *singular* pronoun to replace an indefinite pronoun like "one" as the writer of this sentence has failed to do:

> *Incorrect*:
> *One* should be careful about pronoun agreement, or *their* teacher will certainly point out the error to *them*.

In the sentence below, a singular pronoun replaces the singular antecedent "one"—but the sentence is incorrect because the possessive adjective "his" and the personal pronoun "him" refer to only one gender. In the next section, we discuss problems that can arise when you want to replace an indefinite pronoun or a generic singular noun by a singular pronoun.

> *Also Incorrect*:
> *One* should be careful about pronoun agreement, or *his* teacher will certainly point out the error to *him*.

Problematic Pronouns: Inclusive Language

In recent years, the efforts of many to avoid gender bias have driven them to a gender-neutral, but grammatically incorrect, use of *their* with the singular indefinite pronoun. The inclusion of both correct pronouns in the form *him or her* or *his or her* is awkward compared to the inclusive *him*, but is preferable to an incorrect *their* and better than a form that may appear sexist. In the sentence below, the writer has used both singular forms to replace the antecedent "student."

> A student must footnote *his or her* references, or the teacher will expect *him or her* to correct the oversight.

The problem of pronoun–antecedent agreement is especially common among student writers when the antecedent noun is either an indefinite pronoun or a singular noun referring to a person where gender is unspecified—a generic noun such as *reader, writer, student, teacher, individual, character,* or *person*. Here are three options to consider when you have used an indefinite pronoun or a generic singular noun and want to follow with a pronoun.

> When an antecedent is either a generic singular noun or an indefinite pronoun, the personal pronoun that follows must be singular *and* gender-inclusive. This often means using two personal pronouns, such as *he or she*, etc.

Option 1: Replace the plural pronoun with *both* singular personal pronouns (or possessive adjectives). This option is nearly always acceptable in academic writing, but can be seen as awkward and repetitive in journalistic and workplace writing.

> *Incorrect:*
> Anybody not willing to put in long hours for little pay should give up *their* idea of becoming a writer.
> *Correct:*
> Anybody not willing to put in long hours for little pay should give up *his or her* idea of becoming a writer.

Option 2: Change the singular antecedent into the equivalent plural form and use the plural pronoun.

> *Those* not willing to put in long hours should give up *their* ideas of becoming writers. (Note the plural "ideas" to agree with "those" and "their.")

Option 3: Revise the sentence so that you don't need a pronoun to replace the noun. This option is not always possible and may occasionally sound too informal for academic writing.

> If you are not willing to put in long hours for little pay, you should give up *the idea* of becoming a writer.

Exercise 16.1

In the short paragraph below, fix pronoun–antecedent agreement errors, using at least one of each of the three options discussed above.

> If a child begins to perform poorly at school nowadays, they will likely be sent to a school counsellor to deal with the situation. Everyone assumes that attention deficit disorder is the culprit, and they just as automatically assume that drugs are the answer. On the other hand, perhaps the child is just not interested in a particular subject, or they do not understand the material. Parents, in turn, treat the child as if he is the problem instead of listening to him to find out how he can be helped.

Exercise 16.2

Chose the correct form of the verb and/or pronoun in the sentences and make any other necessary changes in agreement. Rewrite the sentence if that will produce a better result.

1. Everybody who supported the motion raised (his/her/their) hand.

2. Neither the film's director nor its producers (was/were) on hand to receive (his/her/their) prestigious award.

3. The instructor as well as the students (thinks/think) the room is too small.

4. It is unfortunate when a person no longer cares what others think about (him/her/them).

5. One should never expect to succeed unless (one/they) (is/are) willing to persist—even against the odds.

6. It is the tried and true that (provides/provide) the ultimate refuge in mediocrity.

7. Everyone who works during the year (is/are) obliged to file (his/her/their) income tax return.

8. Her set of baby teeth (was/were) complete when she was only eighteen months old.

9. He was one of those few candidates who (was/were) able to win re-election.

10. None of the company's products (requires/require) testing on animals.

11. Lining the side of the highway (is/are) a lot of billboards advertising fast food restaurants.

12. Every specimen of the horned grebe (has/have) a distinctive tuft on each side of (its/their) head.

13. Media and information technology training (provides/provide) students today with important communication skills.

14. Neither team members nor their coach (expects/expect) the season to last another game.

15. The maximum number of people allowed on this elevator (is/are) 30.

Exercise 16.3

Most of the following sentences contain one or more subject–verb agreement and/or pronoun–antecedent agreement errors. Correct the sentences as needed.

1. Every person in the community should have the right to attend a university and create new opportunities for themselves.

2. Especially unique to adolescent depression are physical symptoms, such as headaches.

3. The tonal quality of Amati's violins are excellent, but not perfect.

4. Over the past week, there has been some unexplained occurrences on the girls' floor of the residence.

5. Small class sizes and a low student population means few opportunities to meet new people.

6. A typical poem by Emily Dickinson leaves the reader searching for another line or even another stanza to satisfy their craving for closure.

7. Use of the leaves of the coca plant for its stimulant effects dates back thousands of years.

8. A coalition of neighbourhood organizations, students, and unions are currently forming to oppose the university's proposed plan.

9. Everyone who has purchased tickets is eligible for the grand prize, but they must be residents of Canada to claim their prize.

10. If a child is denied the opportunity to play, how can they develop emotionally and physically?

11. Participation and public education is necessary in a true democracy.

12. When a person contracts jaundice, their skin as well as the white part of their eyes turn yellow.

13. Another round of intense labour negotiations have not produced a settlement, so each union member has been told to do his duty on the strike line.

14. Before rendering its unanimous verdict, the jury was polled individually.

15. Almost nothing shapes a person's true character as much as their home.

16. The nature and role of human resources in organizations have undergone tremendous change in the last two decades.

17. In P.K. Page's poem, it is apparent that the landlady's prying nature and lonely life has made her forget her place.

18. Stereotyping and the use of degrading language in the book serves to reinforce its theme.

19. His overriding concern with rules and regulations, together with his excessive neatness and demand for order, suggests a mild obsessive-compulsive complex.

20. A person who continually disregards others' feelings will pay for their neglect sooner or later.

21. The encouragement of curiosity, questioning, and discussion is vital to the success of today's school environment.

22. In Japanese culture, a person's reputation along with their social standing depend on the concept of "saving face."

23. Medieval universities established a system of education and academic credentials that continue to function in today's universities.

24. The give and take in any relationship is the most important factor in sustaining it.

25. Although the Canadian Forces is still one of the best-trained military in the world, the training standards and morale of the forces is declining, according to some people.

◎ Other Problems with Pronouns

In addition to agreement problems, there are other potential pronoun pitfalls: errors in *pronoun reference, pronoun case,* and *pronoun consistency*.

Pronoun Reference

For a moment, consider life without pronouns.

> The principle for pronoun reference is simple: each pronoun should refer clearly to a specific antecedent.

A Lost Loonie Leads to a Lesson Learned

Alex and Alex's lawyer, Alan, left in Alex's limousine for Loonies Unlimited to buy Alex's landlady, Alice, a litre of light lemonade. Alice told Alex and Alan to also buy a litre of light lemonade for Alice's long-time lodger, Alison. When Alex and Alan alighted at Loonies Unlimited, Alex and Alan were alarmed that Alex had left Alex's loonie in Alex's loft. So Alphonse, of Loonies Unlimited, allowed Alex and Alan only one litre of lemonade, along with a length of limp licorice, and Alphonse loudly lamented Alex's and Alan's laxness.

Exercise 16.4

Newsflash: the pronoun has just been invented! Rewrite the above paragraph, replacing as many nouns as possible with pronouns, ensuring that it is clear what noun (antecedent) the pronoun is referring to. If in doubt about the clarity of antecedents, refer to the section that follows.

> The antecedent is the noun that the pronoun replaces in the sentence.

As discussed, most pronouns take the place of nouns, and the noun that the pronoun replaces is called the antecedent—literally, the one that "goes before" the pronoun. *Each pronoun you use in your writing should refer clearly to its antecedent.* In formal writing, you must pay attention to this principle. Pronouns replace specific nouns; *the relationship between pronoun and antecedent must always be clear.*

You can test for pronoun reference errors in your writing by seeing whether you can replace a pronoun by a specific noun that precedes the pronoun in the sentence (i.e., its antecedent):

Pronoun replaced by specific noun:

As reality shows become more popular, they (*reality shows*) have become more and more bizarre.

Unclear which noun acts as antecedent:

Reality shows have become more popular while their participants have become more and more bizarre; consequently, they (*reality shows? participants?*) can no longer be believed.

There are four kinds of pronoun reference errors, which can be repaired in different ways.

1. No reference (missing antecedent). This error occurs where the pronoun has no apparent noun antecedent. Consider this sentence:

Following the prime minister's speech, *he* took several questions from reporters.

The personal pronoun *he* apparently replaces *prime minister's*, which is a possessive adjective. Pronouns replace nouns, not adjectives. In the following sentence, the noun antecedent is implied but not actually stated; grammatically, the reference is missing:

One thing that Canadians are especially proud of is *its* national health-care system.

Where there is no antecedent, one must be provided or the pronoun changed into an appropriate noun.

After the *prime minister* spoke, *he* took several questions from reporters.
Or:
After speaking, *the prime minister* took several questions from reporters.
One thing that *Canadians* are especially proud of is *their* national health-care system.

A tendency in speaking, and sometimes in informal writing, is the use of the impersonal third-person pronoun *it* or *they* to refer vaguely to some unmentioned authority. In formal writing, you should avoid this habit:

They say there's nothing like a nice car to make you popular.

Don't begin a sentence with a preposition, such as *at, by, for, in, on,* or *with,* and then follow it with a pronoun with an antecedent that is the object of the preposition. The grammatical antecedent will be missing, and the sentence will have to be revised to include an antecedent/subject of the clause. The examples below illustrate this problem (and its solutions), which sometimes occurs in rough drafts when you try to get ideas down quickly.

> If the antecedent is missing, the sentence can be revised so the pronoun has an antecedent.

Incorrect:

With the new Formula One scoring system, it keeps fans excited throughout the season.

Correct:

The new Formula One scoring system keeps fans excited throughout the season.

Or:

With the new Formula One scoring system, fans remain excited throughout the season.

2. Remote reference. A reader should not be expected to connect a pronoun to a noun when they are separated by more than a sentence.

> In George Orwell's prophetic book *1984*, people's lives were watched over by television screens. These screens, along with brainwashing techniques, enabled people to be kept under firm control. *It* is an example of dystopian fiction.

The personal pronoun *It*, in sentence three, takes up the thread too late. Many nouns have intervened, causing the reader to have to hunt for the antecedent. Repetition of the noun is often the best solution where the antecedent is far away from the pronoun.

3. Ambiguous (squinting) reference. This error occurs when the pronoun seems to refer to two or more nouns, either of which could be the antecedent.

> When *Peter* gave *Paul his* driver's licence, *he* was very surprised to see that it had expired.

Who was surprised in this sentence? The pronoun *he* could refer to either Peter or Paul.

> *Other examples:*
>
> The problem for readers aspiring to look like the models in women's magazines is that their photos have been airbrushed. (*Their* has two grammatical antecedents: *readers and models.*)
>
> In 1916, a member of the Russian parliament denounced Rasputin before his colleagues. (Does his refer to the member's colleagues or to Rasputin's?)

While it is sometimes possible to correct ambiguous reference by repeating the noun intended to act as the antecedent, the result is not always pleasing:

> When *Peter* gave *Paul* his driver's license, *Peter* was surprised to see that it had expired.

Rewriting may be the better solution:

> On giving his driver's license to Paul, Peter was surprised to see that it had expired.
>
> The problem for readers aspiring to look like the models in women's magazines is that the models' photographs have been airbrushed.
>
> In 1916, a member of the Russian parliament denounced Rasputin before the house.

If the antecedent could grammatically be one of two possible nouns, you may need to rewrite the sentence so the antecedent is clear.

4. Broad reference (vague reference). This error occurs when the pronoun (often *this, that,* or *which*) refers to a group of words, an idea, or concept, rather than *one specific noun.*

> Children these days are too prone to lazy habits, such as watching television. *This* shows we have become too permissive.

This replaces too much—in effect, the whole preceding clause. The following, though, would be quite acceptable in anything but the most formal writing, even though the pronoun *which* doesn't replace a specific noun here, but rather the fact that she *received top marks.* The meaning of the sentence, however, is clear.

> She received top marks for her final dive, *which* gave her the gold medal in that competition.

In the following sentence the pronoun *this* refers to an idea, rather than a noun antecedent, making the meaning of the second independent clause unclear.

> Many older drivers are retested if they have had medical problems, but *this* needs to go further.

Broad reference often requires a sentence rewrite. Sometimes, the easiest way is to provide a noun and change the demonstrative pronoun into a demonstrative adjective. (Demonstrative adjectives have the same form as demonstrative pronouns—*this, that, these, those*—but, as adjectives, they precede nouns as modifiers, rather than take their place.)

> Children these days are too prone to lazy habits, such as watching television. *This tendency* shows that we have become too permissive.

> Many older drivers are re-tested if they have had medical problems, but *this re-testing* needs to go further.

While there is perhaps a "broad" allowance for broad reference error, depending on the level of formality required, *it* is a personal pronoun, and, like all personal pronouns, should always have a clear noun referent.

> *Poor:*
> We try not to mention specific businesses by name in our article; however, it can't be avoided in some situations.
> *Better:*
> We try not to mention specific businesses by name in our article; however, we can't avoid names in all situations.

> If the antecedent appears to be an idea rather than a specific noun, you need to add a noun that sums up the idea to the part of the sentence where the error occurs.

Exercise 16.5

Broad pronoun reference errors are particularly distracting when they occur repeatedly as a writer tries to develop a point. After reading the following paragraph, revise it to fix the errors in broad pronoun reference:

> Genetically modified foods have been engineered to flourish in harsh environments. *This* will help alleviate the need for usable farmland as *this* will enable farming to occur on lands once considered unsuitable for growing crops. *This* will be a major benefit to many nations in Africa, Asia, and South America where there is a shortage of food and available land.

Exercise 16.6

Working backward: To reinforce the principle that pronouns require clear antecedents, make up antecedent nouns for the pronouns to replace and construct sentences/clauses containing the nouns to precede these sentences/clauses.

Example: He just shrugged off all she had to say in her defence.

Preceding sentence: Lucinda explained her behaviour to Ted, but he just . . . .

1. She had long, brown hair down to her waist. (antecedent for She)

2. He found him sleeping soundly on the kitchen floor the next morning. (He, him)

3. They lived as if nobody else mattered but themselves. (They)

4. This will be her chance to prove whether she is good enough to make the team. (she)

5. They have a responsibility to educate the public. (They)

6. His attorney decided on a "not guilty" plea. (antecedent for possessive adjective His)

7. She awoke suddenly to the sound of gunfire. (She)

8. They make a delightfully odd couple. (They)

9. She will eat only the most expensive kind of deluxe cat food. (She)

10. After hearing their protests for a long time, he finally agreed to take them along. (their, he, them)

Exercise 16.7

Identify the kind of pronoun reference errors in the following sentences; then, correct the errors by making necessary revisions. In the first five sentences, the pronoun that needs to be changed is italicized.

1. *It* says in my textbook that pronouns should always have a clear referent.

2. Whenever a staff meeting is called, *they* are required to attend.

3. Racism is a disease that will continue to plague society until *it* is non-existent.

4. Sixty per cent of our pesticides are used on cotton, and *this* is our major ground water pollutant.

5. During Roosevelt's Pearl Harbor speech, *he* identified the US as a peaceful and tolerant nation.

6. I know it said No Parking, but I went ahead and parked there anyway. They gave me a $20 fine.

7. Her second novel was far different from her first. It was set in the remote Hebrides.

8. Previous Afghan successes were significant victories; for example, they last waged war against the powerful Soviet Union.

9. Some psychologists and researchers believe in the "innate" theory of prejudice. According to this theory, ingrained prejudice is cross-cultural and awareness of race is one of the earliest social characteristics to develop in children. These findings may help account for its popularity.

10. During the dinosaur age, they lived in a rapidly changing environment.

After you've checked your answers, complete the exercise by doing questions 11–20.

11. It is the right of everybody to have access to knowledge, and this means access to the education of choice.

12. In Chapter 21 of my textbook, it analyzes the success of the Liberal Party in Canada.

13. Supervisors may discourage workers from reporting injuries since they receive annual bonuses for low injury rates.

14. Children often hide their compulsive behaviours from friends and family due to feelings of shame, causing them to remain undiagnosed.

15. To experienced "gamers," the quality of the video card is crucial; this is because the latest games require a high standard of video card.

16. The Catholic kings of Spain rallied the country to fight their enemies, the Moors. This became known as the "Reconquista."

17. Huck Finn was the physically abused son of Pap, who harasses Judge Thatcher when he is drunk. This creates sympathy in the reader, which makes him more likeable.

18. By teaching today's youth safe and healthy approaches to sexuality, it will elevate their self-esteem.

19. Part of the appeal of driving an SUV is that they are big and look impressive beside the "merely mortal" car.

20. Japanese smokers consume more than twice the number of cigarettes as American smokers do, and it continues to increase steadily.

Pronoun Case

Some personal, relative, and interrogative pronouns change their form to reflect their function in the sentence. The grammatical term for this form is *case*. You need to be aware of those situations in which you look at the pronoun's function in order to use the correct form.

Personal Pronouns

Personal pronouns refer to persons. The *first person* refers to the one *doing* the speaking or writing; *second person* refers to the one *spoken to*; *third person* refers to the one *spoken about*. Most nouns can be considered third person and can be replaced by third-person pronouns.

Table 16.1 can be used to distinguish between one group of pronouns and another group. It's important to be able to distinguish between them because the role that a personal pronoun plays in a sentence will determine whether you use the pronoun form from the first group (subjective) or from the second one (objective). Notice that the second-person pronoun *you* doesn't change its form, so it's the first- and third-person pronouns you will be concerned about.

On the chart, consider the pronoun forms under Subjective–Singular and Subjective–Plural:

He was swimming in the pool.

He is subject of the sentence, the third-person singular masculine form of the pronoun. *He* is correct because it is the subject of the clause/sentence, so it is said to be in the subjective case. The following sentence illustrates what happens when the pronoun plays a different grammatical role from that of subject:

I was swimming in the pool with *her*.

Table 16.1   Personal Pronoun Chart

PRONOUN PERSON	SUBJECTIVE-SINGULAR	SUBJECTIVE-PLURAL	OBJECTIVE-SINGULAR	OBJECTIVE-PLURAL
First person	I	we	me	us
Second person	you	you	you	you
Third person	he, she, it	they	him, her, it	them

Personal pronouns refer to persons. The *first person* refers to the one *doing* the speaking or writing; *second person* refers to the one *spoken to*; *third person* refers to the one *spoken about*.

The first and third forms of the personal pronoun and two other pronouns (*who* and *whom*) change their form, or *case*, to express their grammatical function in the sentence.

The subject *I* is first-person singular. But the other pronoun in the sentence is acting as object of the preposition *with*. When it acts as the object of a verb or of a preposition, it is in the objective case

If you are in doubt about the correct form of a personal pronoun, determine the grammatical role it is playing in the sentence and then use the corresponding case form.

She spoke so softly to the teacher that it was difficult for *him* to understand *her*.

She is *subject* of the verb *spoke*; *him* is *object* of the preposition *for*; *her* is *object* of the infinitive *to understand*.

Notice the different pronouns in these two sentences:

Anna, the King, and *I* are going out for Chinese food tonight. (*I* is part of the subject.)

Anna arrived late for her dinner with the King and *me*. (*Me* is part of a prepositional phrase; it is object of the preposition *with*.)

The way to decide which form to use is

1. determine the grammatical relationship involved: Is the pronoun subject of a clause/sentence, or the object of a verb, preposition, or infinitive? Then,
2. choose the appropriate form (subjective or objective). Until the forms become familiar, you can refer to the pronoun chart above.

Although the principle of pronoun case with personal pronouns is quite straightforward, it can be tricky to apply in compounds.

Tina and (*I? me?*) plan to attend Mavis's wedding on May 15.

Strategy: isolate the pronoun from the noun to determine the correct form:
~~Tina and~~ I plan to attend Mavis's wedding on May 15.
Mavis's wedding will be a joyous occasion for ~~Tina and~~ me.
We ~~students~~ believe firmly that our rights should be given back to us.
Our rights should be given back to us ~~students~~.

Possessive pronoun. Another example in which pronouns change their form is the possessive (adjectival) form of nouns and pronouns (e.g., my *uncle's* pet alligator; *his* pet alligator).

> Never use an apostrophe when you use a form like *hers* ("belonging to her") or *theirs* ("belonging to them").

The book doesn't belong to Anthony but to Kristy; it is *hers*.

Hers is the noun form of the possessive pronoun replacing the antecedent *Kristy*. The adjectival form is seen in the following sentence:

The book doesn't belong to Anthony but to Kristy; it is *her* book.

Table 16.2 Personal Pronoun Chart with Adjectival and Noun Forms

PRONOUN PERSON	ADJECTIVAL-SINGULAR	ADJECTIVAL-PLURAL	SUBJECT COMPLEMENTS, SINGULAR	SUBJECT COMPLEMENTS, PLURAL
First person	my	our	mine	ours
Second person	your	your	yours	yours
Third person	his, her, its	their	his, hers, its	theirs

Table 16.2 completes Table 16.1 by including the possessive forms of pronouns and the noun (complement) forms.

Relative pronouns *relate* the dependent clause they introduce to the noun that they follow. A relative clause, then, usually functions as an adjective, modifying the preceding noun. Of the major relative pronouns (*who, whoever, which, whichever, that*), only *who* and *whoever* change their form depending on whether they are being used as the subject of the clause or as object of either the verb or a preposition in the clause.

> Relative pronouns introduce dependent clauses and usually function adjectivally, modifying the preceding noun.

To determine the case of a relative pronoun, look at *the role the relative pronoun plays within the clause*; in other words, the answer to whether you use *who* or *whom* will be found *in the clause that the relative pronoun introduces*.

If either the pronoun *who* or *whoever* is subject of the clause or is the subjective completion, use the subjective form. If the pronoun is acting as an object of the verb or of a preposition in the clause, use the objective form: *whom* (*whomever*). Consider these two sentences; italics indicate the dependent (relative) clause:

> If the pronoun is the subject of the clause, use *who*; if it is object of the verb or of the preposition in the clause, use *whom*.

1. The old man shouted at *whoever happened to be within listening distance.*
2. The old man should be free to shout at *whomever he chooses.*

In sentence 1, *whoever* is the *subject* of the clause it introduces (*whoever happened to be within listening distance*). In sentence 2, *he* is subject of the clause, and the relative pronoun is in the objective case. If you see that the relative clause has a subject, you can be certain that the relative pronoun will *not* be the subject of the clause. In sentence 2, *he* does the choosing and is the subject of the verb; *whomever* is the object of the verb.

One test for case is to substitute the third-person form of the personal pronoun for the relative pronoun in the relative clause. *Whoever* (relative pronoun) *happened to be within listening distance* would become *he/she* (personal pronoun) *happened to be within listening distance.* In sentence 2, the relative clause would read, *he chooses he,* which sounds, and is, incorrect.

Determining pronoun case with relative pronouns always involves determining the function of the relative pronoun that begins the clause. Which is correct?

1. Jeong-Gyu is someone who, we firmly believe, will go far.
2. Jeong-Gyu is someone whom, we firmly believe, will go far.

Answer: sentence 1 is correct. *Who* is the subject of the relative clause *who will go far.* *[W]e firmly believe* is not part of the relative clause but part of another clause (with another subject) that interrupts the relative clause.

Jeong-Gyu is someone who ~~, we firmly believe,~~ will go far.

Interrogative Pronouns

The **interrogative pronouns** (*who, whoever, which, whichever, what*) are always asking questions. Once you know how to determine the case of the relative pronouns *who/whom,* the interrogatives shouldn't give you too much trouble. Again, you need to determine their function to determine pronoun case. Of the three interrogatives, it is *who* and *whoever* that change, depending on their function in the sentence.

> The interrogative pronouns, *who, which,* and *what,* introduce questions.

With whom did you go out on Saturday night? (object of the preposition)
Who says you should never reveal your feelings? (subject of the verb)
Whom would you recommend for the new opening? (object of the verb)

If a pronoun is part of a prepositional phrase, it will normally follow the preposition. However, it's possible to structure the sentence so the pronoun precedes the preposition (e.g., "Whom is the note for?") If you end a sentence with a preposition, you can rearrange the sentence so the preposition comes *before* the pronoun. It is then clearer to see that the *objective case* should be used for the pronoun.

> The function of the interrogative pronoun in the sentence determines whether *who* (subjective form) or *whom* (objective form) is used.

Whom did Professor LeGuin direct the question *to*?

The more formal usage makes it easier to determine case:

Rearranged sentence:
To whom did Professor LeGuin direct the question?

It is now clear that *whom* is the object of the preposition *to*.

Exercise 16.8

Choose the correct form of the pronoun.

1. Management often forgets about the needs of (we/us) wage-earners.

2. (Who/whom) should run for office this election?

3. I have no intention of speaking to (they/them).

4. The person (who/whom) finishes first will be rewarded.

5. You recommend (who/whom) for the position?

6. As she entered the room, a mysterious feeling came over (she/her).

7. Margaret Laurence was a novelist (who/whom) entertained her readers with well-developed plots and realistic characters.

8. People (who/whom) use memory aids tend to be better spellers.

9. The instructor explained the different cases of pronouns to Gail and (I/me).

10. "Hey, buddy, (who/whom) did you mean to refer to when you used that insulting term?"

After you've checked your answers, complete the exercise by doing questions 11–25.

11. (Whoever/whomever) fails to address the most important issue—unemployment—will find themselves among the unemployed.

12. The last person (who/whom) she wanted to see at the track meet was her former coach.

13. My fifth grade teacher always let her favourite students—Mallory, Cindy, and (I/me)—help her with clean-up.

14. I wanted to ask her (who/whom) the note should be addressed to.

15. The young narrator's goal is to bring back a present for his friend's sister (who/whom) he admires from afar.

16. Chris's rival, Mike, lasted longer in the ring than (he/him).

17. We were allowed to invite (whoever/whomever) we wanted to the party.

18. I proposed that Geordie and (I/me) would stack chairs after the meeting.

19. The only "mother" (who/whom) the kitten has known is Madeline, (who/whom) rescued it from traffic.

20. The newly renovated house is a very pleasant place for my brother and (I/me) to live.

21. During his career, Jackie Robinson was subjected to racial hatred from many people (who/whom) he came in contact with.

22. Prejudices decrease when children observe non-prejudiced behaviour by peers (who/whom) children associate with during their pre-teen years.

23. Christy so drastically changes his personality that his own father can barely believe it is (he/him).

24. "[I]n these fits I leave them, while I visit / young Ferdinand, (who/whom) they suppose is drowned." —Shakespeare

25. Choose the grammatical poem:

a) Roses are red,

   Butterflies are free;

   You must choose

   Between him and me.

b) Roses are red,

   Birds can fly;

   You must choose

   Between he and I.

Pronoun Consistency

A pronoun must agree in number, gender, and person with its antecedent. In many instances, you will refer to different persons in the same sentence, and it's acceptable to do so, as long as the change isn't arbitrary. On the other hand, if you want simply to replace a preceding noun with a pronoun, the pronoun should be the same *person* as its antecedent. Nouns are usually treated as third-person and are replaced by third-person pronouns.

> Do not needlessly switch from one person of pronoun to another. If an antecedent is a noun, use the third-person form to replace it.

Incorrect:

During final exams, if *students* must go to the washroom, raise *your* hand so *you* can be escorted there. (*Students* is third-person; *your* and *you* are second-person.)

Correct:

During final exams, if *students* need to go to the washroom, *they* should raise their hands....

Or, more informally:

During final exams, if *you* need to go to the washroom, raise *your* hand....

Further examples:

Incorrect:

It is possible that *our* desire to make life easier for *ourselves* will, in fact, make *humans* redundant.

Our and *ourselves* are first-person; *humans* is third-person.

Exercise 16.9

The following paragraph contains errors in pronoun consistency, along with some awkward use of third-person pronouns. When you rewrite the paragraph, strive for correctness and effectiveness. First decide which person you want to refer to consistently. This decision might be based on the level of formality you want to use (first- and second-person pronouns, such as *I /me* and *you*, are considered more informal than third-person pronouns, such as *he/she* and *him/her*).

> You can definitely learn a lot from educational TV; we can learn things that we cannot learn from written texts. If one is a major in Commerce, for example, and if he or she watches the business news, he or she can understand the commerce textbook better by applying what he or she learns from the news. Similarly, I think that watching sports programs can provide people with excitement. Watching sports can also give us a better understanding of the game. On the other hand, if one chooses to watch comedy all the time, people are not going to gain any real benefits. I feel comedies are generally meaningless.

Correct:

It is possible that *our* desire to make life easier for *ourselves* will, in fact, make *us* redundant.

It is possible that the desire to make life easier for *humans* will, in fact, make *them* redundant.

Incorrect:

Educators today should teach *students* learning skills, such as how to manage your money.

Correct:

Educators today should teach *students* learning skills, such as how to manage *their* money.

◎ Sentence Construction Errors

Writing in complete sentences and using the appropriate conjunctions to join clauses will help you form grammatical sentences. However, there are other potential problems in constructing sentences. Major sentence construction errors are discussed below under four categories: (1) misplaced modifiers, (2) dangling modifiers, (3) faulty parallelism, and (4) faulty comparisons.

Misplaced modifiers and dangling modifiers are examples of errors that can result when the first principle is not adhered to. Faulty parallelism and faulty comparisons result when the second principle is not followed (see note in margin).

> Sentence construction errors result from forgetting two basic principles in English grammar:
>
> 1. Modifiers should be placed as close as possible to the words they are intended to modify.
> 2. Coordinate (equal) elements in a sentence must be grammatically parallel and complete.

Misplaced Modifiers

The main function of adjectives is to modify nouns, while the main function of adverbs is to modify verbs. Prepositional phrases can also function as adjectives or adverbs. Misplaced modifiers, then, can be either adjectives or adjectival phrases, or adverbs or adverbial phrases. They are misplaced when mistakenly placed next to a part of speech they are not intended to modify.

The meaning of a sentence in English is heavily dependent on word order, or **syntax**; it is partly through syntax that writers communicate their meaning and that the reader understands the message.

Adjectival Modifiers

The usual position for a one-word adjective is immediately before the noun it is intended to modify, but adjectival phrases and clauses usually *follow* the noun they modify. Most misplaced adjectival modifiers are phrases or clauses. Consider the following examples of misplaced modifiers:

Incorrect:

They headed for a child in the front row *with a long overcoat*.

It is the child, not the front row, wearing the long overcoat. The adjectival phrase should follow the noun *child*.

They headed for a child with a long overcoat in the front row.

Consider:
The furnace thermostat is located upstairs, *which displays the temperature settings.*

In this sentence, the adjectival (relative) clause, *which displays the temperature settings*, is placed next to the adverb *upstairs* instead of the noun *thermostat*.

The furnace thermostat, which displays the temperature settings, is located upstairs.

Adverbial Modifiers

Misplaced adverbs and adverbial phrases are more common than misplaced adjectives and adjectival phrases because adverbs can often be moved in a sentence without affecting meaning. However, moving them does sometimes affect meaning, and it is safest to place them right before or after the word or phrase they are supposed to modify.

The meaning of the following sentence could be misconstrued:

Students should buy this book because it will give them all the information they need to know about writing *in a convenient form.*

Presumably, the writer did not want to highlight "convenience in writing," but that the book "will give them...information...in a convenient form." Correctly,

Students should buy this book because it will give them, *in a convenient form*, all the information they will need to know about writing.

Consider:
The conviction carries a penalty of 8 to 10 years *in two provinces.*

Because of the misplaced prepositional phrase, the writer seems to be saying that on being convicted, the criminal will have to "do time" in two provinces. Either of the following rephrased sentences is correct:

In two provinces the conviction carries a penalty of 8 to 10 years.
The conviction carries a penalty in two provinces of 8 to 10 years.

Fixing Misplaced Modifiers

When the misplaced modifier *in two provinces* in the last sentence is placed before or after the verb it should modify, *carries*, the problem is fixed. The solution to misplaced modifiers, whether an entire clause, a phrase, or a single word, is simple: move them.

The following misplaced modifier makes the sentence awkward or misleading:

Incorrect:
The instructor marked the essay I wrote *unfairly*.
Correct:
The instructor *unfairly marked* the essay I wrote.
Or:
I thought the instructor *marked my essay unfairly*.

Misplaced modifiers should be placed as close as possible to the word(s) they are intended to modify.

When you are writing quickly, trying to get your ideas down, misplaced modifiers can occur anywhere in a sentence; however, they often occur at the end, almost as an afterthought. That is the place to begin checking:

Incorrect:
Cars today produce large amounts of toxic chemicals that can damage human cells *if inhaled*.
Correct:
Cars today produce large amounts of toxic chemicals that, if inhaled, can damage human cells.

One-Word Modifiers

You need to be especially careful in placing one-word modifiers in the sentence, especially with limiting adverbs like *only, almost, just, even, nearly, barely, merely*, and the like.

Does one little word out of place *really* affect the meaning of the sentence? Consider how the meaning of the following statement changes, depending on where the "little" word *only* is put:

Jared didn't do his homework yesterday.

Six Answers to the Question: Is Jared a Lazy Student or a Conscientious One?

1. *Only Jared* didn't do his homework yesterday.

Everyone but Jared did his or her homework; *only* is an adjective modifying *Jared*.

2. Jared *only didn't do* his homework.

The meaning of this sentence is unclear. It could mean the same as sentence 1 or that Jared did other things—but not his homework. It could also mean that the fact Jared didn't do his homework wasn't important.

3. Jared didn't *only do* his homework yesterday.

Now *only* is an adverb modifying the verb *do* and suggests that Jared did do his homework and other things as well.

4. Jared didn't do *only his homework* yesterday.

Placing *only* before *his homework* means that Jared definitely did his homework and other things as well. It might also mean that Jared was involved in doing someone else's homework in addition to his own.

5. Jared didn't do his *only homework* yesterday.

Placing only between *his* and *homework* implies that Jared didn't have much homework, but he didn't do it.

6. Jared didn't do his homework *yesterday only*.

Perhaps Jared is not such a lazy student after all: the only day he didn't do his homework was yesterday!

Dangling Modifiers

Misplaced and dangling modifiers can be the grammatical equivalent of life's most embarrassing moments: modifiers that are misplaced or dangling can give the communication a quite different, sometimes humorous, meaning from the intended one. The sentence below seems to refer to precocious parents:

When only seven years old, my parents decided to enroll me in a Highland dancing course.

Now, consider the following sentence from a résumé, which never mentions the applicant at all:

When not working or attending classes, my hobbies are gardening, doing macramé, and bungie-jumping.

As dangling modifiers are often "–ing" participle (adjectival) phrases, they are sometimes called **dangling participles**. Grammatically, they modify the closest noun. These adjectival phrases, then, are dangling because the intended noun or noun phrase is not in the sentence. That's why it doesn't help to move the modifier.

The way to correct dangling modifiers is (1) to provide the noun or noun phrase in the independent clause to give the modifier something to modify, or (2) to turn the dangling phrase into a dependent clause with a subject.

> Grammatically, dangling modifiers modify the closest noun, often giving the sentence an unintended meaning.

When only seven years old, I was enrolled by my parents in a Highland dancing course. (method 1)

When I was only seven years old, my parents decided to enroll me in a Highland dancing course. (method 2)

When not working or attending classes, I enjoy several hobbies, including gardening, doing macramé, and bungie-jumping. (1)

When I am not working or attending classes, my hobbies include gardening, doing macramé, and bungie-jumping. (2)

While misplaced modifiers frequently appear at the end of a sentence, dangling modifiers usually are found at the beginning—somewhat less often at the end—of a sentence, and even occasionally in the middle. With misplaced modifiers, the needed information is in the sentence, and the modifier needs to be moved as close as possible to the word or phrase it is intended to modify. With dangling modifiers, the essential information *is not in the sentence*. The examples below will show you how to identify dangling modifiers by asking the appropriate questions.

In this example, poetic description is undercut by the statement that the clouds are arriving in Calgary, when more likely the writer is describing his or her arrival.

When arriving in Calgary, the clouds had scattered, and the sky was aglow with bands of pink and red.

In the next example, the book seems to have written itself.

Though a well-known writer, his latest book failed to make the best-seller's list.

The question to ask in the first example is, *Who is arriving in Calgary?* In the second, we can ask, *Who is the well-known writer?* Since the answers are not in the sentences, the modifiers must be dangling. In both cases, the missing information needs to be provided in the independent clause, or the dangling phrase needs to be turned into a dependent clause that can modify the independent clause that follows.

Corrected: When arriving in Calgary, I saw that the clouds had scattered, and the sky was aglow with bands of pink and red. (1—information has been provided in the independent clause)

When I arrived in Calgary, the clouds had scattered, and the sky was aglow with bands of pink and red. (2—dangling phrase has been changed to a dependent clause)

Corrected: Though a well-known writer, he failed to make the best-seller's list with his latest book. (1)

Though he was a well-known writer, his latest book failed to make the best-seller's list. (2)

In the following example, the dangling modifier is at the end of the sentence:

Incorrect: Verbal and non-verbal skills are greatly enhanced when living in a foreign country.

Who is living in a foreign country? This information is missing, so the participial phrase *when living* is dangling. To correct it, add information:

Corrected: When living in a foreign country, you are able to enhance your verbal and non-verbal skills. (1)

Verbal and non-verbal skills are greatly enhanced when you live in a foreign country.

Exercise 16.10

The intended meanings of the following sentences are obscured or distorted due to modifier problems. Working in groups, identify the particular problem (misplaced or dangling modifier) and determine the grammatical (incorrect or ambiguous) meaning(s) of the sentences. Then, fix the sentences using one of the methods above.

1. A striped hat was on his head that came to a point.

2. As we were leaving, he promised to visit us with tears in his eyes.

3. Although unambitious and downright lazy, I have never known Sam to break his word.

4. His ego was further inflated by being awarded first prize in the Ben Affleck look-alike contest.

5. Every character has a purpose in Shakespeare's play, big or small.

6. When asked what my favourite sport is, I usually say that it is running without any hesitation.

7. Stepping out of the airplane, the fresh air was most invigorating.

8. Gabriel Kolko describes peace in Vietnam after the war in his book.

9. Opening the door unexpectedly, his eyes fell upon two of his employees sleeping in front of their computers.

10. Teacher Laurie McNamara posed for the photographer with Principal Dan Saunders, who gave her a kidney last month, in the Cloverdale Elementary School hallway.

Exercise 16.11

Correct the following sentences, each of which contains a modifier error. In some instances, it will be necessary to reword the sentence for clarity and correctness.

1. In our city, shady characters lurk on quiet corners that offer a variety of drugs.

2. Over the years, several world-class cyclists have had spectacular careers, such as Eddie Merckx and Greg LeMond.

3. Running down the street without a care in the world, two pedestrians had to quickly move out of his way.

4. Being a member of the Sikh community, my paper will be given a strong personal focus.

5. Built in mere minutes, you will have a fully interactive website for your business or for your personal use.

6. Benefits will only result from a smoke-free environment.

7. Germany has built an extensive network of highways through its countryside, known as the Autobahn.

8. Trying to find a job today, employers are stressing verbal and written communication skills more than ever before.

9. People's rights to privacy should be forfeited when caught in criminal behaviour.

10. This species of snake will eat frogs, mice, and small pieces of meat in captivity.

After you've checked your answers, complete the exercise by doing questions 11–25.

11. Walking through the streets of Srinigar, devastation and fear are immediately evident.

12. As a beginner, my instructor taught me about the respect one karate student must show to another.

13. Tylenol and Aspirin effectively reduce pain when experiencing a fever.

14. Speaking from experience, tans that dye the top layer of the skin last for about one week.

15. Moving to Nebraska at the age of 10, Jim Burden's narrative reveals the reflections of a child.

16. Being an Elizabethan playwright, I am certain that Shakespeare would have been a major influence on Marlowe.

17. Adolescents essentially experience the same depressive symptoms as adults do.

18. As a serious snowboarder, it is exciting to observe the growth of this sport.

19. In John Donne's "Death, Be Not Proud," Death has a personality that is usually only given to a human being.

20. The boy in *Araby* returns home empty-handed without the highly valued object, in this case, a gift for Mangan's sister that most quests require.

21. Darwin's theory of evolution may be contested on the grounds that species may cease to appear abruptly.

22. Another example of imagery of light and dark in *Heart of Darkness* occurs when Marlow encounters an African dying in a clearing with a white scarf.

23. Based primarily on the work of Karl Marx, socialists see the creation of profit as a complex process.

24. Having an emotional personality, Beethoven's music identified him as a nineteenth-century Romantic.

25. A mother and her daughter were recently reunited after 18 years in a checkout line.

The Parallelism Principle

Balanced constructions give a sentence grace and strength, while unbalanced constructions make a sentence weak and unstable, as a misaligned wall in a building undermines a building's stability. A sentence must be constructed so that *words and phrases parallel in the logic of the sentence are parallel in the grammatical structure of the sentence.*

Coordinate elements are *equal* elements. Checking for parallelism is checking to ensure that the elements in a sentence that have the *same grammatical function* are expressed in parallel structures.

When studying paragraph coherence (Chapter 4), you looked at using repetition and balanced structures. Learning the fundamentals of parallelism in this section will help ensure that your writing is both grammatically correct and easy to read.

Experienced writers have mastered the principles of parallel structures and use them routinely in their writing; balanced structures are rhetorically effective structures. Consider, for example, the following excerpt from Francis Bacon's essay "Of Youth and Age" (1601), which is made up almost entirely of parallel words, phrases, and clauses. Without parallel elements, shown by italics, this paragraph would be very hard to follow:

> A man that is *young in years*, may be *old in hours*, if he have lost no time. But that happeneth rarely. Generally, youth is like the *first cogitations*, not so wise as *the second*. For there is a youth *in thoughts*, as well as *in ages*. . . . Young men, in the conduct and manage of actions, *embrace* more than they can hold; *stir* more than they can quiet; *fly* to the end, without consideration of the means and degrees; *pursue* some few principles, which they have chanced upon absurdly; *care not* to innovate, which draws unknown inconveniences; *use* extreme remedies at first; and, that which doubleth all errors, *will not acknowledge or retract* them; like an unready horse, that will neither *stop* nor *turn*. Men of age *object too much, consult too long, adventure too little, repent too soon,* and seldom *drive* business home to the full period, but *content* themselves with a mediocrity of success.

Student writer Allison McClymont was able to use parallel structures to create a dramatic opening for her essay on school uniforms.

> In the hallways of today's high school, students congregate in various cliques, using their dress as an indicator of their conformity: there are the "jocks" in their letterman jackets, the "nerds" in their high pants and suspenders, the "cheerleaders" in their short skirts and sweaters, and the "arties" in their paint-covered hippie clothes. Other easily identifiable cliques include the "gangsters," the "preppies," the "mods," the "punks," the "weirdos," and "the band geeks."

Read the following sentences. Although their meanings are clear, they don't *sound* balanced. In fact, they're not balanced because the important words

Checking for parallelism is checking to ensure that the elements in a sentence that have the *same grammatical function* are expressed in parallel structures.

in the compound or list aren't all the same part of speech: each sentence contains an error in parallel structure. The words you need to pay attention to are italicized:

1. Ian would rather *snack* on some chips than *eating* a regular dinner.

2. The basic human needs are *food, clothes, shelter* and *having a good job.*

3. After her 10-kilometre run, she felt *weak, tired,* and *she badly needed water.*

4. Our cat enjoys *watching* TV, *looking* out the window, and *to sleep* at the foot of our bed.

5. Neither a *borrower* be, nor *lend* to others.

Identifying and Fixing Parallelism Problems

> You should check to see whether all the elements are parallel whenever you use (1) a list (3 or more items), (2) a compound (2 items), (3) correlative (paired) conjunctions, or (4) a comparison (which has two parts).

Use a two-stage approach to identify and fix unparallel structures in your writing:

First, identify structures where there should be parallelism: *lists, compounds, correlative conjunctions,* and *comparisons.* For example, in the following sentence, there is a compound object of the verb *prefer:*

1. Ian would prefer *to snack* on some chips rather than *eating* a regular dinner.

Second, when you have identified the part(s) of the list, etc. that are not grammatically parallel, make them so. The two objects of the verb *prefer* in the sentence 1 above are not expressed in parallel form: *to snack* and *eating.* Either the verbal noun (infinitive form of the verb acting as a noun) or the gerund can function as objects, so either of these changes is correct:

Ian would prefer *to snack* on some chips than *to eat* a regular dinner.
OR,
Ian would prefer *snacking* on chips to *eating* a regular dinner.

Identify in the following sentences the parts of speech that have the same functions:

2. The basic human needs are *food, clothes, shelter,* and *having* a good job.

Now, use four nouns in the list to make it grammatically parallel.

3. After her 10-kilometre run, she felt *weak, tired,* and *she badly needed water.*

Using three predicate adjectives, make this list parallel. You could also fix the sentence by using three independent clauses: *she felt weak,* etc.

4. Our cat enjoys *watching* TV, *looking* out the window, and *to sleep* at the foot of our bed.

Use three gerunds (*–ing* verb forms acting as nouns) to make the list parallel.

Next, correct the sentence using three infinitives.

5. Neither a *borrower* be, nor *lend* to others.

Using two verbs after the correlative (paired) conjunctions *neither* and *nor* makes the sentence parallel. You could also follow Shakespeare's example in his play *Hamlet* and use two nouns after the conjunctions: Neither a *borrower* nor a *lender* be.

When checking for parallel structure, consider first the structurally essential words like nouns and verbs (not their modifiers). But if adjectives or adverbs appear in a list *by themselves* without words to modify, ensure they are in parallel form. Look at any larger grammatical units, such as prepositional phrases, which also should appear in parallel relationships with other prepositional phrases. Similarly, dependent clauses should be parallel with dependent clauses and independent clauses with independent clauses.

The examples below apply the two-step method to lists, compounds, correlative conjunctions, and comparisons.

A List or Series

A list or series comprises three or more items. So, whenever you list something, you need to check for parallel structure. For example, if you use an expanded thesis statement that lists your essay's main points, you need to ensure that all the items in the list are grammatically parallel.

> *Incorrect*:
> Research into cloning should be encouraged as it could lead to cures for diseases, successful organ transplants, and put an end to infertility problems.
> *Correct*:
> Research into cloning should be legalized as it could lead to | *cures* for diseases, | successful organ *transplants*, | and *solutions* to infertility problems.

The elements are now parallel. Notice that to avoid repeating the word *cures*, a word with a similar meaning has replaced it.

Note: Length is not necessarily a factor in parallelism: for example, a simple noun would normally be considered parallel with a noun phrase (but not with a prepositional phrase) because they have the same grammatical function.

The following sentence contains two nouns preceded by adjectives and a noun followed by an adjectival (prepositional) phrase. The important words here are the nouns:

> Discipline in single-sex schools has been shown to directly affect | regular *attendance*, good *grades*, and *standards for dress and behaviour.*

The following thesis statements include lists where the items are not parallel:

Incorrect:
The major forms of eating disorders involve the compulsion to count calories, to constantly exercise, and the need to alter one's appearance.
Correct:
The major forms of eating disorders involve the compulsion | *to count* calories, *to* constantly *exercise*, and *to alter* one's appearance.

Incorrect:
Buddhism teaches that one's karma can be affected by many things: your generosity to those less fortunate, your behaviour to strangers, and if you treat even your enemies with respect.

The list of "noun, noun, clause" needs to be changed to "noun, noun, noun."

Buddhism teaches that one's karma can be affect by many things: your *generosity* to those less fortunate, your *behaviour* to strangers, and *respect* even for your enemies.

You also need to be careful that items in a list are *logically*, as well as grammatically, parallel. The following list contains five nouns/noun phrases, but not all of the items are logically parallel. Which item does not belong in the list? Why?

Common injuries in the meat-packing industry include chemical burns, broken bones, lacerations, amputations, and even death.

More informal lists that use bullets, numbers, or point form also require parallel structure. Choose a set up or starting point; then, ensure that each bulleted item has the same grammatical function and, if necessary, form.

Before choosing a graduate program, a student should investigate

- the number of graduate students who receive financial support

- the expertise of faculty in the student's desired specialty

- course work required

- do research opportunities exist for graduate students?

Starting all items in the list with a noun or noun phrase would make the list grammatically parallel:

- financial support . . .

- expertise of . . .

- course work . . .

- research opportunities . . .

Compounds

A compound consists of two of the same parts of speech acting as a grammatical unit.

You need to apply the principle of parallel structure to **compounds**. Coordinating conjunctions, such as *or*, *and*, or *but*, can signal a compound, as can prepositional phrase joiners such as *as well as*; in comparisons, *than* or *as* may join the two elements of a comparison.

Once you've identified a compound, look at the important word or phrase in the first element of the compound and ensure that the second element that follows the joiner uses the parallel grammatical structure. Several examples of compounds follow.

Incorrect:
It is actually cheaper | *to convert* a used vehicle into an electric vehicle than | *buying* a new gas-powered model.
Correct:
It is actually cheaper | *to convert* a used vehicle into an electric vehicle than | *to buy* a new gas-powered model.

Some compounds that cause trouble are those with helping verbs. In these cases, it may be helpful to draw a line where the first element begins and another where the second begins (after the conjunction). Then, see if both parts line up with the main verb that follows; you can draw a line there too. The main verb in the sentence below is *worked*:

Incorrect:
The prohibition of marijuana and the laws in place for it | *do not* and | *have never* | worked.
Test:
The prohibition of marijuana and the laws in place for it | *do not* . . . worked and *have never* worked.
Correct:
The prohibition of marijuana and the laws in place for it *do not* **work** and *have never* **worked**.

Sometimes compound phrases ending in prepositions don't line up with what follows. Here is an example of a compound in which the words that follow the verbs don't line up with the object. Again, the presence of a coordinating conjunction can alert you to these tricky kinds of compounds:

Incorrect:
Most people under thirty *are familiar or have heard of* the rapper Eminem.
Correct:
Most people under thirty | *are familiar with or* | *have heard of* | the rapper Eminem.

Incorrect:
"We have to change our production methods to make sure the products we sell are *as good or better as* any in the world," said the Minister of Agriculture.
Correct:
"We have to change our production methods to make sure the products we sell are | *as good as* | or *better as than* | any in the world," said the Minister of Agriculture.

Correlative Conjunctions

A specific kind of compound involves correlative conjunctions. These are joiners that work in pairs (*either . . . or, neither . . . nor, both . . . and, not . . . but, not only . . . but also*). Logically, the part of speech that follows the first half of the compound should also follow the second half. It might be helpful to draw a line after each conjunction:

> *Incorrect*:
> A college diploma today is an investment *not only* | in students' financial resources *but also* | their time.

What follows *not only* is a prepositional phrase that begins with *in*; therefore, a prepositional phrase, not just a noun (*time*), must follow the second member of the pair:

> A college diploma today is an investment *not only in* students' financial resources *but also in* their time.

> *Incorrect*:
> The lack of classroom availability means *either* constructing new buildings *or* lower the number of students accepted into programs.
> *Correct*:
> The lack of classroom availability means *either constructing* new buildings *or lowering* the number of students accepted into programs.

Comparisons

Under Compounds we looked at comparisons as compound structures requiring parallelism. However, sometimes faulty comparisons have less to do with grammar than with logic.

Because comparisons are always made between one thing and another thing, both these elements must be fully expressed for the comparison to be complete. Often either the comparison is left incomplete or the terms being compared are incompatible; that is, they cannot be compared because there is no basis for comparison. Note: *Than* is the word for comparisons, not the adverb related to time, *then*. Other words and phrases can also signal comparisons: *compared to, similar (to), different (from), as, like,* etc.

You need to ask if the two parts of a comparison are grammatically parallel, if both parts of the comparison are fully expressed, and if the two objects of the comparison can logically be compared. In this sentence, the reader is left to assume whom males are being compared to.

> *Incomplete*:
> An unfortunate stereotype is that males are more scientific and less intuitive.
> *Complete*:
> An unfortunate stereotype is that males are more scientific and less intuitive *than females*.

> *Incompatible*:
> I have found that students are less judgmental at university compared to high school.

You can ask what precisely is being compared to what and if the comparison is logical; in this case, the writer is comparing a perceived trait of *students* at university to . . . high school. People must be compared to people.

Compatible:

I have found that people are less judgmental at university than they are at high school.

The two sides of the comparison are now complete and compatible.

Incompatible:

In the study, men's running times were recorded for 30 more years than women.

What is being compared here? Are the terms comparable? The writer is comparing running times (for men) to women.

Compatible:

In the study, men's running times were recorded for 30 more years than women's times.

Exercise 16.12

In the word groups that follow, there are three or four main points related to a topic. Build parallel structures in thesis statements for each topic. Make whatever changes are necessary to achieve parallelism and use whatever order of points seems natural.

Topic 1: Why I like toe socks:

- warm and comfortable
- they are the latest fashion in socks
- come in many colours and designs

Topic 2: The advantages of yoga:

- to relax and reduce stress
- to exercise
- also can meet people in yoga classes

Topic 3: The importance of computers to students:

- they provide entertainment
- cutting down on homework time is important
- you can obtain a wealth of information quickly

Topic 4: Living with roommates:

- they can create a lot of mess
- invade your personal space
- you can talk to them about your problems

Topic 5: The benefits of coffee:

- coffee helps you wake up
- its rich, satisfying flavour
- it improves your concentration

Topic 6: The comparison of two recreational drugs:

- their possible dangerous side effects
- who uses them
- the effects they produce in the user

Topic 7: The facts about organically grown food:

- the way organically grown food is farmed
- the cost of these kinds of foods
- their nutritional value

Topic 8: The advantages of home birthing:

- allows the parents to maintain control over their surroundings
- a positive and friendly place for the child to be born
- is as safe as a hospital birth if common sense is used

Topic 9: School uniforms are beneficial:

- promote school identity and school pride
- they save parents money and hassle
- reduce the pressure of students to conform to the latest fashions
- to make it easier for school authorities to enforce discipline

Topic 10: The legalization of marijuana:

- it is less addictive than some other illegal drugs
- the Canadian government has already made it legal under certain circumstances
- governments could increase their revenue by selling it
- making it legal would reduce crime since people wouldn't have to obtain it illegally

Exercise 16.13

The sentences below contain parallelism errors. Identify the kind of error (series, compounds, correlative conjunctions, or comparisons) and fix the errors.

1. A good journalist is inquisitive, persistent, and must be a good listener.
2. Music can directly affect your thoughts, emotions, and how you feel.
3. In this essay, I will be looking and writing about the role of women in the military.
4. Tiddlywinks is not only a game of considerable skill but also strategy.
5. Television can affect children in a variety of negative ways since children often lack judgment, are naturally curious, and easily influenced.

6. There are three main qualities that a leader must possess: a leader must be enthusiastic, organized, and have creativity.

7. Aman never has and never will be good at golf.

8. She was not only the best teacher I have ever had, but also I was impressed by her modesty.

9. Tremors may occur on either or both sides of the body.

10. There are many reasons why people choose to or enjoy watching television.

After you've checked your answers, complete the exercise by doing questions 11–25.

11. A recent study has found that Caucasian children acquire self-awareness at an earlier age than other ethnic groups.

12. Alyssa's trip to London involved such pleasures as Buckingham Palace, feeding the pigeons, visiting her relatives, and those quaint London accents.

13. I enjoyed watching *The Last Samurai*, *The Last of the Mohicans*, and *Braveheart* was also enjoyable.

14. I want to emphasize that my work as MP in this riding has not, and will not, be affected by political developments.

15. When Jim has the choice of either jumping or to stay on the doomed ship, he chooses to jump.

16. Physical education teaches children not only to work well together but also patience and discipline.

17. Smoking should be banned because it raises health-care costs, physically harms both smokers and non-smokers, and because cigarette production damages the environment.

18. Users of ecstasy report feeling euphoric, energized, intensified pleasure, and increased sensory awareness.

19. What made Beethoven's music different from other composers was his expressive style.

20. Recent studies suggest that wellness depends on three main factors: feeling good about yourself, your everyday eating habits, and being comfortably active.

21. Although two very different American writers, Nathaniel Hawthorne's and Mark Twain's works are nevertheless similar in many ways.

22. Differing viewpoints in a work of fiction not only add conflict, but they can also reveal differences in characters' ages, genders, and upbringings.

23. Those who exercise regularly show a decrease in anxiety, depression, fatigue, and elevated vigour.

24. In Sonnet 130, Shakespeare stresses the reality of his mistress rather than portraying her as something she is not.

25. According to a recent poll, the premier has more support among college students than the general public.

Exercise 16.14

The following five paragraphs contain various errors that have been discussed in Chapters 14–16. Identify the errors indicated and then make corrections.

1. Identify and correct the following:

    a)   comma splice

    b)   one comma use error

    c)   error in pronoun case

    d)   broad pronoun reference

    e)   missing pronoun antecedent

    f)   two pronoun–antecedent agreement errors

    g)   apostrophe omitted

    h)   ambiguous pronoun reference

    i)   failure to use gender-neutral language

    In my family, my father and sister play video games as much as me. They have become very complex, and can even improve problem-solving in children. By progressing through increasing difficulty levels, it can help childrens thought processes. On the one hand, if the child goes straight to the hardest setting, they may feel discouraged, on the other, if the child tries to systematically progress through increasing levels, they can learn the mechanics of the game step by step. This can help in the study of math, as the child may learn to persevere until he finds the solution.

2. Identify and correct the following:

    a)   comma error

    b)   subject–verb agreement error

    c)   fragment

    d)   two parallelism errors

    e)   misplaced modifier

    f)   dangling modifier

    g)   pronoun inconsistency

    h)   comma splice

    Having a job and earning one's livelihood is a necessary goal in life, it is one of the reasons you acquire an education. At the place where I work however, many people come in expecting to find a job lacking presentation skills. Many are poorly dressed, do not know how to behave, and they may not speak grammatically. Untidy, disorganized, and unprepared, I still have to match them with a prospective employer. They lack the skills to present themselves to others and knowing what to do in public. Although they may be highly intelligent people.

3. Identify and correct the following:

   a) comma splice

   b) misplaced comma

   c) parallelism error

   d) two apostrophes omitted

   e) fragment

   f) two pronoun–antecedent agreement errors

   Logic can be defined as "the science of the formation and application of a general notion." Meaning that logic is apt to vary according to ones way of seeing certain things as important. A vegetarians logic, asserts that it is completely unnecessary—not to mention cruel—to eat animals in our day and age. Today's meat eater also has their logic. For them, meat is to be enjoyed, the taste of the food and the social interaction involved is to be cherished. We need to allow time in our busy lives to eat more and feeling guilty about it less.

4. Identify and correct the following:

   a) four comma errors

   b) one error in use of a semicolon

   c) comma splice

   d) pronoun case error

   e) error in apostrophe use

   f) dangling modifier

   The Myers-Briggs personality test is based on the work of Swiss psychologist, Carl Jung, and two Americans; Isabel Briggs Myers, and her mother Katharine C. Briggs. Myers developed the tests, and tried them out on thousands of schoolchildren; she wanted to see how the test results would correlate with vocation. Consisting of a series of questions requiring a yes or no response, she tested a group of medical students, who she followed up on 12 years later and who confirmed the test's validity. Variations of Myer's test are sometimes given by employers today, however, the results should not be the sole means for a hiring decision.

5. Identify and correct the following:

   a) comma splice

   b) one other comma error (missing or misplaced)

   c) one punctuation error other than comma

   d) parallelism error

   e) two apostrophe errors

   f) subject–verb agreement error

   g) pronoun–antecedent agreement error

   h) broad pronoun reference error

According to the principle's of Buddhism, neither sensual pleasures nor self-mortification bring about enlightenment, instead, the "Middle Way" is the path between these extremes; this can be understood through the "Four Noble Truths." These truths are: the truths of suffering, of the origins of suffering, of the cessation of suffering, and finding the path to end suffering. The Buddhas teaching asks each individual to examine their own conscience, and to come to a conclusion about the nature of truth.

Exercise 16.15

Identify then correct the error(s) in each sentence. If there is more than one error, choose the "more than one error" option.

1. Written through the eyes of a young boy, one can see the perspective of the indigenous peoples.

    a) dangling modifier

    b) misplaced modifier

    c) pronoun–antecedent agreement

    d) comma error

2. The daily stresses of students, such as project or assignment due dates, teaches you to manage your time wisely.

    a) subject–verb agreement

    b) pronoun inconsistency

    c) more than one error

    d) parallelism

3. Parents sometimes push their children so hard to excel that they lose interest altogether.

    a) error in use of colon

    b) pronoun reference error

    c) more than one error

    d) subject–verb agreement

4. My roommate thinks it would be better for society, if all drugs were decriminalized.

    a) dangling modifier

    b) none of the above

    c) comma error

    d) subject–verb agreement error

5. Contributors to homelessness include the lack of good-paying jobs, increasingly large families and, probably the most important factor, which is the cost of living in a large city.

   a) dangling modifier

   b) more than one error

   c) comma error

   d) parallelism error

6. One of the most tragic events of the twentieth century. The detonation of the atomic bomb over Hiroshima.

   a) sentence fragment

   b) comma splice

   c) pronoun reference

   d) none of the above

7. With the increasing media focus in the 1980s on the plight of homeless women, came the need for more research, unfortunately, this research was not comprehensive.

   a) comma splice

   b) more than one error

   c) pronoun–antecedent agreement

   d) parallelism error

8. Optometrists have been reshaping the cornea in order to correct vision for 50 years.

   a) parallelism error

   b) error in comma use

   c) misplaced modifier

   d) subject–verb agreement error

9. Information on airlines,currency exchange, and other passenger services are available on this website.

   a) subject–verb agreement

   b) comma error

   c) more than one error

   d) run-on sentence

10. Many people are intrigued by the lives movie and TV heroes seem to live; these viewers tending to be teenagers.

   a) more than one error

   b) error in semicolon use

   c) parallelism error

   d) sentence fragment

Exercise 16.16

Identify the error (a, b, c, or d) and correct it in the sentence (there is one error in each sentence).

1. Anorexia <u>starts</u> when <u>a person</u> decides to take control over <u>their</u> <u>body</u> weight.
          a)   b)   c)   d)

2. There <u>are</u> three types of turbine engines used in aircraft<u>;</u> the <u>turbojet</u>, the
        a)   b)   c)
   turbofan<u>,</u> and the turboprop.
          d)

3. Work <u>songs</u> and street <u>vendors</u> <u>cries</u> <u>are</u> examples of traditional African-American
           a)   b)   c)   d)
   music styles.

4. <u>Reforms</u> of the UN Security Council <u>include</u> abolishing the veto or <u>to extend</u> the
    a)   b)   c)
   Council beyond the <u>current five</u> members.
               d)

5. Results from a recent study <u>showed that</u> patients <u>suffering from</u> osteoarthritis,
                        a)   b)
   <u>who listened to music for twenty minutes each day,</u> reported <u>a 66 per cent</u> reduc-
                    c)   d)
   tion in their perception of pain.

6. As a <u>known</u> anarchist<u>,</u> <u>Chomsky's views</u> <u>have been</u> much debated.
        a)   b)   c)   d)

7. The brain of <u>a drug addict</u> <u>is</u> physically <u>different from</u> <u>a non-addict</u>.
           a)   b)   c)   d)

8. The tobacco in cigarettes is not <u>the only</u> problem<u>,</u> <u>cigarettes</u> contain many danger-
                              a)   b)   c)
   ous chemicals <u>as well</u>.
          d)

9. By teaching <u>today's</u> youth safe and healthy approaches to sexuality<u>,</u> <u>it</u> will elevate
           a)   b)c)
   <u>their</u> self-esteem.
    d)

10. Holly Hunter, the actress <u>who</u> <u>I</u> most admire<u>,</u> appeared in several <u>award-winning</u>
                            a) b)   c)   d)
    movies.

Chapter Review Questions

1. How do you find the subject of the sentence?
2. Do prepositional phrases that follow a subject affect the verb form?
3. What is a compound subject? How is a verb form affected by a compound subject?
4. When is a collective noun followed by a plural verb form?
5. Are most indefinite pronouns considered singular or plural? Why?
6. What are the three situations that cause most subject–verb agreement errors?
7. What is the antecedent of a pronoun?
8. Why is the sentence "One should always finish their homework" incorrect?
9. How can you check for pronoun–antecedent errors?
10. What are the four kinds of pronoun reference errors?
11. When is it correct to use "who" in a sentence or clause? When would the use of "whom" be correct?
12. What are misplaced modifiers? Give an example.
13. What are dangling modifiers? Give an example.
14. What is parallelism and why is it important?
15. What is a compound?

17

Achieving Clarity and Depth in Your Writing

In this chapter, you will learn

- the importance of clarity in all your writing
- strategies for cutting unneeded words and phrases
- ways to avoid constructions, including the passive, that weaken your sentence
- the value of using direct and forceful language
- the difference between formal and informal diction
- strategies to introduce variety and emphasis
- successful proofreading techniques

- a format for presenting your essay
- the correct usage of confusing words

Many beginning writers believe that once they have completed their draft, their essay is ready to be turned in. Unfortunately, these students forget about a crucial stage of essay writing—revision. Papers can always be revised for clarity, precision, and concision. This chapter will help you create stronger essays that are clear, direct, and reader-focused.

◎ Effective Style: Clarity

What is style? If you have written a research essay, you will know that the word *style* is applied to documentation formats, such as the rules for citing sources using MLA or APA guidelines. Style is also a term applied to individual writers—say, a dense, sophisticated style versus a spare, terse style. Although every writer has a unique writing style, when you are writing factually with a specific purpose for a specific audience, you need to put *clarity* above your personal writing style. More than a half-century ago, Wendell Johnson stressed its importance:

> For writing to be effective . . . it may or may not be grammatically correct, but it must be both clear and valid. It can be clear without having validity, but if it is unclear its validity cannot well be determined. . . . We ask of the writer, "What do you mean?" before we ask, "How do you know?" Until we reach agreement as to precisely what he is writing about, we cannot possibly reach agreement as to whether, or in what degree, his statements are true.
>
> —Wendell Johnson, "You Can't Write Writing"

Clarity depends on various factors. If you were writing for a general audience on a specialized topic and used words that were unfamiliar to most readers, you would not be writing clearly, though a specialist might understand you. Word choice and level of language, then, are important factors in clear and effective writing. But they are not the only factors discussed in this chapter.

The "art" of writing clearly is really not an art or talent at all; it is the result of hard work and attention to detail. Few writers—experienced or inexperienced— write clearly without making several revisions. Much of the revising process, in fact, consists in making the language reflect the thought behind it.

One of the differences between experienced and inexperienced writers is that the former expect to spend much of their time revising their prose; they ask not just *Is this clear*? but also *Can this be put more clearly?* Student writers should ask themselves the second question, too. If the answer is "yes" or "maybe," try paraphrasing it (putting it in other words). Can you do this easily? Does your paraphrase express the point more clearly? When you paraphrase something you've written, you often find that the second version is closer to what you intended to say.

When you are writing for an audience, it is not enough that *you* understand your ideas. *Your readers* need to understand what is being written. Therefore, revise your work with this thought in mind.

What, then, is clear writing? Writing that is clear is grammatical, concise, direct, precise, and specific. When you revise, you can ask yourself not just *Is the writing clear?* but also the following questions:

- *Is it grammatical*? Chapters 14–16 have provided most of the information you need to write understandable, grammatically correct sentences.

The "art" of writing clearly is really not an art or talent at all; it is the result of hard work and attention to detail. Few writers—experienced or inexperienced—write clearly without making several revisions. Much of the revising process, in fact, consists in making the language reflect the thought behind it.

When you are writing for an audience, it is not enough that *you* understand your ideas. *Your readers* need to understand what is being written. Therefore, revise your work with this thought in mind.

Writing that is clear is grammatical, concise, direct, precise, and specific.

- *Is it concise?* Do you use as many words as you need and no more than you have to? Have you used basic words and simple constructions that reflect what you want to say?
- *Is it direct?* Have you used straightforward language and avoided **circumlocutions**? Is the structure of your sentences as simple as possible given the complexity of the point you are trying to express?
- *Is it precise?* Does it say exactly what you want it to say? When you are writing for a reader, *almost* or *close enough* is *not* enough. Would another word or phrase more accurately reflect your thought?
- *Is it specific?* Is it as detailed as it needs to be? Is it definitive and concrete—not vague or abstract?

Writers who carefully work to make their writing more grammatical, concise, direct, precise, and specific will likely produce an essay that is clear. However, experienced writers aim also for forceful writing. To these ends, they may introduce variety and emphasis in their writing.

Circumlocution, meaning "speak around," refers to using more words than necessary to express an idea.

Exercise 17.1

The following is a paragraph from an argumentative essay. Try to find examples that illustrate stylistic problems summarized above. How could the writer be more concise, direct, precise, and specific?

There are more humane ways to treat veal cows than are currently practised today. There was a resolution passed by the American Veal Association that recommends action by the year 2010. There have also been numerous animal rights organizations that have been working for the rights of these cows for years. You can help by doing simple things such as just not buying veal or not ordering it when you go out. These calves are treated very poorly for the duration of their incredibly short lifetimes. It is true that these calves are raised to be slaughtered, but that is not a legitimate excuse for treating them with a total lack of consideration.

Exercise 17.2

Go to the student essay in Chapter 11, "The Virtual Life: An Overview of the Effects of MMORPGS on Individuals and Countries." Read through the essay and find examples showing how the writer addressed his audience. Also, note any places where the writer used variety in his sentences or paragraphs to make his essay more interesting and his points more forceful.

Why should so much effort be devoted to concise and direct writing? For one thing, such writing will be easy to follow and will keep the reader's interest. Unnecessary repetition and other kinds of clutter may cause a point to lose its sharpness. Think about a novel that was filled with what you considered unnecessary details. How interested were you in the book? If you were like most readers, you probably stopped reading and moved on to another, more interesting book. Redundancy and unnecessary detail cause the same reaction in your readers.

Just as concise and direct writing makes you seem reliable, indirect writing may give the impression that you lack confidence in what you're saying, that you are just trying to impress the reader, or that you are trying to use more words to reach a word limit. Finally, when you use more words than you have to or express yourself in a roundabout way, you increase the odds of making grammatical and mechanical errors.

> When you use more words than you have to or express yourself in a roundabout way, you increase the odds of making grammatical and mechanical errors.

Cutting for Conciseness

To achieve conciseness, cut what is inessential. How do you determine what is unnecessary? The simple test is whether you can leave something out without changing the meaning and the effectiveness of your statement.

Many common stylistic patterns that student writers adopt, especially in their early drafts, are described below under specific categories. Your instructor may indicate problems with conciseness by putting parentheses around what is unneeded or by writing "wordy" or "verbose" in the margin. You should not think of this as criticism so much as advice directing you to more readable writing.

Student writers may also unconsciously shift the stress away from the main nouns and verbs—where it should lie. Certainly it is not always wrong to use two of the same parts of speech consecutively, and to banish all passive constructions would unreasonably limit writers. The pages that follow are intended as guidelines, strategies to consider as you revise your essay.

Doubling Up: The Noah's Ark Syndrome

Writers sometimes suffer from "double vision." When they write, two words automatically pop up: two verbs, two nouns, two adjectives, or two adverbs. Experienced editors offer this formula: one + one = one-half. In other words, when you use two words when one is enough, you are halving the impact of that one word. When you do choose to use two of the same parts of speech, ensure that the two words don't convey the same thing.

> The administrative officer came up with an ~~original~~, innovative suggestion for cost-cutting. (Anything innovative is bound to be original.)

> The event will be held at ~~various~~ different venues.

Ensure that one of the words doesn't include the meaning of the other, as in the second sentence example. This applies to phrases with words that

If a second noun, verb, adjective, or adverb doesn't make your meaning clearer, delete it.

are unnecessary because the meaning of the phrase can be understood without them. Be especially wary of verb–adverb combinations; ensure that the adverb is necessary.

The airport was ~~intentionally~~ designed for larger aircraft. (Can a design be unintentional?)

She ~~successfully~~ accomplished what she had set out to do. (The word *accomplished* implies success.)

Here are some common verb–adverb pairings and other combinations that usually are redundant:

combine/join (together)	unite (as one)
fill (completely)	finish (entirely)
refer/return/revert (back) to	emphasize/stress (strongly)
examine (closely)	sob (uncontrollably)
hurry (quickly)	drawl (lazily)
(anxiously) fear	(suddenly) interrupt
(totally) eradicate/devastate	(eventually) evolve (over time)
(strictly) forbid	dwindle (down)
rely/depend (heavily) on	praise (in favour of)
(harshly) condemn	gaze (steadily)
protest (against)	ponder (thoughtfully)
(symbolically) represent	plan (ahead)
vanish (without a trace)	estimate/approximate (roughly)
descend (down)	gather/assemble (together)
climb (up)	dominate (over)
(clearly) articulate	(carefully) consider
(successfully) prove	progress (forward/onwards)
(completely) surround	(better/further) enhance

Be wary, too, of such repetitive adjective–noun pairings as the following:

powerful blast	sharp needle
fiery blaze	terrible tragedy
dead carcass	positive benefits
advance warning	timeless classic
past memory	future plan
mutual agreement	brief encapsulation
total abstinence	knowledgeable specialist
new beginning	

Redundancies are evident in such familiar phrases as *end result, end product, consensus of opinion, this point in time, time frame, time period, time span, in actual fact, years of age, etc.*

Unnecessary nouns are redundant. These nouns steal the thunder from other parts of speech, including other nouns and verbs.

Exercise 17.3

Listen to your favourite radio station or watch one of your favourite TV shows. Pay attention to the language used by the advertisers and the announcers or actors. How often did you hear examples of "doubling up?" Write down some of the most frequent examples and be prepared to share these with the class.

1. The world of politics demands that you kowtow to the ineptitude of others.
2. The efforts of conservationists in the fields of ecology and biodiversity are leading to renewed efforts to save old-growth forests.

In each sentence above, the most important noun has been displaced by a weaker noun. In sentence 1, we are not really talking about a *world*, but about *politics*. In sentence 2, the noun *fields* is redundant because *ecology* and *biodiversity* are fields of study.

Phony Phrases

Phony phrases are redundant prepositional phrases. Look for them after verbs and nouns.

> *Unnecessary*:
> For now, the patient's kidneys are functioning *at a normal level.*
> *Better:*
> For now, the patient's kidneys are functioning *normally.*

The prepositional phrase *at a normal level* can be replaced by the adverb *normally*.

Here the phony phrase is introduced by the preposition *for*:

> The bill was legislated in 1995 *for a brief period of time.*
> *Better:*
> The bill was *briefly* legislated in 1995.

A cluster of non-specific nouns are connected to phony phrases beginning with *on, to,* or other prepositions. Watch for prepositional phrases that include *level, scale, basis, degree,* and *extent,* for example, *on/at the international level, on a regular basis, on the larger scale, to a great/considerable degree/extent.* The phrase likely can be replaced by an appropriate adverb.

> If you can sum up a prepositional phrase by a one-word adverb or adjective, use the one-word modifier.

> Jindra checks her answering machine *on a regular basis.*
> *Better:*
> Jindra checks her answering machine *regularly.*

Relative clauses are adjectival and may sometimes be replaced by a corresponding adjective preceding the noun.

Most body-builders follow a strict diet that is high in protein.

[T]hat is high in protein is a relative (adjectival) clause modifying *diet*.

Most body-builders follow a strict, high-protein diet.

The Small but Not-So-Beautiful

Even small words, such as prepositions and articles, may be omitted. Writers may think they make an ordinary phrase sound just a little bit more impressive. In the examples below, parentheses indicate words that can be omitted:

He was (the) last out (of) the door.
(The) taking (of) life can never be condoned.

Look at the following passage and consider what can be deleted—big words and small—without changing the meaning of the sentence:

The city of Toronto has one of the most ethnically diverse of cultures in all of North America. The city has a population of 4,700,000 people, and is also the home of a variety of sports teams that play in professional leagues.

If you can delete "clutter words" like *of* or *that*, do so.

The word *that* can be used as a pronoun (demonstrative and relative), an adjective, and a subordinating conjunction. It can often be omitted if the subject of the second clause introduced by *that* is different from the subject of the preceding clause. By methodically checking your first draft for unnecessary *thats*, you can often improve sentence flow.

I thought (that) Silas was going to go to the same school (that) his brother went to.

Unravel the meaning of the following statement:

It's certain that that "that" that that person used was wrong.

Those Un-Intensives

Overused intensives include the following: absolutely, actually, assuredly, certainly, clearly, completely, considerably, definitely, effectively, extremely, fundamentally, highly, in fact, incredibly, inevitably, indeed, interestingly, markedly, naturally, of course, particularly, significantly, surely, totally, utterly, very

Other overused qualifiers include the following: apparently, arguably, basically, essentially, generally, hopefully, in effect, in general, kind of, overall, perhaps, quite, rather, relatively, seemingly, somewhat, sort of, virtually

An *intensive* is a word or phrase that adds emphasis to the word or expression it modifies but has little meaning on its own. In all levels of formal writing, intensives should be avoided if they do not truly add emphasis. The intensives in the following sentence are unneeded:

She is ~~certainly~~ a(n) ~~very~~ impressive speaker.

Words like *certainly* and *very* have been overused and may add nothing to the sentence. Many intensives are adverbs modifying verbs or adjectives. In some instances, you can simply use a stronger verb in place of a weak verb and an intensive, or a stronger adjective in place of the intensive plus a weak adjective; or, a better option may be to get rid of the intensive, as in *it was a ~~very~~ unique idea.*

He was very grateful for his warm reception.
He was gratified by his warm reception. *OR* He appreciated his warm reception.

Words and prepositional phrases that may clutter:

aforementioned	in accordance with	notwithstanding the fact
amidst	in comparison to	that
amongst	in conjunction with	oftentimes
analogous to	in connection with	pertaining to
as a result of	in reference to	so as to
as to	in regard(s) to	subsequent to
at this point in time	in terms of	the majority of
cognizant of	in the final analysis	thusly
consequent to	in view of the fact	whether or not
despite the fact that	that	whilst
due to the fact that	in as much as	with regard(s) to
each and every	irregardless	with respect to

> Instead of using adverbs like *very*, *highly*, *really*, or *extremely* before adjectives, see if you can find a stronger adjective or simply delete the adverb.

Writing Directly

Writing should get straight to the point. Indirect writing stresses the less important parts of the sentence. Passive constructions are indirect because they displace the subject, though they may be acceptable or even preferable when you do not want to stress the subject or if the exact subject is unknown.

Passive Constructions: The Lazy Subject

In a passive construction, the subject of the sentence is *not* doing the action. Ordinarily, the subject *is* acting, as in the following:

Ezra placed the book on the table.

To change the sentence so that the object becomes the (non-active) subject requires changing the word order and adding words:

The book was placed on the table by Ezra.

> In a passive construction, the subject of the sentence is not doing the action. Instead, a less important word is placed at the beginning of the sentence.

Note the differences between these two sentences. The direct object, "book," has become the subject, and the original subject, "Ezra," is now at the end of the sentence, the object of the preposition "by." The verb form has changed too. The sentence now has a subject that is acted on rather than itself acting. The passive

> ## Exercise 17.4
>
> Go to your school's database and find some annual reports distributed by companies. See if you can find any examples of the cluttered language listed above or examples of doubling up mentioned earlier.

subject sentence requires more words to provide the same information. Effective, direct English is geared towards the *active*, not the passive, voice.

The passive voice uses a form of the verb *to be* followed by a past participle. If the actor is named, it will be the object of a prepositional phrase that begins with *by*. Although you can identify the passive by the verb forms that compose it—the past, present, or future form of *to be* plus a past participle—don't confuse the identifying verb forms of the passive with a construction in which a form of the verb *to be* is used along with the past participle as a predicate adjective. For example, in the following sentence, the subjects are clearly the actors; you can't add the preposition *by* after *determined* or after *pleased*. This sentence uses an active construction:

Dana was determined to succeed at any cost; I am pleased to see him succeed.

In the following sentence, there are three indicators of a passive construction:

The door was opened by a tall, sinister man.

1. The subject (*door*) is not doing the action expressed by the verb *open*;
2. The preposition *by* precedes the actor (*man*);
3. The simple past of *to be* combines with the past participle of the main verb to form the passive voice of the verb.

To change a passive to an active construction,

1. Move the subject so that it follows the verb as the direct object;
2. Move the object of the preposition *by*, the actor, to the beginning of the sentence/clause to replace the passive subject;
3. Get rid of the identifying passive forms of the verb and the preposition *by*.

> A fast way to change a passive into an active construction is to move the noun or pronoun that follows *by* to the beginning of the sentence. The other changes will be easier to see once you've done this.

A tall, sinister man ~~was~~ opened the door ~~by~~.

Here's a slightly more complicated example:

Passive:
The special commission was informed of its mandate by a superior court judge last Monday.
Active:
A superior court judge informed the special commission of its mandate last Monday.

In its active form, the sentence contains fewer words, and the thought is expressed more directly. As a general rule, *don't use the passive voice if the active will serve*. However, these are times when the passive is acceptable or is even the better choice:

1. When the subject isn't known or is so well known it doesn't matter.

    > Pierre Trudeau was first elected prime minister in 1968.

    It is unnecessary to mention that *the voters* or *the electorate* elected him.

2. When passivity is implied, or if the context makes it seem natural to stress the receiver of the action.

    > When a cyclist completes a hard workout, massages are usually performed on the affected muscles.

    In this sentence, the massages are more important than the person giving them.

> *Acceptable passive*:
> The woman was kidnapped and held hostage by a band of thugs.
> *Questionable passive*:
> Several of the thugs were picked out of a line-up by the woman.

In the first sentence, the woman obviously is the passive recipient of the action of the thugs; in the second sentence, she is doing the action. Therefore, in the second sentence, the active is preferred:

> *Active*:
> The woman picked several of the thugs out of a line-up.

Occasionally, you may choose the passive voice because the rhythm of the sentence requires it, or because it is rhetorically effective.

> The books obviously had been arranged by a near-sighted librarian.

In this sentence, the librarian's near-sightedness is important; the placement of the adjective near the end of the sentence gives it emphasis.

There are cases in academic writing, especially in the sciences, in which it is unnecessary to mention the author of a study or the researcher; the passive may be used to stress the object of the study or the method of research.

> Through case studies, a comparison of two common methods for treating depression will be made.

In the following examples from academic writing, the passive is preferred either because the actor doesn't matter or because the writer wants to stress the receiver of the action:

> In 1891 the science of embryology was shaken by the work of the cosmopolitan German biologist and vitalist philosopher Hans Driesch (Bowring, 2004, p. 401).

> The emergence of second-hand smoke (SHS) [as a cancer hazard] has been offered as a viable explanation for the increased enactment of local smoking restrictions (Asbridge, 2003, p. 13).

> Don't use a passive construction unless you want to deemphasize the actor (active subject). Passive constructions stress the noun that is acted upon.

Exercise 17.5

The following sentences use passive constructions. Determine which are appropriate and which are inappropriate in the passive voice. Change unnecessary uses of the passive voice to form active constructions. (In some sentences, the actor or "active" subject is not part of the sentence, so you may have to add it to the sentence (see example sentence below). Be prepared to justify your decisions to leave some sentences as passive constructions.

Example: *Passive*:　The suspect's behaviour had been watched for more than one month.

The suspect's behaviour had been watched [by the police] for more than one month.

Active:　The police had watched the suspect's behaviour for more than one month.

Decision:　Leave as passive because "suspect's behaviour" is more important to the meaning than "the police."

1. I was given two choices by my landlord: pay up or get out.

2. It was reported that more than 1000 people were left homeless by recent flooding.

3. The manager's protest was heard by the fairness committee.

4. The tree was buffeted by the wind, which tore off one of its lower branches.

5. Beethoven's Third Symphony, *The Eroica*, originally was dedicated to Napoleon, but the dedication was erased after Napoleon proclaimed himself emperor.

6. Education needs to be seen by the government as the number one priority.

7. Many acts of self-deception were committed by Bertha, the protagonist of "Bliss."

8. The belief in a powerful and infallible Creator is commonly held today.

9. Poverty in First Nations communities must be addressed by the federal, provincial, and First Nations' governments.

10. There are two ways of looking at rights-based ethics that were put forward by Emanuel Kant.

Black Hole Constructions

Inappropriately passive constructions not only use too many words but also place the stress where it doesn't belong, weakening the entire sentence. Other indirect constructions can also weaken a sentence. You can consider them the black holes of writing: they swallow up the substance of the sentence.

1. *It was. . . .*

It was Mary Shelley who wrote *Frankenstein* in 1816.

Avoid starting sentences with "It is. . ." or "There are" types of constructions. Using these weak beginnings may make your reader lose interest.

As simple as this sentence is, it begins weakly by displacing the logical subject, *Mary Shelley*, and substituting *It was*. The sentence is stronger and more direct when the most important noun is made the subject:

> Mary Shelley wrote *Frankenstein* in 1816.

If a relative pronoun (who, which, or that) follows the displaced subject, consider getting rid of the "empty" subject (*It was*, *There is*, *Here is*) and the relative pronoun to make the statement more direct and concise. Occasionally, you may want to use this and similar constructions for rhetorical effect. In such cases, emphasis, rather than directness, may determine your choice.

> *Unnecessary*:
> There are a variety of different strategies that you can use to reduce excess verbiage in your writing.
> *Better*:
> You can use various strategies to reduce verbiage in your writing.

2. *one of*—a redundancy to be avoided:

> *Poor*:
> The path you have chosen is one of danger and uncertainty.
> *Better*:
> The path you have chosen is dangerous and uncertain.
> You have chosen a dangerous, uncertain path.

3. *the reason . . . is because*, which is both illogical and redundant:

> *Incorrect*:
> The reason Jessica is lucky is because she has a horseshoe on her door.
> *Correct*:
> Jessica is lucky because she has a horseshoe on her door.

Numbing Nouns

Writers sometimes fall into the habit of using a weak verb and a corresponding noun rather than a verb that directly expresses the meaning. In these cases, a weak verb phrase replaces the more direct option:

1. I *had a meeting* with my staff, and I am now asking you to *provide a list* of all your clients.

2. Inexperienced writers *have a tendency* to be wordy.

3. She *made changes* to the document, *making clear* what was ambiguous.

4. Sam *offered comfort* to Amanda, who *received a failing grade* on her essay.

5. Canada *made a significant contribution* to the war effort in France and Belgium.

> Notice how many sentences in the sample paragraph in Exercise 17.1 contain weak openings. They affect the entire paragraph, making it hard to read.

> Weak verb + noun constructions begin with common verbs like *have*, *make*, or *take* and follow with a noun object, which can usually be made into a strong verb.

Stronger constructions:

1.   I *met* with my staff, and now ask you *to list* all your clients.

2.   Inexperienced writers *tend* to be wordy.

3.   She *changed* the document, *clarifying* ambiguities.

4.   Sam *comforted* Amanda, who *had failed* her essay.

5.   Canada *contributed significantly* to the war effort in France and Belgium.

Note: in the weak phrase *has an effect on*, where *has* is the verb and effect is the noun, remember that the corresponding verb form is *affect*.

Global warming *affects* shifting major weather patterns. Its *effects* are being widely felt throughout the globe.

> Avoid a succession of long words if shorter, basic words can do the job equally well.

Nouns that pile up in a sentence can create a numbing effect. This is especially true with nominals, nouns formed from verbs. There is nothing wrong with using a polysyllabic noun formed from a verb—unless a more concise and direct alternative exists.

Clear expression in literary essays is sometimes a challenge to students due to their lack of familiarity with terms or to the temptation to make a point sound complex and, thereby, significant.

The conflict between Billy and Claggart ultimately serves as a device in the interruption of the reader's attempts at a coherent interpretation of the novel as an ideological message. In addition to problematizing definitive interpretations, this technique effectively secures a lasting relevance for the novel.

The thought in these sentences can be expressed more directly and clearly by omitting words and reducing the number of nominals.

The conflict between Billy and Claggart challenges a coherent ideological reading of the novel, making definitive readings difficult and ensuring the novel's relevance.

Table 17.1	Verb, Nominal, Example	
VERB	**NOMINAL**	**EXAMPLE**
accumulate	accumulation	The (accumulation of) evidence is overwhelming.
classify	classification	We will now proceed with the classification of Vertebrata; we will now classify Vertebrata.
intend install	intention installation	Our intention is to complete the installation of the new system this month; we plan to finish installing the new system this month.

Writing in academic journals may also be weakened by too many nominals, as this Internet example, featured in a bad writing contest, illustrates:

> It is the moment of non-construction, disclosing the absentation of actuality from the concept in part through its invitation to emphasize, in reading, the helplessness—rather than the will to power of its fall into conceptuality. (Paul Fry *A Defense of Poetry*, 1995)

Euphemisms

Many ancient cultures used **euphemisms** to avoid naming their enemies directly. They believed that naming gave power to those they feared, so they invented ways around saying their names; the word *euphemism* comes from the Greek word that means "to use words for good omen." We sometimes do the same today out of consideration and kindness to those who may be suffering, as a way of speaking about taboo subjects and objects, or as a form of satire or irony. For example, the euphemisms for *die* are numerous, *to pass away* or *pass on* being the most common.

Although euphemisms can be used to protect us from the unpleasant, they can be used also to falsely reassure. For example, *urban renewal* avoids the implications of *slum clearance*, *revenue enhancement* has a more positive ring than *tax increase*, and *collateral losses* attempts to sidestep the fact that civilians have been killed during military action.

We also sometimes use euphemisms to try to give more dignity and a sense of importance to special objects, actions, or vocations: *pre-owned automobile* for *used car* and *job action* for *strike*. The Plain English Campaign once awarded a Golden Bull Award to the writers of a document that described the act of laying a brick in a wall as "install[ing] a component into the structural fabric."

The following classified ad uses some wordy and euphemistic language:

> We are seeking an individual who possesses demonstrated skills and abilities, a sound knowledge base coupled with the experience to provide service to mentally challenged teenagers with "unique" and significant challenging behaviours.

The requirements of the position could have been written in half the words:

> Applicants need proven skills, knowledge, and experience to serve mentally challenged teenagers with challenging behaviours.

A special category of "acceptable euphemisms" are those that we, as a society, agree should be substituted for expressions that have acquired inappropriate connotations. For example, to refer to someone in a wheelchair as a "cripple" inappropriately stresses the disability and its limitations. More sensitively and more accurately, this person is *physically disabled* or *physically challenged*.

A euphemism is a word or phrase substituted for the actual name of something—usually in order to make it more acceptable or to give it dignity. It is an example of indirect writing.

Exercise 17.6

In groups, think of 10 euphemisms (they can be ones you've heard of or made-up ones). Then, read them to the rest of the class and have them guess what they are meant to describe.

Exercise 17.7

The following sentences can be revised for concision and directness. Make whatever changes you think are necessary and be prepared to justify them.

1. Tanya has been invited to provide us with a summary of the significant main points of her findings.

2. The unexpected eruption of the volcano changed the Western Samoan island into a fiery, blazing inferno.

3. Gretta was decidedly overjoyed after being the unexpected recipient of an income tax refund in excess of $1000.

4. The protagonist of *Life of Pi* was confronted with the necessity of making the decision about whether he wanted to continue on living or not.

5. It was in 1964 that the Beatles first made their inaugural tour of the North American continent.

6. The disappearance of even one single species at the lower end of the food chain can have dire adverse effects in many instances on the survival of various other species.

7. Although Copernicus's radical idea that the earth made revolutions around the sun was once considered an extreme heresy and was ridiculed mercilessly by his peers, the idea eventually gained gradual acceptance.

8. The fact is that for a great many years now antibiotics have been utilized on a regular basis by many people as a cure for each and every symptom that they develop over the course of their entire lifetimes.

9. Perhaps in the heat of emotion the act of capital punishment would seem to be a feasible idea, but when you come to think of it rationally, this act would accomplish virtually next to nothing at all.

10. In protest of their salary freeze, all of the teachers who teach at the high school in Oak Bay have made the unanimous decision not to undertake any tasks of a supervisory nature until the school board has conducted a fair and impartial salary review.

11. Vehicles that have the four-way drive feature option are an extremely practical and pragmatic form of transportation for the majority of the Canadian population in this day and age.

12. There are many people in our society today who have serious drug addictions that take complete and utter control over their lives.

13. From the beginning of its conception, Canada has been a country concerned with promoting an active multicultural society, although the reality of unity within the country is still a large, unanswered question in the minds of most of the people of Canada.

14. A French scientist by the name of Louis Pasteur was the first individual to make the discovery that microbes were harmful menaces to the well-being and healthy functioning of the human body.

15. The reason yoga allows us to live a healthy lifestyle is due to the fact that it provides a strong basis for the efficient functioning of the body's endocrine system.

Exercise 17.8

Rewrite the following paragraph, aiming for concise, direct writing.

Dear Employers,

The Youth Resource Centre, in conjunction with the Federal Human Resource Department of Canada, has opened the Hire-A-Student office once again this summer, staffing Summer Employment Officers working towards finding the best possible student employees for any jobs that you may have available to post with us at the Centre.

Our service, conveniently situated at 147 High Street, is a totally free service to both employers posting jobs in the Centre and to students and youths trying to secure employment opportunities throughout the community. The service is a means for you the employer to help advertise any positions you may have available, and is additionally a way to assist students who are showing initiative in finding possible long-term or limited-term seasonal employment.

We are not a solicitation firm, and this is the point that we need to emphasize to the greatest extent. Our service is absolutely free of charge, and our intention is first and foremost to try and find employment for students who seem serious about working, as well as to offer a free alternative to posting jobs in newspapers and ad agencies that could end up costing you an excessive amount of money through advertising ventures.

Working Toward Precision: Wise Word Choices

For most writing assignments in college and university, you will be required to use formal writing. Because you may be used to writing informally when using the Internet or when text messaging—even, perhaps, from your high school English courses—you may puzzle over the ways that informal writing differs from formal writing. In informal writing

> Colloquialisms are words and expressions acceptable in conversation but not in formal writing.

- language may be close to speech or chatty with colloquialisms, idiom, or even slang
- contractions are acceptable (e.g., don't, can't, shouldn't, it's)
- the first-person ("I," "me") and second-person ("you") voice may be used
- sentence fragments may be used occasionally for dramatic effect
- short paragraphs are the rule rather than the exception
- citations for research sources are not given

> An idiom is a phrase whose meaning is understood only within the context of the phrase itself. For example, "his bark is worse than his bite" can be understood only by looking at the overall meaning and not by the meanings of the individual words.

In your essays, you should avoid contractions, unless your instructor tells you otherwise. Certainly, unless you are quoting someone, you should always avoid slang, colloquialisms, and jargon. For example, you would not use any of the following in a formal essay: *mindset, price tag, quick fix, down side, upfront,*

Avoid using informal verbs such as *saw, has seen*, etc., when you mean *resulted in or occurred*. E.g., The policy that was implemented two years ago has seen a 40 per cent drop in violent crime. *Revised*: The policy that was implemented two years ago has resulted in a 40 per cent drop in violent crime.

stressed (out), okay, do drugs, give the green light, grab the reader's attention, put (someone) down, fall for, obsess (about something), pan out, put on hold, put a positive spin (on something), opt for, tune out, no way, the way to go, go to great lengths, go overboard, way more (of something—*a lot* is also colloquial). Avoid merely quantitative words and phrases, such as *great, incredible, beautiful, terrible*, and the like; they are non-specific. You also should refrain from using words and expressions that might suggest to some readers a gender, sexual, racial, cultural, or other kind of bias.

Of course, your word choices involve much more than thinking about the level of formality. Effective writers choose their words and phrases carefully. In the following three examples from student essays, the writers did not choose carefully:

The mass production of plastics and ready-to-use products is growing at a *stagnating* [sic *staggering*] rate.

Note: *staggering* is informal; the writer could have used *rapid*, *rapidly increasing*, or *exponential*, or a specific number, such as *doubling every five years*.

The Shakespearean sonnet is an *oppressed* [sic *compressed*] form of poetry.

After successfully completing police officer training camp, the applicant can finally *swear* [sic *be sworn in*] and become a police officer.

Exercise 17.9

Read the following paragraphs taken from the essay "An Enviro's Case for Seal Hunt," found in Chapter 3. Highlight or underline examples of informal language use and then try to provide more concise wording for these examples.

There was an article about a campaign that a group called Respect for Animals is waging to convince consumers to boycott Canadian seafood products. The magazine also carried two huge advertisements from the same organization.

The Newfoundland seal hunt is transparently and demonstrably sustainable and humane. There are roughly half a million people in Newfoundland and Labrador, and nearly six million harp seals, which is almost three times as many seals as when I was a kid.

Here's one of those obligatory disclosures: over the years, several environmental organizations—the Sierra Club, the David Suzuki Foundation, Greenpeace, etc.—have subsidized my preoccupation with things that move in the water by having me do research projects for them and so on. With that out of the way, I can now say, if it isn't obvious already, that it's the seal hunt's opponents who turn my stomach.

Rather than making extreme blunders, more often you choose a word that is not quite precise for your purpose. These kinds of "near misses" can distract or confuse the reader. You should not let the search for the exact word prevent you from fully expressing your ideas in a first draft. But when revising, you should look up the meanings of all words you're in doubt about—even if you're only a little unsure.

You can use a thesaurus to look for words similar in meaning to avoid repeating a word too often. But a thesaurus should always be used along with a reliable dictionary. Most thesauruses, such as the ones that come with word-processing programs, simply list words similar in meaning; they do not provide connotations for the words.

Some dictionaries help you to be precise not only by defining the main entry but also by providing distinctions among similar words. In addition to illustrating the way a word is used by making examples, many mid-sized dictionaries distinguish the main entry from other words with similar meanings. For example, the *Gage Canadian Dictionary,* which lists more than six meanings for the adjective *effective,* also defines two words similar to *effective* in meaning but different in connotation:

> *Syn. adj.* **1. Effective, effectual, efficient** = producing an effect. **Effective,** usually describing things, emphasizes producing a wanted or expected effect: *several new drugs are effective in treating serious diseases.* **Effectual,** describing people or things, emphasizes having produced or having the power to produce the exact effect or result intended: *his efforts are more energetic than effectual.* **Efficient,** often describing people, emphasizes being able to produce the effect wanted or intended without wasting energy, time, etc.: *A skilled surgeon is highly efficient.*

Similarly, the *Student's Oxford Canadian Dictionary,* which lists seven meanings for the adjective *nice,* offers the following examples of words that may be more appropriate or more forceful than *nice* in certain contexts:

> we had a **delightful/splendid/enjoyable** time
> a **satisfying/delicious/exquisite** meal
> a **fashionable/stylish/elegant/chic** outfit
> this is a **cozy/comfortable/attractive** room
> she is **kind/friendly/likeable/amiable**
> our adviser is **compassionate/understanding/sympathetic**
> a **thoughtful/considerate/caring** gesture

Precision and Logic

Choosing your words carefully will help make your writing precise. But sometimes, imprecision may result from illogical thinking or from writing down an idea quickly. To be sure whether something you've written really makes sense, you need to look carefully at the relationship among the parts of the sentence, especially at the relationship between the subject and predicate. **Faulty predication** exists if a verb cannot be logically connected to its subject. In general, avoid the phrases *is when* and *is where* after a subject in sentences that *define* something. For example, in the following sentence *faulty predication,* which is a thing, is illogically referred to as a time or a place:

Writers often use words that have specific associations or implications. A word's *connotation* includes its possible meanings in its given context.

When you read an unfamiliar work, it is a good idea to try to guess a word's meaning by its context and then check it in a dictionary if you need to. As a writer, you should *always* check a word's meaning if you're even a little unsure whether it's the right word.

Incorrect:
Faulty predication is when/where a verb cannot be logically connected to its subject.
Correct:
Faulty predication *occurs where* [i.e., in a sentence] a verb is not logically connected to its subject.
Faulty predication *is* an illogical juxtaposing of a subject and a verb.

Consider this comment on the setting of Joseph Conrad's *Heart of Darkness*:

The Congo represents an inward journey for the character Marlow.

The Congo is a country as well as a river. How can a country or a river represent a journey? Of course, a *trip* through a country or on a river could represent an inner journey.

In one kind of faulty predication, an inanimate object is falsely linked to a human action.

Some opponents claim that PE programs are unwilling to accommodate the needs of all students.

The programs aren't "unwilling," since this implies a will, though teachers or administrators may be "unwilling."

Some opponents claim that the administrators of PE programs are unwilling to accommodate the needs of all students.

Sound should also play a role in word choice. You should avoid placing words with similar sounds in close proximity (the "echo effect").

Endorphins enable the body to heal itself and *gain pain* relief.

You should also be wary of unintentional puns in a work of scholarship:

The first experiments in music therapy were *noted* during World War I.

Also, do not write ironically or sarcastically, though you may be tempted to do so in argumentative essays. Your reader may not share your attitude. Besides, the hallmark of both expository and argumentative writing is an objective voice, one that is unbiased.

Inappropriate tone:
It is well-known that college students under stress need to exercise their livers on the occasional Friday night.

> When checking whether a subject fits with its predicate, ensure that the subject can perform the action that the verb describes.

Exercise 17.10

Circle every example of informal diction in the following paragraph; then, rewrite the paragraph using formal diction. There may be one or two places where the word or phrase is colloquial but necessary due to context or the fact it can't be rephrased easily.

Having the winter Olympic Games held in Vancouver is a once-in-a-lifetime opportunity, and it seems like a great idea. It will create world recognition for this world-class city, helping to really put it on the map. On top of that, it will be a fun and exciting time for the citizens of BC. However, after sober second thought, it is clear that while the Games might pay for themselves, who will pay for the upgrades necessary to get Vancouver in good shape for the Games? Even with both the provincial and federal governments chipping in for a fair amount of the costs, because we are dealing in billions of dollars, even a small chunk of that cost is a lot of money. These small chunks will come from the pockets of the taxpayer, some of whom are not big fans of the Games at all. But although these direct costs are bound to be steep, it is the hidden costs of the Games that will be the real killer.

Verbs with Vitality

Verbs are the action words in a sentence. Look at the verbs in your sentences. Could you replace them with stronger, more descriptive verbs? Could you replace verbs, like *be* and *have*, which convey a state or condition, with verbs of action? Common verbs, such as *do*, *make*, *go*, and *get*, are not specific. Could you replace them with more precise or emphatic verbs?

The most common verb in English, *to be*, takes many different forms as an irregular verb: *am*, *is*, *are*, *was*, *were*, *will be*, etc. and appears frequently as a helping verb. Your writing will be more concise if you omit the forms *being* or *to be* whenever they are unnecessary.

> The results of the study can be interpreted as ~~being~~ credible.
> She dreamed of a carriage ~~being~~ pulled by two fine horses.
> Hypnosis has been proven ~~to be~~ an effective therapy for some people.
> In 313 BCE Christianity was declared ~~to be~~ the official religion of Rome.

If you can easily omit a form of *to be*, do so.

As people put on the spot by journalists and the public, politicians have sometimes chosen vague language to avoid committing themselves to statements they may regret later. A more cynical view suggests that taking refuge in abstract, indefinite language enables them to say little while appearing informed and in control. Notice the lack of specificity in the following comment by former American politician Colin Powell, reported by the Associated Press:

> "We knew that the ICRC had concerns, and in accordance with the matter in which the ICRC does its work, it presented those concerns directly to the command in Baghdad. And I know that some corrective action was taken with respect to those concerns."

Verbs and nouns are the two most important parts of speech. The verbs you choose can weaken or strengthen your prose. Choose verbs carefully, preferring active to static ones and deleting verb forms like *being* and *to be* when they are unneeded.

Exercise 17.11

Read the following paragraph and underline places where you would revise verbs to make them more expressive and descriptive.

> By the 1800s, inventions were beginning to put people out of work. One of the first inventions that resulted in rebellion was in the craft guild. In 1801, Joseph Jacquard became known as the inventor of the Jacquard loom. This loom was capable of being programmed by pre-punched cards, which made it possible to create clothing design patterns. This invention led to the creation of the Luddites, who were a group made up from the craft guild. These people were against any type of manufacturing technology and went about burning down several factories that were using this new technology. The Luddites were around only for a couple of years, but the name Luddite is still used to describe people who are resistant to new technologies. The Jacquard loom was, in effect, an invention that replaced people. It could do great designs quickly and without making any errors. The replacement of people by machines was beginning.

Exercise 17.12

Suggest how the following passage could be improved by using more specific language and by omitting unnecessary words and phrases.

> The time period between 1985 and 1989 was a difficult one for graffiti artists in New York City. This was a time when graffiti barely stayed alive because of the harsh laws and efforts of the Metropolitan Transit Authority, which is known as the MTA. This period was called the period of the "Die Hards" because of the small number of die-hard artists who were able to keep graffiti from dying out completely. As a result of the measures of the MTA against graffiti art and artists, there was a lack of paint available for use and the level of enforcement was extremely high. The only important thing that was happening during these years was the use of markers for tagging. These tags were usually small, of poor artistic quality, and were finished quickly by the artists. These tags can be seen today at some bus stops and in some washrooms throughout the city.

Prepackaged Goods: Clichés

Expressions considered clichés today were in their prime a veritable breath of fresh air. If commentary on the cliché were to be made in clichés, you would find the prose wordy and confusing:

> However, with the passage of time (more years than you can shake a stick at), they became the stuff of idle minds until after time immemorial they assumed the mantle of respectability and were accepted verbatim as par for the course. Writers worth their salt should avoid clichés like the plague or they will stop all readers with a good head on their shoulders dead in their tracks (to call a spade a spade and to give the devil his due).

Exercise 17.13

In this short passage adapted from a travel feature, find evidence of tired and predictable writing, citing particular words and phrases that could be made more effective or accurate. Although newspaper features use informal writing, it should be descriptive and concrete. How could you make this passage more interesting?

We're up and about at the crack of dawn, and from outside our cabin we can see the peak of a small mountain looming in the distance. Our ship glides effortlessly over the fathomless blue sea, and soon the mountain's craggy features come into view.

"It's breakfast, honey," my wife, Jen, sings from inside the cabin, and soon our impeccably dressed waiter knocks softly on our door. As we sit down to partake of the delectable repast, I feel as though I could pinch myself. Yes, here we are, aboard a luxurious liner, about to drop anchor off the coast of one of the world's most fabled isles.

Clichés are overworked and unoriginal phrases. Inexperienced writers may reach for them in a vain attempt to "spice up" their writing. Clichés may be *dead metaphors*: expressions drained of their novelty through overuse. Although they may appear in some informal writing, they are poor substitutes for informative, imaginative words.

Providing Depth: Variety and Emphasis

When you revise an early draft to improve clarity, you will likely find opportunities to make your prose more interesting. Variety and emphasis in your writing will make what is competent also *compelling*. Variety and emphasis are worthwhile goals in all forms of essays: personal, literary, argumentative, and expository.

Sentence Variety

Length

You can vary the lengths of sentences for rhetorical effect. Just as short paragraphs suggest underdeveloped points, short, choppy sentences could suggest a lack of content. On the other hand, several long sentences in a row could confuse a reader.

That doesn't mean you should write only sentences that are between 15 and 20 words long. Although sentence length alone is no measure of readability, consider revision if you find you have written more than two very short or very long sentences in a row.

> You should avoid writing too many overly short or overly long sentences. If you see you've done this, you can use the grammatical rules to combine short sentences or break longer sentences into shorter ones.

Coordinating conjunctions are introduced on p. 307; subordinating conjunctions are introduced on p. 308.

Using semicolons to separate independent clauses is discussed on pp. 342–3. Using colons to separate independent clauses is discussed on pp. 346–7.

To review rules for joining sentences and clauses, see pp. 321–3.

The rule for punctuating appositives is on pp. 346–7.

To connect short sentences you can use appropriate conjunctions. Simple sentences can be joined by one of the seven coordinating conjunctions. If the idea in one sentence is less important than the idea in the sentence before or after it, use the subordinating conjunction that best expresses the relationship between the sentences. You can join independent clauses by using a semicolon or a colon.

You can also join independent clauses by using a conjunctive adverb or transitional phrase, ensuring that a semicolon precedes the connecting word or phrase. You may be able to grammatically connect phrases or clauses through a parallel relationship, such as one of apposition. The second phrase or clause could also modify the preceding word, phrase, or clause—for example, a relative (adjectival) clause could give information about a preceding noun clause.

Generally speaking, you waste space when you begin a new sentence by repeating part of the previous sentence, or by beginning a new paragraph by recapitulating part of the previous one. Although repetition can be used to build coherence, it should not create redundancy.

Exercise 17.14

The following paragraph consists of too many short sentences. Using the strategies mentioned above, revise the paragraph to make it more effective.

(1) During the earth's long history, there have been various periods of glaciation. (2) This fact is well known. (3) There is also evidence of one great glacial event. (4) It is possible that the earth was once completely covered by ice and snow. (5) Skeptics argue this is impossible. (6) They say that the earth could never have become this cold. (7) The idea of the tropics being frozen over is unlikely, they believe.

Exercise 17.15

The following paragraph consists of sentences that are too long. Using the strategies mentioned above, revise the paragraph to make it more effective.

(1) Finding a definition for "the homeless" is difficult, but the most common definition, which is used both in the media and in current research, defines the homeless as those who lack visible shelter or use public shelters. (2) Literature about homelessness is sparse, and it was not until the 1980s that the incidence of homelessness began to be reported in the media, but homelessness has existed for centuries, and literature on the subject dates back to the feudal period in Europe.

In 1970, Gordon O. Gallup created the mirror test ~~This test was~~, designed to determine whether ~~or not~~ animals are self-aware.

When checking your work for overly long sentences, consider breaking up sentences with more than two independent clauses or one independent clause and more than two dependent clauses. See if the relationships between the clauses are clear. If they are not, divide the sentences where clauses are joined by conjunctions, by transitional words and phrases, or by relative pronouns.

Relative clauses are discussed on pp. 335–6.

Structural Variety

You can experiment with phrasal openings to sentences. Consider beginning the occasional sentence with a prepositional phrase, a verbal phrase, or an absolute phrase instead of the subject of the sentence.

Prepositional phrases begin with a preposition followed by a noun or pronoun; they are adjectival or adverbial and modify the closest noun (adjectival) or verb (adverbial). A **participial phrase**, which ends in *–ing*, *–ed*, or *–en*, is a verbal phrase acting as an adjective. An **infinitive phrase**, which is preceded by *to*, can act adjectivally or adverbially. An **absolute phrase**, consisting of a noun/pronoun and a partial verb form, modifies the entire sentence.

Prepositional phrases are discussed on pp. 319–20.

In this short excerpt from an essay about the death of a moth, Virginia Woolf uses a prepositional phrase opening, an absolute phrase that introduces an independent clause, and two verbal phrase openings:

> *After a time*, <u>tired by his dancing</u> apparently, he settled on the window ledge in the sun, and **the queer spectacle being at an end**, I forgot about him. Then, <u>looking up</u>, my eye was caught by him. He was trying to resume his dancing, but seemed either so stiff or so awkward that he could only flutter to the bottom of the window-pane; and when he tried to fly across it, he failed.

Make sure that when you use a participial phrase at the beginning of a sentence that you include the word it is intended to modify so that it does not dangle. (See Dangling Modifiers pp. 385–7.)

Note the types of modifiers: *After a time*: prepositional phrase; <u>tired by his dancing</u>; <u>looking up</u>: verbal phrases; **the queer spectacle being at an end**: absolute phrase.

Creating Emphasis

Writers may create emphasis by presenting main points or details in a particular order. Two kinds of sentences vary in the order in which they present the main idea: periodic and cumulative sentences.

Periodic sentences begin with modifiers—words, phrases, or clauses—before the independent clause. **Cumulative sentences** work the other way: they begin with an independent clause and are followed by modifying or parallel words, phrases, or clauses. While periodic sentences delay the main idea, creating anticipation, cumulative sentences develop the main idea by drawing it out. Many sentences are slightly or moderately periodic or cumulative, depending on whether the writer has

You can begin a sentence with detail and follow with the main idea or begin with the main idea and follow with detail. These two different orders will produce contrastive effects.

begun with modifiers or ended with them. However, a writer can employ either periodic or cumulative sentences to create a specific effect. Independent clauses are shown by italics below.

> *Periodic*:
> Unlike novelists and playwrights, who lurk behind the scenes while distracting our attention with the puppet show of imaginary characters—and unlike the scholars and journalists, who quote the opinions of others and take cover behind the hedges of neutrality—*the essayist has nowhere to hide* (Scott Russell Sanders, "The Singular First Person").
> *Cumulative*:
> *The root of all evil is that we all want this spiritual gratification*, this flow, this apparent heightening of life, this knowledge, this valley of many-colored grass, even grass and light prismatically decomposed, giving ecstasy (D.H. Lawrence, *Studies in Classic American Literature*).

A writer can delay the main idea generating tension also by beginning with a prepositional phrase:

> Behind the deconstructionists' dazzling cloud of language lie certain more or less indisputable facts (John Gardner, *The Art of Fiction*).

When the subject is delayed in this kind of construction, ensure that the verb agrees with the subject, which will follow the verb rather than precede it. (See Delayed Subjects, pp. 360–1.)

Other ways to achieve emphasis include parallel structures and repetition—techniques that also help in paragraph coherence—and rhythms that call the reader's attention to important ideas. The end of a sentence in itself provides emphasis, since a reader naturally slows down when approaching the last part of a sentence and pauses slightly between sentences.

The two paragraphs below employ parallel structures, repetition, and rhythm for emphasis.

> A.
> My professors, many of whom were to become very famous, did not tend to be philosophic and did not dig back into the sources of the new language and categories they were using. They thought that these were scientific discoveries like any others, which were to be used in order to make further discoveries. They were very much addicted to abstractions and generalizations, as Tocqueville predicted they would be. They believed in scientific progress and appeared (there may have been an element of boasting and self-irony in this) to be convinced that they were on the verge of a historic breakthrough in the social sciences, equivalent to that scored in the sixteenth and seventeenth centuries in the natural sciences. . . . These teachers were literally inebriated by the unconscious and values. And they were also sure that scientific progress would be related to social and political progress (Allan Bloom, *The Closing of the American Mind*).

Bloom employs the most common structural pattern of subject-verb-object in all his sentences, establishing a predictable rhetorical pattern that complements the predictability and uniformity of his professors that he wants to stress. Thus, *My professors*, the subject in the first sentence, is replaced by the pronoun *they* in the following three sentences; in the fourth sentence, *they* is the subject of two clauses. To avoid too many identical openings, Bloom continues with the same rhythm but varies the subject slightly: the last two sentences begin with *These teachers* and *And they*, respectively.

B.
Tales about Pythagoras flew to him and stuck like iron filings to a magnet. He was said, for example, to have appeared in several places at once and to have been reincarnated many times. Taken literally, this idea can be consigned to the same overflowing bin which contains the story that he had a golden thigh; but taken figuratively, it is an understatement. Pythagoras—or at least Pythagoreanism—was everywhere and still is (Anthony Gottlieb, *The Dream of Reason* 21).

The most obvious technique in paragraph B is the use of figurative language: Gottlieb uses a simile in the first sentence (*like iron filings to a magnet*) and a metaphor in the third sentence (*overflowing bin*). However, he effectively uses sentence length and rhythm to make the paragraph more appealing still. The paragraph is framed by short simple sentences that stress Pythagoras's importance. The middle sentences develop the main idea through examples. Gottlieb's final sentence, though the shortest, contains strong stresses: the use of dashes allows the writer to repeat the name Pythagoras without seeming redundant, while heavy accents fall on the final two words.

◎ Proofreading: Perfection *Is* Possible

In publishing, *editing* refers to the revising of a work before it is formatted, whether for a book, a newspaper, a magazine or journal, or other medium. Proofreading refers to the final check of the formatted material—either done on screen or in the form of paper "proofs" printed from the formatter's electronic files.

While someone who edits and suggests revisions to a document is mainly concerned with improving it, the proofreader is looking for errors. The proofreader is the document's last line of defence before it falls under the public eye. Ironically, poor proofreading may be the *first* thing noticed in the published document.

In spite of its importance, the last proofreading to ensure that the i's are dotted and the t's are crossed is usually one of the neglected stages for student writers working under deadline to submit an essay. Exhausted from the final efforts of putting the essay together, students may think that tiny errors are unimportant compared to other parts of the process stressed throughout the term. However, distracting errors may strike your instructor in a completely different light. They could be seen as careless, a sign of a lack of effort. Your instructor could become annoyed by many small mistakes and even become more critical of other parts of the essay.

When you *edit* or revise, you try to improve your work's structure and readability, or solidify your ideas; when you *proofread*, you try to catch all mistakes to provide a clean copy for your reader. Doing so will make a favourable first impression.

You may think that tiny errors are unimportant compared to other parts of the process stressed throughout the term. However, your instructor could see them as careless, a sign of a lack of effort.

Whether or not proofreading is seen as tedious, it is best performed as a mechanical process. By taking a thorough and systematic approach to the essay at this stage, you can be more confident that the work of many hours, days, or even weeks will be more readable to the person marking it.

Proofreading Methods

Documents may be read **in teams** with one person reading aloud while the other follows the printed copy silently. When it is your work being proofread, it is best if you read aloud since you may more easily catch errors you've missed as a writer. This method works on the principle that two readers are twice as likely to spot errors as one person. It may also be more enjoyable than working alone. Clearly, it works only if a second reader is available and both readers are knowledgeable about writing and committed to the task.

Reading forward is the method of reading the paper aloud or to yourself but more slowly and carefully than you would usually do, paying attention both to the words and to the punctuation. Because it can be hard to concentrate solely on the words apart from the meaning, it's best to read through the essay at least once for meaning and then at least once again for spelling and other errors.

Reading backward is the method by which you start at the end and read to the beginning word by word or sentence by sentence. This technique forces your attention on the writing; it works well for catching spelling errors. However, it is time-consuming, and you may miss some punctuation and other "between the words" errors, as well as words that are dependent on their context.

Reading syllabically, you read from the beginning, breaking every word into syllables. This is faster than reading backward, works well for catching internal misspellings, and is quite effective for catching missing and extra words and for correcting word endings (which may be overlooked when you read forward). However, it is a slower method than reading forward word by word, requires some discipline to master, and can be hard on the eyes if done for a long time.

Guidelines for Proofreading

- Probably the main reason for essays with careless errors is that not enough time was allotted for proofing. The half hour *not* set aside for proofreading can undo the work of several hours.
- Plan to let at least a few hours pass before you look at the essay for the final time (overnight is recommended).
- Having someone else go over the essay can be helpful but is no substitute for your own systematic proofing. Instructors are not likely to be sympathetic to the cry of baffled frustration, "But I had my roommate read it over!"
- Use a spell checker but don't rely on it. Remember the poem that made the rounds on the Internet a few years ago: *Eye halve a spelling chequer / It came with my pea sea / It plainly marques for my revue / miss steaks eye kin knot sea. . . .*

A spell checker will not see any difference between *there house is over their two* and *their house is over there too.*

- Experiment with the different proofreading methods discussed above and use the one(s) you feel most comfortable with and works best for you. When you start proofreading using one particular method, though, you should use it until you finish reading.

Common Errors

Here are categories of typical errors to watch for and correct in your writing.

- All areas where consistency is required—spelling, capitalization, abbreviations, hyphenation, numbers, internal punctuation, and other places where choices pertaining to the mechanics of writing may be involved
- Proper nouns (especially unfamiliar names), acronyms, etc. Are all references to authors and titles spelled correctly?
- Middles and endings of words, for spelling and for agreement
- Small words, such as articles and prepositions (*a, an, the, of, to, in, at, and, or, as, if, it*, etc.)
- Words that have different spellings but the same pronunciation (homophones)— e.g., to/too, their/there/they're, role/roll, cite/site, led/lead, manor/manner
- Font style (italic, bold, Roman: applied correctly and consistently? applied to *all* necessary words?) Have you used italics for complete works, such as books and films, and placed works contained in larger works, such as essays, articles, short stories, and poems, contained in quotation marks?
- End punctuation (periods and question marks)
- Quotation marks applied appropriately? Both opening and closing quotation marks present? Have double and single quotation marks been alternated correctly? Periods and commas inside; colons and semicolons outside? Similar checks can be made for parentheses.
- All citations, both in-text and on the final page of the essay. Check both for accuracy (author, title, journal name, date, and page numbers) and for consistency. Are all citations documented according to the style of your discipline— including capitalization, punctuation, and other conventions?

◎ Essay Presentation

Your audience and purpose are relevant to how you present your essay; for example, a scientific or engineering report probably would look quite different from an essay for English class—for one thing, it might have headings, whereas the English essay would probably not. A research essay, too, must conform to the documentation style of your discipline; on the other hand, if you are writing a personal essay and not using references, presenting your essay may mostly be a matter of following directions for title, typeface, margins, spacing, indentation, page numbering, and identifying information.

Although document design can vary, you can be sure of one thing: if your instructor asks you to format your essay a certain way, he or she will look to see that you followed these instructions. Therefore, if you are unsure about essay presentation, ask for help.

Unless you are told otherwise, you can refer to the following; it is based on MLA guidelines:

- Most instructors require essays to be typed. Use good-quality white paper, printing on one side. If you wish to conserve paper by printing on both sides, check with your instructor first.
- Leave 1–inch margins (2.5 cm) on all sides. The first page should include identification information positioned flush left (i.e., starting at the left margin). List information in the following order: your name and student ID if applicable; instructor's name (use the title that your instructor prefers—e.g., Professor Robert Mills, Dr. M. Sonik, Ms. J. Winestock, etc.); course number and section, if applicable; submission date. Double space, then insert the essay's title, centred.
- Double space the text of your essay; this makes it much easier for the instructor to correct errors and add comments. Also double space any Notes, the Works Cited page, and block quotations.
- Indent each paragraph one-half inch—do *not* use additional spaces to separate paragraphs, and leave a single space (not two spaces) after each period before beginning the next sentence.
- Number pages using Arabic numerals in the upper right-hand corner preceded by your last name; place about one-half inch (1.25 cm) from top and flush right; you can probably create this kind of header automatically using the "Insert" or a similar function on your computer. If you need to include prefatory pages (such as a Contents page or a formal outline), use lower-case Roman numerals (i., ii., iii.) for those pages.
- Title pages are usually optional, though some instructors require them. Position the essay's title down one-third of the page with your name about half-way down; near the bottom of the page include course number, instructor's name, and submission date. All items should be centred. Begin your essay on the second page (numbered 1) under the centred title.
- No illustrations or colours, other than black and white, should be on any pages unless you use graphics directly relevant to your essay—for example, charts or diagrams for a scientific study. Use a paper clip to attach the pages (some instructors ask for stapled pages)—especially, don't dog-ear them. Don't use folders, clear or coloured, unless asked for. (If you do use a folder, the left-hand margin should be slightly wider than the other margins to enhance readability.)
- Prefer common fonts, such as Times New Roman, Arial, or Garamond (not Courier New or cursive ones). Use 10- to 12-point type size. *Do not* justify lines to the margins in academic papers or reports (i.e., set the paragraphing for flush left and use an uneven right line at the margin). Finally, ensure that

Ensure that the text of your essay is easy to read. An essay printed in draft mode or from a cartridge that is almost out of ink will not be easy to read.

the text of your essay is easy to read. An essay printed in draft mode or from a cartridge that is almost out of ink will not be easy to read.

◎ Common Words That Confuse

English has many word pairs that are confusing either because the two words look similar (for example, *affect* and *effect*) or because they have similar, but not identical, uses (for example, *amount* and *number*)—or both. In most cases, the dictionary is best for problems related to meaning, but usage can be more complicated. The words below are the "Top Twenty-five" that continue to give student writers the most trouble. Hints and examples are provided to help you distinguish them.

For a guide to spelling, there is no better resource than the dictionary; if you have the slightest doubt about the spelling of a word, consult a dictionary—don't rely on a spell checker.

1. accept, except. Accept is a verb meaning "to receive, to take what is offered." **Except** is a preposition meaning "other than" or "leaving out."

> *Hint*:
> Think of the "crossing out" connotation of "x" in "except" to remind you that "except" means "leaving out."
> *Example*:
> The bargaining committee accepted all the terms except the last one.

2. affect, effect. Affect is a verb meaning "to influence or have an effect on." **Effect**, a noun, means "a result." As a verb, effect is less often used; it means "to bring about" or "to cause"—not "to have an effect on."

> *Hint*:
> Try substituting "influence" in the sentence; if it fits your intended meaning, "affect" is the word you want.
> *Example*:
> The news of Michael Jordan's return to basketball greatly affected his fans. The effect was also felt at the box office; an immediate hike in ticket prices was effected.

3. allot, a lot. Allot, a verb, means "to portion out"; **a lot** can be an adverb (I sleep a lot) or a noun (I need a lot of sleep) meaning "a great deal." "A lot" is too informal for most academic writing; you should use the more formal "a great deal," "much," "many," or similar substitutes. The one-word spelling, "alot," is incorrect.

> *Example*:
> My parents allotted me $500 spending money for the term, which was not a lot considering my shopping habit. (informal)

4. all right, alright. All right is all right, just as "a lot" is a lot better than "alot"; **alright** and "alot" are not words.

5. allude, elude. Both are verbs, but they mean different things. **Allude** (to) means "to refer to something briefly or indirectly"; **elude** means "to avoid or escape, usually through a clever manoeuvre or strategy." "Allude" should be followed by "to": e.g., "In the poem, Hardy alluded to the end of the century."

> *Hint*:
> "Allude" is the verb from which the noun "allusion" (a kind of reference, see **allusion**) is formed; you can associate the "e" in "elude" with the "e" in "escape."
> *Example*:
> In his prison memoirs, the bank robber alluded to the time in the desert when he eluded capture by disguising himself as a cactus.

6. allusion, illusion. You may have come across the literary use of **allusion**, meaning an historical, religious, mythic, literary, or other kind of outside reference used to reveal character or theme in a work. An **illusion** is something apparently seen that is not real or is something that gives a false impression.

> *Hint*:
> Since the most common mistake is misspelling "allusion" as "illusion" in literary essays, you could remember that "allusion," meaning an outside reference, *always* begins with "*al*."
> *Examples*:
> The title of Nathanael West's novel *The Day of the Locust* is an allusion to the Book of Exodus in the Bible.
>
> Optical illusions often use graphics to fool our senses.

7. among, between. The simple distinction is that **between** refers to two persons or things and **among** to more than two.

> *Examples*:
> The senator found himself between a rock and a hard place.
>
> Ms. O'Grady stood among her adoring students for the school picture.

"Between" may be the obvious choice even if more than two things are involved. For example, "Interlibrary loans are permitted between campuses." Even though a number of campuses may be part of the interlibrary loan system, any one exchange takes place between two campuses.

8. amount, number. Use **amount** to refer to things that can't be counted; **number** refers to countable objects.

> *Hint*:
> Think of using numbers when you count.
> *Example*:
> The number of errors in this essay reveals the amount of care you took in writing it.

9. beside, besides. Beside is a preposition meaning "next to," "adjoining"; **besides** has several meanings as a preposition; as an adverb, **besides** means "in addition (to)."

> *Hint*:
> Think of the extra "s" in besides as an additional letter to remind you of "in addition to."
> *Example*:
> Beside the telephone was the telephone book, besides which she had an address book.

10. bias, biased. Bias is a noun that refers to a "tendency to judge unfairly"; **biased** is an adjective that means "having or showing a preferential attitude." A person can have a bias (a thing); be a biased person (adjective modifying "person"); or can be biased (predicate adjective after a linking verb). A person cannot be bias. Also, a person is biased or has a bias *against* (not *to* or *for*) something or someone.

> *Example*:
> His bias against the Rastafarian lifestyle caused him to overlook some of its ideals.

11. cite, sight, site. To cite, a verb, is "to refer to an outside source." (The complete naming of the source itself is a citation.) **Sight** (noun or verb) refers to seeing, one of the five senses. **Site**, when used as a noun, is a location or place (usually of some importance). The most common error in essays is the use of "site" when "cite" is meant.

> *Hint*:
> Remember that "cite" is a verb referring to "the act of giving a citation"; "site" is "where something is situated or sits."
> *Example*:
> She said the ruins were excavated in 1926, citing as proof the historical plaque that commemorated the site.

12. e.g., i.e. E.g. is an abbreviation for the Latin *exempli gratia*, meaning "for the sake of example"; **i.e.** is an abbreviation for the Latin *id est* meaning "that is." Use "e.g." before one or more examples; use "i.e." if you want to elaborate on or clarify a preceding statement. In both cases, use a period after each letter and a comma after the abbreviation. Because they are abbreviations, they should be avoided in formal writing.

> *Hint*:
> The first letter in "example" tells you that examples should follow "e.g.".
> *Examples*:
> J.K. Rowling defied the common formula for success in the children's book market by writing long novels, e.g., *Harry Potter and the Goblet of Fire, Harry Potter and the Order of the Phoenix*. Some of Rowling's novels have episodic plots that contain many well-developed characters, i.e., they tend to be long.

13. fewer, less. Fewer is the quantitative adjective of comparison and refers to things that can be counted; **less** is the qualitative adjective of comparison, referring to amount and things that can be measured.

> *Examples*:
> Don't believe the notice on the mayonnaise jar: "Contains 40% less calories." Calories can be counted.
>
> There were fewer than a dozen people at the nomination meeting.
>
> The less said about his defection, the better.

14. good, well. Good may be an adjective, noun, or adverb. When used as an adjective, it should clearly modify a noun (e.g., a good story) or be used as a subject complement (predicate adjective, e.g., the child was good until bed-time). It cannot be used as a predicate adjective after verbs that express an action, although it is frequently heard in speech, especially in sports ("I was hitting the ball good").

> *Incorrect*:
> She beat the batter good.
> *Correct*:
> She is a good cook and beat the batter well.

As an adjective, **well** means "in good health" or "satisfactory." As an adverb, it has several meanings, including "thoroughly" and "satisfactorily."

> *Hint*:
> Do not use "good" as a predicate adjective after an action verb; you may use it before a noun or right after an intransitive (linking) verb.
> *Examples*:
> Making a good donation to the Children's Hospital made the corporation look good (i.e., "appear altruistic" *not* "appear good-looking").
>
> Although just having come out of the hospital, she looked well and continued to feel well during her recovery. (i.e., "well" is used as an adjective after linking verbs and means "healthy.")

15. its, it's. Its is a possessive adjective meaning "belonging to it and is formed from the personal pronoun *it*." Remember that personal pronouns are never spelled with an apostrophe. **It's** is the contraction for "it is," the apostrophe indicating that the letter "i" is left out.

> *Hint*:
> Try substituting "it is" if you're having problems identifying the correct form; if it fits, then use it's; if it doesn't, use its. ("Its" is usually followed by a noun.)
> *Example*:
> It's foolish to judge a book by its cover.

16. lay, lie. Both are verbs. **Lay** is a transitive verb, which must always be followed by a direct object (either a noun or a pronoun). It is *incorrect* to say, "I'm going to lay down to rest." **Lie** is an intransitive verb; it is not followed by an object.

> *Hint*:
> You always *lay* something down, as a hen does an egg. Then it *lies* there.
> *Examples*:
> He lay the baby in the crib before going to lie down.
> *Contrast*:
> He had *lain* on the ground for twenty minutes before someone noticed him. (*lain* is the past participle of *lie*)
> Kim Campbell *laid* to rest the notion that a woman couldn't be prime minister. (*laid* is the past participle of *lay*)

17. led, lead. **Led** and **lead** are forms of the irregular verb **to lēad** (long); the present tense is also **lead**. However, the past tense and the past participle are **lĕd** (short). Writers may become confused by the noun "lead," the metal, which looks like "to lead," but is pronounced like "led." Therefore, when they come to write the past tense "led," they may wrongly substitute the noun "lead," rather than the verb.

> *Hint*:
> Don't be led astray by thinking there is an "a" in "led."
> *Example*:
> Although she led in the polls by a 2:1 margin three months ago, today she leads by only a slight margin.

18. loose, lose. **Loose** is the adjective meaning "not tight"; **lose** is a verb meaning "not to be able to find," or "to be defeated."

> *Hint*:
> When you lose something, it is lost. "Lost" is spelled with one "o."
> *Example*:
> If you don't tighten that loose button, you're going to lose it.

19. onset, outset. Both are nouns that mean a "beginning." **Outset** means "setting out," for example, on a journey or to do something; you can also use the phrase "at the outset" to refer to the early events of a narrative or play. **Onset** refers to a force or condition that comes upon one.

> *Example*:
> At the outset of my fourth decade, I experienced the onset of mild osteoarthritis.

20. than, then. Than is a conjunction used in comparisons (He's happier than he knows). **Then** is an adverb with temporal connotations meaning "consequently," "at that time," "after that," etc.

> *Hint*:
> If you're comparing one thing to another, use "than." "Then 'tells when.'"
> *Example*:
> Warren said he was better at darts than Mark, and then he challenged him to a game to prove it.

21. their, there, they're. Their is a possessive adjective meaning "belonging to them"; **there** is an adverb meaning "in that place"; **they're** is the contraction of "they are," the apostrophe indicating that the letter "a" is left out.

> *Hint*:
> If you're uncertain about "they're," substitute "they are"; "there" (meaning "in that place") is spelled the same as here ("in this place") with the letter "t" added.
> *Example*:
> There is no excuse for the rowdy behaviour in there; they're supposed to be in their rooms.

22. to, too. To is a preposition indicating "direction towards"; **too** is an adverb meaning "also."

> *Hint*:
> "To" will usually be followed by a noun or pronoun as part of a prepositional phrase; substitute "also" for "too."
> *Example*:
> The next time you go to the store, may I come along, too?

23. usage, use. Many writers overuse **usage,** which refers to "a customary or habitual pattern or practice." It applies to conventions of groups of people, such as "language usage of the English." Usage shouldn't be used simply to mean a repeated action.

> *Incorrect*:
> The usage of fax machines and e-mail has allowed businesses to increase their efficiency.
> *Example*:
> I have no use for people who are always correcting my usage of "whom."

24. who's, whose. Who's is the contraction of "who is," the apostrophe indicating the omission of the letter "i." **Whose** is the possessive adjective meaning "belonging to whom".

Hint:

Try substituting "who is." If it fits, then "who's" is the correct form.

Example:

Whose turn is it to do the dishes?

Who's going to do the dishes tonight?

25. you're, your. You're is the contraction of "you are"; **your** is a possessive adjective that means "belonging to you."

Hint:

Try substituting "you are." If it fits, then "you're" is the correct form.

Example:

You're going to be sorry if you don't take your turn and do the dishes tonight.

Here is a list of 50 additional words that often give students trouble:

Don't Say. . . .	When You Mean
adolescents	adolescence (the time one is an adolescent)
aforementioned	this/previously stated
around	about (in reference to numbers)
associated to	associated with
attribute to	contribute to
avoid	prevent
base off/around	base on
conscience	conscious
continuous	continual
council	counsel
could of/would of	could have/would have
different than	different from
downfall	disadvantage
downside	disadvantage
entirety of	all
farther	further ("farther" applies to physical distance)
half to	have to
imply	infer
insure	ensure
irregardless	regardless
lifestyle	life
like	as
locality/location	place
majority of	most
man	human/humanity
manpower	resources
mindset	belief
misfortunate	unfortunate

multiple	many
none the less	nonetheless
obsess about	to be obsessed about
obtain	attain
overexaggerate	exaggerate
passed	past
popular	common
principal	principle
prior/prior to	before
references	refers to ("references" is a plural noun)
reoccur	recur
seize	cease
so	very
thanks to	due to
that	who/whom/where, etc.
thru	through
till	until
to transition	to change
upon	on
weather	whether
were	where
which	who/whom

As you progress through your course, you may find other groupings of words that you have problems with. Add them, along with definitions and correct usage, to the list above.

Exercise 17.16

Choose ten of the words from the lists above that you know give you trouble. Find the definitions of these words and then write sentences using the words correctly.

Example:

Amount: the quantity of something; used for non-count nouns

The amount of rain that fell in June this year is equal to all the rain that fell last year.

Number: the quantity of something; used for count nouns

It is hard to count the number of raindrops that fall into a cup.

Chapter Review Questions

1. Why is clarity important in writing?
2. Why is formal writing clearer than informal writing?
3. How is concision different from precision?
4. Find examples from business writing (such as advertising) that illustrate concepts discussed in this chapter, such as doubling up. Can you rewrite the samples so they are more formal and could be used in academic writing?
5. When should you use passive sentence constructions?
6. What are clichés? List some examples. Why should you avoid clichés in formal writing?
7. What is euphemistic language? Why are euphemisms confusing?
8. How are editing and proofreading different? Why are both important?
9. What are some things to look for when you proofread?
10. What message do you send to the reader if your paper has spelling mistakes or typos?

Appendix A
Tense Encounters with Verbs: A Summary

"Tense" refers to time when the action or condition expressed by the verb took place (or is taking place, or will take place). Each tense can take one of four *forms*: **simple, progressive, perfect,** and **perfect progressive**. These forms further describe the aspect of the verb, as to when its action began, and its duration or completion.

The auxiliary (helping) verb for most forms determines the complete form of the verb. The auxiliary verb for the progressive tenses is "to be" (is, was, will be); for the perfect tenses, it is "to have" (has, had, will have).

1. Present Tenses

Simple Present (action or situation exists now or exists on a regular basis):

I call	We call
You call	You call
He/she/it calls	They call

    I usually *call* for the pizza; you *call* for it this time.

Present Progressive (action is in progress):

I am sending	We are sending
You are sending	You are sending
He/she/it is sending	They are sending

    Mr. Kahn *is sending* the package to you by courier.

Present Perfect (action began in the past and is completed in the present):

I have eaten	We have eaten
You have eaten	You have eaten
He/she/it has eaten	They have eaten

    I *have eaten* the apple you gave me.

Present Perfect Progressive (action began in the past, continues in the present, and may continue into the future):

I have been hoping	We have been hoping
You have been hoping	You have been hoping
He/she/it has been hoping	They have been hoping

We *have been hoping* to receive news from the Philippines.

2. Past Tenses

Simple Past (action or situation was completed in the past):

I saw	We saw
You saw	You saw
He/she/it saw	They saw

Garfield *saw* the moon rise last night over his burrow.

Past Progressive (action was in progress in the past):

I was talking	We were talking
You were talking	You were talking
He/she/it was talking	They were talking

James and Beth *were talking* about storms when the hurricane warning flashed onto their computer screen.

Past Perfect (action was completed in the past prior to another action in the past):

I had finished	We had finished
Your had finished	You had finished
He/she/it had finished	They had finished

Alex *had finished* the second assignment when the storm knocked out power to his computer.

Past Perfect Progressive (action in progress in the past):

I had been practising	We had been practising
You had been practising	You had been practising
He/she/it had been practising	They had been practising

The golf team sophomores *had been practising* for the tournament all summer, but when school, started their coach announced his resignation.

3. Future Tenses

Simple Future (action will occur in the future):

I will see	We will see
You will see	You will see
He/she/it will see	They will see

I *will see* the Rocky Mountains on my way to Vancouver.

Future Progressive (action will be continuous in the future):

I will be walking	We will be walking
You will be walking	You will be walking
He/she/it will be walking	They will be walking

Norm and Martee *will be walking* in the Marathon of Hope next Saturday morning.

Future Perfect (action in the future will be completed):

I will have gone	We will have gone
You will have gone	You will have gone
He/she/it will have gone	They will have gone

Sally *will have gone* around the moon several times before the ship leaves its lunar orbit.

Future Perfect Progressive (actions are ongoing up to a specific future time):

I will have been studying	We will have been studying
You will have been studying	You will have been studying
He/she/it will have been studying	They will have been studying

With the completion of this assignment they *will have been studying* verbs for 13 years.

Remember that verbs can reflect mood (conditional, subjunctive) and voice (active, passive), and auxiliary verbs can be used to indicate conditions, such as necessity (I should go), obligation (you must go), possibility (he may go).

Exercise

In the following passages, some of the verb forms are correct, but others need to be changed. All verbs are underlined; correct those that are incorrect.

A.

Nature <u>was</u> a precious gift. It <u>provide</u> energies that <u>affect</u> society today. Although it <u>is</u> a gift, nature <u>needs</u> our attention and care because it <u>is</u> fragile and easily destroyed. I never <u>paid</u> much attention to nature because I <u>thought</u> humanity's impact on the natural world <u>was</u> not important. A few years ago, an encounter with a squirrel <u>has changed</u> my view. I <u>walk</u> home one day, and I <u>saw</u> a gray squirrel picking up loose pine cones in the garden. I <u>am watching</u> the squirrel hopping joyfully around the yard. Suddenly, it <u>starts</u> to run across the street. But before it <u>reached</u> the other side of the street, a car <u>hit</u> it and <u>killed</u> it. I <u>am devastated</u> that the driver <u>didn't even slow down</u>, as if the life of a squirrel is worthless.

We <u>should always respect</u> what nature <u>has offered</u> us. The natural world <u>is</u> an important factor in maintaining a healthy life cycle. If this life cycle <u>is</u> not protected, the balance in the life cycle <u>is</u> destroyed, which <u>will bring</u> serious consequences to the lives of all human beings.

B.

I <u>remember</u> a camping trip that I <u>was going on</u> with a few of my friends. We <u>were</u> very unprepared and <u>run</u> into a few mishaps along the way. The trip <u>occurred</u> during the rainy season, and we <u>have not brought</u> any firewood. We <u>have</u> a hard time getting the fire to start, even after we <u>borrowed</u> wood and an axe from the campers next door. Of course, we <u>forgot</u> to bring a can opener, so we <u>had</u> to try stabbing at the tins with a Swiss army knife to get them open. We <u>spend</u> the night around our Coleman stove, trying to keep warm.

That night <u>made</u> us realize how much we <u>took</u> nature for granted. In our homes everyday we <u>had</u> many household appliances that <u>made</u> our lives easier for us. It <u>is</u> easy to forget that some people <u>live</u> in the world without these conveniences and <u>relied</u> on nature from dawn to dusk. This camping trip <u>occurred</u> a long time ago when I <u>am</u> much younger. But the memory of that long night in the nature <u>stays</u> with me ever since.

Appendix B
A Checklist for EAL Writers

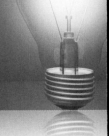

The following are some English idiomatic expressions and rules for usage. The first section is organized alphabetically by the major parts of speech. This section also includes articles. Although they are not a major part of speech, their usage can be confusing for EAL writers, so they have been allotted a separate section, beginning on page 449.

The second section (beginning on page 464) is an alphabetical list of commonly confused words and other usage errors.

For more complete information, many useful references, including OUP's general ESL dictionaries, can be consulted.

Adjectives

One-word adjectives usually precede the word(s) they modify, except predicate adjectives that follow linking verbs (see page 305); also, see **Ago**. However, **relative** (adjectival) **clauses** follow the noun they modify and present special challenges for writers.

Adjectives as participles

When a participle ending in *−ed* or *−en* precedes a noun and acts as an adjective, don't drop the ending it requires as a past participle:

> Although Patrick lived a *fast-paced* [not fast-pace] life, he had the *old-fashioned* [not old-fashion] habit of stopping and reading a newspaper every day before work.

Adjectives and present versus past participles

When participles are used to modify nouns, it can be confusing knowing whether to use the present (*−ing*) form or the past (*−ed* or *−en* form), especially after a linking verb like "was." In verbs related to feeling or emotion, the present participle is used when the subject *causes* the feeling; the past participle is used when the subject *experiences* the feeling.

Dennis felt *embarrassed* to receive a "C" on his essay; the mark was *depressing*.

Dennis experiences embarrassment; the mark causes him to feel depressed.

The surprise ending of the football game was *exciting*; the few fans left in the stadium were *excited*.

Comparatives and superlatives

Use the comparative of adjectives and adverbs when you want to compare one person or thing to another person or thing. Usually, the suffix *–er* is added if the quality being compared is one syllable, while the word *more* precedes a word of two or more syllables:

In BC, summers are usually *drier* than they are in Ontario.
According to *the most recent* statistics, it is *more dangerous* to drive a car than to take an airplane.

Use the superlative of adjectives and adverbs when you want to compare more than two of something. The definite article is usually not used with comparisons, but it is used with superlatives (see Articles, below).

In my opinion, BC is a *better* province than Alberta (there are two); in my friend's opinion, Alberta is *the best* of the western provinces (there are four).

Few vs. a few

Both can precede nouns that can be counted, but few means "not many," and a few means "some." So, *few* usually refers to fewer of something than *a few*! (Since "a few" has more letters than "few," you can associate it with more of something than "few.")

Few Canadians know how to play cricket. However, *a few* people on my listserv said they would be interested in learning how to play it.

Much vs. many

Use *much* before nouns that cannot be counted and *many* before countable nouns. Similarly, use *amount* before uncountable nouns and *number* before countable nouns (see page 434); use *less* before uncountable nouns and *fewer* before countable nouns (see page 436).

The Canadian television channel *MuchMusic* features *many* different kinds of music.

Plurals as adjectival phrases concerning distance, money, and time

When these kinds of plural nouns appear in hyphenated phrases before other nouns, they drop the final "s," as in the following examples:

a *10-kilometre* run (*not* a 10-kilometres run), a *30-day* refund policy (*not* a 30-days refund policy), a *70-year-old* man (*not* a 70-years-old man).

Relative (adjectival) clauses

A relative clause modifies the noun it follows (known as the *antecedent*). These clauses begin with a relative pronoun (usually *who*, *that*, or *which*, but sometimes *whom*, *whose*, *when*, *in which*, or *where*). Make sure you include the introductory relative pronoun at the beginning of the clause. Below, the complete relative clause is underlined, the relative pronoun is bolded, and the antecedent is italicized:

> Sushan looked everywhere for the *sweater* **that** she lost yesterday.

> In China, there is a *high school* **that** was painted green because green is considered a relaxing colour. The *students* **who** attended the school reported better study habits.

When you use a phrase like "in which" to introduce a clause, do not repeat the preposition at the end of the clause:

> Happiness for some people is measured by their success in the society in which they live ~~in~~.

Relative clauses, agreement

The relative pronoun that introduces the relative clause refers back to the noun antecedent, as mentioned above. The antecedent determines whether the verb in the relative clause is singular or plural. The relative pronoun is bolded in the sentence below, the verb is underlined, and the antecedent is italicized:

> The Hyundai hybrid car has a small *engine* **that** consumes less fuel than ordinary cars.

Adverbs

Adverbs with adjectives

Adverbs can modify adjectives and other adverbs, along with verbs. Ensure you always use the correct adverbial form. In the sentence below, "environmental" is the adjectival form; "environmentally" is the adverbial one:

> The average Canadian household has become more environmental*ly* conscious than in the past.

Although many adverbs end in *−ly*, some do not; furthermore, some adjectives end in *−ly* and modify nouns: a *friendly* neighbour, some *fatherly* advice, a *cowardly* act. These adjectives cannot be made into adverbs.

Comparative and superlative of adverbs

See Comparatives and Superlatives, under Adjectives, above.

Articles—*A, An*, and *The*

Indefinite articles precede some singular nouns, and definite articles precede some singular and plural nouns. Context often determines whether an article precedes a noun or whether it is omitted; idiom also can determine usage. However, there are general guidelines that can be used when you're in doubt about whether to include the article or not.

The indefinite article

General rule: Use the indefinite article *a* or *an* if you want to identify a general or nonspecific noun. Use *an* rather than *a* if the noun begins with a vowel that is not pronounced or with a silent "h."

> When I was bird watching, I looked for *a* Rufus hummingbird. (no specific bird is referred to)
> When *the* hummingbird saw me, it darted off into the trees. (a specific bird is referred to)

The indefinite article is *not* used before most uncountable concrete nouns, nor do these nouns form plurals. It is easier to remember these nouns if you divide them into categories:

Kinds of liquids: beer, blood, coffee, milk, oil, soup, water, wine, etc.
Kinds of food: bread, cheese, corn, flour, food, fruit, lettuce, meat, pasta, popcorn, rice, sugar, etc.
Names of languages: Arabic, Mandarin, Dutch, French, Japanese, Vietnamese, etc.
Names of areas of study: biology, economics, geography, mathematics, etc.
Names of gases: hydrogen, methane, ozone, oxygen, etc.; air, fire, smoke, and steam also belong here
Sports and games: baseball, bowling, football, hockey, jogging, surfing, tennis, etc. But, baseballs and footballs (the objects, not the sports) are countable.
Others: chalk, clothing, equipment, feedback, furniture, health, help, homework, housework, laughter, luggage, mail, money, research, scenery, soap, software, weather, wood, work, etc.

However, if preceded by a word like "piece" or "item," such nouns may be countable: *a piece* (or *pieces*) *of chalk, an item* (or *items*) *of furniture, a glass of water.* As well, many nouns can be used adjectivally before countable nouns: *a cheese stick, a hockey game…*
Some of the nouns above can be used in a countable sense if they can be divided into different types:

Red *wine* in moderation can be beneficial to one's health.
Different *wines* are classified by their place of origin.

Note: Although *mail* is an uncountable noun, *email* can be used as a countable noun; thus, you can talk about receiving *an* email. As a noun, email can also be pluralized:

Flora was shocked to see that she had received more than 100 *emails* over the weekend; as a result, she vowed to get rid of her *email* by the end of the week.

See also Uncountable and countable nouns under Nouns.

The definite article

General rule: Nouns that refer to a specific person, place, or object are usually preceded by the definite article, *the*:

Please give me *the* pen on *the* table.

A specific pen (distinct from other pens) on a specific table is requested.

Please give me *a* pen on *the* table.

This request implies that there is more than one pen on the specific table.

Please give me *a* pen.

Any pen from anywhere will do.

Young children, especially in *the* 3–5 age group, are always asking questions.

Other age groups exist, making the reference specific.

Including definite articles before nouns:

a) *First versus second reference*: Use *a* when something is first mentioned, *the* when the same noun is mentioned again (it can now be identified). Several examples are shown in the brief story below:

Mike, who was 18 and lived in Canada, had *a strange experience* as he was walking on *a beach*: he found *a brown bottle* that had washed ashore. When he cleaned it up, he saw that *the bottle* had *a note* inside. With much effort he was able to dislodge *the note*, which was from *a person* in another country. *The person* had written simply "Hi, I'm Mike. I'm 18, and I live in Australia."

b) *Nouns that refer to a species or class of objects*: Use the definite article before this group; an example is "the definite article" in this sentence. Here is another example:

In her English class, Izumi studied *the argumentative essay* before *the research essay*.

c) *Unique nouns*: If the noun has a unique identity, precede it by the definite article.
Examples:

- specific eras or time periods: *the* Industrial Revolution, *the* Age of Reason, in *the* twentieth century, etc.
- *the* Sun, *the* Moon, *the* North Star (unique celestial objects)
- *Newspapers, museums, theatres, and hotels*: *The* Vancouver Sun (newspaper), *the* Royal Ontario Museum, *the* Imax theatre, *The* Banff Springs Hotel

d) *Superlatives* could also be considered unique, in a category by themselves; the definite article precedes superlatives (see also Comparatives and Superlatives). The sentence below includes three superlatives.

I have found that *the best courses* at college are usually *the most challenging ones*, and they are taught by *the best teachers*.

Compare with:
I have found that *courses* at college are usually *challenging*, and they are taught by good *teachers*.

e) *Ordinals*: *the first, the second,* etc. (vs. cardinal numbers: one, two, etc.)

Maria was *the first* to cross the finishing line; Linden was *the second*. They finished one and two, respectively.

Omitting definite articles before nouns. When using nouns that fall into the following groups, omit the definite article. However, there are exceptions to the guidelines.

a) Omit before most *plural nouns*:

If animals have no consciousness, it is meaningless to discuss whether eating meat is immoral.

"Animals" is a plural noun; "meat" is an uncountable noun.

b) Omit before *proper nouns*, though there are many exceptions to this general rule. For example, the article is used before some geographical names:

- *Bodies of water*: Hudson Bay, Lake Ontario, but *the* Pacific Ocean, *the* Fraser River
- *Countries and continents*: Canada, China, Japan, Asia, Africa, North America; but *the* United States, *the* Philippines, *the* Arctic. Omit before Nunavut and

all the *provinces and American states*; but *the Province of Quebec, Ontario,* etc., *The* Northwest Territories, *the* Yukon, *the* District of Columbia (in the US). Omit before Hawaii, but *the Hawaiian Islands.*

- *National, social, and cultural groups*: Canadians, Americans; but *the* English, *the* Japanese, *the* middle class, *the* Inuit peoples

Lonnie is a member of *the* Chipewyan First Nations and lives near Prince Albert in northern Saskatchewan.

c) Omit before *abstract nouns* unless a prepositional phrase follows the noun; abstract nouns are usually uncountable and also cannot be pluralized:

It is said that while truth is relative, reality is what we perceive through our senses.

"Truth" and "reality" are abstractions.

The reality of the situation, unfortunately, is that *justice* does not always prevail.

A prepositional phrase follows "reality" but not the abstract noun "justice."

Other abstract nouns include *advice, anger, curiosity, employment, enjoyment, evidence, freedom, fun, health, information, intelligence, knowledge, love, music, peace, pollution, research, respect, wealth, weather,* etc.

d) Common nouns that often result in errors in article use include *government, nature, society, Internet,* and *media*:

- *Government*: if you are referring to a *specific* government, use the definite article; otherwise, do not use "the":

The *government* (meaning, for example, the government of Ontario) has no right to raise student tuition fees.

- *Nature*: If you are referring to the natural world, the noun *nature* is *not* preceded by "the." If the sense is of a quality, essence, or habit, "the" may be required. The noun *environment*, which has a similar meaning to *nature*, is usually preceded by an article.

The wonders of *nature* surround us every day. It has been *the nature* of previous generations [their habit] to take *nature* [the natural world] for granted.

Evidence of damage to *the environment* is all around us.

- *Society*: It is *not* preceded by "the" if the reference is a general one. Note that *society* is usually singular and requires the singular verb form. If the reference is specific, "the" may be required (for example, if it is followed by a phrase that particularizes society):

Society does not look kindly on those who fail to respect *its* rules.
I find *the society of like-minded individuals* boring and unrewarding.

- When used as a noun, *Internet* is preceded by "the" as is *media* when it refers to *the news media* as a form of mass communication, such as television, radio, newspapers, and magazines; it usually takes a singular verb form when used this way.

With the rise of *the Internet, the media has* become even a more powerful influence on *society*.

For article use with gerunds, see Gerunds, under Nouns, below.

Nouns

Every + noun

"Every one of," like "each one of," "either one of," etc., will be followed by a plural noun but a *singular* verb form. But when one of these words is followed directly by a noun, that noun will be *singular*, not plural (and the verb will be singular, too):

Almost *every* drafting *course* in schools *involves* computers.
Almost *every kind* of species *has its* own social group.
Many high school students in China are not allowed to use calculators, so they have to do *every* mathematical *step* in their heads.

Using "every one of" would result in a plural noun in the "of" phrase: *Every one of the* drafting *courses*; They have to do *every one of the* mathematical *steps* in their heads.

Gerunds

Gerunds are incomplete verb forms that act as nouns in a sentence (they end in *–ing*). They are *always singular* and *are usually not preceded by articles*.

Having a computer *is* necessary for almost all students nowadays.
Learning many new skills *is* enjoyable if you have the time for *it*.

Fast foods have quickly *become* a part of our stressful lives today.

The subject, "fast foods" is plural, so the verb is plural.

Eating fast foods *has* quickly *become* a part of our stressful lives today.

The subject "eating," a gerund, is singular.

Kind(s) of/type(s) of + noun

What follows *kind of* and *type of* will be a singular noun; what follows *kinds of* and *types of* will be a plural countable noun (uncountable nouns could be used with either) since more than one kind/type will be referred to. Often, a demonstrative adjective will precede *kind/type*: "this" or "that" (both are singular) can precede kind/type; "these" or "those" (plural) can precede kinds/types.

What *type of car was* Natalie driving?
Many *kinds of cars are* on the market today.
That *type of incident* occurs every day.

Uncountable and countable nouns

For a list of common uncountable nouns, see The indefinite article, above. The following uncountable nouns are responsible for many writing errors and may require your particular attention:

- *Clothing:* As an uncountable noun, it will never be preceded by the indefinite article and will never form a plural. "Clothes," however, is a countable noun. "Cloth" is a material that is sometimes used in the manufacture of clothing; it does not mean the same thing as "clothing."

People have used *clothing* to cover their body for thousands of years; however, we often choose our *clothes* today for their fashion rather than their practicality.

At lululemon, you can buy *various kinds of clothing*; at a store that sells sewing supplies, you can buy *different kinds of cloths*.

- *Information* and similar nouns, such as *knowledge*, *evidence*, and *advice*, are uncountable abstract nouns: they are not preceded by "a" or "an" and are never plural.
- *Importance*: You can never say "an importance" or "importances." You can say "*the* importance" if a prepositional phrase beginning with "of" follows. As with a few other noun-adjective pairs, the noun ends in *–ance* or *–ence* and the adjective ends in *–ant* or *–ent* (*important*).

I am going to discuss *the importance of getting a good job* in today's society.
The most *important* thing about a job is that it will make you *confident* and *independent*.

- *Research*: A non-count noun, it is never plural. However, *researcher*, a person who *does* or *conducts* research, is a countable noun. As a verb, "research" is usually followed by a direct object (not by "about").

The Journal of Wildlife Management has been covering *research* in the field for more than 30 years. I *am researching* the topic of wildlife management by looking for articles from this journal.

As an adjective, "research" can be followed by a plural noun: *research projects, research studies*.

Some nouns can be either countable or uncountable depending on context.

In their youth, most people have at least 100,000 *hairs* on their head.

If you're determined, you could count the number of hairs!

Shaving your *hair* today is more often a matter of personal choice than of hygiene.

The sense here is of hair as a mass, therefore uncountable.

For examples of countable and uncountable nouns with articles, see Articles, above.

Prepositions

See Verbs and prepositions.

Verbs

Modal auxiliaries

Modals can be considered a special category of helping verb that make the meaning of a main verb more precise. They are usually followed by the bare infinitive, which does not include "to." Some common uses of modals are listed below.

- *Can* expresses capability:

Clothing *can* really say a lot about a person.

Compare the following sentences and note their different meanings:

In the summer, Nina *swims* every day.

The simple present tense is used to show a repeated action (see Appendix A).

In the summer, Nina *can swim* every day.

The modal "can" is used with the bare infinitive to show ability or capability; "is able to" can be substituted for "can."

- *Could* expresses capability in the past tense:

When she lived near a lake, Nina *could* swim every day.

- *Should* expresses necessity or obligation. Compare the following sentences and note their different meanings:

Incorrect statement (i.e., not factually true):
There *are* gun laws in all states in the US that prevent people from killing each other.

Correct but weak:
There *have to be* gun laws in all states in the US.
Correct and effective:
There *should be* (or *must be*) gun laws in all states in the US.

- *May* and *might* express possibility. *May* often conveys a stronger possibility than *might*:

Since she has the prerequisites, Bianca *may* enroll in the second-year course.
Although she worked late, she *might* decide to go to the party.

- *May* also expresses permission:

Students *may* bring beverages into the study area but not food items.

- *Will* expresses probability:

Since she has the prerequisites, Bianca *will* enroll in the second-year anthropology course.

- *Would* expresses a repeated action in the past:

When she lived near a lake, Nina *would* swim every day. (Compare with Could, above.)

Verbs and nouns

Because nouns are sometimes formed from verbs and often look like them, they can be confused. Use a dictionary to ensure you have used a verb where one is required and a noun where one is required. Here are three sets of commonly confused words:

Belief, believe: *belief* is a noun; *believe* is a verb. *Believe* is often followed by *in* or *that*, depending on whether a word/phrase (*in*) or a clause (*that*) follows:

She firmly *believed in* his innocence.
She firmly *believed that* he was innocent; this was her true *belief.*

Breath, breathe: *breath* is a noun; *breathe* (pronounced with a long ē) is a verb. You can *take* or *draw a breath*, meaning "breathe in." Somewhat idiomatically, to *take a deep breath* can mean to prepare yourself for a difficult task (whether or not a deep breath is actually taken).

The guest speaker, Madeleine, *took a deep breath* before she entered the crowded room. After she began speaking, she *breathed* normally again.

Effect, affect: see page 433.

Life, live: *life* is a noun; *live* (pronounced with a short ĭ) is a verb; *live* (long ī) is an adjective meaning "alive." Like many English nouns, *life*, the noun, can precede another noun and act as an adjective.

> While someone born today in Canada can expect to *live* about 81 years, in Botswana the quality of *life* is much lower, and the average lifespan is about 51 years.

Verbs and prepositions

The following alphabetical list includes verbs that have become confusing, usually due to idiomatic prepositional use.

Access: This verb means to get information from (e.g., the Internet); *to have access to* means to be able to obtain information from, or to be able to use something or go somewhere to get it.

> She *accesses* her bank account every day.
> Thanks to the Internet she *has access to* her bank account every day.
> Although she has no stove or refrigerator in her room, she *has access to* a shared kitchen at the end of the hallway.

Agree/Disagree with: You agree or disagree *with* someone or with a person's views or opinions on something. There are other prepositions that can follow both these verbs, but in most essays where you argue a thesis, you will use *with* following *agree* and *disagree*.

> I agree *with* space exploration in general, but I disagree *with* those who want us to spend billions of dollars per year on something with no practical benefit for humanity.

> Hassan and I agreed *on* the issue of space exploration.

> *Agreed* followed by *to* means "to consent" (to).

> I agreed *to* give a speech on the merits of space exploration to my philosophy class.

Apply for a loan, a scholarship, a position, a job; **to apply to** (a place or situation) a school, etc.; **to be accepted to** is usually followed by an object (a place or position):

Joshua *applied to* several Ontario colleges before he *applied for* a student loan.

After he was *accepted to* the business program at Conestoga College, Joshua learned that loans don't *apply to* scholarship students.

Attend (a university, class, concert, wedding, *etc.*; this means "to be present at"); **to study at** (a university). To *attend to* means to apply oneself to something.

The school counsellor told Braden he would have to *attend to* academic matters, which included *attending* tutorials.

Before he decided *to study at* Red Deer College he had been considering the business program at the University of Alberta.

See **Graduate from**.

Avoid vs. to prevent: To *avoid* indicates a passive activity, but to *prevent* is to take an active course to stop something from happening. When you *avoid* something, you stay away from it; the verb is usually followed by a direct object (the thing that is avoided). When you *prevent* something, you take an action so that it does not occur; *prevent* can be followed by a direct object or by a direct object + *from* and a gerund phrase (a gerund is a noun ending in −*ing*):

Inoculations are designed to *prevent the flu*.
You should *avoid people* when you are sick as this will *prevent others from catching* your virus.

Call/draw attention to: To *call/draw attention* to is followed by a noun and means to point something out. A noun or possessive adjective often precedes *attention*, as in the following sentence:

The *Intergovernmental Panel on Climate Change* (IPCC) was founded in 1988 in order to *draw* world *attention to* the link between climate change and human activity.

To *pay attention to* means to take note of or to look at closely.

All Canadians should *pay attention to* the next IPCC report in 2014.

To *get attention*, meaning to attract notice, is not usually followed by a preposition:

After failing to *get* the teacher's *attention* any other way, Harmon shouted "fire!"

See **Pay**; **Point out**.

Care: To care *about* means to be concerned about (see **Concern**):

> She cares *about* good grades.

To *care for* or *take care of* means to look after:

> Thomas *took care of* his sister when his mother was working.

Commit: A person can *commit* a crime, a murder, *an* error, but a person *commits suicide* (no article). Another meaning of the verb *commit* is "to dedicate to" or "resolve to do something"; it is often followed by the reflexive pronoun and the preposition *to*.

> After *committing a* serious crime, he thought briefly about *committing suicide*, but decided instead to *commit himself to* a life of helping others.

Compare and contrast: It can be tricky to use these verbs correctly, but they are very common, and some guidelines can be applied. When you compare, you focus on similarities; when you contrast, you focus on differences. *Compare* is usually followed by *to* or *with*:

> In our class assignment, we were asked to *compare* the Canadian system of government *with* the system in another country.

Note that what follows *compare* (or *contrast*) is the direct object; *with* or *to* then follows, and the indirect object follows *with* or *to*.

If you use the verb phrase *make a comparison*, the preposition you use is *between*:

> He made a comparison *between* one political system *and* another.

Compared to/with: In this construction, the grammatical subject is what is being compared:

> *Compared to* the small town that I grew up in, Victoria seems like a big city.

"Victoria" is the subject as it is being compared to the small town.

> The author *compares and contrasts* two different time periods by analyzing the standards of dress in each one.

The writer will look at similarities and differences.

> The transitional phrase is *by contrast*.

Compete for (something); Compete *against* (someone):

> They *competed for* the honour of being named captain of the team.
> Siblings often *compete for* attention from their parents.
> Mohammed *competed against* his friend to see who could get the higher mark.

Concern: The meaning you want determines the preposition to use:

> *To be concerned about* means to be troubled or worried about *something*
> *To be concerned for* means to be worried about *someone* (or, occasionally, *something*)
> *To concern oneself about* means to take an active interest in something or someone.

When it is not followed by a preposition, *concern* means "applies to" or "is relevant to":

> She *was concerned about* the implications of the new driving regulations; specifically, she *was concerned for* her daughter, who would soon be getting her licence.

> The matter I have to discuss, Yuto, *concerns* your future with this organization.

Consider, Discuss, Mention: When you consider something, you think carefully about it, usually in order to take some kind of action. *Consider*, like *discuss* and *mention*, is followed by a direct object—not by *about*. Unlike *discuss*, however, *consider* and *mention* may be followed by a clause beginning with *that*.

> Before Yoshi decided to get married, he *considered the matter* by talking it over with his married friend Eizad. Then he *discussed it with* Sanjeet.

> Before Yoshi *discussed* his marriage plans with his fiancée, he *mentioned* to Eizad and Sanjeet *that* he was considering marriage.

See **Think**.

Depend, Rely, Count: These verbs can mean "have confidence in someone or something" and are followed by *on* + a noun that states who or what is depended/relied on. They may then be followed by *for* + another noun that expands on the first noun:

> Shaun *depends on* email *for* most of his business.
> Maheen *relies on* her friend Amy *for* fashion advice.

Discriminate *between*: This means "to tell differences between"; two nouns must follow. **Discriminate** *against*: This means to treat the individual(s) or group(s) unfairly; one or more nouns could follow.

It is good to be able to *discriminate between* a true friend and somebody who only wants you to do something for him or her.

We often unconsciously *discriminate against* groups like the homeless by not seeing them when we walk downtown, even when they are a few feet away.

Discrimination is the noun that means "the practice of discriminating."

Discuss: See Consider.

Encourage/discourage: You encourage someone *to* do something, but you discourage someone *from* doing something. You can also *offer encouragement to* someone (which means to actively encourage him/her), but you cannot offer discouragement.

Raising tuition may *discourage* students *from* enrolling in other courses.
The president of the students' union is *encouraging* all students *to* protest the tuition increase.

Note that an infinitive follows *to*, but a gerund follows *from*.

Annie *offered encouragement to* John, who was worried about the tuition increase.

Graduate *from* university, etc.; **to be a graduate** *of* (this is the noun; the second ă is a short vowel); to have/get/obtain/pursue *an* education:

After Kasey *graduated from* college, she went to graduate school and became a *graduate of* UBC.

Hire (someone; *employers* hire); **to be hired by** (someone, a company, etc.; *employees* are hired):

After applying for several positions during the summer, Teh *was hired by* another company.

See **Apply for**.

Know *something*: This means to have information or expertise *about* something; **to know** *someone*: the person's name should follow the verb as the direct object.

When I got *to know Tey*, I learned about computers, and I now *know* everything *about* them; Shelley *knows* that she has a test tomorrow.

Lack: As a verb, it is followed by a direct object; as a noun, it is usually preceded by an article or other determiner (e.g., *its*, *that*, *this*, *your*) and followed by *of*:

> The first thing she noticed about the bedroom was *its lack of* privacy. The kitchen also *lacked* dishes and other utensils.

Lead to: This means the same as *result in* (see below). In both cases, a result or consequence follows the preposition.

> The cloning of animals, according to many people, is certain *to lead to* (or, result in) the eventual cloning of humans.

Look at/around/for/into/over:

> *look at* (examine): In my essay, I will *look at* solutions to the problem of homeless people.
> *around*: Dazed by the accident, he slowly sat up and *looked around*.
> *for* (search): Simon *looked for* his lost notes on his messy desk.
> *into* (investigate): After being laid off for the second time this year, Natalie began to *look into* self-employment.
> *over* (scan): She *looked over* her notes from the previous class.

Mention: See Consider.

Participate *in*: You participate in something—activities, sports, etc.:

> Dong Hun often *participates in* classroom discussions.

Pay (for): *Pay* means to give (usually money) what is due for goods, services, or work, etc. *For* + a noun may follow if you want to indicate what was purchased:

> She *paid* less than $80 *for* all her textbooks since she bought them used.

Point out: This verb means to call attention to (something). It is generally followed by a noun/pronoun or a clause beginning with *that*. One of the meanings of *to point* is to indicate, to single out, using a finger; it is followed by *to*.

> Ruji *pointed out* her sister among the bystanders.
> Ruji *pointed out that* her sister was always late for a meeting.
> Ruji *pointed to* her sister, who was standing in a crowd.

Refer: *Refer* is followed by *to* when the meaning is "to make a reference or to make mention of something." If a clause beginning with *that* follows, a noun such as *fact*, *idea*, etc. should intervene between the verb *refer* and the clause.

> In his letter of recommendation, he *referred to* the many occasions in which Duy had demonstrated his sense of humanity and compassion.

> Specifically, he *referred to the fact that* Duy had often volunteered for work in local hospices.

Result in/result from: When you use the verb *result*, you must be careful about the preposition you use after it. To result *in* means that what follows the verb will be a *result* or consequence; to result *from* means that what follows the verb will be a *cause*.

> Most murders in the US *result from* the use of guns.

Guns are a cause.

> Being convicted of the crime of murder *usually results in* long prison terms.

Prison terms are the consequence.

Stress and **emphasize**: They mean the same thing and are usually followed by direct objects (not prepositions). But if you want to use the verb phrase "put stress/ emphasis *on*," note the preposition that is required. A *that* clause may also follow these verbs.

> The writer *emphasized* the main point of her argument by providing examples.
> The writer *put emphasis on* the main point of her argument by providing examples.
> The instructor *stressed that* all students should arrive on time for class.

Avoid informal expressions like "stress out," meaning to experience feelings of stress.

Think is a verb with many uses. To think *about* means to "reflect on," and to think *over* means to "consider"; note the word order of *it* in the sentence below. Use *think* + a clause beginning with *that* if you want to refer to a belief or opinion.

> William originally *thought that he would take a commerce class* in the second term, but when he thought *about it* (or *thought it over*), he decided to enroll right away.

Verbs and their subjects (subject–verb agreement)

Always ensure that you use the singular form of any verb that has a singular subject. But if the subject is plural (indicating more than one of something or someone), the verb should be plural.

- Remember that the third-person *singular* form of a *verb* usually ends in "s." This can be confusing because it is the *plural* form of most *nouns* that ends in "s."
- See Every + noun, above. *Each, either,* and *neither* are singular and require a singular verb form. For agreement rules, see Chapter 16.
- See Gerunds, under Nouns, above, for agreement with gerund subjects.
- See Relative clauses**,** agreement, above, and **Criteria** and **Data**, below (the last two nouns are plural and require the plural verb form).

Verb tenses

See Appendix A for a summary of verb tenses.

Additional Commonly Confused Words and Idioms

The following list includes words and phrases that present challenges to EAL writers. For more examples of commonly confused word pairs, see Chapter 17.

Advantages/disadvantages: The safest preposition to use after these is *to*, though other situations can make *in, of,* or *for* applicable.

> There are a few *advantages to* cloning, but there are far more *disadvantages to* this controversial practice.

Ago: When you want to refer to a time in the past and relate this time to today, you can use the adjective *ago*; it follows the noun. To refer to a *specific* point in the past, you can give the date (month, day, year) preceded by *on*. See **Times and dates**, below.

> The first truly successful cloning of an animal occurred more than *ten years ago*. The first truly successful cloning of an animal occurred *on July 5, 1996*.

Always, **Usually**, **Often**: Be careful to distinguish between these three adverbs. Use *always* if you want to describe something done *all the time*; use *usually* if you want to describe something done *more often than not*; use *often* if you want to describe something done *many times*. Sometimes, just by using the present tense you are suggesting that something is always done; if that's not what you want to convey, it's *often* better to use the modal of capability (*can*) in front of the bare infinitive.

The sun *always* rises in the east and sets in the west. The sun is *usually* hotter in summer than in spring. In the rainy season, we don't see the sun very *often*.

Await/Wait: The first verb is usually followed by a direct object—an expected person or an event; the second verb means to stay inactive until something happens or someone comes:

They *awaited* the professor's arrival. They *waited* for 20 minutes before they gradually filed out of the room.

Compose, **Comprise**, **Consist**: The verb *compose* means "to make up"; *comprise* means "to consist of." *Compose* is often followed by "of".

A good backpack is *composed* of an inner frame, a shoulder harness, a sternum strap, and a hip belt.

The course practicum *comprises* (or *consists of*) 25 hours of learning theory, teaching practice as a TA, and the completion of a teaching dossier.

Conclusions: There are a few ways to express a conclusion. In most cases, a clause should follow the verb:

One can *conclude that* commercialism destroys culture; *one can come to the conclusion [or draw the conclusion] that commercialism destroys culture.* You can also write *In conclusion,* or *To conclude* + clause.

To announce the conclusion of your essay, don't say, "As a conclusion." Instead, say, "In conclusion." However, no phrase may be needed as your reader can assume it is your conclusion by the fact it is the final paragraph.

Criteria: The noun refers to *more than one* rule or standard for a judgment, whereas *criterion* refers to *one* such standard:

The officer explained the *criteria* for Canadian citizenship to Terry, who satisfied all except the last *criterion*: he had not yet taken the citizenship test.

Data: The noun refers to a collection of facts, such as statistics, from which conclusions are drawn. Because it appears as a plural in formal writing (the singular is *datum*), it usually requires a plural verb form.

The *data led* to the inescapable conclusion that, as a species, we are becoming more intelligent over time.

Despite; **in spite** *of*: Both act as prepositions, so a *noun*—not a clause—needs to follow each.

> *In spite of* her best efforts to create interest in the performance, only a few people attended it.

You can also say, "*Despite* her best efforts...."

Et cetera (abbreviated **etc.**), means "and so forth." You can use it as a substitute for "and more of the same," as the last item in a list. It is *not* preceded by "and."

For example: Use *for example* or *for instance* before providing one or more examples of something. Do not use *As an example....*

Human: This noun can be used in the singular or the plural, but possessive forms should be avoided. Instead, consider using *humanity*, an adjectival form, or *our*.

> It is a *human* [*not* a human's] need to aim for perfection.

> *Humanity's* [*not* Humans'] need for perfection is boundless. OR, *Our* need for perfection is boundless.

Humanity: Humanity refers to humans collectively. Don't use "man" or "mankind" to refer broadly to human beings: many consider these words sexist as, by implication, they exclude women. *Humanity* is not preceded by the definite article (or possessive adjective) unless it refers to an inner quality (see **Nature**, above).

> One quality that *humanity* shares with other organisms is the need to solve problems. She demonstrated *her humanity* (an inner quality) by forgiving her enemies.

The **humanities**: This plural noun refers to the division of knowledge or education that deals with ideas or values. Used collectively to refer to the specific disciplines that explore ideas, the noun is sometimes capitalized.

> *The humanities* may include English, Philosophy, History, Greek and Roman Studies, Women's Studies, and Religious Studies, as well as various language studies.

In fact: It is, *in fact*, two words, not one.

Make vs. **enable**: *Make* is a useful verb, but it can also be overused. To *enable* means to "make possible" or to "allow," so it's often the better choice where something is possible or can happen as a result.

The outlet of laughter often *enables* people to respond to stressful situations in a healthy way.

In the example above, laughter doesn't "make" people respond to stress, but it "allows" them to do so.

Most of: The phrase *most of* is followed by *the* plus a specific group of objects or people. In a general reference using *most*, do not include the preposition *of*:

> *Most of the* women in my class are thinking about entering university, but *most people* at my college just want to complete their diploma or degree.

Movies: You speak generally about *going to the movies*; but you can also say you are *going to see a movie*. If you mean a specific movie, then you would use the definite article before *movie*.

> One of Mohammed's favorite activities is *going to (the) movies*; the *last movie* he saw was *Iron Man 2*.

Nowadays: Used as an adverb, it often is placed at the beginning of a clause and means "at the present time" or "in these times"; it can usually be replaced by *today*. When used as a noun, it is not preceded by *the*.

> *Nowadays*, people seem lost without their BlackBerry clutched in their hand, which has led to a disorder known as "BlackBerry thumb."

On the one hand; **on the other hand**: The preposition *on* introduces these transitional phrases of contrast. If you use the first phrase, you must use the second one when you come to discuss the contrasting element. There are several other transitions that can be used for contrast (e.g., *by contrast, in contrast* [*to*], *conversely, but*).

Opinion, express an opinion: Don't say, "In my point of view," "As for myself," or "As far as I am concerned…." The most direct way of stating your opinion is simply to say, "In my opinion…" or, "I believe that…", and follow with a clause that states your opinion. However, it is often more objective just to express your opinion without announcing that it is your opinion.

If you want to express someone else's opinion, you can say: "According to the point of view of people who smoke…"; "according to smokers…", etc., or simply, "Scientists believe that…."

Unless you are writing about your personal experience, check with your instructor before using the first-person in formal essays.

So: Do not use this adverb as a substitute for *very*; *so* must be followed by a clause beginning with *that*. (When *so* is a coordinating conjunction, it is usually followed by an independent clause).

wrong: Johnny was *so long* at the fair; **right**: Johnny was *so long* at the fair *that* he didn't have time to go shopping before picking me up; Johnny was *very* long at the fair; Johnny spent *a long time* at the fair.

Raise vs. **rise**: *Rise* is an irregular verb (he *rises*; she *rose*; they *have risen*); raise is a regular verb. *To rise* means "to increase" or "go up/go higher"; *to raise* means "to cause to increase." So, the rent you are paying *rises* every year, but your landlord *raises* the rent every year (he or she is the cause). One can, therefore, speak about the government raising student tuition fees; more generally, one would say there has been a rise (not a "raise")—both are nouns—in tuition fees; in other words, the fees have gone up.

Remember: When you are remembering something now (for example, when you're writing about an incident in the past), *remember* is put in the present tense, though the action described will be in the past tense.

> I *remember* when I was little how I *thought* my parents *knew* everything.

Some time, **Sometime**, **Sometimes**: *Some time* refers to an indefinite period of time; *sometime* refers to an indefinite point in time. *Sometimes* is a synonym for "occasionally."

> *Some time* has passed since the deadline for dropping the course.
> The drop deadline was *sometime* in September.
> *Sometimes* I wonder if I should have dropped the course.

Statistics: Use this noun to refer to the subject area that deals with gathering and assessing information and using it numerically (as percentages, raw numbers, etc.). **Statistics** and **mathematics** are *subjects* studied at university; when you refer to either of these as a *subject*, it is considered *singular*; otherwise, it is considered *plural*. Use **statistic** to refer to a particular fact.

> *Statistics show* that people spend less time with their family than they did 20 years ago.

> Less than 10 per cent of parents who work spend more than one hour a day with their children, according to a recent *statistic*.

> My favorite subject at school this year *is Statistics*.

Times and dates, referring to: The preposition used for time expressions will vary according to context: e.g., I will be there *for* Christmas. (I will arrive sometime *on* or *before* Christmas); I will be there *during* Christmas (I will be there for the entire time).

For specific times:
He will arrive *at* 9 a.m. *on* Tuesday; *on* December 24
For less specific times:
He will arrive *in* the morning (*in* the evening, but *at* night); *in* December; *in* 2010.

Throughout: It should be one word, not two, when you use it *throughout* your essay.

Way: Don't use *way* as a synonym for *much*:

It is much [*not* "way"] more interesting to discuss important issues in class than to just watch a PowerPoint lecture.

Appendix C
Peer Edit Forms

◎ Peer Edit Form: Formal Outline

The essay outline provides the structure on which the essay itself will be built. Therefore, as an editor, you should pay special attention to the relation among the parts (Introduction, body paragraphs, Conclusion), to the order of arguments (weakest to strongest? strongest to weakest? some other logical order?), as well as to the strength and effectiveness of each main point. Is each adequately developed? Is the claim supported?

Instructions

Use the check boxes below to record the fact that you have considered and evaluated the criteria. Use the space following to add suggestions, comments, questions, and advice.

Introduction

❏ What kind of formal outline has been used? Topic or Sentence? Other (such as Graphic)?
❏ Does the introduction attract your interest?
❏ Does it announce the topic?
❏ Does it contain a two-part direct thesis statement announcing the topic and commenting on the topic?
❏ Is the claim one of fact, value, or policy?
❏ Is the thesis statement interesting, specific, manageable, and clearly expressed?
  ❏ interesting
  ❏ specific

❏ manageable

❏ clearly expressed

❏ Does each paragraph contain at least one main idea that can be easily identified as such? If not, which paragraph(s) don't do this?

❏ Does each paragraph contain at least two sub-points that help develop the main point? If not, which paragraph(s) don't?

❏ Has the writer been able to provide support for his/her argument? If not, suggest ways that he/she could use kinds of evidence to do this (e.g., examples, facts/statistics, personal experience, outside sources, etc.)

❏ Do the paragraphs appear to be organized using any of the rhetorical patterns discussed in Chapter 6 (e.g., definition, cause/effect, problem solution, compare and contrast)?

❏ Are the main points ordered in a logical and persuasive way? If not, what could you suggest as an alternate arrangement?

❏ Are there at least two levels represented in the outline (main points and sub-points)? Is parallel structure applied to main points and the levels of sub-points?

Conclusion

❏ Does it successfully summarize or restate the argument without sounding repetitious?

❏ Does it go beyond the introduction by enlarging on the implications of the thesis, by urging a change in thought or call to action, or by making an ethical or emotional appeal?

Final Comments or Suggestions?

Writer's Name: _____

Editor's Name: _____

◎ Peer Edit Form: Argumentative Essay First Draft

Your first draft is the stage at which you make the transition from large-scale structural concerns to those focusing on your developing argument—in your final draft, you will work further on these areas, along with clear expression, grammatically sound prose, etc., responding to editorial suggestions as well as your clearer idea of your argument as a result of having written the draft.

Instructions

Use the check boxes below to record the fact that you have considered and evaluated the criteria. Use the space following to add suggestions, comments, questions, and advice. In addition, *underline places in the essay where you would like to draw the writer's attention to possible grammatical problems* (such as fragments, comma splices, apostrophe problems, lack of parallelism, misplaced or dangling modifiers, pronoun agreement, case, and/or consistency), *or stylistic problems* (such as passive constructions or other instances where the writing could be made more concise, direct, or forceful—you should also note possible spelling errors along with errors in mechanics and presentation).

Introduction

❑ Does the Introduction function successfully?

    ❑ interesting?

    ❑ announces subject and contains thesis statement; **is the claim arguable**?

    ❑ suggests the main way the argument will be organized? (e.g., definition, cause/effect, time order, division, compare and contrast, question/answer, etc.)

❑ Does the writer establish him/herself as credible and trustworthy? How?

Body Paragraphs

❑ Does the argument seem complete, and does the order of the paragraphs appear logical?

❑ Look at paragraphs individually. Are any too short? Too long?

❑ Is each paragraph unified (relates to one main idea)? If not, which one(s) aren't?

❑ Is each paragraph coherent? If not, which one(s) aren't?

❑ Do paragraphs contain topic sentences?

❑ Is the order of the sentences natural?

❑ Are there appropriate transitions between sentences, enabling you to see the relationship between consecutive sentences?

❑ Does the writer successfully use repetition, rephrasing, synonyms or other devices to achieve coherence?

❑ Does each paragraph seem developed adequately?

❑ Are there different organizational methods used to develop the argument? Which ones? Are they effective?

❑ What kinds of evidence are produced? Are they used effectively? You don't have to refer to specific paragraphs—only note if they appear to be present to help support the thesis:

   ❑ examples, illustrations?

   ❑ personal experience?

   ❑ analogies?

   ❑ precedents?

   ❑ outside authorities/secondary sources?

   ❑ other?

❑ Are there points where the argument seems strained, weak, incomplete, and/or illogical? Are there any fallacies (e.g., cause/effect fallacies, fallacies of irrelevance, emotional/ethical fallacies)?

Conclusion

❑ Is the conclusion satisfying? Does it summarize and/or generalize?

Other Criteria

❑ Has the arguer presented him/herself credibly?

❑ Conveyed knowledge?

❑ Seems trustworthy and reliable?

❑ Appears to be fair?

❑ Is the opposing view acknowledged?

❑ Is the writer's voice objective?

❑ Are there any examples of slanted language?

❑ Is the opposing view successfully refuted (as in the point by point method)?

❑ **Are specific argumentative strategies used?** Common ground? Appeal to reader interest? Concessions? Emotional appeals? If not, could any of these be helpful?

❑ Are there any places in the draft where the language seemed unclear or where a point was unclear due to the way it was expressed?

❑ If the writer used sources, are they integrated smoothly and grammatically? Are all direct quotations, summaries, paraphrases, and ideas acknowledged?

Final Comments or Suggestions?

Writer's Name: _____

Editor's Name: _____

◎ Peer Edit Form: Research Essay First Draft

Your first draft is the stage at which you make the transition from large-scale structural concerns to those focusing on integrating your research with your own ideas—in your final draft, you will work further on these areas, along with the attempt to achieve conciseness, clear expression, grammatically sound prose, etc.

Instructions

Use the check boxes below to record the fact that you have considered and evaluated the criteria. Use the space following to add suggestions, comments, questions, and advice. In addition, *underline places in the essay where you would like to draw the writer's attention to possible grammatical problems* (such as fragments, comma splices, apostrophes, lack of parallelism, misplaced or dangling modifiers, pronoun agreement and/ or consistency), or stylistic problems (such as passive constructions or other instances where the writing could be made more concise, direct, or forceful—you should also note possible spelling errors along with errors in mechanics and presentation).

Introduction

❏ Is the Introduction successful?

   ❏ interesting?

   ❏ announces the subject and contains a thesis statement with a *claim of fact*, a hypothesis to be tested, or a question to be answered?

   ❏ suggests the main way the argument will be organized?

❏ Does the writer establish him/herself as credible and trustworthy? How?

Body Paragraphs

❏ Does the essay seem complete, and does the order of the paragraphs appear logical?

❏ Look at paragraphs individually. Are any too short? Too long?

❏ Is each paragraph unified (relates to one main idea)? If not, which one(s) aren't?

❏ Is each paragraph coherent? If not, which one(s) aren't?

❏ Do paragraphs contain topic sentences?

❏ Is the order of the sentences natural?

❏ Are there appropriate transitions between sentences, enabling you to see the relationship between consecutive sentences?

❏ Does the writer successfully use repetition, rephrasing, synonyms, or other devices to achieve coherence?

❏ Does each paragraph seem well-developed?

❑ Has the writer used secondary sources effectively? Note any exceptions.

❑ Do all the sources seem reliable?

❑ Does the writer use a sufficient number of sources? Is there an over-reliance on one source? Which one?

❑ Does the writer show familiarity with the sources used?

❑ Do the secondary sources appear to be relevant to the points discussed?

❑ Is each reference integrated smoothly into the essay?

   ❑ stylistically?

   ❑ grammatically?

❑ Has the context been made sufficiently clear in each instance?

❑ Do brackets and ellipses appear to have been used correctly?

❑ Have all sources been cited? (Identify any that may not be.)

❑ Do the citations appear correct and consistent?

❑ Are any other kinds of evidence present in addition to secondary sources (for example, analogies, personal experience, illustrations, or examples)?

❑ Does the essay appear to be fundamentally focused on exposition (explaining) rather than argumentation (persuasion)?

Conclusion

❑ Is the conclusion satisfying? Does it summarize and/or generalize?

Other Criteria

❑ Has the writer presented him/herself credibly?

❑ Conveyed knowledge?

❑ Seems trustworthy and reliable?

❑ Is the writer's voice objective?

❑ Are there any places in the draft where the language seemed unclear or where a point was unclear due to the way it was expressed?

Final Comments or Suggestions?

Writer's Name: _____

Editor's Name: _____

Appendix D
Partial Answer Key

◎ Chapters 14, 15, 16 Exercise Answers

Exercise 14.4. Read the following paragraph and identify the following:

- **5 nouns:** road, street, slum, car, stop, house, bungalow, garden, fountain, middle, arrangement, flamingoes, penguins, windows, bars, door, grandmother, driver, horn, woman
- **2 pronouns:** we, that, any, it, them, she
- **6 verbs:** left, turned, were, came, was, had, did, toot, stepped, saw, nodded, smiled, went
- **3 adjectives:** main, narrow, extended, better, well-kept, cemented, garish, marble, plastic, heavy, iron, front
- **2 adverbs:** far, out, imperiously, immediately, back, inside
- **4 prepositions:** in, in front of, from, around, across, with, of
- **2 conjunctions:** and, once, when

Once we left the main road and turned down a narrow side street, we were in nothing more than an extended slum. The car came to a stop in front of a house that was far better than any of the others around it. Set back a little from the street, it was a well-kept bungalow. The cemented front garden had a garish marble fountain in the middle, with an arrangement of plastic flamingoes and penguins around it. The windows had heavy bars across them, and even the front door had an extra door of iron bars in front of it. My grandmother did not get out; instead she had the driver toot his horn imperiously. A woman stepped out of the front door, and when she saw the car, she immediately nodded and smiled and went back inside.

Exercise 14.5. Which of the following are complete sentences? Draw a line between the subject and the predicate. Mark with an "S" those that contain only a subject and with a "P" those that contain only a predicate. Indicate an "N" if there is neither subject nor predicate.

1. The cat on the window ledge. S
2. Wanted to bury his treasure where it would never be found. P
3. A door in the wall. S
4. Dropped the ball with only ten yards to go. P
5. A sweet-smelling fragrance. S
6. Opportunity | knocks. Complete sentence
7. Is willing to give a presentation. P
8. The high levels of stress of today's students. S
9. Can schizophrenia be cured? Complete sentence (question structure)
   Schizophrenia | can be cured (rearranged as statement)
10. Hundreds of geese in the field. S
11. (You) | send in the clowns! Complete sentence (imperative sentence)
12. An enemy of the people. S
13. (You) | pay attention to the number of times that you end a sentence with a preposition. Complete sentence (imperative sentence)
14. All dressed up with no place to go. N
15. This term | will be my most successful one ever. Complete sentence

Exercise 14.7. To the remaining fragments in Exercise 14.5 add a subject and/or predicate to create grammatically complete sentences. Other options exist than the ones below.
Questions 1–5:

1. The cat on the window ledge basked in the sun all morning;
   I was surprised to see the cat on the window ledge.
2. The imaginative child wanted to bury his treasure where it would never be found.
3. A door in the wall opened to a secret passageway;
   If you look carefully, you can see a door in the wall.
4. The wide receiver dropped the ball with only ten yards to go.
5. A sweet-smelling fragrance floated in the breeze.
   I slowly became aware of a sweet-smelling fragrance.

Exercise 14.8. The following may or may not be sentences. If they are not, identify what kind of fragment they illustrate (lacks subject or predicate, add-on fragment, –ing fragment, dependent clause fragment). If they are fragments, make them into complete sentences with a subject and a predicate and needing nothing else to complete them.

Italics **show material added to make complete sentences. Other options exist for turning the fragments into complete sentences.**

1. Ensuring that you write in complete sentences *will make you a better writer.* (–ing).
2. Huge tears rolled down his cheeks.

3. Being that she was insured as the principal driver *she was responsible when her car was in a minor accident.* (–ing). A better sentence: Because she was insured as the principal driver, *she was responsible when her car was in a minor accident.*

4. Whenever they called her into work, *she was about to leave town for a holiday.* (dependent clause)

5. He promised to call on her tomorrow *to* see if she was still all right. (add–on)

6. He must be guilty *since* he's already confessed. (dependent clause).

7. I won't vote tomorrow *unless* I hear something that makes me change my mind. (dependent clause).

8. *The party president is* introducing our next prime minister. (–ing)

9. A row of stately elms interspersed with sprightly cedars *lined the driveway.* (no predicate)

10. Swimming on her back, *she eventually reached the shore.* (–ing)

Exercise 14.9. Each of the following passages contains four sentence fragments. Underline them. Then, correct them by joining them to complete sentences or by adding information. Each passage contains three *kinds* of fragment error, as discussed above. Which kind of fragment error is *not* present in each passage?

1. <u>Although it is known that the people who inhabited the island were of Polynesian descent</u> (dependent). In 1994, DNA was extracted from 12 skeletons found on the island, and it was proven to be from people of Polynesian descent. Furthermore, it was suggested that these Polynesians came from Southeast Asia. <u>From the fact that the crops grown by the indigenous people were native to Southeast Asia</u> (add-on). <u>For example, bananas, sugarcane, taro, and sweet potato</u> (add-on). For more than 30,000 years prior to human settlement of the island, the area was a subtropical forest of trees and woody bushes. <u>Towering over a ground layer of shrubs, herbs, and grasses</u> (–ing). Fragment 1 (lacks subject or predicate) is not represented here.

Exercise 14.10. First identify the word groups in parentheses as adverbial, adjectival, noun, or verb phrases. Then, identify the subject of the sentence.

1. Yesterday, (the price of food) was the main item (in the news).
          noun phrase   adjectival
               S

2. (Some of my favourite books) (have gone) out of print.
        noun   verb
         S

3. The room (with the two computers) (has been locked) (from the inside).
   S   adjectival   verb   adverbial

4. A search (of the abandoned house) (turned up) several cartons (of
      S   adjectival   verb

   stolen goods).
      adjectival

5. The best player (on our paintball team) broke his arm and (will be lost)
      S   adjectival   verb

   (for the season).
      adverbial

Exercise 14.11. Identify all independent and dependent clauses in the following sentences by underlining independent clauses and placing parentheses around any dependent clauses. Remember that pronouns, such as "I" or "it," can serve as subjects.

1. (While drug testing has become more common,) <u>athletes are still taking drugs</u>.
2. (Although I think winter is here,) <u>the temperature is not cold enough for snow</u>.
3. <u>I became hooked on reality shows</u> (when I began watching them with my roommate.)
4. In most parts of North America, <u>Daylight Saving Time begins in March</u>. "In most parts of North America" is a phrase modifying the verb in the independent clause.
5. <u>The battle against cancer will continue</u> (until a cure is found.)

Exercise 14.12. Examples of the simple, compound, and complex sentence types appear below. For compound and complex sentences, underline independent clauses, circle conjunctions, and put parentheses around dependent clauses. Identify each sentence type.

1. <u>The class average was low in the first semester,</u> (but) <u>it has gone up this semester</u>. **compound**
2. Since the beginning of time, <u>people have worn fur for warmth</u>. **simple—"Since" is a preposition in this sentence, not a subordinating conjunction**
3. <u>The mosquitoes are biting again,</u> (and) <u>the BBQs are being fired up</u>. **compound**
4. <u>She ran the race in record time</u> (but) <u>collapsed at the finish line</u>. **simple—"but" is joining "ran" and "collapsed," two verbs. You can see that it is not joining two independent clauses as "collapsed" has no separate subject from "ran."**
5. <u>Salmon oil is a supplement</u> (that) lowers cholesterol). **complex**
6. <u>Expository writing explains or informs the reader about something</u>. **simple (see number 4)**

7. Snowboarding began in the early 70s, (and) it has grown in popularity ever since. **compound**
8. His library privileges have been suspended (until) he pays his fines). **complex**
9. The committee began its search in September (and) has not yet found a suitable candidate. **simple (see numbers 4 and 6)**
10. She is convinced (that) she will get an "A" in the course). **complex**

Exercise 14.13. To demonstrate your familiarity with the different kinds of clauses and joiners, construct compound, complex, and compound-complex sentences from the independent clauses (simple sentences) below. After you have joined the clauses in the most logical way, identify the sentence type: compound, complex, or compound-complex. Ensure that you have at least one example of each type of sentence. Suggestion: Students could be permitted to make small changes so that it is easier to make up complex sentences; they could also be permitted to change sentence order.

1. They intended to eat at Benny's Bistro.
   They saw a long line-up outside Benny's.
   They went to Kenny's Kitchen instead.

   They intended to eat at Benny's Bistro, but they saw a long line-up outside Benny's, so they went to Kenny's Kitchen instead. (compound)

   Alternative with minor changes: As soon as they saw a long line-up outside Benny's Bistro, they went to Kenny's Kitchen instead, even though they had intended to eat at Benny's. (complex)

2. There may be nearly two million kinds of plants in the world.
   There are likely at least as many different kinds of animals.
   No one can know how many species have evolved, flourished, and become extinct.

   Although there may be nearly two million kinds of plants in the world, and there are likely at least as many different kinds of animals, no one can know how many species have evolved, flourished, and become extinct. (compound-complex)

Exercise 14.14. Fix the sentences by using a period to make two separate sentences, or if you already know the rules for using other forms of punctuation to join independent clauses, you can use them. Also, identify whether the sentence is a run-on or a comma splice.

1. I took two buses to get downtown. It was a long way. (run-on)
2. Our neighbour's dog howled all last night. It was just impossible to get a night's sleep. (comma splice)
3. I was frightened during my first driving lesson: the instructor yelled at me. (run-on)

4. It's easy to punctuate sentences: just put a comma whenever you pause. (comma splice)

5. Janne ate as quickly as he could. Then he went upstairs to finish his homework. (run-on)

6. The incidence of breast cancer has increased. It takes the lives of many women today. (comma splice)

7. Homelessness has existed for centuries. Literature on the subject dates back to the feudal period in Europe. (comma splice)

8. Humans are imitators. Conforming is something they are good at. (comma splice)

9. Mozart composed his first minuet at the age of five; he wrote his first symphony before he turned nine. (run-on)

10. Asthma is a common problem among Canadians. Exposure to secondhand smoke in public places can intensify this condition. (comma splice)

Exercise 14.15. Determine what is wrong in the following sentences. It could be a fragment, a run-on sentence, or a comma splice; then, make the correction.

1. He managed to pass the year though he seldom did his homework. What will happen to him next year is anyone's guess. (comma splice)

2. The opening ceremonies were delayed on account of rain. (fragment)

3. She went to France for the summer. It was a fine opportunity to learn another language. (fragment)

4. Though they both liked to read, they usually read different books: she read adventure stories while he liked detective stories. (comma splice)

5. While books are still the main source for acquiring knowledge, they are usually not as current as magazine articles. (fragment)

6. The only way a person can learn is to pay attention to what is going on in class. (fragment)

7. He was too tall and thin to excel at sports—except basketball, of course. (fragment)

8. The concept that "bigger is better" is part of our culture. It is promoted by both advertisers and the media these days. (comma slice)

9. I have trouble understanding the theory of relativity and its impact on our daily lives. (fragment)

10. Martin Luther King led protests during the civil rights movement. His enthusiasm and his will to end discrimination made him a leader. (comma splice)

Exercise 14.16. Identify the sentence errors in the following paragraph; they may include fragments, run-on sentences, and comma splices. Then, correct them.
In recent decades, our society has become obsessed with body image through fitness and weight loss this infatuation can be seen in the popularity of fad diets. (run-on sentence)

Such as the Atkins diet and its many variants. (fragment)

Fitness routines popular today include yoga and Pilates, there has also been a marked increase in the number of women having plastic surgery. (comma splice)

Since many women are socialized to equate self-worth with physical appearance. (fragment)

Which often portrays unrealistic standards of the ideal body type. (fragment)

In recent decades, our society has become obsessed with body image through fitness and weight loss. This infatuation can be seen in the popularity of fad diets, such as the Atkins diet and its many variants. Fitness routines popular today include yoga and Pilates. There has also been a marked increase in the number of women having plastic surgery. In general, the obsession with body image is a greater concern for females than for males since many women are socialized to equate self-worth with physical appearance. One of the causes of this socialization is the popular media, which often portrays unrealistic standards of the ideal body type.

Exercise 15.1. Add commas to the following sentences, if and where required. Also name the rule category discussed above. There is one comma rule to apply in each sentence.

1. After her inaugural speech, several members of the house rose to congratulate her. (independent clause: introductory phrase)
2. The optional package includes bucket seats, dual speakers, and air-conditioning. (items in a series)
3. We have collected more than $20,000, and there is a week remaining in our campaign. (independent clauses)
4. Metaphors, similes, and personification all are examples of figurative language. (series)
5. As one can see, the tower is leaning some four-and-one-half metres to the south. (independent clause: introductory dependent clause)
6. Hardly daring to breathe, Nelson took a quick look at the valley far below him. (independent clause: introductory phrase)
7. Although many are called, few are chosen. (independent clause; introductory dependent clause)
8. The magnificent country estate is hidden behind a long, elegant row of silver birches. (miscellaneous: coordinate adjectives)
9. "We can't achieve peace in our time if we assume war is inevitable," he said. (miscellaneous: quotations)
10. Her house was a newer one with dark wood trim and large, open rooms. (miscellaneous: coordinate adjectives)

Exercise 15.2. Add commas to the following sentences, if and where required. There is more than one comma rule to apply in most sentences.

1. I had planned to go to Calgary, but my bus was delayed for more than four hours, so I decided to go back home.
2. Juliet studied medicine at The University of Western Ontario in London, Ontario, before becoming a doctor near Prince Albert, Saskatchewan.
3. Like Jane Austen's character, Emma, the heroine of *Clueless*, Cher, is less superficial than she first appears. **If the context suggested that the reader would know what Austen character is being referred to, "Emma" would be considered non-essential information (an appositive); if not, only the comma *after* "Emma" would be correct.**
4. Nick and Nicole were married on April 20, 1995, but they separated two years later.
5. Jessica Julep, the mayor of Nowhere, Nova Scotia, provided inspirational leadership.
6. The simple sentence, as we've seen, is easily mastered by students, but compound sentences necessitate an understanding of various forms of punctuation.
7. The waste of our resources, including the most precious resource, water, is the major environmental problem that Canada is facing today.
8. British general Sir Frederick Morgan established an American-British headquarters, which was known as COSSAC.
9. The book with the fine red binding on the highest shelf is the particular one I want.
10. Agnes Campbell Macphail, the first woman elected to Canadian Parliament, served for 19 years, beginning her career in 1921.

Exercise 15.3. Add commas in the paragraph below, following the rule categories as discussed above and avoiding comma splices. A few commas have been included to help with comprehension, but they may be incorrect.

1. If you asked people to name the most gruelling and challenging race in the world, most of them would probably say that it was an auto race, such as the Indianapolis 500. Few people would name the Tour de France, which is a bicycle race. Thousands of cyclists, however, vie for an elite position in this annual event. Even with the modern advances in bicycle technology, cyclists still find the course very challenging. It offers a variety of climbs, including slight inclines, hills, and steep grades. The Tour de France has a history that dates back about one hundred years. In the years to come, the race will continue to challenge, inspire, and glorify new riders.

Exercise 15.4. The following sentences are punctuated correctly. The italicized word or phrase is either an ordinary adverb acting as an interrupter or a conjunctive adverb (joiner). Rewrite the sentence by moving this word/phrase to another place in the second clause in which its function will be different. Punctuate accordingly.

1. One of my roommates rode her bicycle to school most of the time; **as a result,** she was more physically fit than my other roommate, who didn't even own a bicycle.
2. SPCA officers work for but are not paid by the government; **in fact,** it is donations that provide their salary.

Exercise 15.5. Using the rule categories discussed above, replace commas in the sentences below with the most appropriate form of punctuation (semicolon, colon, dash, parentheses). In some cases, the commas are correct and should not be replaced.

1. April showers bring May flowers; May flowers bring on my asthma.
2. A developing salmon goes through four stages: the alevin, the fry, the smolt, and the adult.
3. Every essay needs three parts: an introduction, a body, and a conclusion.
4. He paused to admire the splendid sight before his eyes: the ruins of Montgomery Castle.
5. Mayumi tended to look on the good side of things; Glenn usually saw the bad side.
6. The following is not a rule for comma use: put a comma wherever you pause.
7. It is probable (though not certain) that she will be promoted to the rank of corporal next year.
8. It was the best of times; it was the worst of times.
9. Marselina has a fine ear for music; unfortunately, she can't sing a note.
10. In my health sciences class, we studied the four main food groups: dairy products, meats, carbohydrates, and fruits and vegetables.
11. Whenever I order designer clothing for my boutique, I shop in Toronto, Canada; Buffalo, New York; and London, England.
12. The Online Dictionary defines animal cruelty this way: "treatment or standards of care that cause unwarranted or unnecessary suffering or harm to animals."
13. The tuition increase has affected many lower income families; therefore, there is an even greater demand for student loans.
14. Brian never tired of misquoting Shakespeare: "the quality of mercy is not stained."
15. Virginia Woolf had this to say about the essay: "Of all forms of literature it is the one which least calls for the use of long words."

Exercise 15.6. The poem that follows is Edward Lear's nonsense poem "The New Vestments." Write it in paragraph form, making sense out of nonsense

by punctuating it for correctness and effectiveness. Most of the original end-of-line punctuation has been taken out, and some internal punctuation also has been omitted. Some of the nineteenth-century spellings have been changed. Of course, there are punctuation options for the first fifteen lines shown below.

There lived an old man in the kingdom of Tess, who invented a purely original dress, and when it was perfectly made and complete, he opened the door and walked into the street. By way of a hat, he'd a loaf of brown bread, in the middle of which he inserted his head. His shirt was made up of no end of dead mice, the warmth of whose skins was quite fluffy and nice. His drawers were of rabbit-skins (but it is not known whose). His waistcoat and trousers were made of pork chops; his buttons were jujubes and chocolate drops. His coat was all pancakes with jam for a border and a girdle of biscuits to keep it in order. And he wore over all, as a screen from bad weather, a cloak of green cabbage leaves stitched all together.

Exercise 15.7. Correct or add commas in the following passages. Among your changes and additions, include *at least* one semicolon and one colon (two semicolons and two colons are shown below). Some commas have been included to help with reading; however, they may not be correct.

1. Cocaine, an alkaloid obtained from coco leaves, is a stimulant to the nervous system; unfortunately, it is one of the most addictive drugs, and it is possible to overdose and die on first use. Among the 3 million users today, 500,000 are highly addicted. Cocaine users describe the high as a euphoric feeling: they feel energetic and mentally alert; however, this feeling wears off in as little as 20 minutes. User responses to the drug vary but may include the following: hyperactivity, elevated blood pressure and heart rate, and increased sexual interest. Large amounts of cocaine, such as more than 100 milligrams, can cause bizarre, erratic, and violent behaviours.

Exercise 15.8. Decide which nouns in the following sentences require the possessive; then add apostrophes and make any other necessary changes.

1. In South Africa, the current crime rate is using up much of the country's GDP.
2. Parents and teachers often complain about television's influence in today's society.
3. The Crosses' house is up for sale, and its list price is $179,000. (The last name is Cross.)
4. One's education should not depend on the financial resources of one's parents.
5. The school's biggest draw for new students was the brand new recreation complex.
6. The course I took required two hours' homework a day.
7. The mayor's biggest asset is her commitment to the city's future growth.

8. In anorexia nervosa, a patient's fingernails and teeth may be damaged due to a lack of calcium.
9. Ryan's and Jessica's birthday is on the same day.
10. Apples, oranges, mangoes, and tomatoes are the store's specials today.

Exercise 15.9. Punctuate for correctness and effectiveness, using commas and other forms of punctuation as appropriate. Minimal punctuation has been provided in places to aid in understanding; however, some punctuation may be incorrect. Correct all errors in apostrophe use. The first two paragraphs, corrected for punctuation and apostrophe use, appear below.

Reader reaction was swift and impassioned. The site's traffic, which averages 65 to 70 million views each month, experienced an additional 50,000 page views within the first 10 days of the posting. The investigation drew more than 400 letters to the editor, hundreds of emails to the message boards, and more than 16,000 responses to an online poll.

The intensity of the response surprised veteran investigative journalist Wayne MacPhail, the article's author. Although the sheer volume of letters was unexpected, it proved to him that there was an audience for online journalism in Canada. MacPhail has experimented with hypertext reporting since the late 1980s, but, outside of "Spin Doctors," he believes that, by and large, newspapers have done a "woeful job" of building an audience for Web-based investigative reporting . . . .

Exercise 16.1. In the short argumentative paragraph below, fix pronoun–antecedent agreement errors, using at least one of each of the three options discussed above.

If a child begins to perform poorly at school nowadays, he or she [option 1] will likely be sent to a school counsellor to deal with the situation. Everyone assumes that attention deficit disorder is the culprit, and ~~they~~ [option 3] just as automatically assume that drugs are the answer. On the other hand, perhaps the child is just not interested in a particular subject, or he or she does [option 1] not understand the material. Parents, in turn, treat their children as if they are [option 2] the problem instead of listening to them [option 2] to find out how they [option 2] can be helped.

Exercise 16.2. Chose the correct form of the verb and/or pronoun in the sentences and make any other necessary changes in agreement. Rewrite the sentence if that will produce a better result. (In some sentences, there may be other options than the one given.)

1. Those who supported the motion raised their hands.
2. Neither the film's director nor its producers were on hand to receive their prestigious award.
3. The instructor as well as the students thinks the room is too small.
4. It is unfortunate when a person no longer cares what others think about him or her.

5. One should never expect to succeed unless one is willing to persist—even against the odds.

6. It is the tried and true that provides the ultimate refuge in mediocrity.

7. Everyone who works during the year is obliged to file an income tax return.

8. Her set of baby teeth was complete when she was only eighteen months old.

9. He was one of those few candidates who was able to win re-election.

10. None of the company's products require testing on animals.

Exercise 16.3. Most of the following sentences contain one or more subject–verb agreement and/or pronoun–antecedent agreement errors. Correct the sentences. Alternatives are given in some cases, but other alternatives may be possible.

1. Every person in the community should have the right to attend a university and create new opportunities for himself or herself.
   Alternative: All people in the community should have the right to attend a university and create new opportunities for themselves.

2. Especially unique to adolescent depression are physical symptoms, such as headaches. (correct)

3. The tonal quality of Amati's violins is excellent, but not perfect.

4. During the past week, there have been some unexplained occurrences on the girls' floor of the residence.

5. Small class sizes and a low student population mean few opportunities to meet new people.

6. A typical poem by Emily Dickinson leaves the reader searching for another line or even another stanza to satisfy his or her craving for closure.
   Alternative: A typical poem by Emily Dickinson leaves readers searching for another line or even another stanza to satisfy their craving for closure.

7. Use of the leaves of the coca plant for its stimulant effects dates back thousands of years. (correct)

8. A coalition of neighbourhood organizations, students, and unions is currently forming to oppose the university's proposed plan.

9. Everyone who has purchased tickets is eligible for the grand prize, but he or she must be a resident of Canada to claim his or her prize.
   Alternatives: Everyone who has purchased tickets is eligible for the grand prize but must be a resident of Canada to claim the prize.
   Those who have purchased tickets are eligible for the grand prize, but they must be residents of Canada to claim their prize.

10. If a child is denied the opportunity to play, how can he or she develop emotionally and physically?
    Alternative: If children are denied the opportunity to play, how can they develop emotionally and physically?

Exercise 16.4. Rewrite the above paragraph, replacing as many nouns as possible with pronouns, ensuring that it is clear what noun (antecedent) the pronoun is referring to.

Alex and his lawyer, Alan, left in Alex's limousine for Loonies Unlimited to buy Alex's landlady, Alice, a litre of light lemonade. She told them to also buy a litre of light lemonade for her long-time lodger, Alison. When they alighted at Loonies Unlimited, they were alarmed that Alex had left his loonie in his loft. So Alphonse, of Loonies Unlimited, allowed them only one litre of lemonade, along with a length of limp licorice, and he loudly lamented their laxness.

Exercise 16.7. Identify the kind of pronoun reference errors in the following sentences; then, correct the errors by making necessary revisions. In the first five sentences, the pronoun that needs to be changed is italicized.

1. According to my textbook, pronouns should always have a clear referent. (no reference)
2. Whenever a staff meeting is called, employees are required to attend. (no reference)
3. Racism is a disease that will continue to plague society until the disease is cured. (ambiguous reference)
4. Sixty per cent of our pesticides, our major ground water pollutant, are used on cotton. (ambiguous reference)
5. During Roosevelt's Pearl Harbor speech, the president identified the US as a peaceful and tolerant nation. (no reference); During his Pearl Harbor speech, Roosevelt identified the US as a peaceful and tolerant nation.
6. I know the sign indicated *No Parking*, but I went ahead and parked there anyway. An officer gave me a $20 fine. (no reference in both sentences)
7. Her second novel, set in the remote Hebrides, was far different from her first one. (ambiguous reference)
8. Previous Afghan successes were significant victories; for example, the country last waged war against the powerful Soviet Union. (no reference)
9. Some psychologists and researchers believe in the "innate" theory of prejudice. According to this theory, ingrained prejudice is cross-cultural and awareness of race is one of the earliest social characteristics to develop in children. These findings may help account for the theory's popularity. (remote reference)

10. During the dinosaur age, dinosaurs lived in a rapidly changing environment. (no reference)

Exercise 16.8. Choose the correct form of the pronoun.

1. Management often forgets about the needs of us wage-earners.
2. Who should run for office this election?
3. I have no intention of speaking to them.
4. The person who finishes first will be rewarded.
5. You recommend whom for the position?
6. As she entered the room, a mysterious feeling came over her.
7. Margaret Laurence was a novelist who entertained her readers with well-developed plots and realistic characters.
8. People who use memory aids tend to be better spellers.
9. The instructor explained the different cases of pronouns to Gail and me.
10. "Hey, buddy, whom did you mean to refer to when you used that insulting term?"

Exercise 16.9. The following paragraph contains errors in pronoun consistency, along with some awkward use of third-person pronouns. When you rewrite the paragraph, strive for correctness and effectiveness. First decide which person you want to refer to consistently. This decision might be based on the level of formality you want to use (first- and second-person pronouns, such as *I/me* and *you*, are considered more informal than third-person pronouns, such as *he/she* and *him/her*).

Informal: You can definitely learn a lot from educational TV; you can learn things that cannot be learned from written texts. If you are a major in Commerce, for example, and if you watch the business news, you can understand the commerce textbook better by applying what you learn from the news. Similarly, watching sports programs can be exciting and can also give you a better understanding of the game. On the other hand, if you choose to watch comedy all the time, you are not going to gain any real benefits. In general, I think that comedies are meaningless.

Formal: Educational TV has many benefits and can teach people things they cannot learn from written texts. If a person is a major in Commerce, for example, and watches the business news, he or she can understand the commerce textbook better by applying what is learned from the news. Similarly, watching sports programs can provide people with excitement and also give them a better understanding of the game. On the other hand, if people choose to watch comedy all the time, they will not gain any real benefits as comedies, generally, are meaningless.

Exercise 16.10. The intended meanings of the following sentences are obscured or distorted due to modifier problems. Working in groups, identify the particular problem (misplaced or dangling modifier) and determine the grammatical (incorrect or ambiguous) meaning(s) of the sentences. Then, fix the sentences using one of the methods above.

1. A striped, pointed hat was on his head. (misplaced)
2. As we were leaving, he tearfully promised to visit us. (misplaced)
3. Although Sam is unambitious and downright lazy, I have never known him to break his word. (dangling)
4. His ego was further inflated when he was awarded first prize in the Ben Affleck look-alike contest. (dangling)
5. Every character has a purpose, big or small, in Shakespeare's play. (misplaced)
6. When asked what my favourite sport is, without any hesitation I usually say that it is running. (misplaced)
7. Stepping out of the airplane, she thought the fresh air was most invigorating. (dangling)
8. In his book, Gabriel Kolko describes peace in Vietnam after the war. (misplaced)
9. As he opened the door unexpectedly, his eyes fell upon two of his employees sleeping in front of their computers. (dangling)
10. Teacher Laurie McNamara posed for the photographer in the Cloverdale Elementary School hallway with Principal Dan Saunders, who gave her a kidney last month. (misplaced)

Exercise 16.11. Correct the following sentences, each of which contains a modifier error; in some instances, it will be necessary to reword the sentence for clarity and correctness. Note: Only one of the options for correcting dangling modifiers is shown below.

1. In our city, shady characters who offer a variety of drugs lurk on quiet corners.
2. Over the years, several world-class cyclists, such as Eddie Merckx and Greg LeMond, have had spectacular careers.
3. As he ran down the street without a care in the world, two pedestrians had to quickly move out of his way.
4. As I am a member of the Sikh community, my paper will be given a strong personal focus.
5. You will have a fully interactive website, built in mere minutes, for your business or for your personal use.
6. Benefits will result only from a smoke-free environment.
7. Germany has built an extensive network of highways, known as the Autobahn, through its countryside.
8. When they look for employees today, employers are stressing verbal and written communication skills more than ever before.
9. If people are caught in criminal behaviour, their rights to privacy should be forfeited.

10. In captivity, this species of snake will eat frogs, mice, and small pieces of meat.

Exercise 16.12. In the word groups that follow, there are three or four main points related to a topic. Build parallel structures in thesis statements for each topic. Make whatever changes are necessary to achieve parallelism and use whatever order of points seems natural. Other options exist in the five sentences below.

Topic 1: I like toe socks because they are warm and comfortable, come in many colours and designs, and are the latest in sock fashions.

Topic 2: Yoga offers many benefits: it enables you to relax and reduce stress, to exercise regularly, and, through yoga classes, to meet people with similar interests.

Topic 3: Computers are important to students as they provide entertainment, cut down on homework time, and enable you to obtain a wealth of information quickly.

Topic 4: One disadvantage of having roommates is that they can create a lot of mess and invade your personal space, but having a roommate gives you someone to talk to about your problems.

Topic 5: The benefits of coffee include helping you wake up, enjoying its rich, satisfying flavour, and improving your concentration.

Exercise 16.13. The sentences below contain parallelism errors. Identify the kind of error (series, compounds, correlative conjunctions, or comparisons) and fix the errors.

1. A good journalist is inquisitive, persistent, and attentive. (series)
2. Music can directly affect your thoughts, emotions, and feelings. (series)
3. In this essay, I will be looking at and writing about the role of women in the military. (compounds)
4. Tiddlywinks is a game not only of considerable skill but also of strategy. (correlative conjunctions)
5. Television can affect children in a variety of negative ways since children often lack judgment, are naturally curious, and are easily influenced. (series)
6. There are three main qualities that a leader must possess: a leader must be enthusiastic, organized, and creative. (series)
7. Aman never has been and never will be good at golf. (compounds)
8. She not only was the best teacher I have ever had but also was very modest. (correlative conjunctions)
9. Tremors may occur on either side or both sides of the body. (compounds)
10. There are many reasons why people choose to watch or enjoy watching television. (compounds)

Exercise 16.14. The following five paragraphs contain various errors that have been discussed in Chapters 14 to 16. Identify the errors indicated and then make corrections. Two paragraphs with errors identified and then corrected appear below.

1.   Identify and correct the following:
   a) comma splice
   b) one comma use error
   c) error in pronoun case
   d) broad pronoun reference
   e) missing pronoun antecedent
   f) two pronoun–antecedent agreement errors
   g) apostrophe omitted
   h) ambiguous pronoun reference
   i) failure to use gender-neutral language

Identify the problems: In my family, my father and sister play video games as much as me **c)**. They **h)** have become very complex, **b)** and can even improve problem-solving in children. By progressing through increasing difficulty levels, it **e)** can help childrens **g)** thought processes. On the one hand, if the child goes straight to the hardest setting, they **f)** may feel discouraged, **a)** on the other, if the child tries to systematically progress through increasing levels, they **f)** can learn the mechanics of the game step by step. This **d)** can help in the study of math, as the child may be more likely to persevere with a problem until he **i)** finds the solution.

Rewritten with corrections: In my family, my father and sister play video games as much as I (do). Video games have become very complex and can even improve problem-solving in children. Progressing through increasing difficulty levels can help children's thought processes. On the one hand, if the child goes straight to the hardest setting, he or she may feel discouraged; on the other, if the child tries to systematically progress through increasing levels, he or she can learn the mechanics of the game step by step. This method can help in the study of math, as the child may be more likely to persevere with a problem until a solution is found.

2.   Identify and correct the following:
   a) comma error
   b) subject–verb agreement error
   c) fragment
   d) two parallelism errors
   e) misplaced modifier
   f) dangling modifier
   g) pronoun inconsistency
   h) comma splice

Identify the problems: Having a job and earning one's livelihood is **b)** a necessary goal in life, **h)** it is one of the reasons you **g)** acquire an education. At the place where I work **a)** however, many people come in expecting to find a job lacking presentation skills **e)**. Many are poorly dressed, do not know how to behave, and they may not speak grammatically **d)**. Untidy, disorganized, and unprepared, **f)** I still have to match them with a prospective employer. They lack the skills to present themselves to others and knowing **d)** what to do in public. Although they may be highly intelligent people. **c)**

Rewritten with corrections: Having a job and earning one's livelihood are necessary goals in life. They are one of the reasons one acquires an education. At the place where I work, however, many people lacking presentation skills come in, expecting to find a job. Many are poorly dressed, do not know how to behave, and may not speak grammatically. They are untidy, disorganized, and unprepared, yet I still have to match them with a prospective employer. They lack the skills to present themselves to others and to know what to do in public, though they may be highly intelligent people.

Exercise 16.15. Identify then correct the error(s) in each sentence. If there is more than one error, choose the "more than one error" option.

1. Written through the eyes of a young boy, one can see the perspective of the indigenous peoples.
    a) dangling modifier. Sentence corrected: Written through the eyes of a young boy, the narrative shows us the perspective of the indigenous peoples.
2. The daily stresses of students, such as project or assignment due dates, teaches you to manage your time wisely.
    c) more than one error (subject–verb agreement: the subject, "stresses," should agree with the verb, "teach"; pronoun inconsistency: "you" is not the same person as the noun antecedent, "students.") Sentence corrected: The daily stresses of students, such as project or assignment due dates, teach them to manage their time wisely.
3. Parents sometimes push their children so hard to excel that they lose interest altogether.
    b) pronoun reference error. Sentence corrected: Parents sometimes push their children so hard to excel that these children lose interest altogether.
4. My roommate thinks it would be better for society, if all drugs were decriminalized.
    c) comma error. Sentence corrected: My roommate thinks it would be better for society if all drugs were decriminalized.
5. Contributors to homelessness include the lack of good-paying jobs, increasingly large families and, probably the most important factor, which is the cost of living in a large city.
    d) parallelism error. Sentence corrected: Contributors to homelessness include the lack of good-paying jobs, increasingly large families and, probably the most important factor, the cost of living in a large city.

Exercise 16.16. Identify the error (a, b, c, or d) and correct it in the sentence (there is one error in each sentence).

1. c) (their) Anorexia starts when a person decides to take control of his or her body weight.
2. b) (the semicolon) There are three types of turbine engines used in aircraft: the turbojet, the turbofan, and the turboprop.
3. b) (vendors) Work songs and street vendors' cries are examples of traditional African–American music styles.
4. c) (to extend) Reforms of the UN Security Council include abolishing the veto or extending the Council beyond the current five members.
5. c) (who listened...) Results from a recent study showed that patients suffering from osteoarthritis reported a 66 per cent reduction in their perception of pain by listening to music for twenty minutes each day.

Appendix E
Glossary of Important Terms

The 166 terms below are used in *The Empowered Writer*. They may also occur in chapters other than the ones specified; for page references, consult the Index. Italicized items below indicate a separate entry for the term; bolded items indicate the terms are defined within the entry itself.

Abstract, Chapter 9   in sciences and social sciences, a condensed *summary* placed before the essay begins; gives overview of purpose, methods, and results.

Adjective, Chapter 14   word that modifies (describes or qualifies) and precedes a noun/pronoun or follows a linking verb; it answers the questions "which?," "what kind?," or "how many?"; *phrases* may also function adjectivally.

Adverb, Chapter 14   word that modifies a *verb*, *adjective*, *adverb*, or an entire sentence; it often ends in *−ly* and answers the questions "when?," "where?," "how?," "to what degree?," or "how much?"; *phrases* may also function adverbially.

Agreement, Chapter 16   matching a *verb* with its subject (*subject–verb agreement*) in number, person, or gender, or a pronoun with its antecedent (*pronoun–antecedent agreement*).

Analogy, Chapters 6, 13   comparison between two objects that are not usually associated in order to explain or clarify one of the objects.

Analysis, Chapters 1, 5   process of breaking down in order to take a closer look at something; many of the patterns of *development* involve analysis; plays an important role in *critical thinking*.

Anecdote, Chapter 7   informal story that introduces or illustrates a point; used because it is interesting or striking.

Annotated bibliography, Chapter 9 expanded bibliography that concisely summarizes similar works in the same field of study as the writer's.

Antecedent, Chapter 16 grammatical term: *noun* (or *indefinite pronoun*) that the *pronoun* replaces in a sentence and that comes before it.

APA style, Chapter 12 American Psychological Association *citation style* used in the social sciences and the sciences; APA uses parenthetical in-text citations and alphabetical list of *sources* on References page.

Apostrophe, Chapter 15 used to show the *possessive* of *nouns* and some *indefinite pronouns*; also can show that letter(s) have been omitted in contractions.

Appeals, Chapter 13 appeals to reason, emotion, and ethics are used to support an argumentative *claim* and persuade a reader/listener.

Appositive, Chapter 15 noun or noun *phrase* grammatically parallel to the *noun* it follows and (re)names; example of **parenthetical** (non-essential) information that usually requires two commas.

Argument, Chapters 3, 13 rhetorical mode; unlike *exposition*, argument attempts to convince a reader to change his/her mind or take an action; uses *claims* of value or policy.

Article, Chapter 14, Appendix B *a, an* (**indefinite articles**) and *the* (**definite article**) may precede nouns and can be considered to function adjectivally.

Audience, Chapters 2, 13 whom you are writing to and their expectations; considerations include *diction, tone*, sentence structure, page design and formats, etc.; audience factors include knowledge/interest level, and in the case of *argument*, orientation to the topic (agree, disagree, neutral).

Authority, Chapters 7, 10 person whose findings or opinion carries weight; an authority may be an *expert* in the field or just a respected person/group whose words lend *credibility*.

Block quotation, Chapter 11 format for integrating long quotations in your essay (more than 40 words or four lines); quotations are indented and double-spaced; quotation marks are not used.

Body paragraphs, Chapter 4 middle paragraphs in an essay that help prove the *thesis* by presenting facts, arguments, or other support; many college/university essays have at least 3 body paragraphs, each having one main point expanding on the thesis.

Brainstorming, Chapter 2 *pre-writing* strategy of listing associations with a *topic* in order to come up with ideas and, perhaps, a *thesis* and main points.

Brackets (square brackets [ ]), Chapter 11 used to indicate a change or addition to a *direct quotation*, such as a necessary grammatical or stylistic change; contrast *Parentheses*.

Case study, Chapters 7, 13 kind of *evidence*; carefully selected example that is analyzed as a testing ground for the writer's *claim*.

Cause–effect analysis, Chapter 6 pattern of *development* for essays and paragraphs common in the (social) sciences; looks at why or how something happened (causes) or the outcomes or consequences (effects) of something.

Chronology, Chapter 6 pattern of *development* for essays and paragraphs tracing the topic's development over time.

Citation, Chapter 12 means of acknowledging *sources* in academic and student essays; parenthetical citations may consist of author name, year, page number, or other detail in *parentheses* in text of the essay; complete information is alphabetized by author last name on **References** (*APA*) or **Works Cited** (*MLA*) page.

Claim, Chapters 7, 13 assertion about a *topic* that appears in the *introduction*, usually as the *thesis statement*; a claim could also appear as the main idea in a *topic sentence*; **claims of fact** are proven by facts and figures; **claims of value** appeal to one's ethics; **claims of policy** call for action to fix a problem or improve a situation; claims may be tentative or conclusive.

Clarity, Chapter 17 dependent on factors such as *diction*, level of language, and sentence structure; also refers to whether the writing is grammatical, concise, direct, precise, and specific.

Classification, Chapter 6 pattern of *development* for essays and paragraphs in which items are organized into manageable groups and analyzed; see *Division*.

Clause, Chapters 14–16 group of words containing both a *subject* and a *predicate*; types are *independent* and *dependent clauses*.

Cliché, Chapter 17 phrase or expression that has been overused, such as "he swims like a fish" or "green with envy."

Clustering, Chapter 2 *pre-writing* strategy in which you graphically link your ideas or thoughts by circling words and phrases and connecting them to other words; enables you to visualize the interrelations among your thoughts; also called **mapping.**

Coherence (paragraph), Chapter 4   ideas that are expressed clearly and are connected to one another; specific strategies can create a coherent paragraph that is easy to follow.

Colloquialism, Chapter 17   Word/expression acceptable in conversation but not in *formal writing.*

Comma splice, Chapter 14   major grammatical error in which a comma alone is used to separate two complete thoughts (*independent clauses*); see *Run-on sentence.*

Common ground, Chapter 13   strategy in *argument* in which you show that you and your opponent share common concerns or basic values.

Comparison and contrast, Chapters 6, 8   pattern of *development* for essays and paragraphs in which you systematically draw similarities and/or differences between two things; two main patterns for organizing compare–contrast essays are **point-by-point** and **block.**

Composing, Chapter 2   getting your ideas down in paragraph form; working from *outline* to rough draft; also called **drafting**; see *Revising.*

Compound, Chapters 14–16   grammatical unit comprised of two of something usually joined by a coordinating *conjunction*; e.g., a **compound sentence** contains two *independent clauses*; see *Compound subject/predicate.*

Compound subject/predicate, Chapters 14–15   compound *subject*: contains two *nouns*, two *pronouns*, or noun and pronoun acting as one *subject*; compound *predicate*: contains two *verbs* connected to one subject.

Concession, Chapter 13   strategy in *argument* in which you give up a point, acknowledging its validity; enables you to come across as fair and reasonable.

Concision, Chapter 17   efficient writing achieved by using effective sentence structures and omitting unnecessary words; in concise writing, *emphasis* falls on important words.

Conclusion, Chapter 5   (1) final paragraph in an essay that sums up what was said in the *body paragraphs*; conclusions can be **circular** (remind reader of thesis) or **spiral** (refer to thesis but also lead beyond it); see *Wrap (paragraph)*; (2) in reasoning, truth or likelihood arrived at through *deductive* or *inductive* methods.

Conjunction, Chapters 14–16 like *prepositions*, function as joiners; **coordinating conjunctions** join equal units, such as *independent clauses*; **subordinating conjunctions** join *dependent* to independent clauses; see page 321 for list of coordinating conjunctions; see page 323 for list of common subordinating conjunctions; **correlative conjunctions** join in pairs.

Conjunctive adverb, Chapter 15 adverb used as *conjunction* to join *independent clauses*; examples include "however," "therefore," "thus," "unfortunately"; preceded by semicolon and usually followed by comma.

Connotation, Chapters 1, 13, 17 implications or associations with a word; may be different from a word's *denotation*, as it depends on the context in which the word is used.

Cost–benefit, Chapter 6 pattern of *development* for essays and paragraphs in which you consider the advantages and disadvantages of something.

Credibility, Chapter 7 along with *support* helps to develop a claim; a writer's credibility includes **knowledge**, **reliability** (trustworthiness), and **fairness** (absence of bias).

Critical response, Chapter 3 writing that uses *critical thinking* and *analysis*—and often, personal experience and knowledge about the *topic*—to engage with a text and share your views with others.

Critical thinking, Chapter 1 process of engagement with a text in which you weigh the *evidence* and come to a *conclusion*; can involve *analyzing*, comparing, evaluating, questioning, rethinking, and other activities. *See Inference.*

Dangling modifier, Chapter 16 grammatical error in which the word the *modifier* is intended to modify is not in the sentence, often giving the sentence an unintended meaning; dangling modifiers are often –ing *phrases*. *See Misplaced modifier.*

Database, Chapter 10 collection of related data organized for efficient access; college/university databases include *journals* in searchable interfaces, enabling you to retrieve articles linked to various kinds of search criteria, such as title, author, or *keyword*.

Deductive reasoning, Chapter 13 form of reasoning that uses a *generalization* and a specific example or subset to form a *conclusion*; compare *Inductive reasoning*.

Definition, Chapters 6, 8 pattern of *development* for essays and paragraphs in which you explain the characteristics of something in order to tell the reader precisely what you will be talking about.

Delayed subject, Chapters 16, 17   in this construction, a *prepositional phrase* is followed by a *verb*, delaying the *subject* to later in the sentence.

Denotation, Chapters 1, 13   literal meaning of a word; the way it is defined in a dictionary; contrast *Connotation*.

Dependent clause, Chapter 14   contains a *subject* and *predicate*, but lacks needed information; dependent clauses begin with subordinating *conjunctions* or relative *pronouns*; see *Clause*.

Description, Chapters 3, 6   pattern of *development* for both essays and paragraphs; gives concrete/sensuous detail by using *adjectives* and *adverbs*.

Determiner, Chapter 14   word such as "this" and "her," along with the *articles*; may precede *nouns* and can be considered to function adjectivally.

Development, patterns of, Chapter 6   essays and paragraphs are often developed (organized) by specific patterns, such as *comparison and contrast*, *definition*, and *division*; also called **organizational patterns** and **rhetorical patterns.**

Diction, Chapter 17   choice of words; level of language (e.g., *formal*, informal); see *Usage*.

Digital Object Identifier (DOI), Chapters 10, 12   number-alphabet sequence that begins with the number 10 often found on documents obtained electronically through *databases*; required where available by *APA style*; see *Uniform resource locator*.

Direct quotation, Chapter 11   using the exact wording of a source, usually to provide support for a point in your essay; direct quotations, like *paraphrases*, require *citations;* see *Block quotation, Brackets, Citation, Ellipses*.

Division, Chapter 6   pattern of *development* for both essays and paragraphs; breaks a subject down into parts in order better to understand or explain the subject; see *Classification*.

Editing, Chapters 1, 17   stage of *revising* an essay where you work on improving your work's structure and readability, or solidifying your ideas; also focuses on *diction, syntax,* sentence structure, and grammatical correctness; contrast *Proofreading*.

Ellipses, Chapter 11   three or four spaced dots indicating words, phrases, or sentences omitted from a *direct quotation*.

Emphasis, Chapter 17   controlling the placement of stress in sentences or paragraphs; **periodic** sentences begin with *modifiers*, delaying the *independent clause*; **cumulative** sentences begin with the independent clause and are followed by modifying or *parallel* words, phrases, or clauses, which add further detail.

Empirical method, Chapters 11, 13   sometimes called the **scientific method**; involves observing and measuring data under controlled conditions in order to reach a *conclusion* about a phenomenon; uses *inductive reasoning*.

Euphemism, Chapter 17   word/phrase substituted for the actual name of something—usually in order to make it more acceptable or to give it dignity; example of indirect writing.

Evidence, Chapter 7   used for *support* in most kinds of essays; includes "hard" evidence, like facts, statistics, and *journal* studies, and "soft" evidence, like *examples, anecdotes, analogies, case studies,* and *precedents*.

Example, Chapters 6, 7, 13   pattern of paragraph *development* in which you use concrete details to translate an abstract claim into something the reader can understand; also, a kind of "soft" *evidence* used to support a point.

Expert, Chapters 7, 10   specialist in a particular field, who has published or produced significant work about a subject, such as books or *journal* articles; see *Authority*.

Exposition, Chapters 3, 8   rhetorical mode concerned with informing, explaining, describing, or defining a topic; expository essays use *claims* of fact.

Fallacy, Chapter 13   means of categorizing a misleading or unsound *argument* or a misuse of emotion.

Faulty predication, Chapter 17   makes illogical connection between a *verb* and its *subject*; e.g., "Marijuana has often been prosecuted in our society" (it is marijuana <u>smokers</u> who are prosecuted).

Faulty reasoning, Chapter 13   occurs when the writer (1) has not created a valid argument, (2) has not provided proof for a *claim*, or (3) has failed to clearly separate fact from opinion; *fallacies* are categories of faulty reasoning.

Focused reading, Chapter 1   close and detailed reading of a specific, relevant passage for comprehension and/or *analysis*; see *Selective reading*.

Formal writing, Chapters 12, 17   level of writing designed for educated readers, such as readers of academic prose; formal *usage* and correct grammar are applied.

Fragment (or Sentence fragment), Chapter 14   major grammatical error; incomplete thought that is punctuated as a complete *sentence*; e.g., "Because I saw a UFO."

Freewriting, Chapter 2   *pre-writing* strategy in which you write without stopping for five to ten minutes.

Generalization, Chapters 5, 13   broad statement; when a writer generalizes, the statement must apply to everyone/everything in the category or it will be invalid; in *deductive reasoning*, the generalization is called the **major premise**.

Gender-inclusive language, Chapter 16   careful use of language and grammatical forms that include both genders, thereby avoiding **sexism**; also called gender-neutral prose.

Hypothesis, Chapter 7   prediction or expected result of an experiment or other research study.

Idiom, Chapter 17   word group whose meaning is understood only within the context of the phrase itself.

Illustration, Chapter 7   detailed *example* that often takes the form of an *anecdote* or other brief *narrative*.

Imperative sentence, Chapter 14   issues a command; consists only of a *verb* with the *subject* understood but not expressed; e.g., "(you) stop"; it is, therefore, a complete *sentence*.

Incomplete verb form, Chapter 14   verb form that cannot be joined to a *subject* as it lacks a helping verb; e.g., "speaking," "spoken"; complete forms are italicized: the dog *is missing*; she *has spoken*; incomplete verb forms, or **verbals**, cannot act as verbs in a *sentence*.

Independent clause, Chapter 14   equivalent to a **simple sentence** as it has a *subject* and *predicate* and needs nothing else to complete it.

Indefinite pronoun, Chapters 14, 16   refers to nonspecific individuals or objects; usually considered singular and take a singular form in agreement; examples include "each," "either," "one," "everyone," "everybody"; see *Pronoun*.

Inference, Chapter 1   *conclusion* the reader draws based on *evidence* presented; the corresponding verb is *infer*; see *Critical thinking*.

Indirect source, Chapter 12 place where you obtained "second-hand" information as opposed to the original source of the information; requires specific methods for citing in *APA* and *MLA styles*.

Introduction, Chapter 5 part of essay that presents the main idea (*thesis statement*) and, often, main organizational pattern; designed to create reader interest; can be developed through **logical**, **dramatic**, or **mixed** methods.

Inductive reasoning, Chapter 13 form of reasoning that relies on specific facts, details, or observations to form *conclusions*; compare *Deductive reasoning*.

Jargon, Chapters 10, 17 (1) words/expressions used among members of a group or in a particular discipline that its members (specialists) would understand, but which might be unclear to non-specialists; (2) indirect, unclear *diction*.

Journal (academic), Chapters 10, 12 category of *periodical* where *experts* publish the results of their *research*; journal articles provide examples of reliable *sources*.

Keyword, Chapter 10 word identified by author and/or cataloguer as important in an article; used in online and *database* searches.

Linear process of writing, Chapter 1 writing process that involves defining a purpose or goal, *pre-writing*, *research*, *outlining*, *composing*, and *revising*.

Mechanics, Chapter 17 applied to format, includes margin size, space between lines, font size and type, and page numbers; applied to writing, includes abbreviations, capital letters, hyphenation, and numbers.

Misplaced modifier, Chapter 16 *adjective/adverb* or adjectival/adverbial *phrase* that is too far away from the word it should *modify*, possibly giving the sentence an unintended meaning; see *Dangling modifier*.

Mixed format, Chapters 9, 11 refers to method of integrating *sources* by combining significant words of the source with your own phrasing; see *Paraphrase*.

MLA style, Chapter 12 The Modern Language Association of America *citation style* used in the humanities; MLA uses parenthetical in-text citations and alphabetical list of *sources* on **Works Cited** page.

Modal, Chapter 14, Appendix B *verb* form placed before main verb to express necessity, obligation, possibility, probability, and similar conditions; compare *Tense*.

Modifiers, Chapters 14, 16, 17   words/phrases that describe or limit other words; *adjectives* modify *nouns/pronouns*; *adverbs* modify *verbs*, adjectives, or other adverbs; see *Dangling modifier*, *Misplaced modifier*.

Narration, Chapter 3   pattern of *development* for a paragraph, such as the *introduction*, in which you relate a scene or incident and perhaps include dialogue.

Noun, Chapter 14, Appendix B   name of a person, place, thing, or idea; for noun categories and functions, see pages 302–3; see also *Subject*.

Outline, Chapters 2, 5, 11, 13   vertical representation of your points and *support*; three types are **scratch**, **graphic**, and **formal**, the last of which can be subdivided into **topic** and **sentence** outlines.

Parallelism, Chapter 16   matching grammatical form and/or function to achieve balance and *coherence* in a sentence; applies to lists (three or more items), *compounds*, correlative *conjunctions*, and comparisons.

Paraphrase, Chapters 9, 11   putting someone else's ideas in your own words but keeping length the same as the original; contrast with *Summary*; note: paraphrasing a *source* requires a *citation*.

Parentheses (round brackets), Chapters, 12, 14   (1) used to include less important information in a sentence; (2) following a reference in *APA* and *MLA* styles, used to convey basic information about a *source* (e.g., name, year, page number).

Parts of speech, Chapter 14   sentences can be divided into individual words, which can be categorized into the major parts of speech: *nouns*, *pronouns*, *verbs*, *adjectives*, *adverbs*, *prepositions*, and *conjunctions*.

Passive voice/construction, Chapter 17   *subject* of the sentence is not doing the action, and a less important word is placed at the beginning of the sentence; active constructions are usually stronger than passive ones.

Peer-reviewed, Chapter 10   article reviewed by *experts* before publication in an academic *journal*; can be considered reliable *source*.

Periodical, Chapter 10   publication issued regularly in magazine format; examples are magazines and academic *journals*.

Personal experience, Chapter 6   personal essays are focused on the writer—an aspect of his or her life that is made relevant to the reader's experience; writers may also use personal experience as a kind of *evidence* to support a point.

Personal pronoun, Chapters 14, 16 group of *pronouns* that refer to people: first person ("I," "me," "we," "us") does the "speaking"; second person ("you") is spoken to; third person ("he," "she," "it," "they," "them") is spoken about; see *Pronoun consistency*.

Phrase, Chapter 14 group of grammatically linked words that lack *subject* and/or *predicate* and function as a single *part of speech*; see *Prepositional phrase*.

Plagiarism, Chapter 11 includes but is not confined to (1) borrowing someone else's words or ideas without acknowledging the *source*, (2) not placing quotation marks around words taken from the source, or (3) following the structure of the source too closely.

Possessive (case), Chapters 14–16 in *nouns* and *indefinite pronouns* indicates relationships like ownership, e.g., the first noun belongs to or is associated with the second noun (indicated by adding an apostrophe + "s" to the first noun if it is singular, and an apostrophe after the "s" in a plural noun); some pronouns change their spelling to show possession, e.g., her book, their dinner (do not add *apostrophes*).

Pre-writing, Chapter 2 stage in linear writing process concerned with generating ideas; sometimes called **inventing**; see *brainstorming, freewriting, clustering*.

Precedent(s), Chapter 7 kind of *example* often used in *argument*; refers to the way that a particular situation was dealt with in the past to argue for its similar use in the present.

Predicate, Chapter 14 part of the *sentence* that includes the main *verb* and its *modifiers*; tells what the *subject* is doing or what is being observed about it.

Premise, Chapter 7 statement assumed to be true; in *deductive reasoning*, the major premise is a *generalization* that must be true or the *conclusion* will be invalid.

Proposal (research proposal), Chapter 10 announces topic, purpose, and (often) research *sources*; may precede *research* stage and include interest in the subject, tentative *thesis*, main points or important questions to ask, and projected completion dates.

Preposition, Chapter 14 short word/phrase that often refers to place or time; joins a noun/pronoun to the rest of the sentence; for list of common prepositions, see page 307.

Prepositional phrase, Chapter 14   consists of a *preposition* and a *noun* and *pronoun*, which is the **object of the preposition**; modifies a *noun* (as an *adjective*) or *verb* (as an *adverb*).

Problem–solution, Chapter 6   pattern of *development* for essays and paragraphs that focuses on a problem, a solution to a problem, or both a problem and solutions.

Process analysis, Chapters 6, 8   pattern of *development* for essays and paragraphs in which you describe the chronological steps in a sequence.

Process-reflective writing, Chapter 1   approach to writing that reflects the back-and-forth process of *composing* between thinking and writing, and re-thinking and re-writing.

Proofreading ("proofing"), Chapter 17   final stage in essay preparation where you try to catch all your errors to provide a clean copy for the reader.

Pronoun, Chapters 14, 16   most pronouns replace *nouns* (*antecedent*) in a sentence; see *Pronoun–antecedent agreement*, *Pronoun reference*, *Pronoun case*, and *Relative clause*; for kinds of pronouns, see pages 303–4; for functions of pronouns, see page 304.

Pronoun–antecedent agreement, Chapter 16   principle that a *pronoun* must agree in number with (i.e., match) its *antecedent*, for which there are several rules; see *Agreement*.

Pronoun case, Chapter 16   grammatical principle whereby a *pronoun* changes its form (case) to reflect its function in a sentence or *clause*; e.g., I/me, we/us, he/him, she/her, they/them, who/whom.

Pronoun consistency, Chapter 16   consistency in use of the "person" of *pronouns* in a sentence; i.e., do not needlessly change from first to second or third person of pronoun; see *Personal pronoun*.

Pronoun reference, Chapter 16   grammatical principle requiring a *pronoun* to refer clearly to its *antecedent*.

Purpose, Chapter 2   refers to your reason for writing; could include many related areas, such as the skills that the assignment is intended to develop or your *audience*.

Question–answer, Chapter 6   pattern of paragraph *development* in which you ask a question in the *topic sentence* and answer it in the paragraph; *thesis statements* may occasionally take the form of a question or questions.

Rebuttal, Chapter 13   the part of your *argument* in which you raise points on the other side, mainly in order to show that your points are stronger; also called the **refutation.**

Relative clause, Chapters 14–16, Appendix B   type of *dependent clause* that acts adjectivally by *modifying* preceding *noun*; usually begins with relative *pronouns* "who," "which," or "that."

Research, Chapters 1, 10–13   stage of essay writing in which you explore a topic to find out what others, especially *experts*, have written/said about it in order to use these *sources* in your essay; at college/university level usually requires use of libraries and/or reliable online sources.

Revising, Chapters 1, 17   final stage in essay writing in which you make necessary changes to the first draft to produce a polished final version; see *Editing*, *Proofreading*.

Run-on sentence, Chapter 14   "fused sentence"; major grammatical error in which nothing is used to join two *subject-predicate* units (*independent clauses*); one "sentence" simply continues into the next; compare *Comma splice*.

Scanning, Chapter 1   reading strategy in which you look for identifiable words or sections of a text rather than read a passage closely; contrast *Focused reading*.

Selective reading, Chapter 1   reading strategy designed to meet a specific objective, such as *scanning* for main points or reading for details (*focused reading*).

Sentence, Chapters 14–16   group of words containing a *subject* and *predicate* and needing nothing else to complete it; sometimes defined as a complete thought.

Signal phrase, Chapters 9, 11   introduces a reference by naming the author and including a signal *verb*; the reference then follows with (usually) a page/paragraph number at the end.

Slanted language, Chapter 13   language that reveals writer's bias; should be avoided in most writing, such as *argument*.

Source, Chapters 10, 11 (Source integration), 12 (Source documentation)   place where information is found, such as an article, book, or website; sources can be divided into (1) **primary**, or original sources, such as stories, poems, interviews, old newspapers and documents, and raw data generated from an experiment; (2) **secondary** sources interpret or comment on primary sources, e.g., *journal* studies; use only reliable sources in your essays.

Style, Chapter 17 (1) specific aspects or areas of the text, such as document formats, citation guidelines (e.g., *MLA* or *APA styles*), or (2) way one writes; e.g., an effective writing style is clear, direct, concise, and precise.

Subject, Chapters 2, 14, 16 (1) broad category that contains many potential *topics*; (2) grammatically, the subject performs the action of the *verb* in an active construction; a "complete subject" includes both the main *noun* (subject) and its *modifiers*; see *Predicate*.

Subject–verb agreement, Chapter 16 principle that a *verb* must agree in number with (i.e., match) its *subject*, for which there are several rules; see *Agreement*.

Support, Chapter 7 used in *body paragraphs* to help prove a *claim*; can be divided into *evidence* and *credibility*.

Summary, Chapters 9, 11 shorter version of original passage or essay that uses only its main ideas put in your own words; compare *Paraphrase*.

Synonym, Chapters 4, 17 word that means the same as, and can therefore replace, another word; see *Connotation*.

Syntax, Chapters 16, 17 grammatical term for word order in a sentence.

Synthesis, Chapter 10 in research essays involves putting together the ideas and words of *sources* with your own ideas and words.

Tense (of verbs), Appendix A conveys the time (simple tenses: present, past, future) that the action of the *verb* occurs.

Thesis (statement), Chapter 5 main point of your essay or what you will be attempting to prove; placed at the end of the *introduction*; can be **simple** (announces topic and comments on it) or **expanded** (lists main points in order they will occur in the *body paragraphs*).

Tone, Chapter 17 writer's attitude to the subject matter expressed partly through language; e.g., familiar, objective, detached, casual, humorous, ironic, formal, informal.

Topic, Chapter 2 what the essay is about; a topic is narrower and more focused than a *subject* but less focused than a *thesis statement*.

Topic sentence, Chapter 4 usually the first sentence of the paragraph, introducing its main idea; see *Unity*.

Transition, Chapter 4   word or phrase that links sentences within a paragraph or ideas between paragraphs, contributing to a paragraph's or essay's *coherence*.

Uniform Resource Locator (URL), Chapters 10, 12   location of a file or content on the Internet; typing in the URL in your browser's address window will lead to the website containing the content; consists of protocol (http), host name (usually preceded by www), path, and file/document name; see *Digital object identifier*; some *citation* formats include URL.

Unity (paragraph), Chapter 4   a unified paragraph is focused on one idea, usually announced in the *topic sentence*.

Usage, Chapter 17   customary and accepted ways words are used; see *Diction*.

Verb, Chapter 14 (kinds of/functions of verbs), Appendix A, (tenses)   conveys an action, state, or condition, or precedes another (main) verb; main verbs combine with **helping verbs** to indicate *tense*, mood, and voice; **transitive verbs** take a direct object; **intransitive verbs** do not; **linking verbs** connect *subject* to complement (adjective or noun).

Working bibliography, Chapter 10   a list of potential *sources* for a research essay that may be revised as you research further.

Wrap (paragraph), Chapter 4   last sentence of a paragraph that sums up the main point, recalling the *topic sentence*.

Index

3-D (Dimensional) reading, 9–10

a, an, 301, 449
absolute phrase, 427
abstract, 19, 21, 154, 165, 177, 253
abstract language, 423
academic writing: conclusion, 259–60;
    grammar, 299–301; interpretation
    and analysis, 259–60; introduction,
    91, 253–4, 292; sample essay,
    252–63; tables, graphs, and charts,
    256–8
accept, except, 433
access, 457
acknowledgement of opposing
    argument, 280, 286, 287, 289
active reading, 10, 18–21
add-on fragments, 313–14
adjectival modifiers, 382–3
adjectival phrase, 319, 447–8
adjectives, 305–6, 338–9, 446–48;
    comparatives and superlatives, 447;
    one-word, 384, 446; as participles,
    446–7; plurals as adjectival phrases
    concerning distance, money, and
    time, 447–8; relative clauses, 446,
    448
advantages/disadvantages, 464
adverbial modifiers, 383
adverbial phrase, 319–20, 337
adverbs, 305–6, 337, 448–9
a few vs. few, 447
affect, effect, 433
aggregator databases, 183
ago, 464
agree/disagree with, 457
agreement: pronoun–antecedent, 365–9;
    subject–verb, 360–5, 464

allot, a lot, 433
all right, alright, 434
allude, elude, 434
allusion, illusion, 434
a lot of, 364
alternative information sources,
    187
always, usually, often, 464–5
ambiguous reference, 372
American Psychological Association. *See*
    APA style
among, between, 434
amount, number, 434
analogy, 24, 25, 118, 127, 273
analysis. *See also* critical reading; critical
    thinking: academic essay, 259–60;
    of claims, 122–3; paragraph
    development using, 111; of
    supporting evidence, 123–31
anecdote, 24, 25
annotated bibliography, 154, 166
annotation, 21
antecedent, 365. *See also* pronoun–
    antecedent agreement
antecedent–consequent organizational
    method, 115–16
a number of, 364
any of, 364
APA style, 213–31; authors, 216–17,
    219–20; citations in reference
    section, 218–25, 230; citation style,
    213–25; disciplines using, 212;
    electronic sources, 217, 223–4;
    government documents, 222;
    indirect source, 215, 226; in-text
    citation, 214–18; multiple sources
    in one citation, 215; non-specific
    reference, 215; non-textual sources,

216, 225; periodicals, 221–2, 231;
    personal communication, 215,
    222; quotation, 201, 214–15;
    sample student essays, 225–31,
    291–3; source type, 220–2; specific
    reference, 215; style manual,
    213–14
apostrophe, 353–5; contractions, 355;
    with indefinite pronoun, 355; joint
    ownership, 355; misused, 355; plural
    nouns, 354; possessive case, 354–5;
    proper nouns ending in *s,* 354;
    singular nouns, 354
apply for, to apply to, to be accepted to,
    457–8
appositives, 229, 302, 303, 336–7
argument: claims, 273–6; emotional *vs.*
    logical arguments, 265–6; facts,
    266, 273; faulty reasoning, 267–70;
    objectivity, 270; opinion and,
    265–6; rebuttals, 278–86; slanted
    language, 271–2
argumentative essay, 264–97; definition
    in, 141, 273; introduction and
    conclusion compared, 106–7;
    outlining, 287–8; peer edit form
    for first draft, 472–3; purpose, 279;
    rhetorical mode, 56–7; sample
    professional essay, 285–6; sample
    student essays, 288–96; template,
    287–8
articles (part of speech), 301, 449–53;
    definite, 450–3; with gerunds,
    453; indefinite, 449–50; rules for
    omitting definite articles,
    451–2
assimilation, 172–3
attend, 458

audience, 32–41; defined, 33; expectations of, 36; explicit, 36; factors, 35–6; general, 36; implicit, 36; and interesting claims, 275–6; knowledge and interest, 36–7; orientation, 38–41; profile, 41; reader-based prose, 33–5; rebuttals, 281; revising final draft, 52–3; silencing, 271; topic/audience table, 39; topic/purpose/audience assessment, 40; writer-based prose, 33; writer-reader relationship, 37–8; and writing purpose, 30, 52–3

authorities and experts, 125, 175–6, 187

auxiliary verbs, 304, 305

a variety of, 364

avoid vs. to prevent, 458

await/wait, 465

bandwagon fallacy, 269

beside, besides, 435

between, among, 434

bias, biased, 435

biased language. *See* slanted language

biased sources, 125

bibliography: annotated, 154, 166; bibliographic information, 178; working, 177

BioMed Central, 184

block method of comparison, 144–5

block quotation, 198, 214–15, 227

both, 365

brackets, 202–3

brainstorming, 45–6

Business Source Elite, 184

call/draw attention, 458

can, could, 455–6

CANSIM (Canadian Socio-economic Information Management), 184

care, 459

case studies, 126, 273, 281–4

cause–effect organizational method, 112, 115–16

certain consequences fallacy, 269

chronological method, 112–13, 254

circular conclusion, 105, 230, 291

circumlocution, 406

citation, 182, 195. *See also* documentation

cite, sight, site, 435

claims: analyzed, 122–3; arguable, 274; conclusive, 123; defined, 122; empirical, 122; of fact, 122; interesting, 275–6; manageable, 276; of policy, 123, 276; specific, 274–5; and support, 273–6; tentative, 123; of value, 122–3, 273, 279

clarity, 407–9; conciseness, 407–17; logic, 421–2; precision, 419–25; word choice, 419–21

classification/division organizational method, 115, 227

clauses, 314–16, 318, 321, 335–6

clichés, 424–5

climax order, 101, 287

clustering, 47

coherent paragraph, 78–85, 110; logical sentence order, 80, 83; parallel structures, 80, 84, 226, 428–9; patterns of development, 79, 82–3; selective repetition, 80, 84; synonyms, 80; transitions, 80–1; word choice, 79

collective nouns: pronoun–antecedent agreement with, 366; subject–verb agreement with, 363

colloquialism, 419

colon, 290, 345–7; elaboration of independent clause, 346–7; with list or series, 346; with quotation, 345–6

comma, 290, 332–42; in addresses, 338; with adverbs and adverbial phrases, 337; with appositive, 336–7; with concluding word or phrase, 334–5; conventional uses, 337–9; with coordinate adjectives, 338–9; in dates, 338; with degrees, titles, and similar designations, 338; and flow of sentence, 337; with independent clauses, 333–5; with introductory word, phrase, or clauses, 334; with non-restrictive phrases or clauses, 335–6; in numbers, 338; with quotation, 338; within quotation marks, 339; rule exceptions, 334, 335; sensible usage, 339; with series, 332–3; setting off parenthetical information, 335–7

comma splice, 326–7

commit, 459

common ground, 279

commonly confused words, 433–40, 456–69

common noun, 452–3

comparatives, 447

compare and contrast, 459–60

comparison and contrast, 118, 226, 274, 286

comparison and contrast essay, 143–6; block method, 144–5; point-by-point method, 144–5; sample student essay, 145–6

compete for, 460

complete subject, 311

complex sentence, 323

compose/comprise/consist, 465

composing process, 4–7. *See also* essay-writing; computer method, 51–2; first draft, 50–2, 173; linear model, 4–5; process-reflective writing, 5–7

compound, 333, 392–5

compound-complex sentence, 324

compound sentence, 321–2, 333–4

compound subjects: linked by conjunctions, 362; with prepositional phrases joining two nouns, 362–3; pronoun case, 377

computer: composing with, 51–2; cross-referencing systems, 179; electronic research, 176–7, 183–5, 186–7; organizing research notes, 178–9

concern, 460

concessions, 279

concision, 407–11. *See also* wordiness; cutting for conciseness, 407–11; verb choice, 423; writing directly, 411–13

conclusion: in argumentative essay, 106–7; circular, 105, 230, 392; essay, 104–8; idiomatic prepositional use with, 467; paragraph, 74–5; in process analysis essay, 138; spiral, 105

conclusive claims, 123

conjunctions, 306–8; coordinating, 307, 318, 321; correlative, 308, 393–4; subordinating, 308, 316, 318, 321, 323

connotation, 26, 141, 226, 271

consider, discuss, mention, 460

context clues, 26–8, 228

contractions, 355, 419

contrast. *See compare and contrast;* comparison and contrast; comparison and contrast essay

coordinating conjunctions, 307, 318, 321, 333–4

correlative conjunctions, 308, 393–4

cost–benefit analysis, 117–18

could, can, 455–6

Council of Science Editors. *See* CSE style

count, depend, rely, 460

countable nouns, 449–50, 454–5

credibility, 91–2, 123, 127–8

criteria, criterion, 465

critical reading, 9

critical response, 64–71; function of, 65; objectives and conventions of, 65; sample student essay, 70–1

critical thinking, 12–25; analyzing arguments, 14; applied, 13–14; argument, 170; defined, 12, 14; inference, 9, 13–16, 27–8; reading and, 14–18

cross-referencing, 179

CSE style, 212–13

cumulative sentence, 427–28

dangling modifiers, 385–6

dashes, 345–7

data, datum, 465

databases, 183–5

dates, 338, 468–9

deductive reasoning, 276, 277–8

definite articles, 450–3

definition, 247; in argumentative essay, 141, 273–4; denotation, 28; as organizational method, 112

definition essay, 141–3

demonstrative pronouns, 303

denotation, 28

depend, rely, count, 460

dependent clause, 321

dependent clause fragment, 315–16

description, 24, 25; and argument, 273; as evidence, 127; organizational method, 113; rhetorical mode, 56, 57–8

desk-thumping (dogmatism), 270

despite, in spite of, 466

digital object identifier (DOI), 178, 224, 230

direct object, 302

discriminate between, discriminate against, 461

discuss, consider, mention, 460

distance: plurals as adjectival phrases concerning money, time, and, 447–8; subject–verb agreement with, 364

documentation, 174. *See also under* specific style of documentation; avoiding plagiarism, 194–5; citation styles, 212–13; journal citation, 182, 221–2, 231; necessary *vs.* unnecessary citations, 195–6, 203; parenthetical citations, 195; purposes, 212

document design, 432–3

doubtful causes fallacy, 269

dramatic introductions, 89–90

dramatic-logical introduction, 91

each of, 363

EBSCOhost, 184

editing, 54, 429. *See also* revising

effect, affect, 433

e.g., i.e., 435

either/neither of, 363

either/or (false dilemma) fallacy, 269

ellipses, 201–2, 249

elude, allude, 434

emotional appeals, 263–4, 285

emotional fallacies. *See* logical fallacies

emphasize, 463

empirical claim, 122

encourage/discourage, 461

endnotes. *See* footnotes

ERIC (Educational Resources Information Center), 185

essay presentation, 432–3

essay-writing: final draft, 52–4; first draft, 50–2, 173; organization, 48–50, 101–4; outline, 48–50; pre-writing, 42–7; research, 47–8; stages in, 41–54

et cetera (etc.), 466

ethical fallacies. *See* logical fallacies

ethics, appeal to, 263, 290, 291

euphemisms, 417

every one of, 363

evidence: analyzed, 123–31; biased sources, 125; contradictory, 180–1; hard, 124–5; kinds of, 124–8; organization of, 123–4; suggestive, 127

examination essay, 58–64; discernment and adaptability, 60–1; examples and illustrations, 61; organization, 59; sample student essay, 61–3; studying for, 59; time management, 59–60

examples and illustrations, uses of, 61, 116, 126, 248

except, accept, 433

expanded thesis statement, 94

experts. *See* authorities and experts

explicit audiences, 36

exposition, 56–7, 137–52; comparison and contrast essay, 143–6; defined, 133; definition essay, 141–3; essay templates, 133–5; introduction and conclusion compared, 106; objective tone, 147; process analysis essay, 136–40; purpose of, 133; research essay, 170; sample professional essay, 148–52; types of expository essays, 133–5

expository essay. *See* exposition

extended summary, 157–60, 160–4; length, 157; main features of, 157; outline, 162–3; samples, 160–4; steps in writing, 157–8

facts, 266, 273

factual claims, 122

factual evidence, 124–5

fairness: and credibility, 128

false analogy, 269

false causes, 269

false universal claim, 94

faulty predication, 421–2

faulty reasoning, 267–70

few, 365

fewer, less, 436

few vs. a few, 447

final draft, 52–4

finite categories fallacy, 270

first draft, 50–2, 173, 472–3

first reading, 21–4

five-paragraph essay, 4

focused reading, 10–11

FOCUS (mnemonic), 52

footnotes, 244

for example, 466

formal outline, 48–9

formal prose, 33–4

fortune-telling fallacy, 270

fragment. *See* sentence fragment

freewriting, 46–7

future perfect progressive tense, 444

future perfect tense, 444

future progressive tense, 444

future tenses, 443–4

general audiences, 36
generalization. *See* hasty generalization
general knowledge, 196
gerund, 453
good, well, 436
graduate from, to be a graduate of, 461
grammar: adjectives, 305–6, 338–9; adverbs, 305–6; conjunctions, 306–8; in formal writing, 299–300; nouns, 301–3; parts of speech, 300–1; preposition, 306–7; pronouns, 301–4; usage guidelines, 299–300; verbs, 304–5
graphic outline, 49
guilt by association, 268

half of, 364
hard evidence, 124–5
hasty generalization, 265, 268, 269
Health Source Nursing/Academic Edition, 185
helping verbs, 304, 305, 314
here is/here are sentence, 360
hey, 301
hire, to be hired by, 461
holding back the claim, 287
human, 466
humanities, the, 466
humanity, 466
hyperlink, 223, 241
hypothesis, 126

idiomatic prepositional use, 457–63. *See also* commonly confused words
i.e., e.g., 435
IEL (IEEE/IEE Electronic Library), 185
Igenta, 185
illusion, allusion, 434
illustrations. *See* examples and illustrations, uses of
imperative sentence, 312
implicit audiences, 36
in-class essay. *See* examination essay
including, 336
incomplete verb forms, 314–15
indefinite article, 449–50
indefinite pronouns, 303, 355, 366–7
independent clause, 314
indirect evidence, 125–7
indirect object, 302
inductive reasoning, 276–7
in fact, 466
inference, 9, 13–16, 27–8
infinitive phrase, 427

informal prose, 33–4, 299–300
InfoTrac, 185
–*ing* fragment, 314–15
in spite of, despite, 466
intensive pronouns, 304
interjections, 301
Internet: searches, 183–5; sources, 176–7
interpretation, 259. *See also* analysis
interrogative pronouns, 303, 379
interviewing, 187
introduction: in academic writing, 91, 294; in argumentative essay, 106–7, 290; dramatic approach, 89–90; functions of, 88–92; inverted pyramid structure of, 88; length, 92–4; logical approach, 88–9; mixed approach, 90–1; opening sentence, 92–3; in process analysis essay, 138; thesis statement in, 91
inverted climax (dramatic) order, 102, 287
inverted pyramid structure, 88–9
irony, 40
"it does not follow" fallacy, 269
it is sentence, 414–15
its, it's, 436

jargon, 22, 419
joint ownership, 355
journals, 165, 182–3, 221–2, 231, 254

keywords, 10
kind(s) of/type(s) of + noun, 454–5
knowledgeability, 128
know something, 461

lack, 462
lay, lie, 437
lead to, 462
led, lead, 437
less, fewer, 436
Lexis-Nexis Academic Universe, 185
library resources, 177, 181, 186–7
lie, lay, 437
linear model of writing, 4–5
linking verbs, 304, 305
loaded language. *See* slanted language
logical-dramatic introduction, 91
logical fallacies, 247, 267–71, 277, 278
logical introductions, 88–9
look at/around/for/into/over, 462
loose, lose, 437
–*ly* ending, 448

main idea, 158. *See also* thesis statement
main verbs, 304
major premise, 276, 277–78
make vs. enable, 466–7
many, 365
many vs. much, 447
mapping. *See* clustering
mathematics, 468
may, might, 456
mention, discuss, consider, 460
middle ground fallacy, 269
minor premise, 276, 277–8
misplaced modifiers, 382–89; adjectival modifiers, 382–3; adverbial modifiers, 383; dangling modifiers, 385–6; fixing, 383–4; one-word modifiers, 384
mixed approach introductions, 90–1
mixed format (quotation and paraphrasing), 199–200, 227
mixed order outlines, 102
MLA style, 231–50; authors, 233–4, 236–8; citation in Works Cited section, 235–44, 249–50; citation style, 231–44; disciplines using, 212; document design, 432–3; electronic sources, 234–5, 241–2; footnotes and endnotes, 244; government documents, 241; indirect source, 232–3, 246; in-text citations, 232–5; multiple sources in one citation, 233; non-textual sources, 235, 242–4; periodicals, 236, 240; personal communication, 233, 241; quotation, 200, 232; sample student essays, 203–8, 245–50, 292–6; style handbook, 213
modals, 305, 321, 455–6
Modern Language Association. *See* MLA style
money: plurals as adjectival phrases concerning distance, time, and, 447–48; subject–verb agreement with, 364
more of, 364
most of, 364, 467
movies, 467
much vs. many, 447

narration: paragraph development with, 113–14; rhetorical mode, 24, 25, 56, 57–8
Newspaper Source, 185

none of, 364

non-restrictive, 335–6

note-taking: reading and, 21; research, 178

noun phrases, 320

nouns, 301–3, 453–5; as appositive, 302, 303; common, 452–3; countable and uncountable, 449–50, 454–5; as direct object, 302; *every* + noun, 453; gerund, 453; as indirect object, 302; *kind(s) of/type(s) of* + noun, 454–5; proper, 451; as subject, 301–2; as subjective complement, 302–3

nowadays, 467

number, amount, 434

numbering nouns, 415–16

object: direct, 302; indirect, 302; pronoun case, 377

often, usually, always, 464–5

oh!, 301

one of, 363, 415

one-way reading. *See* passive reading

one-word modifiers, 384, 446

onset, outset, 437

on the one hand, on the other hand, 467

opening sentence, 92–3

opinion, 265–6

opinion, express an opinion, 467–68

organization: of evidence, 123–4; in-class essay, 59; outlining, 48–50, 101–4; research notes, 178–9

organizational patterns of development, 79, 82–3, 92. *See also* paragraph development

or or *nor:* antecedents joined by, 365

outline: argumentative essay, 287–8; climax order, 101; defined, 101; developed with thesis statement, 102–4; essay, 48–50, 101–4; formal, 48–9; guidelines, 102; headings, 191; informal, 49; inverted climax (dramatic) order, 102; mixed order, 102; organization, 101–2; peer edit form for formal outline, 470–1; research essay, 173, 180, 190–4; sample, 190–4; scratch (sketch), 48; summary, 158, 162–3; value of, 101

outset, onset, 437

overstated claim, 94

paragraph: body, 53; coherence, 78–85; conclusion, 74–5; length, 77; structure of, 74; transition between

paragraphs, 75–6; unity, 76–8, 82, 110, 229; wrap, 74–5, 229

paragraph development, 110; analogy method, 118; by analyzing, 111; cause–effect method, 112, 115–16; chronological method, 112–13, 254; classification/division method, 115, 227; comparison and contrast method, 118, 226; with cost–benefit analysis, 117–18; by defining, 112; descriptive method, 56, 57–8, 113; example/illustration method, 116; narrative method, 24, 25, 56, 57–8, 113–14; in personal essays, 113–14; problem–solution method, 112, 117; by process analysis, 114, 136; question–answer method, 116; question/method of, 111

parallelism, 389–95; comparison, 394–5; compounds, 392–5; correlative conjunctions, 393–4; identifying and fixing faulty, 390–1; list or series, 391–2; parallel structures, 80, 84, 226, 428–9; principle, 389–90

paraphrase, 154, 164–5, 197–8, 199, 232

parentheses, 202, 347–8

parenthetical citations, 195. *See also* APA style; MLA style

participate in, 462

participial phrase, 427

participles, 446–7

part of, 365

parts of speech, 300–1. *See also* grammar

passive construction, 411–12

passive reading, 7–8

past participle, 446–7

past perfect progressive tense, 443

past perfect tense, 443

past progressive tense, 443

past tenses, 443

patterns of development. *See* organizational patterns of development; paragraph development

pay (for), 462

peer edit forms, 470–5; argumentative essay first draft, 472–3; formal outline, 470–1; research essay first draft, 474–5

peer-reviewed journals, 165, 182–3

periodicals, 182. *See also* journals

periodic sentence, 427–8

personal communication, 215, 222, 233, 241

personal essay, 113–14

personal experience, 127, 273, 290

personal pronouns, 303, 365, 376–7

phony phrases, 409–10

phrase, 318–21; absolute, 427; adjectival, 319; adverbial, 319–20, 337; defined, 318; infinitive, 427; noun, 320; participial, 427; phony, 409–10; prepositional, 311, 319–20, 427; verb, 320–1

plagiarism, 194–7

plenty of, 364

point-by-point: comparing and contrasting, 144–5; rebuttal, 280–6, 287

point out, 462

policy, claims of, 123, 276

portions and fractions: pronoun–antecedent agreement with, 366; subject–verb agreement with, 364

possessive case, 354–5, 377–8

precedents, 126–7, 289

precision, 419–25

predicate: faulty predication, 421–2; of sentence, 310

predicate noun. *See* subjective complement

premises, 123, 276, 277–8

preparatory reading, 30, 32

preposition, 302, 306–7

prepositional phrase, 311, 319–20, 427

prepositional use: idiomatic, 457–63

pre-reading questions, 18–21

present participle, 446–7

present perfect progressive tense, 443

present perfect tense, 442

present progressive tense, 442

present tenses, 442–3

pre-writing, 42–7; brainstorming, 45–6; clustering, 47; defined, 42; freewriting, 46–7; looping, 46; strategies, 44–7; subjects *vs.* topics, 42–4; topic hunting, 43

primary sources, 170, 181

problem–solution method of development, 112, 117

process analysis, 114, 136

process analysis essay, 136–40; composing, 137–8; planning, 137; sample student essay, 139–40; topics, 138

process-reflective writing, 5–7

Project Muse, 185

pronoun–antecedent agreement, 365–9; with antecedents joined by *or* or *nor,* 365; with collective noun antecedents, 366; with compound antecedent, 365; and inclusive language, 367; with indefinite pronoun antecedent, 366–7

pronoun consistency, 381

pronoun reference, 370–5; ambiguous reference, 372; broad reference, 373; no reference (missing antecedent), 371–2; remote reference, 372

pronouns, 301–4. *See also* nouns; case, 376–80; defined, 302; demonstrative, 303; indefinite, 303, 355, 366–7; intensive, 304; interrogative, 303, 379; personal, 303, 365, 376–7; possessive, 377–8; reciprocal, 304; reflexive, 304; relative, 303, 316, 323, 378–9, 448

proofreading, 54, 429–1; common errors, 431; and editing compared, 429; guidelines, 430–1; method, 430

Psyc INFO, 185

publication date, 176, 227

punctuation: apostrophe, 353–5; colon, 290, 345–7; comma, 290, 332–42; dashes, 347–48; no-comma rule, 352–3; no-semicolon rules, 353; parentheses, 290, 347–48; prohibitions, 352–3; semicolon, 245, 290, 342–5

purpose. *See* writing purpose

qtd., 232

question/answer organizational method, 116

questioning strategy: in assimilating information, 172–3; in creating outline, 173; in critical reading, 18–25; in critical response, 65–6; in determining audience orientation, 39–40; in generating methods of development, 111–12; in pre-writing, 44, 45; in referencing, 174; in topic selection, 171–2; in writing first draft, 173

questions: interrogative pronouns, 303; sentences phrased as, 360–1

quotation: block format, 198, 214–15; bracket in, 202–3; comma with, 338, 339; direct, 198–200, 214–15,

248; ellipses, 201–2, 249; mixed format, 199–200, 227; signal phrases and verbs with, 200–1, 214

quotation marks, 198, 245

raise vs. rise, 468

reader-based prose, 33–5

reader interest, creating, 88

reading: 3-D (Dimensional), 9–10; abstract, 19, 21, 253; active, 10, 18–21; critical, 9; and critical thinking, 14–18; first, 21–4; focused, 10–11; passive, 7–8; preparatory, 30, 32; pre-reading questions, 18–21; second, 21–5; selective, 10–11; writing and, 3–4

reading-thinking-writing process, 9–10

reason, reasoning, 123, 266, 270, 276–8

rebuttal, 278–80

reciprocal pronouns, 304

red herring, 268

redundancy, 407–9. *See also* wordiness

refer, 463

reflexive pronouns, 304

relative clauses: adjectival clause, 446, 448; agreement, 448

relative pronouns, 303, 316, 323, 378–9, 448

reliability, 128

rely, count, depend, 460

remember, 468

remote reference, 372

repetition, selective, 80, 84, 428–9

research, 47–8; alternative information sources, 187; contradictory evidence, 180–1; exploring stage, 177; Internet searches, 183–5; library, 186–7; meaning of, 170; note-taking, 178; organizing notes, 178–9; strategies, 179–80

research essay: documentation, 174; first draft, 173; organization, 174–5; outline, 173; peer edit for first draft, 474–5; sample student essay, 203–8; synthesis, 170, 173; topic selection, 171–2; using evidence, 170

research notes, 178–9

research proposal, 171–2

restrictive clauses, 335–6

result in/result from, 463

reviewer, feedback of, 53

revising, 52–4; clarifying meaning, 53; for clarity, 405–25; for concision,

407–11; fine-tuning, 54; for precision, 419–25; reviewing purpose and audience, 52–3; solidifying structure, 53–4; underscoring ideas, 53; for variety and emphasis, 425–9

rhetorical (patterns) modes, 56–8. *See also* paragraph development; argument, 56–7; description, 56, 57–8; exposition, 56–7; narration, 56, 57–8

rhythm, 428–9

run-on sentence, 325–6

scanning, 10–11

scientific reasoning. *See* inductive reasoning

scratch outline, 48

search limiters/expanders, 183

secondary sources, 159, 170, 181–2, 197–8

second reading, 21–5

selective reading, 10–11

selective repetition, 80, 84, 428–9

self-survey: assessing writing purpose, 31–2

semicolon, 245, 290, 342–5

sentence, 309–18; active form, 413; comma splice, 326–7; complex, 323; compound, 321–2, 333–4; compound-complex, 324; cumulative, 427–28; defined, 310; emphasis in, 427–9; flow of, 337; generating tension in, 427–8; imperative, 312; length, 425–7; passive construction, 411–12; patterns, 321–4; periodic, 427–8; predicate, 310; run-on, 325–6; simple, 322–3; structural variety, 427; subject of, 310–11, 360–2; syntax, 382; topic, 74, 158, 191, 246; variety, 425–7; weak verb + noun construction, 415

sentence construction errors, 382–402. *See also* sentence fragment; misplaced modifiers, 382–89; parallelism problems, 389–95

sentence fragment, 310, 312–18; add-on fragments, 313–14; dependent clause fragment, 315–16; –ing fragment, 314–15; missing subject or predicate, 313

sentence summaries, 155–6

serial comma, 333

[sic], 202

sight, site, cite, 435

signal phrases, 159–60, 200–1, 214, 216, 227, 248

silencing, 271

simple future tense, 443

simple past tense, 443

simple present tense, 442

simple subject, 311

simple thesis statement, 94

single quotation marks, 198, 249

sketch outline. *See* scratch outline

slang, 419

slanted language, 271–2

slippery slope, 269. *See also* certain consequences

soft evidence, 125–6, 273

some of, 364

some time, sometime, sometimes, 468

sources: authorities and experts, 125, 175–6, 187; evaluating, 20–1, 125, 175–7; primary, 170, 181; reference, 177, 181; of research material, 181–3; secondary, 159, 170, 181–2, 197–8

spiral conclusion, 105

square brackets. *See* brackets

squinting reference, 372

statistical evidence, 124–5, 255–7, 273, 289

statistics, statistic, 468

stereotyping, 278

straw man, 268

stress, 463

structure: reviewing, 53–4

subject: complete, 311; compound subjects, 362–3; noun as, 301–2; of sentence, 310–11, 360–2; simple, 311

subject complement, 302–3

subject–verb agreement, 360–5; with *both, few, many, parts of,* 365; with collective nouns, 363; with compound subjects, 362–3; with distance, time, money, weight or mass, 364; with *every* + noun, 453; finding the subject, 360–1; with indefinite pronouns, 363–4; mistaking the subject, 361–2; with nouns ending in *s,* 364; with phrases involving portions and fractions + *of,* 364; rules, 362–5, 464

subordinating conjunctions, 308, 316, 318, 321, 323

such as, 337

suggestive evidence, 127

summaries: abstract, 19, 21, 154, 165, 253; annotated bibliography, 154, 166; and argument, 159; defined, 154; extended, 160–4; job-related, 166–7; length, 155, 157; main features, 155, 157; outline, 158, 162–3; paraphrase, 154, 164–5; of secondary sources, 159, 197–8; sentence, 155–6; signal phrases in, 159–60; uses of, 154, 155, 166–7, 227, 230, 246, 253

superlatives, 447, 451

synonyms, 26, 80, 248

syntax, 382

synthesis, 12, 170, 172–3, 249

tense: future tenses, 443–4; past tenses, 443; present tenses, 442–3

tentative claims, 123

than, then, 438

that, which, who, 336

the, 301, 449

their: with singular indefinite pronoun, 367

their, there, they're, 438

the majority/minority of, 364

the number of, 364

the reason sentence, 415

there is/there are sentence, 360, 415

thesaurus, 421

thesis, 42, 43

thesis statement, 94–101, 190, 245; checklist, 100–1; effective statements, 95; essay outline with, 102–4; ineffective statements, 96; in introduction, 74, 91; kinds of, 94–5; specific claims, 274–5; summarizing, 158

think, 463

three-way reading. *See* 3-D (Dimensional) reading

throughout, 469

time: plurals as adjectival phrases concerning distance, money, and, 447–8; referring to, 468–9; subject–verb agreement with, 364

time management, 59–60

title: of summary, 158; of works, 19, 253

to, too, 438

tone, 22; and audience, 33–4; objective, 147

topic, 42–4, 138

topic selection, 171–2

topic sentence, 74, 158, 191, 246

tradition (that is the way we have always done it) fallacy, 270

transitions, 75–6, 80–1, 226; of cause and effect, 80; coherent paragraphs through, 80–1, 83–4; of contrast or qualification, 81; of emphasis, 80; of illustration, 80; of limit or concession, 80; between paragraphs, 75–6; of sequence and addition, 80; of summary or conclusion, 81

treadmill logic, 268

two-way reading. *See* critical reading

uncountable nouns, 449–50, 454–5

unified paragraph, 76–8, 82, 110, 229

Universal Resource Locator (URL), 177, 223

usage, use, 438

usually, always, often, 464–5

value, claims of, 122–3, 273, 279

verb phrases, 320–1

verbs, 304–5. *See also* subject–verb agreement; confused with nouns, 456–7; expressing state of being, 310; helping, 304, 305, 314; with idiomatic prepositional use, 457–63; incomplete forms, 314–15; linking, 304, 305; main, 304; modal auxiliaries, 455–6; modals, 305, 321; object of verb, 302; with vitality, 423

wait/await, 465

way, 469

weight or mass: subject–verb agreement with, 364

well, good, 436

which one of, 363

who, which, that, 336

who's, whose, 438–9

who/whom, 378–9

word choice, 79, 419–21, 423–5

wordiness, 407–11; black hole constructions, 414–15; euphemisms, 417; intensives, 410–11; numbering nouns, 415–16; phony phrases, 409–10;

prepositional phrases, 411; redundancy, 407–9; unnecessary prepositions and articles, 410
word meanings, 25–8; context clues, 26–8, 228; denotation, 28; dictionary use, 253, 421; grammar and, 300; inference, 27–8; jargon, 22
working bibliography, 177

WorldCat, 185
wrap, paragraph, 74–5, 229
writer: establishing credibility of, 91–2
writer-based prose, 33
writer-reader relationship, 37–8
writing. *See also* essay-writing: composing process, 4–7; explorative stage, 5; formal *vs.* informal prose, 33–4, 301–2; and reading, 3–4; reading-thinking-writing process, 9–10
writing purpose, 30–2

you (pronoun): used in informal prose, 34
you're, your, 439

Some Irregular Verb Forms

Basic form	3rd-person singular	Past tense	Past participle	Present participle
be	is	was, were	been	being
bear	bears	bore	borne, born	bearing
beat	beats	beat	beaten	beating
begin	begins	began	begun	beginning
bite	bites	bit	bitten	biting
bleed	bleeds	bled	bled	bleeding
blow	blows	blew	blown	blowing
break	breaks	broke	broken	breaking
bring	brings	brought	brought	bringing
broadcast	broadcasts	broadcast	broadcast	broadcasting
build	builds	built	built	building
buy	buys	bought	bought	buying
catch	catches	caught	caught	catching
choose	chooses	chose	chosen	choosing
come	comes	came	come	coming
cost (have as a price)	costs	cost	cost	costing
cut	cuts	cut	cut	cutting
deal	deals	dealt	dealt	dealing
dig	digs	dug	dug	digging
dive	dives	dived, dove	dived	diving
do	does	did	done	doing
draw	draws	drew	drawn	drawing
drink	drinks	drank	drunk	drinking
drive	drives	drove	driven	driving
eat	eats	ate	eaten	eating
fall	falls	fell	fallen	falling
feel	feels	felt	felt	feeling
fight	fights	fought	fought	fighting
find	finds	found	found	finding
fly	flies	flew	flown	flying
forbid	forbids	forbade	forbidden	forbidding
forget	forgets	forgot	forgotten	forgetting
get	gets	got	got, gotten	getting
give	gives	gave	given	giving
go	goes	went	gone	going
grow	grows	grew	grown	growing
have	has	had	had	having
hear	hears	heard	heard	hearing
hide (conceal)	hides	hid	hidden	hiding
hit	hits	hit	hit	hitting
hold	holds	held	held	holding
hurt	hurts	hurt	hurt	hurting
input	inputs	input, inputted	input, inputted	inputting
keep	keeps	kept	kept	keeping
know	knows	knew	known	knowing
lay	lays	laid	laid	laying
lead	leads	led	led	leading
learn	learns	learned, learnt	learned, learnt	learning
leave	leaves	left	left	leaving
lend	lends	lent	lent	lending
let	lets	let	let	letting